9th Workshop on Computational Approaches to Subjectivity, Sentiment and Social Media Analysis (WASSA 2018)

Brussels, Belgium
31 October 2018

ISBN: 978-1-5108-7429-9

WASSA 2018

**The 9th Workshop on Computational Approaches to
Subjectivity, Sentiment and Social Media Analysis**

Proceedings of the Workshop

October 31, 2018
Brussels, Belgium

Order copies of this and other ACL proceedings from:

Association for Computational Linguistics (ACL)
209 N. Eighth Street
Stroudsburg, PA 18360
USA
Tel: +1-570-476-8006
Fax: +1-570-476-0860
acl@aclweb.org

Introduction

Research in automatic Subjectivity and Sentiment Analysis (SSA), as subtasks of Affective Computing and Natural Language Processing (NLP), has flourished in the past years. The growth in interest in these tasks was motivated by the birth and rapid expansion of the Social Web that made it possible for people all over the world to share, comment or consult content on any given topic. In this context, opinions, sentiments and emotions expressed in Social Media texts have been shown to have a high influence on the social and economic behaviour worldwide. SSA systems are highly relevant to many real-world applications (e.g. marketing, eGovernance, business intelligence, social analysis) and also to many tasks in Natural Language Processing (NLP) - information extraction, question answering, textual entailment, to name just a few. The importance of this field has been proven by the high number of approaches proposed in research in the past decade, as well as by the interest that it raised from other disciplines (Economics, Sociology, Psychology, Marketing, Crisis Management disciplines (Economics, Sociology, Psychology, Marketing, Crisis Management, and Behavioral Studies, Digital Humanities) and the applications that were created using its technology.

Next to the growth in the diversity of applications, task definitions change towards more complex challenges: Subjectivity, polarity recognition and opinion mining has been enriched with fine-grained aspect and target level predictions. Polarity as a concept is complemented by emotion models as defined from psychological research.

In spite of the growing body of research in the area in the past years, dealing with affective phenomena in text has proven to be a complex, interdisciplinary problem that remains far from being solved. Its challenges include the need to address the issue from different perspectives and at different levels, depending on the characteristics of the textual genre, the language(s) treated and the final application for which the analysis is done.

The aim of the 9th Workshop on Computational Approaches to Subjectivity, Sentiment and Social Media Analysis (WASSA 2018) was to continue the line of the previous editions, bringing together researchers in Computational Linguistics working on Subjectivity and Sentiment Analysis and researchers working on interdisciplinary aspects of affect computation from text.

This year, we also organized a track on implicit emotion recognition: http://implicitemotions.wassa2018.com/

Participants were given a tweet from which a certain emotion word is removed. That word is one of the following: "sad", "happy", "disgusted", "surprised", "angry", "afraid" or a synonym of one of them. The task was to predict the emotion the excluded word expresses: Sadness, Joy, Disgust, Surprise, Anger, or Fear.

With this formulation of the task, we provided data instances which are likely to express an emotion. However, the emotion needs to be inferred from the causal description, which is typically more implicit than an emotion word.

For the main workshop, we accepted 15/60 papers as long (25%) and another 17 as short, giving a total of 32/60 papers accepted - 53%. For the Implicit Emotions Shared Task, we got 19 system description paper submissions, out of which we accept 17. 49 papers in total will be presented at the workshop, together with the additional contribution from the invited speaker, Dr. Ellen Riloff.

Accepted papers deal with overcoming issues like language and domain dependence of sentiment analysis, irony and sarcasm and adaptation of sentiment and emotion detection systems to work in real-life scenarios.

We would like to thank the EMNLP 2018 Organizers and Workshop Chairs for the help and support at the different stages of the workshop organization process. We are also especially grateful to the Program Committee members and the external reviewers for the time and effort spent assessing the papers. We would like to extend our thanks to our invited speaker – Dr. Ellen Riloff - for accepting to deliver the keynote talks, opening new horizons for research and applications of sentiment and emotion detection from text.

Alexandra Balahur, Saif Mohammad, Veronique Hoste, Roman Klinger

WASSA 2018 Chairs

Organizers:

Alexandra Balahur - European Commission Joint Research Centre

Saif M. Mohammad - National Research Council Canada

Veronique Hoste - University of Ghent, Belgium

Roman Klinger - University of Stuttgart, Germany

Program Committee:

Muhammad Abdul-Mageed - University of British Columbia, Canada

Hassan Alhuzali - University of British Columbia, Canada

Jorge Balazs - University of Tokyo, Japan

Jeremy Barnes - University Pompeu Fabra, Spain

Sabine Bergler - Concordia University, Canada

Cristina Bosco - University of Torino, Italy

Felipe Bravo-Marquez - University of Waikato, New Zealand

Nicoletta Calzolari - CNR Pisa, Italy

Erik Cambria - Nanyang Technological University, Singapore

Alexandra Chronopoulou, University of Illinois at Urbana Champaign, U.S.A.

Montse Cuadros - Vicomtech, Spain

Lingjia Deng - University of Pittsburg, U.S.A.

Yunxia Ding - Yunnan University, China

Daniel Fleischer - Amobee Inc., Tel Aviv, Israel

Lorenzo Gatti - University of Twente, The Netherlands

Vachagan Gratian - University of Stuttgart, Germany

Carlos Iglesias - Universidad Politecnica de Madrid, Spain

Aditya Joshi - CSIRO Data61

Manfred Klenner - University of Zuerich, Switzerland

Isa Maks - Vrije Universiteit Amsterdam, The Netherlands

Edison Marrese-Taylor - University of Tokyo, Japan

Jiří Martínek - University of West Bohemia, Czech Republic

Maite Martin Valdivia – University of Jaen, Spain

Diana Maynard - University of Sheffied, U.K.

Karo Moilanen - University of Oxford, U.K.

Behzad Naderalvojoud - Hacettepe University, Turkey

Günter Neumann - DFKI, Germany

Malvina Nissim - University of Groningen, The Netherlands

Constantin Orasan - University of Wolverhampton, U.K.

Gustavo Paetzhold - Universidade Tecnológica Federal do Parana, Brazil

Samuel Pecar - Slovak University of Technology in Bratislava, Slovakia

Viktor Pekar - University of Wolverhampton, U.K.

Flor Miriam Plaza del Arco - University of Jaén, Spain

Daniel Preotiuc-Pietro - University of Pennsylvania, U.S.A.

Thomas Proisl - Friedrich-Alexander-Universität Erlangen-Nürnberg, Germany

Pavel Přibáň - University of West Bohemia, Czech Republic

Prabod Rathnayaka - University of Moratuwa, Sri Lanka

Esteban Rissola - USI, Switzerland

Mike Thelwall - University of Wolverhampton, U.K

Lyle Ungar - University of Pennsylvania, U.S.A.

Alfonso Ureña - University of Jaén, Spain

Piek Vossen - Vrije Universiteit Amsterdam, The Netherlands

Bin Wang - Yunnan University, China

WenTing Wang - Alibaba Group, Hangzhou City, China

Michael Wiegand - Saarland University, Germany

Wojciech Witon - Disney Research Los Angeles, U.S.A.

Taras Zagibalov - Brantwatch, U.K.

Additional Reviewers:

Luna De Bruyne; Orphée De Clercq; Bart Desmet; Michal Farkas; Aitor Garcia Pablos; Salud maria Jímenez-Zafra; Zohar Kelrich; Sergei Kulikov; Els Lefever; Cui Leyang; Eugenio Martínez Cámara; Alon Rozental; Toh Zhiqiang

Invited Speaker:

Ellen Riloff, University of Utah, U.S.A.

Table of Contents

ix

x

Workshop Program

Wednesday, October 31, 2018

08:30–08:45   **Opening Remarks**

08:45–09:20   **Invited talk**

08:45–09:20   *Identifying Affective Events and the Reasons for their Polarity*
Ellen Riloff

09:20–10:35   **Session 1: Resources and representations for affect detection from text**

09:20–09:40   *Deep contextualized word representations for detecting sarcasm and irony*
Suzana Ilić, Edison Marrese-Taylor, Jorge Balazs and Yutaka Matsuo

09:40–10:00   *Implicit Subjective and Sentimental Usages in Multi-sense Word Embeddings*
Yuqi Sun, Haoyue Shi and Junfeng Hu

10:00–10:20   *Language Independent Sentiment Analysis with Sentiment-Specific Word Embeddings*
Carl Saroufim, Akram Almatarky and Mohammad AbdelHady

10:20–10:35   *Creating a Dataset for Multilingual Fine-grained Emotion-detection Using Gamification-based Annotation*
Emily Öhman, Kaisla Kajava, Jörg Tiedemann and Timo Honkela

10:35–11:00   *Tea/Coffee Break*

Identifying Affective Events and the Reasons for their Polarity

Ellen Riloff
University of Utah
`riloff@cs.utah.edu`

1 Abstract of invited talk

Many events have a positive or negative impact on our lives (e.g., "I bought a house" is typically good news, but "My house burned down" is bad news). Recognizing events that have affective polarity is essential for narrative text understanding, conversational dialogue, and applications such as summarization and sarcasm detection. We will discuss our recent work on identifying affective events and categorizing them based on the underlying reasons for their affective polarity. First, we will describe a weakly supervised learning method to induce a large set of affective events from a text corpus by optimizing for semantic consistency. Second, we will present models to classify affective events based on Human Need Categories, which often explain people's motivations and desires. Our best results use a co-training model that consists of event expression and event context classifiers and exploits both labeled and unlabeled texts. We will conclude with a discussion of interesting directions for future work in this area.

Proceedings of the 9th Workshop on Computational Approaches to Subjectivity, Sentiment and Social Media Analysis, page 1
Brussels, Belgium, October 31, 2018. ©2018 Association for Computational Linguistics
https://doi.org/10.18653/v1/P17

Deep contextualized word representations for detecting sarcasm and irony

Suzana Ilić[1], Edison Marrese-Taylor[2], Jorge A. Balazs[2], Yutaka Matsuo[2]
University of Innsbruck, Austria[1]
suzana.ilic@student.uibk.ac.at
Graduate School of Engineering, The University of Tokyo, Japan[2]
{emarrese,jorge,matsuo}@weblab.t.u-tokyo.ac.jp

Abstract

Predicting context-dependent and non-literal utterances like sarcastic and ironic expressions still remains a challenging task in NLP, as it goes beyond linguistic patterns, encompassing common sense and shared knowledge as crucial components. To capture complex morpho-syntactic features that can usually serve as indicators for irony or sarcasm across dynamic contexts, we propose a model that uses character-level vector representations of words, based on ELMo. We test our model on 7 different datasets derived from 3 different data sources, providing state-of-the-art performance in 6 of them, and otherwise offering competitive results.

1 Introduction

Sarcastic and ironic expressions are prevalent in social media and, due to the tendency to invert polarity, play an important role in the context of opinion mining, emotion recognition and sentiment analysis (Pang and Lee, 2006). Sarcasm and irony are two closely related linguistic phenomena, with the concept of meaning the opposite of what is literally expressed at its core. There is no consensus in academic research on the formal definition, both terms are non-static, depending on different factors such as context, domain and even region in some cases (Filatova, 2012).

In light of the general complexity of natural language, this presents a range of challenges, from the initial dataset design and annotation to computational methods and evaluation (Chaudhari and Chandankhede, 2017). The difficulties lie in capturing linguistic nuances, context-dependencies and latent meaning, due to richness of dynamic variants and figurative use of language (Joshi et al., 2015).

The automatic detection of sarcastic expressions often relies on the contrast between positive and negative sentiment (Riloff et al., 2013). This incongruence can be found on a lexical level with sentiment-bearing words, as in *"I love being ignored"*. In more complex linguistic settings an action or a situation can be perceived as negative, without revealing any affect-related lexical elements. The intention of the speaker as well as common knowledge or shared experience can be key aspects, as in *"I love waking up at 5 am"*, which can be sarcastic, but not necessarily. Similarly, verbal irony is referred to as saying the opposite of what is meant and based on sentiment contrast (Grice, 1975), whereas situational irony is seen as describing circumstances with unexpected consequences (Lucariello, 1994; Shelley, 2001).

Empirical studies have shown that there are specific linguistic cues and combinations of such that can serve as indicators for sarcastic and ironic expressions. Lexical and morpho-syntactic cues include exclamations and interjections, typographic markers such as all caps, quotation marks and emoticons, intensifiers and hyperboles (Kunneman et al., 2015; Bharti et al., 2016). In the case of Twitter, the usage of emojis and hashtags has also proven to help automatic irony detection.

We propose a purely character-based architecture which tackles these challenges by allowing us to use a learned representation that models features derived from morpho-syntactic cues. To do so, we use deep contextualized word representations, which have recently been used to achieve the state of the art on six NLP tasks, including sentiment analysis (Peters et al., 2018). We test our proposed architecture on 7 different irony/sarcasm datasets derived from 3 different data sources, providing state-of-the-art performance in 6 of them and otherwise offering competitive results, showing the effectiveness of our proposal. We make our code available at https://github.com/epochx/elmo4irony.

Proceedings of the 9th Workshop on Computational Approaches to Subjectivity, Sentiment and Social Media Analysis, pages 2–7
Brussels, Belgium, October 31, 2018. ©2018 Association for Computational Linguistics
https://doi.org/10.18653/v1/P17

2   Related work

Apart from the relevance for industry applications related to sentiment analysis, sarcasm and irony detection has received great traction within the NLP research community, resulting in a variety of methods, shared tasks and benchmark datasets. Computational approaches for the classification task range from rule-based systems (Riloff et al., 2013; Bharti et al., 2015) and statistical methods and machine learning algorithms such as Support Vector Machines (Joshi et al., 2015; Tungthamthiti et al., 2010), Naive Bayes and Decision Trees (Reyes et al., 2013) leveraging extensive feature sets, to deep learning-based approaches. In this context, Tay et al. (2018). delivered state-of-the-art results by using an intra-attentional component in addition to a recurrent neural network. Previous work such as the one by Veale (2016) had proposed a convolutional long-short-term memory network (CNN-LSTM-DNN) that also achieved excellent results. A comprehensive survey on automatic sarcasm detection was done by Joshi et al. (2016), while computational irony detection was reviewed by Wallace (2015).

Further improvements both in terms of classic and deep models came as a result of the SemEval 2018 Shared Task on Irony in English Tweets (Van Hee et al., 2018). The system that achieved the best results was hybrid, namely, a densely-connected BiLSTM with a multi-task learning strategy, which also makes use of features such as POS tags and lexicons (Wu et al., 2018).

3   Proposed Approach

The wide spectrum of linguistic cues that can serve as indicators for sarcastic and ironic expressions has been usually exploited for automatic sarcasm or irony detection by modeling them in the form of binary features in traditional machine learning.

On the other hand, deep models for irony and sarcasm detection, which are currently offer state-of-the-art performance, have exploited sequential neural networks such as LSTMs and GRUs (Veale, 2016; Zhang et al., 2016) on top of distributed word representations. Recently, in addition to using a sequential model, Tay et al. (2018) proposed to use intra-attention to compare elements in a sequence against themselves. This allowed the model to better capture word-to-word level interactions that could also be useful for detecting sarcasm, such as the *incongruity* phenomenon (Joshi et al., 2015). Despite this, all models in the literature rely on word-level representations, which keeps the models from being able to easily capture some of the lexical and morpho-syntactic cues known to denote irony, such as all caps, quotation marks and emoticons, and in Twitter, also emojis and hashtags.

The usage of a purely character-based input would allow us to directly recover and model these features. Consequently, our architecture is based on Embeddings from Language Model or ELMo (Peters et al., 2018). The ELMo layer allows to recover a rich 1,024-dimensional dense vector for each word. Using CNNs, each vector is built upon the characters that compose the underlying words. As ELMo also contains a deep bidirectional LSTM on top of this character-derived vectors, each word-level embedding contains contextual information from their surroundings. Concretely, we use a pre-trained ELMo model, obtained using the 1 Billion Word Benchmark which contains about 800M tokens of news crawl data from WMT 2011 (Chelba et al., 2014).

Subsequently, the contextualized embeddings are passed on to a BiLSTM with 2,048 hidden units. We aggregate the LSTM hidden states using max-pooling, which in our preliminary experiments offered us better results, and feed the resulting vector to a 2-layer feed-forward network, where each layer has 512 units. The output of this is then fed to the final layer of the model, which performs the binary classification.

4   Experimental Setup

We test our proposed approach for binary classification on either sarcasm or irony, on seven benchmark datasets retrieved from different media sources. Below we describe each dataset, please see Table 1 below for a summary.

Twitter: We use the Twitter dataset provided for the SemEval 2018 Task 3, Irony Detection in English Tweets (Van Hee et al., 2018). The dataset was manually annotated using binary labels. We also use the dataset by Riloff et al. (2013), which is manually annotated for sarcasm. Finally, we use the dataset by Ptáček et al. (2014), who collected a user self-annotated corpus of tweets with the *#sarcasm* hashtag.

Reddit: Khodak et al. (2017) collected SARC, a corpus comprising of 600.000 sarcastic comments on Reddit. We use main subset, *SARC 2.0,*

Reference	Dataset	Train	Valid	Test	Total	Source
Van Hee et al., 2018	SemEval-2018	3,067	306	784	3,834	Twitter
Ptáček et al., 2014	Ptáček	48,007	6,858	13,717	68,582	Twitter
Riloff et al., 2013	Riloff	1,327	189	381	1,897	Twitter
Khodak et al., 2017	SARC 2.0	205,665	51,417	64,666	321,748	Reddit
Khodak et al., 2017	SARC 2.0 pol	10,934	2,734	3,406	17,074	Reddit
Oraby et al., 2016	SC-V1	1,396	199	400	1,995	Dialogues
Oraby et al., 2016	SC-V2	3,284	469	939	4,692	Dialogues

Table 1: Benchmark datasets: Tweets, Reddit posts and online debates for sarcasm and irony detection.

and the political subset, *SARC 2.0 pol.*

Online Dialogues: We utilize the *Sarcasm Corpus V1* (SC-V1) and the *Sarcasm Corpus V2* (SC-V2), which are subsets of the Internet Argument Corpus (IAC). Compared to other datasets in our selection, these differ mainly in text length and structure complexity (Oraby et al., 2016).

In Table 1, we see a notable difference in terms of size among the Twitter datasets. Given this circumstance, and in light of the findings by Van Hee et al. (2018), we are interested in studying how the addition of external soft-annotated data impacts on the performance. Thus, in addition to the datasets introduced before, we use two corpora for augmentation purposes. The first dataset was collected using the Twitter API, targeting tweets with the hashtags *#sarcasm* or *#irony*, resulting on a total of 180,000 and 45,000 tweets respectively. On the other hand, to obtain non-sarcastic and non-ironic tweets, we relied on the SemEval 2018 Task 1 dataset (Mohammad et al., 2018). To augment each dataset with our external data, we first filter out tweets that are not in English using language guessing systems. We later extract all the hashtags in each target dataset and proceed to augment only using those external tweets that contain any of these hashtags. This allows us to, for each class, add a total of 36,835 tweets for the Ptáček corpus, 8,095 for the Riloff corpus and 26,168 for the SemEval-2018 corpus.

In terms of pre-processing, as in our case the preservation of morphological structures is crucial, the amount of normalization is minimal. Concretely, we forgo stemming or lemmatizing, punctuation removal and lowercasing. We limit ourselves to replacing user mentions and URLs with one generic token respectively. In the case of the SemEval-2018 dataset, an additional step was to remove the hashtags *#sarcasm*, *#irony* and *#not*, as they are the artifacts used for creating the dataset.

For tokenizing, we use a variation of the Twokenizer (Gimpel et al., 2011) to better deal with emojis.

Our models are trained using Adam with a learning rate of 0.001 and a decay rate of 0.5 when there is no improvement on the accuracy on the validation set, which we use to select the best models. We also experimented using a slanted triangular learning rate scheme, which was shown by Howard and Ruder (2018) to deliver excellent results on several tasks, but in practice we did not obtain significant differences. We experimented with batch sizes of 16, 32 and 64, and dropouts ranging from 0.1 to 0.5. The size of the LSTM hidden layer was fixed to 1,024, based on our preliminary experiments. We do not train the ELMo embeddings, but allow their dropouts to be active during training.

5 Results

Table 2 summarizes our results. For each dataset, the top row denotes our baseline and the second row shows our best comparable model. Rows with FULL models denote our best single model trained with all the development available data, without any other preprocessing other than mentioned in the previous section. In the case of the Twitter datasets, rows indicated as AUG refer to our the models trained using the augmented version of the corresponding datasets.

For the case of the SemEval-2018 dataset we use the best performing model from the Shared Task as a baseline, taken from the task description paper (Van Hee et al., 2018). As the winning system is a voting-based ensemble of 10 models, for comparison, we report results using an equivalent setting. For the Riloff, Ptáček, SC-V1 and SC-V2 datasets, our baseline models are taken directly from Tay et al. (2018). As their pre-processing includes truncating sentence lengths at 40 and 80

Dataset		Model	Accuracy	Precision	Recall	F1-Score
Twitter	SemEval-2018	Wu et al. (2018)	**0.735**	0.630	**0.801**	**0.705**
		ELMo-BiLSTM	0.708	**0.696**	0.697	0.696
		ELMo-BiLSTM-FULL	0.702	0.689	0.689	0.689
		ELMo-BiLSTM-AUG	0.658	0.651	0.657	0.651
	Riloff	Tay et al. (2018)	0.823	0.738	0.732	0.732
		ELMo-BiLSTM	0.842	0.759	**0.750**	**0.759**
		ELMo-BiLSTM-FULL	**0.858**	**0.778**	0.735	0.753
		ELMo-BiLSTM-AUG	0.798	0.684	0.708	0.694
	Ptáček	Tay et al. (2018)	0.864	0.861	0.858	0.860
		ELMo-BiLSTM	**0.876**	0.868	0.869	0.869
		ELMo-BiLSTM-FULL	0.872	**0.872**	**0.872**	**0.872**
		ELMo-BiLSTM-AUG	0.859	0.859	0.858	0.859
Dialog	SC-V1	Tay et al. (2018)	0.632	0.639	0.637	0.632
		ELMo-BiLSTM	**0.646**	**0.650**	**0.646**	**0.644**
		ELMo-BiLSTM-FULL	0.633	0.633	0.633	0.633
	SC-V2	Tay et al. (2018)	0.729	0.729	0.729	0.728
		ELMo-BiLSTM	0.748	0.748	0.747	0.747
		ELMo-BiLSTM-FULL	**0.760**	**0.760**	**0.760**	**0.760**
Reddit	SARC 2.0	Khodak et al. (2017)	0.758	-	-	-
		ELMo-BiLSTM	**0.773**	-	-	-
		ELMo-BiLSTM-FULL	0.702	0.760	0.760	0.760
	SARC 2.0 pol	Khodak et al. (2017)	0.765	-	-	-
		ELMo-BiLSTM	**0.785**	-	-	-
		ELMo-BiLSTM-FULL	0.720	0.720	0.720	0.720

Table 2: Summary of our obtained results.

tokens for the Twitter and Dialog datasets respectively, while always removing examples with less than 5 tokens, we replicate those steps and report our results under these settings. Finally, for the Reddit datasets, our baselines are taken from Khodak et al. (2017). Although their models are trained for binary classification, instead of reporting the performance in terms of standard classification evaluation metrics, their proposed evaluation task is predicting which of two given statements that share the same context is sarcastic, with performance measured solely by accuracy. We follow this and report our results.

In summary, we see our introduced models are able to outperform all previously proposed methods for all metrics, except for the SemEval-2018 best system. Although our approach yields higher Precision, it is not able to reach the given Recall and F1-Score. We note that in terms of single-model architectures, our setting offers increased performance compared to Wu et al. (2018) and their obtained F1-score of 0.674. Moreover, our system does so without requiring external features or multi-task learning. For the other tasks we are able to outperform Tay et al. (2018) without requiring any kind of intra-attention. This shows

the effectiveness of using pre-trained character-based word representations, that allow us to recover many of the morpho-syntactic cues that tend to denote irony and sarcasm.

Finally, our experiments showed that enlarging existing Twitter datasets by adding external soft-labeled data from the same media source does not yield improvements in the overall performance. This complies with the observations made by Van Hee et al. (2018). Since we have designed our augmentation tactics to maximize the overlap in terms of topic, we believe the soft-annotated nature of the additional data we have used is the reason that keeps the model from improving further.

6 Conclusions

We have presented a deep learning model based on character-level word representations obtained from ELMo. It is able to obtain the state of the art in sarcasm and irony detection in 6 out of 7 datasets derived from 3 different data sources. Our results also showed that the model does not benefit from using additional soft-labeled data in any of the three tested Twitter datasets, showing that manually-annotated data may be needed in order to improve the performance in this way.

References

S. K. Bharti, B. Vachha, R. K. Pradhan, K. S. Babu, and S. K. Jena. 2016. Sarcastic sentiment detection in tweets streamed in real time: a big data approach. *Digital Communications and Networks*, 2(3):108–121.

Santosh Kumar Bharti, Korra Sathya Babu, and Sanjay Kumar Jena. 2015. Parsing-based Sarcasm Sentiment Recognition in Twitter Data. *Proceedings of the 2015 IEEE/ACM International Conference on Advances in Social Networks Analysis and Mining 2015 - ASONAM '15*, pages 1373–1380.

Pranali Chaudhari and Chaitali Chandankhede. 2017. Literature Survey of Sarcasm Detection. pages 2041–2046.

Ciprian Chelba, Tomas Mikolov, Mike Schuster, Qi Ge, Thorsten Brants, Phillipp Koehn, and Tony Robinson. 2014. One billion word benchmark for measuring progress in statistical language modeling. *Proceedings of the Annual Conference of the International Speech Communication Association, INTERSPEECH*, pages 2635–2639.

Elena Filatova. 2012. Irony and Sarcasm: Corpus Generation and Analysis Using Crowdsourcing. *Lrec*, pages 392–398.

Kevin Gimpel, Nathan Schneider, Brendan O'Connor, Dipanjan Das, Daniel Mills, Jacob Eisenstein, Michael Heilman, Dani Yogatama, Jeffrey Flanigan, and Noah A. Smith. 2011. Part-of-speech tagging for twitter: Annotation, features, and experiments. In *Proceedings of the 49th Annual Meeting of the Association for Computational Linguistics: Human Language Technologies*, pages 42–47, Portland, Oregon, USA. Association for Computational Linguistics.

H. Paul Grice. 1975. Logic and Conversation. In Peter Cole and Jerry L. Morgan, editors, *Syntax and Semantics*, volume 3, pages 41–58. Academic Press, New York.

Jeremy Howard and Sebastian Ruder. 2018. Universal language model fine-tuning for text classification. In *Proceedings of the 56th Annual Meeting of the Association for Computational Linguistics (Volume 1: Long Papers)*, pages 328–339. Association for Computational Linguistics.

Aditya Joshi, Pushpak Bhattacharyya, and Mark James Carman. 2016. Automatic Sarcasm Detection: A Survey. 50(5).

Aditya Joshi, Vinita Sharma, and Pushpak Bhattacharyya. 2015. Harnessing Context Incongruity for Sarcasm Detection. *Proceedings of the 53rd Annual Meeting of the Association for Computational Linguistics and the 7th International Joint Conference on Natural Language Processing (Short Papers)*, 51(4):757–762.

Mikhail Khodak, Nikunj Saunshi, and Kiran Vodrahalli. 2017. A Large Self-Annotated Corpus for Sarcasm.

Florian Kunneman, Christine Liebrecht, Margotvan Mulken, and Antalvan den Bosch. 2015. Signalling sarcasm : From hyperbole to hashtag. *Information Processing & Management*.

Joan Lucariello. 1994. Situational Irony: A Concept of Events Gone Awry. *Journal of Experimental Psychology: General*, 123(2):129–145.

Saif M. Mohammad, Felipe Bravo-Marquez, Salameh Mohammad, and Svetlana Kiritchenko. 2018. SemEval-2018 Task 1 : Affect in Tweets. In *Proceedings of the 12th International Workshop on Semantic Evaluation (SemEval-2018)*, pages 1–17.

Shereen Oraby, Vrindavan Harrison, Lena Reed, Ernesto Hernandez, Ellen Riloff, and Marilyn Walker. 2016. Creating and Characterizing a Diverse Corpus of Sarcasm in Dialogue. *Proceedings of the 17th Annual Meeting of the Special Interest Group on Discourse and Dialogue*, (September):31–41.

Bo Pang and Lillian Lee. 2006. Opinion Mining and Sentiment Analysis. *Foundations and Trends in Information Retrieval*, 1(2):91–231.

Matthew E. Peters, Mark Neumann, Mohit Iyyer, Matt Gardner, Christopher Clark, Kenton Lee, and Luke Zettlemoyer. 2018. Deep contextualized word representations.

Tomáš Ptáček, Ivan Habernal, and Jun Hong. 2014. Sarcasm Detection on Czech and English Twitter. *Proceedings of the 25th International Conference on Computational Linguistics: Technical Papers (COLING 2014), Citeseer*, pages 213–223.

Antonio Reyes, Paolo Rosso, and Tony Veale. 2013. A multidimensional approach for detecting irony in Twitter. *Language Resources and Evaluation*, 47(1):239–268.

Ellen Riloff, Ashequl Qadir, Prafulla Surve, Lalindra De Silva, Nathan Gilbert, and Ruihong Huang. 2013. Sarcasm as Contrast between a Positive Sentiment and Negative Situation. *Emnlp*, (Emnlp):704–714.

Cameron Shelley. 2001. The bicoherence theory of situational irony. *Cognitive Science*, 25(5):775–818.

Yi Tay, Anh Tuan Luu, , Siu Cheung Hui, and Jian Su. 2018. Reasoning with sarcasm by reading in-between. In *Proceedings of the 56th Annual Meeting of the Association for Computational Linguistics (Volume 1: Long Papers)*, pages 1010–1020. Association for Computational Linguistics.

Piyoros Tungthamthiti, Kiyoaki Shirai, and Masnizah Mohd. 2010. Recognition of Sarcasm in Microblogging Based on Sentiment Analysis and Coherence

Identification. *Journal of Natural Language Processing*, 23(5):383–405.

Cynthia Van Hee, Els Lefever, and Veronique Hoste. 2018. SemEval-2018 Task 3: Irony Detection in English Tweets. *Proceedings of the 12th International Workshop on Semantic Evaluation (SemEval-2018)*, pages 39–50.

Tony Veale. 2016. Fracking Sarcasm using Neural Network Fracking Sarcasm using Neural Network. *Acl*, (May):161–169.

Byron C. Wallace. 2015. Computational irony: A survey and new perspectives. *Artificial Intelligence Review*, 43(4):467–483.

Chuhan Wu, Fangzhao Wu, Sixing Wu, Junxin Liu, Zhigang Yuan, and Yongfeng Huang. 2018. THU NGN at SemEval-2018 Task 3 : Tweet Irony Detection with Densely THU NGN at SemEval-2018 Task 3 : Tweet Irony Detection with Densely Connected LSTM and Multi-task Learning. (March):51–56.

Meishan Zhang, Yue Zhang, and Guohong Fu. 2016. Tweet sarcasm detection using deep neural network. In *Proceedings of COLING 2016, the 26th International Conference on Computational Linguistics: Technical Papers*, pages 2449–2460. The COLING 2016 Organizing Committee.

Implicit Subjective and Sentimental Usages in Multi-sense Word Embeddings

Yuqi Sun [1]   Haoyue Shi [1,*]   Junfeng Hu[1,2,†]

1: School of EECS, Peking University, Beijing, China
2: MOE Key Lab of Computational Linguistics, School of EECS, Peking University
{sun_yq, hyshi, hujf}@pku.edu.cn

Abstract

In multi-sense word embeddings, contextual variations in corpus may cause a univocal word to be embedded into different sense vectors. Shi et al. (2016) show that this kind of *pseudo multi-senses* can be eliminated by linear transformations. In this paper, we show that *pseudo multi-senses* may come from a uniform and meaningful phenomenon such as subjective and sentimental usage, though they are seemingly redundant.

In this paper, we present an unsupervised algorithm to find a linear transformation which can minimize the transformed distance of a group of sense pairs. The major shrinking direction of this transformation is found to be related with subjective shift. Therefore, we can not only eliminate *pseudo multi-senses* in multi-sense embeddings, but also identify these subjective senses and tag the subjective and sentimental usage of words in the corpus automatically.

1   Introduction

Multi-sense word embeddings are popular choices to represent polysemous words (Reisinger and Mooney, 2010; Huang et al., 2012; Neelakantan et al., 2014; Cheng and Kartsaklis, 2015; Lee and Chen, 2017). These methods learn senses of words automatically by clustering contexts they appear in. However, contextual variation in corpus may cause a univocal word be embedded into different senses (Shi et al., 2016). For example, the context of "another" in this sentence is normal and narrative:

> "South Trust, another large bank headquartered in Birmingham, was acquired by Wachovia in 2004."

---

*Now at Toyota Technological Institute at Chicago, freda@ttic.edu.

† Corresponding author.

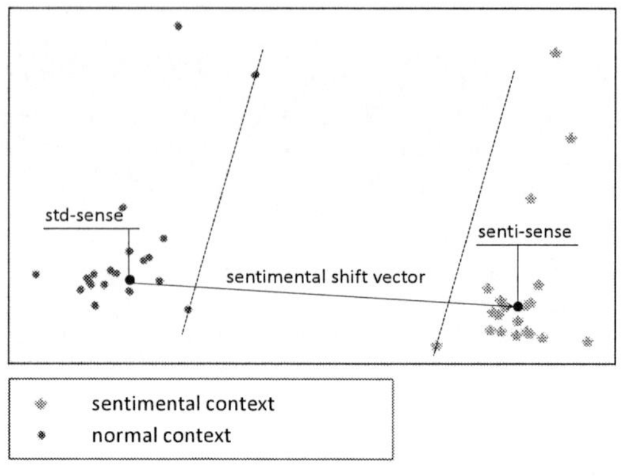

Figure 1: The relation between sentimental sense (senti-sense) and normal sense (std-sense) of a word. The vector differences are considered as sentimental shift vectors.

In the second sentence, the word "another" locates in subjective and emotional context with intense feelings:

> "He committed suicide after the woman he loved married another man."

The word "another" in these two sentences have the same meaning, but they are often embedded into two different senses by existing multi-sense word embedding models.

Shi et al. (2016) used linear transformation to eliminate the vector differences between corresponding sense pairs with the same meaning, and improved the performance on downstream tasks such as contextual word similarity (Huang et al., 2012). Such pairs were called *pseudo multi-sense pairs*. However, they did not give any explicit explanation of the eliminated vector difference in a pseudo multi-sense pair.

In this paper, we propose to explain the so-called pseudo multi-senses by slightly modifying

Proceedings of the 9th Workshop on Computational Approaches to Subjectivity, Sentiment and Social Media Analysis, pages 8–13
Brussels, Belgium, October 31, 2018. ©2018 Association for Computational Linguistics
https://doi.org/10.18653/v1/P17

the linear transformation proposed by Shi et al. (2016). We find that a large number of pseudo multi-senses can be viewed as pairs of i) a normal sense and ii) a subjective or sentimental sense. In addition, as shown in Figure 1, a group of words may have similar normal-subjective/sentimental difference vector, indicating subjectivity and sentiment are general sources of pseudo multi-senses.

In the first step of our approach, we identify the multi-sense pairs that are generated by an uniform contextual variation. Then we regress a linear transformation which can minimize the average Euclidean distance between two opposite groups in embedding space. We analyze the major shrinking directions in the embedding space *w.r.t.* the linear transformation, and find it consistent that one of such directions is relevant to subjective and sentimental usage.

The motivation of our approach is that a group of pseudo multi-senses is often generated systematically, *i.e.*, pseudo multi-senses in the same group come from the same reason. Therefore, a linear transformation that eliminate the shift and minimize distance between senses may reflect a salient language phenomenon. In addition to giving explicit explanation to pseudo multi-senses, experimental results also show that our approach can contribute to some NLP tasks such as subjective and sentimental analysis.

In Section 2, we introduce some related work. In Section 3, we present a method to mine a linear transformation that eliminates *semantic shift* generating *'pseudo multi-senses'*. In Section 4, we analyze the language phenomenon represented and eliminated by that linear transformation, namely subjective and sentimental usage, and do some evaluations on the subjective shift. Finally in Section 6 we draw conclusions and propose future work left to be done.

2 Related Work

Subjectivity and sentiment analysis have been investigated by many researches with different methods(Turney, 2002; Wiebe, 2000; Pang and Lee, 2004, 2008; Liu, 2010; Cambria et al., 2013; Maas et al., 2011; Lin and He, 2009; Abdul-Mageed et al., 2014; Dasgupta and Ng, 2009; Pak and Paroubek, 2010). Many works contribute to language resources for subjectivity and sentimental analysis. (Baccianella et al., 2010) Recent works also provide many training methods to per-

fect the language models' performance on benchmark datasets (Kouloumpis et al., 2011; Maas et al., 2011; Taboada et al., 2011; Wang and Manning, 2012; Labutov and Lipson, 2013; Lan et al., 2016; Ren et al., 2016; Tang et al., 2016). Our work provides a unsupervised method of subjectivity analysis based on multi-sense word embedding.

Multi-sense word embedding is also a popular way to represent polysemous words(Reisinger and Mooney, 2010; Huang et al., 2012; Neelakantan et al., 2014; Guo et al., 2014; Li and Jurafsky, 2015; Iacobacci et al., 2015; Cheng and Kartsaklis, 2015; Lee and Chen, 2017). However, these method using contextual difference for sense clustering to decide senses are so sensitive to contextual variation and usage of word, therefore may embed a single sense into several vectors. We aim to mine such contextual variations. While supervised methods rely on external knowledge with manually definition of senses(Chen et al., 2014; Cao et al., 2017).

Singular value decomposition is used on latent semantic indexing by factorizing a term-document matrix and constructing a "semantic space"(Deerwester et al., 1990). We use a similar approach to extract language phenomena we mine.

3 Methodology

The general framework of our method includes the following four steps:

1. We start with random selected "pseudo multi-senses" as initial seeds, training a linear transformation to minimize transformed distance of these sense pairs.

   Let M denote the transformation matrix and (x, y) denote a vector pair of pseudo multi-sense. Define the set of pairs sharing a uniform *semantic shift* as $\mathbf{P}$. Ideally, we expect M to transform x closer to y and keep y unmoved for all $(x, y) \in \mathbf{P}$. Therefore we derive the following loss function:

$$\mathcal{L}(M) = \sum_{(x,y) \in \mathbf{P}} \|Mx - y\|_2^2 + \|My - y\|_2^2$$

2. Update pseudo multi-senses iteratively *w.r.t.* the loss function.

According to the hypothesis that a systematical contextual variation may generate a group of pseudo multi-senses, the linear transformation that eliminate this variation can be used to pick out most typical pseudo multi-senses. We define *shrinking rate*, which reveals the degree of a pair of senses being combined by transformation M:

$$\rho_M(\boldsymbol{x}, \boldsymbol{y}) = \frac{\|M\boldsymbol{x} - M\boldsymbol{y}\|_2}{\|\boldsymbol{x} - \boldsymbol{y}\|_2} \quad (1)$$

The smaller $\rho_M(\boldsymbol{x}, \boldsymbol{y})$ is, the more likely $(\boldsymbol{x}, \boldsymbol{y})$ are generated by this contextual variation. Thus we optimize the set of pseudo multi-senses, and use it to retrain transformation matrix. This algorithm can eventually converge to an optimal solution.

3. Extract eigen-directions of linear transformation M with a singular value decomposition algorithm.

   The major shrinking directions are semantic directions shrunk and eliminated by the linear transformation. If there exists an obvious explanation of such directions, they can be viewed as the representative directions for specific language phenomena (*e.g.*, subjective or sentimental usage) in the embedding space.

4. Observe KNN of major shrinking directional vectors so as to reveal the language phenomena corresponding to contextual variations.

The pseudo code of this procedure is shown in Algorithm 1.

4 Intuitive Results

Our experiments are based on the multi-sense skip-gram(MSSG) model (Neelakantan et al., 2014) and Wikipedia Corpus, training a 50-dimensional multi-sense embedding space.

With this method, we train a linear transformation with random seeds. Results show that transformation will converge to a stable point, which verifies the existence of systematical contextual variation in corpus.

Furthermore, to understand the language phenomena that generate *'pseudo' mutli-senses*, we observe nearest neighbours of eigen-directional vectors. We find each eigen-direction is meaningful. The eigenvalues of these eigen-directions are

---

Algorithm 1 Train a transformation matrix.

Require: The multi-sense embedding space V; Set of random selected sense pairs, S_0; Loss function, $\mathcal{L}(M)$; Shrinking rate function $\rho_M(\boldsymbol{x}, \boldsymbol{y})$; Size of word set k.

Ensure: Transformation matrix, M; Set of candidate sense pairs, S

1: Initialize S with S_0
2: **while** not converged **do**
3:   Train transformation matrix M by minimizing $\mathcal{L}(M)$ using gradient descent algorithm
4:   Choose the k-most shrunk pairs as S
5: **end while**
6: **return**M, S

---

subj-vec's KNN	feelings, song, strange, love, everything, emotional, never,something, girlfriend, always, eyes, smell, dialogue, smile, really, movie, sounds, things, sexual, mind, script
Reversed *subj-vec*'s KNN	regional, administrative, township, located, racial, lies, avenue, virginia, approximately, historic, register, pennsylvania, municipality, served, delaware, situated, politician, operates, terminus, unincorporated

Table 1: Top 20 KNN for *subj-vec* are shown in '*subj-vec*'s KNN'. Top 20 KNN for reversed *subj-vec* are shown in 'Reversed *subj-vec*'s KNN'.

expansion multipliers of these dimensions. Therefore the eigen-direction with smallest eigenvalue represents the most salient language phenomenon. Interestingly, nearest neighbours are words about sentiments and emotions. Under our observation, this major shrinking directional vector is likely to be the vector representing subjective usage. We denote this vector as *subj-vec*. The KNN of *subj-vec* is shown in Table 1.

Therefore we found that the subjective usage of words is a salient language phenomenon in multi-sense embedding space. Interestingly, we also observe that the reversed direction of *subj-vec* is related to some regional and political topics, which is matched with human intuition.

5 Evaluations

5.1 Sentence Classification

We take subjectivity and sentiment analysis tasks to evaluate the function of *subj-vec*.

We take two text classification tasks: SUBJ

(Pang and Lee, 2004), a subjectivity status detection task and MPQA (Wiebe et al., 2005), an opinion polarity classification task. We use the LR(logistic regression) classifier and sentence level features to do the classification tasks. We use word/sense embedding as encoder, and decide the sense of every instance by Equation2 .

$$Sense(C(w)) = \underset{sense}{\arg\max} \ cos(V_{context}, V_{sense}) \quad (2)$$

We express the sentence-level features with contextual vector, denoted as *context-vec*, which is the sum of sense embeddings in a sentence. We provide four groups of evaluation results with different encoders:

1. *context-vec* with original embeddings.

2. *context-vec* with the embedding space whose subjective direction is stretched. We stretch subjective direction by Equation 3, in which embedding of a sense s is denoted as $v(s)$, and embedding in the stretched space is denoted as $v'(s)$.

$$v'(s) = v(s) + v(s) \cdot subj\text{-}vec * subj\text{-}vec \quad (3)$$

In Equation 3, *subj-vec* is the directional vector of subjective usage. Each embedding is added by a bias in subjective direction.

3. *context-vec* with the embedding space whose subjective direction is eliminated by Equation 4.

$$v'(s) = v(s) - v(s) \cdot subj\text{-}vec * subj\text{-}vec \quad (4)$$

4. *context-vec* + *context-vec* · *subj-vec* * *subj-vec*. We extract information about subjective usage by combining *context-vec* and the dot product of *context-vec* and *subj-vec* of every sentence.

The results are shown in Table 2.

Obviously subjective direction of embedding space improves its performance on subjective and sentimental analysis. Such improvement doesn't appear on single-sense embeddings. Meanwhile eliminating subjective direction worsen the performances on every listed tasks.

Li and Jurafsky (2015) argued that multi-senses word embedding does not outperform single-sense word embedding in several language tasks. In fact, we found by add features on the sentimental dimension, multi-sense embeddings can achieve better performance on subjectivity and sentimental analysis tasks.

Sense Space	SUBJ-multi	SUBJ-single
Original Space	88.36	**88.73**
Subj-Stretched	88.39	88.72
Subj-Eliminated	87.22	88.35
Context + Subj	**88.4**	88.73

Sense Space	MPQA-multi	MPQA-single
Original Space	82.05	**82.73**
Subj-Stretched	82.07	82.23
Subj-Eliminated	81.79	82.13
Context + Subj	**83.05**	82.29

Table 2: The performance of the original MSSG50D on Wiki Corpus embeddings(Original Space), the sentimental-stretched space('Subj-stretched'), the sentimental-eliminated space('Subj-eliminated') and the original contextual vector in combination with its projection on sentimental direction('Context + Subj') on text classification tests including MPQA (Wiebe et al., 2005), an opinion polarity classification task, and SUBJ (Pang and Lee, 2004), a subjectivity detection task. We use equation 2 to decide the sense of every instance.

words	KNN
science	astronomy, psychology, librarianship, research, anthropology, sciences, parapsychology, literature
+*subj-vec*	science, **literature**, journalism, parapsychology, **photography**, **filmmaking**, literary, **graphic**, writing
fight	fights, duel, fighting, confrontation, battling, surprise, revenge, vengeance, foe
+ *subj-vec*	**revenge**, fights, confrontation, vengeance, **furious**, grodd, surprise, **vicious**, **infuriated**
rich	cultivated, lush, cultivating, shady, landscapes, growing, alfalfa, abundance, herb, landscape
+ *subj-vec*	**delight**, **shady**, **good**, riches, immensely, arth, **charm**, curious, little-known, **wonderful**
country	nation, scandinavia, europe, america, countries, turkey, uk, sweden, internationally, ireland
+*subj-vec*	nation, clubbers, **welcome**, coming, **enjoying**, **mam**, wigwam, **pride**, europe, americ

Table 3: KNN for words before and after adding a subjective bias.

5.2 Analogies

Moreover, since *subj-vec* represents subjective usage, we add it to some embeddings in multi-sense embedding space to observe the effect of *subj-vec* on semantic shift. Table 3 illustrates the KNN for the original words and the words with a subjective bias. The table shows that by adding subjective *subj-vec*, the subjective and sentimental properties for words are changed. In general, more emotional and subjective words appear in the KNNs of the new location. This is another interesting property of *subj-vec*.

6 Conclusions And Future Work

In this article we propose a methodology to represent language phenomena such as subjective usage by a uniform bias vector of sense pairs, and provide an unsupervised approach to mine it. We also use evaluations to explore its functions and find *subj-vec* can relatively improve multi-sense embeddings performance on subjective and sentimental analysis tasks. Furthermore, there are many linguistic phenomena left to be mined.

Acknowledgements

We thank the anonymous reviewers for their valuable feedback. This work is supported by National Natural Science Foundation of China (61472017).

References

Muhammad Abdul-Mageed, Mona Diab, and Sandra Kübler. 2014. Samar: Subjectivity and Sentiment Analysis for Arabic Social Media. *Computer Speech & Language*.

Stefano Baccianella, Andrea Esuli, and Fabrizio Sebastiani. 2010. Sentiwordnet 3.0: An Enhanced Lexical Resource for Sentiment Analysis and Opinion Mining. In *Proc. of LREC*.

Erik Cambria, Bjorn Schuller, Yunqing Xia, and Catherine Havasi. 2013. New Avenues in Opinion Mining and Sentiment Analysis. *IEEE Intelligent Systems*.

Yixin Cao, Lifu Huang, Heng Ji, Xu Chen, and Juanzi Li. 2017. Bridge Text and Knowledge by Learning Multi-prototype Entity Mention Embedding. In *Proc. of ACL*.

Xinxiong Chen, Zhiyuan Liu, and Maosong Sun. 2014. A Unified Model for Word Sense Representation and Disambiguation. In *Proc. of EMNLP*.

Jianpeng Cheng and Dimitri Kartsaklis. 2015. Syntax-aware multi-sense word embeddings for deep compositional models of meaning. *arXiv preprint arXiv:1508.02354*.

Sajib Dasgupta and Vincent Ng. 2009. Mine the Easy, Classify the Hard: a Semi-supervised Approach to Automatic Sentiment Classification. In *Proc. of ACL-IJCNLP*.

Scott Deerwester, Susan T. Dumais, George W Furnas, Thomas K Landauer, and Richard Harshman. 1990. Indexing by latent semantic analysis. *Journal of the American society for information science*.

Jiang Guo, Wanxiang Che, Haifeng Wang, and Ting Liu. 2014. Learning Sense-Specific Word Embeddings by Exploiting Bilingual Resources. In *Proc. of COLING*.

Eric H. Huang, Richard Socher, Christopher D. Manning, and Andrew Y. Ng. 2012. Improving Word Representations via Global Context and Multiple word Prototypes. In *Proc. of ACL*.

Ignacio Iacobacci, Mohammad Taher Pilehvar, and Roberto Navigli. 2015. Sensembed: Learning Sense Embeddings for Word and Relational Similarity. In *Proc. of ACL-IJCNLP*.

Efthymios Kouloumpis, Theresa Wilson, and Johanna D Moore. 2011. Twitter Sentiment Analysis: The Good the Bad and the OMG! In *Proc. of the AAAI Conference on Weblogs and Social Media*.

Igor Labutov and Hod Lipson. 2013. Re-embedding Words. In *Proc. of ACL*.

Man Lan, Zhihua Zhang, Yue Lu, and Ju Wu. 2016. Three convolutional neural network-based models for learning sentiment word vectors towards sentiment analysis. In *Proc. of IJCNN*.

Guang-He Lee and Yun-Nung Chen. 2017. MUSE: Modularizing Unsupervised Sense Embeddings. In *Proc. of EMNLP*.

Jiwei Li and Dan Jurafsky. 2015. Do Multi-sense Embeddings Improve Natural Language Understanding? In *Proc. of EMNLP*.

Chenghua Lin and Yulan He. 2009. Joint Sentiment/Topic Model for Sentiment Analysis. In *Proc. of CIKM*.

Bing Liu. 2010. Sentiment Analysis and Subjectivity. *Handbook of Natural Language Processing*.

Andrew L. Maas, Raymond E. Daly, Peter T. Pham, Dan Huang, Andrew Y. Ng, and Christopher Potts. 2011. Learning word vectors for sentiment analysis. In *Proc. of ACL*.

Arvind Neelakantan, Jeevan Shankar, Alexandre Passos, and Andrew McCallum. 2014. Efficient Non-parametric Estimation of Multiple Embeddings per Word in Vector Space. In *Proc. of EMNLP*.

Alexander Pak and Patrick Paroubek. 2010. Twitter as a Corpus for Sentiment Analysis and Opinion Mining. In *Proc. of LREC*.

Bo Pang and Lillian Lee. 2004. A Sentimental Education: Sentiment Analysis using Subjectivity Summarization based on Minimum Cuts. In *Proc. of ACL*.

Bo Pang and Lillian Lee. 2008. *Opinion Mining and Sentiment Analysis*. Now Publishers, Inc.

Joseph Reisinger and Raymond J Mooney. 2010. Multi-prototype Vector-Space Models of Word Meaning. In *Proc. of NAACL-HLT*.

Yafeng Ren, Yue Zhang, Meishan Zhang, and Donghong Ji. 2016. Improving Twitter Sentiment Classification using Topic-Enriched Multi-Prototype Word Embeddings. In *AAAI*, pages 3038–3044.

Haoyue Shi, Caihua Li, and Junfeng Hu. 2016. Real multi-sense or pseudo multi-sense: An approach to improve word representation. *Proc. of the Workshop on Computational Linguistics for Linguistic Complexity*.

Maite Taboada, Julian Brooke, Milan Tofiloski, Kimberly Voll, and Manfred Stede. 2011. Lexicon-based Methods for Sentiment Analysis. *Computational Linguistics*.

Duyu Tang, Furu Wei, Bing Qin, Nan Yang, Ting Liu, and Ming Zhou. 2016. Sentiment embeddings with applications to sentiment analysis. *IEEE Trans. on Knowledge and Data Engineering*.

Peter D. Turney. 2002. Thumbs Up or Thumbs Down?: Semantic Orientation applied to unsupervised classification of reviews. In *Proc. of ACL*.

Sida Wang and Christopher D Manning. 2012. Baselines and Bigrams: Simple, Good Sentiment and Topic Classification. In *Proc. of ACL*.

Janyce Wiebe. 2000. Learning Subjective Adjectives from Corpora. In *Proc. of AAAI*.

Janyce Wiebe, Theresa Wilson, and Claire Cardie. 2005. Annotating Expressions of Opinions and Emotions in Language. *Language Resource and Evaluation*.

Language Independent Sentiment Analysis with Sentiment-Specific Word Embeddings

Carl Saroufim, Akram Almatarky, Mohamed Abdel Hady
Microsoft Corporation, Redmond WA
{casarouf, akrgab, mohabdel}@microsoft.com

Abstract

Data annotation is a critical step to train a text model but it is tedious, expensive and time-consuming. We present a language independent method to train a sentiment polarity model with limited amount of manually-labeled data. Word embeddings such as Word2Vec are efficient at incorporating semantic and syntactic properties of words, yielding good results for document classification. However, these embeddings might map words with opposite polarities, to vectors close to each other. We train Sentiment Specific Word Embeddings (SSWE) on top of an unsupervised Word2Vec model, using either Recurrent Neural Networks (RNN) or Convolutional Neural Networks (CNN) on data auto-labeled as "Positive" or "Negative". For this task, we rely on the universality of emojis and emoticons to auto-label a large number of French tweets using a small set of positive and negative emojis and emoticons. Finally, we apply a transfer learning approach to refine the network weights with a small-size manually-labeled training data set. Experiments are conducted to evaluate the performance of this approach on French sentiment classification using benchmark data sets from SemEval 2016 competition. We were able to achieve a performance improvement by using SSWE over Word2Vec. We also used a graph-based approach for label propagation to auto-generate a sentiment lexicon.

1 Introduction

Text sentiment analysis is defined as the computational study of documents, sentences or phrases (aspect level), to detect opinions, sentiments, emotions, etc. It is particularly useful for companies to collect feedback about their products, analyze the public opinion about their brand, for political parties to monitor the population support, etc. Document-level sentiment analysis corresponds to assigning an overall sentiment polarity to a document. It can be formulated as a two-class classification problem: positive or negative, excluding the neutral case of documents with no polarity (Zhang et al., 2018).

For this task, both supervised and unsupervised learning approaches have been used. Supervised learning methods typically use bag-of-words (which ignores word orders and semantics and suffers from high dimensionality and sparsity), or, more recently, word embeddings, which requires unsupervised training on a big corpus of data. It provides a mapping of words to dense vectors of fixed length, encoding semantic and syntactic properties of those words. The document can then be represented by the average embedding vector of the words it contains. Language-dependent features such as Part of Speech, grammatical analysis, lexicons of opinions and emotions have also been applied successfully (Zhang et al., 2018).

While the use of standard word embedding techniques such as Word2Vec (Mikolov et al., 2013) or C&W (Collobert et al., 2011) can enhance the performance of prediction models and perform well on general classification task, sentiment is not properly encoded in those vectors. According to Tang (2014), words such as "good" and "bad" might be close in the embeddings space, although they have opposite polarities, because of similar usage and grammatical rules. We show in this paper that training Sentiment Specific Word Embeddings (SSWE) by updating an initial Word2Vec model trained on a big corpus of tweets provides better word embeddings for the task of sentiment classification. SSWE training is performed by updating word embeddings as part of a supervised deep learning framework, by training a model on sentiment-labeled data. Through backpropagation, the weights of the Embedding Layer will be adjusted and incorporate sentiment. At the end of the training, the embedding matrix can be extracted from the model and will be used

14

Proceedings of the 9th Workshop on Computational Approaches to Subjectivity, Sentiment and Social Media Analysis, pages 14–23
Brussels, Belgium, October 31, 2018. ©2018 Association for Computational Linguistics
https://doi.org/10.18653/v1/P17

to featurize words and documents. As a result, this process needs a big amount of data labeled with "Positive" and "Negative". While labeled data sets and sentiment lexicons exist in English and can be used to label a big number of documents to build the SSWE (e.g. SentiWordNet or ANEW in English as lexicons), they are scarce in other languages (Pak and Paroubek, 2011). Hence the need to find a systematic way of labeling a big number of documents without any language knowledge, then let prediction models "learn" from them.

One way to do it, is to rely on a universal opinion lexicon that would hold true in any language. With the rise of social media, the widespread use of emojis[1] provide us with such a tool. In particular, Twitter is one of the biggest online social media where users post over 500 million "tweets" every day, with a frequent use of emojis[2]. A tweet is a short (up to 140 characters) user-generated text, typically noisy and written in a very casual language.

By accessing and querying a big number of tweets of a specific language and which have specific emojis, we can auto-label them based on the polarity of those emojis. The assumption is that if emojis are found in a tweet, then it expresses a sentiment (ie. it is not neutral) which has the same polarity as the emoji. This method is called distant-supervised learning and has been applied successfully in several similar scenarios (Pak and Paroubek, 2011; Tang et al., 2014; Narr et al., 2012).

In this paper, we focus on French, assuming no language knowledge. The SSWE we get through the described methodology is then used to featurize documents when training a prediction model on a new French data set for sentiment analysis. The major contributions of the work presented in this paper are:

- We develop SSWE models by updating Word2Vec embeddings trained on tweets, through supervised learning with Recurrent Neural Networks (RNN) and Convolutional Neural Networks (CNN), on a big data set of tweets auto-labeled through emojis.

- We show that SSWE perform better than the underlying Word2Vec embeddings, even

on data sets different and much less noisy than tweets. SSWE trained with auto-labeled tweets from which the emojis were removed, improve the sentiment prediction on data sets that have no or little emojis.

- We show that transfer learning starting with the deep learning model used to train the SSWE performs better than training a new traditional ML prediction model from scratch and using SSWE as features.

In Section 2, we present a literature review. In Section 3, we present the methodology used to auto-label tweets, train a Word2Vec model and update it into SSWE. Section 4 describes the experiment we conducted and discusses results. Finally, in section 5 we summarize our results and present directions for future work.

2 Related Work

We present here a brief review of previous work for sentiment classification. Most early research follows Pang (2002) who uses bag of words and one-hot-encoding to represent words in movie reviews, using linguistic features and various classifiers. Work by Pang (2008), and Owoputi (2013) focused on the features for learning and their effectiveness, such as part-of-speech, syntax, negation handling and topic-oriented features. Mohammad (2013), achieved the best results for the sentiment classification task of the SemEval competition by using sentiment lexicons and hand-crafted rules. Gamon (2004) investigated the sentiment analysis task on noisy data collected from customer feedback surveys, using lexical (lemmatized n-gram) and linguistic features (part-of-speech tagging, context free phrase structure patterns, transitivity of a predicate, tense information etc.). They also tried feature reduction and applied SVM model for classification.

Another approach for features representation is to use low-dimensional real-valued vectors (word embeddings) to represent the words, such as Word2Vec or C&W. Maas (2011) proposed the use of probabilistic document models with a sentiment predictor function for each word. Bespalov (2012) relied on latent semantic analysis to initialize embeddings. Labutov (2013) relies on pre-trained word embeddings which are re-embedded in a supervised task using labeled data by performing unconstrained optimization of a convex objective.

---

[1]In this paper, we will use the word "emojis" to refer to both "emojis" and "emoticons".

[2]Twitter statistics: `http://www.internetlivestats.com/twitter-statistics`

Tang (2014) proposed to update word embeddings specifically for sentiment classification, arguing that words with opposite polarities might end up being neighbors. They learn word embeddings from a massive number of tweets collected by a distant-supervised way based on the existence of positive and negative emojis. They propose a sentiment-specific word embedding (SSWE) model that is a modification of C&W to predict not just the lexical form (n-gram) but also the sentiment of the word in that context. They were able to produce comparable results to the top system (rule-based) in the SemEval 2013 competition.

Ren (2016) extended the work of Tang (2014), arguing that the topic information of a tweet affects the sentiment of its words. They modified the learning objective of the C&W model to also incorporate the sentiment information as well as the topic distribution provided by LDA models. They also tackle the problem of word polysemy (words that have multiple meanings based on their context) by creating context representation for each word occurrence (environment vector) and cluster these vectors into ten groups using k-means algorithm. The words get their meaning by their distance to the centroids of the clusters. Finally, they train a CNN for sentiment classification.

In terms of classification models, with the regained interest in deep learning, recent work shifted to the use of RNNs. These networks process every element of a sequence in a way depending of all previous computations, keeping track of previous information across the sequence. In particular, LSTM (Long Short-Term Memory) can learn long-term dependencies and is thus popular for sentiment classification of sentences. Gugilla (2016) uses both LSTM and CNN with Word2Vec and linguistic embeddings to distinguish between neutral and sentiment documents. Qian (2017) uses LSTM with linguistic resources such as sentiment lexicon, negation and intensity words, to help identify the sentiment effect in sentences. Xu (2016) proposed the use of cached LSTM model to further enhance the capabilities of LSTM to capture the global semantic features and the local semantic features for long text sentiment classification.

For Twitter sentiment classification using distant supervision, while some research used lexicon-based approaches with positive and negative sentiment words (Taboada et al., 2011; Thel-

	# Raw Tweets (in M)	# Tweets cleaned (in M)	% Positive in cleaned
April 18	4,14	2,62	51.29
May 18	3,89	2,44	49.20
June 18	2,83	1,76	50.94
Total	10,86	6,82	50.43

Table 1: Characteristics of the auto-labeled tweets used in this paper.

wall et al., 2012), other studies leveraged emojis for distant supervision (Pak and Paroubek, 2011; Zhao et al., 2012). To ensure repeatability of experiments in many languages without any language knowledge, we will also take this direction even though it means we are neglecting precious language-dependent features that would have increased the prediction power of our models.

3 SSWE Training

3.1 Auto-Labeled Tweets and Preprocessing

Having access to a big database of tweets, we first queried three months of French tweets: April, May and June 2018 (partial). Only tweets containing one or more of a specified list of emojis are considered, but all emojis in a tweet should have the same polarity (confusing tweets are discarded). This polarity will correspond to the label of the tweet. For example, :) is a positive emoji, while :(is negative. To avoid dealing with class imbalance, we downsample the majority class to get a 1:1 ratio of positive to negative auto-labeled tweets.

We perform the following operations on the auto-labeled tweets (**Preprocessing 0**). Using regular expression (Regex), we remove "RT" (corresponding to Retweets), "@" and name mentions, tweet links and duplicate tweets. We also separate emojis when there is no space between them. Otherwise, multiple stacked emojis would be seen as one word instead of a succession of emojis by standard open-source tokenizers. Finally, we replace emojis involving punctuation by "Emoji_01", "Emoji_02", etc. Otherwise, standard tokenizers would separate punctuation marks and break emojis. For example: ":P" would be tokenized into [":", "P"].

Figures 1 and 2 respectively show the positive and negative emojis used for auto-labeling.

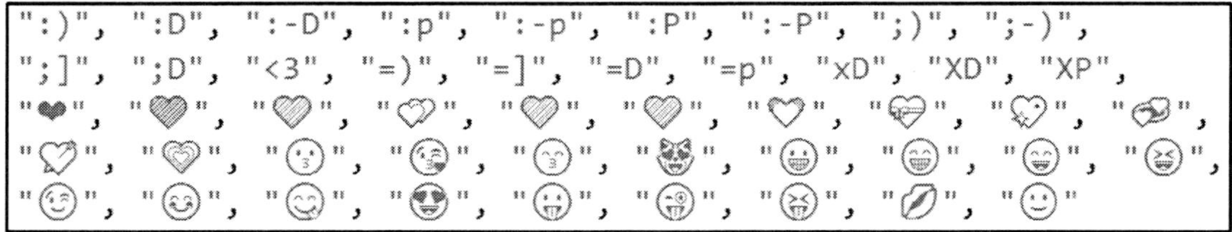

Figure 1: List of positive emojis used for auto-labeling.

Figure 2: List of negative emojis used for auto-labeling.

Table 1 summarizes statistics about the cleaned data sets.

We explored two additional preprocessing methods to study their impact on sentiment prediction.

- **Preprocessing A**: Remove emojis after auto-annotation to avoid biasing the prediction models into classifying mostly based on emojis.

- **Preprocessing B**: Replace every occurrence of three or more successive characters into two of them.

The reasoning behind **Preprocessing B** is as follows: since tweets contain casual language, users sometimes repeat the same character many times to stress out an emotion. For example, the word "aime" could appear as "aime", "aiime", "aiiime", "aiiiiiime", etc. As a result, the number of features will increase when using ngrams, and the dictionary size of word embeddings would also increase. This would dilute the word embeddings because the same word would be considered as different ones which will carry a lower weight than the case where all words with repetitions are assumed to be one. Assuming that when the letter is repeated 2 or more times, the number of repetitions is random and expresses the same meaning, we experiment with replacing any occurrence of two or more successive characters with two occurrences.

3.2 Word2Vec Model Training

Twitter sentiment classification has traditionally been conducted through machine learning models using labor intensive features. A less labor-intensive feature engineering approach has been to rely on word embeddings such as Word2Vec, which incorporates syntactic context of words. After preprocessing the autolabeled tweets, we trained two Word2Vec models on them in an unsupervised way. One where only standard preprocessing is applied to autolabeled data (**Preprocessing 0**), and the second on autolabeled data where characters repetitions above three are removed (**Preprocessing B**). Note that since the autolabeled data is divided in three files, and to avoid loading all the tweets in-memory at once, Word2Vec is trained incrementally on the three files.

3.3 Sentiment Specific Word Embeddings Training

While Word2Vec typically performs well on general classification tasks, it might not be effective enough for sentiment classification because it ignores word sentiments. Hence the need to update the trained Word2Vec embeddings to incorporate sentiment. We train a deep learning network (either RNN or CNN) using first an Embedding layer, initialized with the trained Word2Vec embeddings. During training on the autolabeled tweets, network weights, including word embeddings, are updated. At the end of training, we extract the embedding matrix: it has the same vocabulary as the original Word2Vec, but weights now incorporate sentiment information. We call this embedding matrix a "Sentiment Specific Word Embeddings" (SSWE) (Tang et al., 2014). The assumption to test is if indeed, SSWE used as features would perform better than Word2Vec for the task of sentiment analysis.

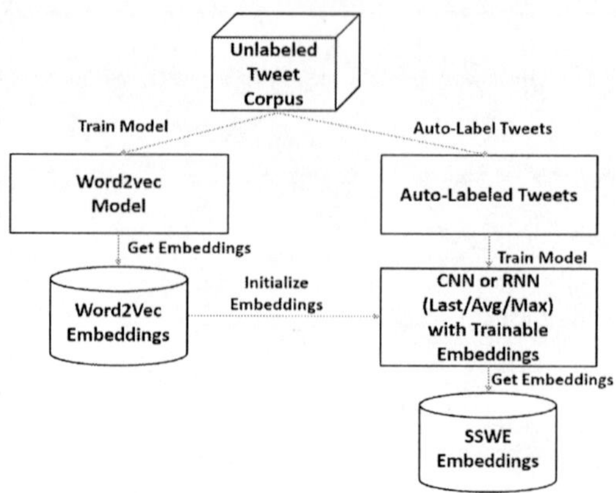

Figure 3: Methodology used to train the SSWE.

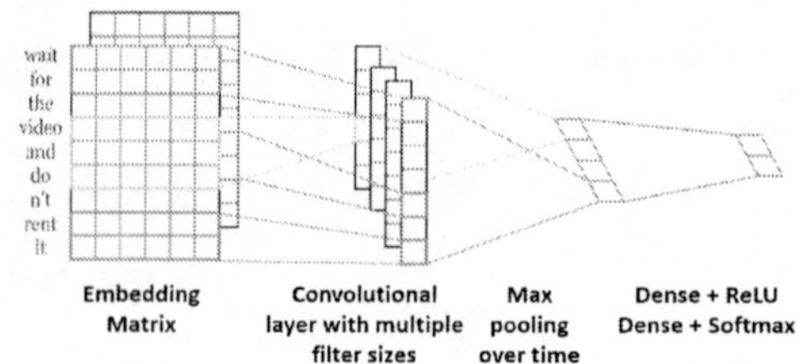

Figure 4: CNN architecture.

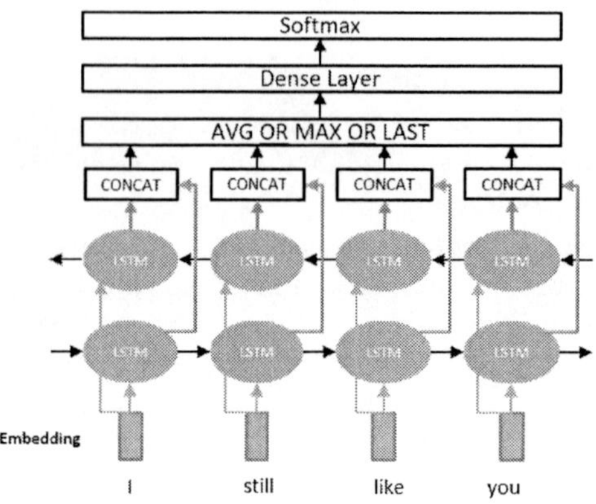

Figure 5: RNN architecture.

We trained four different types of models:

- SSWE_C trained using a CNN structure (three parallel convolutional layers and global max pooling, then dense layer with ReLu, then dense layer with softmax).

- SSWE_R, SSWE_R_avg, and SSWE_R_max trained using an RNN structure (two bidirectional LSTM from which respectively the last output, average of outputs or max of outputs goes through a dense layer with softmax).

After performing **Preprocessing A**, we can train four additional models by removing emojis from the autolabeled data when updating the embeddings of Word2Vec. Note that in this case, emojis still have embeddings but they are not updated during the training of SSWE in order to avoid biasing the weights into relying mostly on emojis.

After performing **Preprocessing B**, we can get an additional eight models by using the apropriate trained Word2Vec (without character repetitions).

Note that since the auto-labeled data is divided in three files, and to avoid loading all the tweets in memory at once, SSWE is trained incrementally on the three files. For each one, we used three epochs and a batch size of 500.

Figure 3 summarizes the methodology used to train the SSWE.

Figure 4[3] and Figure 5 summarize the architectures of the deep learning models used.

3.4 Graph-Based Label Propagation

We used the method introduced by Hamilton (2016) to create a dictionary of positive and negative words from Word2Vec embeddings in an unsupervised way. The idea revolves around building word embeddings (the paper uses Vector Space Model instead of Word2Vec), then creating a graph of words connected to their k-nearest neighbors in the embeddings space with edges weighted by the cosine similarity. Using a short list of "seed words" for positive and negative polarities, sentiment is propagated through the network through a random walk method. This idea was implemented by Hamilton et al. in a Python package called SENTPROP.

We use emojis as seed words and Word2Vec trained on tweets from which we only kept a specific short set of positive and negative emojis (so the focus is on actual words that are neighbors to the seed emojis instead of other emojis).

4 Experiments and Results

4.1 Setup

We conduct experiments to evaluate the validity of using SSWE over Word2Vec for French sentiment classification. In addition to the auto-labeled tweets, four manually labeled French data sets were used. The first three data sets come from the SemEval 2016 competition (International Workshop on Semantic Evaluation). It is an ongoing series of evaluations of computational semantic analysis systems, organized under the umbrella of SIGLEX, the Special Interest Group on the Lexicon of the Association for Computational Linguistics. The first data set (Train) corresponds to French Restaurant Reviews. The two others correspond to French Restaurant Reviews (Test1; i.e. Same domain as the training set) and French Museum Reviews (Test2). The latter being out-of-domain, it is a good gauge of how generalizable a model trained on the training set is to different French data sets. Those three data sets have been labeled for Aspect Based Sentiment Analysis. It is the task of mining and summarizing opinions from text about specific entities and their aspects (Apidianaki et al., 2016) they are annotated with relevant entities, aspects and polarity values. In order to use those three data sets in the context of document level sentiment classification, we ungrouped documents into sentences, then filtered them:

- We reject the sentences with mixed polarity values.

- We keep the rest of the sentences and label them as "Positive" if all polarity values are positive and as "Negative" if all polarity values are negative.

Note that we were not able to download all the reviews as some of them were not available anymore[4]. The fourth data set is comprised of manually labeled French tweets that are not publicly available (Test3). These tweets do not contain emojis, and thus the performance on this data set will solely rely on the understanding that our trained models will have of the French language. The four French data sets (after processing) and their characteristics are summarized in Table 2. We can see that they are all relatively well-balanced, so no special treatment for class imbalance will be performed.

<hr>

[4]The data can be downloaded from `http://alt.qcri.org/semeval2016/task5/index.php?id=data-and-tools`

Data Set	Naming	# Doc	% Positive
SemEval 2016 Restaurant Train	Train	1338	47.80
SemEval 2016 Restaurant Test	Test1	515	47.60
SemEval 2016 Museum Test	Test2	529	54.25
Tweets Manually Labeled	Test3	3296	48.90

Table 2: Characteristics of the training and testing sets used.

4.2 Experiments

The experiments conducted and their results are summarized in Table 3.

In order to establish the importance of the SSWE for sentiment analysis, we trained multiple models using standard features (word ngrams, character ngrams) or more advanced features (Word2Vec, SSWE: average sentence embedding) with standard classifiers (logistic regression (LR), SVM, Random Forest) or deep learning frameworks (CNN or RNN with transfer learning on the data set Train), then evaluated them on Test1, Test2, and Test3. More precisely, we used the following approaches as baselines, training a Logistic Regression (LR), SVM and Random Forest with word and character ngrams, Word2Vec, or both (experiments 1-3).

The three baselines were compared to four methods using SSWE trained with either RNN (taking the last output of the recurrent sequence) or CNN trained on the auto-labeled data and used for feature extraction on Train. We compared the performance with SSWE trained on auto-labeled data cleaned from the emojis to prevent the model from giving a high weight to emojis (experiments 4-7).

We compared those approaches with the use of average or maximum of the output sequences of the RNN (trained on auto-labeled data without emoji, then used for feature engineering on Train) (experiments 8-9).

We then add the character and ngrams features (experiments 10-15).

Finally, we compared them with deep learning and transfer learning. Keeping the same network that was used to train the SSWE, we fix the SSWE and let the last layer(s) be trainable on Train. For the RNN, the dense layer and softmax are trainable. For the CNN, training only the dense layer and softmax as part of transfer learning yields poor results, so we train the dense layer and ReLu as well as the last dense layer and softmax during transfer learning. The reason why transfer learning is used instead of direct training on Train is the lack of data: Train having only 1338 unique documents, this is not enough to tune a deep learning model which has a much larger number of parameters. (experiments 16-21)

We also explored two additional methods that do not require any knowledge of the language and that will be detailed in subsequent sections:

1) using a dictionary auto-built by label propagation using specific emoji seeds on the Word2Vec model (experiments 22-24).

2) repeating the experiment on data for which two or more repetitions of characters are replaced with two characters.

All approaches with Logistic Regression, SVM or Random Forest used the Scikit-Learn Python package. Word2Vec models were built using genism, while SSWE and deep learning frameworks used Keras with Tensorflow backend.

4.3   Evaluation Methods

For models trained with Logistic Regression, SVM and Random Forest, we decided to report and compare only results obtained with Logistic Regression for fair comparison. The reported results correspond to those achieved with a set of parameters giving the best results on part of the training set, through sweeping. The parameters that were swept on in Logistic Regression are: size of word ngrams, size of character ngrams, lowercasing of words, maximum number of iterations for the 'lbfgs' solver, inverse of regularization strength for 'l2' penalty. For models trained with Deep Learning, multiple combinations of epochs and batch sizes were used, and we report here the best results obtained.

While F-score and Accuracy (since there is no class imbalance) can be fair ways of evaluating the performance, we decided to rely mainly on the AUC (Area under the Curve) since it is independent of the classification threshold choice and is a good indicator of the ability of the models to distinguish between Positive and Negative examples.

4.4   Results and Analysis

With Logistic Regression, using only ngram features (1) give the worse results on Test2 and Test3. This is probably because ngrams obtained on a specific training set fail to general-

	Features	Test1	Test2	Test3
	LOGISTIC REGRESSION			
1	ngram	86.27	75.36	72.49
2	Word2Vec	86.03	79.00	86.75
3	ngram + Word2Vec	90.18	83.3	86.71
4	SSWE_R_last	86.11	79.25	84.28
5	SSWE_R_last_no_emoji	87.86	83.12	86.52
6	SSWE_C	85.34	78.91	83.72
7	SSWE_C_no_emoji	89.15	83.59	87.83
8	SSWE_R_avg_no_emoji	88.01	83.07	87.17
9	SSWE_R_max_no_emoji	86.29	82.49	85.40
10	ngram + SSWE_R_last	89.86	83.10	85.06
11	ngram + SSWE_R_last_no_emoji	90.79	84.72	85.82
12	ngram + SSWE_C	89.05	83.62	84.24
13	ngram + SSWE_C_no_emoji	**91.42**	**85.67**	**87.50**
14	ngram + SSWE_R_avg_no_emoji	90.84	84.53	86.90
15	ngram + SSWE_R_max_no_emoji	91.20	85.75	87.37
	TRANSFER LEARNING			
16	SSWE_R_last	90.17	84.2	83.89
17	SSWE_R_last_no_emoji	**92.78**	**91.02**	**90.59**
18	SSWE_C	81.31	76.87	79.91
19	SSWE_C_no_emoji	89.97	87.65	89.27
20	SSWE_R_avg_no_emoji	91.86	90.71	90.03
21	SSWE_R_max_no_emoji	91.61	91.13	90.34
	WITH DICTIONARY (Dict)			
22	Dict	63.52	63.86	64.85
23	LR + ngram + Dict	88.95	76.97	77.73
24	LR + ngram + Dict + SSWE_C_no_emoji	91.21	85.73	87.38

Table 3: Experiments Results with Logistic Regression, Transfer Learning and Dictionary Lookup in terms of AUC (in %).

ize well to out-of-domain data sets (Test2 and Test3). Using Word2Vec only (2) is slightly worse on Test1 but generalizes better on out-of-domain data sets. Using both Word2Vec and ngram (3) considerably improves the results compared to (1) and (2), showing the importance of Word2Vec in adding context information in word features, which ngram does not. This will be the main baseline to compare to the use of SSWE.

We notice that SSWE trained on the auto-labeled data where emojis were kept (4), (6), yields results similar or slightly lower than using Word2Vec only (2). The same comparison holds when we add ngrams: (10) and (12) vs. (3). This is probably because the labels of the auto-labeled data are directly correlated to specific positive and negative emojis since they were used for autolabeling. As a result, training SSWE on the auto-labeled data without removing emojis likely biased the embeddings into giving higher weights to emojis. Since all the test sets have little to no emojis, the use of these SSWE yields poor results.

SSWE trained on auto-labeled data cleaned from the emojis (without ngrams) in (5), (7), (8) and (9) provides similar or better performance than Word2Vec only (2). Adding ngrams to these SSWE in (11), (13), (14) and (15) gives the best results with Logistic Regression compared to the best baseline (3). While beating the performance of (3) on Test3 seems hard (likely due to the fact that Word2Vec was trained on data similar to Test3 since they are both tweets), ngrams and SSWE trained as part of a CNN model on auto-labeled data without emojis (13) gives on average the best results on the three data sets when using Logistic Regression, compared to (3): 1.34%, 2.37%, and 0.79% improvement on Test1, Test2, Test3 respectively. These results already confirm that SSWE improves the prediction performance in sentiment analysis over Word2Vec, likely because it incorporates sentiment polarity.

These results were even more confirmed with deep learning. SSWE trained on auto-labeled data with emojis also perform less good than their counterpart trained without emojis: (16) vs. (17) and (18) vs. (19). The best results are obtained on average across the three test sets when transfer learning is applied with the RNN, using the last output from the bidirectional LSTM. Compared to the best baseline (3), we achieve: 2.6%, 7.72%, and 3.88% improvement on Test1, Test2, Test3 respectively.

We also used the scores of the auto-generated dictionary with a 0.5 threshold to assign a polarity to the words. We then classify the documents by comparing the distribution of negative and positive words. This gave worse results than ngram with logistic regression ((1) vs. (22)). We also used the word scores to create a dictionary with 10 labels: if the word has a score between 0 and 0.1, it is assigned to the sentiment_bin_1 class; between 0.1 and 0.2, it is assigned to sentiment_bin_2, etc. The distribution among those ten classes is then used as an additional feature in our experiments with logistic regression. However, this feature does not improve the results((1) vs. (23) and (13) vs. (24)).

Finally, we did not notice an improvement when removing repetition of characters above three. This might be explained by the fact that character repetition can be important for emphasis: the same word with more character repetitions might have a higher polarity. For example, "heureuxxxxx" might show more excitement and be "more positive" than "heureuxx".

4.5 Discussion

Given those results, multiple conclusions can be drawn:

- Word2Vec boosts performance of ngrams, especially on out-of-domain testing set.

- SSWE trained on data autolabeled with emojis and where emojis were not removed, negatively impacts the performance of the model on data that have little or no emojis.

- SSWE trained on data autolabeled with emojis and where emojis were removed, provides an improvement over Word2Vec.

- Transfer Learning in deep learning by fixing the network structure (including SSWE trained without emojis) on the training set, yields the best improvements over the baseline with an increase of more than 7% AUC on Test2 for example. This is the most noticeable when using RNN and taking the last output of the bidirectional LSTM sequence.

5 Conclusion and Future Work

In this paper, we propose to label a big number of tweets in any language (here French) using a small set of positive and negative emojis, train a Word2Vec model on the tweets, then update the embeddings through deep learning with bidirectional LSTM on the autolabeled data. The embeddings we get are then enriched with sentiment information and can be used as features for new data sets in the same language. If those data sets have little or no emoji, the embeddings enrichment should be performed using autolabeled data filtered from emojis in order to avoid biasing the embeddings and relying mostly on emojis. We show that these sentiment specific word embeddings perform better than plain Word2Vec using SemEval 2016 French data of restaurant reviews (Train) to train a model, another SemEval 2016 testing set of restaurant reviews (Test1), another of museum reviews (Test2) and a manually labeled data set of French tweets (Test3). It provides an AUC improvement of 1.34%, 2.37%, and 0.79% on Test1, Test2, Test3 respectively with Logistic Regression. The improvement gets to 2.6%,

7.72%, and 3.88% with transfer learning using RNN with the network used to train the SSWE. This methodology can be applied to any language since it does not rely on linguistic features.

This work has a few limitations, which could be better addressed in future work. This includes the use of sentiment lexicons, stemming, normalization, and negation handling. Our work did not explore the graph propagation technique with different embeddings models such as Vector Space Models. In addition, distant-supervised learning was applied on tweets to get labeled data and then train the SSWE. Tweets being written in a very casual language, the results on SemEval data (which is clean) might improve if the SSWE were trained on a more general data set. An area for future work would be to explore distant supervised learning on movie or product reviews, then compare the results with the created SSWE on SemEval data with those obtained using the Twitter SSWE. Finally, our work excludes the case of neutral text. We can specify two thresholds for the polarity prediction and assign a document to the neutral class when the model yields a predicted probability between those two thresholds. Another method is to train a subjectivity classifier followed by a polarity classifier for subjective documents.

References

Marianna Apidianaki, Xavier Tannier, and Cécile Richart. 2016. Datasets for aspect-based sentiment analysis in french. In *Proceedings of the Tenth International Conference on Language Resources and Evaluation (LREC 2016)*, Paris, France. European Language Resources Association (ELRA).

Dmitriy Bespalov, Yanjun Qi, Bing Bai, and Ali Shokoufandeh. 2012. Sentiment classification with supervised sequence embedding. In *Proceedings of the 2012 European Conference on Machine Learning and Knowledge Discovery in Databases - Volume Part I*, ECML PKDD'12, pages 159–174, Berlin, Heidelberg. Springer-Verlag.

Ronan Collobert, Jason Weston, Léon Bottou, Michael Karlen, Koray Kavukcuoglu, and Pavel P. Kuksa. 2011. Natural language processing (almost) from scratch. *CoRR*, abs/1103.0398.

Michael Gamon. 2004. Sentiment classification on customer feedback data: Noisy data, large feature vectors, and the role of linguistic analysis. In *Proceedings of the 20th International Conference on Computational Linguistics*, COLING '04, Stroudsburg, PA, USA. Association for Computational Linguistics.

Chinnappa Guggilla, Tristan Miller, and Iryna Gurevych. 2016. Cnn- and lstm-based claim classification in online user comments. In *COLING 2016, the 26th International Conference on Computational Linguistics: Technical Papers*, pages 2740–2751.

William L. Hamilton, Kevin Clark, Jure Leskovec, and Dan Jurafsky. 2016. Inducing domain-specific sentiment lexicons from unlabeled corpora. *CoRR*, abs/1606.02820.

Igor Labutov and Hod Lipson. 2013. Re-embedding words. In *Proceedings of the 51st Annual Meeting of the Association for Computational Linguistics*, pages 489–493.

Andrew L. Maas, Raymond E. Daly, Peter T. Pham, Dan Huang, Andrew Y. Ng, and Christopher Potts. 2011. Learning word vectors for sentiment analysis. In *Proceedings of the 49th Annual Meeting of the Association for Computational Linguistics: Human Language Technologies - Volume 1*, HLT '11, pages 142–150, Stroudsburg, PA, USA. Association for Computational Linguistics.

Tomas Mikolov, Ilya Sutskever, Kai Chen, Greg Corrado, and Jeffrey Dean. 2013. Distributed representations of words and phrases and their compositionality. *CoRR*, abs/1310.4546.

Saif M. Mohammad, Svetlana Kiritchenko, and Xiaodan Zhu. 2013. Nrc-canada: Building the state-of-the-art in sentiment analysis of tweets. *CoRR*, abs/1308.6242.

Sascha Narr, Michael Hulfenhaus, and Sahin Albayrak. 2012. Language-independent twitter sentiment analysis. *Knowledge discovery and machine learning (KDML), LWA*, pages 12–14.

Olutobi Owoputi, Brendan O'Connor, Chris Dyer, Kevin Gimpel, Nathan Schneider, and Noah A. Smith. 2013. Improved part-of-speech tagging for online conversational text with word clusters. In *Proceedings of the 2013 Conference of the North American Chapter of the Association for Computational Linguistics: Human Language Technologies*, pages 380–390. Association for Computational Linguistics.

Alexander Pak and Patrick Paroubek. 2011. Twitter for sentiment analysis: When language resources are not available. In *Proceedings of the 2011 22Nd International Workshop on Database and Expert Systems Applications*, DEXA '11, pages 111–115, Washington, DC, USA. IEEE Computer Society.

Bo Pang and Lillian Lee. 2008. Opinion mining and sentiment analysis. *Found. Trends Inf. Retr.*, 2(1-2):1–135.

Bo Pang, Lillian Lee, and Shivakumar Vaithyanathan. 2002. Thumbs up? sentiment classification using machine learning techniques. In *Proceedings of EMNLP*, pages 79–86.

Qiao Qian, Minlie Huang, Jinhao Lei, and Xiaoyan Zhu. 2017. Linguistically regularized lstm for sentiment classification. In *Proceedings of the Annual Meeting of the Association for Computational Linguistics (ACL 2017*.

Yafeng Ren, Yue Zhang, Meishan Zhang, and Donghong Ji. 2016. Improving twitter sentiment classification using topic-enriched multi-prototype word embeddings.

Maite Taboada, Julian Brooke, Milan Tofiloski, Kimberly D. Voll, and Manfred Stede. 2011. Lexicon-based methods for sentiment analysis. 37:267–307.

Duyu Tang, Furu Wei, Nan Yang, Ming Zhou, Ting Liu, and Bing Qin. 2014. Learning sentiment-specific word embedding for twitter sentiment classification. In *52nd Annual Meeting of the Association for Computational Linguistics, ACL 2014 - Proceedings of the Conference*, volume 1, pages 1555–1565.

Mike Thelwall, Kevan Buckley, and Georgios Paltoglou. 2012. Sentiment strength detection for the social web. *J. Am. Soc. Inf. Sci. Technol.*, 63(1):163–173.

Jiacheng Xu, Danlu Chen, Xipeng Qiu, and Xuanjing Huang. 2016. Cached long short-term memory neural networks for document-level sentiment classification. In *Proceedings of the 2016 Conference on Empirical Methods in Natural Language Processing*, pages 1660–1669. Association for Computational Linguistics.

Lei Zhang, Shuai Wang, and Bing Liu. 2018. Deep learning for sentiment analysis : A survey. *CoRR*, abs/1801.07883.

Jichang Zhao, Li Dong, Junjie Wu, and Ke Xu. 2012. Moodlens: An emoticon-based sentiment analysis system for chinese tweets. In *Proceedings of the 18th ACM SIGKDD International Conference on Knowledge Discovery and Data Mining*, KDD '12, pages 1528–1531, New York, NY, USA. ACM.

Creating a Dataset for Multilingual Fine-grained Emotion-detection Using Gamification-based Annotation

Emily Öhman   Kaisla Kajava   Jörg Tiedemann   Timo Honkela

University of Helsinki
firstname.lastname@helsinki.fi

Abstract

This paper introduces a gamified framework for fine-grained sentiment analysis and emotion detection. We present a flexible tool, *Sentimentator*, that can be used for efficient annotation based on crowd sourcing and a self-perpetuating gold standard. We also present a novel dataset with multi-dimensional annotations of emotions and sentiments in movie subtitles that enables research on sentiment preservation across languages and the creation of robust multilingual emotion detection tools. The tools and datasets are public and open-source and can easily be extended and applied for various purposes.

1 Introduction

Sentiment analysis and emotion detection is a crucial component in many practical applications but also defines a great challenge in natural language processing and artificial intelligence. Detecting emotions is crucial in human-computer interaction, and human behavior in communication is to a large degree affected by the emotional states that are created in a message. These states are typically fine-grained and fuzzy covering various dimensions of human feelings and attitudes. Nevertheless, it is often the practice to consider sentiments and emotions as very coarse and discrete features that can be detected with simple classifiers on a small scale of a few classes.

In our work, we focus on a high-dimensional model of emotions that allows a more natural and fine-grained classification and, furthermore, we tackle emotion detection in a multilingual setting. One of the biggest issues that stand in the way of creating reliable emotion detection algorithms is the lack of properly annotated datasets for training and testing purposes, especially in the case of the dimensionality that we consider and the multilingual support that we envision. This is the reason why we created *Sentimentator*, a new annotation tool that facilitates the efficient creation of appropriate datasets (Öhman and Kajava, 2018).

The main contribution of the paper is the framework based on a gamified environment that we develop to efficiently build large-scale resources. Our setup results in a *self-perpetuating* gold standard, which is initialized by seed sentences that are annotated by experts and augmented by crowd annotators. A combination of correlation-based scoring and ranking makes it possible to build datasets with weighted judgments based on the annotator confidence that we measure. Initial rankings are based on the comparison to seed annotation only but they will be adjusted dynamically once the correlation between crowd annotators allows to estimate further reliability scores. The main idea is that we can trust annotators that provide identical or at least similar judgments as other reliable annotators. With this scheme, we can move away from the use of limited seed sentences for confidence estimation to a more dynamic and self-perpetuating gold standard.

Another fundamental decision in our setup is the use of multilingual material on which to base our annotations. We are interested in the cross-lingual use of emotions and the development of multilingual classifiers (see Öhman et al., 2016). Therefore, we start with sentences extracted from movie subtitles (English originals in our case) for which we also have plenty of translations into a large number of languages. Movies contain a lot of emotional content and, as a side effect, it is interesting to see how that is reflected in subtitles and their translations.

Before presenting *Sentimentator* itself, we will first discuss related work and the theoretical framework we work with. The presentation of the seed/pilot dataset and its application for emotion detection follows the description of the tool and

Proceedings of the 9th Workshop on Computational Approaches to Subjectivity, Sentiment and Social Media Analysis, pages 24–30
Brussels, Belgium, October 31, 2018. ©2018 Association for Computational Linguistics
https://doi.org/10.18653/v1/P17

ends with a concluding discussion.

2 Related Work

Sentiment analysis is a widely studied task in natural language processing. Most of the existing datasets applied in sentiment analysis use binary or ternary annotation schemes (positive-negative, or positive, negative, and neutral) (Andreevskaia and Bergler, 2007), or some kind of combination of these (i.e. the addition of e.g. "mixed" (Saif et al., 2013)). This is not enough if the aim is to detect emotions rather than overarching sentiment (de Albornoz et al., 2012; Li and Hovy, 2017; Cambria et al., 2013). Furthermore, many of the existing datasets or tools (Munezero et al., 2015; Eryigit et al., 2013; Musat et al., 2012; Kakkonen and Kakkonen, 2011; Calefato et al., 2017; Saif et al., 2013; Abdul-Mageed and Ungar, 2017) are domain-dependent (often Twitter data) and/or document-level. Very few of these are also open data or open source.

An important questions is whether to show wider context or not. Boland et al. (2013) show that context can lead to the effect of double weighting for fine-grained annotations. For that reason, we also opted for the annotation of isolated sentences even though our tools would easily support other setups.

2.1 Crowd-sourcing Annotations

The annotation of datasets can be very costly and time consuming (Andreevskaia and Bergler, 2007; Devitt and Ahmad, 2008) if done by expert annotators. Crowd-sourcing can often be a cheaper alternative to hiring expert annotators, and has been used successfully by several researchers to create different types of datasets (Turney, 2002; Greenhill et al., 2014; Mohammad and Turney, 2013).

However, one issue with using non-experts to solicit annotations is that there is a risk of the quality suffering. Our solution to annotation-reliability related issues is gamification, which will be discussed in detail in section 3.

2.2 Theory of Emotion

The underlying theory of emotion for *Sentimentator* is Plutchik's theory of emotion (Plutchik, 1980). The eight core emotions he proposes are *anger*, *anticipation*, *disgust*, *fear*, *joy*, *sadness*, *surprise*, and *trust*. He uses a wheel, or flower, to illustrate these emotions. For a more intuitive

interface, we have inverted the wheel (see figure 1).

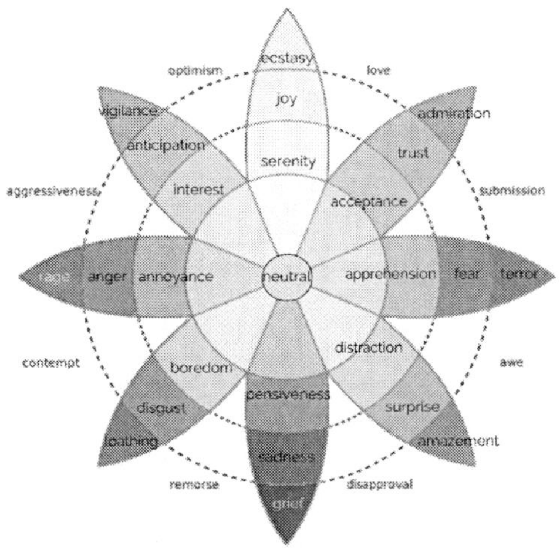

Figure 1: Inverted wheel of emotions

Although *Sentimentator* takes into account the intensity of the emotions, the complexity of the annotation task does not increase linearly with the number of classes this produces. It is possible to annotate for all 24+1 emotions, but only use the eight core emotions for classification, which was done very successfully by Abdul-Mageed and Ungar (2017).

Using Euclidean distance on the inverted wheel to calculate the similarity of annotations, we can see that annotations for *neutral* and low intensity emotions are in fact quite similar. This means we can avoid unnecessarily dismissing an annotation as noise, as might be the case if a more traditional interface was used where *neutral* was a separate category from low-intensity emotions.

2.3 Classification

Table 1 shows the accuracies achieved by a few other multidimensional approaches (generally those of Ekman (1971)) using various classification methods such as SVMs, neural networks, maximum entropy, Naïve Bayes, and k-Nearest Neighbor to name a few. When more classes are included in a model, accuracies achieved are typically lower than what binary or ternary models of sentiment analysis achieve (Purver and Battersby, 2012; Tokuhisa et al., 2008), with the exception of Abdul-Mageed and Ungar (2017) who apply a gated recurrent neural network model.

---

[1]Quoted in Purver and Battersby (2012)

Study	classes	accuracy
Go et al. (2009)	2	82.2-83%
Danisman and Alpkocak (2008)	6	32%
Chuang and Wu (2004)	6+1	56-74%
Chuang and Wu (2004)	6+1, audio	81.5%
Ansari 2010[1]	6	81%
Purver and Battersby (2012)	6	varies
Seol et al. (2008)	8	45-65%
Abdul-Mageed and Ungar (2017)	8	95.68%
Tokuhisa et al. (2008)	10	up to 80%
Abdul-Mageed and Ungar (2017)	24	87.58%

Table 1: Accuracies achieved by previous studies

Although the data and methods are different, it seems reasonable to expect accuracies between 30-70% depending on the category for an initial multiclass classification. Depending on the availability, we will try to apply our model to the same datasets that have been used in the studies listed in table 1 in order to directly compare results.

3 Gamifying the Annotation Platform

Our goal is to implement efficient crowd-sourcing through *gamification*. Gamification refers the use of game elements in environments that are not typically games (Deterding et al., 2011; Hamari and Koivisto, 2013). Previous research shows that one can achieve a high number of quality annotations by non-experts by using carefully considered gamified aspects such as (1) Relatedness (connected to other players), (2) Competence (mastering the game problems), and (3) Autonomy (control of own life) (Musat et al., 2012).

Robson et al. (2015) posits that gamification can change behavior by tapping into motivational drivers of human behavior: reinforcements and emotions. The emotions we want to elicit are of course enjoyment, but negative emotions such as disappointment can also increase commitment and a desire to increase one's competence. Similarly, both positive and negative reinforcements increase repetitive behavior in players (Robson et al., 2015).

Our platform offers players leaderboards and statistics about both their immediate and longterm progress (relatedness). Progress, rank and prestige are important measures that help players feel compensated for the work they are doing within the game (competence). Rank has an additional function in our platform; as we lack a gold standard against which to compare the annotations we receive, we use rank to determine noisy annotations and noisy annotators. Furthermore, the player can see how each of their choice affects their standing in the ranks.

The dataset that the experiments in this paper rely on is our validated seed sentences. These sentences will be used as a type of seeded gold standard. What this means is that annotators will annotate both non-seed sentences and seed sentences. They receive a score from their annotation based on similarity with gold annotations that determines their rank. In practice, rank is equivalent with confidence level. With enough participants, players will also be ranked according to how closely their annotations match those of high-ranked annotators. We, thus, have the option to include only the least noisy, highest quality annotations in our dataset.

In order to compare annotations, we map them on the inverted Plutchik's wheel we propose in Figure 1 projected on a standard two-dimensional space with coordinates $[x, y]$, where the least intense emotions are at the center and the most intense at the tips of the petals. The origin of our emotion space is located in the center of the wheel and represents the case of a neutral expression.

We can then calculate the distance $D(G_x, G_y)$ between any pair of points corresponding to emotion labels G_X and G_y by computing the Euclidean distance normalized by the maximum distance that can be observed between opposite emotions with maximum intensity. Assuming that geometric location expresses the relatedness of emotions, this distance metric takes into account all different types of similarities/dissimilarities between annotations, including labels that combine neighboring emotions.

The distance metric is the basis for the computation of annotation confidence C_x for new annotation G_x that we obtain. We define annotation confidence as

$$C_x = R_{annotator} * \frac{1}{N} \sum_{n=1}^{n} \left(1 - C_n * D(G_x, G_n)\right)$$

where $G_n \in \{G_1, .., G_N\}$ are annotations of the same instance (sentence) from the current gold standard with corresponding confidence scores $\{C_1, .., C_N\}$.[2] In other words, we add an averaged penalty for annotations that differ from existing gold annotations weighted by their confidence scores. Note that our seed annotations G_s obtain

---

[2] Note that we set $C_x = R_{annotator}$ if $N = 0$.

a perfect confidence $C_s = 1$. Another component of the confidence score is the rank of the annotator based on the score $R_{annotator}$. This score is initialized with one and will be updated by each submitted annotation. Currently, we use a simple average over annotation confidence scores of that particular annotator:

$$R_{annotator} = \frac{1}{M} \sum_{m=1}^{M} C_m$$

Our self-perpetuating gold standard with ranking-based confidence ratings will reduce the need for manual screening and will ensure that we can receive consistent emotion annotations with a measurable confidence attached to them.

4 Creating the Dataset

For the seed data, we used the following procedure: On completed expert annotation, another expert annotates the same sentences with the data order randomized. Ambiguous sentences were reviewed and the correct class was agreed upon. In some cases where no agreement could be reached the sentence was excluded from the seed dataset.

Our data collection will be unique in that it will provide a fine-grained multi-dimensional open source dataset for sentiment analysis and emotion detection in various languages. Annotation is on-going and the first real dataset will be available later in 2018. For now we have a set of sentences with validated annotations that we will use as our seed data to get the gamified annotation started. This dataset has already been used to investigate sentiment preservation in Finnish, French, and Italian (Kajava, 2018).

We wanted to make the dataset as useful as possible to as many researchers as possible from the beginning. This is why we selected an open parallel corpus, namely the OPUS movie subtitles corpus (Tiedemann, 2012; Lison and Tiedemann, 2016). From this collection, approximately 9,000 English sentences were annotated into the following emotion classes: *anger, anticipation, disgust, joy, fear, sadness, surprise,* and *trust*. This yielded a preliminary dataset of between 649 to 908 sentences per class (see table 4). For the classification experiments, we did not take into account the measure of emotion intensity that we introduce later in our annotation framework, which is also part of the seed sentence annotation.

	ang	ant	dis	fea	joy	sad	sur	tru	Total
train	816	739	775	615	876	633	583	737	5,774
test	92	84	87	70	99	72	66	83	653

Table 2: Emotion distribution in seed data

We also keep the metadata and therefore all sentences can be paired with a particular movie, genre, time period, as well as its counterpart in another language. This is valuable information for future research avenues.

We expect to have a full dataset by the end of the year as we will be collecting at least 100 000 annotations in September-October of 2018 from crowd annotators (students). Snow et al. (2008) suggest using four non-experts to match the quality of one expert annotator, however, gamification, seed sentences, and rank-validation means that fewer annotations per sentence might be sufficient using our platform. Inter-annotator agreement is on average around 70-90% depending on the type of annotation and who is doing the annotation work (expert vs. non-expert) (Nowak and Rüger, 2010), and this is where annotator agreement was for our data as well, varying between classes.

Based on initial timed annotations, a typical annotator can be expected to annotate up to 10 sentences per minute. This means that it only takes just over one hour to annotate around 600 sentences. If every annotator is asked to annotate 1000 sentences, this should not take more than a few hours each on average taking the learning curve into account. The students are encouraged to annotate in languages other than English as well, resulting in at least two or three separate datasets with an expected minimum of 40 000 annotations each. We currently have preliminary datasets for English, Italian, French, and Finnish.

5 Validation of the Data Quality

In order to test the quality of the data for the purpose of developing an automatic emotion detector we ran some initial experiments using our annotated seed data for training, and evaluating standard multi-class classifiers. The data was tokenized and lowercased as a preprocessing step. We selected Multinomial Naïve Bayes (NB) and Multilayer Perceptron (MLP) classifiers for our experiments. For the classifiers we use the scikit-learn (Pedregosa et al., 2011) machine learning toolkit. In both classification scenarios, the data was split into class-stratified training and test sets of 90%

and 10%, respectively.

The MLP network used in this work is a three-layer network. The model creates a lexicon from the dataset using a bag-of-words approach, employing it for extracting a set of features for each class. We use Adam for training the network and apply Rectified Linear Unit (ReLu) activiation functions in the hidden layers of feed-forward network.

Classifier	Accuracy
NB	0.5069
MLP	0.5023

Table 3: Overall classification accuracy

As can be seen in table 3, the baseline classifiers perform reasonably well for such a small data set and such a fine-grained task. Note that we did spend any time on optimizing features and hyper-parameters to obtain a better performance. The purpose of this study is entirely to test the feasibility of fine-grained classification and validity of our seed data.

In the confusion matrix for the best performing classifier (see Table 4), we can see that there is some significant confusion between anger and fear, between disgust and sadness and also surprisingly between trust and fear. These are the same classes that others have struggled to distinguish (e.g. (Purver and Battersby, 2012)), which is re-assuring that our data is in good shape. With this promising performance on our pilot data set (despite its limited size) we are encouraged to proceed with future experiments and the more fine-grained distinctions we propose that take intensity into account.

These experiments also demonstrate that the seed data is sufficient for initial classifications and that we can go ahead in developing our gamified strategy of getting more annotations based on correlations between annotators and their level of trust, which will initially be based on the comparison to the validated seed sentences.

6 Conclusions

In this paper, we present an open annotation tool for fine-grained emotion detection and a dataset of seed sentences that can be used to gamify the annotation efforts. The classification results show that the dataset is reliable enough to be used as seed sentences, indicating that gamification based

ang	ant	dis	fea	joy	sad	sur	tru	<- classified as
62	3	10	3	5	1	3	5	anger
9	**43**	6	1	5	1	5	14	anticipation
25	6	**29**	5	9	3	3	7	disgust
11	8	6	**20**	2	6	5	12	fear
2	4	5	1	**77**	2	3	5	joy
7	2	8	5	12	**30**	2	6	sadness
5	4	10	4	13	1	**25**	4	surprise
5	3	5	3	16	3	2	**45**	trust

Table 4: Confusion matrix for NB-based classification of the test set.

on the seed data is a viable option for compiling sentiment datasets, and that multidimensional classification yields acceptable results even with a small dataset. However, already with our limited validation experiments we can see that the choice of model and learning algorithm influences the quality of the resulting classifier. This is an important outcome that needs to be considered when designing tools with scarce resources. We will continue to monitor performance to measure the impact of gamification and cross-lingual transfer on classification performance.

7 Discussion and Future Work

As our system collects both coarse (ternary) sentiment annotations, and fine-grained emotion annotations, a future option could be to apply the successful approach demonstrated by Tokuhisa et al. (2008), and utilize the coarser sentiment polarity to pre-classify data before emotion classification, and then implement a k-nearest neighbors algorithm on the larger dataset. Our platform does not show context by default, however, it is easy to add the context of the target segment to be annotated if required for a different type of project.

It might be valuable to re-annotate parts of the data showing additional context to check the impact on annotation and annotator confidence. Tokuhisa et al. (2008) found that in their data, context-dependent samples were useful for training their classifier and yielded slightly higher accuracies than their non-context-dependent data. Finally, we will also consider models that make use of sentence-internal relations to improve the classification results. In particular, we will investigate the use of sequence models and gated recurrent networks as proposed by Abdul-Mageed and Ungar (2017).

References

Muhammad Abdul-Mageed and Lyle Ungar. 2017. Emonet: Fine-grained emotion detection with gated recurrent neural networks. In *Proceedings of the 55th Annual Meeting of the Association for Computational Linguistics (Volume 1: Long Papers)*, volume 1, pages 718–728.

Jorge Carrillo de Albornoz, Laura Plaza, and Pablo Gervás. 2012. Sentisense: An easily scalable concept-based affective lexicon for sentiment analysis.

Alina Andreevskaia and Sabine Bergler. 2007. Clac and clac-nb: Knowledge-based and corpus-based approaches to sentiment tagging. In *Proceedings of the 4th international workshop on semantic evaluations*, pages 117–120. Association for Computational Linguistics.

Katarina Boland, Andias Wira-Alam, and Reinhard Messerschmidt. 2013. Creating an annotated corpus for sentiment analysis of german product reviews.

Fabio Calefato, Filippo Lanubile, and Nicole Novielli. 2017. Emotxt: a toolkit for emotion recognition from text. *arXiv preprint arXiv:1708.03892*.

Erik Cambria, Björn Schuller, Yunqing Xia, and Catherine Havasi. 2013. New avenues in opinion mining and sentiment analysis. *IEEE Intelligent Systems*, 28(2):15–21.

Ze-Jing Chuang and Chung-Hsien Wu. 2004. Multimodal emotion recognition from speech and text. *International Journal of Computational Linguistics & Chinese Language Processing, Volume 9, Number 2, August 2004: Special Issue on New Trends of Speech and Language Processing*, 9(2):45–62.

Taner Danisman and Adil Alpkocak. 2008. Feeler: Emotion classification of text using vector space model. In *AISB 2008 Convention Communication, Interaction and Social Intelligence*, volume 1, page 53.

Sebastian Deterding, Miguel Sicart, Lennart Nacke, Kenton O'Hara, and Dan Dixon. 2011. Gamification. using game-design elements in non-gaming contexts. In *CHI'11 extended abstracts on human factors in computing systems*, pages 2425–2428. ACM.

Ann Devitt and Khurshid Ahmad. 2008. Sentiment analysis and the use of extrinsic datasets in evaluation. In *LREC*.

Paul Ekman. 1971. Universals and cultural differences in facial expressions of emotion. In *Nebraska symposium on motivation*. University of Nebraska Press.

Gülsen Eryigit, Fatih Samet Cetin, Meltem Yanik, Tanel Temel, and Ilyas Çiçekli. 2013. Turksent: A sentiment annotation tool for social media. In *LAW@ ACL*, pages 131–134.

Alec Go, Richa Bhayani, and Lei Huang. 2009. Twitter sentiment classification using distant supervision. *CS224N Project Report, Stanford*, 1(12).

Anita Greenhill, Kate Holmes, Chris Lintott, Brooke Simmons, Karen Masters, Joe Cox, and Gary Graham. 2014. Playing with science: Gamised aspects of gamification found on the online citizen science project-zooniverse. In *GAMEON'2014*. EUROSIS.

Juho Hamari and Jonna Koivisto. 2013. Social motivations to use gamification: An empirical study of gamifying exercise. In *ECIS*, page 105.

Kaisla Kajava. 2018. Cross-lingual sentiment preservation in binary and multi-dimensional classification.

Tuomo Kakkonen and Gordana Galić Kakkonen. 2011. Sentiprofiler: creating comparable visual profiles of sentimental content in texts. *Language Technologies for Digital Humanities and Cultural Heritage*, 62:189–204.

Jiwei Li and Eduard Hovy. 2017. Reflections on sentiment/opinion analysis. In *A Practical Guide to Sentiment Analysis*, pages 41–59. Springer.

Pierre Lison and Jörg Tiedemann. 2016. Opensubtitles2016: Extracting large parallel corpora from movie and tv subtitles.

Saif M. Mohammad and Peter D. Turney. 2013. Crowdsourcing a word-emotion association lexicon. 29(3):436–465.

Myriam Munezero, Calkin Suero Montero, Maxim Mozgovoy, and Erkki Sutinen. 2015. Emotwitter–a fine-grained visualization system for identifying enduring sentiments in tweets. In *International Conference on Intelligent Text Processing and Computational Linguistics*, pages 78–91. Springer.

Claudiu-Cristian Musat, Alireza Ghasemi, and Boi Faltings. 2012. Sentiment analysis using a novel human computation game. In *Proceedings of the 3rd Workshop on the People's Web Meets NLP: Collaboratively Constructed Semantic Resources and Their Applications to NLP*, pages 1–9, Stroudsburg, PA, USA. Association for Computational Linguistics.

Stefanie Nowak and Stefan Rüger. 2010. How reliable are annotations via crowdsourcing: a study about inter-annotator agreement for multi-label image annotation. In *Proceedings of the international conference on Multimedia information retrieval*, pages 557–566. ACM.

Emily Öhman, Timo Honkela, and Jörg Tiedemann. 2016. The challenges of multi-dimensional sentiment analysis across languages. *PEOPLES 2016*, page 138.

Emily Öhman and Kaisla Kajava. 2018. Sentimentator: Gamifying fine-grained sentiment annotation. In *Digital Humanities in the Nordic Countries 2018*. CEUR Workshop Proceedings.

F. Pedregosa, G. Varoquaux, A. Gramfort, V. Michel, B. Thirion, O. Grisel, M. Blondel, P. Prettenhofer, R. Weiss, V. Dubourg, J. Vanderplas, A. Passos, D. Cournapeau, M. Brucher, M. Perrot, and E. Duchesnay. 2011. Scikit-learn: Machine learning in Python. *Journal of Machine Learning Research*, 12:2825–2830.

Robert Plutchik. 1980. A general psychoevolutionary theory of emotion. *Theories of emotion*, 1:3–31.

Matthew Purver and Stuart Battersby. 2012. Experimenting with distant supervision for emotion classification. In *Proceedings of the 13th Conference of the European Chapter of the Association for Computational Linguistics*, pages 482–491. Association for Computational Linguistics.

Karen Robson, Kirk Plangger, Jan H. Kietzmann, Ian McCarthy, and Leyland Pitt. 2015. Is it all a game? understanding the principles of gamification. *Business Horizons*, 58(4):411 – 420.

Hassan Saif, Miriam Fernandez, Yulan He, and Harith Alani. 2013. Evaluation datasets for twitter sentiment analysis: a survey and a new dataset, the sts-gold.

Yong-Soo Seol, Dong-Joo Kim, and Han-Woo Kim. 2008. Emotion recognition from text using knowledge-based ann. In *ITC-CSCC: International Technical Conference on Circuits Systems, Computers and Communications*, pages 1569–1572.

Rion Snow, Brendan O'Connor, Daniel Jurafsky, and Andrew Y Ng. 2008. Cheap and fast—but is it good?: evaluating non-expert annotations for natural language tasks. In *Proceedings of the conference on empirical methods in natural language processing*, pages 254–263. Association for Computational Linguistics.

Jorg Tiedemann. 2012. Parallel data, tools and interfaces in opus. In *Proceedings of the Eight International Conference on Language Resources and Evaluation (LREC'12)*, Istanbul, Turkey. European Language Resources Association (ELRA).

Ryoko Tokuhisa, Kentaro Inui, and Yuji Matsumoto. 2008. Emotion classification using massive examples extracted from the web. In *Proceedings of the 22nd International Conference on Computational Linguistics-Volume 1*, pages 881–888. Association for Computational Linguistics.

Peter D. Turney. 2002. Thumbs up or thumbs down?: Semantic orientation applied to unsupervised classification of reviews. In *Proceedings of the 40th Annual Meeting on Association for Computational Linguistics*, pages 417–424, Stroudsburg, PA, USA. Association for Computational Linguistics.

IEST: WASSA-2018 Implicit Emotions Shared Task

Roman Klinger[1], Orphée De Clercq[2], Saif M. Mohammad[3], and Alexandra Balahur[4]

[1] Institut für Maschinelle Sprachverarbeitung, Universität Stuttgart, Germany
`klinger@ims.uni-stuttgart.de`
[2] LT3, Language and Translation Technology Team, Ghent University, Belgium
`orphee.declercq@ugent.be`
[3] National Research Council Canada, Ottawa, Ontario, Canada
`saif.mohammad@nrc-cnrc.gc.ca`
[4] Text and Data Mining Unit, European Commission Joint Research Centre, Ispra, Italy
`alexandra.balahur@ec.europa.eu`

Abstract

Past shared tasks on emotions use data with both overt expressions of emotions (*I am so happy to see you!*) as well as subtle expressions where the emotions have to be inferred, for instance from event descriptions. Further, most datasets do not focus on the cause or the stimulus of the emotion. Here, for the first time, we propose a shared task where systems have to predict the emotions in a large automatically labeled dataset of tweets without access to words denoting emotions. Based on this intention, we call this the Implicit Emotion Shared Task (IEST) because the systems have to infer the emotion mostly from the context. Every tweet has an occurrence of an explicit emotion word that is masked. The tweets are collected in a manner such that they are likely to include a description of the cause of the emotion – the stimulus. Altogether, 30 teams submitted results which range from macro F_1 scores of 21 % to 71 %. The baseline (MaxEnt bag of words and bigrams) obtains an F_1 score of 60 % which was available to the participants during the development phase. A study with human annotators suggests that automatic methods outperform human predictions, possibly by honing into subtle textual clues not used by humans. Corpora, resources, and results are available at the shared task website at http://implicitemotions.wassa2018.com.

1 Introduction

The definition of emotion has long been debated. The main subjects of discussion are the origin of the emotion (physiological or cognitive), the components it has (cognition, feeling, behaviour) and the manner in which it can be measured (categorically or with continuous dimensions). The Implicit Emotion Shared Task (IEST) is based on Scherer (2005), who considers emotion as "an episode of interrelated, synchronized changes in the states of all or most of the five organismic subsystems (information processing, support, executive, action, monitor) in response to the evaluation of an external or internal stimulus event as relevant to major concerns of the organism".

This definition suggests that emotion is triggered by the interpretation of a stimulus event (*i. e.*, a situation) according to its meaning, the criteria of relevance to the personal goals, needs, values and the capacity to react. As such, while most situations will trigger the same emotional reaction in most people, there are situations that may trigger different affective responses in different people. This is explained more in detail by the psychological theories of emotion known as the "appraisal theories" (Scherer, 2005).

Emotion recognition from text is a research area in natural language processing (NLP) concerned with the classification of words, phrases, or documents into predefined emotion categories or dimensions. Most research focuses on *discrete emotion recognition*, which assigns categorical emotion labels (Ekman, 1992; Plutchik, 2001), *e. g.*, *Anger, Anticipation, Disgust, Fear, Joy, Sadness, Surprise* and *Trust*.[1] Previous research developed statistical, dictionary, and rule-based models for

---

[1] Some shared tasks on fine emotion intensity include the SemEval-2007 Task 14, WASSA-2017 shared task EmoInt (Mohammad and Bravo-Marquez, 2017), and SemEval-2018 Task 1 (Mohammad et al., 2018).

Proceedings of the 9th Workshop on Computational Approaches to Subjectivity, Sentiment and Social Media Analysis, pages 31–42
Brussels, Belgium, October 31, 2018. ©2018 Association for Computational Linguistics
https://doi.org/10.18653/v1/P17

several domains, including fairy tales (Alm et al., 2005), blogs (Aman and Szpakowicz, 2007) and microblogs (Dodds et al., 2011). Presumably, most models built on such datasets rely on emotion words (or their representations) whenever accessible and are therefore not forced to learn associations for more subtle descriptions. Such models might fail to predict the correct emotion when such overt words are not accessible. Consider the instance "when my child was born" from the ISEAR corpus, a resource in which people have been asked to report on events when they felt a specific predefined emotion. This example does not contain any emotion word itself, though one might argue that the words "child" and "born" have a positive prior connotation.

Balahur et al. (2012b) showed that the inference of affect from text often results from the interpretation of the situation presented therein. Therefore, specific approaches have to be designed to understand the emotion that is generally triggered by situations. Such approaches require common sense and world knowledge (Liu et al., 2003; Cambria et al., 2009). Gathering world knowledge to support NLP is challenging, although different resources have been built to this aim – *e. g.*, Cyc[2] and ConceptNet (Liu and Singh, 2004).

On a different research branch, the field of distant supervision and weak supervision addresses the challenge that manually annotating data is tedious and expensive. Distant supervision tackles this by making use of structured resources to automatically label data (Mintz et al., 2009; Riedel et al., 2010; Mohammad, 2012). This approach has been adapted in emotion analysis by using information assigned by authors to their own text, with the use of hashtags and emoticons (Wang et al., 2012).

With the *Implicit Emotion Shared Task (IEST)*, we aim at combining these two research branches: On the one hand, we use distant supervision to compile a corpus of substantial size. On the other hand, we limit the corpus to those texts which are likely to contain descriptions of the cause of the emotion – the *stimulus*. Due to the ease of access and the variability and data richness on Twitter, we opt for compiling a corpus of microposts, from which we sample tweets that contain an emotion word followed by 'that', 'when', or 'because'. We then mask the emotion word and ask systems to predict the emotion category associated with that word.[3] The emotion category can be one of six classes: *anger, disgust, fear, joy, sadness*, and *surprise*. Examples from the data are:

> (1) "It's [#TARGETWORD#] when you feel like you are invisible to others."

> (2) "My step mom got so [#TARGET-WORD#] when she came home from work and saw that the boys didn't come to Austin with me."

In Example 1, the inference is that feeling invisible typically makes us sad. In Example 2, the context is presumably that a person (mom) expected something else than what was expected. This in isolation might cause anger or sadness, however, since "the boys are home" the mother is likely happy. Note that such examples can be used as source of commonsense or world knowledge to detect emotions from contexts where the emotion is not explicitly implied.

The shared task was conducted between 15 March 2018 (publication of train and trial data) and the evaluation phase, which ran from 2 to 9 July. Submissions were managed on CodaLab[4]. The best performing systems are all ensembles of deep learning approaches. Several systems make use of external additional resources such as pretrained word vectors, affect lexicons, and language models fine-tuned to the task.

The rest of the paper is organized as follows: we first review related work (Section 2). Section 3 introduces the shared task, the data used, and the setup. The results are presented in Section 4, including the official results and a discussion of different submissions. The automatic system's predictions are then compared to human performance in Section 5, where we report on a crowdsourcing study with the data used for the shared task. We conclude in Section 6.

2   Related Work

Related work is found in different directions of research on emotion detection in NLP: resource creation and emotion classification, as well as modeling the emotion itself.

Modeling the emotion computationally has been approached from the perspective of humans needs

---

[3]This gives the shared task a mixed flavor of both text classification and word prediction, in the spirit of distributional semantics.

---

[2]http://www.cyc.com

[4]https://competitions.codalab.org/competitions/19214

and desires with the goal of simulating human reactions. Dyer (1987) presents three models which take into account characters, arguments, emotion experiencers, and events. These aspects are modeled with first order logic in a procedural manner. Similarly, Subasic and Huettner (2001) use fuzzy logic for such modeling in order to consider gradual differences. A similar approach is followed by the OCC model (Ortony et al., 1990), for which Udochukwu and He (2015) show how to connect it to text in a rule-based manner for implicit emotion detection. Despite of this early work on holistic computational models of emotions, NLP focused mostly on a more coarse-grained level.

One of the first corpora annotated for emotions is that by Alm et al. (2005) who analyze sentences from fairy tales. Strapparava and Mihalcea (2007) annotate news headlines with emotions and valence, Mohammad et al. (2015) annotate tweets on elections, and Schuff et al. (2017) tweets of a stance dataset (Mohammad et al., 2017). The SemEval-2018 Task 1: Affect in Tweets (Mohammad et al., 2018) includes several subtasks on inferring the affectual state of a person from their tweet: emotion intensity regression, emotion intensity ordinal classification, valence (sentiment) regression, valence ordinal classification, and multi-label emotion classification. In all of these prior shared tasks and datasets, no distinction is made between implicit or explicit mentions of the emotions. We refer the reader to Bostan and Klinger (2018) for a more detailed overview of emotion classification datasets.

Few authors specifically analyze which phrase triggers the perception of an emotion. Aman and Szpakowicz (2007) focus on the annotation on document level but also mark emotion indicators. Mohammad et al. (2014) annotate electoral tweets for semantic roles such as emotion and stimulus (from FrameNet). Ghazi et al. (2015) annotate a subset of Aman and Szpakowicz (2007) with causes (inspired by the FrameNet structure). Kim and Klinger (2018) and Neviarouskaya and Aono (2013) similarly annotate emotion holders, targets, and causes as well as the trigger words.

One of the oldest resources nowadays used for emotion recognition is the ISEAR set (Scherer, 1997) which consists of self-reports of emotional events. As the task of participants in a psychological study was not to express an emotion but to report on an event in which they experienced a given emotion, this resource can be considered similar to our goal of focusing on implicit emotion expressions.

With the aim to extend the coverage of ISEAR, Balahur et al. (2011, 2012a) build EmotiNet, a knowledge base to store situations and the affective reactions they have the potential to trigger. They show how the knowledge stored can be expanded using lexical and semantic similarity, as well as through the use of Web-extracted knowledge (Balahur et al., 2013). The patterns used to populate the database are of the type "I feel [emotion] when [situation]", which was also a starting point for our task.

Finally, several approaches take into consideration distant supervision (Mohammad and Kiritchenko, 2015; Abdul-Mageed and Ungar, 2017; De Choudhury et al., 2012; Liu et al., 2017, *i. a.*). This is motivated by the high availability of user-generated text and by the challenge that manual annotation is typically tedious or expensive. This contrasts with the current data demand of machine learning, and especially, deep learning approaches.

With our work in IEST, we combine the goal of the development of models which are able to recognize emotions from implicit descriptions without having access to explicit emotion words, with the paradigm of distant supervision.

3 Shared Task

3.1 Data

The aim of the Implicit Emotion Shared Task is to force models to infer emotions from the context of emotion words without having access to them. Specifically, the aim is that models infer the emotion through the causes mentioned in the text. Thus, we build the corpus of Twitter posts by polling the Twitter API[5] for the expression 'EMOTION-WORD (that|because|when)', where EMOTION-WORD contains a synonym for one out of six emotions.[6] The synonyms are shown in Table 1. The requirement of tweets to have either 'that', 'because', or 'when' immediately after the emotion word means that the tweet likely describes the cause of the emotion.

The initially retrieved large dataset has a distribution of 25 % *surprise*, 23 % *sadness*, 18 % *joy*, 16 % *fear*, 10 % *anger*, 8 % *disgust*. We discard tweets

---

[5] https://developer.twitter.com/en/docs.html

[6] Note that we do not check that there is a white space before the emotion word, which leads to tweets containing ..."unEMOTION-word...".

Emotion	Abbr.	Synonyms
Anger	A	angry, furious
Fear	F	afraid, frightened, scared, fearful
Disgust	D	disgusted, disgusting
Joy	J	cheerful, happy, joyful
Sadness	Sa	sad, depressed, sorrowful
Surprise	Su	surprising, surprised, astonished, shocked, startled, astounded, stunned

Table 1: Emotion synonyms used when polling Twitter.

Emotion	Train	Trial	Test
Anger	25562	1600	4794
Disgust	25558	1597	4794
Fear	25575	1598	4791
Joy	27958	1736	5246
Sadness	23165	1460	4340
Surprise	25565	1600	4792
Sum	153383	9591	28757

Table 2: Distribution of IEST data.

Gold Labels		Predicted Labels					
		A	D	F	J	Sa	Su
	A	2431	476	496	390	410	426
	D	426	2991	245	213	397	522
	F	430	249	3016	327	251	518
	J	378	169	290	3698	366	345
	Sa	450	455	313	458	2335	329
	Su	411	508	454	310	279	2930

Table 3: Confusion Matrix on Test Data for Baseline.

Gold Labels		Predicted Labels					
		A	D	F	J	Sa	Su
	A	3182	313	293	224	329	453
	D	407	3344	134	102	336	471
	F	403	129	3490	196	190	383
	J	297	67	161	4284	220	217
	Sa	443	340	171	240	2947	199
	Su	411	367	293	209	176	3336

Table 4: Confusion Matrix on Test Data of Best Submitted System

with more than one emotion word, as well as exact duplicates, and mask usernames and URLs. From this set, we randomly sample 80 % of the tweets to form the training set (153,600 instances), 5 % as trial set (9,600 instances), and 15 % as test set (28,800 instances). We perform stratified sampling to obtain a balanced dataset. While the shared task took place, two errors in the data preprocessing were discovered by participants (the use of the word unhappy as synonym for sadness, which lead to inconsistent preprocessing in the context of negated expressions, and the occurrence of instances without emotion words). To keep the change of the data at a minimum, the erroneous instances were only removed, which leads to a distribution of the data as shown in Table 2.

3.2 Task Setup

The shared task was announced through a dedicated website (http://implicitemotions.wassa2018. com/) and computational-linguistics-specific mailing lists. The organizers published an evaluation script which calculates precision, recall, and F_1 measure for each emotion class as well as micro and macro average. Due to the nearly balanced dataset, the chosen official metric for ranking submitted systems is the macro-F_1 measure.

In addition to the data, the participants were provided a list of resources they might want to use[7] (and they were allowed to use any other resources they have access to or create them-

selves). We also provided access to a baseline system.[8] This baseline is a maximum entropy classifier with L2 regularization. Strings which match `[#a-zA-Z0-9_=]+|[^ ]` form tokens. As preprocessing, all symbols which are not alphanumeric or contain the # sign are removed. Based on that, unigrams and bigrams form the Boolean features as a set of words for the classifier.

4 Results

4.1 Baseline

The intention of the baseline implementation was to provide participants with an intuition of the difficulty of the task. It reaches 59.88 % macro F_1 on the test data, which is very similar to the trial data result (60.1 % F_1). The confusion matrix for the baseline is presented in Table 3; the confusion matrix for the best submitted system is shown in Table 4.

4.2 Submission Results

Table 5 shows the main results of the shared task. We received submissions through CodaLab from thirty participants. Twenty-six teams responded to a post-competition survey providing additional information regarding team members (56 people in total) and the systems that were developed. For the remaining analyses and the ranking, we only report on these twenty-six teams.

---

[7]http://implicitemotions.wassa2018.com/resources/

[8]https://bitbucket.org/rklinger/simpletextclassifier

id	Team	F_1	Rank	B
1	*Amobee*	*71.45*	*(1)*	3
2	IIDYT	71.05	(2)	3
3	NTUA-SLP	70.29	(3)	4
4	UBC-NLP	69.28	(4)	6
5	Sentylic	69.20	(5)	7
6	HUMIR	68.64	(6)	8
7	nlp	68.48	(7)	9
8	DataSEARCH	68.04	(8)	10
9	YNU1510	67.63	(9)	11
10	EmotiKLUE	67.13	(10)	11
11	wojtek.pierre	66.15	(11)	15
12	hgsgnlp	65.80	(12)	15
13	UWB	65.70	(13)	15
14	NL-FIIT	65.52	(14)	15
15	TubOslo	64.63	(15)	17
16	YNU_Lab	64.10	(16)	17
17	Braint	62.61	(17)	19
18	EmoNLP	62.11	(18)	19
19	RW	60.97	(19)	20
20	Baseline	59.88		21
21	USI-IR	58.37	(20)	22
22	THU_NGN	58.01	(21)	23
23	SINAI	57.94	(22)	24
24	UTFPR	56.92	(23)	26
25	CNHZ2017	56.40		27
26	lyb3b	55.87		27
27	Adobe Research	53.08	(24)	28
28	Anonymous	50.38		29
29	dinel	49.99	(25)	30
30	CHANDA	41.89	(26)	31
31	NLP_LDW	21.03		

Table 5: Official results of IEST 2018. Participants who did not report on the system details did not get assigned a rank and are reported in gray. Column B provides the first row in the results table to which the respective row is significantly different (confidence level 0.99), tested with bootstrap resampling.

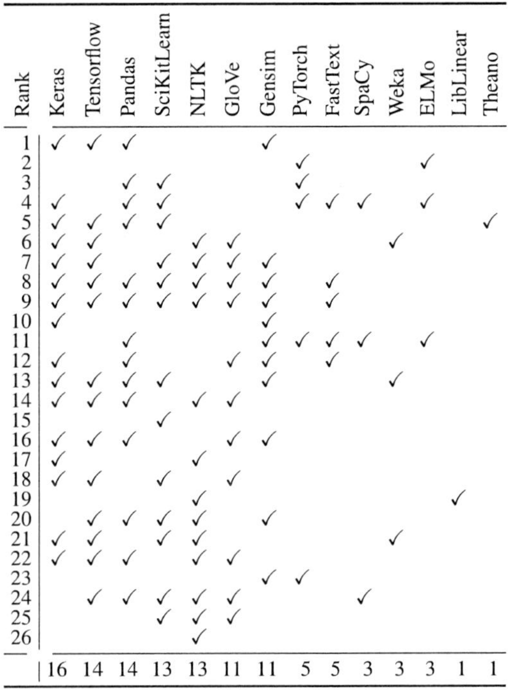

Rank	Keras	Tensorflow	Pandas	SciKitLearn	NLTK	GloVe	Gensim	PyTorch	FastText	SpaCy	Weka	ELMo	LibLinear	Theano
1	✓	✓	✓				✓							
2								✓				✓		
3			✓	✓				✓						
4	✓		✓	✓				✓	✓	✓		✓		
5	✓	✓	✓	✓										✓
6	✓	✓			✓	✓					✓			
7	✓	✓		✓	✓	✓	✓							
8	✓	✓	✓	✓	✓	✓	✓		✓					
9	✓	✓	✓	✓	✓	✓	✓		✓					
10	✓						✓							
11			✓				✓	✓	✓	✓		✓		
12	✓		✓			✓	✓		✓					
13	✓	✓	✓	✓			✓				✓			
14	✓	✓	✓		✓	✓								
15				✓										
16	✓	✓	✓			✓	✓							
17	✓				✓									
18	✓	✓		✓		✓								
19					✓								✓	
20		✓	✓	✓	✓		✓							
21	✓	✓		✓	✓						✓			
22	✓	✓	✓		✓	✓								
23							✓	✓						
24		✓	✓	✓	✓	✓				✓				
25				✓	✓	✓								
26					✓									
	16	14	14	13	13	11	11	5	5	3	3	3	1	1

Table 6: Overview of tools employed by different teams (sorted by popularity from left to right).

contain labels not present in the gold data, which reduced the macro-F_1 dramatically. With an evaluation only taking into account 6 labels, id 22 would be on rank 9 and id 28 would be on rank 10.

4.3 Review of Methods

Table 6 shows that many participants use high-level libraries like Keras or NLTK. Tensorflow is only of medium popularity and Theano is only used by one participant. Table 7 shows a summary of machine learning methods used by the teams, as reported by themselves. Nearly every team uses embeddings and neural networks; many teams use an ensemble of architectures. Several teams use language models showing a current trend in NLP to fine-tune those to specific tasks (Howard and Ruder, 2018). Presumably, those are specifically helpful in our task due to its word-prediction aspect.

Finally, Table 8 summarizes the different kinds of information sources taken into account by the teams. Several teams use affect lexicons in addition to word information and emoji-specific information. The incorporation of statistical knowledge from unlabeled corpora is also popular.

The table shows results from 31 systems, including the baseline results which have been made available to participants during the shared task started. From all submissions, 19 submissions scored above the baseline. The best scoring system is from team *Amobee*, followed by *IIDYT* and *NTUA-SLP*. The first two results are not significantly different, as tested with the Wilcoxon (1945) sign test ($p < 0.01$) and with bootstrap resampling (confidence level 0.99).

Table 10 in the Appendix shows a breakdown of the results by emotion class. Though the data was nearly balanced, joy is mostly predicted with highest performance, followed by fear and disgust. The prediction of surprise and anger shows a lower performance.

Note that the macro F_1 evaluation took into account all classes which were either predicted or in the gold data. Two teams submitted results which

Rank	Embeddings	LSTM/RNN/GRU	Ensemble	CNN/Capsules	Attention	Linear Classifier	Transfer Learning	Language model	MLP	Autoencoder	Random Forrest	k-Means	Bagging	LDA
1	✓	✓	✓	✓	✓		✓	✓						
2	✓	✓	✓						✓					
3	✓	✓	✓		✓		✓	✓						
4	✓	✓	✓		✓		✓	✓						
5	✓	✓	✓	✓										
6	✓	✓	✓				✓					✓	✓	
7	✓	✓	✓		✓									
8	✓	✓		✓										
9	✓	✓	✓	✓	✓									
10	✓	✓												✓
11	✓	✓		✓										
12	✓		✓	✓							✓			
13	✓	✓												
14	✓	✓					✓							
15						✓								
16	✓	✓			✓									
17	✓	✓			✓	✓								
18	✓	✓	✓	✓										
19						✓								
20	✓	✓												
21	✓	✓	✓	✓		✓								
22	✓	✓												
23	✓	✓												
24	✓		✓	✓					✓					
25	✓					✓				✓				
26														
	23	20	12	9	7	5	5	3	2	1	1	1	1	1

Table 7: Overview of methods employed by different teams (sorted by popularity from left to right).

Rank	Words	Lexicons	Characters	Emoji	Unlabeled Corpora	Emotion Emb.	Sentence/Document	SemEval
1	✓	✓			✓	✓	✓	✓
2	✓		✓	✓				
3	✓				✓		✓	✓
4	✓				✓			
5	✓							
6	✓	✓				✓		
7	✓							
8	✓		✓	✓				
9	✓							
10	✓				✓		✓	
11	✓	✓	✓					
12	✓	✓	✓		✓			
13	✓			✓				
14	✓			✓			✓	
15	✓		✓					
16	✓							
17	✓			✓				
18	✓	✓	✓	✓	✓	✓		
19	✓							
20	✓		✓	✓				
21	✓	✓	✓					
22	✓	✓						
23	✓	✓						
24	✓	✓				✓		✓
25	✓							
26	✓							
	26	9	8	7	6	4	4	3

Table 8: Overview of information sources employed by different teams (sorted by popularity from left to right).

4.4 Top 3 Submissions

In the following, we briefly summarize the approaches used by the top three teams: Amobee, IIIDYT, and NTUA-SLP. For more information on these approaches and those of the other teams, we refer the reader to the individual system description papers. The three best performing systems are all ensemble approaches. However, they make use of different underlying machine learning architectures and rely on different kinds of information.

4.4.1 Amobee

The top-ranking system, Amobee, is an ensemble approach of several models (Rozental et al., 2018). First, the team trains a Twitter-specific language model based on the transformer decoder architecture using 5B tweets as training data. This model is used to find the probabilities of potential missing words, conditional upon the missing word describing one of the six emotions. Next, the team applies transfer learning from the trained models they developed for SemEval 2018 Task 1: Affect in Tweets (Rozental and Fleischer, 2018). Finally, they directly train on the data provided in the shared task while incorporating outputs from DeepMoji

(Felbo et al., 2017) and "Universal Sentence Encoder" (Cer et al., 2018) as features.

4.4.2 IIIDYT

The second-ranking system, IIIDYT (Balazs et al., 2018), preprocesses the dataset by tokenizing the sentences (including emojis), and normalizing the USERNAME, NEWLINE, URL and TRIGGER-WORD indicators. Then, it feeds word-level representations returned by a pretrained ELMo layer into a Bi-LSTM with 1 layer of 2048 hidden units for each direction. The Bi-LSTM output word representations are max-pooled to generate sentence-level representations, followed by a single hidden layer of 512 units and output size of 6. The team trains six models with different random initializations, obtains the probability distributions for each example, and then averages these to obtain the final label prediction.

4.4.3 NTUA-SLP

The NTUA-SLP system (Chronopoulou et al., 2018) is an ensemble of three different generic models. For the first model, the team pretrains Twitter embeddings with the word2vec skip-gram model using a large Twitter corpus. Then, these pretrained embeddings are fed to a neural classifier with 2 layers, each consisting of 400 bi-LSTM units with attention. For the second model, they use transfer learning of a pretrained classifier on a 3-class sentiment classification task (Semeval17 Task4A) and then apply fine-tuning to the IEST dataset. Finally, for the third model the team uses transfer learning of a pretrained language model, according to Howard and Ruder (2018). They first train 3 language models on 3 different Twitter corpora (2M, 3M, 5M) and then they fine-tune them to the IEST dataset with gradual unfreezing.

4.5 Error Analysis

Table 11 in the Appendix shows a subsample of instances which are predicted correctly by all teams (marked as +, including the baseline system and those who did not report on system details) and that were not predicted correctly by any team (marked as −), separated by correct emotion label.

For the positive examples which are correctly predicted by all teams, specific patterns reoccur. For *anger*, the author of the first example encourages the reader not to be afraid – a prompt which might be less likely for other emotions. For several emotions, single words or phrases are presumably associated with such emotions, *e. g.*, "hungry" with anger, "underwear", "sweat", "ewww" with disgust, "leaving", "depression" for sadness, "why am i not" for surprise.

Several examples which are all correctly predicted by all teams for *joy* include the syllable "un" preceding the triggerword – a pattern more frequent for this emotion than for others. Another pattern is the phrase "fast and furious" (with furious for *anger*) which should be considered a mistake in the sampling procedure, as it refers to a movie instead of an emotion expression.

Negative examples appear to be reasonable when the emotion is given but may also be valid with other labels than the gold. For *disgust*, respective emotion synonyms are often used as a strong expression actually referring to other negative emotions. Especially for *sadness*, the negative examples include comparably long event descriptions.

5 Comparison to Human Performance

An interesting research question is how accurately native speakers of a language can predict the emotion class when the emotion word is removed from

	Predicted Labels					
	A	D	F	J	Sa	Su
A	349	40	34	55	95	43
D	195	92	30	84	157	69
F	94	20	265	92	120	42
J	39	6	22	398	36	13
Sa	88	37	23	89	401	46
Su	123	25	29	132	53	183

(Row labels A, D, F, J, Sa, Su under the group label "Gold Labels".)

Table 9: Confusion Matrix Sample Annotated by Humans in Crowdsourcing

a tweet. Thus we conducted a crowdsourced study asking humans to perform the same task as proposed for automatic systems in this shared task.

We sampled 900 instances from the IEST data: 50 tweets for each of the six emotions in 18 pair-wise combinations with 'because', 'that', and 'when'. The tweets and annotation questionnaires were uploaded on a crowdsourcing platform, Figure Eight (earlier called CrowdFlower).[9] The questionnaire asked for the best guess for the emotion (Q1) as well as any other emotion that they think might apply (Q2).

About 5 % of the tweets were annotated internally beforehand for Q1 (by one of the authors of this paper). These tweets are referred to as gold tweets. The gold tweets were interspersed with other tweets. If a crowd-worker got a gold tweet question wrong, they were immediately notified of the error. If the worker's accuracy on the gold tweet questions fell below 70 %, they were refused further annotation, and all of their annotations were discarded. This served as a mechanism to avoid malicious annotations.

Each tweet is annotated by at least three people. A total of 3,619 human judgments of emotion associated with the trigger word were obtained. Each judgment included the best guess for the emotion (response to Q1) as well as any other emotion that they think might apply (response to Q2). The answer to Q1 corresponds to the shared task setting. However, automatic systems were not given the option of providing additional emotions that might apply (Q2).

The macro F_1 for predicting the emotion is 45 % (Q1, micro F_1 of 0.47). Observe that human performance is lower than what automatic systems reach in the shared task. The correct emotion was present in the top two guessed emotions in 57 % of the cases. Perhaps, the automatic systems are honing

---

[9]https://www.figure-eight.com

in to some subtle systematic regularities in hope that particular emotion words are used (for example, the function words in the immediate neighborhood of the target word). It should also be noted, however, that the data used for human annotations was only a subsample of the IEST data.

An analysis of subsets of Tweets containing the words *because*, *that*, and *when* after the emotion word shows that Tweets with "that" are more difficult (41 % accuracy) than with "when" (49 %) and "because" (51 %). This relationship between performance and query string is not observed in the baseline system – here, accuracy on the test data (on the data used for human evaluation) for the "that" subset is 61 % (60 %), for "when" 62 % (53 %), and for "because" 55 % (50 %) – therefore, the automatic system is most challenged by "because", while humans are more challenged by "that". Please note that this comparison on the test data is somewhat unfair since for the human analysis, the data was sampled in a stratified manner, but not for the automatic prediction. The test data contains 5635 "because" tweets, 13649 with "that" and 9474 with "when".

There are differences in the difficulty of the task for different emotions: The accuracy (F_1) by emotion is 57 % (46 %) for anger, 15 % (21 %) for disgust, 42 % (51 %) for fear, 77 % (58 %) for joy, 59 % (52 %) for sadness and 34 % (39 %) for surprise. The confusion matrix is depicted in Table 9. Disgust is often confused with anger, followed by fear being confused with sadness. Surprise is often confused with anger and joy.

6 Conclusions & Future Work

With this paper and the Implicit Emotion Shared Task, we presented the first dataset and joint effort to focus on causal descriptions to infer emotions that are triggered by specific life situations on a large scale. A substantial number of participating systems presented the current state of the art in text classification in general and transferred it to the task of emotion classification.

Based on the experiences during the organization and preparation of this shared task, we plan the following steps for a potential second iteration. The dataset was now constructed via distant supervision, which might be a cause for inconsistencies in the dataset. We plan to use crowdsourcing as applied for the estimation of human performance to improve preprocessing of the data. In addition,

as one participant noted, the emotion words which were used to retrieve the data were removed, but, in a subset of the data, other emotion words were retained.

The next step, which we suggest to the participants and future researchers is introspection of the models – carefully analyse them to prove that the models actually learn to infer emotions from subtle descriptions of situations, instead of purely associating emotion words with emotion labels. Similarly, an open research question is how models developed on the IEST data perform on other data sets. Bostan and Klinger (2018) showed that transferring models from one corpus to another in emotion analysis leads to drops in performance. Therefore, an interesting option is to use transfer learning from established corpora (which do not distinguish explicit and implicit emotion statements) to the IEST data and compare the models to those directly trained on the IEST and vice versa.

Finally, another line of future research is the application of the knowledge inferred to other tasks, such as argument mining and sentiment analysis.

Acknowledgments

This work has been partially supported by the German Research Council (DFG), project SEAT (Structured Multi-Domain Emotion Analysis from Text, KL 2869/1-1). We thank Evgeny Kim, Laura Bostan, Jeremy Barnes, and Veronique Hoste for fruitful discussions.

References

Muhammad Abdul-Mageed and Lyle Ungar. 2017. Emonet: Fine-grained emotion detection with gated recurrent neural networks. In *Proceedings of the 55th Annual Meeting of the Association for Computational Linguistics (Volume 1: Long Papers)*, pages 718–728, Vancouver, Canada. Association for Computational Linguistics.

Cecilia Ovesdotter Alm, Dan Roth, and Richard Sproat. 2005. Emotions from text: Machine learning for text-based emotion prediction. In *Proceedings of Human Language Technology Conference and Conference on Empirical Methods in Natural Language Processing*, pages 579–586, Vancouver, British Columbia, Canada. Association for Computational Linguistics.

Saima Aman and Stan Szpakowicz. 2007. Identifying expressions of emotion in text. In *Text, Speech and Dialogue*, pages 196–205, Berlin, Heidelberg. Springer Berlin Heidelberg.

Alexandra Balahur, Jesus Hermida, and Andres Montoyo. 2012a. Building and exploiting emotinet, a knowledge base for emotion detection based on the appraisal theory model. *IEEE Transactions on Affective Computing*, 3:88–101.

Alexandra Balahur, Jesús M. Hermida, Andrés Montoyo, and Rafael Muñoz. 2011. EmotiNet: A knowledge base for emotion detection in text built on the appraisal theories. In *Natural Language Processing and Information Systems*, pages 27–39, Berlin, Heidelberg. Springer Berlin Heidelberg.

Alexandra Balahur, Jesús M. Hermida, and Hristo Tanev. 2013. Detecting implicit emotion expressions from text using ontological resources and lexical learning. In *New Trends of Research in Ontologies and Lexical Resources: Ideas, Projects, Systems*, pages 235–255, Berlin, Heidelberg. Springer Berlin Heidelberg.

Alexandra Balahur, Jess Hermida, and Andrs Montoyo. 2012b. Detecting implicit expressions of emotion in text: A comparative analysis. *Decision Support Systems*, 53(4):742753.

Jorge A. Balazs, Edison Marrese-Taylor, and Yutaka Matsuo. 2018. IIIDYT at IEST 2018: Implicit Emotion Classification with Deep Contextualized Word Representations. In *Proceedings of the 9th Workshop on Computational Approaches to Subjectivity, Sentiment and Social Media Analysis*, Brussels, Belgium. Association for Computational Linguistics.

Laura Ana Maria Bostan and Roman Klinger. 2018. A survey on annotated data sets for emotion classification in text. In *Proceedings of COLING 2018, the 27th International Conference on Computational Linguistics*, Santa Fe, USA.

Erik Cambria, Amir Hussain, Catherine Havasi, and Chris Eckl. 2009. Affectivespace: Blending common sense and affective knowledge to perform emotive reasoning. In *WOMSA09: 1st Workshop on Opinion Mining and Sentiment Analysis. WOMSA'09: 1st Workshop on Opinion Mining and Sentiment Analysis*, pages 32–41, Seville, Spain.

Daniel Cer, Yinfei Yang, Sheng-yi Kong, Nan Hua, Nicole Limtiaco, Rhomni St. John, Noah Constant, Mario Guajardo-Cespedes, Steve Yuan, Chris Tar, Yun-Hsuan Sung, Brian Strope, and Ray Kurzweil. 2018. Universal sentence encoder. *CoRR*, abs/1803.11175.

Alexandra Chronopoulou, Aikaterini Margatina, Christos Baziotis, and Alexandros Potamianos. 2018. NTUA-SLP at IEST 2018: Ensemble of neural transfer methods for implicit emotion classification. In *Proceedings of the 9th Workshop on Computational Approaches to Subjectivity, Sentiment and Social Media Analysis*, Brussels, Belgium. Association for Computational Linguistics.

Munmun De Choudhury, Scott Counts, and Michael Gamon. 2012. Not all moods are created equal! exploring human emotional states in social media. In *Sixth international AAAI conference on weblogs and social media*, pages 66–73.

Peter S. Dodds, Kameron D. Harris, Isabel M. Kloumann, Catherine A. Bliss, and Christopher M. Danforth. 2011. Temporal patterns of happiness and information in a global social network: Hedonometrics and twitter. *PloS one*, 6(12).

Michael G. Dyer. 1987. Emotions and their computations: Three computer models. *Cognition and Emotion*, 1(3):323–347.

Paul Ekman. 1992. An argument for basic emotions. *Cognition & emotion*, 6(3-4):169–200.

Bjarke Felbo, Alan Mislove, Anders Søgaard, Iyad Rahwan, and Sune Lehmann. 2017. Using millions of emoji occurrences to learn any-domain representations for detecting sentiment, emotion and sarcasm. In *Proceedings of the 2017 Conference on Empirical Methods in Natural Language Processing*, pages 1615–1625, Copenhagen, Denmark. Association for Computational Linguistics.

Diman Ghazi, Diana Inkpen, and Stan Szpakowicz. 2015. Detecting emotion stimuli in emotion-bearing sentences. In *Computational Linguistics and Intelligent Text Processing*, pages 152–165, Cham. Springer International Publishing.

Jeremy Howard and Sebastian Ruder. 2018. Universal language model fine-tuning for text classification. In *Proceedings of the 56th Annual Meeting of the Association for Computational Linguistics (Volume 1: Long Papers)*, pages 328–339, Melbourne, Australia. Association for Computational Linguistics.

Evgeny Kim and Roman Klinger. 2018. Who feels what and why? annotation of a literature corpus with semantic roles of emotions. In *Proceedings of COLING 2018, the 27th International Conference on Computational Linguistics*, Santa Fe, USA.

Hugo Liu, Henry Lieberman, and Ted Selker. 2003. A model of textual affect sensing using real-world knowledge. In *Proceedings of the 8th International Conference on Intelligent User Interfaces*, IUI '03, pages 125–132, New York, NY, USA. ACM.

Hugo Liu and Push Singh. 2004. Conceptnet – a practical commonsense reasoning tool-kit. *BT Technology Journal*, 22(4):211–226.

Vicki Liu, Carmen Banea, and Rada Mihalcea. 2017. Grounded emotions. In *2017 Seventh International Conference on Affective Computing and Intelligent Interaction (ACII)*, pages 477–483, San Antonio, Texas.

Mike Mintz, Steven Bills, Rion Snow, and Dan Jurafsky. 2009. Distant supervision for relation extraction without labeled data. In *Conference of the Association for Computational Linguistics and the International Joint Conference on Natural Language Processing of the Asian Federation of Natural Language Processing*.

Saif Mohammad. 2012. #emotional tweets. In **SEM 2012: The First Joint Conference on Lexical and Computational Semantics – Volume 1: Proceedings of the main conference and the shared task, and Volume 2: Proceedings of the Sixth International Workshop on Semantic Evaluation (SemEval 2012)*, pages 246–255, Montréal, Canada. Association for Computational Linguistics.

Saif M. Mohammad and Felipe Bravo-Marquez. 2017. WASSA-2017 shared task on emotion intensity. In *Proceedings of the Workshop on Computational Approaches to Subjectivity, Sentiment and Social Media Analysis (WASSA)*, Copenhagen, Denmark.

Saif M. Mohammad, Felipe Bravo-Marquez, Mohammad Salameh, and Svetlana Kiritchenko. 2018. Semeval-2018 Task 1: Affect in tweets. In *Proceedings of International Workshop on Semantic Evaluation (SemEval-2018)*, New Orleans, LA, USA.

Saif M. Mohammad and Svetlana Kiritchenko. 2015. Using hashtags to capture fine emotion categories from tweets. *Computational Intelligence*, 31(2):301–326.

Saif M. Mohammad, Parinaz Sobhani, and Svetlana Kiritchenko. 2017. Stance and sentiment in tweets. *ACM Trans. Internet Technol.*, 17(3):26:1–26:23.

Saif M. Mohammad, Xiaodan Zhu, Svetlana Kiritchenko, and Joel Martin. 2015. Sentiment, emotion, purpose, and style in electoral tweets. *Information Processing & Management*, 51(4):480–499.

Saif M. Mohammad, Xiaodan Zhu, and Joel Martin. 2014. Semantic role labeling of emotions in tweets. In *Proceedings of the 5th Workshop on Computational Approaches to Subjectivity, Sentiment and Social Media Analysis*, pages 32–41, Baltimore, Maryland. Association for Computational Linguistics.

Alena Neviarouskaya and Masaki Aono. 2013. Extracting causes of emotions from text. In *Proceedings of the Sixth International Joint Conference on Natural Language Processing*, pages 932–936.

Andrew Ortony, Gerald L. Clore, and Allan Collins. 1990. *The cognitive structure of emotions*. Cambridge University Press.

Robert Plutchik. 2001. The nature of emotions human emotions have deep evolutionary roots, a fact that may explain their complexity and provide tools for clinical practice. *American Scientist*, 89(4):344–350.

Sebastian Riedel, Limin Yao, and Andrew McCallum. 2010. Modeling Relations and Their Mentions without Labeled Text. In *Proceedings of the European Conference on Machine Learning and Principles and Practice in Knowledge Discovery from Databases*.

Alon Rozental and Daniel Fleischer. 2018. Amobee at semeval-2018 task 1: GRU neural network with a CNN attention mechanism for sentiment classification. *CoRR*, abs/1804.04380.

Alon Rozental, Daniel Fleischer, and Zohar Kelrich. 2018. Amobee at IEST 2018: Transfer Learning from Language Models. In *Proceedings of the 9th Workshop on Computational Approaches to Subjectivity, Sentiment and Social Media Analysis*, Brussels, Belgium. Association for Computational Linguistics.

Klaus R Scherer. 1997. Profiles of emotion-antecedent appraisal: Testing theoretical predictions across cultures. *Cognition & Emotion*, 11(2):113–150.

Klaus. R. Scherer. 2005. What are emotions? and how can they be measured? *Social Science Information*, 44(4):695–729.

Hendrik Schuff, Jeremy Barnes, Julian Mohme, Sebastian Padó, and Roman Klinger. 2017. Annotation, modelling and analysis of fine-grained emotions on a stance and sentiment detection corpus. In *Proceedings of the 8th Workshop on Computational Approaches to Subjectivity, Sentiment and Social Media Analysis*, Copenhagen, Denmark. Workshop at Conference on Empirical Methods in Natural Language Processing, Association for Computational Linguistics.

Carlo Strapparava and Rada Mihalcea. 2007. Semeval-2007 task 14: Affective text. In *Proceedings of the Fourth International Workshop on Semantic Evaluations (SemEval-2007)*, pages 70–74, Prague, Czech Republic. Association for Computational Linguistics.

Pero Subasic and Alison Huettner. 2001. Affect analysis of text using fuzzy semantic typing. *IEEE Transactions on Fuzzy Systems*, 9(4):483–496.

Orizu Udochukwu and Yulan He. 2015. A rule-based approach to implicit emotion detection in text. In *Natural Language Processing and Information Systems*, pages 197–203, Cham. Springer International Publishing.

Wenbo Wang, Lu Chen, Krishnaprasad Thirunarayan, and Amit P. Sheth. 2012. Harnessing twitter "big data" for automatic emotion identification. In *SocialCom/PASSAT*, pages 587–592. IEEE.

Frank Wilcoxon. 1945. Individual comparisons by ranking methods. *Biometrics bulletin*, 1(6):80–83.

A Results by emotion class

Table 10 shows breakdown of the results by emotion class.

	Joy			Sadness			Disgust			Anger			Surprise			Fear		
Team	P	R	F_1	P	R	F_1	P	R	F_1	P	R	F_1	P	R	F_1	P	R	F_1
Amobee	**82**	**82**	**82**	70	**68**	69	**73**	70	**72**	62	**66**	64	**66**	70	68	**77**	73	**75**
IIIDYT	79	81	80	**71**	67	69	70	**71**	71	**66**	63	64	**66**	**71**	**68**	76	**74**	75
NTUA-SLP	81	77	79	71	66	69	72	70	71	63	64	63	62	71	67	75	73	74
UBC-NLP	79	79	79	67	67	67	69	68	69	62	63	62	65	67	66	73	73	73
Sentylic	80	77	79	68	66	67	69	69	69	63	61	62	63	69	66	73	73	73
HUMIR	77	78	78	70	64	66	70	68	69	61	63	62	61	69	65	74	70	72
nlp	77	78	78	68	62	65	70	67	69	62	63	62	62	68	65	72	72	72
DataSEARCH	77	77	77	66	64	65	69	68	68	61	62	62	64	65	65	72	71	71
YNU1510	78	75	76	64	64	64	68	68	68	60	63	62	64	65	64	73	71	72
EmotiKLUE	77	78	77	69	59	64	67	67	67	60	61	60	60	68	64	72	69	71
wojtek.pierre	77	75	76	67	61	64	66	68	67	57	60	58	62	63	62	69	70	69
hgsgnlp	75	75	75	66	59	62	67	66	67	59	59	59	59	67	63	69	69	69
UWB	74	77	75	61	68	64	74	59	65	57	63	60	66	56	61	65	73	69
NL-FIIT	76	74	75	62	64	63	69	63	66	61	57	59	58	65	61	68	70	69
TubOslo	82	67	74	62	63	62	62	68	65	59	56	58	57	66	62	68	66	67
YNU_Lab	74	74	74	66	56	61	63	67	65	55	61	58	63	56	60	66	70	68
Braint	77	70	73	61	60	60	60	68	64	56	55	55	60	57	59	63	66	65
EmoNLP	73	72	73	62	57	60	63	62	63	55	56	56	56	61	58	64	64	64
RW	71	72	72	60	57	59	62	63	62	55	52	53	56	60	58	62	63	63
Baseline	69	71	70	58	54	56	62	62	62	54	51	52	55	59	57	63	63	63
USI-IR	71	69	70	58	51	54	59	59	59	49	58	53	57	50	53	59	62	61
THU_NGN	77	78	77	69	63	66	68	68	68	60	63	62	61	66	64	71	68	70
SINAI	68	68	68	52	52	52	59	60	59	52	51	52	56	55	55	61	61	61
UTFPR	64	53	58	54	60	57	59	58	58	50	53	52	51	62	56	66	56	61
CNHZ2017	65	70	67	58	47	52	58	59	59	51	48	50	49	58	53	58	57	58
lyb3b	72	64	68	58	46	52	55	62	58	46	53	50	47	50	49	60	58	59
AdobeResearch	62	65	63	52	52	52	52	51	52	48	45	46	49	52	50	56	54	55
Anonymous	76	77	76	64	67	65	70	64	67	62	59	60	59	69	64	74	68	71
dinel	61	61	61	52	37	43	52	49	50	44	50	47	44	54	48	51	50	50
CHANDA	46	64	54	39	36	38	54	42	47	38	37	37	51	20	29	39	58	46
NLP_LDW	33	38	36	18	12	14	20	31	25	22	26	24	18	7	10	18	17	18

Table 10: Results by emotion class. Note that this table is limited to the six emotion labels of interest in the data set. However, other labels predicted than these six were taken into account for calculation of the final macro F_1 score. Therefore, the macro F_1 calculated from this table is different from the results in Table 5 in two cases (THU_NGN and Anonymous, who would be on rank 9 and rank 10, when predictions for classes outside the labels were ignored.).

B Examples

Table 11 shows examples which have been correctly or wrongly predicted by all instances. They are discussed in Section 4.5.

Emo.	+/−	Instance
Anger	+	You can't spend your whole life holding the door open for people and then being TRIGGER when they dont thank you. Nobody asked you to do it.
	+	I get impatient and TRIGGER when I'm hungry
	+	Anyone have the first fast and TRIGGER that I can borrow?
	−	I'm kinda TRIGGER that I have to work on Father's Day
	−	@USERNAME she'll become TRIGGER that I live close by and she will find me and punch me
	−	This has been such a miserable day and I'm TRIGGER because I wish I could've enjoyed myself more
Disgust	+	I find it TRIGGER when I can see your underwear through your leggings
	+	@USERNAME ew ew eeww your weird I can't I would feel so TRIGGER when people touch my hair
	+	nyc smells TRIGGER when it's wet.
	−	I wanted a cup of coffee for the train ride. Got ignored twice. I left TRIGGER because I can't afford to miss my train. #needcoffee :(
	−	So this thing where other black people ask where you're "really" from then act TRIGGER when you reply with some US state. STAHP
	−	I'm so TRIGGER that I have to go to the post office to get my jacket that i ordered because delivering it was obviously rocket science
Fear	+	@USERNAME & explain how much the boys mean to me but I'm too TRIGGER that they'll just laugh at me bc my dad laughed after he
	+	I threw up in a parking lot last night. I'm TRIGGER that's becoming my thing. #illbutmostlymentally
	+	When you holding back your emotions and you're TRIGGER that when someone tries to comfort you they'll come spilling out http://url.removed
	−	It's so funny how people come up to me at work speaking Portuguese and they get TRIGGER when I respond in Portuguese
	−	@USERNAME it seems so fun but i haven't got to try it yet. my mom and sis are always TRIGGER when i try do something new with food.
	−	@USERNAME It's hard to be TRIGGER when your giggle is so cute
Joy	+	maybe im so unTRIGGER because i never see the sunlight?
	+	@USERNAME you're so welcome !! i'm super TRIGGER that i've discovered ur work ! cant wait to see more !!
	+	@USERNAME Im so TRIGGER that you guys had fun love you
	−	@USERNAME Not TRIGGER that your show is a rerun. It seems every week one or more your segments is a rerun.
	−	I am actually TRIGGER when not invited to certain things. I don't have the time and patience to pretend.
	−	This has been such a miserable day and I'm TRIGGER because I wish I could've enjoyed myself more
Sadness	+	this award honestly made me so TRIGGER because my teacher is leaving http://url.removed
	+	It is very TRIGGER that people think depression actually does work like that... http://url.removed
	+	@USERNAME @USERNAME @USERNAME It's also TRIGGER that you so hurt about it :'(
	−	Some bitch stole my seat then I had to steal the seat next to me. The boy looked TRIGGER when he saw me, and he was smart! #iwasgonnapass
	−	I was so TRIGGER because I was having fun lol then i slipped cus I wasn't wearing shoes
	−	@USERNAME I wipe at my eyes next, then swim a bit. "I'm sorry." I repeat, TRIGGER that I made him worry.
Surprise	+	why am i not TRIGGER that cal said that
	+	@USERNAME why am I not TRIGGER that you're the founder
	+	@USERNAME I'm still TRIGGER when students know my name. I'm usually just "that guy who wears bow ties" =) (and there are a few at WC!)
	−	It's TRIGGER when I see people that have the same phone as me no has htcs
	−	There is a little boy in here who is TRIGGER that he has to pay for things and that we won't just give him things
	−	totally TRIGGER that my fams celebrating easter today because my sister goes back to uni sunday

Table 11: Subsample of Tweets that were correctly predicted by all teams and of Tweets that were not correctly predicted by any team.

Amobee at IEST 2018: Transfer Learning from Language Models

Alon Rozental[*]**, Daniel Fleischer**[*]**, Zohar Kelrich**[*]
Amobee Inc., Tel Aviv, Israel
`alon.rozental@amobee.com`
`daniel.fleischer@amobee.com`
`zohar.kelrich@amobee.com`

Abstract

This paper describes the system developed at Amobee for the WASSA 2018 implicit emotions shared task (IEST). The goal of this task was to predict the emotion expressed by missing words in tweets without an explicit mention of those words. We developed an ensemble system consisting of language models together with LSTM-based networks containing a CNN attention mechanism. Our approach represents a novel use of language models—specifically trained on a large Twitter dataset—to predict and classify emotions. Our system reached 1st place with a macro F_1 score of 0.7145.

1 Introduction

Sentiment analysis (SA) is a sub-field of natural language processing (NLP) that explores the automatic deduction of feelings and attitudes from textual data. One popular choice of source to study is Twitter, a social network website where people publish short messages, called tweets, with a maximum length of 280 characters. People write on various topics, including global and local events, public figures, brands and products. Twitter data has attracted the interest of both academia and industry for the last several years. It contains some unique features, such as emojis, misspelling and slang that are of interest to NLP researchers while also containing insights relevant for business intelligence, marketing and e-governance.

The implicit emotions shared task (IEST) is part of the WASSA 2018 workshop, and is concerned with classifying tweets into one of 6 emotions—anger, disgust, fear, joy, sadness and surprise—without an explicit mention of emotion words. There were 30 teams who participated in the task; for a description and analysis of the task and the datasets, see Klinger et al. (2018).

This paper describes our specially developed system for the shared task; it comprises several ensembles, where our new contribution is the use of a language model as an emotion classifier. A language model, based on the Transformer-Decoder architecture (Vaswani et al., 2017) was trained using a large Twitter dataset, and used to produce probabilities for each of the 6 emotions.

The paper is organized as follows: Sections 2 and 3 describe our data sources and the embedding training, Section 4 describes the training and usage of the language models. In Section 5 we describe the resources that are used as features; Section 6 describes the architecture, broken into smaller components. Finally, we review and conclude in Section 7.

2 Data Sources

We used several data sources for the shared task:

1. Twitter Firehose: we took a random sample of 5 billion unique tweets using the Twitter Firehose service. The tweets were used to train language models and word embeddings; in the following, we will refer to this as the Tweets_5B dataset.

2. Semeval 2018 shared task 1 datasets, specifically subtasks 1 and 5 in which tweets are classified into one of 4 emotions (anger, fear, joy and sadness; subtask 1) and a multi-label classification of tweets into 11 emotions (sub-task 5). We used both the datasets and our trained models; Rozental and Fleischer (2018) describes the system and Mohammad et al. (2018) describes the shared task.

3. The official IEST 2018 task datasets; the missing emotion words are replaced by the

---

Proceedings of the 9th Workshop on Computational Approaches to Subjectivity, Sentiment and Social Media Analysis, pages 43–49
Brussels, Belgium, October 31, 2018. ©2018 Association for Computational Linguistics
https://doi.org/10.18653/v1/P17

---

[*]These authors contributed equally to this work.

Label	Train	Dev	Test
Anger	25562	1600	4794
Disgust	25558	1597	4794
Fear	25575	1598	4791
Joy	27958	1736	5246
Sad	23165	1460	4340
Surprise	25565	1600	4792
Total	153383	9591	28757

Table 1: Distributions of labels in the train, dev and test datasets.

keyword [#TRIGGERWORD#]. Table 1 presents the label distributions; refer to the task paper for a description of the dataset.

We used different pre-processing procedures on the aforementioned tweets for our different learning algorithms. Those procedures ranged from no pre-processing at all (for language models), through a simple cleanup (for word embeddings) to an extensive pre-processing, used with our Semeval (2018) system to produce predictions, with the following processing steps: word tokenization, part of speech tagging, regex treatment, lemmatization, named entity recognition, synonym replacement and word replacement using a wikipedia-based dictionary.

3 Embeddings Training

Word embeddings are a set of algorithms designed to encode a large vocabulary using low-dimensional real vectors. Depending on the algorithm, the vectors carry additional semantic information, and are used in down-stream NLP tasks. We trained word embeddings specifically for the task; first, starting with the Tweets_5B dataset, we removed exact duplicates. Then we used a regex process: URLs, emails and Twitter usernames were replaced with special keywords. Next we removed tweets by using a text similarity threshold[1]. Finally, we replaced rare words with a special token; the criterion was to have a vocabulary of 300K unique tokens in total. We used the Gensim package (Řehůřek and Sojka, 2010) to train 4 embeddings with sizes of 300, 500, 700 and 1000 with the Word2vec (Mikolov et al., 2013) algorithm. Similarly, we trained 4 embeddings using the FastText

algorithm (Bojanowski et al., 2017). We found that for the purpose of downstream tasks, the Word2vec embeddings outperformed the FastText embeddings for each of the 4 sizes. In addition, the Word2vec embedding of size 1000 performed better than the others, provided that the training set is large enough. The size of the IEST 2018 train set was sufficiently large for us to use that single word embedding. The embeddings usage is described in the architecture section 6.

4 Language Models

We trained a language model (LM) using the Transformer-Decoder architecture, introduced in Vaswani et al. (2017). We used the Tensor2Tensor library (Vaswani et al., 2018) with the built-in `transformer-big` parameter set, where we only set the tweet maximum length to be 64 tokens. The model was trained for 2 days using the Tweets_5B dataset on 8 Nvidia Tesla V100 GPUs. We will refer to this model as LM1. We built a pipeline around the trained model, such that given a sentence, its probability to be randomly generated by the model is returned. For example, under LM1 the probability of the text *"I was surprised to see you here"* (S1) being generated is $\exp(-25.76)$ and the text *"I was afraid to see you here"* (S2) has a probability of $\exp(-27.86)$. One can then calculate the conditional probability of having S1 given only S1 or S2 were generated, with a resulting value of 0.89.

In order to use LM1 to predict the correct label for a tweet, we created a list of possible words for each of the six emotions, presented in appendix A. For each tweet, we replaced the trigger word with each of the words from the list and then selected the most probable version of each emotion. The resulting 6 normalized probabilities are considered to be the probabilities assigned by the LM for the possible labels. See table 2 for a more detailed example with 3 emotions.

In addition to LM1, we trained another language model, denoted by LM2; it was generated by taking LM1 and continuing its training using just the tweets of the shared task dataset, where the trigger word was replaced by the most probable word (according to LM1 predictions) in the emotional category matching the label. LM2 was trained for a day using a single V100 GPU. The prediction procedure was the same as for LM1. For the purposes of downstream analysis,

---

[1] Using the `SequenceMatcher` module in Python.

Emotion	Possible Tweet	Log Probability	Max	Final Probability
Joy	I'm **happy** than you.	-24.38	-19.7	0.89995
	I'm **happier** than you.	-19.7		
Angry	I'm **angry** than you.	-26.8	-21.9	0.09972
	I'm **angrier** than you.	-21.9		
Surprise	I'm **surprise** than you.	-27.6	-27.6	0.00033
	I'm **surprised** than you.	-31.5		

Table 2: Probability calculation of the sentence "I'm #{TRIGGERWORD} than you." with 3 emotions using the language models. Notice that the sentences which are grammatically incorrect have much lower probabilities.

the features we extracted from these models are the final 6 probabilities $p_i\,(s)$, the log probability to generate the most likely candidate tweet by random—referred to as tweet complexity—given by $\mathrm{comp}\,(s) = \max_{w \in \mathrm{W}} \log p_w\,(s)$, where W is the set of possible replacement words and finally, for each candidate tweet, its shifted log probability, given by $\log \tilde{p}_w\,(s) = \log p_w\,(s) - \mathrm{comp}\,(s)$.

5 Features

We used 4 types of features in our system: first we used predictions from the language models; we took both the log probabilities of the tweets with the trigger words replaced by each word from appendix A, as well as the final 6 probabilities for each tweet, for each of the two language model. Next, we used our system for the Semeval 2018 task 1 competition to generate features and predictions for sub-tasks 1 and 5 (as mentioned in section 2). Next we used 2 external resources for tweets embedding: Universal Sentence Embedding (Cer et al., 2018), using the Tensorflow Hub service and the DeepMoji package (Felbo et al., 2017). We created 7 versions of each tweet by replacing the trigger word with one of the 6 emotions and an unrecognized word, thus creating 7 Universal Sentence Embedding of dimension 512. The DeepMoji embedding size is 2304 and only one was produced for each tweet. Finally, we added a binary feature that captures whether the trigger word has a prefix in each tweet. These features are used in the 1st (6.2) and 2nd (6.3) ensembles.

6 Architecture Overview

The system comprises of a multi-level soft-voting ensemble. Each building block described in this section is a classifier by itself and is presented as such. For our submitted solution, the building blocks were trained jointly in the manner described in the next section, using a single Nvidia GTX 1080 Ti GPU. We used the Keras library (Chollet et al., 2015) and the TensorFlow framework (Abadi et al., 2016).

6.1 Mini ASC Modules

This component consists of a bi-LSTM layer with a CNN-based attention mechanism, similar to a single module in the Amobee Sentiment Classifier (ASC) architecture described in (2018). A Dropout layer (Srivastava et al., 2014) of 0.5 was applied between each 2 consecutive layers except for the word embedding layer; for an illustration, see figure 1. The input was the official dataset, transformed using our trained embeddings, where the trigger word was embedded as an unknown word using the rare-words token. We concatenated an additional bit to each word vector, denoting whether it is the missing trigger-word, differentiating it from other unknown words. There are three key differences from our original work:

1. The GRU layer was replaced by an LSTM layer.

2. Residual connections were added from the output of the max-pooling layer to the network output.

3. Hyper parameters values were in the following ranges: embedding size=1000, LSTM hidden size=[128, 512], number of filters=[128, 512] and dense layer size=[16, 32].

Training a single mini-ASC module on the IEST 2018 training set using the Adam optimizer (Kingma and Ba, 2014), categorial cross entropy

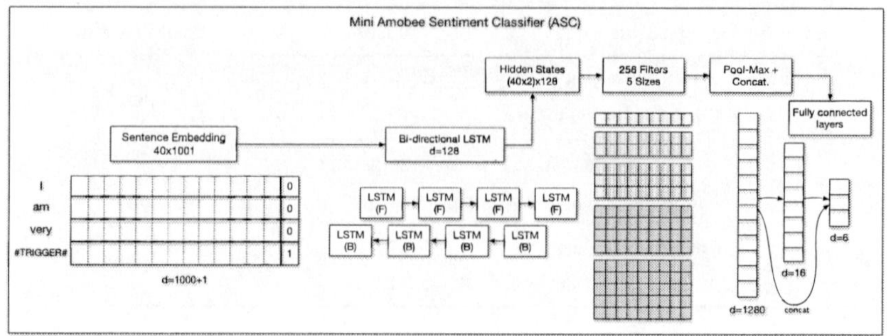

Figure 1: Architecture of the mini Amobee sentiment classifier.

loss function and a batch size of 32, results in an average accuracy of 0.669 on the official validation set.

6.2 First Ensemble

The first level ensemble incorporates 4 mini ASC modules and 3 identical sub-networks (see figure 2). The sub-networks share the same architecture and their inputs are the following:

1. Universal + DeepMoji embeddings; this network reaches an average F_1 score of 0.587 by itself on the validation set.

2. The LM1 + LM2 predictions; this network reaches an average F_1 score of 0.637 by itself on the validation set.

3. The Semeval 2018 predictions, together with the LM1 predictions; this network reaches an average F_1 score of 0.646 by itself on the validation set.

These networks share the same structure: the input is connected to a dense layer of dimension 16 and then concatenated with the input going into a final dense layer of size 6 with a softmax activation function. Dropout layers of 0.5 are applied after the input and before the output layers.

The other 4 models are copies of the architecture described in 6.1. All orange layers of size 6 are outputs of the model and are trained against the labels with equal contribution to the total loss. We used the Adam optimizer with a batch size of 32, a learning rate of $5 \cdot 10^{-4}$ and a decay of $5 \cdot 10^{-5}$ (decay in Adam is introduced in Keras, and is not part of the original algorithm; it represents decay between batches). This network reaches an average F_1 score of 0.700 on the validation set. This first ensemble is denoted by E1.

6.3 Second Ensemble

In the second level ensemble (figure 3), we started with 8 copies of the aforementioned E1 models (with different parameters for the Mini ASC modules in the ranges described in section 6.1) and combined them with a concatenation of the following features (described in section 5): two external embeddings (Universal Sentence Embedding, DeepMoji) and our Semeval 2018 pipeline predictions.

We have used a dense layer of size 16 over the outputs of the 8 E1 models and a dense layer of size 100 over all of the above features (including the E1 outputs). These two layers were concatenated into a softmax layer of size 6 which was the output of the second ensemble; we denote this by E2. This E2 network reaches an average F_1 score of 0.702 on the validation set. The final model is a soft voting ensemble, comprising 128 networks of type E2; this probability averaging is meant to decrease the variance of the model which reaches an average F_1 score of 0.705 on the validation set.

Since the final model is an ensemble, where some models are somewhat overfitted with respect to the training dataset (e.g. E1) and some models are not overfitted at all (LM1), we decided to use the validation dataset to train the final model for an additional 4 epochs using a large batch size of 900. After this procedure, the system scored an F_1 of 0.7145 on the test dataset.

7 Review and Conclusions

In this paper we described the system developed for the WASSA 2018 implicit emotion shared task. It consists of a multi-level ensemble, combining a novel use of language models to predict the right emotion word, together with

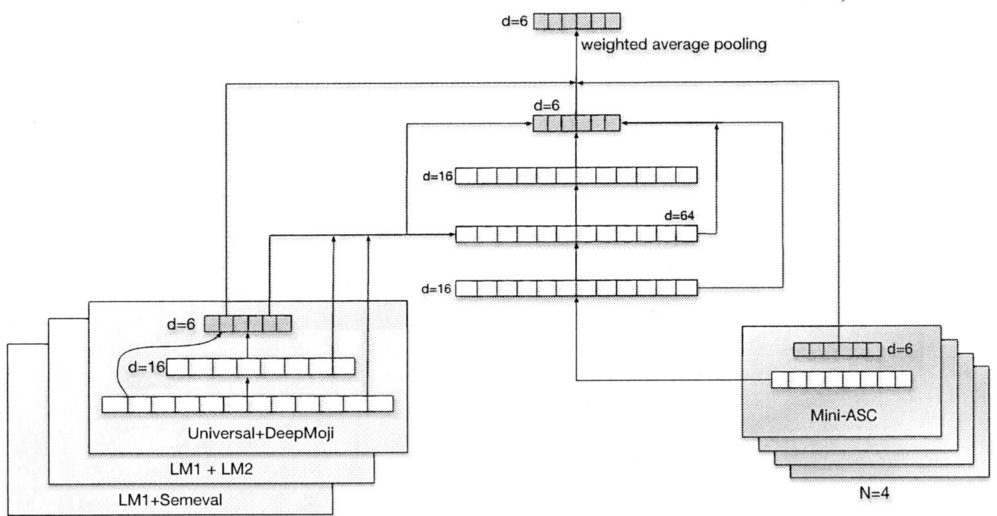

Figure 2: Architecture of the first-level ensemble.

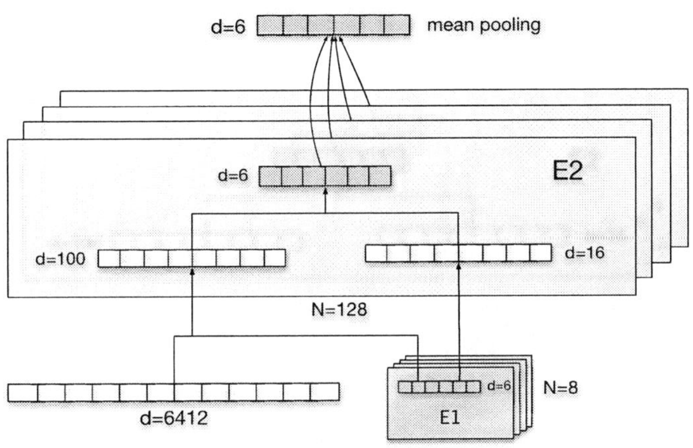

Figure 3: Architecture of the second-level ensemble.

previous high-ranking architecture, used in the Semeval 2018 sentiment shared task, and two external embeddings. The system reached 1st place with macro F_1 of 0.7145, with the next system scoring 0.7105. Examining the nature of the this task, it is a combination of both sentiment classification and word prediction; this was the motivation of using the Semeval 2018 models, which were designed to classify emotions. On the other hand, the language model is specifically trained to maximize the likelihood of matching a word to a given sentence, thus naturally lending itself to the word prediction aspect of the task.

We have seen that splitting the dataset into two parts, one for training our models and the other for the ensembling process (in this case the second part is the validation set) is much more beneficial than training our models on the combined bigger dataset, in cases when some of the models are expected to be much less generalizable than others.

It is interesting to note the task organizers have tested human performance on a subset sample, achieving macro F_1 of 0.45, which is much lower than the automated systems.

We plan to release the word embeddings and language models as open-source in the near future to benefit further research and increase sharing of resources.

References

Martín Abadi, Paul Barham, Jianmin Chen, Zhifeng Chen, Andy Davis, Jeffrey Dean, Matthieu Devin, Sanjay Ghemawat, Geoffrey Irving, Michael Isard, et al. 2016. Tensorflow: A system for large-scale machine learning. In *OSDI*, volume 16, pages 265–283.

Piotr Bojanowski, Edouard Grave, Armand Joulin, and Tomas Mikolov. 2017. Enriching word vectors with subword information. *Transactions of the Association for Computational Linguistics*, 5:135–146.

Daniel Cer, Yinfei Yang, Sheng-yi Kong, Nan Hua, Nicole Limtiaco, Rhomni St. John, Noah Constant, Mario Guajardo-Cespedes, Steve Yuan, Chris Tar, Yun-Hsuan Sung, Brian Strope, and Ray Kurzweil. 2018. Universal sentence encoder. *CoRR*, abs/1803.11175.

François Chollet et al. 2015. Keras. `https://github.com/keras-team/keras`.

Bjarke Felbo, Alan Mislove, Anders Søgaard, Iyad Rahwan, and Sune Lehmann. 2017. Using millions of emoji occurrences to learn any-domain representations for detecting sentiment, emotion and sarcasm. In *Conference on Empirical Methods in Natural Language Processing (EMNLP)*.

Diederik P Kingma and Jimmy Ba. 2014. Adam: A method for stochastic optimization. *arXiv preprint arXiv:1412.6980*.

Roman Klinger, Orphée de Clercq, Saif M. Mohammad, and Alexandra Balahur. 2018. Iest: Wassa-2018 implicit emotions shared task. In *Proceedings of the 9th Workshop on Computational Approaches to Subjectivity, Sentiment and Social Media Analysis*, Brussels, Belgium. Association for Computational Linguistics.

Tomas Mikolov, Ilya Sutskever, Kai Chen, Greg S Corrado, and Jeff Dean. 2013. Distributed representations of words and phrases and their compositionality. In C. J. C. Burges, L. Bottou, M. Welling, Z. Ghahramani, and K. Q. Weinberger, editors, *Advances in Neural Information Processing Systems 26*, pages 3111–3119. Curran Associates, Inc.

Saif M. Mohammad, Felipe Bravo-Marquez, Mohammad Salameh, and Svetlana Kiritchenko. 2018. Semeval-2018 Task 1: Affect in tweets. In *Proceedings of International Workshop on Semantic Evaluation (SemEval-2018)*, New Orleans, LA, USA.

Radim Řehůřek and Petr Sojka. 2010. Software Framework for Topic Modelling with Large Corpora. In *Proceedings of the LREC 2010 Workshop on New Challenges for NLP Frameworks*, pages 45–50, Valletta, Malta. ELRA. `http://is.muni.cz/publication/884893/en`.

Alon Rozental and Daniel Fleischer. 2018. Amobee at semeval-2018 task 1: GRU neural network with a CNN attention mechanism for sentiment classification. *CoRR*, abs/1804.04380.

Nitish Srivastava, Geoffrey Hinton, Alex Krizhevsky, Ilya Sutskever, and Ruslan Salakhutdinov. 2014. Dropout: a simple way to prevent neural networks from overfitting. *The Journal of Machine Learning Research*, 15(1):1929–1958.

Ashish Vaswani, Samy Bengio, Eugene Brevdo, Francois Chollet, Aidan N. Gomez, Stephan Gouws, Llion Jones, Łukasz Kaiser, Nal Kalchbrenner, Niki Parmar, Ryan Sepassi, Noam Shazeer, and Jakob Uszkoreit. 2018. Tensor2tensor for neural machine translation. *CoRR*, abs/1803.07416.

Ashish Vaswani, Noam Shazeer, Niki Parmar, Jakob Uszkoreit, Llion Jones, Aidan N. Gomez, Lukasz Kaiser, and Illia Polosukhin. 2017. Attention is all you need. *CoRR*, abs/1706.03762.

A Emotions Lexicon

Emotion	Words
Anger	Anger, angry, fuming, angrily, angrier, angers, angered, furious.
Disgust	Disgust, disgusted, disgusting, disgustedly, disgusts.
Fear	Fear, feared, fearing, fearfully, frightens, fearful, afraid, scared.
Joy	Joy, happy, thrilling, joyfully, happily, happier, delights, joyful, joyous.
Sad	Sad, sadden, depressing, depressingly, sadder, depresses, sorrowful, saddened.
Surprise	Surprise, surprised, surprising, surprisingly, surprises, shocked.

Table 3: Emotion lexicon used to produce predictions using the language models.

IIIDYT at IEST 2018: Implicit Emotion Classification With Deep Contextualized Word Representations

Jorge A. Balazs, Edison Marrese-Taylor and **Yutaka Matsuo**

Graduate School of Engineering

The University of Tokyo

{jorge, emarrese, matsuo}@weblab.t.u-tokyo.ac.jp

Abstract

In this paper we describe our system designed for the WASSA 2018 Implicit Emotion Shared Task (IEST), which obtained 2nd place out of 30 teams with a test macro F1 score of 0.710. The system is composed of a single pre-trained ELMo layer for encoding words, a Bidirectional Long-Short Memory Network BiLSTM for enriching word representations with context, a max-pooling operation for creating sentence representations from them, and a Dense Layer for projecting the sentence representations into label space. Our official submission was obtained by ensembling 6 of these models initialized with different random seeds. The code for replicating this paper is available at https://github.com/jabalazs/implicit_emotion.

1 Introduction

Although the definition of emotion is still debated among the scientific community, the automatic identification and understanding of human emotions by machines has long been of interest in computer science. It has usually been assumed that emotions are triggered by the interpretation of a stimulus event according to its meaning.

As language usually reflects the emotional state of an individual, it is natural to study human emotions by understanding how they are reflected in text. We see that many words indeed have affect as a core part of their meaning, for example, *dejected* and *wistful* denote some amount of sadness, and are thus associated with sadness. On the other hand, some words are associated with affect even though they do not denote affect. For example, *failure* and *death* describe concepts that are usually accompanied by sadness and thus they denote some amount of sadness. In this context, the task of automatically recognizing emotions from text has recently attracted the attention of re-

searchers in Natural Language Processing. This task is usually formalized as the classification of words, phrases, or documents into predefined discrete emotion categories or dimensions. Some approaches have aimed at also predicting the degree to which an emotion is expressed in text (Mohammad and Bravo-Marquez, 2017).

In light of this, the WASSA 2018 Implicit Emotion Shared Task (IEST) (Klinger et al., 2018) was proposed to help find ways to automatically learn the link between situations and the emotion they trigger. The task consisted in predicting the emotion of a word excluded from a tweet. Removed words, or *trigger-words*, included the terms "sad", "happy", "disgusted", "surprised", "angry", "afraid" and their synonyms, and the task was to predict the emotion they conveyed, specifically sadness, joy, disgust, surprise, anger and fear.

From a machine learning perspective, this problem can be seen as sentence classification, in which the goal is to classify a sentence, or in particular a tweet, into one of several categories. In the case of IEST, the problem is specially challenging since tweets contain informal language, the heavy usage of emoji, hashtags and username mentions.

In this paper we describe our system designed for IEST, which obtained the second place out of 30 teams. Our system did not require manual feature engineering and only minimal use of external data. Concretely, our approach is composed of a single pre-trained ELMo layer for encoding words (Peters et al., 2018), a Bidirectional Long-Short Memory Network (BiLSTM) (Graves and Schmidhuber, 2005; Graves et al., 2013), for enriching word representations with context, a max-pooling operation for creating sentence representations from said word vectors, and finally a Dense Layer for projecting the sentence representations into label space. To the best of our knowledge,

Proceedings of the 9th Workshop on Computational Approaches to Subjectivity, Sentiment and Social Media Analysis, pages 50–56

Brussels, Belgium, October 31, 2018. ©2018 Association for Computational Linguistics

https://doi.org/10.18653/v1/P17

our system, which we plan to release, is the first to utilize ELMo for emotion recognition.

2 Proposed Approach

2.1 Preprocessing

As our model is purely character-based, we performed little data preprocessing. Table 1 shows the special tokens found in the datasets, and how we substituted them.

Original	Replacement
[#TRIGGERWORD#]	_TRIGGERWORD_
@USERNAME	_USERNAME_
[NEWLINE]	_NEWLINE_
http://url.removed	_URL_

Table 1: Preprocessing substitutions.

Furthermore, we tokenized the text using a variation of the `twokenize.py`[1] script, a Python port of the original `Twokenize.java` (Gimpel et al., 2011). Concretely, we created an emoji-aware version of it by incorporating knowledge from an emoji database,[2] which we slightly modified for avoiding conflict with emoji sharing unicode codes with common glyphs used in Twitter,[3] and for making it compatible with Python 3.

2.2 Architecture

Figure 1 summarizes our proposed architecture. Our input is based on Embeddings from Language Models (ELMo) by Peters et al. (2018). These are character-based word representations allowing the model to avoid the "unknown token" problem. ELMo uses a set of convolutional neural networks to extract features from character embeddings, and builds word vectors from them. These are then fed to a multi-layer Bidirectional Language Model (BiLM) which returns context-sensitive vectors for each input word.

We used a single-layer BiLSTM as context fine-tuner (Graves and Schmidhuber, 2005; Graves et al., 2013), on top of the ELMo embeddings, and then aggregated the hidden states it returned by using max-pooling, which has been shown to perform well on sentence classification tasks (Conneau et al., 2017).

Finally, we used a single-layer fully-connected network for projecting the pooled BiLSTM output into a vector corresponding to the label logits for each predicted class.

2.3 Implementation Details and Hyperparameters

ELMo Layer: We used the official AllenNLP implementation of the ELMo model[4], with the official weights pre-trained on the 1 Billion Word Language Model Benchmark, which contains about 800M tokens of news crawl data from WMT 2011 (Chelba et al., 2014).

Dimensionalities: By default the ELMo layer outputs a 1024-dimensional vector, which we then feed to a BiLSTM with output size 2048, resulting in a 4096-dimensional vector when concatenating forward and backward directions for each word of the sequence[5]. After max-pooling the BiLSTM output over the sequence dimension, we obtain a single 4096-dimensional vector corresponding to the tweet representation. This representation is finally fed to a single-layer fully-connected network with input size 4096, 512 hidden units, output size 6, and a ReLU nonlinearity after the hidden layer. The output of the dense layer is a 6-dimensional logit vector for each input example.

Loss Function: As this corresponds to a multiclass classification problem (predicting a single class for each example, with more than 2 classes to choose from), we used the Cross-Entropy Loss as implemented in PyTorch (Paszke et al., 2017).

Optimization: We optimized the model with Adam (Kingma and Ba, 2014), using default hyperparameters ($\beta_1 = 0.9$, $\beta_2 = 0.999$, $\epsilon = 10^{-8}$), following a slanted triangular learning rate schedule (Howard and Ruder, 2018), also with default hyperparameters ($cut\_frac = 0.1$, $ratio = 32$), and a maximum learning rate $\eta_{max} = 0.001$, over $T = 23,970$ iterations[6].

Regularization: we used a dropout layer (Srivastava et al., 2014), with probability of 0.5 after both the ELMo and the hidden fully-connected layer, and another one with probability of 0.1 af-

---

[1] https://github.com/myleott/ark-twokenize-py
[2] https://github.com/carpedm20/emoji/blob/e7bff32/emoji/unicode_codes.py
[3] For example, the hashtag emoji is composed by the unicode code points U+23 U+FE0F U+20E3, which include U+23, the same code point for the # glyph.

[4] https://allenai.github.io/allennlp-docs/api/allennlp.modules.elmo.html
[5] A BiLSTM is composed of two separate LSTMs that read the input in opposite directions and whose outputs are concatenated at the hidden dimension. This results in a vector double the dimension of the input for each time step.
[6] This number is obtained by multiplying the number of epochs (10), times the total number of batches, which for the training dataset corresponds to 2396 batches of 64 elements, and 1 batch of 39 elements, hence $2397 \times 10 = 23,970$.

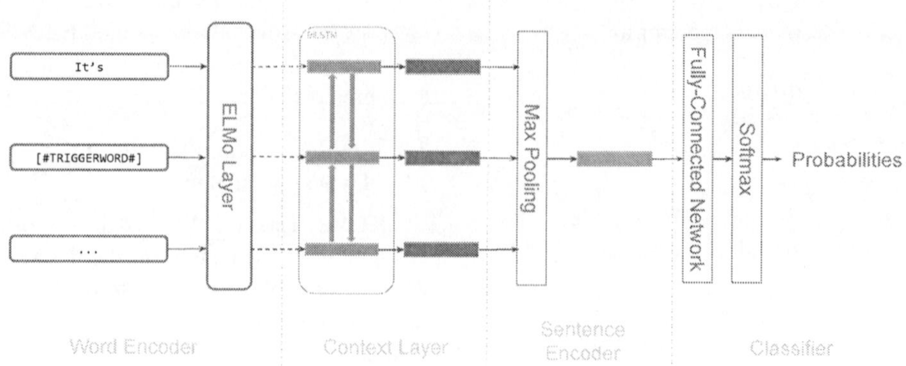

Figure 1: Proposed architecture.

ter the max-pooling aggregation layer. We also reshuffled the training examples between epochs, resulting in a different batch for each iteration.

Model Selection: To choose the best hyperparameter configuration we measured the classification accuracy on the validation (trial) set.

2.4 Ensembles

Once we found the best-performing configuration we trained 10 models using different random seeds, and tried averaging the output class probabilities of all their possible $\sum_{k=1}^{9} \binom{9}{k} = 511$ combinations. As Figure 2 shows, we empirically found that a specific combination of 6 models yielded the best results (70.52%), providing evidence for the fact that using a number of independent classifiers equal to the number of class labels provides the best results when doing average ensembling (Bonab and Can, 2016).

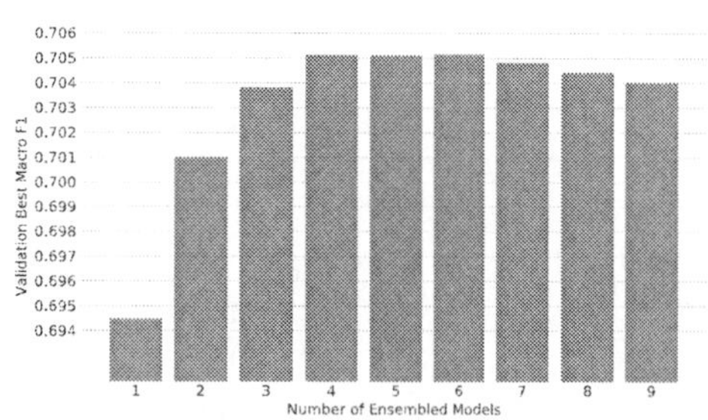

Figure 2: Effect of the number of ensembled models on validation performance.

3 Experiments and Analyses

We performed several experiments to gain insights on how the proposed model's performance inter-

acts with the shared task's data. We performed an ablation study to see how some of the main hyperparameters affect performance, and an analysis of tweets containing hashtags and emoji to understand how these two types of tokens help the model predict the trigger-word's emotion. We also observed the effects of varying the amount of data used for training the model to evaluate whether it would be worthwhile to gather more training data.

3.1 Ablation Study

We performed an ablation study on a single model having obtained 69.23% accuracy on the validation set. Results are summarized in Table 2.

We can observe that the architectural choice that had the greatest impact on our model was the ELMo layer, providing a 3.71% boost in performance as compared to using GloVe pre-trained word embeddings.

We can further see that emoji also contributed significantly to the model's performance. In Section 3.4 we give some pointers to understanding why this is so.

Additionally, we tried using the concatenation of the max-pooled, average-pooled and last hidden states of the BiLSTM as the sentence representation, following Howard and Ruder (2018), but found out that this impacted performance negatively. We hypothesize this is due to tweets being too short for needing such a rich representation. Also, the size of the concatenated vector was $4096 \times 3 = 12,288$, which probably could not be properly exploited by the 512-dimensional fully-connected layer.

Using a greater BiLSTM hidden size did not help the model, probably because of the reason

Variation	Accuracy (%)	Δ%
Submitted	**69.23**	-
No emoji	68.36	- 0.87
No ELMo	65.52	- 3.71
Concat Pooling	68.47	- 0.76
LSTM hidden=4096	69.10	- 0.13
LSTM hidden=1024	68.93	- 0.30
LSTM hidden=512	68.43	- 0.80
POS emb dim=100	68.99	- 0.24
POS emb dim=75	68.61	- 0.62
POS emb dim=50	69.33	+ 0.10
POS emb dim=25	69.21	- 0.02
SGD optim lr=1	64.33	- 4.90
SGD optim lr=0.1	66.11	- 3.12
SGD optim lr=0.01	60.72	- 8.51
SGD optim lr=0.001	30.49	- 38.74

Table 2: Ablation study results.

Accuracies were obtained from the validation dataset. Each model was trained with the same random seed and hyperparameters, save for the one listed. "No emoji" is the same model trained on the training dataset with no emoji, "No ELMo" corresponds to having switched the ELMo word encoding layer with a simple pre-trained GloVe embedding lookup table, and "Concat Pooling" obtained sentence representations by using the pooling method described by Howard and Ruder (2018). "LSTM hidden" corresponds to the hidden dimension of the BiLSTM, "POS emb dim" to the dimension of the part-of-speech embeddings, and "SGD optim lr" to the learning rate used while optimizing with the schedule described by Conneau et al. (2017).

mentioned earlier; the fully-connected layer was not big or deep enough to exploit the additional information. Similarly, using a smaller hidden size neither helped.

We found that using 50-dimensional part-of-speech embeddings slightly improved results, which implies that better fine-tuning this hyperparameter, or using a better POS tagger could yield an even better performance.

Regarding optimization strategies, we also tried using SGD with different learning rates and a stepwise learning rate schedule as described by Conneau et al. (2018), but we found that doing this did not improve performance.

Finally, Figure 3 shows the effect of using different dropout probabilities. We can see that having higher dropout after the word-representation layer and the fully-connected network's hidden layer, while having a low dropout after the sentence encoding layer yielded better results overall.

3.2 Error Analysis

Figure 4 shows the confusion matrix of a single model evaluated on the test set, and Table 3 the

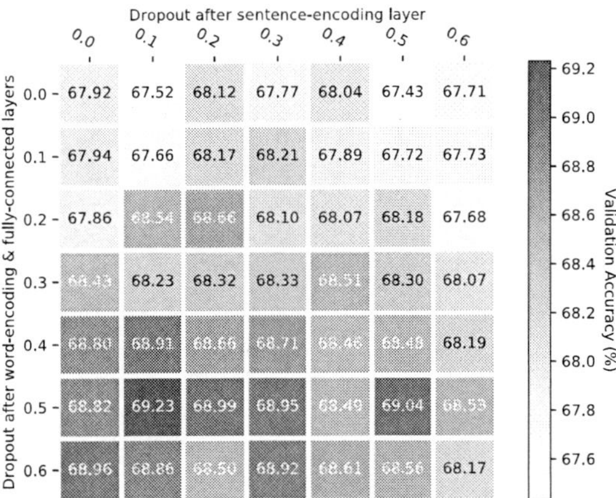

Figure 3: Dropout Ablation.

Rows correspond to the dropout applied both after the ELMo layer (word encoding layer) and after the fully-connected network's hidden layer, while columns correspond to the dropout applied after the max-pooling operation (sentence encoding layer.)

corresponding classification report. In general, we confirm what Klinger et al. (2018) report: anger was the most difficult class to predict, followed by surprise, whereas joy, fear, and disgust are the better performing ones.

To observe whether any particular pattern arose from the sentence representations encoded by our model, we projected them into 3d space through Principal Component Analysis (PCA), and were surprised to find that 2 clearly defined clusters emerged (see Figure 6), one containing the majority of datapoints, and another containing joy tweets exclusively. Upon further exploration we also found that the smaller cluster was composed only by tweets containing the pattern un __TRIGGERWORD__, and further, that all of them were correctly classified.

It is also worth mentioning that there are 5827 tweets in the training set with this pattern. Of these, 5822 (99.9%) correspond to the label joy. We observe a similar trend on the test set; 1115 of the 1116 tweets having the un __TRIGGERWORD__ pattern correspond to joy tweets. We hypothesize this is the reason why the model learned this pattern as a strong discriminating feature.

Finally, the only tweet in the test set that contained this pattern and did not belong to the joy class, originally had *unsurprised* as its triggerword[7], and unsurprisingly, was misclassified.

---

[7]We manually searched for the original tweet.

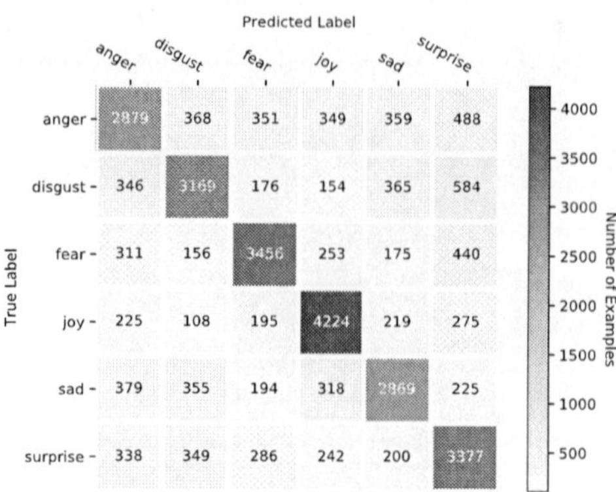

Figure 4: Confusion Matrix (Test Set).

	Precision	Recall	F1-score
anger	0.643	0.601	0.621
disgust	0.703	0.661	0.682
fear	0.742	0.721	0.732
joy	0.762	0.805	0.783
sad	0.685	0.661	0.673
surprise	0.627	0.705	0.663
Average	0.695	0.695	0.694

Table 3: Classification Report (Test Set).

3.3 Effect of the Amount of Training Data

As Figure 5 shows, increasing the amount of data with which our model was trained consistently increased validation accuracy and validation macro F1 score. The trend suggests that the proposed model is expressive enough to learn from more data, and is not overfitting the training set.

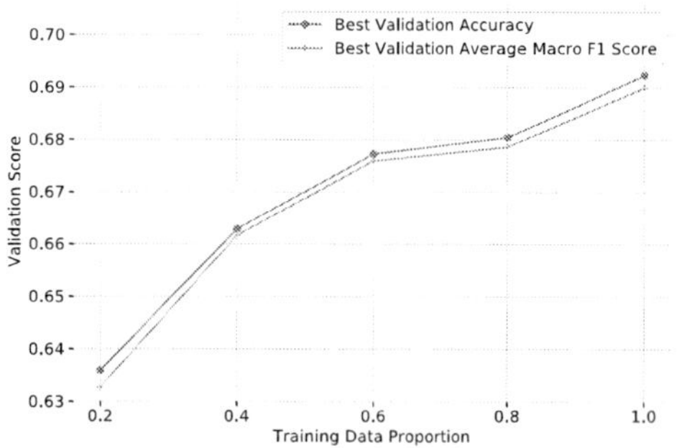

Figure 5: Effect of the amount of training data on classification performance.

3.4 Effect of Emoji and Hashtags

Table 4 shows the overall effect of hashtags and emoji on classification performance. Tweets con-

	Present	Not Present
Emoji	4805 (76.6%)	23952 (68.0%)
Hashtags	2122 (70.5%)	26635 (69.4%)

Table 4: Number of tweets on the test set with and without emoji and hashtags. The number between parentheses is the proportion of tweets classified correctly.

taining emoji seem to be easier for the model to classify than those without. Hashtags also have a positive effect on classification performance, however it is less significant. This implies that emoji, and hashtags in a smaller degree, provide tweets with a context richer in sentiment information, allowing the model to better guess the emotion of the *trigger-word*.

Emoji alias	N	emoji		no-emoji		$\Delta\%$
		#	%	#	%	
mask	163	154	94.48	134	82.21	- 12.27
two_hearts	87	81	93.10	77	88.51	- 4.59
heart_eyes	122	109	89.34	103	84.43	- 4.91
heart	267	237	88.76	235	88.01	- 0.75
rage	92	78	84.78	66	71.74	- 13.04
cry	116	97	83.62	83	71.55	- 12.07
sob	490	363	74.08	345	70.41	- 3.67
unamused	167	121	72.46	116	69.46	- 3.00
weary	204	140	68.63	139	68.14	- 0.49
joy	978	649	66.36	629	64.31	- 2.05
sweat_smile	111	73	65.77	75	67.57	1.80
confused	77	46	59.74	48	62.34	2.60

Table 5: Fine grained performance on tweets containing emoji, and the effect of removing them.
N is the total number of tweets containing the listed emoji, **#** and **%** the number and percentage of correctly-classified tweets respectively, and $\Delta\%$ the variation of test accuracy when removing the emoji from the tweets.

Table 5 shows the effect specific emoji have on classification performance. It is clear some emoji strongly contribute to improving prediction quality. The most interesting ones are mask, rage, and cry, which significantly increase accuracy. Further, contrary to intuition, the sob emoji contributes less than cry, despite representing a stronger emotion. This is probably due to sob being used for depicting a wider spectrum of emotions.

Finally, not all emoji are beneficial for this task. When removing sweat_smile and confused accuracy increased, probably because they represent emotions other than the ones being predicted.

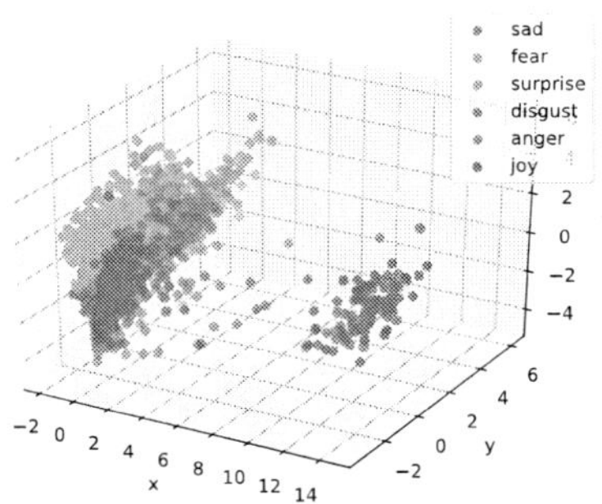

Figure 6: 3d Projection of the Test Sentence Representations.

4 Conclusions and Future Work

We described the model that got second place in the WASSA 2018 Implicit Emotion Shared Task. Despite its simplicity, and low amount of dependencies on libraries and external features, it performed almost as well as the system that obtained the first place.

Our ablation study revealed that our hyperparameters were indeed quite well-tuned for the task, which agrees with the good results obtained in the official submission. However, the ablation study also showed that increased performance can be obtained by incorporating POS embeddings as additional inputs. Further experiments are required to accurately measure the impact that this additional input may have on the results. We also think the performance can be boosted by making the architecture more complex, concretely, by using a BiLSTM with multiple layers and skip connections in a way akin to (Peters et al., 2018), or by making the fully-connected network bigger and deeper.

We also showed that, what was probably an annotation artifact, the `un __TRIGGERWORD__` pattern, resulted in increased performance for the `joy` label. This pattern was probably originated by a heuristic naïvely replacing the ocurrence of *happy* by the trigger-word indicator. We think the dataset could be improved by replacing the word *unhappy*, in the original examples, by `__TRIGGERWORD__` instead of `un __TRIGGERWORD__`, and labeling it as `sad`, or `angry`, instead of `joy`.

Finally, our studies regarding the importance of hashtags and emoji in the classification showed that both of them seem to contribute significantly to the performance, although in different measures.

5 Acknowledgements

We thank the anonymous reviewers for their reviews and suggestions. The first author is partially supported by the Japanese Government MEXT Scholarship.

References

Hamed R. Bonab and Fazli Can. 2016. A theoretical framework on the ideal number of classifiers for online ensembles in data streams. In *Proceedings of the 25th ACM International on Conference on Information and Knowledge Management*, CIKM '16, pages 2053–2056, New York, NY, USA. ACM.

Ciprian Chelba, Tomas Mikolov, Mike Schuster, Qi Ge, Thorsten Brants, Phillipp Koehn, and Tony Robinson. 2014. One billion word benchmark for measuring progress in statistical language modeling. *Proceedings of the Annual Conference of the International Speech Communication Association, INTERSPEECH*, pages 2635–2639.

Alexis Conneau, Douwe Kiela, Holger Schwenk, Loïc Barrault, and Antoine Bordes. 2017. Supervised Learning of Universal Sentence Representations from Natural Language Inference Data. In *Proceedings of the 2017 Conference on Empirical Methods in Natural Language Processing*, pages 670–680, Copenhagen, Denmark. Association for Computational Linguistics.

Alexis Conneau, Germán Kruszewski, Guillaume Lample, Loïc Barrault, and Marco Baroni. 2018. What you can cram into a single vector: Probing sentence embeddings for linguistic properties. In *Proceedings of the 56th Annual Meeting of the Association for Computational Linguistics (Volume 1: Long Papers)*, pages 2126–2136. Association for Computational Linguistics.

Kevin Gimpel, Nathan Schneider, Brendan O'Connor, Dipanjan Das, Daniel Mills, Jacob Eisenstein, Michael Heilman, Dani Yogatama, Jeffrey Flanigan, and Noah A. Smith. 2011. Part-of-speech tagging for twitter: Annotation, features, and experiments. In *Proceedings of the 49th Annual Meeting of the Association for Computational Linguistics: Human Language Technologies*, pages 42–47, Portland, Oregon, USA. Association for Computational Linguistics.

Alex Graves, Abdel-rahman Mohamed, and Geoffrey Hinton. 2013. Speech Recognition with Deep Recurrent Neural Networks. In *Proceedings of the 2013 International Conference on Acoustics, Speech and Signal Processing (ICASSP)*, pages 6645–6649, Vancouver, Canada. IEEE.

Alex Graves and Jürgen Schmidhuber. 2005. Framewise Phoneme Classification with Bidirectional LSTM and Other Neural Network Architectures. *Neural Networks*, 18(5-6):602–610.

Jeremy Howard and Sebastian Ruder. 2018. Universal Language Model Fine-tuning for Text Classification. *ArXiv e-prints*.

Diederik P. Kingma and Jimmy Ba. 2014. Adam: A method for stochastic optimization. *CoRR*.

Roman Klinger, Orphée de Clercq, Saif M. Mohammad, and Alexandra Balahur. 2018. IEST: WASSA-2018 Implicit Emotions Shared Task. In *Proceedings of the 9th Workshop on Computational Approaches to Subjectivity, Sentiment and Social Media Analysis*, Brussels, Belgium. Association for Computational Linguistics.

Saif M. Mohammad and Felipe Bravo-Marquez. 2017. WASSA-2017 Shared Task on Emotion Intensity. In *Proceedings of the EMNLP 2017 Workshop on Computational Approaches to Subjectivity, Sentiment, and Social Media (WASSA)*, Copenhagen, Denmark.

Adam Paszke, Sam Gross, Soumith Chintala, Gregory Chanan, Edward Yang, Zachary DeVito, Zeming Lin, Alban Desmaison, Luca Antiga, and Adam Lerer. 2017. Automatic differentiation in pytorch. In *NIPS Autodiff Workshop*.

Matthew Peters, Mark Neumann, Mohit Iyyer, Matt Gardner, Christopher Clark, Kenton Lee, and Luke Zettlemoyer. 2018. Deep contextualized word representations. In *Proceedings of the 2018 Conference of the North American Chapter of the Association for Computational Linguistics: Human Language Technologies, Volume 1 (Long Papers)*, pages 2227–2237, New Orleans, Louisiana. Association for Computational Linguistics.

Nitish Srivastava, Geoffrey Hinton, Alex Krizhevsky, Ilya Sutskever, and Ruslan Salakhutdinov. 2014. Dropout: A simple way to prevent neural networks from overfitting. *Journal of Machine Learning Research*, 15:1929–1958.

NTUA-SLP at IEST 2018: Ensemble of Neural Transfer Methods for Implicit Emotion Classification

Alexandra Chronopoulou[1]*, Aikaterini Margatina[1]*
Christos Baziotis[1,2], Alexandros Potamianos[1,3]

[1]School of ECE, National Technical University of Athens, Athens, Greece
[2] Department of Informatics, Athens University of Economics and Business, Athens, Greece
[3] Signal Analysis and Interpretation Laboratory (SAIL), USC, Los Angeles, USA

`el12068@central.ntua.gr`, `el12108@central.ntua.gr`
`cbaziotis@mail.ntua.gr`, `potam@central.ntua.gr`

Abstract

In this paper we present our approach to tackle the Implicit Emotion Shared Task (IEST) organized as part of WASSA 2018 at EMNLP 2018. Given a tweet, from which a certain word has been removed, we are asked to predict the emotion of the missing word. In this work, we experiment with neural Transfer Learning (TL) methods. Our models are based on LSTM networks, augmented with a self-attention mechanism. We use the weights of various pretrained models, for initializing specific layers of our networks. We leverage a big collection of unlabeled Twitter messages, for pretraining word2vec word embeddings and a set of diverse language models. Moreover, we utilize a sentiment analysis dataset for pretraining a model, which encodes emotion related information. The submitted model consists of an ensemble of the aforementioned TL models. Our team ranked 3rd out of 30 participants, achieving an F_1 score of 0.703.

1 Introduction

Social media, especially micro-blogging services like Twitter, have attracted lots of attention from the NLP community. The language used is constantly evolving by incorporating new syntactic and semantic constructs, such as emojis or hashtags, abbreviations and slang, making natural language processing in this domain even more demanding. Moreover, the analysis of such content leverages the high availability of datasets offered from Twitter, satisfying the need for large amounts of data for training.

Emotion recognition is particularly interesting in social media, as it has useful applications in numerous tasks, such as public opinion detection about political tendencies (Pla and Hurtado, 2014; Tumasjan et al., 2010; Li and Xu, 2014), stock market monitoring (Si et al., 2013; Bollen et al., 2011b), tracking product perception (Chamlertwat et al., 2012), even detection of suicide-related communication (Burnap et al., 2015).

In the past, emotion analysis, like most NLP tasks, was tackled by traditional methods that included hand-crafted features or features from sentiment lexicons (Nielsen, 2011; Mohammad and Turney, 2010, 2013; Go et al., 2009) which were fed to classifiers such as Naive Bayes and SVMs (Bollen et al., 2011a; Mohammad et al., 2013; Kiritchenko et al., 2014). However, deep neural networks achieve increased performance compared to traditional methods, due to their ability to learn more abstract features from large amounts of data, producing state-of-the-art results in emotion recognition and sentiment analysis (Deriu et al., 2016; Goel et al., 2017; Baziotis et al., 2017).

In this paper, we present our work submitted to the WASSA 2018 IEST (Klinger et al., 2018). In the given task, the word that triggers emotion is removed from each tweet and is replaced by the token `[#TARGETWORD#]`. The objective is to predict its emotion category among 6 classes: *anger, disgust, fear, joy, sadness* and *surprise*. Our proposed model employs 3 different TL schemes of pretrained models: word embeddings, a sentiment model and language models.

---

*These authors contributed equally to this work.

Proceedings of the 9th Workshop on Computational Approaches to Subjectivity, Sentiment and Social Media Analysis, pages 57–64
Brussels, Belgium, October 31, 2018. ©2018 Association for Computational Linguistics
https://doi.org/10.18653/v1/P17

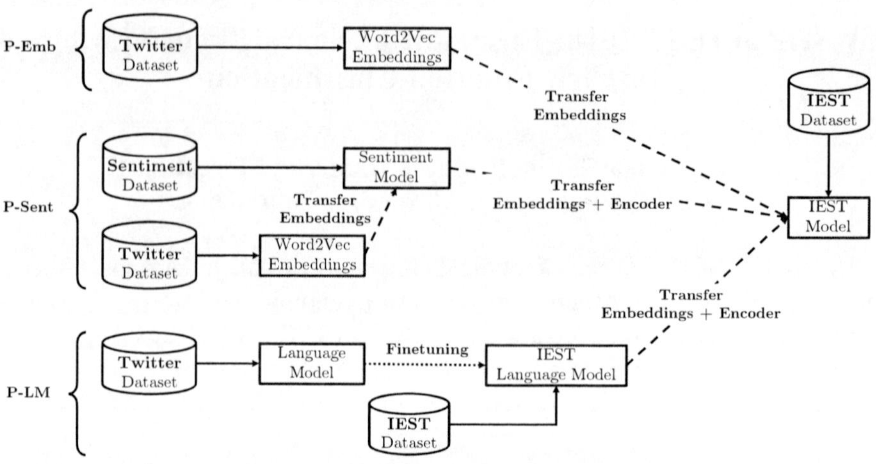

Figure 1: High-level overview of our TL approaches.

2 Overview

Our approach is composed of the following three steps: (1) *pretraining*, in which we train word2vec word embeddings (P-Emb), a sentiment model (P-Sent) and Twitter-specific language models (P-LM), (2) *transfer learning*, in which we transfer the weights of the aforementioned models to specific layers of our IEST classifier and (3) *ensembling*, in which we combine the predictions of each TL model. Figure 1 depicts a high-level overview of our approach.

2.1 Data

Apart from the IEST dataset, we employ a Se-mEval dataset for sentiment classification and other manually-collected unlabeled corpora for our language models.

Unlabeled Twitter Corpora. We collected a dataset of 550 million archived English Twitter messages, from 2014 to 2017. This dataset is used for calculating word statistics for our text preprocessing pipeline and training our *word2vec* word embeddings presented in Sec. 4.1.

For training our language models, described in Sec. 4.3, we sampled three subsets of this corpus. The first consists of 2M tweets, all of which contain emotion words. To create the dataset, we selected tweets that included one of the six emotion classes of our task (*anger, disgust, fear, joy, sadness* and *surprise*) or synonyms. We ensured that this dataset is balanced by concatenating approximately 350K tweets from each category. The second chunk has 5M tweets, randomly selected from the initial 550M corpus. We aimed to create

a general sub-corpus, so as to focus on the structural relationships of words, instead of their emotional content. The third chunk is composed of the two aforementioned corpora. We concatenated the 2M emotion dataset with 2M generic tweets, creating a final 4M dataset. We denote the three corpora as *EmoCorpus* (2M), *EmoCorpus+* (4M) and *GenCorpus* (5M).

Sentiment Analysis Dataset. We use the dataset of SemEval17 Task4A (Sent17) (Rosenthal et al., 2017) for training our sentiment classifier as described in Sec. 4.2. The dataset consists of Twitter messages annotated with their sentiment polarity (*positive, negative, neutral*). The training set contains 56K tweets and the validation set 6K tweets.

2.2 Preprocessing

To preprocess the tweets, we use *Ekphrasis* (Baziotis et al., 2017), a tool geared towards text from social networks, such as Twitter and Facebook. *Ekphrasis* performs Twitter-specific tokenization, spell correction, word normalization, segmentation (for splitting hashtags) and annotation.

2.3 Word Embeddings

Word embeddings are dense vector representations of words which capture semantic and syntactic information. For this reason, we employ the *word2vec* (Mikolov et al., 2013) algorithm to train our word vectors, as described in Sec. 4.1.

2.4 Transfer Learning

Transfer Learning (TL) uses knowledge from a learned task so as to improve the performance of a related task by reducing the required training data (Torrey and Shavlik, 2010; Pan et al., 2010). In computer vision, transfer learning is employed in order to overcome the deficit of training samples for some categories by adapting classifiers trained for other categories (Oquab et al., 2014). With the power of deep supervised learning, learned knowledge can even be transferred to a totally different task (i.e. *ImageNet* (Krizhevsky et al., 2012)).

Following this logic, TL methods have also been applied to NLP. Pretrained word vectors (Mikolov et al., 2013; Pennington et al., 2014) have become standard components of most architectures. Recently, approaches that leverage pretrained language models have emerged, which learn the compositionality of language, capture long-term dependencies and context-dependent features. For instance, ELMo contextual word representations (Peters et al., 2018) and ULMFiT (Howard and Ruder, 2018) achieve state-of-the-art results on a wide variety of NLP tasks. Our work is mainly inspired by ULMFiT, which we extend to the Twitter domain.

2.5 Ensembling

We combine the predictions of our 3 TL schemes with the intent of increasing the generalization ability of the final classifier. To this end, we employ a pretrained word embeddings approach, as well as a pretrained sentiment model and a pretrained LM. We use two ensemble schemes, namely unweighted average and majority voting.

Unweighted Average (UA). In this approach, the final prediction is estimated from the unweighted average of the posterior probabilities for all different models. Formally, the final prediction p for a training instance is estimated by:

$$p = \arg\max_{c} \frac{1}{C} \sum_{i=1}^{M} \vec{p_i}, \quad p_i \in \mathbb{R}^C \quad (1)$$

where C is the number of classes, M is the number of different models, $c \in \{1, ..., C\}$ denotes one class and $\vec{p_i}$ is the probability vector calculated by model $i \in \{1, ..., M\}$ using softmax function.

Majority Voting (MV). Majority voting approach counts the votes of all different models and chooses the class with most votes. Compared to UA, MV is affected less by single-network decisions. However, this schema does not consider any information derived from the minority models. Formally, for a task with C classes and M

different models, the prediction for a specific instance is estimated as follows:

$$v_c = \sum_{i=1}^{M} F_i(c)$$

$$p = \arg\max_{c \in \{1, ..., C\}} v_c \quad (2)$$

where v_c denotes the votes for class c from all different models, F_i is the decision of the ith model, which is either 1 or 0 with respect to whether the model has classified the instance in class c or not and p is the final prediction.

3 Network Architecture

All of our TL schemes share the same architecture: A 2-layer LSTM with a self-attention mechanism. It is shown in Figure 2.

Embedding Layer. The input to the network is a Twitter message, treated as a sequence of words. We use an embedding layer to project the words $w_1, w_2, ..., w_N$ to a low-dimensional vector space R^W, where W is the size of the embedding layer and N the number of words in a tweet.

LSTM Layer. An LSTM takes as input a sequence of word embeddings and produces word annotations $h_1, h_2, ..., h_N$, where h_i is the hidden state at time-step i, summarizing all the information of the sentence up to w_i. We use bidirectional LSTM to get word annotations that summarize the information from both directions. A bi-LSTM consists of a forward $\overrightarrow{f}$ that parses the sentence from w_1 to w_N and a backward $\overleftarrow{f}$ that parses it from w_N to w_1. We obtain the final annotation for each word h_i, by concatenating the annotations from both directions, $h_i = \overrightarrow{h_i} \parallel \overleftarrow{h_i}, \quad h_i \in R^{2L}$, where $\parallel$ denotes the concatenation operation and L the size of each LSTM. When the network is initialized with pretrained LMs, we employ unidirectional instead of bi-LSTMs.

Attention Layer. To amplify the contribution of the most informative words, we augment our LSTM with an attention mechanism, which assigns a weight a_i to each word annotation h_i. We compute the fixed representation r of the whole input message, as the weighted sum of all the word annotations.

$$e_i = tanh(W_h h_i + b_h), \quad e_i \in [-1, 1] \quad (3)$$

$$a_i = \frac{exp(e_i)}{\sum_{t=1}^{T} exp(e_t)}, \quad \sum_{i=1}^{T} a_i = 1 \quad (4)$$

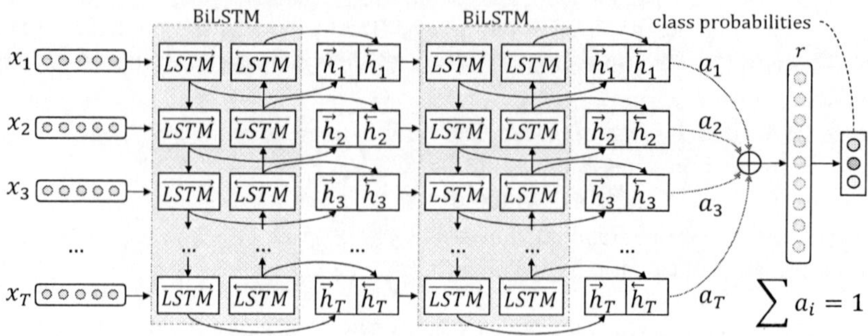

Figure 2: The proposed model, composed of a 2-layer bi-LSTM with a deep self-attention mechanism. When the model is initialized with pretrained LMs, we use unidirectional LSTM instead of bidirectional.

$$r = \sum_{i=1}^{T} a_i h_i, \quad r \in R^{2L} \qquad (5)$$

where W_h and b_h are the attention layer's weights. **Output Layer**. We use the representation r as feature vector for classification and we feed it to a fully-connected softmax layer with L neurons, which outputs a probability distribution over all classes p_c as described in Eq. 6:

$$p_c = \frac{e^{Wr+b}}{\sum_{i \in [1,L]} (e^{W_i r + b_i})} \qquad (6)$$

where W and b are the layer's weights and biases.

4 Transfer Learning Approaches

4.1 Pretrained Word Embeddings (*P-Emb*)

In the first approach, we train *word2vec* word embeddings with which we initialize the embedding layer of our network. The weights of the embedding layer remain frozen during training. The *word2vec* word embeddings are trained on the 550M Twitter corpus (Sec. 2.1), with negative sampling of 5 and minimum word count of 20, using Gensim's (Řehůřek and Sojka, 2010) implementation. The resulting vocabulary contains $800,000$ words.

4.2 Pretrained Sentiment Model (*P-Sent*)

In the second approach, we first train a sentiment analysis model on the Sent17 dataset, using the architecture described in Sec. 3. The embedding layer of the network is initialized with our pretrained word embeddings. Then, we fine-tune the network on the IEST task, by replacing its last layer with a task-specific layer.

4.3 Pretrained Language Model (*P-LM*)

The third approach consists of the following steps: (1) we first train a language model on a generic Twitter corpus, (2) we fine-tune the LM on the task at hand and finally, (3) we transfer the embedding and RNN layers of the LM, we add attention and output layers and fine-tune the model on the target task.

LM Pretraining. We collect three Twitter datasets as described in Sec. 2.1 and for each one we train an LM. In each dataset we use the 50,000 most frequent words as our vocabulary. Since the literature concerning LM transfer learning is limited, especially in the Twitter domain, we aim to explore the desired characteristics of the pretrained LM. To this end, our contribution in this research area lies in experimenting with a task-relevant corpus (EmoCorpus), a generic one (GenCorpus) and a mixture of both (EmoCorpus+).

LM Fine-tuning. This step is crucial since, albeit the diversity of the general-domain data used for pretraining, the data of the target task will likely have a different distribution.

We thus fine-tune the three pretrained LMs on the IEST dataset, employing two approaches. The first is simple fine-tuning, according to which all layers of the model are trained simultaneously. The second one is a simplified yet similar approach to *gradual unfreezing*, proposed in (Howard and Ruder, 2018), which we denote as *Simplified Gradual Unfreezing* (SGU). According to this method, after we have transfered the pretrained embedding and LSTM weights, we let only the output layer fine-tune for $n - 1$ epochs. At the nth epoch, we unfreeze both LSTM layers. We let the model fine-tune, until epoch $k - 1$. Finally, at epoch k, we also unfreeze the embed-

60

ding layer and let the network train until convergence. In other words, we experiment with pairs of numbers of epochs, {n, k}, where n denotes the epoch when we unfreeze the LSTM layers and k the epoch when we unfreeze the embedding layer. Naive fine-tuning poses the risk of catastrophic forgetting, or else abruptly losing the knowledge of a previously learnt task, as information relevant to the current task is incorporated. Therefore, to prevent this from happening, we unfreeze the model starting from the last layer, which is task-specific, and after some epochs we progressively unfreeze the next, more general layers, until all layers are unfrozen.

LM Transfer. This is the final step of our TL approach. We now have several LMs from the second step of the procedure. We transfer their embedding and RNN weights to a final target classifier. We again experiment with both simple and more sophisticated fine-tuning techniques, to find out which one is more helpful to this task.

Furthermore, we introduce the *concatenation method* which was inspired by the correlation of language modeling and the task at hand. We use pretrained LMs to leverage the fact that the task is basically a cloze test. In an LM, the probability of occurrence of each word, is conditioned on the preceding context, $P(w_t|w_1, \ldots, w_{t-1})$. In RNN-based LMs, this probability is encoded in the hidden state of the RNN, $P(w_t|h_{t-1})$. To this end, we concatenate the hidden state of the LSTM, right before the missing word, $h_{implicit}$, to the output of the self-attention mechanism, r:

$$r' = r \parallel h_{implicit}, \quad h_i \in R^{2L} \tag{7}$$

where L is the size of each LSTM, and then feed it to the output linear layer. This way, we preserve the information which implicitly encodes the probability of the missing word.

5 Experiments and Results

5.1 Experimental Setup

Training. We use Adam algorithm (Kingma and Ba, 2014) to optimize our networks, with mini-batches of size 64 and clip the norm of the gradients (Pascanu et al., 2013) at 0.5, as an extra safety measure against exploding gradients. We also used PyTorch (Paszke et al., 2017) and Scikit-learn (Pedregosa et al., 2011).

Hyperparameters. For all our models, we employ the same 2-layer attention-based LSTM ar-

chitecture (Sec. 3). All the hyperparameters used are shown in Table 1.

Layer	P-Emb	P-Sent	P-LM
Embedding	300	300	400
Embedding noise	0.1	0.1	0.1
Embedding dropout	0.2	0.2	0.2
LSTM size	400	400	600/800
LSTM dropout	0.4	0.4	0.4

Table 1: Hyper-parameters of our models.

5.2 Official Results

Our team ranked 3rd out of 30 participants, achieving 0.703 F1-score on the official test set. Table 2 shows the official ranking of the top scoring teams.

Rank	Team Name	Macro F1
1	Amobee	0.714
2	IIIDYT	0.710
3	**NTUA-SLP**	**0.703**
4	UBC-NLP	0.693
5	Sentylic	0.692

Table 2: Results of the WASSA IEST competition.

5.3 Experiments

Baselines. In Table 5 we compare the proposed TL approaches against two strong baselines: (1) a Bag-of-Words (BoW) model with TF-IDF weighting and (2) a Bag-of-Embeddings (BoE) model, where we retrieve the *word2vec* representations of the words in a tweet and compute the tweet representation as the centroid of the constituent *word2vec* representations. Both *BoW* and *BoE* features are then fed to a linear SVM classifier, with tuned $C = 0.6$. All of our reported F1-scores are calculated on the evaluation (*dev*) set, due to time constraints.

P-Emb and *P-Sent* **models (4.1, 4.2)**. We evaluate the *P-Emb* and *P-Sent* models, using both bidirectional and unidirectional LSTMs. The F1 score of our best models is shown in Table 5. As expected, bi-LSTM models achieve higher performance.

P-LM **(4.3)**. For the experiments with the pretrained LMs, we intend to transfer not just the first layer of our network, but rather the whole model, so as to capture more high-level features of language. As mentioned above, there are three distinct steps concerning the training procedure of this TL approach: (1) *LM pretraining*: we train three LMs on the EmoCorpus, EmoCorpus+ and

LM Fine-tuning	LM Transfer			F1
	Simple FT	SGU	Concat.	
Simple FT	✓			0.672
	✓		✓	0.667
		✓		0.676
		✓	✓	0.673
SGU	✓			0.673
	✓		✓	0.667
		✓		0.678
		✓	✓	**0.682**

Table 3: Results of the P-LM, trained on the Emo-Corpus. The first column refers to the way we fine-tune each LM on the IEST dataset and the second to the way we finally fine-tune the classifier on the same dataset.

Dataset	F1
EmoCorpus	0.682
EmoCorpus+	0.680
GenCorpus	0.675

Table 4: Comparison of the P-LM models, all fine-tuned with *SGU* and *Concat.* methods.

GenCorpus corpora, (2) *LM fine-tuning*: we fine-tune the LMs on the IEST dataset, with 2 different ways. The first one is simple fine-tuning, while the second one is our simplified gradual unfreezing (SGU) technique. (3) *LM transfer*: We now have 6 LMs, fine-tuned on the IEST dataset. We transfer their weights to our final emotion classifier, we add attention to the LSTM layers and we experiment again with our 2 ways of fine-tuning and the *concatenation method* proposed in Sec. 4.3.

In Table 3 we present all possible combinations of transferring the *P-LM* to the IEST task. We observe that SGU consistently outperforms Simple Fine-Tuning (Simple FT). Due to the difficulty in running experiments for all possible combinations, we compare our best approach, namely *SGU + Concat.*, with *P-LM*s trained on our three unlabeled Twitter corpora, as depicted in Table 4. Even though EmoCorpus contains less training examples, *P-LM*s trained on it learn to encode more useful information for the task at hand.

5.4 Ensembling

Our submitted model is an ensemble of the models with the best performance. More specifically, we leverage the following models: (1) TL of pre-trained word embeddings, (2) TL of pretrained sentiment classifier, (3) TL of 3 different LMs, trained on 2M, 4M and 5M respectively. We use Unweighted Average (UA) ensembling of our best

Model	F1
Bag of Words (BoW)	0.601
Bag of Embeddings (BoE)	0.605
P-Emb	0.668
P-Sent	0.671
P-LM	**0.675**
P-Emb + bidir.	0.684
P-Sent + bidir.	0.674
P-LM + SGU	0.679
P-LM + SGU + Concat.	0.682
Ensembling (UA) P-Emb + P-Sent	0.684
Ensembling (UA) P-Sent + P-LM	0.695
Ensembling (UA) P-Emb + P-LM	0.701
Ensembling (MV) All	0.700
Ensembling (UA) All	**0.702**

Table 5: Results of our experiments when tested on the evaluation (*dev*) set. *BoW* and *BoE* are our baselines, while *P-Emb*, *P-Sent* and *P-LM* our proposed TL approaches. *SGU* stands for Simplified Gradual Unfreezing, *bidir.* for bi-LSTM, *Concat.* for the concatenation method, *UA* for Unweighted Average and *MV* for Majority Voting ensembling.

models from all aforementioned approaches. Our final results on the evaluation data are shown in Table 5.

5.5 Discussion

As shown in Table 5, we observe that all of our proposed models achieve individually better performance than our baselines by a large margin. Moreover, we notice that, when the three models are trained with unidirectional LSTM and the same number of parameters, the *P-LM* outperforms both the *P-Emb* and the *P-Sent* models. As expected, the upgrade to bi-LSTM improves the results of *P-Emb* and *P-Sent*. We hypothesize that *P-LM* with bidirectional pretrained language models would have outperformed both of them. Furthermore, we conclude that both SGU for fine-tuning and the concatenation method enhance the performance of the *P-LM* approach. As far as the ensembling is concerned, both approaches, *MV* and *UA*, yield similar performance improvement over the individual models. In particular, we notice that adding the *P-LM* predictions to the ensemble contributes the most. This indicates that *P-LM*s encode more diverse information compared to the other approaches.

6 Conclusion

In this paper we describe our deep-learning methods for missing emotion words classification, in the Twitter domain. We achieved very competitive results in the IEST competition, ranking 3rd/30 teams. The proposed approach is based on an ensemble of Transfer Learning techniques. We demonstrate that the use of refined, high-level features of text, as the ones encoded in language models, yields a higher performance. In the future, we aim to experiment with subword-level models, as they have shown to consistently face the OOV words problem (Sennrich et al., 2015; Bojanowski et al., 2016), which is more evident in Twitter. Moreover, we would like to explore other transfer learning approaches.

Finally, we share the source code of our models [1], in order to make our results reproducible and facilitate further experimentation in the field.

References

Christos Baziotis, Nikos Pelekis, and Christos Doulkeridis. 2017. Datastories at semeval-2017 task 4: Deep lstm with attention for message-level and topic-based sentiment analysis. In *Proceedings of the 11th International Workshop on Semantic Evaluation (SemEval-2017)*, pages 747–754.

Piotr Bojanowski, Edouard Grave, Armand Joulin, and Tomas Mikolov. 2016. Enriching word vectors with subword information. *arXiv preprint arXiv:1607.04606*.

Johan Bollen, Huina Mao, and Alberto Pepe. 2011a. Modeling public mood and emotion: Twitter sentiment and socio-economic phenomena. *Icwsm*, 11:450–453.

Johan Bollen, Huina Mao, and Xiaojun Zeng. 2011b. Twitter mood predicts the stock market. *Journal of computational science*, 2(1):1–8.

Pete Burnap, Walter Colombo, and Jonathan Scourfield. 2015. Machine classification and analysis of suicide-related communication on twitter. In *Proceedings of the 26th ACM conference on hypertext & social media*, pages 75–84. ACM.

Wilas Chamlertwat, Pattarasinee Bhattarakosol, Tippakorn Rungkasiri, and Choochart Haruechaiyasak. 2012. Discovering consumer insight from twitter via sentiment analysis. *J. UCS*, 18(8):973–992.

Jan Deriu, Maurice Gonzenbach, Fatih Uzdilli, Aurelien Lucchi, Valeria De Luca, and Martin Jaggi. 2016. Swisscheese at semeval-2016 task 4: Sentiment classification using an ensemble of convolutional neural networks with distant supervision. In *Proceedings of the 10th international workshop on semantic evaluation*, EPFL-CONF-229234, pages 1124–1128.

Alec Go, Richa Bhayani, and Lei Huang. 2009. Twitter sentiment classification using distant supervision. *CS224N Project Report, Stanford*, 1(12).

Pranav Goel, Devang Kulshreshtha, Prayas Jain, and Kaushal Kumar Shukla. 2017. Prayas at emoint 2017: An ensemble of deep neural architectures for emotion intensity prediction in tweets. In *Proceedings of the 8th Workshop on Computational Approaches to Subjectivity, Sentiment and Social Media Analysis*, pages 58–65.

Jeremy Howard and Sebastian Ruder. 2018. Fine-tuned language models for text classification. *CoRR*, abs/1801.06146.

Diederik Kingma and Jimmy Ba. 2014. Adam: A method for stochastic optimization. *arXiv preprint arXiv:1412.6980*.

Svetlana Kiritchenko, Xiaodan Zhu, and Saif M. Mohammad. 2014. Sentiment analysis of short informal texts. *Journal of Artificial Intelligence Research*, 50:723–762.

Roman Klinger, Orphée de Clercq, Saif M. Mohammad, and Alexandra Balahur. 2018. Iest: Wassa-2018 implicit emotions shared task. In *Proceedings of the 9th Workshop on Computational Approaches to Subjectivity, Sentiment and Social Media Analysis*, Brussels, Belgium. Association for Computational Linguistics.

Alex Krizhevsky, Ilya Sutskever, and Geoffrey E Hinton. 2012. Imagenet classification with deep convolutional neural networks. In *Advances in neural information processing systems*, pages 1097–1105.

Weiyuan Li and Hua Xu. 2014. Text-based emotion classification using emotion cause extraction. *Expert Systems with Applications*, 41(4):1742–1749.

Tomas Mikolov, Ilya Sutskever, Kai Chen, Greg S. Corrado, and Jeff Dean. 2013. Distributed representations of words and phrases and their compositionality. In *Advances in Neural Information Processing Systems*, pages 3111–3119.

Saif M. Mohammad, Svetlana Kiritchenko, and Xiaodan Zhu. 2013. NRC-Canada: Building the state-of-the-art in sentiment analysis of tweets. *arXiv preprint arXiv:1308.6242*.

Saif M Mohammad and Peter D Turney. 2010. Emotions evoked by common words and phrases: Using mechanical turk to create an emotion lexicon. In *Proceedings of the NAACL HLT 2010 workshop on computational approaches to analysis and generation of emotion in text*, pages 26–34. Association for Computational Linguistics.

---

[1] /github.com/alexandra-chron/wassa-2018

Saif M Mohammad and Peter D Turney. 2013. Crowdsourcing a word–emotion association lexicon. *Computational Intelligence*, 29(3):436–465.

Finn Årup Nielsen. 2011. A new anew: Evaluation of a word list for sentiment analysis in microblogs. *arXiv preprint arXiv:1103.2903*.

Maxime Oquab, Leon Bottou, Ivan Laptev, and Josef Sivic. 2014. Learning and transferring mid-level image representations using convolutional neural networks. In *Proceedings of the IEEE conference on computer vision and pattern recognition*, pages 1717–1724.

Sinno Jialin Pan, Qiang Yang, et al. 2010. A survey on transfer learning. *IEEE Transactions on knowledge and data engineering*, 22(10):1345–1359.

Razvan Pascanu, Tomas Mikolov, and Yoshua Bengio. 2013. On the difficulty of training recurrent neural networks. *ICML (3)*, 28:1310–1318.

Adam Paszke, Sam Gross, Soumith Chintala, Gregory Chanan, Edward Yang, Zachary DeVito, Zeming Lin, Alban Desmaison, Luca Antiga, and Adam Lerer. 2017. Automatic differentiation in pytorch.

Fabian Pedregosa, Gaël Varoquaux, Alexandre Gramfort, Vincent Michel, Bertrand Thirion, Olivier Grisel, Mathieu Blondel, Peter Prettenhofer, Ron Weiss, Vincent Dubourg, and others. 2011. Scikit-learn: Machine learning in Python. *Journal of Machine Learning Research*, 12(Oct):2825–2830.

Jeffrey Pennington, Richard Socher, and Christopher D. Manning. 2014. Glove: Global Vectors for Word Representation. In *EMNLP*, volume 14, pages 1532–1543.

Matthew E Peters, Mark Neumann, Mohit Iyyer, Matt Gardner, Christopher Clark, Kenton Lee, and Luke Zettlemoyer. 2018. Deep contextualized word representations. *arXiv preprint arXiv:1802.05365*.

Ferran Pla and Lluís-F Hurtado. 2014. Political tendency identification in twitter using sentiment analysis techniques. In *Proceedings of COLING 2014, the 25th international conference on computational linguistics: Technical Papers*, pages 183–192.

Radim Řehůřek and Petr Sojka. 2010. Software Framework for Topic Modelling with Large Corpora. In *Proceedings of the LREC 2010 Workshop on New Challenges for NLP Frameworks*, pages 45–50, Valletta, Malta. ELRA. http://is.muni.cz/publication/884893/en.

Sara Rosenthal, Noura Farra, and Preslav Nakov. 2017. Semeval-2017 task 4: Sentiment analysis in twitter. In *Proceedings of the 11th International Workshop on Semantic Evaluation (SemEval-2017)*, pages 502–518.

Rico Sennrich, Barry Haddow, and Alexandra Birch. 2015. Neural machine translation of rare words with subword units. *arXiv preprint arXiv:1508.07909*.

Jianfeng Si, Arjun Mukherjee, Bing Liu, Qing Li, Huayi Li, and Xiaotie Deng. 2013. Exploiting topic based twitter sentiment for stock prediction. In *Proceedings of the 51st Annual Meeting of the Association for Computational Linguistics (Volume 2: Short Papers)*, volume 2, pages 24–29.

Lisa Torrey and Jude Shavlik. 2010. Transfer learning. In *Handbook of Research on Machine Learning Applications and Trends: Algorithms, Methods, and Techniques*, pages 242–264. IGI Global.

Andranik Tumasjan, Timm Oliver Sprenger, Philipp G Sandner, and Isabell M Welpe. 2010. Predicting elections with twitter: What 140 characters reveal about political sentiment. *Icwsm*, 10(1):178–185.

Sentiment analysis under temporal shift

Jan Lukes and Anders Søgaard
Dpt. of Computer Science
University of Copenhagen
Copenhagen, Denmark
`smx262@alumni.ku.dk`

Abstract

Sentiment analysis models often rely on training data that is several years old. In this paper, we show that lexical features change polarity over time, leading to degrading performance. This effect is particularly strong in sparse models relying only on highly predictive features. Using predictive feature selection, we are able to significantly improve the accuracy of such models over time.

1 Introduction

Sentiment analysis models often rely on data that is several years old. Such data, e.g., product reviews, continuously undergo shifts, leading to changes in term frequency, for example. We also observe the emergence of novel expressions, as well as the amelioration and pejoration of words (Cook and Stevenson, 2010). Such changes are typically studied over decades or centuries; however, we hypothesize that change is continuous, and small changes can be detected over shorter time spans (years), and that their cumulation can influence the quality of sentiment analysis models. In this paper, we analyze temporal polarity changes of individual features using product reviews data. Additionally, we show that predictive feature selection, trying to counteract shifts in polarity, significantly improves model accuracy over time.

Contributions First, we show deterioration of sentiment analysis model performance over time. We propose rank-based metrics for detecting polarity shifts and identify several examples of lexical features that exhibit temporal drift in our data. Finally, we use our findings to design a predictive feature selection scheme, based on expected polarity changes, and show that models using predictive

Sample positive review:

"Grand daughters really like this movie. Good clean movie for all ages. Would recommend for everyone. Good horse movie for girls."

Sample negative review:

"Not what I expected. Very cheap and chintzy looking for the price. Certainly did not look like a wallet. Very disappointed in the quality."

Figure 1: Examples of reviews

feature selection perform significantly better than models that simply rely on the most predictive features across the training data without estimating temporal shifts.

Training data	Model accuracy			
Runs	1	2	3	Mean
2001-2004	0.858	0.855	0.863	0.859
2008-2011	0.877	0.873	0.878	0.877

Table 1: Classifier accuracy deterioration when using older and newer training sets. Models were trained using random independent data subsets from periods 2001-2004 or 2008-2011 and tested using random independent subsets from 2012-2014. Subset size: $K = 40,000$ with 80/20 split.

2 Sentiment analysis models get worse over time

One way we may observe polarity shifts over time is when we see models trained on older data perform worse than models trained on more recent data. Or, equivalently, by seeing performance degradations over time.

The Amazon product review data, which we

Proceedings of the 9th Workshop on Computational Approaches to Subjectivity, Sentiment and Social Media Analysis, pages 65–71
Brussels, Belgium, October 31, 2018. ©2018 Association for Computational Linguistics
https://doi.org/10.18653/v1/P17

will use in our experiments, is a collection of user product reviews and meta-data crawled from Amazon.com, consisting of 82 million reviews and spanning May 1996 until July 2014 (He and McAuley, 2016; McAuley et al., 2015). Previous work already preprocessed the dataset, removing duplicates and boiler plates. We sample large sub-samples of reviews per year from the original data set ($K = 40000$). Only years 2001 to 2014 were used in this project, as the samples from earlier years were of insufficient size.

Following previous work (Blitzer et al., 2007), we map the user-provided sentiment annotations, ranging from 1 star to 5 stars, into binary labels, where 3 stars and less are replaced by negative class labels, indicating negative or critical review, and 4 or more stars were considered positive reviews and associated with a positive class label.

Experiments with off-the-shelf classifiers In our first set of experiments, we train logistic regression models on data from 2001-2004 and on data from 2008-2011, and test their accuracy on random test samples from years 2012 to 2014. Our results show that models trained on older data performed noticeably worse than models trained on data from years 2008-2011 (see Table 1). The mean accuracies, obtained by averaging accuracies of models trained on three independently selected samples, were 0.859 for models trained on reviews from 2001-2004, and 0.877 for models trained on reviews from 2008-2011, i.e., an average absolute 2% decrease in accuracy.

This model deterioration over time could be attributed to a decrease in vocabulary overlap – as measured by, for example, the Jaccard similarity coefficient over unigrams and bigrams. To measure possible influence of this factor, we monitor the Jaccard index of unigram and bigram features that occur at least 5 times in the data sets: The average Jaccard indices between training and test data were 0.112 for 2001-2004 and 0.154 for 2008-2011.[1] Since the difference is minor, we hypothesize that temporal shifts in polarity are responsible for at least some of the drops in model performance over time. We confirm this hypothesis below by monitoring performance over time with a *fixed* feature set (fixing also the Jaccard index).

---

[1] The relatively low values are due to training and test sets being of different sizes, 32000 and 8000 respectively.

2.1 Experiments with a fixed feature set

The purpose of our second set of experiments is again to see how accuracy changesover time with models being trained on 'older' and 'newer' data subsets, but on *identical* feature sets. Similar to the above experiments, years 2001 to 2004 were selected as our *older* training data subsets, and years 2008 to 2011 were selected as our *newer* data. We again sample $40,000$ reviews per year and create 80/20 train-test splits. The experiment was repeated three times with new samples to obtain the average accuracies seen below in Figure 2. The fixed feature set used was obtained by selecting the 5,000 most frequent unigrams and bigrams present in the training data for year 2001.We use simple count vectors to represent the reviews.

The deterioration of performance over time is clearly visible from the plot in Figure 2, by looking at the gap between the red and the green scatter points. We believe these results support our hypothesis that over time, the polarities of individual features may change, and the cumulation of such changes significantly influences performance of sentiment classifiers.

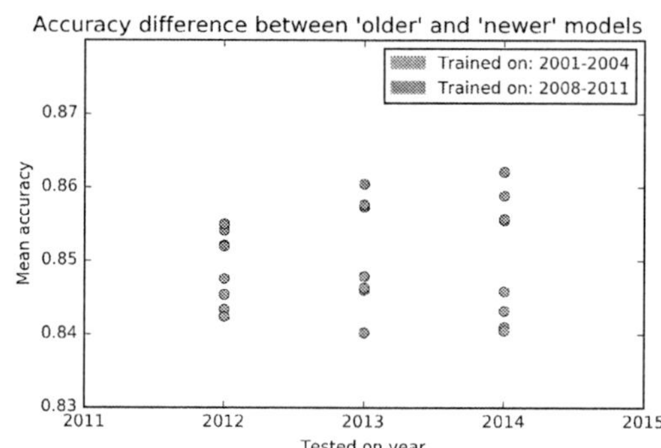

Figure 2: Each dot represents the average accuracy of the model trained on data from year x, where $y \in [2001, .., 2004, 2008, .., 2011]$, and tested on year x, where $x \in [2012, 2013, 2014]$. All possible combinations were run 3 times with different random yearly subsets to compute the average accuracies presented in the figure.

3 Polarity shifts

In this section, we look at individual features in order to detect examples of polarity shifts, i.e., amelioration or pejoration over time. We do so by analyzing the weights of classifiers trained on different years. As in our previous experiments, we use logistic regression classifiers trained with ℓ_1 regularization penalties. For each year in the interval 2001 to 2014, we training a classifier on a training set of 32,000 randomly sampled reviews, and we then inspect the coefficients associated with particular lexical features. These values measure the impact of lexical features on the final predictions of the models; high coefficients associate lexical features with positive sentiment, and low (negative) coefficients associate lexical features with high negative sentiment.

Logistic regression coefficients are not comparable across models, though, because of different scales, and one option would therefore be to use Min-Max scaling to transform coefficient values to the interval $[1, 0]$ for positive values and $[0, -1]$ for negative values. We use such scaling later in the paper; however, for robustly detecting polarity shifts, we instead propose using feature polarity rankings. Such ranking is done by ordering features by their respective coefficients and assigning a rank to each feature. The highest coefficient is rank 1, the second highest rank 2, and so on. This allows us to make direct comparisons between several models trained on different subsets of data.

Year	Positive feature polarity rank		
	'highly'	'great'	'incredible'
2001	1	11	9
2002	4	11	10
2003	4	6	57
2004	1	6	40
2005	3	4	50
2006	3	1	173
2007	6	1	137
2008	3	2	126

Table 2: Example feature ranks obtained by training a logistic regression classifier on 32,000 reviews from each year.

Due to the exponential distribution of coefficient values, as seen in Figure 3, a cap on maximal rank is placed such that $max\{rank\} \leq 3 * f$, where f is the number of positive (or negative) features. If ranks would be uncapped, even the slightest decrease in coefficient value would disproportionately increase feature ranks. As a result, rank and rank averages (used in predictive feature selection) would be much more influenced

by randomness of logistic regression, and hence, less interpretable. We argue that shifts in polarity are more precisely measured this way.

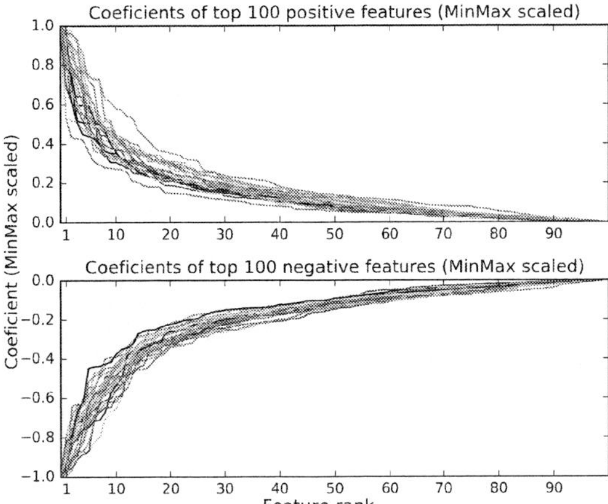

Figure 3: Distribution of coefficient values of 100 most positive and negative features obtained from models trained on data subsets from years 2001 to 2014. Coefficient values were scaled using Min-Max.

Using the feature polarity ranking described above, we analyze what shifts occur in individual unigrams and bigrams. To do so, we again use random data subsets of $40,000$ reviews and 80/20 splits. For each year spanning 2001 to 2014, we again generate three independent subsets to allow for more robust results and less randomness caused by logistic regression. Each subset is used to train a classifier, and we compute the polarity ranks of all lexical features.

Once we have established the ranks of lexical features, we use linear regression to estimate the degree to which polarity has changed. Using the p value of such a linear fit, we filter out non-significant changes where $p > 0.05$. See Figure 4 for examples of significant polarity shifts.

4 Models that are robust over time

Based on our previous findings that sentiment analysis models deteriorate over time, as training data sets get older, combined with observing significant changes in the polarity of lexical features, we hypothesize, that predictive feature selection can, to some extent, counteract the negative effects of polarity shift. In our final set of experiments, we perform predictive feature selection using polarity

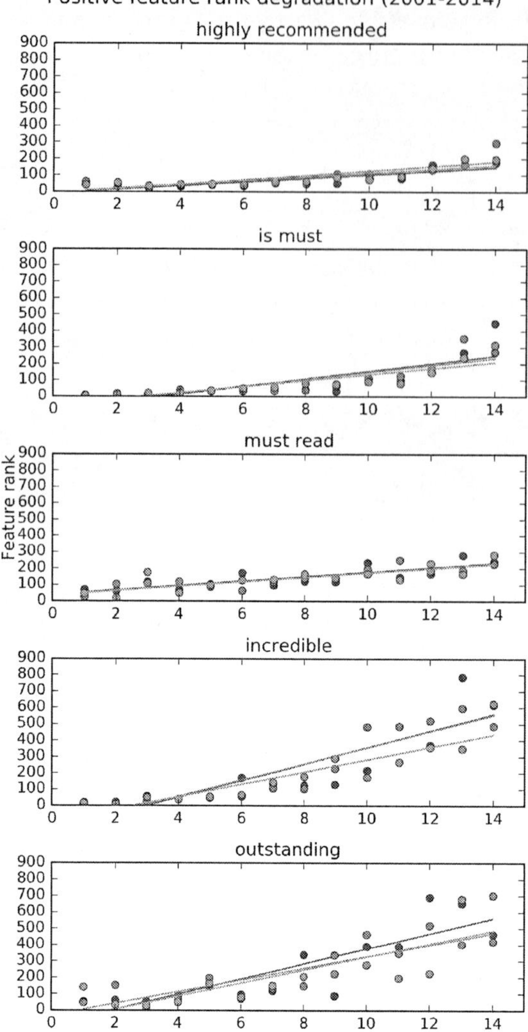

Figure 4: Figure shows a sample of 3 bigrams and 2 unigrams, where significant degradation in positivity was observed. Each color represents an independently selected collection of random yearly subsets of reviews.

rank predictions to select features based on their expected polarity.

We use two methods for predictive feature selection, both relying on the predicted rate (or slope) of change in polarity and a metric of significance that serves as a filtering mechanism. The methods used are:

- **Difference of means:** This method uses two mean polarity ranks - initial and final, to determine rate of change in feature polarity, and

whether the change is significant. Initial and final mean ranks are calculated using polarity ranks from individual years (i.e. how feature ranked in polarity as determined by model trained on data from that year). In our case, the training data spans 2001-2008 and difference of means uses years 2001-2003 for the initial mean rank and 2006-2008 for the final mean rank. Furthermore, each feature to be included has to pass the following significance test:

$$\left| \frac{mean(06-08) - mean(01-03)}{mean(01-03)} \right| > 0.05$$

The exact value can optionally be determined by experimentation, however in this experiment the significance threshold was set to 5% of the initial rank.

- **Linear regression:** We use linear regression to find the trend line of the feature polarity rank and use that in the decision process. As in previous method, yearly polarity ranks are used, however, instead of using only initial or final years we use the whole span of training data to obtain a linear fit. The p-value calculated during the fit is used as the significance threshold, where $p < 0.05$, for the feature polarity shift to be considered significant.

Using the methods described above, if significant temporal shift in polarity occurs, we obtain an expected rank for each such feature. This information is then used in predictive feature selection that is identical with both methods. First, a feature set of fixed size K (e.g. K positive and K negative features) is created by looking at features that have the best average rank. Additionally, an extended supplement feature set is made of features that are in the *next best* category (i.e. mean rank $K + 1$ to mean rank $3K$). This *next best* feature set is then analyzed by one of the predictive methods described above, and expected rank is determined for features with significant temporal polarity shift. The results of such analysis are ordered from the most polar expected rank to the least polar, while any result where the expected rank is larger than the fixed size K is ignored. The next step is to analyze the K-sized original feature set using the same method. Results are then ordered in inverse order, so that features expected to be least polar are first, while also, any feature that is expected to remain polar (i.e. $feature\_rank < K$) is ignored.

This new smaller set of features is then read from least polar expected rank, and while there is a feature in the *next best* set we make a switch. Simply put, this procedure eliminates features predicted to lose polarity and features predicted to gain most polarity are included instead. Experiments show that number of features switched changes based on parameters (i.e. p-values, size of K, etc.) from around 10% of the feature set for $K = 100$ to 30% for $K = 300$.

4.1 Experiments

In the first experiment with temporally robust models, we used the difference of means to implement predictive feature selection. The data used to create baseline accuracy was a random subset of R reviews, where, again, $R = 40,000$ reviews were selected uniformly at random from years 2001 to 2008. After using 80/20 splits, a subset of 32,000 reviews was used to train a logistic regression classifier, and following the training, K most negative and K most positive features were selected. In contrast to the baseline model, the temporally robust model used the difference of means method to select K negative and K positive features using predictive feature selection described in the section above. This setup was run 3 times with different random subsets of data for both the baseline and the temporally robust model. The result obtained from the runs can be seen below in Figure 5 and Table 3.

Average model accuracies using 200 features		
Test years	Baseline	Temp. robust
2010	0.828	0.834
2011	0.821	0.825
2012	0.834	0.839
2013	0.845	0.847
2014	0.845	0.85

Table 3: Each value in the table represents an average accuracy of either a baseline or a temporally robust model tested on a data set of 8,000 reviews from the designated year. Each average is made over 3 experimental runs using different random subsets as training and test data (with no overlap between training and test). Every model used 100 positive and 100 negative features (i.e. $K = 100$). The predictive feature selection was implemented using the difference of means method.

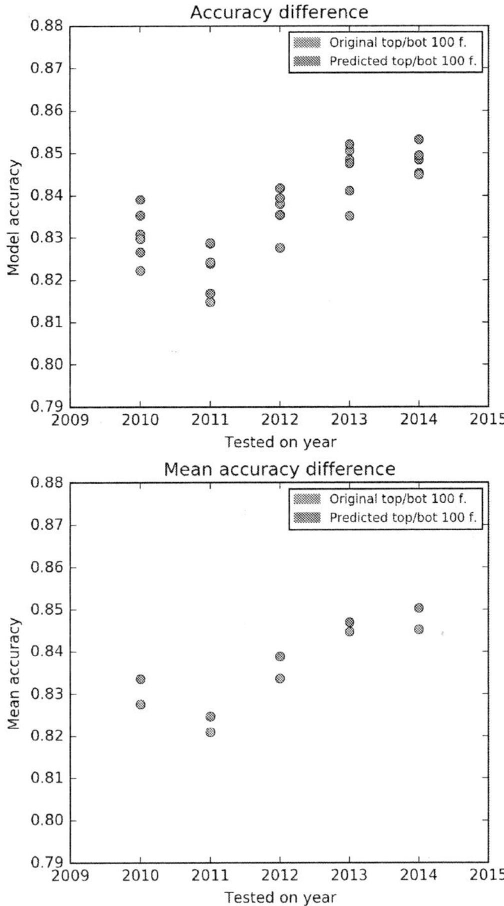

Figure 5: The figure contains results from both the baseline and the temporally robust models trained with 200 features on 32,000 reviews. Upper part of the figure depicts model accuracies for all tested years and all 3 experimental runs; the lower part shows the average accuracy for each tested year. The difference of means method was used for predictive feature selection.

In this particular experiment $K = 100$ (i.e. 200 features in total), however, identical experiments were run also with $K = 200$ and $K = 400$ (see Figure 6). The results indicate that with the number of features limited to 200, the predictive feature selection on average outperforms our baseline model by a significant margin across all tested years, i.e. 2010 to 2014.

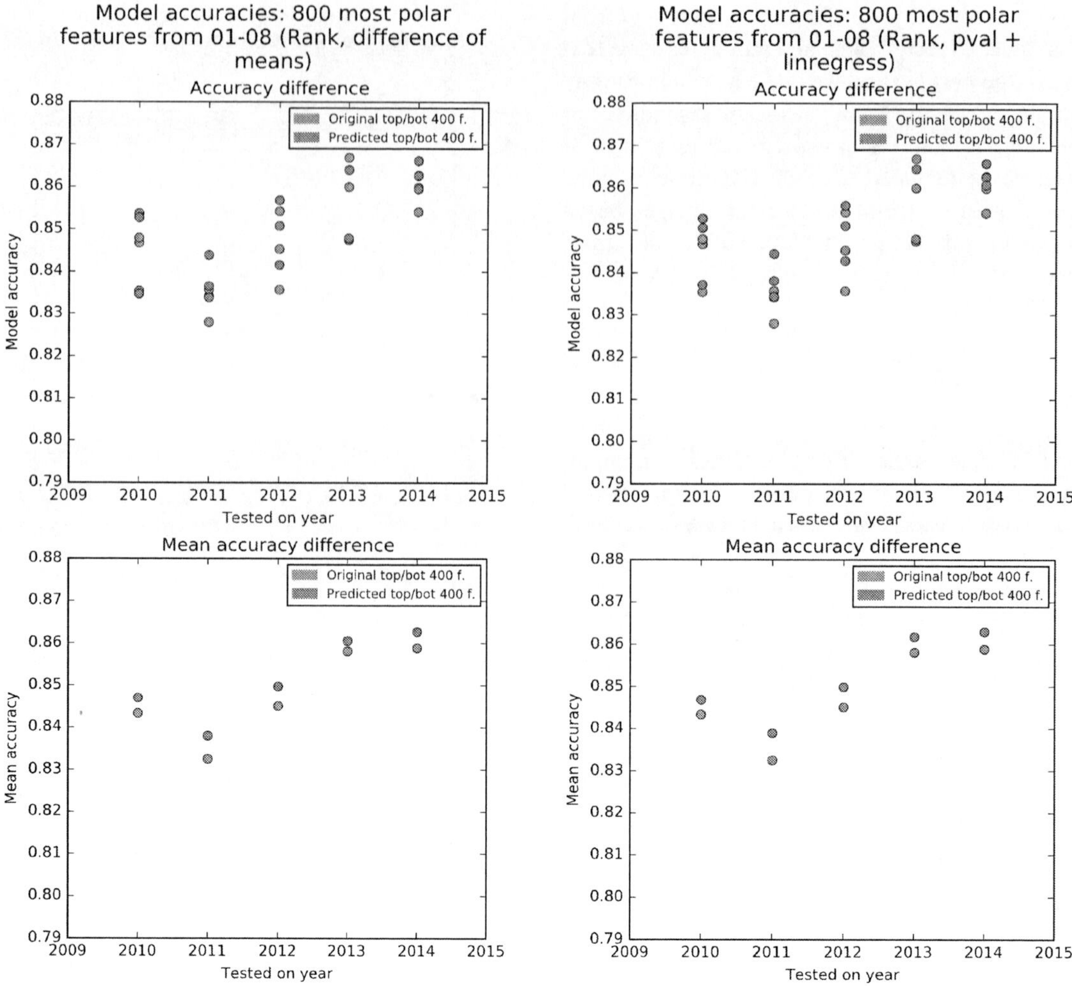

Figure 6: The figure contains results from both the baseline and the temporally robust models trained with 800 features on 32,000 reviews. Upper part of the figure depicts model accuracies for all tested years and all 3 experimental runs; the lower part shows the average accuracy for each tested year. The difference of means method was used for the predictive feature selection.

Figure 7: The figure contains results from both the baseline and the temporally robust models trained with 800 features on 32,000 reviews. Upper part of the figure depicts model accuracies for all tested years and all 3 experimental runs; the lower part shows the average accuracy for each tested year. The linear regression method with p-value filtering was used for the predictive feature selection.

As can be seen above in Figure 6, significantly increased performance is present even in models that use increased number of features, i.e. from $K = 100$ to $K = 400$. Such a result suggests that predictive feature selection increases performance even when more features are used, and not only in the extremely sparse model with 200 features.

Furthermore, additional experiment with an identical experimental setup ($K = 400$) was performed; however, the predictive feature selection was implemented using linear regression method with p-value filter, as described above in the paper. Results, seen in Figure 7, clearly show that this method also performs better than the baseline approach consisting of selecting only most polar features based on training data. In general, both methods - **difference of means** and **linear regression with p-value filter** - achieve a similar performance, which is consistently better than our baseline model for all tested years and all tested numbers of features, i.e. $K \in [100, 200, 400]$.

5 Conclusion

Large data sets for sentiment analysis are costly to create and are quite commonly a few years old. The performance of classifiers trained on such data sets decreases over time, as the interval between creations of test and training sets expands. This is, in part, due to a cumulative effect of individual lexical features going through amelioration, or pejoration, which significantly changes their polarity over time. We call this effect for *temporal polarity shift*.

To counter effects of these shifts, and improve the overall performance of a classifier, we devised two methods that allow us to predict the expected feature polarity. Using these methods, we implemented predictive feature selection, an approach, especially beneficial for sparse models, that selects a better feature set for the classifier using the expected polarity, rather than using the current most polar features in the training data. Temporally robust models, i.e., the models using predictive feature selection, consistently achieve better accuracy than the baseline models, which suggest that negative effects of temporal polarity shifts can be countered to some degree.

References

John Blitzer, Mark Dredze, and Fernando Pereira. 2007. Biographies, Bollywood, Boom-boxes and Blenders: Domain Adaptation for Sentiment Classification. In *Proceedings of ACL*.

Paul Cook and Suzanne Stevenson. 2010. Automatically identifying changes in the semantic orientation of words. In *LREC*.

Ruining He and Julian McAuley. 2016. Ups and downs: Modeling the visual evolution of fashion trends with one-class collaborative filtering. In *proceedings of the 25th international conference on world wide web*, pages 507–517. International World Wide Web Conferences Steering Committee.

Julian McAuley, Christopher Targett, Qinfeng Shi, and Anton Van Den Hengel. 2015. Image-based recommendations on styles and substitutes. In *Proceedings of the 38th International ACM SIGIR Conference on Research and Development in Information Retrieval*, pages 43–52. ACM.

Not Just Depressed: Bipolar Disorder Prediction on Reddit

Ivan Seuklić   Matej Gjurković   Jan Šnajder
Text Analysis and Knowledge Engineering Lab
Faculty of Electrical Engineering and Computing, University of Zagreb
Unska 3, 10000 Zagreb, Croatia
{ivan.sekulic,matej.gjurkovic,jan.snajder}@fer.hr

Abstract

Bipolar disorder, an illness characterized by manic and depressive episodes, affects more than 60 million people worldwide. We present a preliminary study on bipolar disorder prediction from user-generated text on Reddit, which relies on users' self-reported labels. Our benchmark classifiers for bipolar disorder prediction outperform the baselines and reach accuracy and F1-scores of above 86%. Feature analysis shows interesting differences in language use between users with bipolar disorders and the control group, including differences in the use of emotion-expressive words.

1 Introduction

World Health Organization's 2017 and Wykes et al. (2015) report that up to 27% of adult population in Europe suffer or have suffered from some kind of mental disorder. Unfortunately, as much as 35–50% of those affected go undiagnosed and receive no treatment for their illness. To counter that, the WHO's Mental Health Action Plan's (Saxena et al., 2013) lists as one of its main objectives the gathering of information and evidence on mental conditions. At the same time, analysis of texts produced by authors affected by mental disorders is attracting increased attention in the natural language processing community. The research is geared toward a deeper understanding of mental health and the development of models for early detection of various mental disorders, especially on social networks.

In this paper we focus on bipolar disorder, a complex psychiatric disorder manifested by uncontrolled changes in mood and energy levels. Bipolar disorder is characterized by manic episodes, during which people feel abnormally elevated and energized, and depression episodes, manifested in decreased activity levels and a feeling of hopelessness. The two phases are recurrent and differ in intensity and duration, greatly affecting the person's capacity to carry out daily tasks. Bipolar disorder affects more than 60 million people, or almost 1% of the world population (Anderson et al., 2012). The suicide rate in patients diagnosed with bipolar disorder is more than 6% (Nordentoft et al., 2011). There is thus a clear need for the development of systems capable of early detection of this illness.

As a first step toward that goal, in this paper we present a preliminary study on bipolar disorder prediction based on user-generated texts on social media. The main problem in detecting mental disorders from user-generated text is the lack of labeled datasets. We follow the recent strand of research (Gkotsis et al., 2016; De Choudhury et al., 2016; Shen and Rudzicz, 2017; Gjurković and Šnajder, 2018) and use Reddit as a rich and diverse source of high-volume data with self-reported labels. Our study consists of three parts. First, we test benchmark models for predicting Reddit users with bipolar disorder. Second, we carry out a feature analysis to determine which psycholinguistic features are good predictors of the disorder. Lastly, acknowledging that emotional swings are the main symptom of the disorder, we analyze the emotion-expressive textual features in bipolar disorder users and the non-bipolar control group of users.

2 Related Work

Psychologist have long studied the language use in patients with mental disorders, including schizophrenia (Taylor et al., 1994), suicidal tendencies (Thomas and Duszynski, 1985), and depression (Schnurr et al., 1992). Lately, computer-based analysis with LIWC (Linguistic Inquiry and Word Count) (Pennebaker et al., 2001) resource was used to extract features for various studies regarding mental health (Pennebaker and King, 1999). For example, Stirman and Pennebaker (2001) found

Proceedings of the 9th Workshop on Computational Approaches to Subjectivity, Sentiment and Social Media Analysis, pages 72–78
Brussels, Belgium, October 31, 2018. ©2018 Association for Computational Linguistics
https://doi.org/10.18653/v1/P17

the increased use of the first-person singular pronouns (*I, me, my*) in poems to be a good predictor of suicidal behavior, while Rude et al. (2004) detected an excessive use of the pronoun *I* in essays of depressed psychology students. In a recent study, however, Tackman et al. (2018) suggest that first-person singular pronouns may be better viewed as a marker of general distress or negative emotionality rather than as a specific marker of depression.

A number of studies looked into the use of emotion-expressive words. Rude et al. (2004) found that currently depressed students used more negative emotion words than never-depressed students. Halder et al. (2017) tracked linguistic changes of social network users over time to understand the progression of their emotional status. Kramer et al. (2004) found that conversations in bipolar support chat rooms contained more positively valence words and slightly more negatively valenced emotions than casual conversations.

Much recent work has leveraged social media as a source of user-generated text for mental health profiling (Park et al., 2012). Most studies used Twitter data; e.g., De Choudhury et al. (2013) predicted depression in Twitter users, while CLPsych 2015 shared task (Coppersmith et al., 2015b) addressed depression and post-traumatic stress disorder (PTSD). Bipolar disorder on Twitter is usually classified alongside other disorders. E.g., Coppersmith et al. (2014, 2015a) achieved a precision of 0.64 at 10% false alarms, while Benton et al. (2017) used multi-task learning and achieved an AUC-score of 0.752.

Reddit has only recently been used as a source for the analysis of mental disorders. Gkotsis et al. (2016) analyzed the language in different subreddits related to mental health, and showed that linguistic features such as vocabulary use and sentence complexity vary across different subreddits. De Choudhury et al. (2016) explored the methods for automatic detection of individuals which could transit from mental health discourse to suicidal ideas. Shen and Rudzicz (2017) used topic modeling, LIWC, and language models to predict whether a Reddit post is related to anxiety. To our knowledge, there is no previous study on the analysis of bipolar disorder of Reddit users.

3 Dataset

Reddit is one of the largest social media sites in the world, with more than 85 million unique visitors per month.[1] Reddit is suitable for our study not only because of its vast volume, but also because it offers user anonimity and covers a wide range of topics. Registered users can anonymously discuss various topics on more than 1 million subpages, called "subreddits". A considerable number of subreddits is dedicated to mental health in general, and to bipolar disorder in particular. All comments between 2005 and 2018 (more than 3 billion) are available as a Reddit dump database via Google Big Query, which we used to obtain the data.

Bipolar disorder users. To obtain a sample of users with bipolar disorder, we first retrieved all subreddits related to the disorder, i.e., *bipolar, bipolar2, BipolarReddit, BipolarSOs, bipolarart*, as well as the more generic *mentalhealth* subreddit. Then, following Beller et al. (2014) and Coppersmith et al. (2014), we looked for self-reported bipolar users by searching in the user's comments for the string *"I am diagnosed with bipolar"* and its paraphrased versions. In addition, following Gjurković and Šnajder (2018), we inspect users' *flairs* – short descriptive texts that the users can set for certain subreddits to appear next to their names. While a flair is not mandatory, we found that many users with bipolar disorder do use flairs on mental health subreddits to indicate their disorder.

The acquisition procedure yielded a set of 4,619 unique users with self-reported bipolar disorder. The users generated around 5 million comments, totaling more than 163 million tokens. To get an estimate of labeling quality, we randomly sampled 250 users and inspected their labels and text. As we found no false positives (i.e., all 250 users report on being diagnosed a bipolar disorder), we gauge that the dataset is of high precision. The true precision of the dataset depends, of course, on the veracity of the self-reported diagnosis.

To make the subsequent analysis reliable and unbiased, we decided to additionally prune the dataset as follows. To mitigate the topic bias, we removed all comments by bipolar disorder users on bipolar subreddits, as well as on the general mental health subreddit. Additionally, any comment on any subreddit that mentions the words *bipolar* or *BP* (case insensitive) was also excluded. Finally, to increase the reliability, we retained in our dataset only the users who, after pruning, have at least 1000 word remaining. The final number of users in our dataset is 3,488.

---

[1] https://www.alexa.com/siteinfo/reddit.com

Category	# bipolar	# control
Animals	397	898
AskReddit	1797	2767
Gaming	489	1501
Jobs and finance	293	586
Movies/music/books	502	1606
Politics	332	2445
Religion	264	700
Sex and relationships	948	1000
Sports	156	785
All	3488	3931

Table 1: The number of unique bipolar disorder and control group users broken down by topic categories

Control group. The control group was sampled from the general Reddit community, serving as a representative of the mentally healthy population. To ensure that the topics discussed by the control group match those of bipolar disorder users, we sampled users that post in subreddits often visited by bipolar disorder users (i.e., subreddits where posting frequency of bipolar disorder users was above the average). To also ensure that the control group is representative of the mentally healthy Reddit population, we removed all users with more than 1000 words on mental health related subreddits. As before, we only retained users that had more than 1000 words in all of their comments. The final number of users in the control group is 3,931, which is close to the number of bipolar users, with the purpose of having a balanced dataset. The total number of comments is about 20 million, which is four times more than for the bipolar disorder users.

Topic categories. Topic of discussion may affect the language use, including the stylometric variables (Mikros and Argiri, 2007), which means that topic distribution may act as a confounder in our analysis. To minimize this effect, we split the dataset into nine topic categories, each consisting of a handful of subreddits on a similar topic. Table 1 shows the breakdown of the number of unique users from both groups across topic categories. *AskReddit* is the biggest subreddit and not bound to any particular topic; in this category, we also add other subreddits covering a wide range of topics, such as *CasualConversation* and *Showerthoughts*. To be included in a category, the user must have had at least 1000 words on subreddits from that category.

4 Bipolar Disorder Prediction

Feature extraction. For each user, we extracted three kinds of features: (1) psycholinguistic fea-

tures, (2) lexical features, and (3) Reddit user features. For the psycholinguistic features, in line with much previous work, we used LIWC (Pennebaker et al., 2015), a widely used tool in predicting mental health, which classifies the words into dictionary-defined categories. We extracted 93 features, including syntactic features (e.g., pronouns, articles), topical features (e.g., work, friends), and psychological features (e.g., emotions, social context). In addition to LIWC, we used Empath (Fast et al., 2016), which is similar to LIWC but categorizes the words using similarities based on neural embeddings. We used the 200 predefined and manually curated categories, which Fast et al. have found to be highly correlated with LIWC categories (r=0.906).

The lexical features are the tf-idf weighted bag-of-words, stemmed using Porter stemmer from NLTK (Bird et al., 2009). Finally, Reddit user features are meant to model user's interaction patterns. These include post-comment ratio, the number of *gilded* posts (posts awarded with money by other users), average controversiality, the average difference between *ups* and *downs* on user's comments and the time intervals between comments (the mean, median, selected percentiles, and the mode).[2]

Experimental setup. We frame bipolar disorder prediction as a binary classification task, using the above-defined features and three classifiers: a support vector machine (SVM), logistic regression, and random forest ensemble (RF). We evaluated our models and tune the hyperparameters using 10×5 nested cross validation. To mitigate for class imbalance, we use class weighting when training classifiers on the dataset split into categories. As baselines, we used a majority class classifier (MCC) for evaluating the accuracy score and a random classifier with class priors estimated from the training set for evaluating the F1-score (F1-score is undefined for MCC). For implementation, we used Scikit-learn (Pedregosa et al., 2011). We use a two-sided t-test for all statistical significance tests and test at p<0.001 level.

Results. Table 2 shows the accuracy and F1-scores for the different classifiers. Random forest

---

[2]Users with bipolar disorder often experience sleep disturbance, which can make their usage patterns deviate from that of other users. Unfortunately, timestamps in Big Query are in UTC, not in users' local times, thus determining the time zone would require geolocalization. We leave this for future work.

	Acc	F1
MCC	0.529	–
Random	0.546	0.453
SVM	0.865	0.853
LogReg	0.866	0.849
RF	**0.869**	**0.863**

Table 2: Prediction accuracy and F1-scores

	LIWC	Empath	Tf-idf	All
SVM	0.837	0.782	**0.865**	0.838
LogReg	0.841	0.819	**0.866**	0.862
RF	0.829	0.825	0.869	**0.869**

Table 3: Prediction accuracy for the different models and feature sets

	MCC	Our models
Animals	0.693	0.807*
AskReddit	0.606	0.856*
Gaming	0.754	0.777*
Jobs and finance	0.665	0.752*
Movies/music/books	0.761	0.817*
Politics	0.880	0.882*
Religion	0.724	0.784*
Sex and relationships	0.513	0.801*
Sports	0.832	0.837

Table 4: Accuracy of the MCC baseline and our models across topic categories. Accuracies marked with "*" are significantly different from the baseline.

classifier achieved the best results, with accuracy of 0.869 and an F1-score of 0.863. All models outperform the baseline accuracies of 0.529 and 0.546, and the baseline F1-score of 0.453.

Table 3 shows the accuracy of the models using different feature sets. We observe two trends: Empath generally performs worse than LIWC, and tf-idf features perform better than LIWC. However, looking at the scores of the random forest classifier as the best model, we find that there is no significant difference between LIWC and Empath. Tf-idf does perform significantly different than both LIWC and Empath, while all features combined (including Reddit user features) do not differ from tf-idf alone. We speculate that tf-idf might yield better results in this case because essentially all the words that LIWC and Empath detect also exist as individual features in tf-idf. Similarly, Coppersmith et al. (2014) achieve better results using language models than LIWC, arguing that many relevant text signals go undetected by LIWC.

Finally, Table 4 shows the accuracy across topic categories for the MCC baseline and the best classifier in each category. Our models outperform MCC in all categories, and the differences are significant for all categories except *Sports*.

5 Feature Analysis

We analyze the merit of the psycholinguistic features using a two-sided t-test, with the null hypothesis of no difference in feature values between users with bipolar disorder and control users. The lower the p-value, the higher the merit. We analyzed the features separately on the entire dataset and on the dataset split into categories.

Between-group analysis. Ten LIWC features with the lowest p-value on the entire dataset are presented in Table 5, together with feature value means for the two groups. The values in the table are percentages of words in text from each category, except *Authentic* and *Clout*, which are "summary variables" devised by Pennebaker et al. (2015). Personal pronouns, especially the pronoun *I*, are used more often by bipolar disorder users. This observation is in accord with past studies on language of depressed people, which we can compare to because a bipolar depressive episode is almost identical to major depression (Anderson et al., 2012). Coppersmith et al. (2014) also report a significant difference in the use of *I* between Twitter users with bipolar disorder and the control group. The *Authentic* feature of Newman et al. (2003) reflects the authenticity of the author's text: a higher value of this feature in bipolar disorder users may perhaps be explained by them speaking about personal issues more sincerely, though further research would be required to confirm this. We also observe a higher use of words associated with feelings (*feel*), *health*, and biological processes (*bio*). Kacewicz et al. (2014) argue that pronoun use reflects standings in social hierarchies, expressed through *Clout* and *power* features: we observe a lower use of these words in users with bipolar disorder, which might indicate they think of themselves as less valuable members of society. The analysis of Empath features yielded similar findings: *health*, *contentment*, *affection*, *pain*, and *nervousness* have higher values in users with bipolar disorder.

Per-category analysis. Significant features in specific categories follow a pattern similar to the features on the complete dataset. Pronoun *I* is statistically significant in all of the categories, as well as features *Clout* and *Authentic*.

Feature	bipolar μ	control μ
Authentic	52.65	32.92
ppron	10.69	8.66
i	5.84	3.38
health	0.96	0.50
feel	0.69	0.48
power	2.11	2.58
pronoun	16.87	14.86
bio	2.65	1.90
Clout	48.51	58.03
article	5.88	6.55

Table 5: Mean values of most significant LIWC features for both groups

	Bipolar	Control
posemo	3.899 ± 1.02	3.442 ± 0.78
negemo	2.432 ± 0.67	2.569 ± 0.70
anxiety	0.367 ± 0.19	0.266 ± 0.10
anger	0.818 ± 0.39	1.128 ± 0.52
sad	0.455 ± 0.21	0.363 ± 0.11
affect	6.415 ± 1.22	6.074 ± 1.12

Table 6: Means and standard deviations of LIWC emotion categories for bipolar and control group

6 Emotion Analysis

As emotional swings are of the main symptoms of bipolar disorder, we expect that there will be a difference in the use of emotion words between users with bipolar disorder and the control group. We report the results for LIWC, as Empath gave very similar results.

Between-group differences. Table 6 shows means and standard deviations of the values of six LIWC emotion categories (*posemo*, *negemo*, *anxiety*, *anger*, *sad*, and *affect*) for the users with bipolar disorder and the control group. Users with bipolar disorder use significantly more words linked with general affect. Furthermore, we observe increased use of words related to sadness, while the control group uses more anger-related words. The results for *sadness* are in line with previous work on depressed authors. In addition, we find significant use of *anxiety* words in users with bipolar disorder, similar to the findings of Coppersmith et al. (2014). Surprisingly, we find that users with bipolar disorder use more positive emotion words than the control group. This is in contrast to findings of Rude et al. (2004), who report no statistical significance in the use of positive emotion words in depressed authors. We speculate that this difference may be due to the characteristics of manic episodes, which do not occur in clinically depressed people.

	Bipolar	Control	p-value
posemo	0.00272*	0.00166	0.00272
negemo	0.00583*	0.00379	0.00583
anxiety	0.00765*	0.00627	0.00765
anger	0.01745	0.01422	0.01745
sadness	0.00695*	0.00572	0.00695

Table 7: Averages of standard deviations in the use of emotion-expressive words for the two groups. All differences are significant except for "anger".

Per-category differences. The difference between users with bipolar disorders and the control group in *AskReddit*, *Animals*, *Movies/music/books*, and *Sex and relationships* categories is significant in words related to sadness, anxiety, anger, and positive emotions. However, there is no significant difference in positive and negative emotions in categories *Jobs* and *Politics*, while *Sports*, *Gaming*, and *Religion* differ only in positive emotions.

User-level variance. We hypothesize that, due to the alternation of manic and depressive episodes, users with bipolar disorder will have a higher variance across time in the use of emotion words than users from control group. To verify this, we randomly sampled 100 users with bipolar disorder and 100 control users from all the users in our dataset with more than 100K words and split their comments into monthly chunks. For each of the 200 users, we calculated the LIWC features for each month and computed their standard deviations. We then measured the difference between standard deviations for the two groups. Table 7 shows the results. We find that bipolar users have significantly more variance in most emotion-expressive words, which confirms our hypothesis.

7 Conclusion

We presented a preliminary study on bipolar disorder prediction from user comments on Reddit. Our classifiers outperform the baselines and reach accuracy and F1-scores of above 86%. Feature analysis suggests that users with bipolar disorder use more first-person pronouns and words associated with feelings. They also use more affective words, words related to sadness and anxiety, but also more positive words, which may be explained by the alternating episodes. There is also a higher variance in emotion words across time in users with bipolar disorder. Future work might look into the linguistic differences in manic and depressive episodes, and propose models for predicting them.

References

Ian M. Anderson, Peter M. Haddad, and Jan Scott. 2012. Bipolar disorder. *BMJ: British Medical Journal (Online)*, 345.

Charley Beller, Rebecca Knowles, Craig Harman, Shane Bergsma, Margaret Mitchell, and Benjamin Van Durme. 2014. Ima belieber: Social roles via self-identification and conceptual attributes. In *Proceedings of the 52nd Annual Meeting of the Association for Computational Linguistics (Volume 2: Short Papers)*, volume 2, pages 181–186.

Adrian Benton, Margaret Mitchell, and Dirk Hovy. 2017. Multi-task learning for mental health using social media text. *arXiv preprint arXiv:1712.03538*.

Steven Bird, Ewan Klein, and Edward Loper. 2009. *Natural Language Processing with Python: Analyzing Text with the Natural Language Toolkit.* " O'Reilly Media, Inc.".

Glen Coppersmith, Mark Dredze, and Craig Harman. 2014. Quantifying mental health signals in Twitter. In *Proceedings of the Workshop on Computational Linguistics and Clinical Psychology: From Linguistic Signal to Clinical Reality*, pages 51–60.

Glen Coppersmith, Mark Dredze, Craig Harman, and Kristy Hollingshead. 2015a. From ADHD to SAD: Analyzing the language of mental health on Twitter through self-reported diagnoses. In *Proceedings of the 2nd Workshop on Computational Linguistics and Clinical Psychology: From Linguistic Signal to Clinical Reality*, pages 1–10.

Glen Coppersmith, Mark Dredze, Craig Harman, Kristy Hollingshead, and Margaret Mitchell. 2015b. CLPsych 2015 shared task: Depression and PTSD on Twitter. In *Proceedings of the 2nd Workshop on Computational Linguistics and Clinical Psychology: From Linguistic Signal to Clinical Reality*, pages 31–39.

Munmun De Choudhury, Scott Counts, and Eric Horvitz. 2013. Social media as a measurement tool of depression in populations. In *Proceedings of the 5th Annual ACM Web Science Conference*, pages 47–56. ACM.

Munmun De Choudhury, Emre Kiciman, Mark Dredze, Glen Coppersmith, and Mrinal Kumar. 2016. Discovering shifts to suicidal ideation from mental health content in social media. In *Proceedings of the 2016 CHI conference on human factors in computing systems*, pages 2098–2110. ACM.

Ethan Fast, Binbin Chen, and Michael S Bernstein. 2016. Empath: Understanding topic signals in large-scale text. In *Proceedings of the 2016 CHI Conference on Human Factors in Computing Systems*, pages 4647–4657. ACM.

Matej Gjurković and Jan Šnajder. 2018. Reddit: A gold mine for personality prediction. In *Proceedings of the Second Workshop on Computational Modeling of Peoples Opinions, Personality, and Emotions in Social Media*, pages 87–97.

George Gkotsis, Anika Oellrich, Tim Hubbard, Richard Dobson, Maria Liakata, Sumithra Velupillai, and Rina Dutta. 2016. The language of mental health problems in social media. In *Proceedings of the Third Workshop on Computational Lingusitics and Clinical Psychology*, pages 63–73.

Kishaloy Halder, Lahari Poddar, and Min-Yen Kan. 2017. Modeling temporal progression of emotional status in mental health forum: A recurrent neural net approach. In *Proceedings of the 8th Workshop on Computational Approaches to Subjectivity, Sentiment and Social Media Analysis*, pages 127–135.

Ewa Kacewicz, James W. Pennebaker, Matthew Davis, Moongee Jeon, and Arthur C. Graesser. 2014. Pronoun use reflects standings in social hierarchies. *Journal of Language and Social Psychology*, 33(2):125–143.

Adam DI Kramer, Susan R. Fussell, and Leslie D. Setlock. 2004. Text Analysis as a tool for analyzing conversation in online support groups. In *CHI'04 Extended Abstracts on Human Factors in Computing Systems*, pages 1485–1488. ACM.

George K. Mikros and Eleni K. Argiri. 2007. Investigating topic influence in authorship attribution. In *PAN*.

Matthew L. Newman, James W. Pennebaker, Diane S. Berry, and Jane M. Richards. 2003. Lying words: Predicting deception from linguistic styles. *Personality and social psychology bulletin*, 29(5):665–675.

Merete Nordentoft, Preben Bo Mortensen, et al. 2011. Absolute risk of suicide after first hospital contact in mental disorder. *Archives of general psychiatry*, 68(10):1058–1064.

Minsu Park, Chiyoung Cha, and Meeyoung Cha. 2012. Depressive moods of users portrayed in Twitter. In *Proceedings of the ACM SIGKDD Workshop on healthcare informatics (HI-KDD)*, volume 2012, pages 1–8. ACM New York, NY.

Fabian Pedregosa, Gaël Varoquaux, Alexandre Gramfort, Vincent Michel, Bertrand Thirion, Olivier Grisel, Mathieu Blondel, Peter Prettenhofer, Ron Weiss, and Vincent Dubourg. 2011. Scikit-learn: Machine learning in Python. *Journal of machine learning research*, 12(Oct):2825–2830.

James W. Pennebaker, Ryan L. Boyd, Kayla Jordan, and Kate Blackburn. 2015. The development and psychometric properties of LIWC2015. Technical report.

James W. Pennebaker, Martha E. Francis, and Roger J. Booth. 2001. Linguistic inquiry and word count: LIWC 2001. *Mahway: Lawrence Erlbaum Associates*, 71(2001):2001.

James W. Pennebaker and Laura A. King. 1999. Linguistic styles: Language use as an individual difference. *Journal of personality and social psychology*, 77(6):1296.

Stephanie Rude, Eva-Maria Gortner, and James Pennebaker. 2004. Language use of depressed and depression-vulnerable college students. *Cognition & Emotion*, 18(8):1121–1133.

Shekhar Saxena, Michelle Funk, and Dan Chisholm. 2013. World health assembly adopts comprehensive mental health action plan 2013–2020. *The Lancet*, 381(9882):1970–1971.

Paula P. Schnurr, Stanley D. Rosenberg, and Thomas E. Oxman. 1992. Comparison of TAT and free speech techniques for eliciting source material in computerized content analysis. *Journal of personality assessment*, 58(2):311–325.

Judy Hanwen Shen and Frank Rudzicz. 2017. Detecting anxiety on Reddit. In *Proceedings of the Fourth Workshop on Computational Linguistics and Clinical Psychology—From Linguistic Signal to Clinical Reality*, pages 58–65.

Shannon Wiltsey Stirman and James W. Pennebaker. 2001. Word use in the poetry of suicidal and non-suicidal poets. *Psychosomatic medicine*, 63(4):517–522.

Allison M. Tackman, David A. Sbarra, Angela L. Carey, M. Brent Donnellan, Andrea B. Horn, Nicholas S. Holtzman, To'Meisha S. Edwards, James W. Pennebaker, and Matthias R. Mehl. 2018. Depression, negative emotionality, and self-referential language: A multi-lab, multi-measure, and multi-language-task research synthesis. *Journal of personality and social psychology*.

Michael Alan Taylor, Robyn Reed, and Sheri A Berenbaum. 1994. Patterns of speech disorders in schizophrenia and mania. *Journal of Nervous and Mental Disease*.

Caroline B. Thomas and Karen R. Duszynski. 1985. Are words of the Rorschach predictors of disease and death? The case of "whirling.". *Psychosomatic medicine*.

Til Wykes, Josep Maria Haro, Stefano R. Belli, Carla Obradors-Tarragó, Celso Arango, José Luis Ayuso-Mateos, István Bitter, Matthias Brunn, Karine Chevreul, and Jacques Demotes-Mainard. 2015. Mental health research priorities for Europe. *The Lancet Psychiatry*, 2(11):1036–1042.

Topic-Specific Sentiment Analysis Can Help Identify Political Ideology

Sumit Bhatia
IBM Research AI
New Delhi, India
sumitbhatia@in.ibm.com

Deepak P
Queen's University Belfast
Belfast, UK
deepaksp@acm.org

Abstract

Ideological leanings of an individual can often be gauged by the sentiment one expresses about different issues. We propose a simple framework that represents a political ideology as a distribution of sentiment polarities towards a set of topics. This representation can then be used to detect ideological leanings of documents (speeches, news articles, etc.) based on the sentiments expressed towards different topics. Experiments performed using a widely used dataset show the promise of our proposed approach that achieves comparable performance to other methods despite being much simpler and more interpretable.

1 Introduction

The ideological leanings of a person within the *left-right* political spectrum are often reflected by how one feels about different topics and by means of preferences among various choices on particular issues. For example, a left-leaning person would prefer nationalization and state control of public services (such as healthcare) where privatization would be often preferred by people that lean towards the right. Likewise, a left-leaning person would often be supportive of immigration and will often talk about immigration in a positive manner citing examples of benefits of immigration on a country's economy. A right-leaning person, on the other hand, will often have a negative opinion about immigration.

Most of the existing works on political ideology detection from text have focused on utilizing bag-of-words and other syntactic features to capture variations in language use (Sim et al., 2013; Biessmann, 2016; Iyyer et al., 2014). We propose an alternative mechanism for political ideology detection based on sentiment analysis. We posit that adherents of a political ideology generally have similar sentiment toward specific topics (for example, right wing followers are often posi-

tive towards free markets, lower tax rates, etc.) and thus, *a political ideology can be represented by a characteristic sentiment distribution over different topics* (Section 3). This topic-specific sentiment representation of a political ideology can then be used for automatic ideology detection by comparing the topic-specific sentiments as expressed by the content in a document (news article, magazine article, collection of social media posts by a user, utterances in a conversation, etc.).

In order to validate our hypothesis, we consider exploiting the sentiment information towards topics from archives of political debates to build a model for identifying political orientation of speakers as one of right or left leaning, which corresponds to republicans and democrats respectively, within the context of US politics. This is inspired by our observation that the political leanings of debators are often expressed in debates by way of speakers' sentiments towards particular topics. Parliamentary or Senate debates often bring the ideological differences to the centre stage, though somewhat indirectly. Heated debates in such forums tend to focus on the choices proposed by the executive that are in sharp conflict with the preference structure of the opposition members. Due to this inherent tendency of parliamentary debates to focus on topics of disagreement, the sentiments exposited in debates hold valuable cues to identify the political orientation of the participants.

We develop a simple classification model that uses a topic-specific sentiment summarization for republican and democrat speeches separately. Initial results of experiments conducted using a widely used dataset of US Congress debates (Thomas et al., 2006) are encouraging and show that this simple model compares well with classification models that employ state-of-the-art distributional text representations (Section 4).

Proceedings of the 9th Workshop on Computational Approaches to Subjectivity, Sentiment and Social Media Analysis, pages 79–84
Brussels, Belgium, October 31, 2018. ©2018 Association for Computational Linguistics
https://doi.org/10.18653/v1/P17

2 Related Work

2.1 Political Ideology Detection

Political ideology detection has been a relatively new field of research within the NLP community. Most of the previous efforts have focused on capturing the variations in language use in text representing content of different ideologies. Beissmann et al. (2016) employ bag-of-word features for ideology detection in different domains such as speeches in German parliament, party manifestos, and facebook posts. Sim et al. (2013) use a labeled corpus of political writings to infer lexicons of cues strongly associated with different ideologies. These "ideology lexicons" are then used to analyze political speeches and identify their ideological leanings. Iyyer at al. (2014) recently adopted a recursive neural network architecture to detect ideological bias of single sentences. In addition, topic models have also been used for ideology detection by identifying latent topic distributions across different ideologies (Lin et al., 2008; Ahmed and Xing, 2010). Gerrish and Blei (2011) connected text of the legislations to voting patterns of legislators from different parties.

2.2 Sentiment Analysis for Controversy Detection

Sentiment analysis has proved to be a useful tool in detecting controversial topics as it can help identify topics that evoke different feelings among people on opposite side of the arguments. Mejova et al. (2014) analyzed language use in controversial news articles and found that a writer may choose to highlight the negative aspects of the opposing view rather than emphasizing the positive aspects of ones view. Lourentzou et al. (2015) utilize the sentiments expressed in social media comments to identify controversial portions of news articles. Given a news article and its associated comments on social media, the paper links comments with each sentence of the article (by using a sentence as a query and retrieving comments using BM25 score). For all the comments associated with a sentence, a sentiment score is then computed, and sentences with large variations in positive and negative comments are identified as controversial sentences. Choi et al. (2010) go one step further and identify controversial topics and their sub-topics in news articles.

3 Using Topic Sentiments for Ideology Detection

Let $\mathcal{D} = \{\ldots, d, \ldots\}$ be a corpus of political documents such as speeches or social media postings. Let $\mathcal{L} = \{\ldots, l, \ldots\}$ be the set of ideology class labels. Typical scenarios would just have two class labels (i.e., $|\mathcal{L}| = 2$), but we will outline our formulation for a general case. For document $d \in \mathcal{D}$, $l_d \in \mathcal{L}$ denotes the class label for that document. Our method relies on the usage of topics, each of which are most commonly represented by a probability distribution over the vocabulary. The set of topics over $\mathcal{D}$, which we will denote using $\mathcal{T}$, may be identified using a topic modeling method such as LDA (Blei et al., 2003) unless a pre-defined set of handcrafted topics is available.

Given a document d and a topic t, our method relies on identifying the sentiment as expressed by content in d towards the topic t. The sentiment could be estimated in the form of a categorical label such as one of positive, negative and neutral (Haney, 2013). Within our modelling, however, we adopt a more fine-grained sentiment labelling, whereby the sentiment for a topic-document pair is a probability distribution over a plurality of ordinal polarity classes ranging from *strongly positive* to *strongly negative*. Let s_{dt} represent the *topic-sentiment* polarity vector of d towards t such that $s_{dt}(x)$ represents the probability of the polarity class x. Combining the topic-sentiment vectors for all topics yields a document-specific *topic-sentiment matrix* (TSM) as follows:

$$
S_{d,\mathcal{T}} = \begin{bmatrix} \cdots & s_{dt_1}(x) & \cdots \\ \cdots & s_{dt_2}(x) & \cdots \\ \vdots & \vdots & \vdots \end{bmatrix} \tag{1}
$$

Each row in the matrix corresponds to a topic within $\mathcal{T}$, with each element quantifying the probability associated with the sentiment polarity class x for the topic t within document d. The topic-sentiment matrix above may be regarded as a sentiment signature for the document over the topic set $\mathcal{T}$.

3.1 Determining Topic-specific Sentiments

In constructing TSMs, we make use of topic-specific sentiment estimations as outlined above. Typical sentiment analysis methods (e.g., NLTK

Sentiment Analysis[1]) are designed to determine the overall sentiment for a text segment. Using such sentiment analysis methods in order to determine topic-specific sentiments is not necessarily straightforward. We adopt a simple keyword based approach for the task. For every document-topic pair (t, d), we extract the sentences from d that contain at least one of the top-k keywords associated with the topic t. We then collate the sentences in the order in which they appear in d and form a mini-document d_t. This document d_t is then passed on to a conventional sentiment analyzer that would then estimate the sentiment polarity as a probability distribution over sentiment polarity classes, which then forms the $s_{dt}(.)$ vector. We use $k = 5$ and the RNN based sentiment analyzer (Socher et al., 2013) in our method.

3.2 Nearest TSM Classification

We now outline a simple classification model that uses summaries of TSMs. Given a labeled training set of documents, we would like to find the prototypical TSM corresponding to each label. This can be done by identifying the matrix that minimizes the cumulative deviation from those corresponding to the documents with the label.

$$S_{l,\mathcal{T}} = \arg\min_{X} \sum_{d \in \mathcal{D} \wedge l_d = l} ||X - S_{d,\mathcal{T}}||_F^2 \quad (2)$$

where $||M||_F$ denotes the Frobenius norm. It turns out that such a label-specific signature matrix is simply the mean of the topic-sentiment matrices corresponding to documents that bear the respective label, which may be computed using the below equation.

$$S_{l,\mathcal{T}} = \frac{1}{|\{d | d \in \mathcal{D} \wedge l_d = l\}|} \sum_{d \in \mathcal{D} \wedge l_d = l} S_{d,\mathcal{T}} \quad (3)$$

For an unseen (test) document d', we first compute the TSM $S_{d',\mathcal{T}}$, and assign it the label corresponding to the label whose TSM is most proximal to $S_{d',\mathcal{T}}$.

$$l_{d'} = \arg\min_{l} ||S_{d',\mathcal{T}} - S_{l,\mathcal{T}}||_F^2 \quad (4)$$

3.3 Logistic Regression Classification

In two class scenarios with label such as $\{left, right\}$ or $\{democrat, republican\}$ as we have in our dataset, TSMs can be flattened into a vector and fed into a logistic regression classifier that learns weights - i.e., co-efficients for each topic + sentiment polarity class combination. These weights can then be used to estimate the label by applying it to the new document's TSM.

4 Experiments

4.1 Dataset

We used the publicly available Convote dataset[2] (Thomas et al., 2006) for our experiments. The dataset provides transcripts of debates in the House of Representatives of the U.S Congress for the year 2005. Each file in the dataset corresponds to a single, uninterrupted utterance by a speaker in a given debate. We combine all the utterances of a speaker in a given debate in a single file to capture different opinions/view points of the speaker about the debate topic. We call this document the view point document (VPD) representing the speaker's opinion about different aspects of the issue being debated. The dataset also provides political affiliations of all the speakers – Republican (R), Democrat (D), and Independent (I). With there being only six documents for the independent class (four in training, two in test), we excluded them from our evaluation. Table 1 summarizes the statistics about the dataset and distribution of different classes. We obtained 50 topics using LDA from Mallet[3] run over the training dataset. The topic-sentiment matrix was obtained using the Stanford CoreNLP sentiment API[4] (Manning et al., 2014) which provides probability distributions over a set of five sentiment polarity classes.

4.2 Methods

In order to evaluate our proposed TSM-based methods - viz., nearest class (NC) and logistic regression (LR) - we use the following methods in our empirical evaluation.

[1] http://text-processing.com/demo/sentiment/

[2] http://www.cs.cornell.edu/home/llee/data/convote.html
[3] http://mallet.cs.umass.edu/
[4] https://nlp.stanford.edu/sentiment/code.html

	Training Set	Test Set
Republican (R)	530	194
Democrat (D)	641	215
Total	1175	411

Table 1: Distribution of different classes in the Con-Vote dataset.

Method	R	D	Total
GloVe d2v	0.6391	0.6465	0.6430
TSM-NC	**0.6907**	0.4558	0.5672
TSM-LR	0.5258	**0.7628**	**0.6504**
GloVe-d2v + TSM	0.5051	0.7023	0.6088

Table 2: Results achieved by different methods on the ideology classification task.

1. **GloVe-d2v:** We use pre-trained GloVe (Pennington et al., 2014) word embeddings to compute vector representation of each VPD by averaging the GloVe vectors for all words in the document. A logistic regression classifier is then trained on the vector representations thus obtained.

2. **GloVe-d2v+TSM:** A logistic regression classifier trained on the GloVe features as well as TSM features.

4.3 Results

Table 2 reports the classification results for different methods described above. TSM-NC, the method that uses the TSM vectors and performs simple nearest class classification achieves an overall accuracy of 57%. Next, training a logistic regression classifier trained on TSM vectors as features, TSM-LR, achieves significant improvement with an overall accuracy of 65.04%. The word embedding based baseline, the GloVe-d2v method, achieves slightly lower performance with an overall accuracy of 64.30%. However, we do note that the per-class performance of GloVe-d2v method is more balanced with about 64% accuracy for both classes. The TSM-LR method on the other hand achieves about 76% for R class and only 52% for the D class. The results obtained are promising and lend weight to out hypothesis that ideological leanings of a person can be identified by using the fine-grained sentiment analysis of the viewpoint a person has towards different underlying topics.

4.4 Discussion

Towards analyzing the significance of the results, we would like to start with drawing attention to the format of the data used in the TSM methods. The document-specific TSM matrices do *not* contain any information about the topics themselves, but only about the sentiment in the document towards each topic; one may recollect that $s_{dt}(.)$ is a quantification of the strength of the sentiment in d towards topic t. Thus, in contrast to distributional embeddings such as doc2vec, TSMs contain only the information that directly relates to sentiment towards specific topics that are learnt from across the corpus. The results indicate that TSM methods are able to achieve comparable performance to doc2vec-based methods despite usage of only a small slice of informatiom. This points to the importance of sentiment information in determining the political leanings from text. We believe that leveraging TSMs along with distributional embeddings in a manner that can combine the best of both views would improve the state-of-the-art of political ideology detection.

Next, we also studied if there are topics that are more polarizing than others and how different topics impact classification performance. We identified polarizing topics, i.e, topics that invoke opposite sentiments across two classes (ideologies) by using the following equation.

$$dist(t, R, D) = ||s_{R,t} - s_{R,t}||_F \qquad (5)$$

Here, $s_{R,t}$ and $s_{D,t}$ represent the sentiment vectors for topic t for republican and democrat classes. Note that these sentiment vectors are the rows corresponding to topic t in TSMs for the two classes, respectively.

Table 3 lists the top five topics with most distance, i.e., most polarizing topics (top) and five topics with least distance, i.e.,least polarizing topics (bottom) as computed by equation 5. Note that the topics are represented using the top keywords that they contain according to the probability distribution of the topic. We observe that the most polarizing topics include topics related to healthcare (H3, H4), military programs (H5), and topics related to administration processes (H1 and H2). The least polarizing topics include topics related to worker safety (L3) and energy projects (L2). One counter-intuitive observation is topic related to gun control (L4) that is amongst the least polarizing topics. This anomaly could be at-

Most polarizing topics	**H1:** republican congress majority administration leadership n't vote party republicans special
	H2: administration process vote work included find n't true fix carriers
	H3: health programs education funding million program cuts care billion year
	H4: health insurance small care coverage businesses plans ahps employees state
	H5: military center n't students recruiters policy houston men universities colleges
Least polarizing topics	**L1:** enter director march years response found letter criminal paid general
	L2: corps nuclear year energy projects committee project million funding funds
	L3: osha safety workers commission health h.r employers occupational bills workplace
	L4: gun police industry lawsuits firearms dept chief manufacturers dealers guns
	L5: medal gold medals individuals reagan history legislation ronald king limiting

Table 3: List of most polarizing (top) and least polarizing (bottom) topics as computed using equation 5.

tributed to only a few speeches related to this issue in the training set (only 23 out of 1175 speeches mention *gun*) that prevents a reliable estimate of the probability distributions. We observed similar low occurrences of other lower distance topics too indicating the potential for improvements in computation of topic-specific sentiment representations with more data. In fact, performing the nearest neighbor classification ($TSM - NC$) with only top-10 most polarizing topics led to improvements in classification accuracy from 57% to 61% suggesting that with more data, better TSM representations could be learned that are better at discriminating between different ideologies.

5 Conclusions

We proposed to exploit topic-specific sentiment analysis for the task of automatic ideology detection from text. We described a simple framework for representing political ideologies and documents as a matrix capturing sentiment distributions over topics and used this representation for classifying documents based on their topic-sentiment signatures. Empirical evaluation over a widely used dataset of US Congressional speeches showed that the proposed approach performs on a par with classifiers using distributional text representations. In addition, the proposed approach offers simplicity and easy interpretability of results making it a promising technique for ideology detection. Our immediate future work will focus on further solidifying our observations by using a larger dataset to learn better TSMs for different ideologies. Further, the framework easily lends itself to be used for detecting ideological leanings of authors, social media users, news websites, magazines, etc. by computing their TSMs and comparing against the TSMs of different ideologies.

Acknowledgments

We would like to thank the anonymous reviewers for their valuable comments and suggestions that helped us improve the quality of this work.

References

Amr Ahmed and Eric P. Xing. 2010. Staying informed: Supervised and semi-supervised multi-view topical analysis of ideological perspective. In *EMNLP*, pages 1140–1150. ACL.

Felix Biessmann. 2016. Automating political bias prediction. *arXiv preprint arXiv:1608.02195*.

David M Blei, Andrew Y Ng, and Michael I Jordan. 2003. Latent dirichlet allocation. *Journal of machine Learning research*, 3(Jan):993–1022.

Yoonjung Choi, Yuchul Jung, and Sung-Hyon Myaeng. 2010. Identifying controversial issues and their subtopics in news articles. In *Intelligence and Security Informatics, Pacific Asia Workshop, PAISI 2010, Hyderabad, India, June 21, 2010. Proceedings*, volume 6122 of *Lecture Notes in Computer Science*, pages 140–153. Springer.

Sean Gerrish and David M. Blei. 2011. Predicting legislative roll calls from text. In *Proceedings of the 28th International Conference on Machine Learning, ICML 2011, Bellevue, Washington, USA, June 28 - July 2, 2011*, pages 489–496. Omnipress.

Carol Haney. 2013. Sentiment analysis: Providing categorical insight into unstructured textual data. *Social Media, Sociality, and Survey Research*, pages 35–59.

Mohit Iyyer, Peter Enns, Jordan L. Boyd-Graber, and Philip Resnik. 2014. Political ideology detection using recursive neural networks. In *ACL (1)*, pages 1113–1122. The Association for Computer Linguistics.

Wei-Hao Lin, Eric P. Xing, and Alexander G. Hauptmann. 2008. A joint topic and perspective model for ideological discourse. In *Machine Learning and Knowledge Discovery in Databases, European Conference, ECML/PKDD 2008, Antwerp, Belgium, September 15-19, 2008, Proceedings, Part II*, volume 5212 of *Lecture Notes in Computer Science*, pages 17–32. Springer.

Ismini Lourentzou, Graham Dyer, Abhishek Sharma, and ChengXiang Zhai. 2015. Hotspots of news articles: Joint mining of news text & social media to discover controversial points in news. In *Big Data*, pages 2948–2950. IEEE.

Christopher D. Manning, Mihai Surdeanu, John Bauer, Jenny Rose Finkel, Steven Bethard, and David McClosky. 2014. The stanford corenlp natural language processing toolkit. In *ACL (System Demonstrations)*, pages 55–60. The Association for Computer Linguistics.

Yelena Mejova, Amy X. Zhang, Nicholas Diakopoulos, and Carlos Castillo. 2014. Controversy and sentiment in online news. *CoRR*, abs/1409.8152.

Jeffrey Pennington, Richard Socher, and Christopher D. Manning. 2014. Glove: Global vectors for word representation. In *Proceedings of the 2014 Conference on Empirical Methods in Natural Language Processing, EMNLP 2014, October 25-29, 2014, Doha, Qatar, A meeting of SIGDAT, a Special Interest Group of the ACL*, pages 1532–1543. ACL.

Yanchuan Sim, Brice D. L. Acree, Justin H. Gross, and Noah A. Smith. 2013. Measuring ideological proportions in political speeches. In *Proceedings of the 2013 Conference on Empirical Methods in Natural Language Processing*, pages 91–101. Association for Computational Linguistics.

Richard Socher, Alex Perelygin, Jean Wu, Jason Chuang, Christopher D. Manning, Andrew Ng, and Christopher Potts. 2013. Recursive deep models for semantic compositionality over a sentiment treebank. In *Proceedings of the 2013 Conference on Empirical Methods in Natural Language Processing*, pages 1631–1642, Seattle, Washington, USA. Association for Computational Linguistics.

Matt Thomas, Bo Pang, and Lillian Lee. 2006. Get out the vote: Determining support or opposition from congressional floor-debate transcripts. In *EMNLP 2007, Proceedings of the 2006 Conference on Empirical Methods in Natural Language Processing, 22-23 July 2006, Sydney, Australia*, pages 327–335. ACL.

Saying no but meaning yes: negation and sentiment analysis in Basque

Jon Alkorta
Computer Languages
and Systems
IXA group (UPV/EHU)

Koldo Gojenola
Computer Languages
and Systems
IXA group (UPV/EHU)

Mikel Iruskieta
Didactics of Language
and Literature Department
IXA group (UPV/EHU)

{jon.alkorta,koldo.gojenola,mikel.iruskieta}@ehu.eus

Abstract

In this work, we have analyzed the effects of negation on the semantic orientation in Basque. The analysis shows that negation markers can strengthen, weaken or have no effect on sentiment orientation of a word or a group of words. Using the Constraint Grammar formalism, we have designed and evaluated a set of linguistic rules to formalize these three phenomena. The results show that two phenomena, strengthening and no change, have been identified accurately and the third one, weakening, with acceptable results.

1 Introduction

Negation is a morphosyntactic operation in which a lexical item denies or inverts the meaning of another lexical item or language construction (Loos et al., 2004). The effect of the negation can be the change of semantic orientation (SO) and, according to Liu (2012), negation is called sentiment shifters because they change the semantic orientation of a word or a sentence.

With the aim of calculating the semantic orientation, the first step is to build a lexicon, but this is not enough, to grasp the correct SO-value of Example 1.

(1) $[Irabazi_{+2}$ *ezinik* jarraitzen du $Eibarrek]^{+2}$. (KIR17)
[(The soccer team) Eibar continues <u>without</u> winning$_{+2}]^{+2}$.

Following the semantic lexicon Sentitegi (Alkorta et al., 2018)[1], the semantic orientation of the word *irabazi* ("to win") is $+2$, and consequently, of the sentence also is $+2$. But we can notice that the semantic orientation of the sentence is clearly negative. The negator *ezin* ("can not") turns the positive oriented word $irabazi_{+2}$ ("to win") into a negative oriented one. Therefore, we think that addressing this phenomenon is crucial to obtain better results in the calculation of the SO of texts.

The main aim of this work is to study how negation expressions and syntactic structures can change the semantic orientation of words, and to design a set of linguistic rules by means of Constraint Grammar (Karlsson et al., 2011) in order to identify these phenomena. According to our corpus study, different negation language forms can strengthen, weaken or have no effect on semantic orientation. These results go in the same direction as (Jiménez-Zafra et al., 2018b) where effects of negation within its scope are studied. We have centered our study on negation markers that unlike negation in verbs and nouns and negative polarity items, they only share information about negativity while others can share more information like aspect of action (e.g. *they denied going to the city*).

This paper has been organized as follows: after presenting related work in Section 2, Section 3 describes methodological steps. Then, Section 4 presents theoretical framework, while Section 5 gives a linguistic analysis. Section 6 shows results and error analysis, concluding with Section 7 and proposing directions for future work.

2 Related Work

There is a variety of works about negation and sentiment analysis in different languages and from different approaches.

For English, Liu and Seneff (2009) have presented a work where a parse-and-paraphrase paradigm is used to assign sentiment polarity for product reviews. If negation is detected, its polarity will be reversed (switch negation). If it has a value of $+5$, it will be reversed to -5, and vice versa. Following this, they have improved results (recall was improved in 45 %). The treatment of negation has been different in Taboada et al. (2011). In their work, when a negator is identified, the polarity value is not reversed; instead it is shifted toward the opposite polarity by a fixed amount. This approach is called shift negation. In

---

[1] The semantic lexicon is available on the web at: http://ixa.si.ehu.es/node/11438

Proceedings of the 9th Workshop on Computational Approaches to Subjectivity, Sentiment and Social Media Analysis, pages 85–90
Brussels, Belgium, October 31, 2018. ©2018 Association for Computational Linguistics
https://doi.org/10.18653/v1/P17

Text	Text span	Dictionary words	SO value
MUS20	*Pogostkinak [ezin hobeki]*[+] *atera zituen*	*hobeki*	+2
	Pogostkina took them out [in an unbeatable way][+]	best, better	
KIR17	*[Irabazi ezinik]*[−] *jarraitzen du Eibarrek,*	*Irabazi*	+2
	Eibar continues [without winning][−]	to win	

Table 1: Polarity extraction of words (step 2) and linguistic analysis (step 3).

the creation of the semantic orientation calculator (SO-CAL tool), Taboada et al. (2011) have also treated negation in combination with other linguistic phenomena (like irrealis or intensifiers).

In Spanish, there are several works related to negation and sentiment analysis. In the case of Jiménez Zafra et al. (2015), firstly, they have analyzed what the effects of different negators in different sentences are. After that, they have created linguistic rules defined by the previous analysis. Finally, they developed a module that has been included in their polarity classifier system, improving results between 2.25 % and 3.02 % depending on the resource. Vilares et al. (2015) have used a syntactic approach for opinion mining on Spanish reviews. This system treats negation taking into account the scope and polarity flip caused by negation. According to their results, there is an improvement, due to the implementation of negation, among other reasons.

Our work is related to (Taboada et al., 2011) and (Jiménez Zafra et al., 2015) since it is based on a linguistic analysis and also because a set of rules that detect the negation language forms are created. As far as we know, there is not any work which analyzes negation in connection with sentiment analysis in Basque.[2]

3 Methodological steps

1- Negation corpus. We have extracted 359 negation instances of seven[3] negation markers. They were extracted from a total of 96 reviews of six different topics: movies, music, literature, politics, sports and forecast. We have selected those negation markers because they are the most frequent in the corpus.

2- Polarity extraction of every instance. We have created a polarity tagger, based on a POS tagger (Ezeiza et al., 1998) to enrich the corpus with POS information on a se-

mantic oriented lexicon for Basque (Alkorta et al., 2018), to assign the semantic orientation value (SO value, between −5 and +5) to words, as shown in Table 1. There, the adverb *hobeki* ("best", "better") and the verb *irabazi* ("to win"), have a SO value of +2 in the lexicon.

3- Linguistic analysis. We have analyzed whether the negation markers can change the semantic orientation and the SO value of sentences. We have also tried to identify whether there are other phenomena related to negation with or without effects on semantic orientation. In Table 1, in MUS20, the negation marker appears near *hobeki* ("best"), an adverb. The result of this combination is strengthening. In contrast, in KIR17, the verb *irabazi* ("to win") is before the negator and the result is weakening. These two examples show the different performances of *ezin(ik)* ("can not"). Consequently, in Table 1, for example, this negation marker appears in two different groups. The same methodology has been used with other negation markers.

4- Constraint Grammar (CG3) rules for negation. Several rules have been proposed to detect each group, in order to identify the effects of negation based on the linguistic analysis presented in Section 5.

5- Evaluation. We use F_1 to evaluate the results using a different set of 46 reviews from the same corpus (Alkorta et al., 2016)[4].

4 Theoretical framework

In this section, we explain the three most important concepts, regarding our analysis: i) scope (negation analysis) and ii) switch and iii) shift negation (sentiment analysis approach to negation).

(2) *Berez pianorako konposatutako poliptiko txiki honek ez du bere naf kutsua galtzen*$_{-2}$ *bertsio orkestratuan.* (MUS01)
This small polyptych composed for the piano does **not** lose$_{-2}$ its naive sense in the orchestral version.

---

[2]Altuna et al. (2017) also analyze negation but their point of view is different, since they analyze events in Basque texts.

[3]The extracted negation markers from the Basque Opinion Corpus (Alkorta et al., 2016) are the following: *ez* ("not"), *gabe* ("without"), *ezin* ("can not"), *salbu* ("except (for)"), *izan ezik* ("except (for)"), *ezta* ("not even, not either") and *ezean* ("in the absence of" or "unless").

[4]A part of the corpus is available on the web at: http://ixa2.si.ehu.es/diskurtsoa/ fitxategiak.php

(3) —*maitasun istorio konbentzional bat, grazia*$_{+3}$ *handirik*$_{+1}$ **gabea**—. (LIB07)
—a conventional love story, **without** great$_{+1}$ grace$_{+3}$.[5]

According to Huddleston and Pullum (2002), the scope of negation is the part of the meaning that is affected by the negation marker, changing or not their SO value. In the examples above, the scope is underlined. As our study shows, there can be two kinds of semantic orientation in scope and these can be changed by negation markers. In Example 2, the SO value of the verb *galdu* ("to lose") and of its scope is −2. The negation weakens the SO value of the verb, reversing its SO. But, in Example 3, the SO values of the noun *grazia* ("grace") +3 and the adjective *handi* ("great") +1 assign a SO value of +4 to the scope which is positive. The negator *gabe* ("without") weakens the SO value.

According to Taboada et al. (2011), there are two approaches in sentiment analysis to weaken the negative SO value: i) switch negation and ii) shift negation.

(4) This pub is [**not** good$_{+3}$]$^{-3(switch)}_{-1(shift)}$ but the music from there is good$_{+3}$.

In the switch negation approach, the SO value of Example 4 is reversed. The SO value of the adjective *good* is +3 while the reversed SO value is −3. However, this criteria has a problem: if *excellent* is +5; *not excellent* would be more positive (+1) than *not good* (−2), but the SO value points to the contrary (*not excellent* is more negative than *not good*).

Otherwise, in the shift negation, the different negators have their own SO value and the results depend on the interaction of both SO values (the value of negation marker and negated word). Taking into account Example 4, the SO value of the negation *no* is −4 in the dictionary; so, when it modifies the word *good*, which has a SO value of +3, the sum value of scope is −1. This is the way how the shift approach solves the problem we describe in Example 4. We have decided to use the shift negation approach assigning a ±4 SO value to the negators.

5 Linguistic analysis

In the theoretical framework of the shift negation, it has been considered that negation

markers only weakens the SO value. Nevertheless, we have identified two other functions of these negation markers with low frequency, but relevant anyway from our point of view as the works of (Jiménez-Zafra et al., 2018a) and (Jiménez-Zafra et al., 2018b) show. As we observed in this study, the negation markers can strengthen, weaken or have no effect in the SO value of its scope as Figure 1 shows.

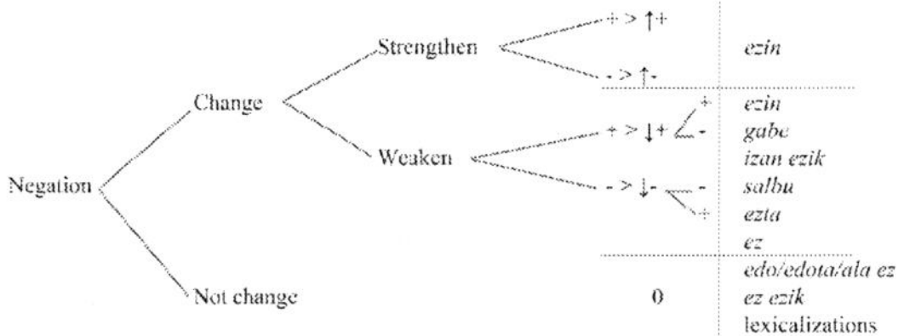

Figure 1: The effects of negation on semantic orientation according to negation markers.

The majority of negation markers usually weaken the semantic orientation of scope. But as we can see in Figure 1, the negation marker *ezin* ("can not"), for example, can strengthen or weaken the semantic orientation of scope. The weakening can be understood in two ways: i) if the word or scope of the semantic orientation is +5, +4, −5 or −4, their semantic orientation will not become negative because according to our methodology (shift negation), due to our SO value of the negators is ±4. In contrast, ii) if the semantic orientation of scope or sentence is between −3 and +3, their semantic orientation will be reversed. iii) Finally, negation with conjunction, contrastive negation and lexicalized structures do not change the SO value of the scope.

5.1 Negation strengthening the SO

Among all the negation instances, we have observed some cases where the semantic orientation has been strengthened (1.96 %: 7 of 359). This happens when the negation marker *ezin* ("can not") modifies adjectives or adverbs.

(5) *Dena nahasten da maisulan* **ezin** *ederragoa*$_{(+4)}$ *osatzeko.* (MUS21)
Everything is mixed to create a masterpiece that can **not** be more beautiful$_{(+4)}$.

In Example 5, the negator modifies the adjective and, in this case, the negation with an adjective in a comparative structure is used to reinforce the positive SO value. The result

---

[5]**Bold** is used to mark the negator, underline means the scope of negation.

Example	Negation marker	Categorization	Instances
6		[(NP +)] *ez* [+ aux. (+ NP) + verb (+ NP)]	214
	ez	[(NP +) verb +] *ez*	18
		[NP +] *ez*	13
		ez [+ NP +] *ez* [+ NP] (...) (repetitive)	2
	gabe	[NP/VP/clause +] *gabe*	41
7	ezin	[(NP) + verb +] *ezin*	19
		ezin [(+ NP) +] verb [(+ NP)]	5
	salbu	[NP] + *salbu*	2
	izan ezik	[NP/clause] + *izan ezik*	1
	ezta	*ezta* + [NP/clause]	1
	ez, ezin	with any clear pattern	7
	Total		**323**

Table 2: Negation weakening the semantic orientation.

of negating a positive chunk *can not be more beautiful* is to be even more positive. In this case, the *masterpiece* is *very beautiful*.

5.2 Negation weakening the SO

In the majority of cases, the SO value is weakened due to negation. Several negation markers can weaken the semantic orientation. In our corpus, 89.98 % of cases (323 of 359) show a weakening of scope.

(6) *Horrek* **ez** *die eragotzi$_{(-2)}$ ordea, 57 milioi euro ematea San Mames klub pribatuari!*. (POL30)
It does **not** prevent$_{(-2)}$ them, however, to give 57 milion euros to San Mames private club!

(7) *Irabazi$_{(+2)}$* **ezin**ik *jarraitzen du Eibarrek, baina oso puntu ona eskuratu du Getaferen zelaian.* (KIR17)
Eibar continues **without** winning$_{(+2)}$, but it has achieved a very good point in Getafe's (football) field.

In Example 6, the default word order of Basque (main verb + auxiliary verb) was reversed in a typical negation structure (*ez* "not" + auxiliary verb + main verb). In this example, the negation marker *ez* ("not") has an effect on all the words of the sentence, including the verb *eragotzi* ("prevent") which has a negative SO value (−2), weakening its SO value. In Example 7, the negation marker *ezin* "can not" negates the verb *irabazi* ("win"). Therefore, the negation marker *ezin* ("can not") works like an intensifier does with adjectives and adverbs (Example 5) while it has the opposite function with verbs and nouns (Example 7). Therefore, weakening negators can have a positive or negative (±4) SO value, if the modified chunk (scope) has a positive or negative SO value. The same happens if the SO value is positive +5, because the result of the weakening (−4) will not change the polarity and

the SO value will still be positive +1. In contrast, if the SO value of the modified chunk +3 or −3 or lower, the SO value will be reversed to a ±1. This happens in Example 6 and Example 7. In the first example, the SO value of the scope is +2 (*eragotzi* ("prevent") −2 + *ez* ("not") +4 = +2). In the second one, the SO value of the scope is −2 (*irabazi* ("win") +2 + *ez* ("not") −4 = −2).

5.3 Negation with no effect

Negation with no effect on semantic orientation has happened in 8.08 % of our sample (27 of 359). In these cases, the negation does not modify any word with a SO value assigned. This can happen due to three reasons: *i*) the negator appears with a conjunction, *ii*) the negator is a part of contrastive negation and *iii*) the negator is part of a lexicalized structure (structures with their own meaning and sometimes also corresponding to dictionary entries). The scope concept is applicable only in the case of contrastive negation and the particle *ez* ("no") with a conjunction.

(8) *Ikuspuntu politikotik$_{(-1)}$ ez ezik, ekonomikotik$_{(+3)}$ ere Greziak esperantza ekarri du Europako hegoaldeko beste herrietara, tartean Euskal Herria.* (POL08)
Not only from the political point of view, but also from the economic point of view, Greece has also hoped for other parts of southern Europe, including the Basque Country.

(9) *Sei puntu baino ez dituela, hamaseigarren postuan da Reala sailkapenean.* (KIR27)
With only six points, Real is in the sixteenth position in the classification.

Example 8 shows a contrastive negation with additive function (Silvennoinen, 2017). In other words, the negation mark does not negate the noun phrase, as in *ikuspuntu politikotik$_{(-1)}$* ("from the political$_{(-1)}$ point of view"), actually it functions as conjunction

Example	Negation marker / lexicalized structure	Instances
	[verb/*bai* "yes"] + *edo/edota/ala ez* (*ez* with conjuction)	3
8	[NP] + *ez ezik* (contrastive negation)	2
9	*baino/besterik ez*	11
	Others lexicalized structures	13
	Total	**29**

Table 3: Negation without effects on semantic orientation.

and adds new information: *ekonomikotik ere* ("also from the economic point of view"). Structures of Table 3 have their own SO value, they can be considered as dictionary entries and they can appear in different positions in the sentence. In Example 9, the structure *baino/besterik ez* ("only") is an adverb.

6 Evaluation

6.1 Evaluation methodology

To tag the negation changes of the SO value, we have created negation rules based on previous studies.Rules have been implemented using Constraint Grammar (CG3) (Karlsson et al., 2011) to assign the correct value to the negated structures. The corpus of 96 texts has been tagged using the Basque morphosyntactic disambiguator based on the CG formalism (Aduriz et al., 1997). Then, a different set of 48 texts of the Basque Opinion Corpus has been used as test dataset to evaluate the rules. After that, the results have been analyzed manually, observing if the words have been annotated or not and, when annotated, whether they have the correct annotation.

Negation effects	Prec.	Rec.	F_1
Strengthen	1.00	1.00	1.00
Weaken	0.93	0.80	0.86
No effect	0.97	1.00	0.98
Total	**0.93**	**0.80**	**0.86**
Negated elements	**Prec.**	**Rec.**	**F_1**
Negation markers	1.00	0.96	0.98
Lexicalized structures	0.96	1.00	0.98
Scope	0.91	0.75	0.82
Total	**0.93**	**0.80**	**0.86**

Table 4: General results of negation effects and negated elements.

Most of the corpus was evaluated by one linguist, but with the aim to know the reliability of this evaluation a piece of the corpus (10 %) has been annotated by two linguists. Both annotators have followed a guideline to evaluate the output of CG3 rules. According to the results, the Cohen's kappa score is 0.93 for the annotation of the words that belong to negation and the kappa score is 0.69 for the annotation of words that have been annotated correctly, badly or is missed (which can be considered as *substantial* in (Landis and Koch, 1977)).

6.2 Results and error analysis

According to general results, the F_1 of the negation rules identifying elements related to negation is 0.86 (Precision is 0.93 while recall is 0.80).

In accordance with weakening and scope error analysis, these elements show lower F_1 score because they behave more irregularly. The components as well as the length in scope are more unpredictable. Moreover, some negators apply to lists of words with comma and, as some constraints in CG3 rules correspond to punctuation marks, they have not been detected. This suggests that the rules need more precision. So, the punctuation mark constraint is not enough. Therefore, some syntactic information is needed to detect these kind of structures.

7 Conclusions and Future Work

This work presents a negation analysis for Basque sentiment analysis based on Constraint Grammar rules. According to this study, the negation can affect the semantic orientation (SO value) in different ways: *i*) strengthening, *ii*) weakening or *iii*) having no effect. According to our evaluation to measure the identified words, the overall precision is 0.93, the recall 0.80 and the F_1 score 0.86. In line with error analysis, the punctuation mark constraint is not enough and more precise rules are needed in the negation weakening. In the near future, *i*) we want to implement these negation rules in a tool for automatic Basque sentiment analysis and *ii*) we want to continue with the analysis of negation: analyzing the scope in a bigger corpus and especially based on the Rhetorical Structure Theory (RST) (Mann and Thompson, 1987), studying if the position of negator in rhetorical structure has any effect on sentiment analysis.

References

Itziar Aduriz, José María Arriola, Xabier Artola, Arantza Díaz de Ilarraza, Koldo Gojenola, and Montse Maritxalar. 1997. Morphosyntactic disambiguation for basque based on the constraint grammar formalism. *Proceedings of Recent Advances in NLP (RANLP97)*, pages 282–288, Tzigov Chark (Bulgary).

Jon Alkorta, Koldo Gojenola, and Mikel Iruskieta. 2016. Creating and evaluating a polarity - balanced corpus for Basque sentiment analysis. In *IWoDA16 Fourth International Workshop on Discourse Analysis*, pages 58–62. Santiago de Compostela (Spain).

Jon Alkorta, Koldo Gojenola, and Mikel Iruskieta. 2018. SentiTegi: building a semantic oriented Basque lexicon. In *Proceedings of the CICLing 2018*. Hanoi (Vietnam).

María Jesus Aranzabe Begoña Altuna and Arantza Díaz de Ilarraza. 2017. Euskarazko ezeztapenaren tratamendu automatikorako azterketa. In *Iñaki Alegria, Ainhoa Latatu, Miren Josu Ormaetxebarria and Patxi Salaberri (pub.), II. IkerGazte, Nazioarteko Ikerketa Euskaraz: Giza Zientziak eta Artea*, pages 127–134. Udako Euskal Unibertsitatea (UEU), Bilbo (Spain).

Nerea Ezeiza, Iñaki Alegria, José María Arriola, Rubén Urizar, and Itziar Aduriz. 1998. Combining stochastic and rule-based methods for disambiguation in agglutinative languages. In *Proceedings of the 17th international conference on Computational linguistics-Volume 1*, pages 380–384. Association for Computational Linguistics.

Rodney Huddleston and Geoffrey Keith Pullum. 2002. The Cambridge grammar of English. *Language. Cambridge: Cambridge University Press.*

Salud María Jiménez-Zafra, M. Teresa Martín-Valdivia, M. Dolores Molina-González, and L. Alfonso Ureña-López. 2018a. Relevance of the SFU Review SP-NEG corpus annotated with the scope of negation for supervised polarity classification in Spanish. *Information Processing & Management*, 54(2):240–251.

Salud María Jiménez Zafra, Eugenio Martínez Cámara, María Teresa Martín Valdivia, and María Dolores Molina González. 2015. Tratamiento de la Negación en el Análisis de Opiniones en Espanol. *Procesamiento del Lenguaje Natural*, (54).

Salud María Jiménez-Zafra, Mariona Taulé, M. Teresa Martín-Valdivia, L. Alfonso Ureña-López, and M. Antónia Martí. 2018b. SFU Review SP-NEG: a Spanish corpus annotated with negation for sentiment analysis. A typology of negation patterns. *Language Resources and Evaluation*, 52(2):533–569.

Fred Karlsson, Atro Voutilainen, Juha Heikkilae, and Arto Anttila. 2011. *Constraint Grammar: a language-independent system for parsing unrestricted text*, volume 4. Walter de Gruyter.

J. Richard Landis and Gary G. Koch. 1977. The measurement of observer agreement for categorical data. *Biometrics*, pages 159–174.

Bing Liu. 2012. Sentiment analysis and opinion mining. *Synthesis lectures on human language technologies*, 5(1):1–167.

Jingjing Liu and Stephanie Seneff. 2009. Review sentiment scoring via a parse-and-paraphrase paradigm. In *Proceedings of the 2009 Conference on Empirical Methods in Natural Language Processing: Volume 1-Volume 1*, pages 161–169. Association for Computational Linguistics.

Eugene Emil Loos, Susan Anderson, Dwight H. Day, Paul C. Jordan, and J. Douglas Wingate. 2004. *Glossary of linguistic terms*, volume 29. SIL International Camp Wisdom Road Dallas.

William C. Mann and Sandra A. Thompson. 1987. *Rhetorical Structure Theory: A theory of text organization*. University of Southern California, Information Sciences Institute.

Olli O. Silvennoinen. 2017. Not only apples but also oranges: Contrastive negation and register. *In Turo Hiltunen, Joe McVeigh and Tanja Sily (edit.), Big and Rich Data in English Corpus Linguistics: Methods and Explorations, VARIENG, Helsinki (Finland).*

Maite Taboada, Julian Brooke, Milan Tofiloski, Kimberly Voll, and Manfred Stede. 2011. Lexicon-based methods for sentiment analysis. *Computational linguistics*, 37(2):267–307.

David Vilares, Miguel A. Alonso, and Carlos Gómez-Rodríguez. 2015. A syntactic approach for opinion mining on Spanish reviews. *Natural Language Engineering*, 21(1):139–163.

Leveraging Writing Systems Change for Deep Learning Based Chinese Emotion Analysis

Rong Xiang[1], Yunfei Long[1], Qin Lu[1], Dan Xiong[1], I-Hsuan Chen[2]
[1]Department of Computing, The Hong Kong Polytechnic University
csrxiang,csylong,csluqin,csdxiong@comp.polyu.edu.hk
[2]Department of Chinese and Bilingual Studies, The Hong Kong Polytechnic University
ihcucb@gmail.com

Abstract

Social media text written in Chinese communities contains mixed scripts including major text written in Chinese, an ideograph-based writing system, and some minor text using Latin letters, an alphabet-based writing system. This phenomenon is called writing systems changes (WSCs). Past studies have shown that WSCs can be used to express emotions, particularly where the social and political environment is more conservative. However, because WSCs can break the syntax of the major text, it poses more challenges in Natural Language Processing (NLP) tasks like emotion classification. In this work, we present a novel deep learning based method to include WSCs as an effective feature for emotion analysis. The method first identifies all WSCs points. Then representation of the major text is learned through an LSTM model whereas the minor text is learned by a separate CNN model. Emotions in the minor text are further highlighted through an attention mechanism before emotion classification. Performance evaluation shows that incorporating WSCs features using deep learning models can improve performance measured by F1-scores compared to the state-of-the-art model.

1 Introduction

Emotion analysis has been studied using different NLP methods from a variety of linguistic perspectives such as semantic, syntactic, and cognitive properties (Barbosa and Feng, 2010; Balamurali et al., 2011; Liu and Zhang, 2012; Wilson et al., 2013; Joshi and Itkat, 2014; Long et al., 2017). In many areas, such as Hong Kong and the Chinese Mainland, social media text is often written in mixed text with major text written in Chinese characters, an ideograph-based writing system. The minor text can be written in En-

glish, emoji, Pinyin[1] (phonetic denotation for Chinese), or other new Internet shorthand notations using Roman characters of some Latin-based writing systems. Using mixed characters in different writing systems is known as WSCs.

Generally speaking, WSCs refers to the use of mixed text which switches between two or more writing systems (Clyne, 2000; Lee and Liu, 2012). A narrower definition, often referred to as code-switching, is the use of more than one linguistic variety in a manner consistent with the syntax and phonology of each variety[2]. The use of alteration of different systems or languages of symbols is rooted in pragmatic and socio-linguistic motivations (Cromdal, 2001; Musk, 2012). The use of WSCs is a case of Economy principle in language (Vicentini, 2003) which is pursued by human being in various activities due to the innate indolence. It aims at the maximum effect with the least input. For instance, *'Good luck'* becomes more popular than the Chinese version of *'祝你好运'* *(Good luck)* because inputting the English version takes shorter time in expressing the same emotion.

Studies in social psychology (Bond and Lai, 1986; Heredia and Altarriba, 2001) also show that WSCs is an effective and commonly used strategy to express emotion or mark emotion change especially in some society where social and political environment is more conservative (Wei, 2003). For instance, a new-born swear word *'zz'* is often used in place of the Chinese version of *'moron'*. This is because *'zz'*, which is the acronym of the Pinyin *'zhi zhang (moron)'*, looks less disrespectful lexically and more acceptable in social networks. With the rapid growth of internationalization, Chinese youngsters like to use English acronyms such as *'wtf' (what the fuck) 'stfu' (shut*

---

[1]https://en.wikipedia.org/wiki/Pinyin
[2]https://en.wikipedia.org/wiki/Code-switching

91

Proceedings of the 9th Workshop on Computational Approaches to Subjectivity, Sentiment and Social Media Analysis, pages 91–96
Brussels, Belgium, October 31, 2018. ©2018 Association for Computational Linguistics
https://doi.org/10.18653/v1/P17

the fuck up). People also use WSCs to express idiosyncrasies written in English or other languages because text in other writing systems is much more difficult to be censored. For example, the sensitive term of democracy in Chinese (民主*'min zhu'*) is often written as an intended misspelled Pinyin *minzu* or the English word *democracy*. This paper studies WSCs related textual features from the orthography perspective to explore their effectiveness as emotion indicators.

Previous studies in emotion analysis mostly rely on emotion lexicon, context information, or semantic knowledge to improve sentence level classification tasks. This linguistic knowledge is often used to transform raw data into feature vector, called feature engineering (Kanter and Veeramachaneni, 2015). However, WSCs can break the syntax of the major text and the switched minor text also lacks linguistic cues in this type of social media data (Dos Santos and Gatti, 2014). This makes feature engineering-based methods difficult to work. Neologism in the Internet forums increases the difficulty for both syntactic and semantic analysis. In particular, newly coined phrases tend to contain different types of symbols. Despite the challenges, this type of datasets is rich in shifts of writing systems orthographically. This characteristic offers reliable clues for emotion classification. Since WSCs is relatively common in real-time on-line platforms like microblog in China [3]. This work adopts a broader scope of WSCs to include switching between two languages, and change of writing systems in the same language such as Chinese characters to Pinyin notations. Notably, the accessibility of different character sets and symbols, as well as the frequent exposures to other languages and cultures characterize the nature of such short and informal text.

This paper presents our work in progress which uses a novel deep learning based method to incorporate textual features associated with WSCs via an attention mechanism. More specifically, the proposed Hybrid Attention Network (HAN) method first identifies all WSCs points. The representation of the major text is learned through a Long-Short Term Memory (LSTM) model whereas the representation of the minority text is learned by a separate Convolution Neural Network (CNN). Emotions expressed in the minor text are further highlighted through an attention mecha-nism before emotion classification. The attention mechanism is achieved by projecting the major text representation into attention vectors while aggregating the representation of the informative words from WSCs context.

2 The Hybrid Attention Network Model

Let D be the dataset as a collection of documents for emotion classification. Each document d_i is an instance in D. The goal of an emotion analysis is to predict the emotion label for each d_i. The set of emotion labels includes {*Happiness, Sadness, Anger, Fear, Surprise*}. Let us use the term WSC segments to refer to the minor WSC text pieces. WSC segments can be easily marked in a pre-processing step using code ranges of Chinese characters and Romanized Pinyin or English text.

To make better use of WSCs scripts, a deep learning based HAN model is proposed to explicitly assemble WSCs information in an attention mechanism. Figure 1 shows the framework of HAN. The LSTM model on the left side is used to learn the representation of a document including the WSC segments. This is because documents with WSCs are generally coherent and intact despite few WSC segments that may break the syntax. The CNN model on the right is used to learn the representation of WSCs segments extracted from the sentence because they often occur discontinuously without syntactic structure. The outputs of both models are integrated into a hybrid attention layer before classification is carried out.

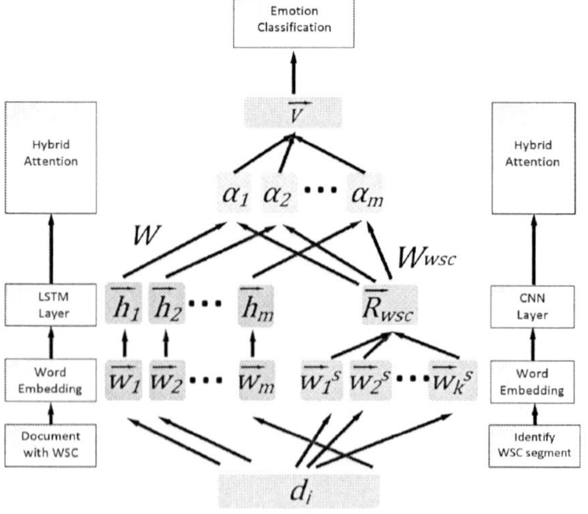

Figure 1: Hybrid attention network framework

---

[3] https://en.wikipedia.org/wiki/Microblogging

Using deep learning methods, the word representation in $d_i = \vec{w}_1, ..., \vec{w}_m$, d_i, is learned using two networks. To distinguish the WSC units, they are given designed switch labels $\vec{w}_j^s$($\vec{w}_j^s \subset d_i$, $j = 1...k$) and are extracted to be fed into the CNN as an extra feature. d_i is fed into LSTM to generate the hidden vector $\vec{h}_1, \vec{h}_2...\vec{h}_m$ from d_i. In Chinese social media, WSCs segments are generally dispersed sporadically. So, for d_i with k WSC segments, the convolution is calculated using a sliding window of size $2n + 1$:

$$\overrightarrow{conv_p} = \sum_{p=k-n}^{k+n} \vec{w}_p^s, \qquad (1)$$

and

$$\vec{R}_{wsc} = \frac{\sum_{p=1}^{k} \overrightarrow{conv_p}}{k}. \qquad (2)$$

The WSC feature vector R_{wsc} is generated by average pooling.

Attention model was introduced by Yang et al.(2016) to show different contribution of different words semantically. To include both the information learned from LSTM and CNN, the consolidated representation, $\vec{u}_p$, includes the representations of both $\vec{h}_p$, and the WSC representation vector $\vec{R}_{wsc}$ into a perceptron defined below:

$$\vec{u}_p = \tanh(W\vec{h}_p + W_{wsc}\vec{R}_{wsc} + b). \qquad (3)$$

In order to re-evaluate the significance of word $\vec{w}_p$, a coefficient vector $\vec{U}$ is introduced as an informative representation of the words in a network memory. The representation of a word $\vec{u}_p$ and the corresponding word-level context vector $\vec{U}$ is integrated to obtain a normalized attention weight:

$$\alpha_p = \frac{\exp(\vec{u}_p \cdot \vec{U})}{\sum_p \exp(\vec{u}_p \cdot \vec{U})}. \qquad (4)$$

The updated document representation $\vec{v}$ can be generated as a weighted sum of the word vectors given below:

$$\vec{v} = \sum_p (\alpha_p \vec{h}_p), \qquad (5)$$

where $\vec{v}$ contains both document information and WSCs representation with attention shall be used in the final SoftMax method, producing the output vector. Lastly, an argmax classifier is used to predict the class label.

3　Performance Evaluation

A Chinese microblog dataset is used for performance evaluation (Lee and Wang, 2015). We first present the dataset with some analysis first and then proceed to make performance comparison to baseline systems on emotion classification.

3.1　Dataset and Statistics

The dataset for WSCs is collected from Chinese microblog by Lee's group (2015). It contains 8,728 instances with an average length of 48.8. Every instance contains at least one WSCs script. In previous studies, half is used as the training set and the rest serves as the testing set.

The major text is written in Chinese characters. The WSC segments contain English words and Pinyin scripts, acronyms of Pinyin or other scripts. The annotation of emotions in each instance allows more than one class label. Each instance is labeled independently by the five emotion classes, happiness, sadness, anger, fear and surprise, based on the Ekman model (1992) except for Disgust. The emotion label can be contributed by Chinese text (E1), WSCs (E2) or Both (E3). Some of the instances have NULL emotion labels (E4). Out of the 6 labels, 25% of all instances has the happiness label, which is the most significant emotion. 16% has the sadness label, the percentages of anger, fear, surprise and NULL labels are 9%, 9%, 11% and 30%, respectively. Below shows four example instances in the three WSC types:

E1 *Emotion: Happiness*
这个年每天都吃好饱！初三来点小朋友的最爱 麦当劳和pizza！！ *(We are so full for every meal during Spring Festival! Will take kids to their favorite, MacDonald and pizza!)*

E2 *Emotion: Anger*
我们会因为金希澈开了微博而看到许多无下限的nc发言。 *(We will see a lot of morons ("nc") comments once Jin Xicheu opens her Weibo.)*("nc" is short for Pinyin "nao-can", which means moron.)

E3 *Emotion: Happiness*
真是速度啊，收到快递了。。happy! *(What a fast delivery, I got the parcel already, happy!)*

E4 *Emotion: None*
我在bean bar *(I am in the bean bar.)*

	Hap	Sad	Anger	Fear	Surprise	Avg. F1	Wgt. F1
SVM	0.693	0.560	0.640	0.549	0.593	0.607	0.623
CNN	0.675	0.618	0.671	0.596	0.603	0.633	0.641
LSTM	0.717	0.642	0.704	0.606	0.628	0.659	0.671
BAN	0.724	0.649	0.712	**0.627**	0.628	0.668	0.678
HAN	**0.729**	**0.658**	**0.729**	0.625	**0.641**	**0.676**	**0.688**

Table 1: Performance evaluation (best result: **marked bold**; 2nd best: underlined.)

3.2 Analysis of WSCs Linked to Emotions

According to the work of Lee and Wang (2015), emotion words often serve as the cues of bilingual context. However, many WSCs segments which are not emotional words can also express emotion. To gain more insight on different types of WSC segments, we examine three types of WSCs: (1) English emotion words found from the NRC emotion lexicon (Mohammad and Turney, 2013), (2) Pinyin/acronym segments, and (3) others which include English words (no emotion), symbolic expressions, and emoji symbols, etc..

Figure 2 depicts their distribution in training dataset in different emotion labels. Note that English emotion words only serve about 1/3 of all WSCs for emotion. The largest group of WSC is in the category of 'Others'. This means non-emotion linked English words and symbols of other orthographic forms place an important part in emotion analysis of text with WSCs.

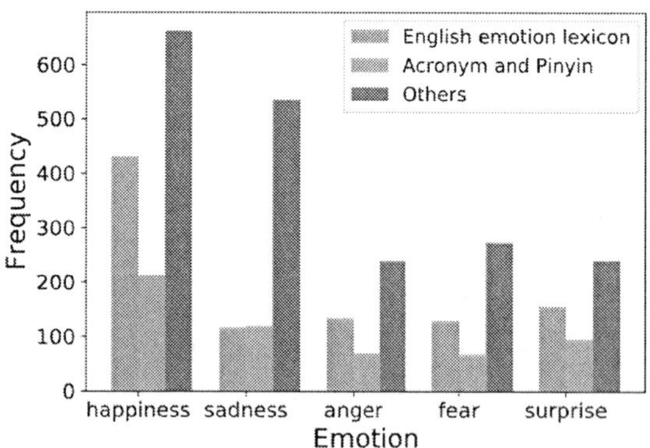

Figure 2: Distribution of different types of WSCs

3.3 Emotion Analysis

A group of experiments are implemented to examine the performance of different emotion classification methods evaluated using average F1-score and weighted F1-score[4]. The baseline algorithms include BAN (Wang et al., 2016), the current state-of-the-art emotion classification algorithm. Others used in the comparison include SVM (Mullen and Collier, 2004), CNN and LSTM (Rosenthal et al., 2017). For all these baseline methods, WSC segments are included in the text. The difference compared to our HAN model is that we also separately extract WSCs segments and feed them into a separate CNN model.

Table 1 shows the performance evaluation result. From Table 1 we can draw a number of observations. Firstly, the performance of SVM is the worst since it lacks phrase level analytical capability because each word is considered independently in SVM. In other words, insufficient amount of information is learned in such a simple method. Secondly, the average weighted F1-score of CNN is lower than that of LSTM, indicating that the memory mechanism is effective in learning semantic information sequentially. The 3.0% gap of weighted F1-score shows that the order of words is valuable in emotion analysis. Thirdly, in addition to the improvement by BAN compared to CNN and LSTM, including WSCs in BAN can give performance gains 0.7% increase in weighted F1 measures. For the largest class Happy, the improvement is over 0.7% increase. Finally, compared to BAN, our proposed HAN which makes additional use of WSCs in a separate CNN gives another 1.0% performance gain.

3.4 Effects of Different Types of Text

In this set of experiments, we investigate the effect of three types of text, CN only (stands for Chinese), WSC segments, and CN+WSCs which are complete instances with both Chinese and WSC segments. We take LSTM and BAN to be compared to our proposed HAN.

Table 2 shows the performance evaluation of

[4]https//en.wikipedia.org/wiki/F1_score

	Hap	Sad	Anger	Fear	Surprise	Avg. F1	Wgt. F1
LSTM(WSCs)	0.631	0.546	0.682	0.589	0.529	0.595	0.598
LSTM(CN)	0.695	0.632	0.671	0.612	0.615	0.645	0.656
LSTM(CN+WSCs)	0.717	0.642	0.704	0.606	0.628	0.659	0.671
BAN(WSCs)	0.631	0.551	0.681	0.589	0.529	0.596	0.599
BAN(CN)	0.698	0.626	0.669	0.613	<u>0.631</u>	0.647	0.658
BAN(CN+WSCs)	<u>0.724</u>	<u>0.649</u>	<u>0.712</u>	**0.627**	0.628	<u>0.668</u>	<u>0.678</u>
HAN(CN+WSCs; WSCs)	**0.729**	**0.658**	**0.729**	<u>0.625</u>	**0.641**	**0.676**	**0.688**

Table 2: Performance using single writing system;best result is **marked bold**; second best is <u>underlined</u>.

	Hap	Sad	Anger	Fear	Surprise	Avg. F1	Wgt. F1
HAN(CN; WSCs)	0.629	0.613	0.682	0.588	0.531	0.606	0.613
HAN(CN+WSCs; CN)	<u>0.720</u>	<u>0.646</u>	<u>0.698</u>	<u>0.624</u>	<u>0.616</u>	<u>0.661</u>	<u>0.673</u>
HAN(CN+WSCs; WSCs)	**0.729**	**0.658**	**0.729**	**0.625**	**0.641**	**0.676**	**0.688**

Table 3: Performance by multiple writing systems;best result is **marked bold**; second best is <u>underlined</u>.

the three systems using different text types. Obviously, Chinese text carries more emotional information than WSCs text. The use of both Chinese and WCSs text gives better performance which shows that both WSCs and Chinese text contribute to the prediction task. However, by extracting WSCs into a separate CNN and re-merging into the attention layer, HAN still gives the best performance. This is because we are able to extract more emotion related information for the WSCs with a separate CNN. The attention model also gives dual consideration to WSCs. Nevertheless, note that BAN(CN+WSCs) can be competitive when both Chinese text and WSCs are learned.

To further analyze the effect of the two sub-models of LSTM and CNN in HAN, we examine the performance of HAN with different types of text to be taken by the two sub-models. In Table 3, the first type of text in the parenthesis denotes the text for the LSTM sub-model. The second text is used by the CNN sub-model. Note that in the first combination, only Chinese text without WSCs is used by the LSTM. Because this will break the syntax of the Chinese text, the result is the worst. In the second evaluation, the CNN sub-model is fed with Chinese text only. Still its performance is about 6% better than the first combination. Comparing HAN(CN+WSCs; CN) with the state-of-the-art method BAN(CN+WSCs), we can see that applying CNN to Chinese text will only introduce more noise and will not help to make performance improvement. Obviously, this gives more justification of using HAN(CN+WSCs; WSCs) as it gives the best performance gain.

4 Conclusion and Future Work

This paper presents a work in progress of an HAN model based on an LSTM model for emotion analysis in the context of WSCs in social media. We argue that WSCs text is potentially informative in emotion classification tasks such that they should be used as additional information contributing to deep learning based emotion classification models. Our proposed method offers a novel way to integrate multiple types of writing systems into an attention-based LSTM model. Along with WSCs text, the descriptive text of the major writing system is informatively valuable and semantic and affective information can be captured by LSTM effectively. Furthermore, WSCs texts indeed contain addition semantic and affective information which can be captured by a CNN model. After combining the representation of both the complete text and the WSCs, the two vectors are incorporated as the final feature.

Future works include two directions. One is to further evaluate the performance of HAN using larger corpora as currently only one public accessible corpus for writing systems for the Chinese communities can be studied. Another direction is to give more detailed study on how people use different types of WSCs to express emotions in censorship detection studies.

Acknowledgments

The work is partially funded by UGC under GRF projects(PolyU 152111/14E & U152006/16E).

References

AR Balamurali, Aditya Joshi, and Pushpak Bhattacharyya. 2011. Harnessing wordnet senses for supervised sentiment classification. In *Proceedings of the conference on empirical methods in natural language processing*, pages 1081–1091. Association for Computational Linguistics.

Luciano Barbosa and Junlan Feng. 2010. Robust sentiment detection on twitter from biased and noisy data. In *Proceedings of the 23rd International Conference on Computational Linguistics: Posters*, pages 36–44. Association for Computational Linguistics.

Michael H Bond and Tat-Ming Lai. 1986. Embarrassment and code-switching into a second language. *Journal of Social Psychology*, 126(2):179–186.

Michael Clyne. 2000. Constraints on code-switching: How universal are they. *The bilingualism reader*, pages 257–280.

Jakob Cromdal. 2001. Overlap in bilingual play: Some implications of code-switching for overlap resolution. *Research on Language and Social Interaction*, 34(4):421–451.

Cícero Nogueira Dos Santos and Maira Gatti. 2014. Deep convolutional neural networks for sentiment analysis of short texts. In *COLING*, pages 69–78.

Paul Ekman. 1992. An argument for basic emotions. *Cognition & emotion*, 6(3-4):169–200.

Roberto R Heredia and Jeanette Altarriba. 2001. Bilingual language mixing: Why do bilinguals codeswitch? *Current Directions in Psychological Science*, 10(5):164–168.

Neha S Joshi and Suhasini A Itkat. 2014. A survey on feature level sentiment analysis. *International Journal of Computer Science and Information Technologies*, 5:5422–5425.

James Max Kanter and Kalyan Veeramachaneni. 2015. Deep feature synthesis: Towards automating data science endeavors. In *Data Science and Advanced Analytics (DSAA), 2015. 36678 2015. IEEE International Conference on*, pages 1–10. IEEE.

Jyh-An Lee and Ching-U Liu. 2012. Forbidden city enclosed by the great firewall: The law and power of internet filtering in china. *Minn. JL Sci. & Tech.*, 13:125.

Sophia Lee and Zhongqing Wang. 2015. Emotion in code-switching texts: Corpus construction and analysis. In *Proceedings of the Eighth SIGHAN Workshop on Chinese Language Processing*, pages 91–99.

Bing Liu and Lei Zhang. 2012. A survey of opinion mining and sentiment analysis. In *Mining text data*, pages 415–463. Springer.

Yunfei Long, Lu Qin, Rong Xiang, Minglei Li, and Chu-Ren Huang. 2017. A cognition based attention model for sentiment analysis. In *Proceedings of the 2017 Conference on Empirical Methods in Natural Language Processing*, pages 473–482.

Saif M. Mohammad and Peter D. Turney. 2013. Crowdsourcing a word-emotion association lexicon. 29(3):436–465.

Tony Mullen and Nigel Collier. 2004. Sentiment analysis using support vector machines with diverse information sources. In *EMNLP*, volume 4, pages 412–418.

Nigel Musk. 2012. Performing bilingualism in wales. *Pragmatics. Quarterly Publication of the International Pragmatics Association (IPrA)*, 22(4):651–669.

Sara Rosenthal, Noura Farra, and Preslav Nakov. 2017. Semeval-2017 task 4: Sentiment analysis in twitter. In *Proceedings of the 11th International Workshop on Semantic Evaluation (SemEval-2017)*, pages 502–518.

Alessandra Vicentini. 2003. The economy principle in language. *Notes and Observations from early modern english grammars. Mots, Palabras, Words*, 3:37–57.

Zhongqing Wang, Yue Zhang, Sophia Lee, Shoushan Li, and Guodong Zhou. 2016. A bilingual attention network for code-switched emotion prediction. In *Proceedings of COLING 2016, the 26th International Conference on Computational Linguistics: Technical Papers*, pages 1624–1634.

Jennifer MY Wei. 2003. Codeswitching in campaigning discourse: The case of taiwanese president chen shui-bian. *Language and Linguistics*, 4(1):139–165.

Theresa Wilson, Zornitsa Kozareva, Preslav Nakov, Sara Rosenthal, Veselin Stoyanov, and Alan Ritter. 2013. Sentiment analysis in twitter. In *Proceedings of the International Workshop on Semantic*.

Zichao Yang, Diyi Yang, Chris Dyer, Xiaodong He, Alex Smola, and Eduard Hovy. 2016. Hierarchical attention networks for document classification. In *Proceedings of the 2016 Conference of the North American Chapter of the Association for Computational Linguistics: Human Language Technologies*.

Ternary Twitter Sentiment Classification with
Distant Supervision and Sentiment-Specific Word Embeddings

Mats Byrkjeland   Frederik Gørvell de Lichtenberg   Björn Gambäck
Department of Computer Science
Norwegian University of Science and Technology
NO—7491 Trondheim, Norway
{matsbyr,frederikgdl}@gmail.com, gamback@ntnu.no

Abstract

The paper proposes the Ternary Sentiment Embedding Model, a new model for creating sentiment embeddings based on the Hybrid Ranking Model of Tang et al. (2016), but trained on ternary-labeled data instead of binary-labeled, utilizing sentiment embeddings from datasets made with different distant supervision methods. The model is used as part of a complete Twitter Sentiment Analysis system and empirically compared to existing systems, showing that it outperforms Hybrid Ranking and that the quality of the distant-supervised dataset has a great impact on the quality of the produced sentiment embeddings.

1 Introduction

Bengio et al. (2003) introduced word embeddings as a technique for representing words as low-dimensional real-valued vectors capturing the words' semantic and lexical properties, based on ideas dating back to the 1950s (Firth, 1957). Collobert and Weston (2008) showed the utility of using pre-trained word embeddings, and after the introduction of *word2vec* (Mikolov et al., 2013), which is much faster to train than its predecessors, word embeddings have become ubiquitous. This effectuated a dramatic shift in 2016 at the International Workshop on Semantic Evaluation (SemEval), with eight of the top-10 Twitter Sentiment Analysis systems using word embeddings.

Word embeddings learn the representation of a word by looking at its contexts (word neighbours in a text), making it difficult to discriminate between words with opposite sentiments that appear in similar contexts, such as "good" and "bad". Hence, Tang et al. (2014) presented Sentiment-Specific Word Embeddings (or *Sentiment Embeddings*), a model employing both context and sentiment information in word embeddings.

Training sentiment embeddings requires large amounts of sentiment annotated data. Manual annotation is too expensive for this purpose, so fast, automatic annotation is used to set low-quality (weak) labels on large corpora; a procedure referred to as *distant supervision*. The traditional approach is to use occurrences of emoticons to guess binary sentiment (positive / negative). Motivated by the possible performance gains of focusing on the ternary task (where tweets can also be classified as neutral), this paper compares distant supervision methods on a large corpus of tweets that can be used to train sentiment embeddings. To this end, a new model architecture was developed with a new loss function trained on three-way classified distant supervised data. Various lexicon-based sentiment classifiers are compared, with their performance as distant supervision methods tested as part of a complete Twitter Sentiment Analysis system, evaluating both prediction quality and speed.

The paper is laid out as follows: Section 2 introduces related work on word and sentiment embeddings. Section 3 describes the proposed model for training ternary sentiment embeddings. Section 4 introduces a set of distant supervision methods and a comparison between them. Section 5 explores the optimal setup for the Ternary Sentiment Embedding Model through hyperparameter searches and dataset comparisons, while Section 6 compares the model against baselines and other methods to establish its performance. Section 7 concludes and suggests future improvements.

2 Related Work

Recent years have seen a vast number of Twitter Sentiment Analysis (TSA) systems, mainly because SemEval since 2013 has featured a TSA task, providing training data and a platform to compare different systems. This data will be uti-

Proceedings of the 9th Workshop on Computational Approaches to Subjectivity, Sentiment and Social Media Analysis, pages 97–106
Brussels, Belgium, October 31, 2018. ©2018 Association for Computational Linguistics
https://doi.org/10.18653/v1/P17

lized here and the results below will be compared to those of SemEval in Section 6.4. First, however, the models most directly related to the present work will be introduced: the Collobert and Weston model (Collobert et al., 2011), three Sentiment Embeddings models by Tang et al. (2014), and their Hybrid Ranking Model (Tang et al., 2016). These can be viewed as sequential refinements of each other and as predecessors of the Ternary Sentiment Embedding Model described in Section 3.

The Collobert and Weston (C&W) Model: Collobert et al. (2011) proposed a task-general multilayer neural network language processing architecture. It starts with a *Lookup Layer*, which extracts features for each word, using a window approach to tag one word at a time based on its context. The input vector is then passed through one or several *Linear Layers* that extract features from a window of words, treated as a sequence with local and global structure (i.e., not as a bag of words). The following layers are standard network layers: a *HardTanh Layer* adds some non-linearity to the model (Collobert and Weston, 2008) and a final *Linear Layer* produces an output vector with dimension equal to the number of classes.

When learning word embeddings from context information, the output vector has size 1. For each context used to train the model, a corrupted context is created by replacing the focus word with a random word from the vocabulary. Both the correct and the corrupted context windows are passed through the model, with the training objective that the original context window should obtain a higher model score than the corrupted by a margin of 1. This can be formulated as a hinge loss function:

$$loss_{cw}(t, t^r) = max(0, 1 - f^{cw}(t) + f^{cw}(t^r))$$

where t and t^r are the original and corrupted context windows, and $f^{cw}(\cdot)$ the model score.

Sentiment Embeddings: To improve word embeddings for sentiment analysis, Tang et al. (2014) introduced Sentiment-Specific Word Embeddings (SSWE). They enhanced the C&W word embedding model by employing massive amounts of distant-supervised tweets, assigning positive labels to tweets containing positive emoticons and negative to those containing negative emoticons. Tang et al. used three strategies to incorporate sentiment information in embeddings: two basic models that only look at sentence sentiment polarity, and a Unified Model which adds word context and C&W's *corrupted context window* training.

Basic Model 1 uses C&W's window-based approach, but with the top linear layer's output vector elements defining probabilities over labels. A *softmax activation layer* is added to predict positive n-grams as $[1, 0]$ and negative as $[0, 1]$. This constraint is relaxed in *Basic Model 2*, which removes the softmax layer to handle more fuzzy distributions and uses a ranking objective function:

$$loss_r(t) = \max\{0, 1 - \delta_s(t) f_0^r(t) + \delta_s(t) f_1^r(t)\}$$

where f_0^r and f_1^r are the predicted positive and negative scores, while $\delta_s(t)$ reflects the gold sentiment polarity of the context window t, with

$$\delta_s(t) = \{1 : f^g(t) = [1, 0]\} \wedge \{-1 : f^g(t) = [0, 1]\}$$

Unified Model uses corrupted context window training with two objectives: the original context should get a higher language model score and be more consistent with the gold polarity annotation than the corrupted one. The loss function combines word contexts and sentence polarity:

$$loss_u(t, t^r) = \alpha \cdot loss_{cw}(t, t^r) + (1-\alpha) \cdot loss_{us}(t, t^r)$$

where $0 \leq \alpha \leq 1$ weights the parts, $loss_{cw}$ is the C&W loss function, and with $\delta_s(t)$ as above:

$$loss_{us}(t, t^r) = \max\{0, 1 - \delta_s(t) f_1^u(t) + \delta_s(t) f_1^u(t^r)\}$$

Hybrid Ranking Model (Tang et al., 2016) splits the top linear layer of the Unified Model into a context-aware layer that calculates a context score f^{cw} and a sentiment-aware layer calculating a sentiment score f^r for the input context window. The objective function only compares the predicted positive and negative score for the correct context window when calculating the loss:

$$loss_{hy} = \alpha \cdot loss_r + (1-\alpha) \cdot loss_{cw}$$

3 Ternary Sentiment Embedding Model

A new neural network model for training word embeddings called the *Ternary Sentiment Embedding Model* is proposed. The model extends the Hybrid Ranking Model by Tang et al. (2016) for training Sentiment-Specific Word Embeddings by also looking at tweets labeled as "neutral", and consists of three bottom (core) layers and two top layers that work in parallel, as shown in Figure 1.

Core Layers: The first layers identical to those of the C&W model. As with that model, the objective of the context part of the Ternary Sentiment Embedding Model is to assign a higher score to a correct context window than a corrupted window:

$$loss_c(t, t^r) = max(0, m - f^c(t) + f^c(t^r)) \quad (1)$$

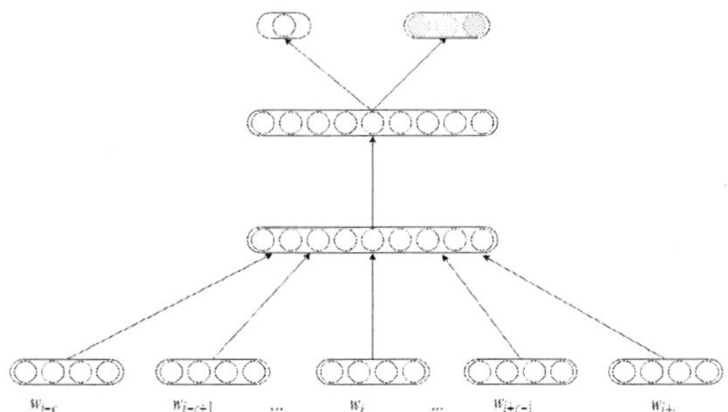

Figure 1: Ternary Sentiment Embedding Model. At the top are the Context Linear Layer and the new Ternary Sentiment Linear Layer; in the middle HardTanh and Linear layers, with the word context Lookup Layer at the bottom.

where m is the margin ($m = 1 \Rightarrow loss_c = loss_{cw}$), t and t^r the correct resp. corrupted context windows, and $f^c(\cdot)$ the context linear layer's score.

Ternary Sentiment Linear Layer: A new top linear layer is introduced to calculate sentiment scores. It outputs a vector of size 3, representing positive, negative and neutral scores for a given context window. The objective is to give a higher score to the value corresponding to the context's label than the other possible labels. A new margin hinge loss function is used to train the model:

$$loss_s(t) = max(0, m - f_c^s(t) + f_{i1}^s(t)) \\ + max(0, m - f_c^s(t) + f_{i2}^s(t)) \quad (2)$$

where t is a context window, m the margin, $f_c^s(\cdot)$ the sentiment score for the currently labelled sentiment of the input context, and $f_{i1}^s(\cdot)$ and $f_{i2}^s(\cdot)$ the sentiment scores for the other two classes.

The model's **total loss function** is a weighted linear combination of the hinge losses for the Sentiment Linear and Context Linear layers:

$$loss(t, t^r) = \alpha \cdot loss_s(t) + (1-\alpha) \cdot loss_c(t, t^r) \quad (3)$$

Model Training: As in the C&W model, parameters of the neural network are trained by taking the derivative of the loss through backpropagation. Stochastic Gradient Descent (SGD) is used to update the model parameters. This means that samples, in this case context windows created from tweets, are randomly drawn from the training corpus, and the parameters are updated for each sample passed through the model, according to:

$$w_t = w_{t-1} - l_r \cdot g_t \quad (4)$$

where w_t is the value of the parameter w at time t, g_t its gradient at time t, and l_r the learning rate.

The model parameters are initialised as in Tang et al. (2016). Lookup layer parameters are initialised with values from the uniform distribution $U(-0.01, 0.01)$, while hidden layer parameters are initialised using *fan-in* (Collobert et al., 2011), i.e., the number of inputs used by a layer, i. The technique draws the initial parameters from a centred distribution with variance $\mathbb{V} = 1/\sqrt{i}$. Fan-in is also used for the learning rate, with l_r for the hidden layers in Eqn. 4 divided by the fan-in, i.

4 Distant Supervision of Tweets

The idea of *distant supervision* is to automatically label data in order to be able to leverage large amounts of it. These data are called *distant supervised* or *weakly annotated*, as the quality is not great, but the quantity is. To train sentiment embeddings, large amounts of weakly annotated tweets are needed. This section describes the approach of extracting weak labels from a corpus of collected tweets (about 547 million), and explains each of the sentiment analysis methods that are compared for distant supervision use.

The outputs are ranked using SemEval's measures F_1^{PN} (the average of the F_1-scores for positive and negative samples) and AvgRec (the average of the recall scores for the three classes). While F_1^{PN} and AvgRec have been used in SemEval for both binary and ternary classification, it is debatable how representative they are for the latter. Hence, the Macro F_1 metric used by Tang et al. (2016) will also be calculated. It extends F_1^{PN} by averaging the F_1-scores of all three classes.

Emoticons and Emojis: Go et al. (2009) automatically classified tweet sentiment using distant supervision based on a few positive (':)', ':-)', ':)', ':D', '=)') and negative (':(', ':-(', ': (') emoticons, while removing tweets containing both a positive and negative emoticon. This method was reimplemented in Python and adapted to the ternary task by classifying tweets containing none of the emoticons as neutral. Further, since the sets of emoticons used by Go et al. are quite sparse compared to the vast amount of emojis and emoticons available today, extended sets ("Emojis+") were also created, as shown in the Appendix.

Dataset	Class.	Dist.	Pos.	Neg.	Neut.
2013-dev	1,228	959	353	198	408
2013-test	2,695	1,839	827	318	694
2013-train	7,109	5,411	2,171	878	2,362
2014-sarcasm	56	52	20	26	6
2014-test	1,460	997	556	134	307
2015-test	1,865	1,363	610	249	504
2015-train	352	281	103	39	139
2016-dev	1,657	1,051	453	207	391
2016-devtest	1,645	1,171	574	193	404
2016-test	16,771	12,072	4,328	1,899	5,845
2016-train	4,893	3,256	1,714	515	1,027
2013-2016-all	39,731	28,452	11,709	4,656	12,087

Table 1: Sentiment distribution in the datasets

Method	F_1	F_1^{PN}	F_1^{POS}	F_1^{NEG}	F_1^{NEU}	ms
LC	**.570**	.532	.593	**.472**	**.646**	0.93
Combo B	.561	.532	.626	.437	.620	2.27
Combo A	.557	.537	.628	.446	.598	2.26
TextBlob	.541	.502	**.643**	.361	.619	0.48
AFINN	.537	**.542**	.620	.465	.526	1.21
VADER	.532	.524	.621	.428	.546	0.63
Emoji+	.259	.130	.101	.159	.517	0.11
Emoticon	.251	.061	.086	.036	.630	**0.09**

Table 2: Distant supervision, SemEval 2013–2016

AFINN, TextBlob and VADER: These methods respectively use the AFINN (Nielsen, 2011),[1] TextBlob,[2] and VADER (Hutto and Gilbert, 2014) libraries to count tweet sentiment scores. For AFINN, tweets with a 0 sentiment score were classified as neutral, while those with scores greater and lower than 0 were classified as positive and negative, respectively. For TextBlob, tweets with subjectivity score less than a threshold θ_s were defined as neutral; a threshold θ_p was set to classify tweets with polarity $< -\theta_p$ as negative and those with polarity $> \theta_p$ as positive. VADER returns a 3D vector where each element represents a score for each sentiment class. The vector is normalized so that $positiveScore + negativeScore + neutralScore = 1$. Setting a confidence threshold $\theta_c > 0.5$ ascertains that the other scores are below 0.5. If no score is $> \theta_c$, the tweet is skipped. VADER also gives a *compound* score, a single sentiment score from -1 to 1 (most positive).

The methods' hyperparameters were tuned through grid searches, testing each value in increasing steps of 0.1. VADER struggled to classify positive and negative tweets as the threshold increased, and performed best at $\theta_c = 0.1$. TextBlob performed best with a low subjectivity threshold, with $\theta_s = 0.1$ and $\theta_p = 0.3$ chosen for the final classifier, as these values gave the best Macro F_1.

Combo Average: An ensemble of the AFINN, TextBlob, and VADER classifiers, with scores normalised to be in the $[-1, 1]$ range. For AFINN, its score is divided by $5 \cdot n$ (the number of words in the tweet), since $|5|$ is the highest score a word can get. For VADER, the *compound* score is used, while TextBlob's score is already normalised. The scores are combined using a weighted average: $(a \cdot afinn + b \cdot vader + c \cdot textblob)/(a + b + c)$. A threshold θ is set so that tweets with score $> \theta$ are classified positive, those with score $< -\theta$ negative, and all others neutral. Running a grid search as above to select the method's four parameters, the combination achieving the top F_1^{PN} score was $\{a = 0.0, b = 0.4, c = 0.4, \theta = 0.2\}$ (this is called *Combo A* below), while the Macro F_1 winner was $\{a = 0.3, b = 0.1, c = 0.1, \theta = 0.1\}$ (*Combo B*).

Lexicon Classifier (LC): A Python port of the Lexicon Classifier of Fredriksen et al. (2018), using their best performing lexicon and parameters.[3]

Evaluation: All manually annotated SemEval datasets from 2013 to 2016 were downloaded. They contain IDs for 50,333 tweets, but 10,251 of those had been deleted, while duplicates were removed,[4] leaving 39,731 tweets for later classifier training (the second column of Table 1). For the distant supervision, further filtering removed retweets (i.e., copies of original tweets; including retweets might lead to over-representation of certain phrases), tweets containing ° symbols (mostly weather data), tweets containing URLs, and tweets ending with numbers (often spam). Then 28,452 tweets remained for evaluating the distant supervision methods, distributed as in Table 1 (note that only 16% of the total tweets are negative).

Comparisons of the methods with tuned parameters on all SemEval datasets merged into one (the *2013-2016-all* dataset of Table 1) are shown in Table 2. We see that the top Macro F_1 score is 0.570, which does not seem very impressive. However, to our knowledge no previous sentiment analysis

---

[1] github.com/fnielsen/afinn
[2] github.com/sloria/textblob
[3] github.com/draperunner/fjlc
[4] If duplicate tweets with the same sentiment label were found, only one was kept. If duplicate tweets were found with different labels, both were deleted.

research has been evaluated against the complete set of SemEval datasets, making the results hard to compare to other work. Evaluating each dataset individually, a trend could be observed with decreasing scores for later data, with a top Macro F_1 score on the *2013-test* set of 0.628 compared to 0.578 on the *2016-test* set. This is consistent with Fredriksen et al. (2018) who noted significantly dropping scores for tests on 2016 data, attributing this to those sets having more noise and annotation errors than earlier datasets.

The runtimes (ms) in Table 2 were obtained on a computer with four AMD Opteron 6128 CPUs and 125 GB RAM running Ubuntu 16.04 (note that the given runtimes do not include saving to file). The emoticon-based methods are very fast (0.09 and 0.11 ms/tweet), but their scores are substantially worse than the others. The ensemble methods are slow (2.26 and 2.27 ms/tweet), since they have to calculate the score of each component method.

5 Optimising the Model

In order to find the best performing configuration of the Ternary Sentiment Embedding Model, the hyperparameters were tested one-by-one through a search of manually selected values.

More than 500 million tweets had been collected at the time of the start of the experiments, with URLs, mentions, reserved words and numbers removed. The tweets were lower-cased and elongated words reduced to contain a maximum of three repeating characters. Using the distant supervision methods described above, the collection was iterated through, and the resulting datasets saved. To create even datasets for each method and label, three sets of 1M tweets from each sentiment class were extracted from the total datasets for each method (except for the Emoticon method, which only annotated 151,538 tweets as negative, so its datasets were limited to 150k tweets for each label). The model hyperparameter searches were performed using the dataset created by the Lexicon Classifier, since it was the top performer in Table 2. The following paragraphs give the results for each of the hyperparameters.

Context Window Size: Testing with window sizes in the range $[1, 9]$ showed the best performing size to be 3 (Macro $F_1 = 0.6325$). Tweets are typically short texts with informal language. It is possible that larger context windows will lead to the model considering excerpts that are too long

for tweet lingo, and would fit better for more formal texts. However, the differences in the results were too small to draw any conclusions.

Embedding Length is the *dimension* of each word embedding vector. The larger the dimension, the more fine-grained information the vectors can hold. $\{50, 75, 100, 125, 150\}$ dimensions were tested, with 150 performing best (Macro $F_1 = 0.6249$), indicating that larger embeddings result in better scores for the model. This is no surprise, as word embeddings as GloVe and word2vec are commonly trained with dimensions of 200 or 300. However, a length of 100 was selected, since larger embeddings only gave minor improvements but severely increased processing time.

Hidden Layer Size: For the Ternary Sentiment Embedding Model, the hidden layers are the Linear Layer and the HardTanh Layer. Experiments show a minimal impact of varying the hidden layer size ($\{10, 20, 30, 50, 100\}$ neurons), having a range on the score values of only 0.0046. The best performance (Macro $F_1 = 0.6201$) was achieved with size 100. These results correspond well to the claim by Collobert et al. (2011) that the size of the hidden layer, given it is of sufficient size, has limited impact on the generalisation performance. However, the size of the hidden layers has a significant impact on training runtime, so since the difference in score values were small, a hidden layer size of 50 was used in the final model.

Alpha is the weighting between the sentiment loss and the context loss in the combined loss function (Eqn. 3) used when training the model. α-values in the range $[0.1, 1.0]$ were explored. The best score (Macro $F_1 = 0.6310$) was achieved for $\alpha = 0.2$. This indicates that the contexts of the words are more important than the sentiment of the tweets. However, leaving out sentiment information altogether ($\alpha = 0$) gave the by far worse score (0.5400). Interestingly, leaving out context information ($\alpha = 1$) did not perform as badly (0.6069).

Learning Rate states how fast the neural network parameters are updated during backpropagation. A small rate makes the network slowly converge towards a possible optimal score, while a large rate can make it overshoot the optimum. Testing on values from 0.001 to 1.1, the best learning rate was 0.01 (Macro $F_1 = 0.6231$), although the total range of the scores was only 0.0412.

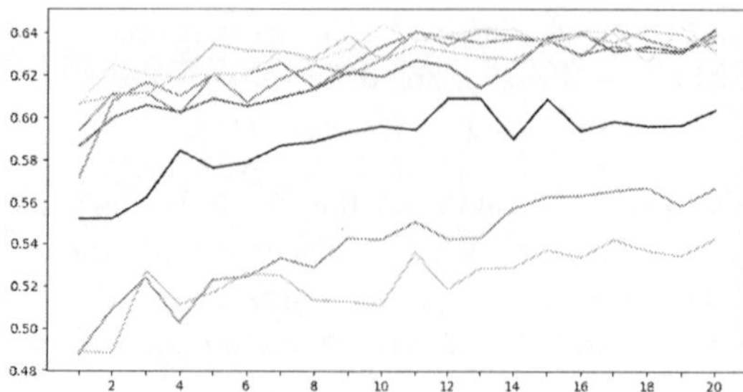

Method	F_1	F_1^{PN}	F_1^{POS}	F_1^{NEG}	F_1^{NEU}
Combo B	.609	.595	.668	.522	.637
Combo A	.608	.596	.667	.524	.633
LC	.604	.587	.665	.509	.637
AFINN	.602	.589	.660	.518	.628
VADER	.596	.583	.656	.511	.623
TextBlob	.584	.571	.657	.486	.608
Emoji+	.548	.525	.630	.419	.594
Emoticon	.504	.481	.595	.368	.550

Table 3: Distant supervision method comparison

Figure 2: Distance supervision scores / epochs
(Colour legend, top-to-bottom: Lexicon Classifier, Combo B, Combo A, VADER, AFINN, **TextBlob**, Emoji+, Emoticon.)

Margin   defines how the scores should be separated in the loss functions of Eqn. 1 and Eqn. 2. Larger margins lead to similar scores for each sentiment class giving a larger total loss, with the model parameters being updated by a larger value during backpropagation. Experimenting with margins in the range $[0.5, 10.0]$, a value of 2.0 obtained the best Macro F_1 (0.6188). It is hard to predict the impact of higher margins, but since the loss is greater when sentiment scores are close, this appears to give a better separation of words from tweets belonging to each sentiment class.

Distant Supervision Method: Using the above-selected hyperparameter values, the Ternary Sentiment Embedding Model was trained on the 3M tweet datasets created by using each distant supervision method (450k tweets for the Emoticon method). Performance over 1–20 epochs is shown in Figure 2. A top Macro F_1 score of 0.6440 was obtained for LC after 10 epochs, but the scores vary notably for each epoch. For a more robust comparison, the Macro F_1 scores were averaged over epochs 10 to 20, with LC again performing best (0.6383), but followed closely by the ensemble methods (Combo B: 0.6361, Combo A: 0.6352), VADER (0.6339), and AFINN (0.6296).

6   Evaluating the Final System

To evaluate the performance of the Ternary Sentiment Embedding Model, it was compared to the Hybrid Ranking Model by Tang et al. (2016) using different distant supervision methods, as well as to a range of baselines, among them other popular word embeddings models. Finally, the performance of the total Twitter Sentiment Analysis system was evaluated against the state-of-the-art.

The Twitter Sentiment Analysis system com-prises the Ternary Sentiment Embedding Model and a linear kernel Support Vector Machine (SVM). The C parameter of the SVM classifier was set through a coarse search on values ranges from 0.001 to 1000 with the word embeddings produced by the Ternary Sentiment Embedding Model using the LC distant supervision dataset and trained for 20 epochs, followed by two finer searches around the best value of 0.01, covering value ranges of $[0.001, 0.009]$ and $[0.01, 0.09]$, with a C value of 0.006 giving the best performing classifier. A small C means the classifier favours more misclassified samples over separating samples by a large margin, indicating that it is hard to avoid misclassifying some samples. However, the differences in scores were very low even for large variations of the parameter, meaning the samples to classify are not easily linearly separable.

6.1   Comparing Distant Supervision Methods

The Ternary Sentiment Embedding Model was trained for 20 epochs using the different distant supervision methods and the produced sentiment embeddings tested using the SVM classifier using 10-fold cross validation on the unfiltered 39,731 tweets from the *2013-2016-all* dataset (i.e., all the combined 2013–2016 SemEval datasets), 15,713 of which were positive (39.5%), 5,945 negative (15.0%), and 18,073 neutral (45.5%). Table 3 shows different metrics for the tests, sorted by descending Macro F_1 score.

The Combo methods perform best in this comparison. By averaging over three methods, they can overcome weaknesses of their components. While the combo methods were not the top performers in the comparison of the distant supervision methods in Table 2, the ability to balance other weak classifiers seems to be important when used as distant supervision method for the proposed model. The results show that the Ternary Sentiment Embedding Model performs best when trained on data from a distant supervision method that is good at classifying all tweets into all three sentiment classes. The emoticon methods and TextBlob have weaknesses when classifying tweets into one or more of the classes, hence yielding the worst results for the total system.

6.2 Comparison to Baselines

In order to see how well the final TSA system performs, it was compared to some existing sentiment analysis methods. The systems were also tested using 10-fold cross-validation on the unfiltered *2013-2016-all* dataset (39,731 tweets). Table 4 shows the results for each TSA system using the Macro F_1 metric.

'Random Uniform' and 'Random Weighted' are two simple baselines, respectively created by picking a random label from a uniform probability distribution and by picking a random label from the same distribution as in the training set. The distant supervision classifiers are as above, except that the Emoticons and Emoji+ methods add the variation that tweets containing both negative and positive emoticons are regarded as neutral.

The word embeddings for Ternary Sentiment Embedding Model, GloVe and word2vec were all trained on the same set of 3M tweets, with 1M from each of the sentiment classes, assigned by the Lexicon Classifier distant supervision method. The GloVe model (Pennington et al., 2014) was used to train word embeddings of dimension 100. The word2vec (Mikolov et al., 2013) embeddings were trained using both the Continuous Bag-of-Words (CBOW) and the Continuous Skip-gram model, also with 100 dimensions. Word embeddings were also produced using the Hybrid Ranking Model of Tang et al. (2016) trained on a set of 3M tweets classified with the LC method, but using only tweets labelled as positive or negative when training word embeddings, with 1.5M tweets of each class. All the word embeddings were fed to the SVM classifier specified above.

As the results in Table 4 shows, the best Macro F_1 scores were achieved by the word embedding systems. The word embeddings produced by the Ternary Sentiment Embedding Model gave slightly better results than the word embeddings produced by the Continuous Bag-of-Words model, however, the difference is small.

One of the strengths of the word2vec models is that they require much less training time than

Model	F_1
Ternary Sentiment Embedding Model	.6036
word2vec (CBOW)	.6015
Hybrid Ranking Model (w/LC)	.5919
word2vec (Skip-gram)	.5886
LC	.5706
GloVe	.5662
Combo B	.5621
Combo A	.5579
AFINN	.5381
VADER	.5286
TextBlob	.3826
Random Weighted	.3315
Random Uniform	.3174
Emoji+	.2542
Emoticon	.2462

Table 4: The final Ternary Sentiment Embedding Model compared to baselines (Macro F_1-scores)

larger neural network models such as the Collobert and Weston model and the Ternary Sentiment Embedding Model. The word2vec models used approximately three minutes, while the Ternary Sentiment Embedding Model used 24 hours to train on 3M tweets. This advantage of the word2vec models means that they could be trained using a much larger dataset, which would likely yield an even better performance.

The word2vec models do not utilise sentiment information of the tweets, which is necessary to create sentiment embeddings with the Ternary Sentiment Embedding Model. This is another advantage of the word2vec models, as they have no need for a separate distant supervision method. The word2vec models are, however, slightly outperformed by the Ternary Sentiment Embedding Model in terms of the final score, and with further optimisation the difference could increase.

6.3 Comparison to Hybrid Ranking Model

In order to compare the distant supervision performance of the sentiment embeddings produced by the Ternary Sentiment Embedding Model and the Hybrid Ranking Model of Tang et al. (2016), both architectures were trained for 20 epochs on 3M tweets weakly annotated using the different distant supervision methods of Section 4. The Ternary Sentiment Embedding Model was trained on tweets labelled as positive, negative or neutral, with 1M of each, with the hyperparameters stated in Section 5. The Hybrid Ranking Model only utilises tweets labelled as positive or neutral, and was as a result trained on 1.5M tweets of each sentiment class, using the hyperparameters

Dataset	Ternary Embedding	Hybrid Ranking
AFINN	**.602**	.578
Combo A	**.608**	.587
Combo B	**.609**	.592
Emoticon	.504	**.528**
Emoji+	**.548**	.536
LC	**.604**	.592
TextBlob	**.584**	.575
VADER	.596	.596
TSA system	**.655**	.634

Table 5: Ternary Sentiment Embedding Model vs. Tang et al.'s Hybrid Ranking (Macro F_1-scores)

Year	Top SemEval result	Ternary Embedding
2013	.6902	$.6178_9$
2016	.633	$.5805_{12}$
2017	.685	$.6291_9$

Table 6: Comparison to top results from different SemEvals (F_1^{PN} scores). Subscripts denote the ranking the system would have achieved each year.

given by Tang et al. (2016). The produced sentiment embeddings were fed to the SVM classifier and tested using 10-fold cross-validation over the *2013-2016-all* SemEval dataset.

The results in Table 5 show that the Ternary Sentiment Embedding Model outperforms the Hybrid Ranking Model using all but two of the eight tested distant supervision methods. The Hybrid Ranking Model only performs significantly better than the proposed model on the Emoticon dataset. The Hybrid Ranking Model is trained using only tweets labelled as positive or negative, while the Ternary Sentiment Embedding Model also utilises neutral tweets. The Emoticon method performs well for classifying tweets as positive or negative, but not for neutral, meaning that the quality of the positive and negative tweets is likely higher than for neutral tweets. This possibly explains why the Hybrid Ranking Model performs better when using this method.

When using the more sophisticated distant supervision methods, the Ternary Sentiment Embedding Model outperforms the Hybrid Ranking Model, with the exception of VADER where the scores are identical. This indicates that the proposed model is able to better take advantage of sentiment information from a larger set of tweets, increasing performance when used for the ternary sentiment classification task.

To compare the entire Twitter Sentiment Analysis system performance to that of Tang et al. (2016), the unfiltered datasets from SemEval 2013 were chosen for the classifier optimisation, with training on the 7,109 tweet *2013-train* set (distributed 2,660-1,010-3,439 positive-negative-neutral) and testing on the *2013-dev* set (1,228 tweets distributed 430-245-553), as this was the validation set of the 2013 workshop.

Tang et al. (2016) trained sentiment embeddings on 5M positive and 5M negative distant-supervised tweets, publishing the results produced by their model when tested with a SVM classifier on the SemEval 2013 test dataset, as presented in the last line of Table 5.[5] The results indicate that the Ternary Sentiment Embedding Model performs better on the ternary classification task than the Hybrid Ranking Model, even though Tang et al.'s embeddings were trained on a much larger dataset than those used in the present work.

6.4 Comparison to SemEval

To see how the final Twitter Sentiment Analysis system fares against the state-of-the-art, its performance was compared to the published results of SemEval 2013 Task 2B (Nakov et al., 2013), SemEval 2016 Task 4A (Nakov et al., 2016), and SemEval 2017 Task 4A (Rosenthal et al., 2017).

The system was trained using the training sets provided by the respective workshop. For 2013, the model was trained on 2013-train-A and tested on 2013-test-A. SemEval 2016 and 2017 allowed training on the training and development datasets of previous years, so for 2016, the model was trained on a combined 2013-2016-train-dev-A dataset and tested on 2016-test-A, while for 2017, the model was trained on all 2013-2016 datasets and tested on 2017-test-A.

The results in Table 6 show that the Ternary Sentiment Embedding Model does not match the top systems of the different years. There are some possible reasons to this: The SemEval systems might have trained on other or more data than here. As tweets have been deleted, not as many could be downloaded as were available at the time of each workshop. Also, the model is optimised for Macro F_1 score. Had it been optimised for F_1^{PN}, better scores for this metric could have been obtained.

---

[5] Only the most similar systems are compared here; Tang et al.'s results improved by using additional lexical features.

7 Conclusion and Future Work

The paper has proposed the Ternary Sentiment Embedding Model, a model for training sentiment-specific word embeddings using distance supervision. The model is based on the Hybrid Ranking Model of Tang et al. (2016), but considers the three classes *positive*, *negative* and *neutral* instead of just *positive* and *negative*. Experiments show the Ternary Sentiment Embedding Model to generally perform better than the Hybrid Ranking Model, and that the quality of the distant-supervised dataset greatly impacts the quality of the produced sentiment embeddings, and transitively the Twitter Sentiment Analysis system.[6]

The Hybrid Ranking Model only performed significantly better than the proposed model on the Emoticon dataset. Tang et al. (2016) use a distant supervision method similar to the Emoticon method, due to the high precision that method can give. For a ternary model, however, it is not sufficient to only find some tweets that are likely positive or negative, and a more sophisticated distant supervision method is essential. This also means that a much larger and more varied corpus of distant supervised tweets can be used for training, since no tweets are discarded. Consequently, the Ternary Sentiment Embedding Model outperformed the Hybrid Ranking Model when using more sophisticated distant supervision methods.

Both Hybrid Ranking and Ternary Sentiment Embedding assume that all senses of a word are synonyms and that all words in a tweet have the same sentiment, ignoring their prior sentiment polarity. Ren et al. (2016) proposed a model for training topic-enriched multi-prototype word embeddings that addresses the issue of polysemy, significantly improving upon the results of SemEval 2013 on the binary classification task. Xiong (2016) addressed the prior polarity problem by exploiting both a sentiment lexicon resource (Hu and Liu, 2004) and distant supervised information in a multi-level sentiment-enriched word embedding learning method. Further work could look at extending the Ternary Sentiment Embedding Model with the ability to discriminate sentiment of polysemous words in three classes, and to use word-sense aware lexica in order to combine the works of Ren et al. (2016) and Xiong (2016).

---

[6]To perform the experiments, several tools and programs were developed, most of these are open sourced. See: `github.com/draperunner`

Acknowledgements

Thanks to Valerij Fredriksen and Brage Ekroll Jahren for providing their classifier code, to the organisers of the different SemEval sentiment analysis tasks for collecting the data, to the anonymous reviewers for comments that helped enrich the discussion of the results, and to Steven Loria, Finn Årup Nielsen, Clayton J. Hutton and Eric Gilbert for respectively providing the TextBlob, AFINN and VADER libraries.

References

Yoshua Bengio, Réjean Ducharme, Pascal Vincent, and Christian Jauvin. 2003. A neural probabilistic language model. *Journal of Machine Learning Research*, 3:1137–1155.

Ronan Collobert and Jason Weston. 2008. A unified architecture for natural language processing: Deep neural networks with multitask learning. In *Proceedings of the 25th International Conference on Machine Learning*, pages 160–167, Helsinki, Finland. ACM.

Ronan Collobert, Jason Weston, Léon Bottou, Michael Karlen, Koray Kavukcuoglu, and Pavel Kuksa. 2011. Natural language processing (almost) from scratch. *Journal of Machine Learning Research*, 12:2493–2537.

John Rupert Firth. 1957. A synopsis of linguistic theory 1930–55. *Studies in Linguistic Analysis*, Special Volume of the Philological Society.

Valerij Fredriksen, Brage Jahren, and Björn Gambäck. 2018. Utilizing large Twitter corpora to create sentiment lexica. In *Proceedings of the 11th International Conference on Language Resources and Evaluation*, pages 2829–2836, Miyazaki, Japan. ELRA.

Alec Go, Richa Bhayani, and Lei Huang. 2009. Twitter sentiment classification using distant supervision. CS224N project report, Stanford University, CA, USA.

Minqing Hu and Bing Liu. 2004. Mining and summarizing customer reviews. In *Proceedings of the Tenth ACM SIGKDD International Conference on Knowledge Discovery and Data Mining*, pages 168–177, New York, NY, USA. ACM.

Clayton J. Hutto and Eric Gilbert. 2014. VADER: A parsimonious rule-based model for sentiment analysis of social media text. In *Proceedings of the Eighth International Conference on Weblogs and Social Media*, pages 216–225, Ann Arbor, MI, USA. The AAAI Press.

Tomas Mikolov, Kai Chen, Greg Corrado, and Jeffrey Dean. 2013. Efficient estimation of word representations in vector space. *CoRR*, abs/1301.3781.

Preslav Nakov, Alan Ritter, Sara Rosenthal, Fabrizio Sebastiani, and Veselin Stoyanov. 2016. SemEval-2016 Task 4: Sentiment analysis in Twitter. In *Proceedings of the 10th International Workshop on Semantic Evaluation (SemEval-2016)*, pages 1–18, San Diego, CA, USA. ACL.

Preslav Nakov, Sara Rosenthal, Zornitsa Kozareva, Veselin Stoyanov, Alan Ritter, and Theresa Wilson. 2013. SemEval-2013 Task 2: Sentiment analysis in Twitter. In *Proceedings of the 7th International Workshop on Semantic Evaluation (SemEval 2013)*, pages 312–320, Atlanta, GA, USA. ACL.

Finn Årup Nielsen. 2011. A new ANEW: Evaluation of a word list for sentiment analysis in microblogs. In *Proceedings of the ESWC2011 Workshop on 'Making Sense of Microposts': Big things come in small packages*, volume 718 of *CEUR Workshop Proceedings*, pages 93–98, Heraklion, Crete.

Jeffrey Pennington, Richard Socher, and Christopher D. Manning. 2014. GloVe: Global vectors for word representation. In *Proceedings of the Conference on Empirical Methods in Natural Language Processing*, pages 1532–1543, Doha, Qatar. ACL.

Yafeng Ren, Ruimin Wang, and Donghong Ji. 2016. A topic-enhanced word embedding for Twitter sentiment classification. *Information Sciences*, 369:188–198.

Sara Rosenthal, Noura Farra, and Preslav Nakov. 2017. SemEval-2017 Task 4: Sentiment analysis in Twitter. In *Proceedings of the 11th International Workshop on Semantic Evaluation (SemEval-2017)*, pages 493–509, Vancouver, Canada. ACL.

Duyu Tang, Furu Wei, Bing Qin, Nan Yang, Ting Liu, and Ming Zhou. 2016. Sentiment embeddings with applications to sentiment analysis. *IEEE Transactions on Knowledge and Data Engineering*, 28(2):496–509.

Duyu Tang, Furu Wei, Nan Yang, Ming Zhou, Ting Liu, and Bing Qin. 2014. Learning sentiment-specific word embedding for Twitter sentiment classification. In *Proceedings of the 52nd Annual Meeting of the Association for Computational Linguistics*, volume 1: Long Papers, pages 1555–1565, Baltimore, MD, USA. ACL.

Shufeng Xiong. 2016. Improving Twitter sentiment classification via multi-level sentiment-enriched word embeddings. *CoRR*, abs/1611.00126.

Appendix:
Positive and negative emoticons and emojis

The character combinations and Unicode characters used in the 'Emoticons' and 'Emojis' distant supervision methods described in Section 4.

Positive		Emojis		Negative		Emojis	
Emoticons				Emoticons			
:)	:-)			:(	DX		
:)	:D			:-(	:-/		
=D	:-]			: (	:/		
:]	:-3			:'(	:-.		
:3	:->			:-(	>:\		
:>	8-)			:(	>:/		
8)	:-}			:-c	:\		
:}	:o)			:c	=/		
:c)	:^)			:-<	=\		
=]	=)			:<	:L		
:-D	8-D			:-[	=L		
8D	x-D			:[	:S		
xD	X-D			:-||	</3		
XD	=D			>:[	<\3		
=3	B-^D			:{	>.<		
:-))	:'-)			:@	v.v		
:')	:-*			>:(			
:*	:×			D-':			
;-)	;)			D:<			
*-)	*)			D:			
;-]	;]			D8			
;^)	:-,			D;			
;D	<3			D=			

Linking News Sentiment to Microblogs: A Distributional Semantics Approach to Enhance Microblog Sentiment Classification

Tobias Daudert and Paul Buitelaar

Insight Centre for Data Analytics, Data Science Institute, National University of Ireland, Galway

`firstname.lastname@insight-centre.org`

Abstract

Social media's popularity in society and research is gaining momentum and simultaneously increasing the importance of short textual content such as microblogs. Microblogs are affected by many factors including the news media, therefore, we exploit sentiments conveyed from news to detect and classify sentiment in microblogs. Given that texts can deal with the same entity but might not be vastly related when it comes to sentiment, it becomes necessary to introduce further measures ensuring the relatedness of texts while leveraging the contained sentiments. This paper describes ongoing research introducing distributional semantics to improve the exploitation of news-contained sentiment to enhance microblog sentiment classification.

1 Introduction

In our increasingly digital society, we are subject to a deluge of unfiltered information not always objective or unbiased. The popularity of social media has made it a gateway to digital news content with 23% of the population in 2017 preferring this medium as a source of news[1]. A particular case is Twitter and with the rise in popularity of this medium, short texts rich in information and/or sentiment are becoming a relevant source of information for the sharing of news stories (Mitchell and Page, 2015). However, traditional news are still important and at least as influential as digital media; in 2017, 32% of the people worldwide accessed digital news directly on a news website[1]. In Twitter, over 85% of the retweets contain news mentions (Kwak et al., 2010). The diffusion of information is also crucial; people view what friends share leading to a fast diffusion of information with 75% of the total retweets occurring within a

---

[1]`https://www.statista.com/chart/10262/`
`selected-gateways-to-digital-news-content/`

day (Lerman and Ghosh, 2010; Kwak et al., 2010). This effect, combined with a higher perceived trust of shared information by friends, can lead to the construction of opinions based on already opinionated content (Zhao et al., 2011; Turcotte et al., 2015).

The importance of microblogs and news articles, their similar instantaneous availability, and their topic intersections lead us to explore how news articles and microblogs affect each other and, in detail, how the sentiments contained in both affect each other. This paper presents ongoing research dealing with this question and utilises distributional semantics, in detail, word embeddings, the cosine similarity, and the word mover's distance, to improve the modeling of the conveyance of news-contained sentiment on microblogs, aiming to enhance microblog sentiment classification.

2 Background

In the financial domain, prior research has shown the connection between sentiments and the market dynamics, exposing the financial domain as a relevant area for sentiment analysis in text (Van De Kauter et al., 2015; Kearney and Liu, 2014). Sentiments are contained in various forms of text including news and microblogs. It has been shown that positive news tend to lift markets whereas bad news tend to lower the markets (Schuster, 2003; Van De Kauter et al., 2015). Past research mainly focuses on news, particularly news titles (i.e headlines) (Nassirtoussi et al., 2014; Kearney and Liu, 2014). However, not only sentiment contained in news is an important factor for the markets. For example, Bollen et al. (2011) linked changes in public mood to value shifts in the Dow Jones Industrial Index three to four days later. With an increasing magnitude of instantly available informa-

Proceedings of the 9th Workshop on Computational Approaches to Subjectivity, Sentiment and Social Media Analysis, pages 107–115
Brussels, Belgium, October 31, 2018. ©2018 Association for Computational Linguistics
https://doi.org/10.18653/v1/P17

tion, factors affecting people's sentiment rise. This includes other people's textually-expressed sentiment since information is not always presented in a neutral manner. However, the relation between sentiments across different data sources, how they affect each other, and how this can be leveraged for sentiment classification has not been investigated yet.

2.1 Linking Sentiments Across Data Sources

Daudert et al. (2018) goes a step in this direction and exploits news sentiment to improve microblog sentiment classification. Their work utilises an **entity-based approach** which, given data annotated with sentiment, an entity e, and a period p, calculates the average sentiment for entity e in period p. The authors used a news dataset and calculated an average sentiment per company for news published between March 11th and 18th 2016 which was then used as additional information. Their assumption that within a certain period sentiments regarding the same entity should be similar across different data sources was examined. Using the average news sentiment performs well in periods when there is an overall sentiment other than neutral; in periods when the overall sentiment is neutral or balanced, a more sophisticated approach is needed. A neutral overall sentiment is achieved when positive and negative sentiment counteract with each other, independently of the number of news where each sentiment is expressed, whilst a balanced overall sentiment is achieved when the number of positive and negative news regarding a certain entity is similar. Given this, it becomes important to take a deeper look at news and microblogs as not all news are equally important to each microblog dealing with the same entity. Therefore, this research employs a distributional semantics approach to remove noise in terms of microblog-unrelated news sentiment although dealing with the same entity. To the best of our knowledge, only the previously mentioned work has started investigating the relations between the sentiments and leveraged them for microblog sentiment classification, hence, there is no research on the use of distributional semantics for sentiment linking. On the other hand, research targeting the field of semantic enrichment is available and it is particularly relevant when addressing the linking of news and microblogs (e.g. Guo et al. (2013); Wei et al. (2014); Abel et al. (2011);

Tsagkias et al. (2011)). Abel et al. (2011) suggests five different approaches of linking news to tweets: 1) a strict URL-based strategy, 2) a lenient URL-based strategy, 3) a bag-of-words strategy, 4) a hashtag-based strategy, and 5) an entity-based strategy. Strategy 5) comes close to what has been explored by Daudert et al. (2018) whereby our approach is inspired by 3), employing it as an add-on to 5). Other related research considering the combination of semantic similarity and sentiment analysis are (Tang et al., 2016; Poria et al., 2016). Poria et al. (2016) developed a Latent Dirichlet Allocation algorithm considering the semantic similarity between word pairs, instead of only utilising a word frequency measure, thus, capable of capturing opinions and sentiments that are implicitly expressed in a text and, overall, contributing to improved clustering. Tang et al. (2016) focused on learning word embeddings defined not only by context but also by sentiment. Their approach is able to better capture nearest neighboring vectors not only through their semantic similarity but also favoring the same sentiment polarity. This novel idea of utilising word embeddings to better capture polarity in documents was initially brought up by Maas et al. (2011).

The work described in this paper aims to address the existing knowledge gap concerning the application of distributional semantics for sentiment linking and assigning.

3 Methodology

The work performed is divided into two parts: the preparation of the data, and its use in a Machine Learning (ML) prediction model. Throughout this paper, we implement the methodology described by Daudert et al. (2018), utilising the same datasets (section 3.1) and experimental setup (section 3.4). We extend their previous work by improving the method to link a news sentiment to a microblog as well as to assign a news sentiment to a microblog (section 3.2).

The aim of this research is to explore the relation of sentiments between news and microblogs, hence, the linking of both data types becomes necessary. To fulfill this task, we leverage a microblog and a complimentary news dataset covering the same period and entities. For each microblog in the dataset, we model the sentiment conveyance between the news sentiment and the microblogs sentiment by assigning one news sentiment according to each of the different methods as described in 3.2; these are then used as additional features for the Support Vector Machine (SVM).

This SVM is trained and tested with the datasets mentioned in section 3.1, aiming to explore whether the consideration of textual similarities for modeling the conveyed news sentiment can add value to the microblog sentiment classification. To investigate this, we compare a classification (1) purely based on microblog messages (table 2, *MT*) with (2) a classification based on microblog messages and entity-based news sentiment (table 2, *ES Agg.*), and (3) classifications based on microblog messages and context-based news sentiment (table 2, columns highlighted in gray).

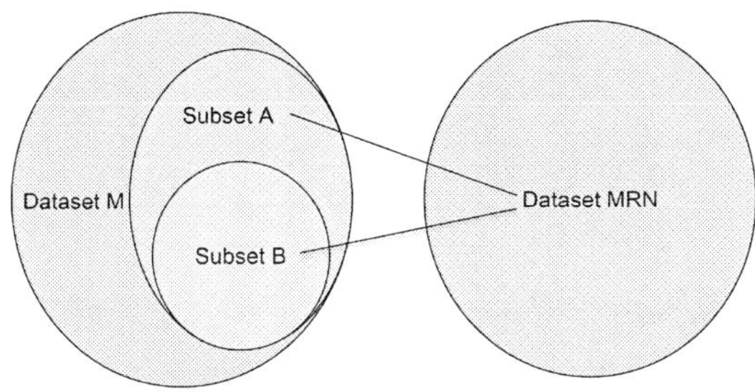

Figure 1: Representation of dataset M and MRN, subset A and B. The two links represent matching entities in the datasets.

3.1 Data

This research makes use of two datasets: a microblog dataset (M) and a microblogs-related news dataset (MRN), represented in Figure 1. Dataset M contains microblogs from Twitter[2] as well as StockTwits[3] and was initially created for the Semeval 2017 Task 5 - subtask 1 (Cortis et al., 2017); dataset MRN contains the news titles, urls, time and date, a sentiment score within the five classes [-1.0, -0.5, 0.0, 0.5, 1.0], and, if available, a description. All news in MRN are related to at least one microblog in dataset M. In total, MRN contains 106 news covering 18 unique entities in 463 microblogs (defined as subset A below). For dataset M, the sentiment scores are processed to cluster data in three classes by transforming sentiment scores above 0.0 to 1.0, and scores lower than 0.0 to -1.0. Moreover, two subsets of dataset M were created according to the microblogs' re-

<hr>

[2]https://twitter.com
[3]https://stocktwits.com

Type	Dataset M	Subset A	Subset B
Training	1,694	298	185
Test	794	165	92
Total	2,488	463	277

Table 1: Number of microblogs in dataset M, subset A, and subset B. Subset A and B are extracted from Dataset M.

lation to dataset MRN (see Table 1 and Figure 1). Subset A contains microblogs which have a relation to one or multiple news; subset B contains microblogs from subset A which are retrieved from Twitter. Subset B is necessary as dataset M contains StockTwits not specifically collected in the same period as the tweets. Figure 2 contains additional information regarding the annotation of both dataset as well as subsets.

3.2 Assigning a News Sentiment to Microblogs

All news in dataset MRN correspond to companies referred to in a minimum of one microblog in dataset M. With this information, our goal is to determine how to model the sentiment conveyance between the news-contained sentiment and each microblog given that news and microblogs might contain the same entities but not be vastly related. Considering the following example of two news articles, one about *Apple* and *Tim Cook's* private life, and another one about *Apple* and the new *iPhone*, the latter one's sentiment should have a higher impact on a microblog's sentiment about Apple's new products since they are more related. Using a purely entity based approach, both news articles would be linked to the microblog and the influence of both news on the assigned sentiment would be equal as they deal with *Apple*.

This work considers the assumption that *"within a certain period, sentiments regarding the same entity should be similar across different data sources"* (Daudert et al., 2018) and refines it with the assumption that *sentiments are particularly similar if the textual context is similar*. To lay the foundation for future research applications and to ensure a coherent understanding of the terminology applied throughout this work, we define core concepts as follows:

Linking - The linking of sentiment describes the creation of relations between sentiments, particularly their literal representations, by

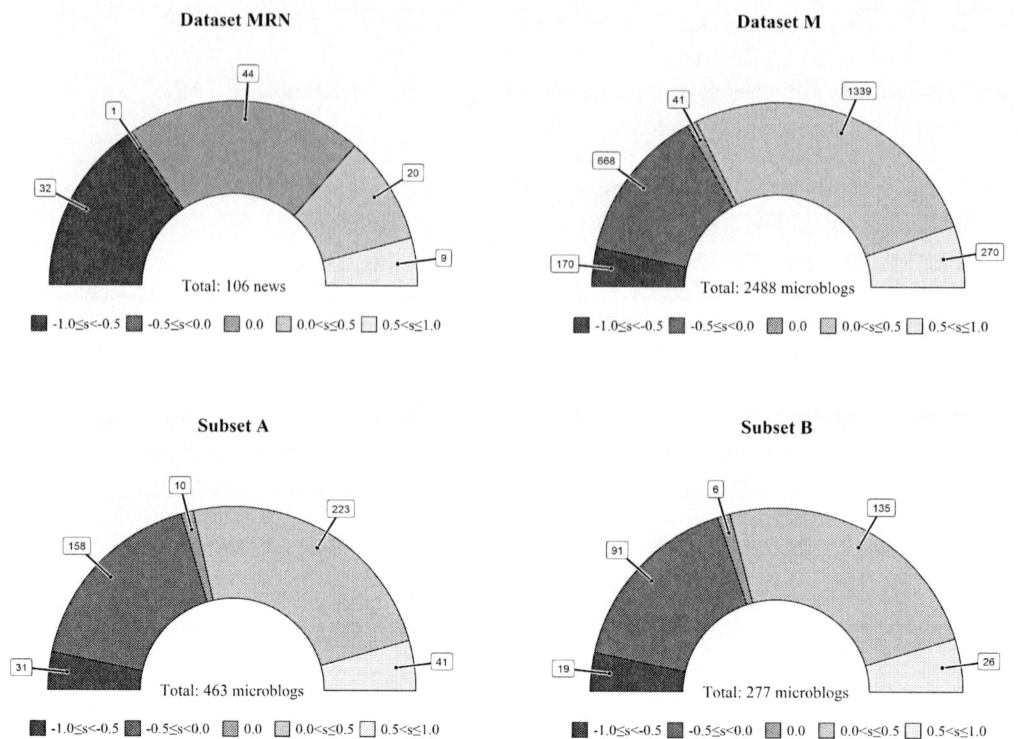

Figure 2: Distribution of the annotated sentiment for dataset MRN, dataset M, subset A, and subset B. The sentiment is represented by *s*.

matching pieces of text according to predefined criteria such entities, text intersections, or a degree of textual similarity. Hereby, we assume that linked sentiments are either influenced by the same cause or affecting each other.

Conveyance - The conveyance of sentiment describes the influence of the sentiment of one text on the sentiment of another. Sentiment is (indirectly) fully or partially transfered from a piece of text A to a piece of text B.

Assigning - The assigning of sentiment models the conveyance of sentiment from a text to another. Given two linked sentiments and the hypothesis that one is affecting the other, or both are affected by the same cause, we model the influence of text A's sentiment on text B's sentiment; improvements of this assignment can be measured by an enhanced sentiment detection for text B.

The aim behind this is the removal of noise in terms of microblog-unrelated news, although dealing with the same entity, as well as the reduction of the impact of less-related news on the assigned sentiment. To explore this, we compare four context-based approaches with the entity-based approach. The two context-based approaches employing a threshold for determining the relevance of a news to a microblog's sentiment (approach 1 and 3) aim at improving the sentiment linking since they fully discard news below a certain similarity value. The remaining two context-based approaches using a weighting scheme are reducing the impact of less relevant news on a microblog's sentiment and are, hence, aiming at improving the assigning of sentiment. This occurs in multiple steps: First, URLs in microblogs as well as news titles and descriptions are removed. Second, microblogs are tokenised employing the NLTK TweetTokenizer (Bird and Loper, 2004); news titles and descriptions are tokenized using the Stanford CoreNLP Tokenizer (Manning et al., 2014).

Measure / Features	MT	ES Agg.	TS Thr.	TS Wgt. Agg.	WMD-S Thr. Agg.	WMD-S Wgt. Agg.
Dataset M						
Micro F1-Score	0.8048	0.8060	**0.8073**	0.8060	0.8060	0.8060
Macro F1-Score	0.6349	0.6357	**0.6369**	0.6357	0.6357	0.6357
Weighted F1-Score	0.8018	0.8030	**0.8044**	0.8030	0.8030	0.8030
Euclidean Distance	23.9165	23.8328	**23.7487**	23.8328	23.8328	23.8328
Mean Error Squared	0.7204	0.7154	**0.7103**	0.7154	0.7154	0.7154
Subset A						
Micro F1-Score	0.6485	0.6545	**0.6606**	0.6545	0.6485	0.6485
Macro F1-Score	0.5547	0.5583	**0.5633**	0.5597	0.5547	0.5547
Weighted F1-Score	0.64167	0.6471	**0.6539**	0.6485	0.6416	0.6416
Euclidean Distance	14.9332	14.7986	**14.6629**	14.7986	14.9332	14.9332
Mean Error Squared	1.3515	1.3273	**1.3030**	1.3272	1.3515	1.3515
Subset B						
Micro F1-Score	0.7283	0.7283	0.7283	0.7391	**0.75**	0.7391
Macro F1-Score	0.6917	0.6917	0.6917	0.701	**0.7077**	0.701
Weighted F1-Score	0.7241	0.7241	0.7241[*]	0.7363	**0.7463**	0.7363
Euclidean Distance	9.8489	9.8489	9.8489	9.6437	**9.434**	9.6437
Mean Error Squared	1.0543	1.0543	1.0543	1.0109	**0.9674**	1.0109

Table 2: Scores obtained by the SVM model for dataset M, subset A, and B. MT abbreviates the message text, ES the entity-based news sentiment, TS the news title and description text similarity, WMD-S the word mover's distance similarity. Thr. represents threshold, Wgt. weighted, and Agg. aggregated. A p-value < 0.01 is achieved for all models with the exception of *TS Thr.* on subset B (marked with [*]) which achieves a p-value < 0.05. The classifications based on microblog messages and context-based news sentiment are represented in gray (columns 4-7).

We choose different tokenizers for microblogs and news as the TweetTokenizer is specifically made for microblogs while news require a tokenizer adapted to a different structure and length. Third, we convert the Stanford GloVe Twitter model (Pennington et al., 2014) to Word2Vec (Mikolov et al., 2013a) and obtain the word embeddings. Having the word embeddings for microblogs and news in place, the subsequent processing varied depending on the context-based approach.

3.3 Context-based Approaches

We define **context-based** as an approach which utilises the textual similarity between two data artifacts as a factor to modify the sentiment of one of these, aiming at the generation of a sentiment to be assigned for the other artifact, necessary to model the sentiment conveyance.

In this work, we use microblog messages and a concatenation of the news titles and descriptions, if available, as our textual information. We then measure the textual similarity and utilise it as a factor to modify the news sentiment and subsequently generate the news sentiment to be assigned (NSTBA). This generated sentiment is then applied to model the sentiment conveyance between a news and a microblog.

$$NSTBA_m = \frac{s(n_1) + s(n_2)}{2} \quad (1)$$

The first context-based approach generates the NSTBA as an average of the sentiments of the microblog-related news articles. Document embeddings are retrieved for each microblog and news by averaging the word embeddings (Kartsaklis, 2014). We employ the cosine similarity as measure since vector offsets have been shown to be effective (Mikolov et al., 2013b). To be considered as context-related, a cosine similarity of at least 0.5 is required. For example, if two news articles (n_1, n_2) are context-related to microblog m, the two news sentiments (s) are added together and then divided by 2.

$$NSTBA_m = \frac{s(n_1) * sim(n_1, m) + s(n_2) * sim(n_2, m)}{2} \quad (2)$$

In contrast, the second context-based approach does not exclude relations with a cosine similarity lower than 0.5 but it uses the similarity score as a weighting factor multiplying it with the respective news sentiment score. Thus, an average of the similarity-weighted sentiments of the related-news is created. As an example, if two news articles (n_1, n_2) are context-related to microblog m, each news sentiment $s(n_x)$ is multiplied with the respective similarity (sim) score of n_x and m and then divided by 2. The NSTBA is then aggregated into the classes [-1.0, 0.0, 1.0] as this enhanced the results.

The third approach utilises the word mover's distance (WMD) as described in (Kusner et al., 2015). We choose the WMD as it is a promising, recently developed function to measure the dissimilarity between two text documents. In our data, the WMDs d are within the range of [3.5, 9.5]. In spirit of equation 1, we use a threshold of 6.5 which is located halfway between both turning points as a requirement to be considered as context-related. As previously, the NSTBA has been aggregated into three classes.

The fourth approach is also based on the WMD. Since the WMD is not a similarity score but a distance theoretically ranging from 0 to unlimited, we transformed it into a similarity score (WMD-S). For WMDs ranging between [3.5, 9.5] in our data, we converted them into a similarity score within [0, 0.955] using the following formula:

$$sim(d) = 1 - \frac{1}{-0.1(d-9.5)^3+1} \qquad (3)$$

Initially, we also experimented with other functions such as $1 - d/9.5$, however, function 3 represented a better approximation of a similarity score for our data. First, word embeddings are used to create the WMD between each microblog and news. Then, this distance is transformed into a similarity score using the formula above. Third and in the spirit of equation 2, news sentiments are weighted with the WMD-based similarity score. However, here we also aggregated the NSTBA.

3.4 Experimental Setup

For consistency, we utilise a similar setup to Daudert et al. (2018) for the preprocessing of the microblog texts, as well as for the SVM, and performance measures. The preprocessing steps are as follows:

1. URLs were replaced with $< url >$

2. Numbers were replaced with $< number >$

3. With $WORD$ representing the original hastag:

    (a) hastags in upper case were replaced with $< hashtag > WORD < allcaps >$

    (b) the remaining cases were replaced with $< hashtag > WORD$

4. Smileys and emoticons were replaced with a description (e.g.☺ becomes $slightly\_smiling\_face$) [4]

The processed text was then transformed into a unigram tf-idf representation.

The SVM model is trained and tested in six distinct approaches whereby approach three to six utilise different methods to model the context-based news sentiment: (1) a feature matrix representing the microblog messages; (2) a feature matrix representing the microblog messages enriched with the assigned entity-based news sentiment for each microblog, and (3)-(6) a feature matrix representing the microblog messages enriched with the assigned context-based news sentiment for each microblog. We chose to balance the class weight to get as close as possible to a *neutral sentiment* setting; the iterations are set to 500 and the random state to 42.

To test for statistical significance of the models, we apply a permutation test under the null hypothesis that the model has no effect in microblog sentiment classification (Ojala and Garriga, 2010).

4   Results

Table 2 shows the classification results on dataset M, subset A, and subset B. Although the use of an entity-based sentiment is already beneficial to the results, the addition of textual similarity measures further improves them. As the table shows, utilising context-based approaches to influence to-microblogs-assigned news sentiments enhances all measures in comparison to only using an entity-based average news sentiment. The weighted F1-Score for dataset M is increased by 0.17% and the Euclidean distance is decreased by 7.04%. In comparison to only using the message text (*MT*), the same scores are improved by 3.13% and 13.99%. For the subsets A and B the weighted F1-Score increases by 1.06% and 3.07%, and the Euclidean distance is decreased by 1.82% and 8.25%, respectively. For subset A, in contrast to only using *MT*, the weighted F1-Score and Euclidean distance are improved by 1.91% and 3.59%. This suggests the benefit of applying distributional semantics to the linking and assigning of news sentiment to microblogs, shown by the improvement on microblog sentiment classifica-

---

[4] `http://www.unicode.org/emoji/charts/full-emoji-list.html`

tion. Additionally, all scores improve on dataset M although only around 18.6% of the microblogs in the dataset are related to news. Surprisingly, utilising WMD-S improves all measures for subset B, whereas the cosine similarity between the document embeddings, together with the application of a threshold of 0.5, delivers the best results for dataset M and subset A. Furthermore, our approach outperforms the best score achieved in the SemEval 2017 Task 5 - Track 1 competition in which microblog sentiment analysis on a continuous scale was performed. Although our focus is to show the benefit of leveraging sentiment across news and microblogs, classifying the sentiment into 3 classes, our model reaches a cosine similarity of 0.869 on dataset M (table 2, column *TS Thr.*) whereas Jiang et al. (2017) reach a cosine similarity of 0.778.

5 Conclusion and Future Work

In this work, we utilise distributional semantics to model the conveyance of sentiment between news and microblogs. The achieved results suggest the benefit of using textual similarities and word embeddings to enhance the sentiment linking and assigning, culminating in an improved microblog sentiment classification. Our contributions are threefold: First, we present novel research utilising distributional semantics, specifically, word embeddings, the cosine similarity, and the word mover's distance, for the linking and assigning of news-contained sentiment to microblogs; second, we explore the use of the word mover's distance as similarity measure and; third, we suggest the benefit of leveraging news sentiment together with similarity methods for microblog sentiment classification. Comparing the additional use of an entity-based news sentiment with only the microblog text as features (columns *MT* versus *ES Agg.*), our results show an improvement on microblog sentiment classification on dataset M and subset A, while achieving a p-value$<$0.01. In case of subset B, which has the most related news but the least news in quantity, the performance remains unchanged (columns *MT* versus *ES Agg.*). However, models utilising context-based news sentiment for an enhanced sentiment linking and assigning (columns *TS Thr.* and *WMD-S Thr. Agg.*) improve the performance for subset B and also reach the best scores for all three datasets. This suggests that applying distributional semantics is particularly fruitful when entity-based news sentiments have less impact on the sentiment analysis on microblogs; this can be true in three cases:

1. The overall sentiments are neutral or balanced. We balanced all sentiment classes, however, the classifiers trained on context-based sentiment outperform the one trained on average entity-based news sentiment.

2. Only sparse related news exist. A classifier utilising the average entity-based sentiment as features achieves better results for dataset M and subset A than one with only the message text as features, however, on the smaller subset B this does not occur. Furthermore, when context-based sentiment is used as feature, the improvement on subset B becomes the largest. This suggests that each misleading news sentiment, present on dataset M and subset A, would have a noticeable impact on the results.

3. Related news are noisy and contain, apart from matching entities, unrelated information. Nonetheless, training our classifier on context-based sentiment outperforms the one trained on the average entity-based sentiment, suggesting that more-related news have a higher influence.

As future work, we aim to create a larger dataset, referring to a single defined period, linking microblogs and news. In addition, hybrid models taking into account not only a threshold for discarding noise but also a weighting scheme could potentially improve the classification. In this paper, we utilise the word mover's distance and the cosine similarity to measure the similarity between two texts, however, other potentially adequate methods for this task still require exploration.

Acknowledgments

This publication has emanated from research conducted with the financial support of Science Foundation Ireland (SFI) under Grant Number SFI/12/RC/2289, co-funded by the European Regional Development Fund.

References

Fabian Abel, Qi Gao, Houben Geert-Jan, and Tao KE. 2011. Semantic Enrichment of Twitter Posts for User Profile Contrunction on the Social Web. In *Proceedings of the Extended Semantic Web Conference*, pages 375 – 389. Springer, Berlin, Heidelberg.

Steven Bird and Edward Loper. 2004. NLTK: The Natural Language Toolkit. In *Proceedings of the ACL 2004 on Interactive poster and demonstration sessions*, volume 1, pages 31 – 34, Morristown, NJ, USA. Association for Computational Linguistics.

Johan Bollen, Huina Mao, and Xiaojun Zeng. 2011. Twitter mood predicts the stock market. *Journal of Computational Science*, 2(1):1–8.

Keith Cortis, Andre Freitas, Tobias Daudert, Manuela Huerlimann, Manel Zarrouk, Siegfried Handschuh, and Brian Davis. 2017. SemEval-2017 Task 5: Fine-Grained Sentiment Analysis on Financial Microblogs and News. In *Proceedings of the 11th International Workshop on Semantic Evaluation (SemEval-2017)*, pages 519–535.

Tobias Daudert, Paul Buitelaar, and Sapna Negi. 2018. Leveraging News Sentiment to Improve Microblog Sentiment Classification in the Financial Domain. In *Proceedings of the First Workshop on Economics and Natural Language Processing*, pages 49–54, Melbourne, Australia. Association for Computational Linguistics.

Weiwei Guo, Hao Li, Heng Ji, and Mona Diab. 2013. Linking Tweets to News: A Framework to Enrich Short Text Data in Social Media. In *Proceedings of the 51st Annual Meeting of the Association for Computational Linguistics*, pages 239–249.

Mengxiao Jiang, Man Lan, and Yuanbin Wu. 2017. ECNU at SemEval-2017 Task 5: An Ensemble of Regression Algorithms with Effective Features for Fine-Grained Sentiment Analysis in Financial Domain. In *Proceedings of the 11th International Workshop on Semantic Evaluation (SemEval-2017)*, pages 888–893.

Dimitri Kartsaklis. 2014. Compositional Operators in Distributional Semantics. *Springer Science Reviews*, 2(1-2):161–177.

Colm Kearney and Sha Liu. 2014. Textual sentiment in finance: A survey of methods and models. *International Review of Financial Analysis*, 33:171–185.

Matt J Kusner, Yu Sun, Nicholas I Kolkin, and Kilian Q Weinberger. 2015. From Word Embeddings To Document Distances. In *Proceedings of The 32nd International Conference on Machine Learning*, volume 37, page 957 966.

Haewoon Kwak, Changhyun Lee, Hosung Park, and Sue Moon. 2010. What is Twitter, a Social Network or a News Media? In *Proceedings of the International World Wide Web Conference Committee (IW3C2)*, pages 591 – 600.

Kristina Lerman and Rumi Ghosh. 2010. Information Contagion: an Empirical Study of the Spread of News on Digg and Twitter Social Networks. In *Proceedings of the Fourth International AAAI Conference on Weblogs and Social Media*, pages 90 – 97.

Andrew L Maas, Raymond E. Daly, Peter T. Pham, Dan Huang, Andrew Y. Ng, and Christopher Potts. 2011. Learning Word Vectors for Sentiment Analysis. In *Proceedings of the 49th Annual Meeting of the Association for Computational Linguistics: Human Language Technologies*, pages 142–150.

Christopher Manning, Mihai Surdeanu, John Bauer, Jenny Finkel, Steven Bethard, and David McClosky. 2014. The Stanford CoreNLP Natural Language Processing Toolkit. In *Proceedings of 52nd Annual Meeting of the Association for Computational Linguistics: System Demonstrations*, pages 55 – 60.

Tomas Mikolov, Kai Chen, Greg Corrado, and Jeffrey Dean. 2013a. Efficient Estimation of Word Representations in Vector Space. *arXiv preprint arXiv:1301.3781*, pages 1–12.

Tomas Mikolov, Wen-tau Yih, and Geoffrey Zweig. 2013b. Linguistic regularities in continuous space word representations. *Proceedings of NAACL-HLT*, (June):746–751.

Amy Mitchell and Dana Page. 2015. The Evolving Role of News on Twitter and Facebook. Technical report, pewresearch.org.

Arman Khadjeh Nassirtoussi, Saeed Aghabozorgi, Teh Ying Wah, and David Chek Ling Ngo. 2014. Text mining for market prediction: A systematic review. *Expert Systems with Applications*, 41(16):7653–7670.

Markus Ojala and Gemma C. Garriga. 2010. Permutation Tests for Studying Classifier Performance. *Journal of Machine Learning Research*, 11(June):1833–1863.

Jeffrey Pennington, Richard Socher, and Christopher D Manning. 2014. GloVe : Global Vectors for Word Representation. In *Proceedings of the 2014 Conference on Empirical Methods in Natural Language Processing (EMNLP)*, page 1532 1543.

Soujanya Poria, Iti Chaturvedi, Erik Cambria, and Federica Bisio. 2016. Sentic LDA: Improving on LDA with semantic similarity for aspect-based sentiment analysis. In *Proceedings of the International Joint Conference on Neural Networks (IJCNN)*, volume 201, pages 4465–4473. IEEE.

Thomas Schuster. 2003. Meta-Communication and Market Dynamics. Reflexive Interactions of Financial Markets and the Mass Media. *SSRN eLibrary*, (July).

Duyu Tang, Furu Wei, Bing Qin, Nan Yang, Ting Liu, and Ming Zhou. 2016. Sentiment Embeddings with Applications to Sentiment Analysis. *IEEE Transactions on Knowledge and Data Engineering*, 28(2):496–509.

Manos Tsagkias, Maarten de Rijke, and Wouter Weerkamp. 2011. Linking online news and social media. In *Proceedings of the fourth ACM international conference on Web search and data mining - WSDM '11*, pages 565–574.

Jason Turcotte, Chance York, Jacob Irving, Rosanne M. Scholl, and Raymond J. Pingree. 2015. News Recommendations from Social Media Opinion Leaders: Effects on Media Trust and Information Seeking. *Journal of Computer-Mediated Communication*, 20(5):520 – 535.

Marjan Van De Kauter, Diane Breesch, and Veronique Hoste. 2015. Fine-grained analysis of explicit and implicit sentiment in financial news articles. *Expert Systems with Applications*, 42(11):4999–5010.

Zhongyu Wei, Hong Kong, and Wei Gao. 2014. Utilizing Microblogs for Automatic News Highlights Extraction. In *Proceedings of COLING 2014, the 25th International Conference on Computational Linguistics*, pages 872 – 883.

Wayne Xin Zhao, Jing Jiang, Jianshu Weng, Jing He, Ee-Peng Lim, Hongfei Yan, and Xiaoming Li. 2011. Comparing Twitter and Traditional Media Using Topic Models. In *Proceedings of the European Conference on Information Retrieval*, pages 338–349. Springer, Berlin, Heidelberg.

Aspect Based Sentiment Analysis into the Wild

Caroline Brun, Vassilina Nikoulina[*]
`firstname.lastname@naverlabs.com`
Naver Labs Europe, 6 chemin de Maupertuis, 38240 Meylan

Abstract

In this paper, we test state-of-the-art Aspect Based Sentiment Analysis (ABSA) systems trained on a widely used dataset on actual data. We created a new manually annotated dataset of user generated data from the same domain as the training dataset, but from other sources and analyse the differences between the new and the standard ABSA dataset. We then analyse the results in performance of different versions of the same system on both datasets. We also propose light adaptation methods to increase system robustness.

1 Introduction

The aim of Aspect Based Sentiment Analysis (ABSA) is to detect fine-grained opinions expressed about different aspects of a given entity, on user-generated comments.

Aspects are attributes of an entity, e.g. the screen of a cell phone, the service for a restaurant, or the picture quality of a camera, and can be described by an ontology associated to the entity. ABSA includes therefore to identify aspects of an entity, and the sentiment expressed by the writer of the comment about different aspects. For example, from a sentence extracted from a review about a museum, an ABSA system could extract the following information: *This museum hosts remarkable collections, however, prices are quite high and the attendants are not always friendly.*

"collections": aspect=museum#collection, polarity=positive;

"prices": aspect=museum#price, polarity=negative;

"attendants": aspect=museum#service, polarity=negative;

ABSA receives now a specific interest from the scientific community, especially with the SemEval dedicated challenges, (Pontiki et al., 2014), (Pontiki et al., 2015), (Pontiki et al., 2016), that provided a framework to design and evaluate ABSA

systems, for different domains, initially on English but for 8 languages in the 2016 (last) edition. Besides SemEval, other challenges focussing on the task have been also launched recently, for example TASS, dedicated to Spanish, (Villena-Román et al., 2015b), (Villena-Román et al., 2015a), (Cumbreras et al., 2016), or GermanEval, dedicated to German ABSA, (Wojatzki et al., 2017).

Following this particular interest, the technology performing ABSA becomes more and more mature, however, experiments and evaluation are restricted to a small number of academic datasets, in relatively favorable settings. The goal of this paper is to test a state-of-the-art ABSA system on actual data, to evaluate the performance loss in real-world application conditions, and to experiment potential solutions to it. To achieve this goal, we've created a new ABSA annotated dataset, developed on Foursquare data. We also performed evaluation of the full ABSA processing chain (as opposed to sub-tasks evaluation which is traditionally performed). We also propose a weakly supervised method for aspect-based lexical acquisition designed to improve the robustness of our initial system.

2 Related Work

Most of the systems dedicated to ABSA use machine learning algorithms such as SVMs (Wagner et al., 2014; Kiritchenko et al., 2014), or CRFs (Toh and Wang, 2014; Hamdan et al., 2015), which are often combined with semantic lexical information, n-gram models, and sometimes more fine-grained syntactic or semantic information. For example, (Kumar et al., 2016) proposed a very efficient system on different languages of SemEval2016. The system use information extracted from dependency graphs and distributional thesaurus learned on the different domains and

---

[*] Both authors contributed equally.

Proceedings of the 9th Workshop on Computational Approaches to Subjectivity, Sentiment and Social Media Analysis, pages 116–122
Brussels, Belgium, October 31, 2018. ©2018 Association for Computational Linguistics
https://doi.org/10.18653/v1/P17

languages of the challenge. Deep Learning methods are also emerging: for example, (Ruder et al., 2016) proposed a method using multiple filters CNNs and obtained competitive results on both polarity and aspect detection tasks. However, ABSA datasets are very costly to annotate by humans, and they are usually small, which is a problem for Deep Learning supervised methods.

3 Datasets

Usually, ABSA systems are tested on the same dataset as they are developped on. One of the widely used ABSA datasets was released in Semeval2016 challenge (Pontiki et al., 2016), in particular the dataset for restaurant domain. It is based on the dataset of (Ganu et al., 2009) who extracted restaurant reviews from City Search New York over year 2006. Since then, the notion of the user review has evolved. Many factors may impact the linguistic structure of a review, e.g. the support it was written on (computer vs. smartphone), the age of the user, the location (US vs. UK English), the user mother tongue (native vs. non-native speakers), etc. How would a system trained on Semeval2016 dataset perform on a new data coming from different sources?

In order to assess ABSA real-world performances, we manually annotated a completely new dataset from Foursquare[1] comments. We have access to about 215K user reviews of restaurants all over the world in English[2]. The reviews were written during the period between 2009 to 2018. From these reviews, we randomly selected 585 samples, which contain 1006 sentences and annotate these sentences with the SemEval2016 annotation guidelines for the restaurant domain. The annotations have been performed by a single annotator, expert linguist with a very good knowledge of the SemEval2016 annotation guidelines, using BRAT, (Stenetorp et al., 2012).

Each sentence contains annotations about: 1. Opinion Target Expression (OTE), i.e. the linguistic expression (term) used in the text to refer to the reviewed entity, annotated as "NULL" if the aspect is implicit; 2. Aspect Categories, i.e. the semantic categories of the opinionated aspects, which are part of a predefined ontology (12 semantic classes for the restaurant domain from

Dataset	#Rev	#S	#W/S	#A/S
Semeval	92	676	12.8	1.27
Foursquare	585	1006	8.0	1.15

Table 1: Dataset statistics: Semeval 2016 test set and Foursquare dataset. #Rev: number of reviews, #S: number of sentences, #W/S : number of words per sentence, #A/S: number of <OTE, Aspect Category, Polarity> tuples per sentence

(Pontiki et al., 2016)); 3. Sentiment Polarities: polarities (positive, negative or neutral) associated to the tuple <OTE, Aspect Category>. An illustration of such annotation is given on figure 1.

```
<text>Their sake list was extensive,
but we were looking for Purple Haze,
which wasn't listed but made for us
upon request!</text>
<Opinions>
<Opinion target="sake list"
        category="DRINKS#STYLE_OPTIONS"
        polarity="positive"/>
<Opinion target="NULL"
        category="SERVICE#GENERAL"
        polarity="positive"/>
</Opinions>
```

Figure 1: ABSA: an annotated sentence from the Semeval-2016 training corpus

Table 1 gives some statistics about the Foursquare and Semeval2016 datasets. One may notice, that in average, Foursquare reviews are shorter and therefore contain less aspects per sentence. We believe this is due to the generalisation of smart-phones (and other mobile devices) usage over the world in the last decade, which influenced the way users write. We release the Foursquare dataset to the community in order to better assess robustness of ABSA systems[3].

4 Evaluation Procedure

We consider different evaluation measures. First, we re-use the SemEval2016 ABSA evaluation paradigm and scripts, where the evaluation was run in two phases, phase A and phase B. In phase A, raw reviews have to be annotated with aspects (slot 1 of the challenge) and OTE (slot 2 of the challenge). In phase B, gold annotations for phase A, i.e. tuples <OTE, aspect>, have to be annotated with polarities (slot 3 of the challenge).

---

[1] https://foursquare.com/

[2] Countries with most of English comments include US, UK, Australia, Canada, Indonesia, Malaysia, Philippines, India, Thailand

[3] http://www.europe.naverlabs.com/Research/Natural-Language-Processing/Aspect-Based-Sentiment-Analysis-Dataset

Thus, we evaluate separately the OTE detection, aspect detection and finally, we evaluate the polarity of opinion detection on the ground truth of phase A. The advantage of this evaluation procedure is of course to assess the quality of the systems on each of the different subtasks involved in the full ABSA system. However, these measures do not reflect the overall results such systems would obtain on the full chain of annotations starting from raw data, in end-to-end application settings. Therefore, we also propose to evaluate the results obtained with the complete annotation chain, i.e. computing F1-measure on the triplets <OTE, Aspect, Polarity>. In addition, we compute the F1-measure on the pairs <Aspect, Polarity> at sentence level. This last measure can be useful to assess ABSA general Aspect-Polarity performance since many ABSA applications may not require the OTE step. In what follows, we refer to these measures as slot1,3 and slot1,2,3 to make connection with the challenge tasks.

5 Baseline ABSA Systems

In our experiments, we use several baseline systems. Each of the systems consists in the following pipeline of different components: 1. Opinionated domain term extraction (OTE); 2. aspect categorization, for opinionated term (OT), and whole sentence level; final aspect is predicted as a combination of both; 3. polarity classification of each aspect identified in the previous step. The difference between baselines lies in the implementation of each component of the pipeline, and the level of external resources involved.

5.1 Baseline-1

The first system is resource-rich system relying on available syntactic and semantic parser, and domain-specific semantic lexicons. It is based on composite models combining sophisticated linguistic features with machine learning algorithms. The linguistic features are extracted via a NLP pipeline (based on in-house parser) comprising lexical semantic information, POS tagging, syntactic parsing and a partial semantic parsing that outputs semantic relations between polarity predicates and their opinionated targets (OTE). These linguistic features are then used by classifiers to perform each step of the pipeline.

The OTE detection is performed with Conditional Random Fields (implemented with CRF++[4] toolkit), trained with some standard features (POS, lemma, presence of upper-case letters, features combining syntactic/semantic dependencies with semantic lexicons, embedding-based features).

Aspect and polarity classification components rely on the same features as for OTE, excluding embedding-based features, but extended with bi-grams features. In addition, polarity classifier feature representation is extended with entity and attribute of aspect category (e.g. RESTAURANT#PRICES results in two additional features: *(restaurant, prices)*). Classification is performed with CoreNLP (Manning et al., 2014) implementation of Maximum Entropy.

5.2 Baseline-2

The second baseline system (*baseline-2*) replaces each component of the previous pipeline with neural network classifiers. Aspect classification and polarity classification components are based on multiple filters CNNs as in (Ruder et al., 2016). OTE component is based on Bidirectional GRU architecture (similar to (Jebbara and Cimiano, 2016)). All the components are implemented with the keras (Chollet et al., 2015) library.

Since the size of the training data is relatively small, we attempt to enrich an input with prior knowledge to help the system to generalize better. In order to do so, we enrich word representation with semantic lexicon features[5], which are encoded as one-hot vector of dimension 100 and concatenated with word embedding. These new word representations are fed to the same pipeline as *baseline-2*. We'll refer to this system as *baseline-2'*.

Both *baseline-2* and *baseline-2'* are initialised with pre-trained word embeddings.

5.3 Baseline Results

Common ressources between all baselines are pre-trained word embeddings and semantic lexicon. We use word2vec (Mikolov et al., 2013) 300-dimensional Google News word embeddings, on which some"noise" filtering has been performed. Semantic lexicon was created semi-automatically using existing polarity lexicons and capitalizing on the annotated vocabulary present in the SemEval

---

[4]https://taku910.github.io/crfpp/

[5]This is close to the idea of *sentic features* (Jebbara and Cimiano, 2016), integrating aspect categories and polarities, rather than *sentics*.

Model	Foursquare				
	s2	s1	s3	s1,3	s1,2,3
baseline-1	68.9	63.8	88.7	56.9	33.6
baseline-2	47.9	62.9	86.0	52.5	9.1
baseline-2'	47.7	62.7	86.1	52.6	8.8
	Semeval				
baseline-1	75.3	70.4	87.3	63.0	37.1
baseline-2	61.1	69.9	80.2	54.9	12.0
baseline-2'	61.0	68.8	78.7	53.8	11.8

Table 2: Performance of various baseline systems. s1: Aspect Category detection (F1), s2: Opinion Target Expression (F1), s3: Sentiment Polarity (Accuracy). s1,3: Aspect,Polarity (F1), s1,2,3: Aspect,OTE,Polarity (F1).

ABSA datasets. It contains ~1000 words with aspect categories and/or polarities associated to each word.

Results for all the baselines are summarized in the table 2. Note, that for *baseline-2,2'*, we report an average performance after executing the whole pipeline 10 times.

First, we observe an important performance drop in aspect prediction (tasks s2, s1) for the new Foursquare dataset for both baselines. This is of course related to the fact that this dataset is different from the one the training has been performed on. Thus, the aspects may not be expressed in the same way, style of the reviews are different[6]. However, for polarity prediction we observe better results on Foursquare dataset than on Semeval dataset. It can be explained by shorter length of Foursquare comments, resulting in less aspect mentions per sentence (rarely more that one opinionated term per sentence), and thus less ambiguity in polarity prediction.

The second observation is a pretty low overall pipeline performance (s1,3 and s1,2,3). Although our *baseline-1* has pretty good performances on each individual task (best, or close to best official SemEval2016 results) when putting all together, it results in 63.0 F1-score on aspect-polarity tuples. The performance on <OTE, Aspect, Polarity> tuples drops down to F1 of 37.1. This evaluation procedure allows us to get an idea on what would be "real-world" system performance, and also indicates the capacities and limitations of the system.

Finally, we note that *baseline-1* ("ressource rich" baseline) has the best performances from all the baselines we explored (as expected). The performances of *baseline-2* and *baseline-2'* are pretty close on the Semeval dataset, but *baseline-2* seems to perform slightly better.

6 Exploring Additional Ressources for Adaptation

One of the natural resources to explore for system adaptation is a set non-annotated reviews. In our case, we exploit all Foursquare reviews in English we have access to.

6.1 Domain Specific Embeddings

First, we learn domain dependent words embeddings (300-dimensional) on the Foursquare restaurant data using Gensim (Řehůřek and Sojka, 2010) implementation of word2vec. We filtered out the words occurring less than 5 times, and used a context window of 10 words, which resulted in 60K word embeddings.

6.2 Weakly Supervised Lexical Acquisition

Among other components, our system relies on semantic lexical ressources encoding domain aspect and polarity vocabulary, that were developed semi-automatically, based on SemEval2016 training datasets. In order to enrich these lexicons, we have adapted a semantic clustering method described in (Pelevina et al., 2016)[7]. The core idea of this approach is to induce a sense inventory from existing word embeddings via clustering of ego-networks of related words. An ego network consists of a single node (ego) together with the nodes they are connected to and the edges between the connected nodes. Words referring to the same sense tend to have a large number of connections, and to be clustered together. The clustering is done with the Chinese Whispers algorithm (Biemann, 2006).

In the case of the present experiments, we initialize the algorithm with a set of seed words together with their semantic aspect (e.g *cider:drink*, *tikka:food*), in order to obtain clusters of aspect words. We used 60 seed words randomly selected from our existing semantic lexicon and learned clusters from Foursquare embeddings. Table 4

---

[6]a lot of emojis are used in Foursquare dataset, but not in Semeval dataset

[7]This method was initially experimented for word sense disambiguation, but we directly adapted it for domain aspect lexicon creation

Model	Foursquare					Semeval				
	s2	s1	s3	s1,3	s1,2,3	s2	s1	s3	s1,3	s1,2,3
baseline-1										
baseline-1	68.9	63.8	88.7	56.9	33.6	75.3	70.4	**87.3**	63.0	37.1
f_lex	**69.2**	64.1	**88.8**	57.1	33.8	**76.4**	70.4	86.6	**63.5**	**38.1**
f_emb	66.7	63.8	88.7	**57.3**	**34.1**	75.3	70.5	87.1	63.4	37.4
f_lex + f_emb	67.1	**64.3**	**88.8**	57.3	33.9	75.8	**70.7**	86.6	**63.5**	37.7
baseline-2										
baseline-2	47.9	62.9	86.0	52.5	9.1	61.1	69.9	80.2	54.9	**12.0**
f_emb	**54.5**	**66.4**	**87.1**	**56.7**	9.1	**61.7**	69.7	**80.6**	54.7	11.3
baseline-2'										
baseline-2'	47.7	62.7	86.1	52.5	8.8	61.1	68.8	78.7	53.8	**11.8**
f_lex	47.7	62.4	86.1	52.6	8.7	61.0	68.9	78.7	53.9	11.4
f_emb	**53.8**	**65.9**	**86.7**	**56.2**	**9.2**	**62.4**	**70.0**	**80.5**	**55.8**	11.4
f_lex + f_emb	**53.8**	65.8	**86.7**	**56.2**	**9.2**	**62.4**	69.9	**80.5**	**55.8**	11.4

Table 3: Experimental results with foursquare embeddings and automatically acquired lexicon

Seed:Aspect	Aspect Cluster
kimchi:food	kimchee, bulgogi, galbi, bibimbap, jigae, chigae, ...
waiter:service	waitress, server, hostess, nikki, melissa, kyle, kelly, ...
expensive:price	over-priced, pricey, costly pricy, cheap, spendy, ...

Table 4: Clusters learnt on Foursquare embeddings

gives some cluster examples. It's interesting to observe that we obtain a cluster of first names, often used to mention a waiter in Foursquare data, with semantic class *service*.

We use these clusters of aspect words by concatenating them to the existing lexicon of the system.

6.3 Experimental Results

We've performed following series of experiments (summarized in table 3): 1. *f_lex*: foursquare lexicon extending existing lexicon (for systems using lexicons); 2. *f_emb*: all baselines with foursquare embeddings replacing generic embeddings (GoogleNews-based) 3. *f_lex +f_emb*: combination of the previous two. We observe light improvements for *baseline-1* which are especially due to lexicon enrichment experiments. We think that Foursquare embeddings didn't bring expected improvements for *baseline-1* (embeddings are used only for OTE/s2 task, which in it's turn impacts s1 task), mostly because these embeddings are much smaller and we lose some non domain-specific knowledge when they replace GoogleNews embeddings.

The impact of embedding is opposite for *baseline-2* experiments. Foursquare pretrained embeddings bring important gains on Foursquare dataset thus moving *baseline-2* system above *baseline-1* for s1 evaluation. It also improves (although less) system performance on Semeval dataset. Automatically acquired lexicon on *baseline-2* systems seems to be very low. We plan to explore other ways to integrate this knowledge into deep learning framework.

7 Conclusion

In this work, we release a new ABSA dataset, in order to better assess state-of-the-art systems robustness; we also evaluate a full ABSA chain of various systems, to reflect end-to-end performances. We show that even for the systems with good performances on individual ABSA subtasks, an overall aspect/polarity F1 score drops down to 63.0. Evaluation of various baselines on the new dataset have shown that standard ABSA systems may suffer a significant decrease in performance, especially for aspect detection. We've experimented with light adaptation methods integrating in-domain embeddings and automatically acquired lexicons, and showed their impact on different systems. Both the new Foursquare ABSA dataset and the evaluation script of the full pipeline are distributed with the paper.

References

Chris Biemann. 2006. Chinese whispers: An efficient graph clustering algorithm and its application to natural language processing problems. In *Proceedings of the First Workshop on Graph Based Methods for Natural Language Processing*, TextGraphs-1, pages 73–80, Stroudsburg, PA, USA. Association for Computational Linguistics.

François Chollet et al. 2015. Keras. `https://keras.io`.

Miguel Ángel García Cumbreras, Julio Villena-Román, Eugenio Martínez Cámara, Manuel Carlos Díaz-Galiano, Maria Teresa Martín-Valdivia, and Luis Alfonso Ureña López. 2016. Overview of TASS 2016. In *Proceedings of TASS 2016: Workshop on Sentiment Analysis at SEPLN co-located with 32nd SEPLN Conference (SEPLN 2016), Salamanca, Spain, September 13th, 2016.*, pages 13–21.

G. Ganu, N. Elhadad, and A. Marian. 2009. Beyond the stars: Improving rating predictions using review text content. In *Proceedings of the 12th International Workshop on the Web and Databases*, Providence, Rhode Island.

Hussam Hamdan, Patrice Bellot, and Frederic Bechet. 2015. Lsislif: Crf and logistic regression for opinion target extraction and sentiment polarity analysis. In *Proceedings of the 9th International Workshop on Semantic Evaluation (SemEval 2015)*, pages 753–758, Denver, Colorado. Association for Computational Linguistics.

Soufian Jebbara and Philipp Cimiano. 2016. Aspect-Based Sentiment Analysis Using a Two-Step Neural Network Architecture. In *Semantic Web Challenges. Third SemWebEval Challenge at ESWC 2016. Revised Selected Papers*, volume 641, pages 153–170. Springer.

Svetlana Kiritchenko, Xiaodan Zhu, Colin Cherry, and Saif Mohammad. 2014. Nrc-canada-2014: Detecting aspects and sentiment in customer reviews. In *Proceedings of the 8th International Workshop on Semantic Evaluation (SemEval 2014)*, pages 437–442, Dublin, Ireland. Association for Computational Linguistics and Dublin City University.

Ayush Kumar, Sarah Kohail, Amit Kumar, Asif Ekbal, and Chris Biemann. 2016. Iit-tuda at semeval-2016 task 5: Beyond sentiment lexicon: Combining domain dependency and distributional semantics features for aspect based sentiment analysis. In *Proceedings of the 10th International Workshop on Semantic Evaluation (SemEval-2016)*, pages 1129–1135, San Diego, California. Association for Computational Linguistics.

Christopher D. Manning, Mihai Surdeanu, John Bauer, Jenny Finkel, Steven J. Bethard, and David McClosky. 2014. The Stanford CoreNLP natural language processing toolkit. In *Association for Computational Linguistics (ACL) System Demonstrations*, pages 55–60.

Tomas Mikolov, Ilya Sutskever, Kai Chen, Greg Corrado, and Jeffrey Dean. 2013. Distributed representations of words and phrases and their compositionality. In *Proceedings of the 26th International Conference on Neural Information Processing Systems - Volume 2*, NIPS'13, pages 3111–3119.

Maria Pelevina, Nikolay Arefyev, Chris Biemann, and Alexander Panchenko. 2016. Making sense of word embeddings. In *Proceedings of the 1st Workshop on Representation Learning for NLP*, pages 174–183.

Maria Pontiki, Dimitrios Galanis, Haris Papageorgiou, Ion Androutsopoulos, Suresh Manandhar, Mohammad AL-Smadi, Mahmoud Al-Ayyoub, Yanyan Zhao, Bing Qin, Orphée De Clercq, Véronique Hoste, Marianna Apidianaki, Xavier Tannier, Natalia Loukachevitch, Evgeny Kotelnikov, Nuria Bel, Salud María Jiménez-Zafra, and Gülşen Eryiğit. 2016. SemEval-2016 task 5: Aspect based sentiment analysis. In *Proceedings of the 10th International Workshop on Semantic Evaluation*, SemEval '16, San Diego, California. Association for Computational Linguistics.

Maria Pontiki, Dimitris Galanis, Haris Papageorgiou, Suresh Manandhar, and Ion Androutsopoulos. 2015. Semeval-2015 task 12: Aspect based sentiment analysis. In *Proceedings of the 9th International Workshop on Semantic Evaluation (SemEval 2015)*, pages 486–495, Denver, Colorado. Association for Computational Linguistics.

Maria Pontiki, Dimitris Galanis, John Pavlopoulos, Harris Papageorgiou, Ion Androutsopoulos, and Suresh Manandhar. 2014. Semeval-2014 task 4: Aspect based sentiment analysis. In *Proceedings of the 8th International Workshop on Semantic Evaluation (SemEval 2014)*, pages 27–35, Dublin, Ireland. Association for Computational Linguistics and Dublin City University.

Radim Řehůřek and Petr Sojka. 2010. Software Framework for Topic Modelling with Large Corpora. In *Proceedings of the LREC 2010 Workshop on New Challenges for NLP Frameworks*, pages 45–50, Valletta, Malta. ELRA. `http://is.muni.cz/publication/884893/en`.

S. Ruder, P. Ghaffari, and J. G. Breslin. 2016. INSIGHT-1 at SemEval-2016 Task 5: Deep Learning for Multilingual Aspect-based Sentiment Analysis. *ArXiv e-prints*.

Pontus Stenetorp, Sampo Pyysalo, Goran Topi, Tomoko Ohta, and Sophia Ananiadou. 2012. Brat: a web-based tool for nlp-assisted text annotation. In *Proceedings of the Association for Computational Linguistics (ACL)*, pages 102–107.

Zhiqiang Toh and Wenting Wang. 2014. Dlirec: Aspect term extraction and term polarity classification system. In *Proceedings of the 8th International Workshop on Semantic Evaluation (SemEval 2014)*, pages 235–240, Dublin, Ireland. Association for Computational Linguistics and Dublin City University.

Julio Villena-Román, Janine García-Morera, Miguel Ángel García Cumbreras, Eugenio Martínez-Cámara, Maria Teresa Martín-Valdivia, and Luis Alfonso Ureña López. 2015a. Overview of TASS 2015. In *Proceedings of TASS 2015: Workshop on Sentiment Analysis at SEPLN co-located with 31st SEPLN Conference (SEPLN 2015), Alicante, Spain, September 15, 2015.*, pages 13–21.

Julio Villena-Román, Eugenio Martínez-Cámara, Janine García-Morera, and Salud M. Jiménez Zafra. 2015b. TASS 2014 - the challenge of aspect-based sentiment analysis. *Procesamiento del Lenguaje Natural*, 54:61–68.

Joachim Wagner, Piyush Arora, Santiago Cortes, Utsab Barman, Dasha Bogdanova, Jennifer Foster, and Lamia Tounsi. 2014. Dcu: Aspect-based polarity classification for semeval task 4. In *Proceedings of the 8th International Workshop on Semantic Evaluation (SemEval 2014)*, pages 392–397, Dublin, Ireland. Association for Computational Linguistics and Dublin City University.

Michael Wojatzki, Eugen Ruppert, Sarah Holschneider, Torsten Zesch, and Chris Biemann. 2017. GermEval 2017: Shared Task on Aspect-based Sentiment in Social Media Customer Feedback. In *Proceedings of the GermEval 2017 Shared Task on Aspect-based Sentiment in Social Media Customer Feedback*, pages 1–12, Berlin, Germany.

The Role of Emotions in Native Language Identification

Ilia Markov[1], Vivi Nastase[2], Carlo Strapparava[3], Grigori Sidorov[4]

[1]INRIA, Paris, France
[2]University of Heidelberg, Heidelberg, Germany
[3]Fondazione Bruno Kessler, Trento, Italy
[4]Instituto Politécnico Nacional, Center for Computing Research, Mexico City, Mexico
`ilia.markov@inria.fr, nastase@cl.uni-heidelberg.de,`
`strappa@fbk.eu, sidorov@cic.ipn.mx`

Abstract

We explore the hypothesis that emotion is one of the dimensions of language that surfaces from the native language into a second language. To check the role of emotions in native language identification (NLI), we model emotion information through polarity and emotion load features, and use document representations using these features to classify the native language of the author. The results indicate that emotion is relevant for NLI, even for high proficiency levels and across topics.

1 Introduction

Native Language Identification (NLI) is the task of identifying the native language (L1) of a person based on his/her writing in the second language (L2). NLI can inform security, marketing and educational applications by tuning pedagogical materials to L1s, and for this it is important to understand the phenomena that get transferred from L1 to L2 (native language interference). Emotion is one of these. Linguistics research (Dewaele, 2010) has focused on the way emotions are encoded in different text types and in different languages. How to express emotion appropriately is related to the origin of the speaker (country, region), situational context in which social norms might be different (formal vs. informal setting), interlocutors (age, gender, social distance), topic.

As emotions are psychological constructions of cultural meaning, there may be a misfit between emotions and social context when individuals change cultural contexts or live two cultural models (Leersnyder et al., 2011). The use of emotions is considered both culture- and language-specific (Wierzbicka, 1994, 1999). We hypothesize that this leads to different emotion signals in writings in a second language, by authors with different native languages.

We test this hypothesis through multi-class classification of the L1 of the authors of essays written in L2 in different experimental set-ups that take into account proficiency levels and topics of the written essays. We encode emotion information using polarity and sentiment information from the NRC Word-Emotion Association Lexicon (NRC emotion lexicon) (Mohammad and Turney, 2013), taking into account not only the fine-grained (word-level) emotion information, but also general aspects of the written material (overall high- or low-emotion load). The results show that emotional information contributes to detecting the native language of the speaker.

2 Related Work

Caldwell-Harris (2014) shows that emotion usage depends on the language by focusing on differences in emotion usage in L1 and L2. The author states that there is a correlation between the usage of emotions and proficiency levels and the age a language is acquired.

While emotion-based features have been used in other NLP tasks, such as sentiment analysis (Sidorov et al., 2013), classification of documents into the corresponding emotion category (Wen and Wan, 2014), deception detection (Newman et al., 2003), among others, they are an underexplored area of second language writing.

Torney *et al.* (2012) use psycholinguistic features extracted by the Linguistic Inquiry and Word Count (LIWC) tool (Pennebaker et al., 2007) to identify the first language of an author, where emotion-based features are included as part of the feature vector, e.g., percentage of positive/negative emotion words. The LIWC feature set used in the paper also contains other types of features, e.g., personal concern categories (work, leisure), paralinguistic dimensions (assents, fillers,

Proceedings of the 9th Workshop on Computational Approaches to Subjectivity, Sentiment and Social Media Analysis, pages 123–129
Brussels, Belgium, October 31, 2018. ©2018 Association for Computational Linguistics
https://doi.org/10.18653/v1/P17

nonfluencies), which obscure the contribution of the actual emotion features.

Rangel and Rosso (2013; 2016) investigate and confirm the hypothesis that the use of emotions depends on author's age and gender. The authors used a graph-based approach, where each node and edge were represented by the corresponding part-of-speech (POS) tag, then the representation was enriched with semantic information, emoticons, and with emotion information, which included polarity of words (polarity of common nouns, adjectives, adverbs or verbs in a sentiment lexicon) and emotionally charged words (replacing common nouns, adjectives, adverbs or verbs with the emotion information from the Spanish Emotion Lexicon (Sidorov et al., 2013)). The representation combining all the features described above was used with a SVM classifier.

Rangel and Rosso (2013; 2016) suggest that there are commonalities in the use of emotions across author age and gender. We examine the hypothesis that there are commonalities in the use of emotions in L2 across different L1s, suggested by the linguistic and psycholinguistic studies (Leersnyder et al., 2011; Wierzbicka, 1999). We test this by evaluating the impact of emotion-based features on classifying the L1 of the authors of essays written in L2.

3 Emotion features for NLI

The best performing features for NLI are word and character n-grams (Jarvis et al., 2013). They cover – and obscure – a wide range of phenomena, because language usage has multiple dimensions that can reveal information such as age, gender, cultural influences. In this study, we investigate the impact of words that have an emotion signal, since studies have shown that emotion is culture specific (Wierzbicka, 1994, 1999), and thus could be indicative of the native language of a speaker.

3.1 Datasets

We conduct experiments on two datasets commonly used in NLI research:

TOEFL11 (Blanchard et al., 2013): the ETS Corpus of Non-Native Written English (TOEFL11) contains 1,100 essays in English (avg. 348 tokens/essay) for each of the 11 L1s: Arabic (ARA), Chinese (CHI), French (FRE), German (GER), Hindi (HIN), Italian (ITA), Japanese (JPN), Korean (KOR), Spanish (SPA), Telugu (TEL), and Turkish (TUR). The essays were written in response to eight different writing prompts, all of which appear in all 11 L1 groups. The dataset contains information regarding the proficiency level (low, medium, high) of the authors.

ICLE (Granger et al., 2009): the ICLEv2 dataset consists of essays written by highly-proficient non-native college-level students of English. We used a 7-language subset of the corpus normalized for topic and character encoding (Tetreault et al., 2012; Ionescu et al., 2014) to which we refer as ICLE. This subset contains 110 essays (avg. 747 tokens/essay after tokenization and removal of metadata) for each of the 7 languages: Bulgarian (BUL), Chinese (CHI), Czech (CZE), French (FRE), Japanese (JPN), Russian (RUS), and Spanish (SPA).

3.2 Experiment setup

We used the (pre-)tokenized version of TOEFL11 and tokenized ICLE with the Natural Language Toolkit (NLTK)[1] tokenizer. ICLE metadata was removed in pre-processing. Each essay was represented through the sets of features described below, using term frequency (tf) and the liblinear scikit-learn (Pedregosa et al., 2011) implementation of Support Vector Machines (SVM) with OvR (one vs. the rest) multi-class strategy. We report classification accuracy on 10-fold cross-validation experiments.

3.3 Features

3.3.1 Part-of-speech tags and function words

POS tag n-grams and function words (FWs) are considered core features in NLI research (Malmasi and Dras, 2015), not susceptible to topic bias, unlike word and character n-grams (Brooke and Hirst, 2011).

POS n-grams, n=1..3 POS features capture the morpho-syntactic patterns in a text, and are indicative of the L1, especially when used in combination with other types of features (Cimino and Dell'Orletta, 2017; Markov et al., 2017). POS tags were obtained with TreeTagger (Schmid, 1999), which uses the Penn Treebank tagset (36 tags).

Function words (FWs) n-grams, n=1..3 Function words clarify the relationships between the content-carrying elements of a sentence, and introduce syntactic structures like verbal complements,

---

[1]http://www.nltk.org

relative clauses, and questions (Smith and Witten, 1993). They are considered one of the most important stylometric features (Kestemont, 2014). The FW feature set consists of 318 English FWs from the scikit-learn package (Pedregosa et al., 2011). With respect to emotion features, FWs can appear as quantifiers, intensifiers (e.g., very good) or modify the emotion expressed in other ways.

3.3.2 Emotion words

We use the 14,182 emotion words and their associations with eight emotions (anger, fear, anticipation, trust, surprise, sadness, joy, and disgust) and two sentiments (negative and positive) from the NRC emotion lexicon (Mohammad and Turney, 2013). Table 1 presents the emotion words statistics for our data.

	TOEFL11			ICLE			
L1	No.	L1	%	L1	No.	L1	%
HIN	96,184	KOR	24.93	CZE	20,162	CHI	26.81
TEL	88,979	HIN	24.62	RUS	20,142	BUL	25.06
GER	88,268	CHI	24.32	BUL	18,939	JPN	24.74
CHI	87,486	TEL	24.19	SPA	17,187	RUS	24.72
TUR	83,945	JPN	24.15	CHI	16,794	FRE	23.88
KOR	82,878	TUR	23.90	FRE	16,750	CZE	23.81
FRE	82,454	FRE	23.30	JPN	16,234	SPA	23.33
SPA	81,497	GER	23.21				
ITA	75,339	ITA	23.16				
JPN	73,740	SPA	22.40				
ARA	69,156	ARA	21.91				

Table 1: Emotion words statistics (absolute number and frequency) sorted from the highest to the lowest.

Before committing to analyzing emotion features, we want to test whether emotion-loaded words have any impact on the NLI task. The bag-of-words (BoW) representation covers a variety of phenomena, without distinguishing them and giving us insight into their individual impact on the task. We represent our data using BoW variations – including and excluding words that have an emotional dimension. To verify that the effect in classification is not just due to a smaller feature set, we match the BoW size by removing a selection of random words. Table 2 presents the 10-fold cross-validation results (accuracy, %) on the TOEFL11 and ICLE datasets, when using emotion words and random words of such that the BoW representations have the same size, as well as the results when excluding emotion words and the random words.[2]

The results in Table 2 show that emotion words have higher impact on classification accuracy than random words when evaluated in isolation. Moreover, the accuracy drop is higher when excluding

<hr>

^[2]Random words accuracy was calculated as average over five experiments with five different sets of random words.

Features	TOEFL11		ICLE	
	Acc., %	No.	Acc., %	No.
BoW	68.65	61,339	80.65	20,032
Random words	36.15	8,187	70.21	6,465
Emotion words	46.75	8,187	72.86	6,465
BoW w/o random words	66.68	53,152	76.83	13,567
BoW w/o emotion words	63.11	53,152	75.19	13,567

Table 2: Performance of emotion words.

emotion words from the BoW approach than when excluding random words, confirming that emotion is a useful dimension for L1 classification, and not just an effect of having additional features.

3.3.3 Emotion features

Having confirmed that due to cultural identity and linguistic habits of an author's native language, we can distinguish the L1 of the author of an essay, we proceed with a deeper analysis, for which we build two types of emotion features.

Emotion polarity features (*emoP*) In the NRC emotion lexicon, binary associations are provided for each emotion word for 8 emotions (anger, fear, anticipation, trust, surprise, sadness, joy, or disgust) and two sentiments (negative or positive) – e.g., *good* = "0100101011". This representation is used as a categorial feature (not a 10-dimensional binary vector). It performed best compared to other ways of encoding the emotion information we tried, e.g., using a 10-dimensional binary vector or excluding the sentiment information.

The *emoP* features are added to the POS and to POS & FW representations: the phrase *This is very good* is represented through POS & emoP unigrams as 'DT', 'VBZ', 'RB', 'JJ-0100101011', or as 3-grams 'DT_VBZ_RB', VBZ_RB_JJ-0100101011', and as POS & FW & emoP 3-grams as 'This_is_very', 'is_very_JJ-0100101011'.

Emotion load features (*emoL*) Speakers of different L1s may use a higher or lower number of emotionally charged words than speakers of other L1s, reflecting cultural customs or linguistic habits of the respective cultures. We modeled this information using three types of emotion load features: (i) two binary features, *emoL* (binary) that capture whether an essay has a high or low emotional load: (a) we compute the average ratio of emotion words in all essays in each dataset: for TOEFL11 this was 0.236 and for ICLE 0.246; (b) if the ratio of emotion words in an essay was higher/lower than the average, assigned it a "highly-emotional"/"low-emotional" feature. We used this representation to examine whether the polarity as such is informative. We also used more fine-grained *emoL* features: (ii) the ratio of the emotion words in each essay as a numeric feature (1 feature, *emoL* (1)), and (iii) the ratio of each emotion/sentiment in each essay (10 numeric features: 8 emotions and 2 sentiments, *emoL* (10)). Overall, three different types of *emoL* features are examined.

4   Results and Discussion

Following previous studies on NLI (Markov et al., 2018) and author profiling (Rangel and Rosso, 2016), we provide the results when adding emotion-based features to POS tag feature set. We also experiment with POS and FW feature sets similarly to, e.g., (Malmasi and Dras, 2015).

The 10-fold cross-validation results in terms of accuracy (%) on the TOEFL11 and ICLE datasets for POS and POS & FW n-gram (n = 1–3) representations are shown in Tables 3 and 4, respectively. The number of features (No.) is included. Statistically significant gains/drops according to McNemar's statistical significance test (McNemar, 1947) with $\alpha < 0.05$ are marked with '*'.

The experimental results show that emotion features, in particular the *emoP* features, significantly contribute to the results for all the considered settings, indicating that different cultures (as defined by the authors' L1) have different emotion word usage. It is very interesting to note that despite being very general, the three types of *emoL* features – 13 features that characterize the emotional load of a document – also improve the results in the majority of settings, including when combined with the *emoP* features. This supports the hypothesis that some cultures use a bigger or smaller emotional vocabulary. More fine grained emotional load features could improve the results further.

To explore whether emotion usage depends on specific topics, we conducted experiments for the topics in the TOEFL11 dataset (Table 5).[3] The improvement brought by the emotion-based features does seem to depend on the topic, as some topics more naturally elicit emotional reactions. The highest improvements were achieved for P5 (car usage) and P7 (young vs. old people comparison). When combined with the POS & FW representation, emotion-based features are less helpful (not

___

[3]We did not conduct this experiment on the ICLE dataset, since it has a higher number of topics, with a fewer number of documents per topic, which would not allow us to learn informative topic-specific models.

statistically significant improvements) for the topics discussing traveling (P1), ideas vs. facts (P3), and education (P4). Overall, adding emotion-based features to POS and POS & FW representations leads to accuracy improvement for all the topics present in the dataset.

The ability to choose the proper words to express oneself increases with the proficiency level. From this perspective, identifying the L1 of authors of essays in L2 using emotion words information should be performed with better results. On the other hand, we expect other linguistic characteristics to become closer to a native L2 speaker, and thus make identifying L1 harder. We experiment with L1 classification separating the data based on the three different proficiency levels in TOEFL11. The results are included in Table 6. With respect to the emotion features, medium and high proficiency levels have a much better performance. As postulated above, this could be explained by the different ability of the L1 speakers to choose the words that express closely the message and nuances they wish to convey.

5   Conclusions

We investigated the hypothesis that the use of emotions is indicative of an author's native language. We used two types of emotion-based features – one that captures the types of sentiments expressed, the other captures the frequency of emotion words in documents. We expected these features to capture cultural characteristics and linguistic habits from the authors' L1. The fact that adding these features to POS and function word n-grams leads to improvements in predicting a text's author's native language leads us to conclude that emotion characteristics from a native language are "imported" into the production of L2.

The overall goal of this paper was to understand the influence of various facets of L1 speakers' language and culture on their acquisition (and production) of L2. These influences from L1 are not under the author's conscious control, and it is very interesting to understand their nature. Emotion is one of these. The fact that we explore the use of emotions on learner corpora ("controlled environment"), with a specific task and specific requirement – and a (implied, not specifically requested) more neutral style – should probably lower the effect of emotional influences from the L1 and its culture. From that point of view, it is even more remarkable that such an effect is detected.

Features	TOEFL11		ICLE	
	Acc., %	**No.**	**Acc., %**	**No.**
POS 1–3-grams (baseline)	40.16	17,483	62.86	11,755
POS 1–3-grams + emoL (binary)	40.60	17,485	62.86	11,757
POS 1–3-grams + emoL (1)	40.19	17,484	62.86	11,756
POS 1–3-grams + emoL (10)	40.41	17,493	62.99	17,765
POS 1–3-grams + emoL (binary) + emoL (1) + emoL (10)	40.65	17,496	62.60	11,768
Difference:	**0.49***		**−0.26**	
POS 1–3-grams + emoP	50.36	216,090	67.66	90,920
Difference:	**10.20***		**4.80***	
POS 1–3-grams + emotion-based features	50.28	216,103	67.79	90,933
Difference (with POS 1–3 + emoP):	**−0.08**		**0.13**	
Difference (with baseline):	**10.12***		**4.93***	

Table 3: 10-fold cross-validation accuracy for POS 1–3-grams combined with emotion-based features. '*' marks statistically significant differences.

Features	TOEFL11		ICLE	
	Acc., %	**No.**	**Acc., %**	**No.**
POS 1–3-grams	40.16	17,483	62.86	11,755
POS & FW 1–3-grams (baseline)	64.06	411,599	74.42	138,170
Difference:	**23.90***		**11.56***	
POS & FW 1–3-grams + emoL (binary)	64.10	411,601	74.42	138,172
POS & FW 1–3-grams + emoL (1)	64.10	411,600	74.42	138,171
POS & FW 1–3-grams + emoL (10)	64.09	411,609	74.42	138,180
POS & FW 1–3-grams + emoL (binary) + emoL (1) + emoL (10)	64.13	411,612	74.42	138,183
Difference:	**0.07**		**0.00**	
POS & FW 1–3-grams + emoP	67.73	880,595	77.92	268,605
Difference:	**3.67***		**3.50***	
POS & FW 1–3-grams + emotion-based features	67.85	880,608	78.31	268,618
Difference (with POS & FW 1–3 + emoP):	**0.12**		**0.39**	
Difference (with baseline):	**3.79***		**3.89***	

Table 4: 10-fold cross-validation accuracy for POS & FW 1–3-grams combined with emotion-based features. '*' marks statistically significant differences.

	P0	P1	P2	P3	P4	P5	P6	P7
POS 1–3-grams	33.74	39.26	38.54	39.89	42.40	38.29	42.08	38.15
POS 1–3-grams + emotion-based features	41.14	47.34	44.79	46.02	49.12	49.55	49.01	47.19
Difference:	**7.40***	**8.08***	**6.25***	**6.13***	**6.72***	**11.26***	**6.93***	**9.04***
POS & FW 1–3-grams	50.54	56.54	53.28	55.62	60.34	56.84	57.79	55.31
POS & FW 1–3-grams + emotion-based features	53.18	57.66	56.56	57.04	62.28	62.40	61.46	58.66
Difference:	**2.64***	**1.12**	**3.28***	**1.42**	**1.94**	**5.56***	**3.67***	**3.35***
No. of emotion words:	99,606	75,308	116,795	118,427	122,741	129,837	107,924	139,288
Ratio:	0.213	0.239	0.222	0.226	0.238	0.239	0.243	0.274

Table 5: 10-fold cross-validation accuracy for each topic in the TOEFL11 dataset. '*' marks statistically significant differences.

	Low		Medium		High	
	Acc., %	No.	Acc., %	No.	Acc., %	No.
POS 1–3-grams	41.10	9,751	43.07	15,334	34.65	14,454
POS 1–3-grams + emotion-based features	44.56	51,108	52.64	152,059	42.58	136,783
Difference:	**3.46***		**9.57***	L	**7.93***	
POS & FW 1–3-grams	52.40	91,340	66.52	288,658	54.25	242,880
POS & FW 1–3-grams + emotion-based features	54.13	155,725	69.09	585,083	57.20	491,342
Difference:	**1.73**		**2.57***		**2.95***	
No. of emotion words:	62,223		475,665		372,025	
Ratio:	0.228		0.235		0.242	

Table 6: 10-fold cross-validation accuracy for each proficiency level. '*' marks statistically significant differences.

References

Daniel Blanchard, Joel Tetreault, Derrick Higgins, Aoife Cahill, and Martin Chodorow. 2013. TOEFL11: A corpus of non-native English. *ETS Research Report Series*, 2013(2):i–15.

Julian Brooke and Graeme Hirst. 2011. Native language detection with 'cheap' learner corpora. In *Proceedings of the Conference of Learner Corpus Research*, pages 37–47, Louvain-la-Neuve, Belgium. Presses universitaires de Louvain.

Catherine Caldwell-Harris. 2014. Emotionality differences between a native and foreign language: Theoretical implications. *Frontiers in Psychology*, 5(1055).

Andrea Cimino and Felice Dell'Orletta. 2017. Stacked sentence-document classifier approach for improving native language identification. In *Proceedings of the 12th Workshop on Building Educational Applications Using NLP*, pages 430–437, Copenhagen, Denmark. ACL.

Jean-Marc Dewaele. 2010. *Emotions in Multiple Languages*. Basingstoke: Palgrave Macmillan.

Sylviane Granger, Estelle Dagneaux, Fanny Meunier, and Magali Paquot. 2009. *International Corpus of Learner English v2 (ICLE)*. Presses Universitaires de Louvain, Louvain-la-Neuve, Belgium.

Radu Tudor Ionescu, Marius Popescu, and Aoife Cahill. 2014. Can characters reveal your native language? A language-independent approach to native language identification. In *Proceedings of the 2014 Conference on Empirical Methods in Natural Language Processing*, pages 1363–1373, Doha, Qatar. ACL.

Scott Jarvis, Yves Bestgen, and Steve Pepper. 2013. Maximizing classification accuracy in native language identification. In *Proceedings of the Eighth Workshop on Innovative Use of NLP for Building Educational Applications*, pages 111–118, Atlanta, GA, USA. ACL.

Mike Kestemont. 2014. Function words in authorship attribution. From black magic to theory? In *Proceedings of the 3rd Workshop on Computational Linguistics for Literature*, pages 59–66, Gothenburg, Sweden. ACL.

Jozefien De Leersnyder, Batja Mesquita, and Heejung S. Kim. 2011. Where do my emotions belong? a study of immigrants' emotional acculturation. *Personality and Social Psychology Bulletin*, 37(4):451–463.

Shervin Malmasi and Mark Dras. 2015. Multilingual native language identification. *Natural Language Engineering*, 23(2):163–215.

Ilia Markov, Lingzhen Chen, Carlo Strapparava, and Grigori Sidorov. 2017. CIC-FBK approach to native language identification. In *Proceedings of the 12th Workshop on Building Educational Applications Using NLP*, pages 374–381, Copenhagen, Denmark. ACL.

Ilia Markov, Vivi Nastase, and Carlo Strapparava. 2018. Punctuation as native language interference. In *Proceedings of the 27th International Conference on Computational Linguistics*, pages 3456–3466, Santa Fe, New Mexico, USA. The COLING 2018 Organizing Committee.

Quinn McNemar. 1947. Note on the sampling error of the difference between correlated proportions or percentages. *Psychometrika*, 12(2):153–157.

Saif Mohammad and Peter Turney. 2013. Crowdsourcing a word-emotion association lexicon. *Computational Intelligence*, 29:436–465.

Matthew Newman, James Pennebaker, Diane Berry, and Jane Richards. 2003. Lying words: Predicting deception from linguistic styles. *Personality and Social Psychology Bulletin*, 29(5).

Fabian Pedregosa, Gaël Varoquaux, Alexandre Gramfort, Vincent Michel, Bertrand Thirion, Olivier Grisel, Mathieu Blondel, Peter Prettenhofer, Ron Weiss, Vincent Dubourg, Jake Vanderplas, Alexandre Passos, David Cournapeau, Matthieu Brucher, Matthieu Perrot, and Édouard Duchesnay. 2011. Scikit-learn: Machine learning in Python. *Journal of Machine Learning Research*, 12:2825–2830.

James Pennebaker, Roger Booth, and Martha Francis. 2007. *Linguistic Inquiry and Word Count: LIWC2007*. Austin, TX: LIWC.net.

Francisco Rangel and Paolo Rosso. 2013. On the identification of emotions and authors' gender in Facebook comments on the basis of their writing style. In *Proceedings of the First International Workshop on Emotion and Sentiment in Social and Expressive Media: Approaches and perspectives from AI*, volume 1096, pages 34–46, Torino, Italy. CEUR-WS.org.

Francisco Rangel and Paolo Rosso. 2016. On the impact of emotions on author profiling. *Information Processing & Management*, 52(1):74–92.

Helmut Schmid. 1999. *Improvements In Part-of-Speech Tagging With an Application to German*. Springer.

Grigori Sidorov, Sabino Miranda-Jiménez, Francisco Viveros-Jiménez, Alexander Gelbukh, Noé Castro-Sánchez, Francisco Velásquez, Ismael Díaz-Rangel, Sergio Suárez-Guerra, Alejandro Treviño, and Juan Gordon. 2013. Empirical study of machine learning based approach for opinion mining in tweets. In *Proceedings of the Mexican International Conference on Artificial Intelligence*, volume 7629, pages 1–14, San Luis Potosí. Mexico. Springer.

Tony C. Smith and Ian H. Witten. 1993. Language inference from function words. Working papers, https://hdl.handle.net/10289/9927.

Joel Tetreault, Daniel Blanchard, Aoife Cahill, and Martin Chodorow. 2012. Native tongues, lost and found: Resources and empirical evaluations in native language identification. In *Proceedings of the 24th International Conference on Computational Linguistics*, pages 2585–2602, Mumbai, India. The COLING 2012 Organizing Committee.

Rosemary Torney, Peter Vamplew, and John Yearwood. 2012. Using psycholinguistic features for profiling first language of authors. *Journal of the Association for Information Science and Technology*, 63(6).

Shiyang Wen and Xiaojun Wan. 2014. Emotion classification in microblog texts using class sequential rules. In *Proceedings of the Twenty-Eighth AAAI Conference on Artificial Intelligence*, pages 187–193, Quebec, Canada. AAAI Press.

Anna Wierzbicka. 1994. Emotion, language, and cultural scripts. *Emotion and culture: Empirical studies of mutual influence*, pages 133–196.

Anna Wierzbicka. 1999. *Emotions across languages and cultures: Diversity and universals*. Cambridge University Press.

Self-Attention: A Better Building Block for Sentiment Analysis Neural Network Classifiers

Artaches Ambartsoumian
School of Computing Science
Simon Fraser University
Burnaby, BC, CANADA
aambarts@sfu.ca

Fred Popowich
School of Computing Science
Simon Fraser University
Burnaby, BC, CANADA
popowich@sfu.ca

Abstract

Sentiment Analysis has seen much progress in the past two decades. For the past few years, neural network approaches, primarily RNNs and CNNs, have been the most successful for this task. Recently, a new category of neural networks, self-attention networks (SANs), have been created which utilizes the attention mechanism as the basic building block. Self-attention networks have been shown to be effective for sequence modeling tasks, while having no recurrence or convolutions. In this work we explore the effectiveness of the SANs for sentiment analysis. We demonstrate that SANs are superior in performance to their RNN and CNN counterparts by comparing their classification accuracy on six datasets as well as their model characteristics such as training speed and memory consumption. Finally, we explore the effects of various SAN modifications such as multi-head attention as well as two methods of incorporating sequence position information into SANs.

1 Introduction

Sentiment analysis, also know as opinion mining, deals with determining the opinion classification of a piece of text. Most commonly the classification is whether the writer of a piece of text is expressing a position or negative attitude towards a product or a topic of interest. Having more than two sentiment classes is called fine-grained sentiment analysis with the extra classes representing intensities of positive/negative sentiment (e.g. very-positive) and/or the neutral class. This field has seen much growth for the past two decades, with many applications and multiple classifiers proposed [Mäntylä et al., 2018]. Sentiment analysis has been applied in areas such as social media [Jansen et al., 2009], movie reviews [Pang et al., 2002], commerce [Jansen et al., 2009], and health care [Greaves et al., 2013b] [Greaves et al., 2013a].

In the past few years, neural network approaches have consistently advanced the state-of-the-art technologies for sentiment analysis and other natural language processing (NLP) tasks. For sentiment analysis, the neural network approaches typically use pre-trained word embeddings such as word2vec [Mikolov et al., 2013] or GloVe[Pennington et al., 2014] for input, which get processed by the model to create a sentence representation that is finally used for a softmax classification output layer. The main neural network architectures that have been applied for sentiment analysis are recurrent neural networks(RNNs) [Tai et al., 2015] and convolutional neural networks (CNNs) [Kim, 2014], with RNNs being more popular of the two. For RNNs, typically gated cell variants such as long short-term memory (LSTM) [Hochreiter and Schmidhuber, 1997], Bi-Directional LSTM (BiLSTM) [Schuster and Paliwal, 1997], or gated recurrent unit (GRU) [Cho et al., 2014] are used.

Most recently, Vaswani et al. [Vaswani et al., 2017] introduced the first fully-attentional architecture, called Transformer, which utilizes only the self-attention mechanism and demonstrated its effectiveness on neural machine translation (NMT). The Transformer model achieved state-of-the-art performance on multiple machine translation datasets, without having recurrence or convolution components. Since then, self-attention networks have been successfully applied to a variety of tasks, including: image classification [Parmar et al., 2018], generative adversarial networks [Zhang et al., 2018], automatic speech recognition [Povey et al., 2017], text summarization [Liu et al., 2018], semantic role labeling [Strubell et al., 2018], as well as natural language inference and sentiment analysis [Shen et al., 2018].

In this paper we demonstrate that self-attention is a better building block compared to recurrence or convolutions for sentiment analysis classifiers. We

Proceedings of the 9th Workshop on Computational Approaches to Subjectivity, Sentiment and Social Media Analysis, pages 130–139
Brussels, Belgium, October 31, 2018. ©2018 Association for Computational Linguistics
https://doi.org/10.18653/v1/P17

extend the work of [Barnes et al., 2017] by exploring the behaviour of various self-attention architectures on six different datasets and making direct comparisons to their work. We set our baselines to be their results for *LSTM*, *BiLSTM*, and *CNN* models, and used the same code for dataset preprocessing, word embedding imports, and batch construction. Finally, we explore the effectiveness of SAN architecture variations such as different techniques of incorporating positional information into the network, using multi-head attention, and stacking self-attention layers. Our results suggest that relative position representations is superior to positional encodings, as well as highlight the efficiency of the stacking self-attention layers.

Source code is publicly available[1].

2 Background

The attention mechanism was introduced by [Bahdanau et al., 2014] to improve the RNN encoder-decoder sequence-to-sequence architecture for NMT [Sutskever et al., 2014]. Since then, it has been extensively used to improve various RNN and CNN architectures ([Cheng et al., 2016]; [Kokkinos and Potamianos, 2017]; [Lu et al., 2016]). The attention mechanism has been an especially popular modification for RNN-based architectures due to its ability to improve the modeling of long range dependencies ([Daniluk et al., 2017]; [Zhou et al., 2018]).

2.1 Attention

Originally [Bahdanau et al., 2014] described attention as the process of computing a context vector for the next decoder step that contains the most relevant information from all of the encoder hidden states by performing a weighted average on the encoder hidden states. How much each encoder state contributes to the weighted average is determined by an alignment score between that encoder state and previous hidden state of the decoder.

More generally, we can consider the previous decoder state as the query vector, and the encoder hidden states as key and value vectors. The output is a weighted average of the value vectors, where the weights are determined by the compatibility function between the query and the keys. Note that the keys and values can be different sets of vectors [Vaswani et al., 2017].

<hr>

[1] https://github.com/Artaches/SSAN-self-attention-sentiment-analysis-classification

The above can be summarized by the following equations. Given a query q, values $(v_1, ..., v_n)$, and keys $(k_1, ..., k_n)$ we compute output z:

$$z = \sum_{j=1}^{n} \alpha_j(v_j) \tag{1}$$

$$\alpha_j = \frac{\exp f(k_j, q)}{\sum_{i=1}^{n} \exp f(k_i, q)} \tag{2}$$

α_j is computed using the softmax function where $f(k_i, q)$ is the compatibility score between k_i and q,

For the compatibility function, we will be using using the scaled dot-product function from [Vaswani et al., 2017]:

$$f(k, q) = \frac{(k)(q)^T}{\sqrt{d_k}} \tag{3}$$

where d_k is the dimension of the key vectors. This scaling is done to improve numerical stability as the dimension of keys, values, and queries grows.

2.2 Self-Attention

Self-attention is the process of applying the attention mechanism outlined above to every position of the source sequence. This is done by creating three vectors (query, key, value) for each sequence position, and then applying the attention mechanism for each position x_i, using the x_i query vector and key and value vectors for all other positions. As a result, an input sequence $X = (x_1, x_2, ..., x_n)$ of words is transformed into a sequence $Y = (y_1, y_2, ..., y_n)$ where y_i incorporates the information of x_i as well as how x_i relates to all other positions in X. The (query, key, value) vectors can be created by applying learned linear projections [Vaswani et al., 2017], or using feed-forward layers.

This computation can be done for the entire source sequence in parallel by grouping the queries, keys, and values in Q, K, V matrices[Vaswani et al., 2017].

$$\text{Attention}(Q, K, V) = \text{softmax}(\frac{QK^T}{\sqrt{d_k}})V \tag{4}$$

Furthermore, instead of performing self-attention once for (Q,K,V) of dimension d_{model}, [Vaswani et al., 2017] proposed multi-head attention, which performs attention h times on projected (Q,K,V) matrices of dimension d_{model}/h. For each head, the (Q,K,V) matrices are uniquely projected to dimension d_{model}/h and self-attetnion is performed to yield an output of dimension d_{model}/h. The outputs of each head are then concatenated, and once again a linear projection layer is applied, resulting in an output of same dimensionality as performing self-attention once on the original (Q,K,V) matrices. This process is described by the following formulas:

$$\text{MultiHead}(Q, K, V) =$$
$$\text{Concat}(\text{head}_1, ..., \text{head}_\text{h})W^O \quad (5)$$

where $\text{head}_\text{i} =$
$$\text{Attention}(QW_i^Q, KW_i^K, VW_i^V) \quad (6)$$

Where the projections are parameter matrices $W_i^Q \in R^{d_{\text{model}} \times d_k}$, $W_i^K \in R^{d_{\text{model}} \times d_k}$, $W_i^V \in R^{d_{\text{model}} \times d_v}$ and $W^O \in R^{hd_v \times d_{\text{model}}}$.

2.3 Position Information Techniques

The attention mechanism is completely invariant to sequence ordering, thus self-attention networks need to incorporate positional information. Three main techniques have been proposed to solve this problem: adding sinusoidal positional encodings or learned positional encoding to input embeddings, or using relative positional representations in the self-attention mechanism.

2.3.1 Sinusoidal Position Encoding

This method was proposed by [Vaswani et al., 2017] to be used for the Transformer model. Here, positional encoding (PE) vectors are created using sine and cosine functions of difference frequencies and then are added to the input embeddings. Thus, the input embeddings and positional encodings must have the same dimensionality of d_{model}. The following sine and cosine functions are used:

$$PE_{(pos,2i)} = sin(pos/10000^{2i/d_{\text{model}}})$$
$$PE_{(pos,2i+1)} = cos(pos/10000^{2i/d_{\text{model}}})$$

where pos is the sentence position and i is the dimension. Using this approach, sentences longer than those seen during training can still have positional information added. We will be referring to this method as PE.

2.3.2 Learned Position Encoding

In a similar method, learned vectors of the same dimensionality, that are also unique to each position can be added to the input embeddings instead of sinusoidal position encodings[Gehring et al., 2017]. There are two downsides to this approach. First, this method cannot handle sentences that are longer than the ones in the training set as no vectors are trained for those positions. Second, the further position will likely not get trained as well if the training dataset has more short sentences than longer ones. Vaswani et al. [2017] also reported that these perform identically to the positional encoding approach.

2.3.3 Relative Position Representations

Relative Position Representations (RPR) was introduced by [Shaw et al., 2018] as a replacement of positional encodings for the Transformer. Using this approach, the Transformer was able to perform even better for NMT. Out of the three discussed, we have found this approach to work best and we will be referring to this method as RPR throughout the paper.

For this method, the self-attention mechanism is modified to explicitly learn the relative positional information between every two sequence positions. As a result, the input sequence is modeled as a labeled, directed, fully-connected graph, where the labels represent positional information. A tunable parameter k is also introduced that limits the maximum distance considered between two sequence positions. [Shaw et al., 2018] hypothesized that this will allow the model to generalize to longer sequences at test time.

3 Proposed Architectures

In this work we propose a simple self-attention (SSAN) model and test it in 1 as well as 2 layer stacked configurations. We designed the SSAN architecture to not have any extra components in order to compare specifically the self-attention component to the recurrence and convolution components of LSTM and CNN models. Our goal is to test the effectiveness of the main building blocks. We compare directly the results of two proposed architectures, *1-Layer-SSAN* and *2-Layer-SSAN*, to the LSTM, BiLSTM, and CNN architectures from [Barnes et al., 2017].

SSAN performs self-attention only once, which is identical to 1-head multi-head attention. SSAN

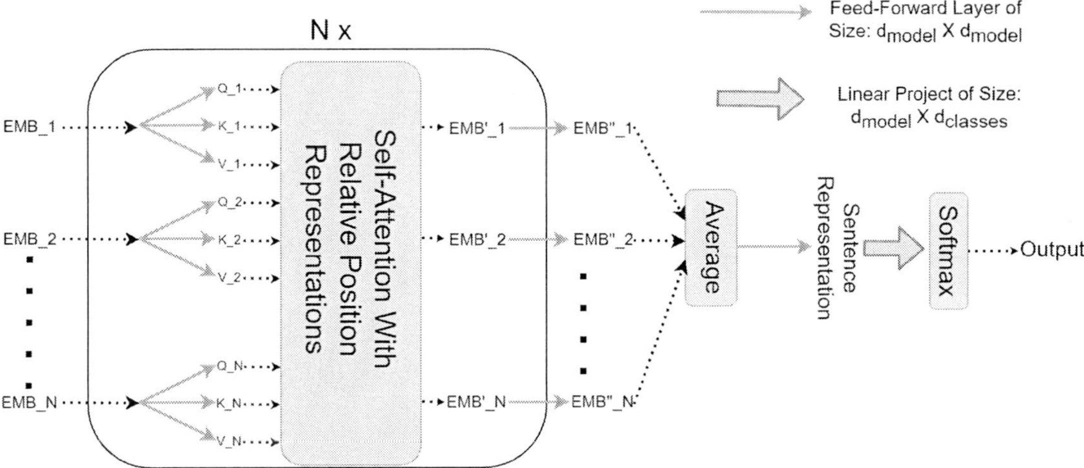

Figure 1: SSAN Model Architecture

takes in input word embeddings and applies 3 feed-forward layers to obtain Q,K,V representations on which self-attention is performed. The output of the self-attention layer is passed through another feed-forward layer. This process is done twice for *2-Layer-SSAN*, using the output of first layer as input for the second. The output of the last self-attention layer is averaged and a feed-forward layer is then applied to create a sentence representation vector of fixed dimension d_{model}. Finally, the sentence representation vector is passed through an output softmax layer that has an output dimension of $d_{classes}$. Dropout [Srivastava et al., 2014] is applied on input word embeddings, output of self-attention layers, on the sentence representation vector. The architecture is visualized in Figure 1. All feed-forward layers use ReLU [Nair and Hinton, 2010] activation functions. For relative positional representation, we set the parameter k=10, which is the maximum relative position considered for each input sequence position.

Finally, we also show results for other, more complex, self-attention architectures that are based on the Transformer. We take a 2 layer Transformer encoder as described by [Vaswani et al., 2017], then just like for SSAN, average the output of the second layer to create a sentence representation and apply a feed-forward layer followed by an output softmax layer. Dropout is applied as described in [Vaswani et al., 2017] as well as on the sentence representation vector.

4 Experiments

To reduce implementation deviations from previous work, we use the codebase from [Barnes et al., 2017] and only replace the model and training process. We re-use the code for batch pre-processing and batch construction for all datasets, accuracy evaluation, as well as use the same word embeddings[2]. All neural network models use cross-entropy for the training loss.

All experiments and benchmarks were run using a single GTX 1080 Ti with an i7 5820k @ 3.3Ghz and 32Gb of RAM. For model implementations: LSTM, BiLSTM, and CNN baselines are implemented in Keras_2.0.8 [Chollet et al., 2015] with Tensorflow_1.7 backend using cuDNN_5.1.5 and CUDA_9.1. All self-attention models are implemented in Tensorflow_1.7 and use the same CUDA libraries.

4.1 Datasets

In order to determine if certain neural network building blocks are superior, we test on six datasets from [Barnes et al., 2017] with different properties. The summary for dataset properties is in Table 1.

The Stanford Sentiment Treebank (*SST-fine*) [Socher et al., 2013] deals with movie reviews, containing five classes [very-negative, negative, neutral, positive, very-positive]. (*SST-binary*) is constructed from the same data, except the neutral class sentences are removed, all negative classes are

---

[2]https://github.com/jbarnesspain/sota_
sentiment

	Train	Dev.	Test	# of Classes	Average Sent. Length	Max Sent. Length	Vocab. Size	Wiki Emb. Coverage	300D Emb. Coverage
SST-fine	8,544	1,101	2,210	5	19.53	57	19,500	94.4%	89.0%
SST-binary	6,920	872	1,821	2	19.67	57	17,539	95.0%	89.6%
OpeNER	2,780	186	743	4	4.28	23	2,447	94.2%	99.3%
SenTube-A	3,381	225	903	2	28.54	127	18,569	75.6%	74.5%
SenTube-T	4,997	333	1,334	2	28.73	121	20,276	70.4%	76.0%
SemEval	6,021	890	2,376	3	22.40	40	21,163	77.1%	99.8%

Table 1: Modified Table 2 from [Barnes et al., 2017]. Dataset statistics, embedding coverage of dataset vocabularies, as well as splits for Train, Dev (Development), and Test sets. The 'Wiki' embeddings are the 50, 100, 200, and 600 dimension used for experiments.

grouped, and all positive classes are grouped. The datasets are pre-processed to only contain sentence-level labels, and none of the models reported in this work utilize the phrase-level labels that are also provided.

The *OpeNER* dataset [y Montse Cuadros y Seán Gaines y German Rigau, 2013] is a dataset of hotel reviews with four sentiment classes: very negative, negative, positive, and very positive. This is the smallest dataset with the lowest average sentence length.

The SenTube datasets [Uryupina et al., 2014] consist of YouTube comments with two sentiment classes: positive and negative. These datasets contain the longest average sentence length as well as the longest maximum sentence length of all the datasets.

The SemEval Twitter dataset (*SemEval*) [Nakov et al., 2013] consists of tweets with three classes: positive, negative, and neutral.

4.2 Embeddings

We use the exact same word embeddings as [Barnes et al., 2017]. They trained the 50, 100, 200, and 600-dimensional word embeddings using the word2vec algorithm described in [Mikolov et al., 2013] on a 2016 Wikipedia dump. In order to compare to previous work, they also used the publicly available Google 300-dimensional word2vec embeddings, which are trained on a part of Google News dataset[3]. For all models, out-of-vocabulary words are initialized randomly from the uniform distribution on the interval [-0.25 , 0.25].

---

[3]https://code.google.com/archive/p/
word2vec/

4.3 Baselines

We take 5 classifiers from [Barnes et al., 2017] and use their published results as baselines. Two of the methods are based on logistic regression, *Bow* and *Ave*, and 3 are neural network based, *LSTM*, *BiLSTM*, and *CNN*.

The (*Bow*) baseline is a L2-regularized logistic regression trained on bag-of-words representation. Each word is represented by a one-hot vectors of size $n = |V|$, where $|V|$ is the vocabulary size.

The (*Ave*) baseline is also a L2-regularized logistic regression classifier except trained on the average of the 300-dimension word embeddings for each sentence.

The *LSTM* baseline, input word embeddings are passed into an LSTM layer. Then a 50-dimensional feed-forward layer with ReLU activations is applied, followed by a softmax layer that produces that model classification outputs. Dropout [Srivastava et al., 2014] is applied to the input word embeddings for regularization.

The *BiLSTM* baseline is the same as *LSTM*, except that a second LSTM layer is used to process the input word embeddings in the reverse order. The outputs of the two LSTM layers are concatenated and passed a feed-forward layer, following by the output softmax layer. Dropout is applied identically as in *LSTM*. This modification improves the networks ability to capture long-range dependencies.

The final baseline is a simple *CNN* network. The input sequence of n embeddings is reshaped to an $n \times R$ dimensional matrix M, where R is the dimensionality of the embeddings. Convolutions with filter size of [2,3,4] are applied to M, following by a pooling layer of length 2. As for *LSTM* networks, a

	Model	Dim.	SST-fine	SST-binary	OpeNER	SenTube-A	SenTube-T	SemEval	Macro-Avg.
Baselines	Bow		40.3	80.7	77.1	60.6	66.0	65.5	65.0
	Ave	300	41.6	80.3	76.3	61.5	64.3	63.6	64.6
	LSTM	50	43.3 (1.0)	80.5 (0.4)	81.1 (0.4)	58.9 (0.8)	63.4 (3.1)	63.9 (1.7)	65.2 (1.2)
		100	44.1 (0.8)	79.5 (0.6)	82.4 (0.5)	58.9 (1.1)	63.1 (0.4)	67.3 (1.1)	65.9 (0.7)
		200	44.1 (1.6)	80.9 (0.6)	82.0 (0.6)	58.6 (0.6)	65.2 (1.6)	66.8 (1.3)	66.3 (1.1)
		300	45.3 (1.9)	81.7 (0.7)	82.3 (0.6)	57.4 (1.3)	63.6 (0.7)	67.6 (0.6)	66.3 (1.0)
		600	44.5 (1.4)	83.1 (0.9)	81.2 (0.8)	57.4 (1.1)	65.7 (1.2)	67.5 (0.7)	66.5 (1.0)
	BiLSTM	50	43.6 (1.2)	82.9 (0.7)	79.2 (0.8)	59.5 (1.1)	65.6 (1.2)	64.3 (1.2)	65.9 (1.0)
		100	43.8 (1.1)	79.8 (1.0)	82.4 (0.6)	58.6 (0.8)	66.4 (1.4)	65.2 (0.6)	66.0 (0.9)
		200	44.0 (0.9)	80.1 (0.6)	81.7 (0.5)	58.9 (0.3)	63.3 (1.0)	66.4 (0.3)	65.7 (0.6)
		300	45.6 (1.6)	82.6 (0.7)	82.5 (0.6)	59.3 (1.0)	66.2 (1.5)	65.1 (0.9)	66.9 (1.1)
		600	43.2 (1.1)	83.0 (0.4)	81.5 (0.5)	59.2 (1.6)	66.4 (1.1)	68.5 (0.7)	66.9 (0.9)
	CNN	50	39.9 (0.7)	81.7 (0.3)	80.0 (0.9)	55.2 (0.7)	57.4 (3.1)	65.7 (1.0)	63.3 (1.1)
		100	40.1 (1.0)	81.6 (0.5)	79.5 (0.9)	56.0 (2.2)	61.5 (1.1)	64.2 (0.8)	63.8 (1.1)
		200	39.1 (1.1)	80.7 (0.4)	79.8 (0.7)	56.3 (1.8)	64.1 (1.1)	65.3 (0.8)	64.2 (1.0)
		300	39.8 (0.7)	81.3 (1.1)	80.3 (0.9)	57.3 (0.5)	62.1 (1.0)	63.5 (1.3)	64.0 (0.9)
		600	40.7 (2.6)	82.7 (1.2)	79.2 (1.4)	56.6 (0.6)	61.3 (2.0)	65.9 (1.8)	64.4 (1.5)
Self-Attention Models	1-Layer SSAN + RPR	50	42.8 (0.8)	79.6 (0.3)	78.6 (0.5)	**64.1** (0.4)	67.0 (1.0)	67.1 (0.5)	66.5 (0.6)
		100	44.6 (0.3)	82.3 (0.3)	81.6 (0.5)	61.6 (1.3)	68.6 (0.6)	68.6 (0.5)	67.9 (0.6)
		200	45.4 (0.4)	83.1 (0.5)	82.3 (0.4)	62.2 (0.6)	68.4 (0.8)	70.5 (0.4)	68.6 (0.5)
		300	**48.1** (0.4)	**84.2** (0.4)	83.8 (0.2)	62.5 (0.3)	68.4 (0.8)	**72.2** (0.8)	**69.9** (0.5)
		600	47.7 (0.7)	83.6 (0.4)	83.1 (0.4)	62.0 (0.4)	**68.8** (0.7)	70.5 (0.8)	69.2 (0.5)
	2-Layer SSAN + RPR	50	43.2 (0.9)	79.8 (0.2)	79.2 (0.6)	63.0 (1.3)	66.6 (0.5)	67.5 (0.7)	66.5 (0.7)
		100	45.0 (0.4)	81.6 (0.9)	81.1 (0.4)	63.3 (0.7)	67.7 (0.5)	68.7 (0.4)	67.9 (0.5)
		200	46.5 (0.7)	82.8 (0.5)	82.3 (0.6)	61.9 (1.2)	68.0 (0.8)	69.6 (0.8)	68.5 (0.8)
		300	**48.1** (0.8)	83.8 (0.9)	83.3 (0.9)	62.1 (0.8)	67.8 (1.0)	70.7 (0.5)	69.3 (0.8)
		600	47.6 (0.5)	83.7 (0.4)	82.9 (0.5)	60.7 (1.4)	68.2 (0.7)	70.3 (0.3)	68.9 (0.6)
	Transformer Encoder + RPR	300	47.3 (0.4)	83.8 (0.4)	**84.2** (0.5)	62.0 (1.4)	68.2 (N1.6)	72.0 (0.5)	69.6 (0.8)
	Transformer Encoder + PE	300	45.0 (0.7)	82.0 (0.6)	83.3 (0.7)	62.3 (2.4)	66.9 (0.8)	68.4 (0.8)	68.0 (1.0)
	1-Layer SSAN	300	47.2 (0.5)	83.9 (0.7)	83.6 (0.6)	62.1 (2.5)	68.7 (1.0)	70.2 (1.2)	69.3 (1.1)
	1-Layer SSAN + PE	300	45.0 (0.3)	82.9 (0.2)	80.7 (0.6)	62.6 (2.3)	67.8 (0.4)	69.1 (0.3)	68.0 (0.7)

Table 2: Modified Table 3 from [Barnes et al., 2017]. Test accuracy averages and standard deviations (in brackets) of 5 runs. The baseline results are taken from [Barnes et al., 2017]; the self-attention models results are ours. Best model for each dataset is given in **bold**.

feed-forward layer is applied followed by an output softmax layer. Here, dropout is applied to input embeddings as well as after the convolution layers.

The *LSTM*, *BiLSTM*, and *CNN* baselines are trained using ADAM [Kingma and Ba, 2014] with cross-entropy loss and mini-batches of size 32. Hidden layer dimension, dropout amount, and the number of training epochs are tuned on the validation set for each (model, input embedding, dataset) combination.

4.4 Self-Attention Architectures

We use *1-Layer SSAN + RPR* and *2-Layer SSAN + RPR* to compare the self-attention mechanism to the recurrence and convolution mechanisms in *LSTM*, *BiLSTM*, and *CNN* models. We compare these models using all word embeddings sizes.

Next, we explore the performance of a modified *Transformer Encoder* described in 3. We do this to determine if a more complex architecture that utilized multi-head attention is more beneficial.

Finally, we compare the performance of using positional encodings (*+PE*) and relative positional

Model	# of Parameters	GPU VRAM Usage (Mb)	Training Time (s)	Inference Time (s)
LSTM	722,705	419Mb	235.9s	7.6s
BiLSTM	1,445,405	547Mb	416.0s	12.7s
CNN	83,714	986Mb	21.1s	0.85s
1-Layer SSAN + RPR	465,600	381Mb	64.6s	8.9s
1-Layer SSAN + PE	453,000	381Mb	58.1s	8.5s
2-Layer SSAN + RPR	839,400	509Mb	70.3s	9.3s
Transformer + RPR	1,177,920	510Mb	78.2s	9.7s

Table 3: Neural networks architecture characteristics. A comparison of number of learnable parameters, GPU VRAM usage (in megabytes) during training, as well as training and inference times (in seconds).

representations (*+RPR*) for the *Transformer Encoder* and *1-Layer-SSAN* architectures. We also test *1-Layer SSAN* without using any positional information techniques.

For the self-attention networks, we simplify the training process to only tune one parameter and apply the same process to all models. Only the learning rate is tuned for every (model, input embedding) pair. We fix the number of batches to train for to 100,000 and pick the model with highest validation accuracy. Each batch is constructed by randomly sampling the training set. Model dimensionality d_{model} is fixed to being the same as the input word embeddings. Learning rate is tuned based on the size of d_{model}. For d_{model} dimensions [50, 100, 200, 300, 600] we use learning rates of [0.15, 0.125, 0.1, 0.1, 0.05] respectively, because the larger d_{model} models tend to over-fit faster. Dropout of 0.7 is applied to all models, and the ADADELTA [Zeiler, 2012] optimizer is used with cross-entropy loss.

5 Analysis

Table 2 contains the summary of all the experimental results. For all neural network models we report mean test accuracy of five runs as well as the standard deviations. Macro-Avg results are the average accuracy of a model across all datasets. We focus our discussion on the Macro-Avg column as it demonstrates the models general performance for sentiment analysis.

Our results show general better performance for self-attention networks in comparison to *LSTM*, *BiLSTM* and *CNN* models. Using the same word embedding, all of the self-attention models receive higher Macro-Avg accuracy than all baseline models. *1-Layer-SSAN+RPR* models generally perform the best for all (input embeddings, dataset) combinations, and getting top scores for five out of six datasets. *Transformer Encoder+RPR* also performs comparatively well across all datasets, and achieves top accuracy for the *OpeNER* dataset.

Using *2-Layer-SSAN+RPR* does not yield better performance results compared to *1-Layer-SSAN+RPR*. We believe that one self-attention layer is sufficient as the datasets that we have tested on were relatively small. This is reinforced by the results we see from *Transformer Encoder + RPR* since it achieves similar accuracy as *2-Layer-SSAN+RPR* and *1-Layer-SSAN+RPR* while having greater architectural complexity and more trainable parameters, see Table 3.

Using relative positional representations for *1-Layer-SSAN+RPR* increases the Macro-Avg accuracy by 2.8% compared to using positional encodings for *1-Layer-SSAN+PE*, and by 0.9% compared to using no positional information at all (*1-Layer-SSAN*). Interestingly enough, we observe that using no positional information performs better than using positional encodings. This could be attributed once again to small dataset size, as [Vaswani et al., 2017] successfully used positional encodings for larger MT datasets.

Another observation is that SenTube dataset trials achieve a low accuracy despite having binary classes. This is unexpected as generally with a low number of classes it is easier to train on the dataset and achieve higher accuracy. We suspect that this is because SenTube contains longer sentences and very low word embedding coverage. Despite this, SSANs perform relatively well on the SenTube-A dataset, which suggests that they are superior at capturing long-range dependencies compared to other models.

Smaller d_{model} *SSAN* models perform worse for lower dimension input embeddings on *SST-fine*, *SST-binary* and *OpeNER* datasets while still performing well on *SenTube* and *SemEval*. This is caused by the limitations of our training process where we forced the network d_{model} to be same size as the input word embeddings and use the same learning rate for all datasets. We found that working with smaller dimensions of d_{model} the learning rate needed to be tuned individually for some datasets. For example, using a learning of 0.15 for 50D models would work well for *SenTube* and *SemEval*, but would under-fit for *SST-fine*, *SST-binary* and *OpeNER* datasets. We decided to not modify the training process for the smaller input embeddings in order to keep our training process simplified.

5.1 Model Characteristics

Here we compare training and test efficiency, memory consumption and number of trainable parameters for every model. For all models, we use the *SST-fine* dataset, hidden dimension size of 300, Google 300D embeddings, batch sizes of 32 for both training and inference, and the ADAM optimizer [Kingma and Ba, 2014]. The *Training Time* test is the average time it takes every model to train on 10 epochs of the SST-fine train set (2670 batches of size 32). The *Inference Time* test is the average time it takes a model to produce predictions for the validation set 10 times (344 batches of size 32). Table 3 contains the summary of model characteristics. The GPU VRAM usage is the amount of GPU video memory that is used during training.

CNN has the lowest number of parameters but consumes the most GPU memory. It also has the shortest training and inference time, which we attributed to the low number of parameters.

Using relative position representations compared to positional encoding for *1-Layer-SSAN* increases the number of trainable parameters by only 2.7%, training time by 11.2%, and inference time by 4.7%. These findings are similar to what [Shaw et al., 2018] reported.

BiLSTM has double the number of parameters as well as near double training and inference times compared to *LSTM*. This is reasonable due to the nature of the architecture being two *LSTM* layers. Much like *BiLSTM*, going from *1-Layer-SSAN* to *2-Layer-SSAN* doubles the number of trainable parameters. However, the training and inference

times only increase by 20.1% and 9.4% respectively. This demonstrates the efficiency of the self-attention mechanism due to it utilizing only matrix multiply operations, for which GPUs are highly-optimized.

We also observe that self-attention models are faster to train than *LSTM* by about 3.4 times, and 5.9 times for *BiLSTM*. However, inference times are slower than *LSTM* by 15.5% and faster than *BiLSTM* by 41%.

6 Conclusion

In this paper we focused on demonstrating that self-attention networks achieve better accuracy than previous state-of-the-art techniques on six datasets. In our experiments, multiple *SSAN* networks performed better than *CNN* and *RNN* architectures; Self-attention architecture resulted in higher accuracy than *LSTMs* while having 35% fewer parameters and shorter training time by a factor of 3.5. Additionally, we showed that SSANs achieved higher accuracy on the *SenTube* datasets, which suggests they are also better at capturing long-term dependencies than *RNNs* and *CNNs*. Finally, we reported that using relative positional representation is superior to both using positional encodings, as well as not incorporating any positional information at all. Using relative positional representations for self-attention architectures resulted in higher accuracy with negligible impact on model training and inference efficiency.

For future work, we plan to extend the *SSAN* networks proposed to achieve state-of-the-art results on the complete *SST* dataset. We are also interested to see the behaviour of the models explored in this work on much larger datasets, we hypothesize that stacked multi-head self-attention architectures will perform significantly better than *RNN* and *CNN* counterparts, all while remaining more efficient at training and inference.

Acknowledgments

We thank the anonymous reviewers for their insightful suggestions.

References

Dzmitry Bahdanau, Kyunghyun Cho, and Yoshua Bengio. Neural machine translation by jointly learning to align and translate. *arXiv:1409.0473*, 2014.

Jeremy Barnes, Roman Klinger, and Sabine Schulte im
Walde. Assessing state-of-the-art sentiment models on state-of-the-art sentiment datasets. In *Proceedings of the 8th Workshop on Computational Approaches to Subjectivity, Sentiment and Social Media Analysis*, Copenhagen, Denmark, 2017.

Jianpeng Cheng, Li Dong, and Mirella Lapata. Long
short-term memory-networks for machine reading.
CoRR, abs/1601.06733, 2016. URL http://
arxiv.org/abs/1601.06733.

Kyunghyun Cho, Bart van Merrienboer, Dzmitry Bahdanau, and Yoshua Bengio. On the properties of
neural machine translation: Encoder–decoder approaches. In *Proceedings of SSST-8, Eighth Workshop on Syntax, Semantics and Structure in Statistical Translation*, pages 103–111. Association for
Computational Linguistics, 2014. doi: 10.3115/v1/
W14-4012. URL http://www.aclweb.org/
anthology/W14-4012.

François Chollet et al. Keras. https://keras.io,
2015.

Michał Daniluk, Tim Rocktäschel, Johannes Welbl,
and Sebastian Riedel. Frustratingly short attention
spans in neural language modeling. *arXiv preprint
arXiv:1702.04521*, 2017.

Jonas Gehring, Michael Auli, David Grangier, Denis Yarats, and Yann N Dauphin. Convolutional
sequence to sequence learning. *arXiv preprint
arXiv:1705.03122*, 2017.

Felix Greaves, Daniel Ramirez-Cano, Christopher Mil-
lett, Ara Darzi, and Liam Donaldson. Harnessing
the cloud of patient experience: using social media
to detect poor quality healthcare. *BMJ Qual Saf*, 22
(3):251–255, 2013a.

Felix Greaves, Daniel Ramirez-Cano, Christopher Mil-
lett, Ara Darzi, and Liam Donaldson. Use of sentiment analysis for capturing patient experience from
free-text comments posted online. *Journal of medical Internet research*, 15(11), 2013b.

Sepp Hochreiter and Jürgen Schmidhuber. Long short-
term memory. *Neural Computation*, 9(8):1735–
1780, 1997.

Bernard J Jansen, Mimi Zhang, Kate Sobel, and Ab-
dur Chowdury. Twitter power: Tweets as electronic
word of mouth. *Journal of the American society for
information science and technology*, 60(11):2169–
2188, 2009.

Yoon Kim. Convolutional neural networks for sentence classification. In *Proceedings of the 2014
Conference on Empirical Methods in Natural Language Processing (EMNLP)*, pages 1746–1751.
Association for Computational Linguistics, 2014.
doi: 10.3115/v1/D14-1181. URL http://www.
aclweb.org/anthology/D14-1181.

Diederik P. Kingma and Jimmy Ba. Adam: A method
for stochastic optimization. *CoRR*, abs/1412.6980,
2014.

Filippos Kokkinos and Alexandros Potamianos. Structural attention neural networks for improved sentiment analysis. *arXiv preprint arXiv:1701.01811*,
2017.

Peter J Liu, Mohammad Saleh, Etienne Pot, Ben
Goodrich, Ryan Sepassi, Lukasz Kaiser, and Noam
Shazeer. Generating wikipedia by summarizing
long sequences. *arXiv preprint arXiv:1801.10198*,
2018.

Jiasen Lu, Jianwei Yang, Dhruv Batra, and Devi
Parikh. Hierarchical question-image co-attention
for visual question answering. In D. D. Lee,
M. Sugiyama, U. V. Luxburg, I. Guyon, and
R. Garnett, editors, *Advances in Neural Information Processing Systems 29*, pages 289–
297. Curran Associates, Inc., 2016. URL
http://papers.nips.cc/paper/6202-
hierarchical-question-image-co-
attention-for-visual-question-
answering.pdf.

Tomas Mikolov, Kai Chen, Greg Corrado, and Jeffrey
Dean. Efficient estimation of word representations
in vector space. *arXiv preprint arXiv:1301.3781*,
2013.

Mika V. Mäntylä, Daniel Graziotin, and Miikka
Kuutila. The evolution of sentiment analysis—a
review of research topics, venues, and top cited
papers. *Computer Science Review*, 27:16 –
32, 2018. ISSN 1574-0137. doi: https://doi.
org/10.1016/j.cosrev.2017.10.002. URL http:
//www.sciencedirect.com/science/
article/pii/S1574013717300606.

Vinod Nair and Geoffrey E Hinton. Rectified linear
units improve restricted boltzmann machines. In
*Proceedings of the 27th international conference on
machine learning (ICML-10)*, pages 807–814, 2010.

Preslav Nakov, Zornitsa Kozareva, Alan Ritter, Sara
Rosenthal, Veselin Stoyanov, and Theresa Wilson.
Semeval-2013 task 2: Sentiment analysis in twitter,
2013.

Bo Pang, Lillian Lee, and Shivakumar Vaithyanathan.
Thumbs up?: Sentiment classification using machine learning techniques. In *Proceedings of the
ACL-02 Conference on Empirical Methods in Natural Language Processing - Volume 10*, EMNLP
'02, pages 79–86, Stroudsburg, PA, USA, 2002.
Association for Computational Linguistics. doi:
10.3115/1118693.1118704. URL https://doi.
org/10.3115/1118693.1118704.

Niki Parmar, Ashish Vaswani, Jakob Uszkoreit, Łukasz
Kaiser, Noam Shazeer, and Alexander Ku. Image transformer. *arXiv preprint arXiv:1802.05751*,
2018.

Jeffrey Pennington, Richard Socher, and Christopher D. Manning. Glove: Global vectors for word representation. In *Empirical Methods in Natural Language Processing (EMNLP)*, pages 1532–1543, 2014. URL http://www.aclweb.org/anthology/D14-1162.

Daniel Povey, Hossein Hadian, Pegah Ghahremani, Ke Li, and Sanjeev Khudanpur. A time-restricted self-attention layer for asr. 2017.

Mike Schuster and Kuldip K Paliwal. Bidirectional recurrent neural networks. *IEEE Transactions on Signal Processing*, 45(11):2673–2681, 1997.

Peter Shaw, Jakob Uszkoreit, and Ashish Vaswani. Self-attention with relative position representations. *CoRR*, abs/1803.02155, 2018.

Tao Shen, Tianyi Zhou, Guodong Long, Jing Jiang, Shirui Pan, and Chengqi Zhang. Disan: Directional self-attention network for rnn/cnn-free language understanding. In *AAAI Conference on Artificial Intelligence*, 2018.

Richard Socher, Alex Perelygin, Jean Wu, Jason Chuang, Christopher D Manning, Andrew Ng, and Christopher Potts. Recursive deep models for semantic compositionality over a sentiment treebank. In *Proceedings of the 2013 conference on empirical methods in natural language processing*, pages 1631–1642, 2013.

Nitish Srivastava, Geoffrey Hinton, Alex Krizhevsky, Ilya Sutskever, and Ruslan Salakhutdinov. Dropout: A simple way to prevent neural networks from overfitting. *The Journal of Machine Learning Research*, 15(1):1929–1958, 2014.

Emma Strubell, Patrick Verga, Daniel Andor, David Weiss, and Andrew McCallum. Linguistically-informed self-attention for semantic role labeling. *CoRR*, abs/1804.08199, 2018.

Ilya Sutskever, Oriol Vinyals, and Quoc V Le. Sequence to sequence learning with neural networks. In Z. Ghahramani, M. Welling, C. Cortes, N. D. Lawrence, and K. Q. Weinberger, editors, *Advances in Neural Information Processing Systems 27*, pages 3104–3112. Curran Associates, Inc., 2014. URL http://papers.nips.cc/paper/5346-sequence-to-sequence-learning-with-neural-networks.pdf.

Kai Sheng Tai, Richard Socher, and Christopher D Manning. Improved semantic representations from tree-structured long short-term memory networks. *arXiv preprint arXiv:1503.00075*, 2015.

Olga Uryupina, Barbara Plank, Aliaksei Severyn, Agata Rotondi, and Alessandro Moschitti. Sentube: A corpus for sentiment analysis on youtube social media. In *Proceedings of the Ninth International Conference on Language Resources and Evaluation*. European Language Resources Association, 2014.

Ashish Vaswani, Noam Shazeer, Niki Parmar, Jakob Uszkoreit, Llion Jones, Aidan N Gomez, Ł ukasz Kaiser, and Illia Polosukhin. Attention is all you need. In I. Guyon, U. V. Luxburg, S. Bengio, H. Wallach, R. Fergus, S. Vishwanathan, and R. Garnett, editors, *Advances in Neural Information Processing Systems 30*, pages 5998–6008. Curran Associates, Inc., 2017. URL http://papers.nips.cc/paper/7181-attention-is-all-you-need.pdf.

Rodrigo Agerri y Montse Cuadros y Seán Gaines y German Rigau. Opener: Open polarity enhanced named entity recognition. *Procesamiento del Lenguaje Natural*, 51(0):215–218, 2013. ISSN 1989-7553. URL http://journal.sepln.org/sepln/ojs/ojs/index.php/pln/article/view/4891.

Matthew D Zeiler. Adadelta: an adaptive learning rate method. *arXiv preprint arXiv:1212.5701*, 2012.

Han Zhang, Ian Goodfellow, Dimitris Metaxas, and Augustus Odena. Self-attention generative adversarial networks. *arXiv preprint arXiv:1805.08318*, 2018.

Yi Zhou, Junying Zhou, Lu Liu, Jiangtao Feng, Haoyuan Peng, and Xiaoqing Zheng. Rnn-based sequence-preserved attention for dependency parsing. 2018. URL https://www.aaai.org/ocs/index.php/AAAI/AAAI18/paper/view/17176.

Dual Memory Network Model for Biased Product Review Classification

Yunfei Long[1*], **Mingyu Ma**[1*], **Qin Lu**[1], **Rong Xiang**[1] and **Chu-Ren Huang**[2]

[1]Department of Computing, The Hong Kong Polytechnic University

csylong,csluqin,csrxiang@comp.polyu.edu.hk, derek.ma@connect.polyu.hk

[2]Department of Chinese and Bilingual Studies, The Hong Kong Polytechnic University

*These two authors contributed equally

churen.huang@polyu.edu.hk

Abstract

In sentiment analysis (SA) of product reviews, both user and product information are proven to be useful. Current tasks handle user profile and product information in a unified model which may not be able to learn salient features of users and products effectively. In this work, we propose a dual user and product memory network (DUPMN) model to learn user profiles and product reviews using separate memory networks. Then, the two representations are used jointly for sentiment prediction. The use of separate models aims to capture user profiles and product information more effectively. Compared to state-of-the-art unified prediction models, the evaluations on three benchmark datasets, IMDB, Yelp13, and Yelp14, show that our dual learning model gives performance gain of 0.6%, 1.2%, and 0.9%, respectively. The improvements are also deemed very significant measured by *p-values*.

1 Introduction

Written text is often meant to express sentiments of individuals. Recognizing the underlying sentiment expressed in the text is essential to understand the full meaning of the text. The SA community is increasingly interested in using natural language processing (NLP) techniques as well as sentiment theories to identify sentiment expressions in the text.

Recently, deep learning based methods have taken over feature engineering approaches to gain further performance improvement in SA. Typical neural network models include Convolutional Neural Network (CNN) (Kim, 2014), Recursive auto-encoders (Socher et al., 2013), Long-Short Term Memory (LSTM) (Tang et al., 2015a), and many more.

Attention-based models are introduced to highlight important words and sentences in a piece of text. Different attention models are built using information embedded in the text including users, products and text in local context (Tang et al., 2015b; Yang et al., 2016; Chen et al., 2016; Gui et al., 2016). In order to incorporate other aspects of knowledge, Qian et al. (2016) developed a model to employ additional linguistic resources to benefit sentiment classification. Long et al.(2017b) and Mishra et al.(2016) proposed cognition-based attention models learned from cognition grounded eye-tracking data.

Most text-based SA is modeled as sentiment classification tasks. In this work, SA is for product reviews. We use the term **users** to refer to writers of text, and **products** to refer to the targets of reviews in the text. A **user profile** is defined by the collection of reviews a user writes. **Product information** defined for a product is the collection of reviews for this product. Note that user profiles and product information are not independent of each other. That is one reason why previous works use unified models. By common-sense we know that review text written by a person may be subjective or biased towards his/her own preferences. Lenient users tend to give higher ratings than finicky ones even if they review the same products. Popular products do receive higher ratings than those unpopular ones because the aggregation of user reviews still shows the difference in opinion for different products. While users and products both play crucial roles in sentiment analysis, they are fundamentally different.

Reviews written by a user can be affected by user preference which is more subjective whereas reviews for a product are useful only if they are from a collection of different reviewers, because we know individual reviews can be biased. The popularity of a product tends to reflect the general impression of a collection of users as an aggregated result. Therefore, sentiment prediction of a

Proceedings of the 9th Workshop on Computational Approaches to Subjectivity, Sentiment and Social Media Analysis, pages 140–148

Brussels, Belgium, October 31, 2018. ©2018 Association for Computational Linguistics

https://doi.org/10.18653/v1/P17

product should give dual consideration to individual users as well as all reviews as a collection.

In this paper, we address the aforementioned issue by proposing to learn user profiles and product review information separately before making a joint prediction on sentiment classification. In the proposed Dual User and Product Memory Network (DUPMN) model, we first build a hierarchical LSTM (Hochreiter and Schmidhuber, 1997) model to generate document representations. Then a user memory network (UMN) and a product memory network (PMN) are separately built based on document representation of user comments and product reviews. Finally, sentiment prediction is learned from a dual model.

To validate the effectiveness of our proposed model, evaluations are conducted on three benchmarking review datasets from IMDB and Yelp data challenge (including Yelp13 and Yelp14) (Tang et al., 2015a). Experimental results show that our algorithm can outperform baseline methods by large margins. Compared to the state-of-the-art method, DUPMN made 0.6%, 1.2%, and 0.9% increase in accuracy with *p-values* 0.007, 0.004, and 0.001 in the three benchmark datasets respectively. Results show that leveraging user profile and product information separately can be more effective for sentiment predictions.

The rest of this paper is organized as follows. Section 2 gives related work, especially memory network models. Section 3 introduces our proposed DUPMN model. Section 4 gives the evaluation compared to state-of-the-art methods on three datasets. Section 5 concludes this paper and gives some future directions in sentiment analysis models to consider individual bias.

2   Related Work

Related work includes neural network models and the use of user/product information in sentiment analysis.

2.1   Neural Network Models

In recent years, deep learning has greatly improved the performance of sentiment analysis. Commonly used models include Convolutional Neural Networks (CNNs) (Socher et al., 2011), Recursive Neural Network (ReNNs) (Socher et al., 2013), and Recurrent Neural Networks (RNNs) (Irsoy and Cardie, 2014). RNN naturally benefits sentiment classification because of its ability to capture sequential information in text. However, standard RNNs suffer from the so-called *gradient vanishing problem* (Bengio et al., 1994) where gradients may grow or decay exponentially over long sequences. LSTM models are adopted to solve the gradient vanishing problem. An LSTM model provides a gated mechanism to keep the long-term memory. Each LSTM layer is generally followed by mean pooling and the output is fed into the next layer. Experiments in datasets which contain sentences and long documents demonstrate that LSTM model outperforms the traditional RNNs (Tang et al., 2015a,c). Attention mechanism is also added to LSTM models to highlight important segments at both sentence level and document level. Attention models can be built from text in local context (Yang et al., 2016), user/production information (Chen et al., 2016; Long et al., 2017a) and other information such as cognition grounded eye tracking data (Long et al., 2017b). LSTM models with attention mechanism are currently the state-of-the-art models in document sentiment analysis tasks (Chen et al., 2016; Long et al., 2017b).

Memory networks are designed to handle larger context for a collection of documents. Memory networks introduce inference components combined with a so called long-term memory component (Weston et al., 2014). The long-term memory component is a large external memory to represent data as a collection. This collective information can contain local context (Das et al., 2017) or external knowledge base (Jain, 2016). It can also be used to represent the context of users and products globally (Tang et al., 2016). Dou uses (2017) a memory network model in document level sentiment analysis and makes comparable result to the state-of-the-art model (Chen et al., 2016).

2.2   Incorporating User and Product Information

Both user profile and product information have crucial effects on sentiment polarities. Tang et al. (2015b) proposed a model by incorporating user and product information into a CNN network for document level sentiment classification. User ids and product names are included as features in a unified document vector using the vector space model such that document vectors capture important global clues include individual preferences and product information.

Nevertheless, this method suffers from high model complexity and only word-level preference is considered rather than information at the semantic level (Chen et al., 2016). Gui et al. (2016) introduce an inter-subjectivity network to link users to the terms they used as well as the polarities of the terms. The network aims to learn writer embeddings which are subsequently incorporated into a CNN network for sentiment analysis. Chen et al. (2016) propose a model to incorporate user and product information into an LSTM with attention mechanism. This model is reported to produce the state-of-the-art results in the three benchmark datasets (IMDB, Yelp13, and Yelp14). Dou (2017) also proposes a deep memory network to integrate user profile and product information in a unified model. However, the model only achieves a comparable result to the state-of-the-art attention based LSTM (Chen et al., 2016).

3 The DUPMN Model

We propose a DUPMN model. Firstly, document representation is learned by a hierarchical LSTM network to obtain both sentence-level representation and document level representation (Sundermeyer et al., 2012). A memory network model is then trained using dual memory networks, one for training user profiles and the other for training product reviews. Both of them are joined together to predict sentiment for documents.

3.1 Task Definition

Let D be the set of review documents for classification, U be the set of users, and P be the set of products. For each document $d(d \in D)$, user $u(u \in U)$ is the writer of d on product $p(p \in P)$. Let $U_u(d)$ be all documents posted by u and $P_p(d)$ be all documents on p. $U_u(d)$ and $P_p(d)$ define the user context and the product context of d, respectively. For simplicity, we use $U(d)$ and $P(d)$ directly. The goal of a sentiment analysis task is to predict the sentiment label for each d.

3.2 Document Embedding

Since review documents for sentiment classification such as restaurant reviews and movie comments are normally very long, a proper method to embed the documents is needed to speed up the training process and achieve better accuracy. Inspired by the work of Chen (Chen et al., 2016), a hierarchical LSTM network is used to obtain embedding representation of documents. The first LSTM layer is used to obtain sentence representation by the hidden state of an LSTM network. The same mechanism is also used for document level representation with sentence-level representation as input. User and product attentions are included in the network so that all salient features are included in document representation. For document d, its embedding is denoted as $\vec{d}$. $\vec{d}$ is a vector representation with dimension size n. In principle, the embedding representation of user context of d, denoted by $\hat{U}(d)$, and product context $\hat{P}(d)$ vary depending on d. For easy matrix calculation, we take m as our model parameter so that $\hat{U}(d)$ and $\hat{P}(d)$ are two fixed $n \times m$ matrices.

3.3 Memory Network Structure

Inspired by the successful use of memory networks in language modeling, question answering, and sentiment analysis (Sukhbaatar et al., 2015; Tang et al., 2016; Dou, 2017), we propose our DUPMN by extending a single memory network model to two memory networks to reflect different influences from users' perspective and products' perspective. The structure of the model is shown in Figure 1 with 3 hops as an example although in principle a memory network can have K computational hops.

The DUPMN model has two separate memory networks: the UMN and the PMN. Each hop in a memory network includes an attention layer $Attention_i$ and a linear addition Σ_k. Since the external memory $\hat{U}(d)$ and $\hat{P}(d)$ have the same structure, we use a generic notation $\hat{M}$ to denote them in the following explanations. Each document vector $\vec{d}$ is fed into the first hop of the two networks ($\vec{d_0}=\vec{d}$). Each $\vec{d}_{k-1}$(k= 1 ...... K-1) passes through the attention layer using an attention mechanism defined by a softmax function to obtain the attention weights $\vec{p}_k$ for document d:

$$\vec{p}_k = Softmax(\vec{d}_{k-1}^T * \hat{M}), \qquad (1)$$

And to produce an attention weighted vector $\vec{a}_k$ by

$$\vec{a}_k = \sum_{i=0}^{m} p_{ki} * \vec{M}_i. \qquad (2)$$

$\vec{a}_k$ is then linearly added to $\vec{d}_{k-1}$ to produce the output of this hop as $\vec{d}_k$.

After completing the Kth hop, the output $\vec{d}_K^u$ in UMN and $\vec{d}_K^p$ in PMN are joined together using

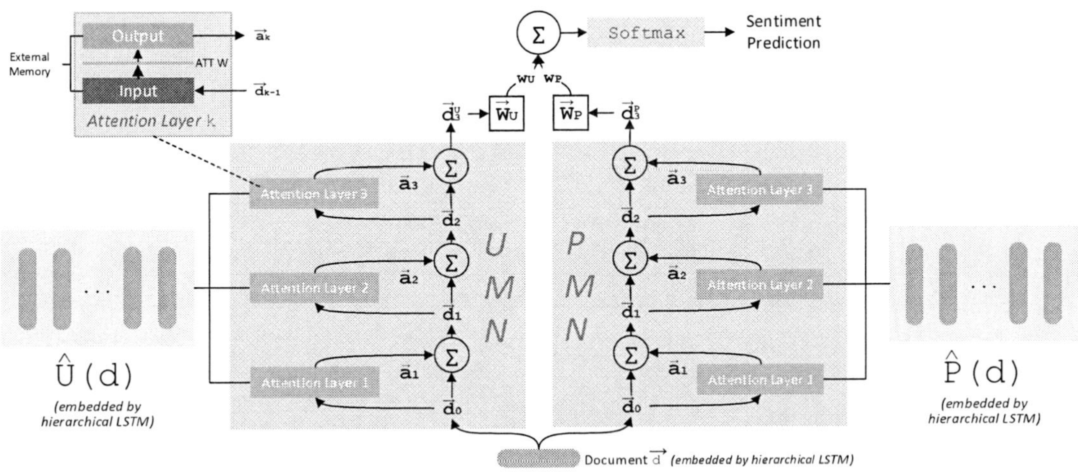

Figure 1: Structure for Proposed DUPMN Model

a weighted mechanism to produce the output of DUPMN, $Output_{DUPMN}$, is given below:

$$Output_{DUPMN} = w_U \vec{W}_U \vec{d}_K^u + w_P \vec{W}_P \vec{d}_K^p. \quad (3)$$

Two different weight vectors $\vec{W}_u$ and $\vec{W}_p$ in Formula 3 can be trained for UMN and PMN. w_U and w_P are two constant weights to reflect the relative importance of user profile $\vec{d}_K^u$ and product information $\vec{d}_K^p$. The parameters in the model including $\vec{W}_U$, $\vec{W}_P$, w_U and w_P. By minimizing the loss, those parameters can be optimized.

Sentiment prediction is obtained through a $Softmax$ layer. The loss function is defined by the cross entropy between the prediction from $Output_{DUPMN}$ and the ground truth labels.

4 Experiment and Result Analysis

Performance evaluations are conducted on three datasets and DUPMN is compared with a set of commonly used baseline methods including the state-of-the-art LSTM based method (Chen et al., 2016; Wu et al., 2018).

4.1 Datasets

The three benchmarking datasets include movie reviews from IMDB, restaurant reviews from Yelp13 and Yelp14 developed by Tang (2015a). All datasets are tokenized using the Stanford NLP tool (Manning et al., 2014). Table 1 lists statistics of the datasets including the number of classes, number of documents, average length of sentences, the average number of documents per user, and the average number of documents per product.

	IMDB	Yelp13	Yelp14
#class	10	5	5
#doc	84,919	78,966	231,163
#users	1,310	1,631	4,818
#products	1,635	1,631	4,194
Av sen. len	24.56	17.37	17.25
Av docs/user	64.82	48.41	47.97
Av docs/prod	51.93	48.41	55.12
#p(0-50)	1,223	1,299	3,150
#p(50-100)	318	254	749
#p(100-150)	72	56	175
#p(150-200)	22	24	120

Table 1: Statistics of the three benchmark datasets

Since postings in social networks by both users and products follow the long tail distribution (Kordumova et al., 2016), we only show the distribution of total number of posts for different products. For example, #p(0-50) means the number of products which have reviews between the size of 0 to 50. We split train/development/test sets at the rate of 8:1:1 following the same setting in (Tang et al., 2015b; Chen et al., 2016). The best configuration by the development dataset is used for the test set to obtain the final result.

4.2 Baseline Methods

In order to make a systematic comparison, three groups of baselines are used in the evaluation. Group 1 includes all commonly used feature sets mentioned in Chen et al. (2016) including Majority, Trigram, Text features (TextFeatures), and AveWordvec. All feature sets in Group 1 except

143

		IMDB			Yelp13			Yelp14		
	Model	Acc	RMSE	MAE	Acc	RMSE	MAE	Acc	RMSE	MAE
	Majority	0.196	2.495	1.838	0.392	1.097	0.779	0.411	1.060	0.744
	Trigram	0.399	1.783	1.147	0.577	0.804	0.487	0.569	0.814	0.513
G1	TextFeature	0.402	1.793	1.134	0.572	0.800	0.490	0.556	0.845	0.520
	AvgWordvec	0.304	1.985	1.361	0.530	0.893	0.562	0.526	0.898	0.568
	SSWE	0.312	1.973	N/A	0.549	0.849	N/A	0.557	0.851	N/A
	RNTN+RNN	0.400	1.734	N/A	0.574	0.804	N/A	0.582	0.821	N/A
G2	CLSTM	0.421	1.549	N/A	0.592	0.729	N/A	0.637	0.686	N/A
	LSTM+LA	0.443	1.465	N/A	0.627	0.701	N/A	0.637	0.686	N/A
	LSTM+CBA	0.489	1.365	N/A	0.638	0.697	N/A	0.641	0.678	N/A
	UPNN	0.435	1.602	0.979	0.608	0.764	0.447	0.596	0.784	0.464
G3	UPDMN	0.465	1.351	0.853	0.613	0.720	0.425	0.639	0.662	0.369
	InterSub	0.476	1.392	N/A	0.623	0.714	N/A	0.635	0.690	N/A
	LSTM+UPA	<u>0.533</u>	<u>1.281</u>	N/A	<u>0.650</u>	<u>0.692</u>	N/A	<u>0.667</u>	<u>0.654</u>	N/A
New	DUPMN	**0.539**	**1.279**	**0.734**	**0.662**	**0.667**	**0.375**	**0.676**	**0.639**	**0.351**

Table 2: Evaluation of different methods; best result/group in accuracy is marked in bold; second best is underlined.

Majority use the SVM classifier.

Group 2 methods include the recently published sentiment analysis models which only use context information, including:

- **SSWE** (Tang et al., 2014) — An SVM model using sentiment specific word embedding.

- **RNTN+RNN** (Socher et al., 2013) — A Recursive Neural Tensor Network (RNTN) to represent sentences.

- **CLSTM** (Xu et al., 2016) — A Cached LSTM model to capture overall semantic information in long text.

- **LSTM+LA** (Chen et al., 2016) — A state-of-the-art LSTM using local context as attention mechanism at both sentence level and document level.

- **LSTM+CBA** (Long et al., 2017b)— A state-of-the-art LSTM model using cognition based data to build attention mechanism.

Group 3 methods are recently published neural network models which incorporate user and product information, including:

- **UPNN** (Tang et al., 2015b) — User and product information for sentiment classification at document level based on a CNN network.

- **UPDMN** (Dou, 2017) — A deep memory network for document level sentiment classification by including user and product information in a unified model. Hop 1 gives the best result, and thus K=1 is used.

- **InterSub** (Gui et al., 2016) — A CNN model making use of user and product information.

- **LSTM+UPA** (Chen et al., 2016) — The state-of-the-art LSTM including both local context based attentions and user/product in the attention mechanism.

For the DUPMN model, we also include two variations which use only one memory network. The first variation only includes user profiles in the memory network, denoted as **DUPMN-U**. The second variation only uses product information, denoted as **DUPMN-P**.

4.3 Performance Evaluation

Four sets of experiments are conducted. The first experiment compares DUPMN with other sentiment analysis methods. The second experiment evaluates the effectiveness of different hop size K of memory network. The third experiment evaluates the effectiveness of UMN and PMN in different datasets. The fourth set of experiment examines the effect of memory size m on the performance of DUPMN. Performance measures include Accuracy (ACC), Root-Mean-Square-Error (RMSE), and Mean Absolute Error (MAE) for our model. For other baseline methods in Group 2 and Group 3, their reported results are used. We also show the p-value by comparing the result of 10 random tests for both our model and the state-of-the-art model [1] in the t-test [2].

Compared to other state-of-the-art models

Table 2 shows the result of the first experiment. DUPMN uses one hop (the best performer) with m being set at 100, a commonly used memory size for memory networks.

Generally speaking, Group 2 performs better than Group 1. This is because Group 1 uses a traditional SVM with feature engineering (Chang and Lin, 2011) and Group 2 uses more advanced deep learning methods proven to be effective by recent studies (Kim, 2014; Chen et al., 2016). However, some feature engineering methods are no worse than some deep learning methods. For example, the TextFeature model outperforms SSWE by a significant margin.

When comparing Group 2 and Group 3 methods, we can see that user profiles and product information can improve performance as most of the methods in Group 3 perform better than methods in Group 2. This is more obvious in the IMDB dataset which naturally contains more subjectivity. In the IMDB dataset, almost all models with user and product information outperform the text-only models in Group 2 except LSTM+CBA (Long et al., 2017b). However, the two LSTM models in Group 2 which include local attention mechanism do show that attention base methods can outperform methods using user profile and product information. In fact, the LSTM+CBA model using attention mechanism based on cognition grounded eye-tracking data in Group 2 outperforms quite a number of methods in Group 3. LSTM+CBA in Group 2 is only inferior to LSTM+UPA in Group 3 because of the additional user profile and production information used in LSTM+UPA.

Most importantly, the DUPMN model with both user memory and product memory significantly outperforms all the baseline methods including the state-of-the-art LSTM+UPA model (Chen et al., 2016). By using user profiles and product information in memory networks, DUPMN outperforms LSTM+UPA in all three datasets. In the IMDB dataset, our model makes 0.6 % improvement over LSTM+UPA in accuracy with $p-value$ of 0.007. Our model also achieves lower RMSE value. In the Yelp review dataset, the improvement is even more significant. DUPMN achieves 1.2% improvement in accuracy in Yelp13 with $p-value$ of 0.004 and 0.9% in Yelp14 with $p-value$ of 0.001, and the lower RMSE obtained by DUPMN also indicates that the proposed model can predict review ratings more accurately.

Effects of different hop sizes

The second set of experiments evaluates the effectiveness of DUPMN using different number of hops K. Table 3 shows the evaluation results. The number in the brackets after each model name indicates the number of hops used. Two conclusions can be obtained from Table 3. We find that more hops do not bring benefit. In all the three models, the single hop model obtains the best performance. Unlike video and image information, written text is grammatically structured and contains abstract information such that multiple hops may introduce more information distortion. Another reason may be due to over-fitting by the additional hops.

Effects of DUPMN-U and DUPMN-P

Comparing the performance of DUPMN-U and DUPMN-P in Table 3, it also shows that user memory and product memory indeed provide different kinds of information and thus their usefulness are different in different datasets. For the movie review dataset, IMDB, which is more subjective, results show that user profile information using DUPMN-U outperforms DUPMN-P as there is a 1.3% gain compared to that of DUPMN-P. However, on restaurant reviews in Yelp datasets, DUPMN-P performs better than DUPMN-U indicating product information is more valuable.

To further examine the effects of UMN and PMN on sentiment classification, we observe the difference of optimized values of the constant weights w_U and w_P between the UMN and the PMN given in Formula 3. The difference in their values indicates the relative importance of the two networks. The optimized weights given in Table 4 on the three datasets show that user profile has a higher weight than product information in IMDB because movie review is more related to personal preferences whereas product information

---

[1] We re-run experiment based on their public available code on GitHub (https://github.com/thunlp/NSC).

[2] http://www.statisticshowto.com/probability-and-statistics/t-test/

[3] Best results are marked in bold; second best are underlined in the table

	IMDB			Yelp13			Yelp14		
	Acc	RMSE	MAE	Acc	RMSE	MAE	Acc	RMSE	MAE
DUPMN-U(1)	0.536	1.273	0.737	0.656	0.687	0.380	0.667	0.655	0.361
DUPMN-U(2)	0.526	1.285	0.748	0.653	0.689	0.382	0.665	0.661	0.369
DUPMN-U(3)	0.524	1.295	0.754	0.651	0.692	0.388	0.661	0.667	0.374
DUPMN-P(1)	0.523	1.346	0.769	0.660	0.668	0.370	0.670	0.649	0.357
DUPMN-P(2)	0.517	1.348	0.775	0.656	0.680	0.380	0.667	0.656	0.364
DUPMN-P(3)	0.512	1.356	0.661	0.651	0.699	0.388	0.661	0.661	0.370
DUPMN(1)	**0.539**	**1.279**	**0.734**	**0.662**	**0.667**	**0.375**	**0.676**	**0.639**	**0.351**
DUPMN(2)	0.522	1.299	0.758	0.650	0.700	0.390	0.667	0.650	0.359
DUPMN(3)	0.502	1.431	0.830	0.653	0.686	0.382	0.658	0.668	0.371

Table 3: Evaluation of different memory network hops and user and product information utilization[3]

IMDB		Yelp13		Yelp14	
w_U	w_P	w_U	w_P	w_U	w_P
0.534	0.466	0.475	**0.525**	0.436	**0.564**

Table 4: Average weight of UMN and PMN in different datasets

has a higher weight in the two restaurant review datasets. This result is consistent with the evaluation in Table 3 on DUPMN-U and DUPMN-P.

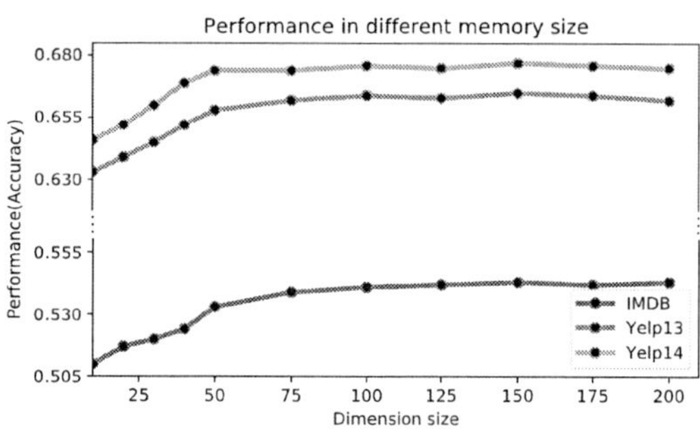

Figure 2: Effect of different memory sizes

Effects of the memory size

Most social network data follows the long tail distribution. If the memory size to represent the data is too small, some context information will be lost. On the other hand, too large memory size which requires more resources in computation and storage may not introduce much benefit. Thus, the fourth set of experiments evaluates the effect of dimension size m in the DUPMN memory networks. Figure 2 shows the result of the evaluation for 1 hop configuration with memory size starting at 1

with 10 points at each increment until size of 75, the increment set to 25 from 75 to 200 to cover most postings. Results show that when memory size increases from 10 to 100, the performance of DUPMN steadily increases. Once it goes beyond 100, DUPMN is no longer sensitive to memory size. This is related to the distribution of document frequency rated by user/product in Table 1 as the average is around 50. With long tail distribution, after 75, not many new documents will be included in the context. To improve algorithm efficiency without much compromise on performance, m can be any value that doubles the average. So, values between 100-200 in our algorithm should be quite sufficient.

4.4 Case Analysis

The review text below is for a sci-fi movie which has the golden label 10 (most positive). However, if it is read as an isolated piece of text, identifying its sentiment is difficult. The LSTM+LA model gives it the rating of 1 (most negative), perhaps because on the surface, there are many negative words like *unacceptable*, *criticize* and *sucks* even though the reviewer is praising the movie. Since our user memory can learn that the reviewer is a fan of sci-fi movies, our DUPMN model indeed gives the correct rating of 10.

okay, there are two types of movie lovers: ... they expect to see a Titanic every time they go to the cinema ... this movie sucks? ... it is definitely better than other sci-fi ..... the audio and visual effects are simply terrific and Travolta's performance is brilliant-funny and interesting. what people expect from sci-fi is beyond me ... the rating for Battlefield Earth is below 2.5, which is unacceptable for a movie with such

*craftsmanship. Scary movie, possibly the worst of all time -
..., has a 6! maybe we should all be a little more subtle when
we criticize movies... especially sci-fi.., since they have become an endangered genre ... give this movie the recognition
it deserves.*

5 Conclusion and Future Work

We propose a novel dual memory network model
for sentiment predictions. We argue that user profile and product information are fundamentally
different as user profiles reflect more on subjectivity whereas product information reflects more
on salient features of products at aggregated level.
Based on this hypothesis, two separate memory
networks for user context and product context are
built at the document level through a hierarchical
learning model. The inclusion of an attention layer
can further capture semantic information more effectively. Evaluation on three benchmark review
datasets shows that the proposed DUPMN model
outperforms the current state-of-the-art systems
with significant improvements shown in p-value
of 0.007, 0.004 and 0.001 respectively. We also
show that single hop memory networks is the most
effective model. Evaluation results show that user
profile and product information are indeed different and have different effects on different datasets.
In more subjective datasets such as IMDB, the inclusion of user profile information is more important. Whereas on more objective datasets such
as Yelp data, collective information of restaurant
plays a more important role in classification.

Future works include two directions. One direction is to explore the contribution of user profiles
and product information in aspects level sentiment
analysis tasks. Another direction is to explore how
knowledge-based information can be incorporated
to further improve sentiment classification tasks.

Acknowledgments

The work is partially supported by the research
grants from Hong Kong Polytechnic University
(PolyU RTVU) and GRF grant (CERG PolyU
15211/14E, PolyU 152006/16E).

References

Yoshua Bengio, Patrice Simard, and Paolo Frasconi.
1994. Learning long-term dependencies with gradient descent is difficult. *IEEE transactions on neural
networks*, 5(2):157–166.

Chih-Chung Chang and Chih-Jen Lin. 2011. Libsvm: a
library for support vector machines. *ACM transactions on intelligent systems and technology (TIST)*,
2(3):27.

Huimin Chen, Maosong Sun, Cunchao Tu, Yankai Lin,
and Zhiyuan Liu. 2016. Neural sentiment classification with user and product attention. EMNLP.

Rajarshi Das, Manzil Zaheer, Siva Reddy, and
Andrew McCallum. 2017. Question answering on knowledge bases and text using universal
schema and memory networks. *arXiv preprint
arXiv:1704.08384*.

Zi-Yi Dou. 2017. Capturing user and product information for document level sentiment analysis with deep
memory network. In *Proceedings of the 2017 Conference on Empirical Methods in Natural Language
Processing*, pages 521–526.

Lin Gui, Ruifeng Xu, Yulan He, Qin Lu, and Zhongyu
Wei. 2016. Intersubjectivity and sentiment: From
language to knowledge. In *IJCAI*, pages 2789–
2795.

Sepp Hochreiter and Jürgen Schmidhuber. 1997.
Long short-term memory. *Neural computation*,
9(8):1735–1780.

Ozan Irsoy and Claire Cardie. 2014. Opinion mining
with deep recurrent neural networks. In *EMNLP*,
pages 720–728.

Sarthak Jain. 2016. Question answering over knowledge base using factual memory networks. In *Proceedings of the NAACL Student Research Workshop*,
pages 109–115.

Yoon Kim. 2014. Convolutional neural networks for sentence classification. *arXiv preprint
arXiv:1408.5882*.

Svetlana Kordumova, Jan van Gemert, and Cees GM
Snoek. 2016. Exploring the long tail of social me-
dia tags. In *International Conference on Multimedia
Modeling*, pages 51–62. Springer.

Yunfei Long, Qin Lu, Rong Xiang, Minglei Li, and
Chu-Ren Huang. 2017a. Fake news detection
through multi-perspective speaker profiles. In *Proceedings of the Eighth International Joint Conference on Natural Language Processing (Volume 2:
Short Papers)*, volume 2, pages 252–256.

Yunfei Long, Lu Qin, Rong Xiang, Minglei Li, and
Chu-Ren Huang. 2017b. A cognition based attention model for sentiment analysis. In *Proceedings of
the 2017 Conference on Empirical Methods in Natural Language Processing*, pages 473–482.

Christopher D Manning, Mihai Surdeanu, John Bauer,
Jenny Rose Finkel, Steven Bethard, and David Mc-
Closky. 2014. The stanford corenlp natural language processing toolkit. In *ACL (System Demonstrations)*, pages 55–60.

Abhijit Mishra, Diptesh Kanojia, Seema Nagar, Kuntal Dey, and Pushpak Bhattacharyya. 2016. Leveraging cognitive features for sentiment analysis. In *Proceedings of The 20th SIGNLL Conference on Computational Natural Language Learning*, pages 156–166.

Qiao Qian, Minlie Huang, Jinhao Lei, and Xiaoyan Zhu. 2016. Linguistically regularized lstms for sentiment classification. *arXiv preprint arXiv:1611.03949*.

Richard Socher, Jeffrey Pennington, Eric H Huang, Andrew Y Ng, and Christopher D Manning. 2011. Semi-supervised recursive autoencoders for predicting sentiment distributions. In *Proceedings of the Conference on Empirical Methods in Natural Language Processing*, pages 151–161. Association for Computational Linguistics.

Richard Socher, Alex Perelygin, Jean Y Wu, Jason Chuang, Christopher D Manning, Andrew Y Ng, and Christopher Potts. 2013. Recursive deep models for semantic compositionality over a sentiment treebank. In *Proceedings of the conference on empirical methods in natural language processing (EMNLP)*, volume 1631, page 1642. Citeseer.

Sainbayar Sukhbaatar, Jason Weston, Rob Fergus, et al. 2015. End-to-end memory networks. In *Advances in neural information processing systems*, pages 2440–2448.

Martin Sundermeyer, Ralf Schlüter, and Hermann Ney. 2012. Lstm neural networks for language modeling. In *Thirteenth Annual Conference of the International Speech Communication Association*.

Duyu Tang, Bing Qin, and Ting Liu. 2015a. Document modeling with gated recurrent neural network for sentiment classification. In *Proceedings of the 2015 Conference on Empirical Methods in Natural Language Processing*, pages 1422–1432.

Duyu Tang, Bing Qin, and Ting Liu. 2015b. Learning semantic representations of users and products for document level sentiment classification. In *Proc. ACL*.

Duyu Tang, Bing Qin, and Ting Liu. 2015c. Learning semantic representations of users and products for document level sentiment classification. In *Proceedings of the 53rd Annual Meeting of the Association for Computational Linguistics and the 7th International Joint Conference on Natural Language Processing (Volume 1: Long Papers)*, pages 1014–1023, Beijing, China. Association for Computational Linguistics.

Duyu Tang, Bing Qin, and Ting Liu. 2016. Aspect level sentiment classification with deep memory network. *arXiv preprint arXiv:1605.08900*.

Duyu Tang, Furu Wei, Nan Yang, Ming Zhou, Ting Liu, and Bing Qin. 2014. Learning sentiment-specific word embedding for twitter sentiment classification. In *ACL (1)*, pages 1555–1565.

Jason Weston, Sumit Chopra, and Antoine Bordes. 2014. Memory networks. *arXiv preprint arXiv:1410.3916*.

Zhen Wu, Xin-Yu Dai, Cunyan Yin, Shujian Huang, and Jiajun Chen. 2018. Improving review representations with user attention and product attention for sentiment classification. *Proceedings of the Thirty-Second AAAI Conference on Artificial Intelligence (AAAI-18)*.

Jiacheng Xu, Danlu Chen, Xipeng Qiu, and Xuangjing Huang. 2016. Cached long short-term memory neural networks for document-level sentiment classification. *arXiv preprint arXiv:1610.04989*.

Zichao Yang, Diyi Yang, Chris Dyer, Xiaodong He, Alex Smola, and Eduard Hovy. 2016. Hierarchical attention networks for document classification. In *Proceedings of the 2016 Conference of the North American Chapter of the Association for Computational Linguistics: Human Language Technologies*.

Measuring Issue Ownership using Word Embeddings [*]

Amaru Cuba Gyllensten
RISE AI
`amaru.cuba.gyllensten@ri.se`

Magnus Sahlgren
RISE AI
`magnus.sahlgren@ri.se`

Abstract

Sentiment and topic analysis are common methods used for social media monitoring. Essentially, these methods answers questions such as, "what is being talked about, regarding X", and "what do people feel, regarding X". In this paper, we investigate another venue for social media monitoring, namely *issue ownership* and *agenda setting*, which are concepts from political science that have been used to explain voter choice and electoral outcomes. We argue that issue alignment and agenda setting can be seen as a kind of semantic source similarity of the kind "how similar is source A to issue owner P, when talking about issue X", and as such can be measured using word/document embedding techniques. We present work in progress towards measuring that kind of conditioned similarity, and introduce a new notion of similarity for predictive embeddings. We then test this method by measuring the similarity between politically aligned media and political parties, conditioned on bloc-specific issues.

1 Introduction

Social Media Monitoring (SMM; i.e. monitoring of online discussions in social media) has become an established application domain with a large body of scientific literature, and considerable commercial interest. The subfields of *Topic Detection and Tracking* (Allan et al., 1998; Sridhar, 2015) and *Sentiment Analysis* (Turney, 2002; Pang and Lee, 2008; Liu, 2012; Pozzi et al., 2016) are both scientific topics spawned entirely within the SMM domain. In its most basic form, SMM entails nothing more than counting occurrences of terms in data; producing frequency lists of commonly used vocabulary, and matching of term sets

related to various topics and sentiments. More sophisticated approaches use various forms of probabilistic topic detection (such as Latent Dirichlet Allocation) and sentiment analysis based on supervised machine learning.

The central questions SMM seeks to answer are *"what do users talk about?"* and *"how do they feel about it?"*. Answers to these questions may provide useful insight for market research and communications departments. It is apparent how product and service companies may use such analysis to gain an understanding of their target audience. It is also apparent how such analysis may be used in the context of elections for providing an indication of citizens' opinions as manifested in what they write in social media. There are numerous studies attempting to use various forms of social media monitoring techniques to predict the outcome of elections, with varying success (Bermingham and Smeaton, 2011; Ceron et al., 2015).

Most notably, the recent examples of the inadequacy of standard opinion measuring techniques to forecast the most recent US election and the Brexit demonstrate that for certain questions related to measuring mass opinion, standard SMM techniques may be inadequate. Political scientists have used the concepts of *agenda setting* and *issue ownership* to explain voter choice and election outcomes (Klüver and naki Sagarzazu, 2016; Kiousis et al., 2015; Stubager, 2018). In short, the issue ownership theory of voting states that voters identify the most credible party proponent of a particular issue and cast their ballots for that issue owner (Bélanger and Meguid, 2008). Agenda setting refers to the media's role in influencing the importance of issues in the public agenda (Mccombs and Reynolds, 2002). Note that current social media monitoring techniques are unable to measure these concepts in a satisfactory manner; it does not suffice to measure the occurrence of cer-

[*]This research was supported by the Swedish Research Council under contract 2017-02429

Proceedings of the 9th Workshop on Computational Approaches to Subjectivity, Sentiment and Social Media Analysis, pages 149–155
Brussels, Belgium, October 31, 2018. ©2018 Association for Computational Linguistics
https://doi.org/10.18653/v1/P17

tain keywords, since most parties tend to use the same vocabulary to discuss issues, and sentiment analysis does not touch upon the issue ownership and agenda setting questions. What is needed for measuring issue ownership and agenda setting is a way to measure *language use*, i.e. when talking about an issue, to which extent does the language used align with issue owner A vs. issue owner B.

We argue that issue alignment can be seen as a kind of semantic source similarity of the kind "how similar is source A to issue owner P, when talking about issue X", and as such can be measured using word/document embedding techniques. To measure that kind of conditioned similarity we introduce a new notion of similarity for predictive word embeddings. This method enables us to manipulate the similarity measure by weighting the set of entities we account for in the predictive scoring function. The proposed method is applied to measure similarity between party programs and various subsets of online text sources, conditioned on bloc specific issues. The results indicate that this conditioning disentangles similarity. We can, for example, observe that while the Left Party representation is, overall, similar to that of nativist media, it differs significantly on nativist issue, while this effect is not seen to the same extent on more mainstream left wing or right wing media.

2   Vector Similarity

Vector similarity has been a foundational concept in natural language processing ever sine the introduction of the *vector space model* for information retrieval by Salton (1971). In this model, queries and document are represented as vectors in term space, and similarity is expressed using cosine similarity. The main reason for using cosine similarity in the vector space model is that it normalizes for vector length; the fact that a document (or query) contains a certain word is more important than how many times it occurs in the document.

The vector space model was the main source of inspiration for early work on *vector semantics*, such as Latent Semantic Analysis (Deerwester et al., 1990; Landauer and Dumais, 1997) and the works on *word space models* by Schütze (1992, 1993). These works continued to embrace cosine similarity as the similarity metric of choice, since length normalization is equally desired when words are represented by vectors whose elements encode (some function of) co-occurrences with other words. Contemporary research on *distributional semantics* (Sahlgren, 2006; Bullinaria and Levy, 2007; Turney and Pantel, 2010; Pennington et al., 2014) still use largely the same mathematical machinery as the vector space model, and cosine similarity is still the preferred similarity metric due to its simplicity and use of length normalization. Even neural language models, which originate from the neural network community, employ cosine similarity to quantify similarity between learned representations (Mikolov et al., 2013; Bojanowski et al., 2017).

Word embeddings, as these techniques are nowadays referred to, have been used extensively in SMM, both for topic detection (Sridhar, 2015) and for sentiment analysis (Severyn and Moschitti, 2015). To the best of our knowledge, only one previous study (Dahlberg and Sahlgren, 2014) has used word embeddings to analyze issue ownership. However, that study relied on simple nearest neighbor analysis using cosine similarity to study language use in the Swedish blogosphere.

We believe that prediction-based word embeddings such as Word2Vec are amenable to another notion of similarity, which we call predictive similarity.

2.1   Predictive Similarity

Given a function $f : A \times B \to \mathbb{R}$, we define the predictive similarity of two items $x, y \in A$ as the correlation of $f(x, \mathbf{b})$, and $f(y, \mathbf{b})$, where $\mathbf{b}$ is a random variable of type B:

$$psim(x, y) = \frac{\mathrm{cov}\left(f\left(x, \mathbf{b}\right), f\left(y, \mathbf{b}\right)\right)}{\sqrt{\mathrm{var}\left(f\left(x, \mathbf{b}\right)\right) \mathrm{var}\left(f\left(y, \mathbf{b}\right)\right)}} \tag{1}$$

At a very general level, prediction based word embeddings such as Word2Vec or FastText consists of a scoring function $s : C \times T \to \mathbb{R}$ with an objective function taking the following form:

$$\sum_{t \times C \in D} \left[\sum_{c \in C} l(s(c, t)) + \sum_{n \in \mathcal{N}_{t,c}} l(-s(n, t)) \right] \tag{2}$$

where l is the logistic loss function $l(x) = \log(1 + e^{-x})$ and s being the model-specific scoring function that relates to the probability of observing the target t in the context c. For the Skipgram variant of Word2Vec, this function s is simply the dot

		orange	
	paint	**juice**	**county**
1	deep-red	cranberry	siskiyou
2	fuschia	lime	calaveras
3	lime-green	caraway	ventura
4	hand-woven	fanta	osceola
5	blue	clove	yolo
6	yellow	zests	mendocino
7	ocher	coconut	bernardino
8	linoleum	peppercorns	okanogan
9	duck-egg	lemons	okfuskee
10	rust-colored	peach	tuolumne

Table 1: Examples of predictive similarity neighborhoods of "orange" conditioned on "paint", "juice", and "county", respectively. [2]

product between a vector representation of the target word t, and a vector representation of the context word c.

The predictive similarity has several interpretations for the Skipgram model, but the simplest one is the one where we let $f = s$, i.e. we say that the similarity of two words x and y is the correlation between the scores they assign to target words $\mathbf{b}$, i.e. $\mathrm{corr}(s(x, \mathbf{b}), s(y, \mathbf{b}))$. Since s is linear, this correlation takes a fairly simple form: [1]

$$\mathrm{cov}(s(x, \mathbf{b}), f(s, \mathbf{b}))$$
$$= \mathbf{E}\left[\left(x^T\mathbf{b} - \overline{x^T\mathbf{b}}\right)\left(y^T\mathbf{b} - \overline{y^T\mathbf{b}}\right)\right]$$
$$= \mathbf{E}\left[\left(x^T\left(\mathbf{b} - \overline{\mathbf{b}}\right)\right)\left(y^T\left(\mathbf{b} - \overline{\mathbf{b}}\right)\right)^T\right]$$
$$= x^T\mathbf{E}\left[\left(\mathbf{b} - \overline{\mathbf{b}}\right)\left(\mathbf{b} - \overline{\mathbf{b}}\right)^T\right]y \qquad (3)$$
$$= x^T\,\mathrm{var}(\mathbf{b})y$$
$$psim(x, y) = \frac{x^T\,\mathrm{var}(\mathbf{b})y}{\sqrt{x^T\,\mathrm{var}(\mathbf{b})x\; y^T\,\mathrm{var}(\mathbf{b})y}}$$

We argue that we can get a a notion of conditioned similarity by estimating a *weighted* correlation, where the weighting acts as the conditioning.

Table 1 shows a small example where we queried the neighborhood of the word "orange", conditioned such that a single word ("paint", "juice", and "county", respectively) accounts for half the weight in var($\mathbf{b}$), with all other words in the vocabulary having equal weights.

Predictive similarity can easily be extended to similar models, and for the purpose of this paper in particular, we extend it to Doc2Vec (Le and Mikolov, 2014), a model where the notion of context is enriched by the source[3] of the utterance. The scoring function s then takes the following form: $s(t, c, d) = t^T(c + d)$, with d being a vector representation of the source in question.

We argue that by using conditioned predictive similarity on document embeddings we can answer questions such as: "how similar is *The BBC* to *The Daily Mail*, when talking about *Climate Change*". The end goal is to measure aggregate similarity in specific issues: "when talking about *health policy*, to which extent does the general language use align with *Source A, Source B, Source C*, et.c.".

3 Experiments

To answer the language similarity question posed by issue ownership we measure aggregate predictive similarity between party platforms and various subsets of online text data, conditioned on words pertaining to left wing issues, right wing issues, nativist issues, and general political topics.

We built Doc2Vec embeddings (Le and Mikolov, 2014) on Swedish online data from 2018 crawled by Trendiction and manually scraped party platforms from the eight parties in parliament and *Feministiskt Initiativ* (Feminist Initiative).[4] Doc2Vec requires us to define a notion of source. For the data crawled by Trendiction, we take the source to be the domain name of the document, e.g. *www.wikipedia.se*, whereas for the manually scraped party platforms, we assign it the appropriate party identifier. The model was trained using the Gensim package (Řehůřek and Sojka, 2010) with embedding dimension 100 and a context window of size 8.

In collaboration with the Political Science department at Gothenburg University we also extracted keywords for each party from their party platform. We use these party specific keywords as a crude proxy for issues: we let left wing issues be defined by the union of left bloc party keywords, right wing issues be defined by right bloc party keywords, and nativist issues be defined by the

---

[1] It might be interesting to note that this coincides with cosine similarity if var($\mathbf{b}$) is a scalar multiple of the identity, i.e. if there is no correlation between dimensions and all dimensions have the same variance.

[3] By source we can mean a paragraph, document, or in our case: domain name from which the utterance originates.

[4] A complete list of parties, their abbreviations, their English translations, and bloc affiliation can be found in Table 2.

Abbr.	Name	Translation	Word count	Bloc
V	Vänsterpartiet	The Left Party	15,383	
S	Socialdemokraterna	The Social Democrats	27,899	Left
MP	Miljöpartiet	The Green Party	19,471	
C	Centern	The Centre Party	68,136	
L	Liberalerna	The Liberals	64,276	Right
KD	Kristdemokraterna	The Christian Democrats	16,494	
M	Moderaterna	The Moderates	12,807	
SD	Sverigedemokraterna	The Swedish Democrats	3,430	N/A (Nativist)
FI	Feministiskt Initiativ	Feminist Initiative	84,424	N/A

Table 2: Party abbreviations, names, translated names, word count, and bloc allegiance.

keywords of Sverigedemokraterna (The Swedish Democrats), we also let the union of all keywords be representative for general political discourse. The parties' bloc alignment and the size of the data used to generate representations for them can be seen in Table 2.

We let the conditioned predictive similarity between sources two x and y be defined by the following equation (Equation 4), i.e. a weighted variant of equation 3, where only words among the given issues keywords are accounted for, as described by Equation 5.

$$psim(x, y) = \frac{x^T \text{var}(\mathbf{t}; w) y}{\sqrt{x^T \text{var}(\mathbf{t}; w) x \; y^T \text{var}(\mathbf{t}; w) y}} \tag{4}$$

$$w_t = \begin{cases} 1, t \in \text{Issue keywords} \\ 0, t \notin \text{Issue keywords} \end{cases} \tag{5}$$

Above, x and y are document vectors and $\text{var}(\mathbf{t}; w_t)$ is the weighted covariance matrix of the target word vectors. This is the equivalent of letting $s(d, c, t) = d^T t$, i.e. the case we ignore the effect of context words.

Table 3 (next side) shows the average predictive similarity between the political party platforms and various online data sources, conditioned on left wing party issues, right wing party issues, nativist party issues, and general political discourse. Average cosine similarity between the sources and parties is also shown as a comparison.

4 Discussion

As can be seen in Table 3, there is a marked difference when conditioning on issues versus using regular document — i.e. cosine — similarity. Furthermore, we observe that conditioned similarity seems to align left wing media with left wing parties, nativist media with the Swedish Democrats, but not align right wing media with right wing parties. This effect can be made more apparent by grouping the parties into blocs and fitting a simple additive model for the similarities along all dimensions (i.e. Media, Issues, and Bloc), as a way to normalize for general Media, Issue, and Bloc similarity. The results of this normalization, i.e. the residuals, can be observed in Table 4. From this one can see a small trend where left wing media is similar to left wing parties, nativist media being similar to the Swedish Democrats, and both left wing media and right wing media being dissimilar to the Swedish Democrats.

Furthermore, we see a strong dissimilarity between nativist media and all parties regarding nativist issues. This is particularly true for parties promoting liberal immigration policy: The Left Party, The Social Democrats, The Green Party, The Centre Party, and The Moderates are all currently or historically promoting liberal immigration policy at odds with nativist sentiment.

A shortcoming of the method used here is the rather limited amount of party specific data: the quality and the quantity of the text data used varies drastically between parties, as can be seen in Table 2. Using, for example, parliamentary debates, opinion pieces, and other official party communication might improve data coverage.

5 Conclusion

In this paper we have introduced some very preliminary results on how to measure similarities in language use, conditioned on discourse, e.g. "how similar is *The BBC* to *The Daily Mail*, when talking about *Climate Change*". The end goal is to

Media	Issues	V	S	MP	C	L	KD	M	SD	FI
Left wing	Left wing	0.43	0.35	0.25	0.20	0.36	0.35	0.45	0.47	0.36
	Right wing	0.44	0.38	0.36	0.34	0.41	0.36	0.45	0.45	0.32
	Nativist	0.43	0.40	0.42	0.36	0.42	0.39	0.42	0.45	0.37
	All	0.42	0.35	0.31	0.28	0.38	0.36	0.42	0.44	0.36
	Cos	0.50	0.48	0.48	0.46	0.51	0.47	0.53	0.49	0.44
Right wing	Left wing	0.25	0.24	0.31	0.25	0.31	0.27	0.35	0.34	0.16
	Right wing	0.28	0.31	0.32	0.32	0.34	0.28	0.36	0.36	0.19
	Nativist	0.29	0.32	0.36	0.34	0.38	0.34	0.36	0.36	0.21
	All	0.26	0.27	0.31	0.30	0.34	0.30	0.35	0.34	0.18
	Cos	0.44	0.45	0.44	0.47	0.51	0.47	0.51	0.45	0.41
Nativist	Left wing	0.36	0.17	0.04	0.05	0.30	0.31	0.34	0.48	0.32
	Right wing	0.28	0.09	0.08	0.17	0.30	0.32	0.30	0.39	0.23
	Nativist	0.05	-0.11	0.02	0.01	0.17	0.16	0.03	0.21	0.08
	All	0.28	0.08	0.06	0.10	0.28	0.31	0.27	0.39	0.29
	Cos	0.51	0.45	0.47	0.45	0.56	0.53	0.56	0.61	0.53
All News	Left wing	0.32	0.26	0.25	0.21	0.33	0.30	0.38	0.40	0.25
	Right wing	0.33	0.30	0.30	0.31	0.36	0.32	0.38	0.40	0.24
	Nativist	0.30	0.28	0.33	0.30	0.36	0.33	0.33	0.36	0.24
	All	0.32	0.27	0.27	0.26	0.34	0.32	0.36	0.38	0.25
	Cos	0.47	0.46	0.46	0.47	0.52	0.48	0.52	0.48	0.44
Social	Left wing	0.07	0.11	0.18	0.06	0.06	0.08	0.09	0.12	0.18
	Right wing	0.20	0.28	0.31	0.22	0.18	0.14	0.20	0.17	0.26
	Nativist	0.12	0.18	0.19	0.08	0.09	0.07	0.12	0.22	0.21
	All	0.13	0.18	0.20	0.14	0.11	0.10	0.13	0.16	0.23
	Cos	0.42	0.42	0.42	0.40	0.39	0.41	0.42	0.45	0.39

Table 3: Average predictive similarity (and cosine similarity) between political parties and various subsets of the online sources.

Media	Bloc Issues	Left	Nativist	Right
Left wing	Left wing	-0.02	-0.02	-0.06
	Nativist	0.09	-0.00	0.03
	Right wing	0.02	-0.05	-0.02
Nativist	Left wing	0.02	0.18	0.04
	Nativist	-0.15	-0.06	-0.08
	Right wing	-0.03	0.08	0.05
Right wing	Left wing	-0.02	-0.06	-0.02
	Nativist	0.07	-0.02	0.07
	Right wing	0.01	-0.06	-0.01

Table 4: Grouped and normalized predictive similarity.

measure aggregate similarity in specific issues, answering questions such as "when talking about *health policy*, to which extent does the general language use align with *Source A*, *Source B*, etc.", and use such an aggregate measure to study issue ownership at scale.

We believe that issue ownership and agenda setting can be explored through the lens of language use and similarity, but deem it necessary to condition similarity to the specific issue at hand. The reason for this is the need to distinguish between level of engagement in an issue and agreement in an issue: two sources that talk a lot about an issue — e.g. health insurance — but in very different ways should not be considered similar. Dually, if a source very rarely talks about an issue, but consistently does so in a way that is very similar to the way some political party talks about it, we consider it reasonable to believe that that source's opinion aligns with the political party in question on that specific issue.

While we have not found a satisfactory, direct, evaluation of this task, we do believe that the examples we put forward show some face validity of the proposed method at measuring ideological alignment.

6 Appendix

6.1 Left wing news sources

- Aftonbladet
- Arbetarbladet
- Dala-Demokraten
- Folkbladet
- ETC
- Arbetaren
- Flamman
- Bang
- Offensiv
- Proletären

6.2 Right wing news sources

- Dagens Industri
- Dalabygden
- Hallands Nyheter
- Axess
- Svensk Tidskrift
- Hemmets Vän
- Dagens Nyheter
- Göteborgs-Posten
- Helsingborgs Dagblad
- Nerikes Allehanda
- Sydsvenskan
- Upsala Nya Tidning
- Expressen
- Svenska Dagbladet
- Smålandsposten
- Norrbottens Kuriren

6.3 Nativist news sources

- Nordfront
- Samhällsnytt
- Fria Tider
- Nya Tider
- Samtiden

References

James Allan, Jaime Carbonell, George Doddington, Jonathan Yamron, Yiming Yang, et al. 1998. Topic detection and tracking pilot study: Final report. In *Proceedings of the DARPA broadcast news transcription and understanding workshop*, volume 1998, pages 194–218. Citeseer.

Éric Bélanger and Bonnie M. Meguid. 2008. Issue salience, issue ownership, and issue-based vote choice. *Electoral Studies*, 27(3):477 – 491.

Adam Bermingham and Alan Smeaton. 2011. On using twitter to monitor political sentiment and predict election results. In *Proceedings of the Workshop on Sentiment Analysis where AI meets Psychology (SAAIP 2011)*, pages 2–10.

Piotr Bojanowski, Edouard Grave, Armand Joulin, and Tomas Mikolov. 2017. Enriching word vectors with subword information. *Transactions of the Association for Computational Linguistics*, 5:135–146.

John A. Bullinaria and Joseph P. Levy. 2007. Extracting semantic representations from word co-occurrence statistics: A computational study. *Behavior Research Methods*, 39(3):510–526.

Andrea Ceron, Luigi Curini, and Stefano M Iacus. 2015. Using sentiment analysis to monitor electoral campaigns: Method mattersevidence from the united states and italy. *Social Science Computer Review*, 33(1):3–20.

Ciprian Chelba, Tomas Mikolov, Mike Schuster, Qi Ge, Thorsten Brants, Phillipp Koehn, and Tony Robinson. 2013. One billion word benchmark for measuring progress in statistical language modeling. *arXiv preprint arXiv:1312.3005*.

Stefan Dahlberg and Magnus Sahlgren. 2014. Issue framing and language use in the swedish blogosphere: Changing notions of the outsider concept. In Bertie Kaal, Isa Maks, and Annemarie van Elfrinkhof, editors, *From Text to Political Positions: Text Analysis across Disciplines*, pages 71–92. John Benjamins.

Scott Deerwester, Susan T. Dumais, George W. Furnas, Thomas K. Landauer, and Richard Harshman. 1990. Indexing by latent semantic analysis. *Journal of the American Society for Information Science*, 41(6):391–407.

Spiro Kiousis, Jesper Strömbäck, and Michael McDevitt. 2015. Influence of issue decision salience on vote choice: Linking agenda setting, priming, and issue ownership. *International Journal of Communication*, 9(0).

Heike Klüver and Iñaki Sagarzazu. 2016. Setting the agenda or responding to voters? political parties, voters and issue attention. *West European Politics*, 39(2):380–398.

Thomas K Landauer and Susan T Dumais. 1997. A solution to plato's problem: The latent semantic analysis theory of acquisition, induction, and representation of knowledge. *Psychological review*, 104(2):211–240.

Quoc Le and Tomas Mikolov. 2014. Distributed representations of sentences and documents. In *International Conference on Machine Learning*, pages 1188–1196.

Bing Liu. 2012. *Sentiment Analysis and Opinion Mining*. Morgan & Claypool Publishers.

Maxwell Mccombs and Amy Reynolds. 2002. News influence on our pictures of the world. In Jennings Bryant and Dolf Zillmann, editors, *Media Effects. Advances in Theory and Research*, pages 1–18. Lawrence Erlbaum Associates.

Tomas Mikolov, Ilya Sutskever, Kai Chen, Greg S Corrado, and Jeff Dean. 2013. Distributed representations of words and phrases and their compositionality. In C. J. C. Burges, L. Bottou, M. Welling, Z. Ghahramani, and K. Q. Weinberger, editors, *Advances in Neural Information Processing Systems 26*, pages 3111–3119. Curran Associates, Inc.

Bo Pang and Lillian Lee. 2008. Opinion mining and sentiment analysis. *Foundations and Trends in Information Retrieval*, 2(1-2):1–135.

Jeffrey Pennington, Richard Socher, and Christopher D Manning. 2014. Glove: Global vectors for word representation. In *EMNLP*, volume 14, pages 1532–1543.

Federico Alberto Pozzi, Elisabetta Fersini, Enza Messina, and Bing Liu. 2016. *Sentiment Analysis in Social Networks*, 1st edition. Morgan Kaufmann Publishers Inc., San Francisco, CA, USA.

Radim Řehůřek and Petr Sojka. 2010. Software Framework for Topic Modelling with Large Corpora. In *Proceedings of the LREC 2010 Workshop on New Challenges for NLP Frameworks*, pages 45–50, Valletta, Malta. ELRA. `http://is.muni.cz/publication/884893/en`.

Magnus Sahlgren. 2006. *The Word-space model*. Ph.D. thesis, University of Stockholm (Sweden).

Gerard Salton. 1971. *The SMART Retrieval System— Experiments in Automatic Document Processing*. Prentice-Hall, Inc., Upper Saddle River, NJ, USA.

Hinrich Schütze. 1992. Dimensions of meaning. In *Proceedings of the 1992 ACM/IEEE Conference on Supercomputing*, Supercomputing '92, pages 787–796, Los Alamitos, CA, USA. IEEE Computer Society Press.

Hinrich Schütze. 1993. Word space. In *Advances in Neural Information Processing Systems 5*, pages 895–902. Morgan Kaufmann.

Aliaksei Severyn and Alessandro Moschitti. 2015. Twitter sentiment analysis with deep convolutional neural networks. In *Proceedings of the 38th International ACM SIGIR Conference on Research and Development in Information Retrieval*, pages 959–962. ACM.

Vivek Kumar Rangarajan Sridhar. 2015. Unsupervised topic modeling for short texts using distributed representations of words. In *Proceedings of the 1st workshop on vector space modeling for natural language processing*, pages 192–200.

Rune Stubager. 2018. What is issue ownership and how should we measure it? *Political Behavior*, 40(2):345–370.

Peter D. Turney. 2002. Thumbs up or thumbs down?: Semantic orientation applied to unsupervised classification of reviews. In *Proceedings of the 40th Annual Meeting on Association for Computational Linguistics*, ACL '02, pages 417–424, Stroudsburg, PA, USA. Association for Computational Linguistics.

Peter D. Turney and Patrick Pantel. 2010. From frequency to meaning: Vector space models of semantics. *Journal of Artificial Intelligence Research*, 37(1):141–188.

Sentiment Expression Boundaries in Sentiment Polarity Classification

Rasoul Kaljahi
ADAPT
School of Computing
Dublin City University
rasoul.kaljahi@adaptcentre.

Jennifer Foster
ADAPT
School of Computing
Dublin City University
jennifer.foster@adaptcentre.ie

Abstract

We investigate the effect of using sentiment expression boundaries in predicting sentiment polarity in aspect-level sentiment analysis. We manually annotate a freely available English sentiment polarity dataset with these boundaries and carry out a series of experiments which demonstrate that high quality sentiment expressions can boost the performance of polarity classification. Our experiments with neural architectures also show that CNN networks outperform LSTMs on this task and dataset.

1 Introduction

Sentiment analysis is a much studied problem in natural language processing research, yet it is far from solved, especially when a fine-grained analysis is required. Aspect-based sentiment analysis (Pontiki et al., 2014, 2015, 2016) is concerned with multi-faceted opinions. Consider, for example, a restaurant review which states that the food was delicious but the place was too noisy. For anyone using such a review to inform a decision about where to dine, this aspect-based information is more useful than one overall sentiment score. In this work, we aim to improve the performance of sentence-level aspect-based sentiment polarity classification. We compare several neural architectures and we investigate whether identifying and highlighting the parts of the sentence which carry the sentiment can be beneficial for this task.

The data that we use in our experiments is an English dataset used in the SemEval 2016 Task on Aspect-Based Sentiment Analysis (Pontiki et al., 2016), which consists of consumer reviews of restaurants and laptops. Each sentence is annotated with the aspect of the restaurant or laptop that is being discussed in the sentence together with the polarity of the sentiment towards that as-

pect. Some aspects are quite general to any product or service, e.g. value for money, but many are domain-specific, e.g. battery life and performance for laptops, and ambience and food quality for restaurants.

We first apply two very widely used neural architectures – CNNs (LeCun et al., 1998) and LSTMs (Hochreiter and Schmidhuber, 1997) – to the problem of predicting the polarity towards an aspect. We show that CNNs work better than LSTMs, and experiment with two ways of combining the two networks, neither of which provide a significant improvement over CNNs. We compare to those SemEval 2016 shared task systems which also used a neural architecture, and confirm that our systems are competitive.

Our next step is to provide a further layer of annotation to the data by marking those words in a sentence which are contributing towards the sentiment. Once the data is annotated with sentiment expressions, we use the annotation to augment our baseline models and show that this information increases polarity classification accuracy by approximately six percentage points on average. We then experiment with multi-task learning (Caruana, 1997; Collobert and Weston, 2008; Bingel and Søgaard, 2017; Ruder, 2017) in order to jointly learn sentiment expression boundaries and polarities. However, we do not see an improvement in polarity classification with our joint architecture.

The paper is organised as follows: in Section 2 we describe our data in more detail; in Section 3 we describe the architectures of our baseline systems and compare to other neural systems; in Section 4, we describe the process of enriching the original dataset with sentiment expression annotations; in Section 5, our sentiment polarity classification experiments involving this enriched dataset are presented; we review related work on senti-

Proceedings of the 9th Workshop on Computational Approaches to Subjectivity, Sentiment and Social Media Analysis, pages 156–166
Brussels, Belgium, October 31, 2018. ©2018 Association for Computational Linguistics
https://doi.org/10.18653/v1/P17

D	Aspect Category	Sentence	Polarity
R	`food#prices`	*But the pizza is way to expensive*	Neg
R	`ambience#general`	*However , go for the ambience, and consider the food just a companion for a trip across the world !*	Pos
R	`food#quality`	*However , go for the ambience, and consider the food just a companion for a trip across the world !*	Neu
L	`laptop#design_features`	*Only two USB ports*	Neg
L	`laptop#general`	*It's a lemon*	Neg
L	`laptop#general`	*My first Mac computer and as many before me I just fall in love with it*	Pos

Table 1: SemEval 2016 Task 5 Dataset Examples (D: domain, R: restaurant, L: laptop)

	Laptop		Restaurant	
	Train	Test	Train	Test
# sentences	2500	808	2000	676
# aspect categories	2909	801	2507	859
% positive	56%	60%	66%	71%
% negative	37%	34%	30%	24%
% neutral	7%	6%	4%	5%

Table 2: Number of sentences, aspect categories and their polarity distributions in the datasets

ment expression annotation and the use of sentiment expressions in sentiment polarity classification in Section 6 before we summarise our findings and provide some pointers for future work in Section 7.

2 Data

The data used in our experiments consists of English consumer reviews (restaurants and laptops) released as part of the SemEval 2016 Shared Task on Aspect-Based Sentiment Analysis (Task 5, Subtask 1) (Pontiki et al., 2016). Each review sentence has been labelled with a sentiment polarity (*positive, negative, neutral*) towards an aspect of the laptop or restaurant under review (so-called *aspect categories*). Examples from the datasets are shown in Table 1. Each aspect category is of the form E#A, where E is an entity and A is some attribute of that entity. There are 11 distinct aspect categories in the restaurant dataset and 31 in the laptop dataset.

The SemEval 2016 shared task, and its previous iterations in 2014 and 2015, were concerned with several sentence-level subtasks including identifying aspect categories, opinion target expres-

sion(s)[1] and sentiment polarities. We focus on the polarity classification subtask, i.e. given a sentence and an aspect category, we attempt to predict the polarity of the sentiment expressed in the sentence towards that aspect category. Table 2 shows the number of sentences and aspect categories together with their polarity distribution in the training and test subsets of each domain. While some sentences contain multiple aspect categories (see the second and third examples in Table 1), most contain only one.

3 Neural Architecture

We build our aspect-based sentiment polarity classification systems using deep neural networks including Long Short-Term Memory (LSTM) networks (Hochreiter and Schmidhuber, 1997) and Convolutional Neural Networks (CNN) (LeCun et al., 1998). The input layer for these systems is the concatenation of an embedding layer, which uses pre-trained *GloVe* (Pennington et al., 2014) word embeddings[2] (1.9M vocabulary *Common Crawl*), concatenated with a one-hot vector which encodes information about aspect categories. At the output layer, we use a softmax function to perform the classification into positive, negative or neutral. The middle layers are then stacks of LSTM or CNN layers, the depth of which is determined via hyper-parameter tuning. A dropout layer follows each LSTM or CNN layer to prevent

---

[1] Opinion target expressions are the words in the sentence which refer to the aspect category, e.g. *pizza* in the first example of Table 1. We do not make use of this information since it is only available for those sentences where the aspect category is explicitly expressed in the sentence, and is not available at all for the laptop dataset.

[2] The embedding weights are not updated during training.

	Laptop		Restaurant	
	Dev	Test	Dev	Test
`lstm`	77.71	75.61	80.42	83.59
`cnn`	78.47	77.82	79.14	84.90
`chcnn+lstm`	77.10	74.45	80.74	83.28
`lstm+cnn`	80.45	76.32	80.68	84.52
`lstm+cnn(gse:aux)`	86.63	83.73	86.12	89.87
`lstm+cnn(gse:filtered)`	84.65	83.98	86.69	87.97
`lstm+cnn(gse:multitask)`	78.47	75.99	81.77	84.71

Table 3: Accuracy of aspect-based sentiment polarity classification models (`gse`: using gold-standard sentiment expressions, `filtered`: filtering non-SE tokens)

System	Type	Laptop	Restaurant
Khalil and El-Beltagy (2016)	CNN	77.40	85.44
Yanase et al. (2016)	RNN	70.29	81.02
Chernyshevich (2016)	MLP	77.90	83.90
Ruder et al. (2016b)	CNN	78.40	82.10

Table 4: Test set accuracy of neural systems who participated in the SemEval 2016 polarity classification task for aspect-based sentiment analysis

the models from overfitting.[3]

To tune the hyper-parameters, a development set is randomly sub-sampled from each training set. The list of tuned hyper-parameters and their selected best values for each domain are given in Appendix A. In addition to the tuned parameters, we use the *Adam* (Kingma and Ba, 2014) algorithm for optimization. The models are built using *Keras*[4] with a *TensorFlow*[5] backend. Note that the evaluation of each architecture is performed by three rounds of training and testing, and averaging the resulting accuracy for each dataset. This is done to handle the randomness introduced throughout the model training.

3.1 LSTM vs. CNN

Due to their ability to remember information over sequences of words, LSTMs are a natural choice for many NLP tasks. Our first model uses one or more (bidirectional) LSTM layers as the middle layers between the input and output layers. Figure 1a shows the architecture of this model. The accuracy of the model on the laptop and restaurant datasets can be found in the first row of Table 3.

Convolutional networks have also shown to be useful in text classification tasks (Kim, 2014). We build another model to investigate their effect in aspect-based sentiment polarity classification. The model is displayed in Figure 1b and its performance is reported in the second row of Table 3 . Comparing the accuracy of the LSTM and CNN models, we can see that the CNN models most of the time outperform LSTM models.

3.2 Combining LSTM and CNN

LSTM and CNN networks can be combined to take advantage of the benefits of both. Ma and Hovy (2016), for example, address sequence tagging problems (POS tagging and Named Entity Recognition) using a CNN at the character level, combining the resulting character embeddings with pre-trained word embeddings and feeding it into a bidirectional LSTM network. The output is then fed into a Conditional Random Field (CRF) classifier to jointly classify labels for all words in the sentence. Their combined architecture outperforms networks built using LSTMs alone, especially on the NER task. In a similar vein, Chiu and Nichols (2016) use CNNs to generate character-level features for NER and then concatenate them with word embeddings before finally inputting them into an LSTM network. They report new state-of-the-art performance using this

---

[3]Note that, to save space, the dropout layers are not shown in the architecture diagrams in Fig. 1 (discussed in subsequent sections).

[4]`https://keras.io/`

[5]`https://www.tensorflow.org/`

architecture, outperforming previous models relying on extensive feature engineering and external resources.

Here, we experiment with two different approaches to combining CNN and LSTM networks. In the first approach, we first apply CNN on the character embeddings to extract the character-level representations of each word. These vectors are then concatenated with the word embeddings and sent to a LSTM. This is similar to the approach used by Ma and Hovy (2016) and Chiu and Nichols (2016), except that our problem is a regular classification one rather than sequence labelling. The architecture is depicted in Figure 1c. Note that *TimeDistributed* is a wrapper used in Keras which applies a layer, with the same weights, to every temporal step of the input. As can be seen in Table 3, the resulting model (`chcnn+lstm`) does not perform better than the individual networks, and in fact has the lowest accuracies on the laptop datasets.

In the second approach, the input data is first fed to a LSTM network and then the output representation is passed to a convolutional network. This is different from the work described above in that it does not use characters and it also places the LSTM before the CNN, in order to allow the LSTM to account for the original word order. Figure 1d shows the architecture of this network. The performance of the model trained with this architecture is shown in Table 3 (`lstm+cnn`). This model outperforms the `chcnn+lstm` one. Compared to the best individual model (`CNN`), the accuracy increases on the laptop development set, degrades on the laptop test set and stays about the same on the restaurant datasets.

3.3 Comparison to Other Systems

Table 4 shows the four neural systems who competed in the sentence-level English polarity classification subtask of the SemEval 2016 aspect-based sentiment analysis task. Two of the four systems employed a CNN, one an LSTM and one a MLP. Specifying just the network type is of course a simplification because there are many differences between the systems including the input embeddings, the hyper-parameters and the training data (some systems combined the domains in training) but it does serve to demonstrate that our neural systems achieve competitive performance. Note, however, that the best system on the restaurant domain (Brun et al., 2016), with 88.13% accuracy, and on the laptop domain (Kumar et al., 2016), with 82.77% accuracy, are non-neural systems which employed a range of linguistic information as features. Ruder et al. (2016a) also show that improvements can be achieved by not focusing just on the sentence level and taking the context sentences in the review into account also.

4 Sentiment Expressions

We define a sentiment expression to be the part of the sentence which conveys the sentiment towards a certain aspect of the item under discussion. Thus, annotating a `<sentence,aspect category,polarity>` triple involves highlighting those words in the sentences which express the sentiment towards the aspect category. Table 5 shows the examples from Table 1 with the sentiment expressions marked. We distinguish between neutral polarities where no opinion is expressed (1) and neutral polarities which represent a "neutral" opinion (2). Only the latter type are considered to contain sentiment expressions.

(1) *We had lunch in that restaurant last week.*

(2) *The food was **OK**.*

The annotation was carried out by two annotators with a background in computational linguistics, using the *brat*[6] annotation tool. In marking the sentiment expression spans, the annotators followed the general rule of thumb of being concise while at the same time respecting phrase boundaries so that the resulting sentiment expression was a self-contained, semantically coherent phrase. In order to avoid annotator disagreement over sometimes somewhat arbitrary span boundaries, rules about what to include in a span were devised and documented in the annotation guidelines. For example, any preceding articles or auxiliaries are included before sentiment-bearing nouns and verbs, e.g. *the ease of setup* versus *ease of setup*, and *is still not working* versus *still not working*. The guidelines were calibrated at three stages. At each stage, 100 items, 50 per domain, were randomly selected and annotated. The disagreements were then discussed and the guidelines were adjusted. After finalising the guidelines, the entire dataset was divided between the two annotators and annotated.

---

[6] `http://brat.nlplab.org`

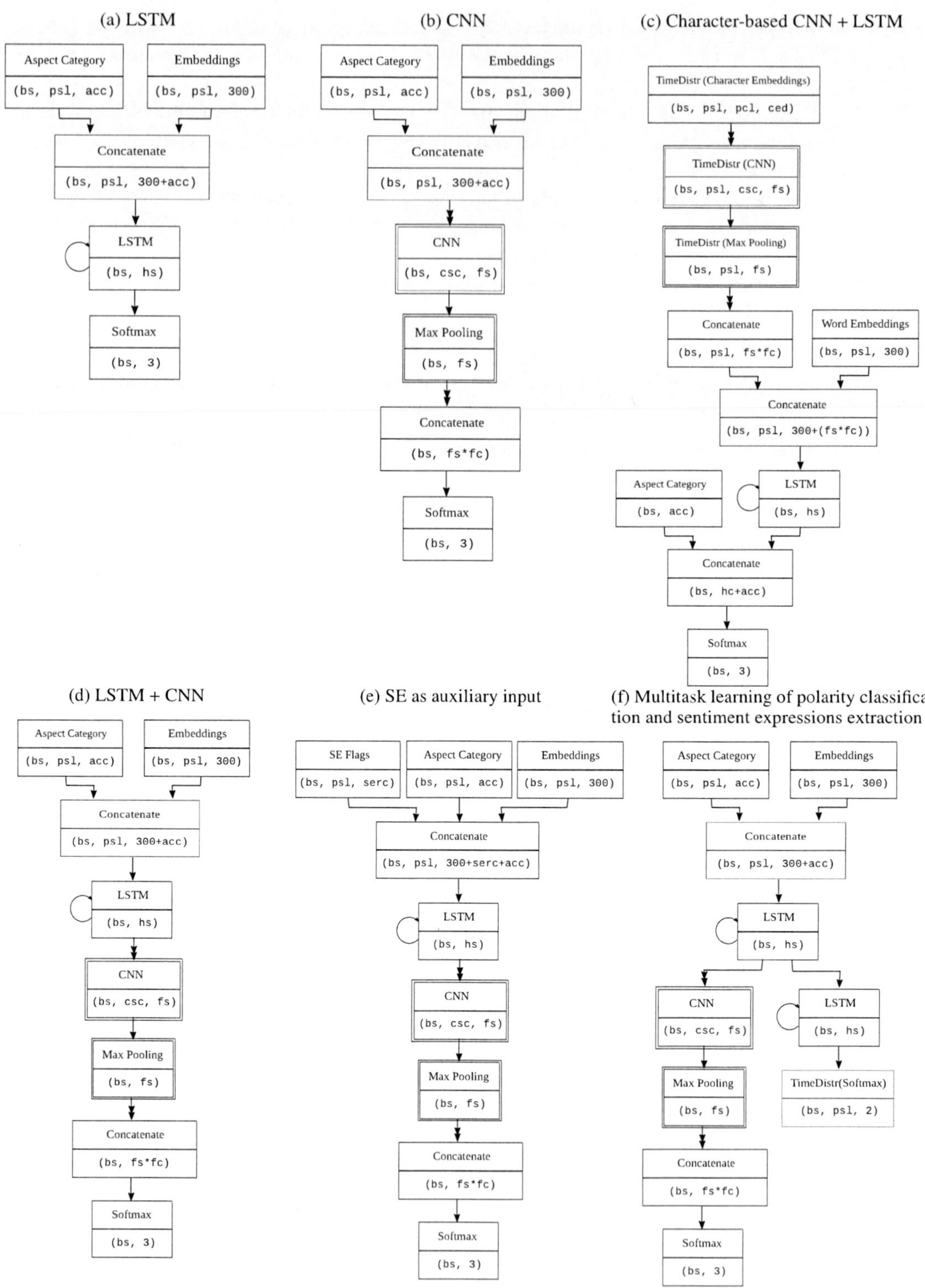

Figure 1: Architectures of the ABSA models; tuples are the shapes of the output tensors (`bs`: batch size, `psl`: padded sequence length, `acc`: aspect category count, `hs`: hidden layer size, `csc`: convolution step count, `fs`: filter size, `fc`: filter count, `TimeDistr`: distributing the layer over temporal steps of the input with the same weights, `CSC`: convolution step count, `serc`: repetition count for the SE flag (0 or 1 per token)). Note that the figures are only illustrative of the models and the middle layers are underrepresented. The double arrows show multiple input and double lines show multiple nodes.

D	Aspect Category	Sentence	Sentiment
R	`food#prices`	*But the pizza is* **way to expensive**	Neg
R	`ambience#general`	*However ,* **go for the ambience**, *and consider the food just a companion for a trip across the world !*	Pos
R	`food#quality`	*However , go for the ambience, and* **consider the food just a companion** *for a trip across the world !*	Neu
L	`laptop#design_features`	**Only two USB ports**	Neg
L	`laptop#general`	**It's a lemon**	Neg
L	`laptop#general`	*My first Mac computer and as many before me* **I just fall in love with it**	Pos

Table 5: SemEval 2016 Task 5 Dataset Examples with Sentiment Expressions (in bold)

Laptop			Restaurant		
P	R	$F1$	P	R	$F1$
81.63	91.58	86.32	89.67	91.61	90.63

Table 6: Inter-annotator agreement of sentiment expression annotation measured using precision, recall and F1 of sentiment expression span intersections

Inter-annotator agreement was calculated on a subset of 200 items, 100 per domain, where 100 items from each annotator's subset was also annotated by the other annotator. We used precision, recall and F_1 based on the intersection of the sentiment expression spans annotated by the two annotators, assuming the first annotator's annotations as gold-standard and the second annotator's as predicted.

The IAA scores, shown in Table 6, show a high level of agreement between the two annotators. The agreement on the restaurant dataset is particularly high, suggesting that the restaurant reviews use more straightforward language than the laptop reviews (also reflected in the polarity classification results - see Section 3). Examining the doubly annotated data, we see that, most of the time, the disputed annotations overlap and the disagreement is over how long the sentiment expression span should be. In fact, 122 out of the 200 samples in the laptop dataset and 142 out of 200 in the restaurant dataset were annotated in exactly the same way by the two annotators.

An example disagreement can be seen in (3) and (4). While the first annotator has decided that *No more Apple devices* is enough to infer the negative sentiment from the sentence, the second annotator deems *in my household* to be also contributing. With a binary overlap metric (correct for any overlap; wrong for no overlap), as used, for example, by Breck et al. (2007) to evaluate expression extraction, this example would have a perfect precision and recall score.

(3) *No more Apple devices in my household.*

(4) *No more Apple devices in my household.*

Concluding that the sentiment expressions have been marked with a reasonable level of consistency, we now go on to use these expression boundaries in more sentiment polarity classification experiments.

5 Using Sentiment Expressions in Polarity Classification

We conduct experiments to examine the degree to which sentiment expressions can help boost polarity classification performance. We first measure the upper bound of the improved performance using gold-standard sentiment expressions and experiment with two alternative ways of encoding the sentiment expression information. We then attempt to use the sentiment expression annotation in a multi-task setup, with the sentiment expression extraction as an auxiliary task and the polarity classification as the main one. For all our experiments we employ the combined LSTM/CNN architecture described in Section 3.2 – `lstm+cnn` in Table 3.

5.1 Using Gold-standard Sentiment Expressions

To exploit sentiment expressions in polarity classification, we experiment with two approaches. In the first approach, the sentiment expression is fed into the model as an auxiliary input, in concatenation with the embeddings and aspect categories. The architecture of this approach is illustrated in Figure 1e. The sentiment expression annotation of a sentence is encoded in a binary-valued vector of size equal to the sentence length. For every token inside the SE boundary, the binary value is 1 and 0 otherwise. In order to give more weight to this information, the vector is vertically replicated n times (seen as `serc` in Figure 1e) to form a matrix. Table 3 shows the performance of this approach (`lstm+cnn(gse:aux)`). It can be seen that the sentiment expressions consistently boost the performance of polarity classification over all four datasets, with an average improvement of six percentage points.

The second approach works by filtering out the non-sentiment-expression tokens in the sentence. In other words, the input to the model is the sequence of sentiment expression tokens. The architecture of this model is the same as that of the combined LSTM and CNN depicted in Figure 1d, since only the input has changed from the entire sentence to filtered tokens. The results for this approach are also shown in Table 3 (`lstm+cnn(gse:filtered)`). According to the accuracy scores, using sentiment expressions as auxiliary input is preferable to this filtering approach, as the latter obtains significantly lower scores on two of the evaluation subsets, suggesting that the sentiment expressions themselves do not carry all the information relevant to the task.

Overall, both sets of results show that knowing which words (if any) in the sentence are part of the sentiment expression is a valuable source of information for polarity classification, which is what one might expect. The SE-augmented models are better at handling the neutral cases, appearing to learn to associate a lack of sentiment expressions with this category. They are also better at handling negative cases, particularly in the restaurant dataset where the sentiment expression information helps the system to move away from the majority positive class (see the polarity class distribution in Table 2).

5.2 Multitask Learning of Polarity and SE

One way to utilize the sentiment expressions in polarity classification is multitask learning of polarity classification and sentiment expression extraction (Caruana, 1997). The idea is that sharing representations between related tasks can help each of them generalize better. Collobert and Weston (2008) build a unified architecture to simultaneously learn several NLP problems including part-of-speech tagging, chunking, named entity recognition, semantic role labelling (SRL), semantic relatedness detection and language modelling. Their model consists of convolutional networks on top of a shared embedding layer along with individual embedding layers for each task. They try various combinations of these tasks and show that, SRL, for example can benefit from other tasks such as language modelling to achieve state-of-the-art performance without the need for syntactic information as is common in conventional SRL models.

We further investigate this approach by designing a model that learns both tasks at the same time, meaning that the two objective functions are optimized simultaneously, but the main focus is learning the polarity classification and the sentiment expression extraction is an auxiliary task. The architecture of this model is displayed in Figure 1f. The model is built by combining LSTM and CNN, where the input is first fed into a shared LSTM layer between the two tasks. The output of the LSTM layer is then sent to a CNN layer which learns the polarity classification and to another LSTM layer which learns to extract sentiment expressions. The sentiment expressions in the output are represented in a vector of length 2 for each token, where being inside the SE is encoded by $[1, 0]$ and being outside by $[1, 0]$. The prediction for both tasks is achieved using a softmax layer at the end.

The results of this approach are shown in Table 3 (`lstm+cnn(gse:multitask)`). The multitask approach fails to reach the level of performance of the systems which uses gold sentiment expression boundaries as auxiliary input (`lstm+cnn(gse:aux)`) or to filter the original input (`lstm+cnn(gse:filtered)`), especially apparent on the laptop dataset. It should however be noted that multitask learning eliminates the need for gold sentiment expression boundaries at prediction time, so its comparison is more meaningful with systems that use automatically obtained sentiment expression boundaries.

6 Related Work

To the best of our knowledge, the only other dataset containing manual annotations of opinion expressions is MPQA (Wiebe et al., 2005). MPQA annotates *private states* (Quirk et al., 1985), which is a general term covering opinions, evaluations, emotions and speculations. The annotations are categorized into two types: *direct subjective expressions* and *expressive subjective expressions*, the former mentioning the opinions explicitly and the latter implicitly. For example, in (5), *said* is a direct subjective and *full of absurdities* is an expressive subjective expression.

(5) *"The report is full of absurdities," Xirao-Nima said.*

Our annotation scheme does not differentiate between these two types, instead aiming at a simpler guideline for annotating sentiment expressions, where the main rule is to find the part of the sentence which independently carries the sentiment. Therefore, *said* in (5) would be ignored in our annotation as it does not help recognize the sentiment towards *The report*. Instead, *full of absurdities* would be annotated as the sentiment expression towards *The report*, as it is clearly the source negative sentiment expressed by the speaker (*Xirao-Nima*). Therefore, our definition of sentiment expression is closer to the MPQA's expressive subjective expression.

A related work in terms of utilizing opinion expressions for other opinion mining tasks is (Johansson and Moschitti, 2013), who use features extracted from MPQA opinion expressions in product attribute identification (i.e. finding sentiment targets) and also document polarity classification. The features used in the second task – which is more relevant to this work – include the individual opinion expression words combined with the polarity or type of the expressions. Their results show that information extracted from opinion expressions can help improve polarity classification compared to when only bag-of-word features and sentiment polarity lexicons are used. Using a different dataset, a different type of opinion expression and a different way of encoding this knowledge (by marking expression *boundaries*), we provide further evidence that isolating the opinion expression in an utterance helps in polarity classification.

7 Conclusion

A major contribution of the paper is an additional set of manual annotations in the English SemEval 2016 Task 5 dataset in which those words in a sentence which are contributing towards the expression of sentiment towards a particular aspect are explicitly marked. In experiments with this dataset, we demonstrate that knowledge of the boundaries of sentiment expressions can simplify the task of polarity classification. This knowledge seems to have the effect of reducing noise for the learner by de-emphasizing words in the input that are not contributing towards the sentiment and providing clues about how subjective a sentence is.

Although the results of our multitasking experiments were somewhat disappointing, our experiments with gold sentiment expressions motivate us to continue exploring ways of using sentiment expressions in polarity classification. A pipeline approach in which the sentiment expression extraction is carried out before polarity classification is also possible, and indeed several sentiment expression extraction systems have been built with the MPQA dataset (Breck et al., 2007; Choi and Cardie, 2010; Yang and Cardie, 2012; İrsoy and Cardie, 2014). We plan to build a sentiment expression extraction system using our new set of annotations and then investigate the effect of substituting gold sentiment expressions with automatically predicted sentiment expressions.

The dataset reported in this work is available for use by other researchers, as a source of train/test data for sentiment expression extraction or joint polarity classification/sentiment expression extraction, as well as a potential source of linguistic insights about expressions of sentiment in this type of text.[7]

In addition to our sentiment expression data and experiments, we have also compared the use of LSTMs and CNNs and their combination for English aspect-based sentiment polarity classification with the SemEval 2016 Task 5 dataset, concluding that CNNs on their own or in combination with an LSTM are a good choice.

Acknowledgments

This research is supported by Science Foundation Ireland in the ADAPT Centre (Grant 13/RC/2106) (www.adaptcentre.ie) at Dublin City University

---

[7] https://opengogs.adaptcentre.ie/rszk/sea

References

Joachim Bingel and Anders Søgaard. 2017. Identifying beneficial task relations for multi-task learning in deep neural networks. *arXiv preprint arXiv:1702.08303*.

Eric Breck, Yejin Choi, and Claire Cardie. 2007. Identifying expressions of opinion in context. In *Proceedings of the 20th International Joint Conference on Artifical Intelligence*, pages 2683–2688.

Caroline Brun, Julien Perez, and Claude Roux. 2016. Xrce at semeval-2016 task 5: Feedbacked ensemble modeling on syntactico-semantic knowledge for aspect based sentiment analysis. In *Proceedings of the 10th international workshop on semantic evaluation (SemEval-2016)*, pages 277–281.

Rich Caruana. 1997. Multitask learning. *Mach. Learn.*, 28(1):41–75.

Maryna Chernyshevich. 2016. Ihs-rd-belarus at semeval-2016 task 5: Detecting sentiment polarity using the heatmap of sentence. In *Proceedings of the 10th International Workshop on Semantic Evaluation (SemEval-2016)*, pages 296–300. Association for Computational Linguistics.

Jason P.C. Chiu and Eric Nichols. 2016. Named entity recognition with bidirectional lstm-cnns. *Transactions of the Association for Computational Linguistics*, 4:357–370.

Yejin Choi and Claire Cardie. 2010. Hierarchical sequential learning for extracting opinions and their attributes. In *Proceedings of the ACL 2010 Conference Short Papers*, pages 269–274.

Ronan Collobert and Jason Weston. 2008. A unified architecture for natural language processing: Deep neural networks with multitask learning. In *Proceedings of the 25th International Conference on Machine Learning*, pages 160–167.

Sepp Hochreiter and Jürgen Schmidhuber. 1997. Long short-term memory. *Neural computation*, 9(8):1735–1780.

Ozan İrsoy and Claire Cardie. 2014. Opinion mining with deep recurrent neural networks. In *Proceedings of the Conference on Empirical Methods in Natural Language Processing*, pages 720–728.

Richard Johansson and Alessandro Moschitti. 2013. Relational features in fine-grained opinion analysis. *Computational Linguistics*, 39(3):473–509.

Talaat Khalil and Samhaa R. El-Beltagy. 2016. Niletmrg at semeval-2016 task 5: Deep convolutional neural networks for aspect category and sentiment extraction. In *Proceedings of the 10th International Workshop on Semantic Evaluation (SemEval-2016)*, pages 271–276.

Yoon Kim. 2014. Convolutional neural networks for sentence classification. In *Proceedings of the 2014 Conference on Empirical Methods in Natural Language Processing (EMNLP)*, pages 1746–1751, Doha, Qatar. Association for Computational Linguistics.

Diederik Kingma and Jimmy Ba. 2014. Adam: A method for stochastic optimization. *arXiv preprint arXiv:1412.6980*.

Ayush Kumar, Sarah Kohail, Amit Kumar, Asif Ekbal, and Chris Biemann. 2016. Iit-tuda at semeval-2016 task 5: Beyond sentiment lexicon: Combining domain dependency and distributional semantics features for aspect based sentiment analysis. In *Proceedings of the 10th international workshop on semantic evaluation (SemEval-2016)*, pages 1129–1135.

Y. LeCun, L. Bottou, Y. Bengio, and P. Haffner. 1998. Gradient-based learning applied to document recognition. *Proceedings of the IEEE*, 86(11):2278–2324.

Xuezhe Ma and Eduard Hovy. 2016. End-to-end sequence labeling via bi-directional lstm-cnns-crf. In *Proceedings of the 54th Annual Meeting of the Association for Computational Linguistics (Volume 1: Long Papers)*, pages 1064–1074, Berlin, Germany. Association for Computational Linguistics.

Jeffrey Pennington, Richard Socher, and Christopher D. Manning. 2014. Glove: Global vectors for word representation. In *Empirical Methods in Natural Language Processing (EMNLP)*, pages 1532–1543.

Maria Pontiki, Dimitris Galanis, Haris Papageorgiou, Ion Androutsopoulos, Suresh Manandhar, AL-Smadi Mohammad, Mahmoud Al-Ayyoub, Yanyan Zhao, Bing Qin, Orphée De Clercq, et al. 2016. Semeval-2016 task 5: Aspect based sentiment analysis. In *Proceedings of the 10th international workshop on semantic evaluation (SemEval-2016)*, pages 19–30.

Maria Pontiki, Dimitris Galanis, Haris Papageorgiou, Suresh Manandhar, and Ion Androutsopoulos. 2015. Semeval-2015 task 12: Aspect based sentiment analysis. In *Proceedings of the 9th International Workshop on Semantic Evaluation (SemEval 2015)*, pages 486–495.

Maria Pontiki, Dimitris Galanis, John Pavlopoulos, Harris Papageorgiou, Ion Androutsopoulos, and Suresh Manandhar. 2014. Semeval-2014 task 4: Aspect based sentiment analysis. In *Proceedings of the 8th International Workshop on Semantic Evaluation (SemEval 2014)*, pages 27–35.

Randolph Quirk, Charles Ewart Eckersley, and Jan Svartvik. 1985. *A Comprehensive Grammar of the English Language*. Longman.

Sebastian Ruder. 2017. An overview of multi-task learning in deep neural networks. *CoRR*, abs/1706.05098.

Sebastian Ruder, Parsa Ghaffari, and John G. Breslin. 2016a. A hierarchical model of reviews for aspect-based sentiment analysis. In *Proceedings of the 2016 Conference on Empirical Methods in Natural Language Processing*, pages 999–1005. Association for Computational Linguistics.

Sebastian Ruder, Parsa Ghaffari, and John G. Breslin. 2016b. Insight-1 at semeval-2016 task 5: Deep learning for multilingual aspect-based sentiment analysis. In *SemEval@NAACL-HLT*.

Janyce Wiebe, Theresa Wilson, and Claire Cardie. 2005. Annotating expressions of opinions and emotions in language. *Language Resources and Evaluation*, 1(2):0.

Toshihiko Yanase, Kohsuke Yanai, Misa Sato, Toshinori Miyoshi, and Yoshiki Niwa. 2016. bunji at semeval-2016 task 5: Neural and syntactic models of entity-attribute relationship for aspect-based sentiment analysis. In *Proceedings of the 10th International Workshop on Semantic Evaluation (SemEval-2016)*, pages 289–295. Association for Computational Linguistics.

Bishan Yang and Claire Cardie. 2012. Extracting opinion expressions with semi-markov conditional random fields. In *Proceedings of the 2012 Joint Conference on Empirical Methods in Natural Language Processing and Computational Natural Language Learning*, pages 1335–1345.

A Model Hyper-parameters

	direction	epochs	batch size	#LSTM layers	LSTM layer size	CNN filter sizes	#CNN filters	learning rate	activation	dropout rate	char. embed. dim.
lstm	bi	100	128	1	50	-	-	0.01	tanh	0.3	-
cnn	-	200	64	-	-	[2,3,4]	128	0.05	tanh	0.5	-
lstm+cnn	bi	100	32	1	50	[3,4,5]	256	0.001	tanh	0.5	-
chcnn+lstm	bi	50	32	2	50	[3]	64	0.001	tanh	0.3	50
lstm+cnn(gse:aux)	bi	100	32	1	100	[2,3,4]	256	0.001	tanh	0.5	-
lstm+cnn(gse:filtered)	bi	100	32	2	100	[3,4,5]	128	0.001	tanh	0.3	-
lstm+cnn(gse:multitask)	uni	100	32	2	100	[3,4,5]	64	0.001	tanh	0.3	-

Hyper-parameters of the polarity classification models tuned on the laptop development set

	direction	epochs	batch size	#LSTM layers	LSTM layer size	CNN filter sizes	#CNN filters	learning rate	activation	dropout rate	char. embed. dim.
lstm	bi	100	128	1	100	-	-	0.005	tanh	0.3	-
cnn	-	200	32	-	-	[2,3,4]	64	0.001	tanh	0.3	-
lstm+cnn	bi	100	64	1	100	[2,3,4]	64	0.001	tanh	0.3	-
chcnn+lstm	bi	50	64	2	100	[3]	32	0.001	tanh	0.3	20
lstm+cnn(gse:aux)	bi	100	32	1	50	[2,3,4]	128	0.001	tanh	0.5	-
lstm+cnn(gse:filtered)	bi	100	64	1	100	[3,4,5]	128	0.001	tanh	0.5	-
lstm+cnn(gse:multitask)	uni	100	32	2	50	[3,4,5]	128	0.001	tanh	0.3	-

Hyper-parameters of the polarity classification models tuned on the restaurant development set

Exploring and Learning Suicidal Ideation Connotations on Social Media with Deep Learning

Ramit Sawhney[1], **Prachi Manchanda**[1], **Puneet Mathur**[1],
Raj Singh[1], and **Rajiv Ratn Shah** [4]

[1]Netaji Subhas Institute of Technology, NSIT-Delhi
`ramits.co, prachim.co, rajs.co`@nsit.net.in, pmathur3k6@gmail.com
[2]Indraprastha Institute of Information Technology, IIIT-Delhi
`rajivratn@iiitd.ac.in`

Abstract

The increasing suicide rates amongst youth and its high correlation with suicidal ideation expression on social media warrants a deeper investigation into models for the detection of suicidal intent in text such as tweets to enable prevention. However, the complexity of the natural language constructs makes this task very challenging. Deep Learning architectures such as LSTMs, CNNs, and RNNs show promise in sentence level classification problems. This work investigates the ability of deep learning architectures to build an accurate and robust model for suicidal ideation detection and compares their performance with standard baselines in text classification problems. The experimental results reveal the merit in C-LSTM based models as compared to other deep learning and machine learning based classification models for suicidal ideation detection.

1 Introduction

The Centre of Disease Control and Prevention[], in the US, reports that, overall, suicide is the eleventh leading cause of death for all US Americans, and is the third leading cause of death for young people 15-24 years. According to the World Health Organisation(WHO)[], in the last 45 years, suicide rates have increased by 60% worldwide. Suicide attempts are up to 20 times more frequent than completed suicides. Cases of suicide occur due to many complex sociocultural factors and is more likely to occur during periods of socioeconomic, family and individual crisis such as loss of a loved one, unemployment, sexual orientation, difficulties with developing one's identity, disassociation from one's community or other social/belief group, and honour.

The Internet is a powerful source that people turn to when seeking help while having any suicidal thoughts. Understanding how people interact with the Internet in such situations can go a long way in an attempt to prevent such suicides. The availability of suicide-related material on the Internet plays an important role in the process of suicide ideation. Due to this increasing availability of content on social media websites (such as Twitter, Facebook and Reddit etc.), there is an urgent need to identify affected individuals and offer help.

In the past, few attempts such as (O'Dea et al., 2015), (Sueki, 2015) and (Jashinsky et al., 2014) have been made to identify patterns in the language used on social media that express suicidal ideation. However, very few attempts have been made to employ deep learning classifiers that separate text not related to suicide from text that clearly indicates the author exhibiting suicidal intent. In this paper, three deep learning based architectures (Vanilla-RNN, LSTM, and C-LSTM) are compared in the task of sentence classification for the crucial task of detecting suicidal ideation.

The main contributions of this paper can be summarized as follows:

1. Generation of a lexicon of suicide-related words and phrases by scraping suicide web forums to gather tweets for dataset creation.

2. The creation of a labeled dataset for learning the patterns in tweets exhibiting suicidal ideation by manual annotation.

3. Exploration of the performance of three deep learning based architectures for the suicide ideation detection task and compared with

Proceedings of the 9th Workshop on Computational Approaches to Subjectivity, Sentiment and Social Media Analysis, pages 167–175
Brussels, Belgium, October 31, 2018. ©2018 Association for Computational Linguistics
https://doi.org/10.18653/v1/P17

three baselines in terms of four evaluation metrics.

2 Related Work

Media communication can have both positive and negative influence on suicidal ideation. A systematic review of all articles in PsycINFO, MEDLINE, EMBASE, Scopus, and CINAH from 1991 to 2011 for language constructs relating to self-harm or suicide by Daine et al. (2013) concluded that internet may be used as an intervention tool for vulnerable individuals under the age of 25. However, not all language constructs containing the word suicide indicate suicidal intent, specific semantic constructs may be used for predicting whether a sentence implies self-harm tendencies or not.

A suicide note analysis method for automated the identification of suicidal ideation was built using binary support vector machine classifiers by Desmet and Hoste (2013) using fine-grained emotion detection for classifier optimization with lexico-semantic features for optimization. In 2014, Huang et al. (2014) used rule-based methods with a hand-crafted unsupervised classification for developing a real-time suicidal ideation detection system deployed over Weibo[1], a microblogging platform. By combining both machine learning and psychological knowledge, they reported an SVM classifier as having the best performance of different classifiers. Some semantic constructs are associated with lifetime suicidal ideation as compared to others. A cross-sectional study of suicidal intent in 220,848 Twitter users in their 20s in Japan (Sueki, 2015) concluded that language framing was important for identifying suicidal markers in the text. For example: *want to suicide* was found to be associated more frequently with a lifetime suicidal intent than *want to die* in similar sentences. Several of these studies emphasized the influencing power of social media and internet in the study of suicide ideation. (Sawhney et al., 2018a) demonstrated the use of ensembles to approach the detection of suicidal mentions on social media.

One of the most concerning issues with suicide-related content on Twitter is the propagation of harmful ideas through social network graphs. A study by Grandjean (2016) performed a classification of users by influence in digital communities based on graph density and vectors of cen-

trality. The study primarily concluded that some users (nodes) in a social network graph had higher influence factor than others. Ueda et al. (2017) collected 1 million tweets following the suicides of 26 prominent figures in Japan between 2010 and 2014 and investigated if media coverage of suicides is correlated with an increase in the actual number of suicides. The reciprocal connectivity between authors of suicidal content suggested a ripple effect in tightly-coupled virtual communities (Colombo et al., 2016) thereby concluding that Twitter is an effective source for investigation of virtual self-harm markers and appropriate intervention. Tweet mining has been successfully been applied in detecting social problems on the web as indicated by Mathur et al. (2018a,b,c) and Mahata et al. (2018).

3 Data

3.1 Data Collection

One of the foremost challenges in the domain of suicidal ideation detection is the lack of availability of a public dataset due to privacy and anonymity concerns borne out of social stigma associated with mental illness and suicide. Motivated by the need to create a fresh dataset, the primary requirement of developing a suicidal language for data collection was identified. Rather than developing a word list to represent this language, a corpus of words and phrases were developed using anonymized data from known Suicide web forums (Burnap et al., 2015). These forums were identified by Recupero et al. (2008) as dedicated for suicidal issues with related discussions in this subject. Between 3rd December 2017 and 31st January 2018, four of these Suicide forums were scraped for the user posts and human annotators were asked to identify if these posts had any suicidal intent. In addition to this, user posts (containing tags of 'suicide') from the micro-blogging websites, Tumblr and Reddit were collected and added to this collection.

This resulted in the following composition of posts: 300 from each of the Suicide forums and 2000 posts randomly selected from the Tumblr and Reddit posts. These were subsequently human annotated based on them having a suicidal intent or not. Then, Term Frequency/Inverse Document frequency (Ramos et al., 2003) (TF-IDF) method was applied to this set of manually annotated texts to identify terms which appear frequently in the

---

[1] http://www.scmp.com/topics/weibo

suicidal	suicide	not worth living	slit my wrist
kill myself	can't go on	ready to jump	cut my wrist
my suicide note	want to die	sleep forever	slash my wrist
my suicide letter	be dead	suicide plan	do not want to be here
end my life	better off without me	bold	want it to be over
never wake up	better off dead	bold	want to be dead
suicide pact	don't want to be here	tired of living	nothing to live for
die alone	go to sleep forever	die now	ready to die
wanna die	wanna suicide	commit suicide	not worth living
why should I continue living	take my own life	thoughts of suicide	I wish I were dead
to take my own life	suicide ideation	depressed	kill me now

Table 1: Words/Phrases linked with Suicidal Intent

Suicidal	Non-suicidal
I want to kill myself	Visit the #SuicideAwarenessCampaign this weekend
I failed again. I can't do this anymore.	The movie was so bad, I wanted to kill myself.
When did I get addicted? Kill me now!	1 girl commits suicide from EY Square Rooftop
My husband has Cancer. I want to die.	Finish this sentence: Before I die I want to —
My mental illness leaves me only to suicide	An honest talk about the recent suicides in the city.
Suicide is my only really option...	My friend attempted suicide. Weeks later I got this mail.
Life sucks. #gonnasuicide #onthebridge	Idk man. Social media is suicide. Please kill urself

Table 2: Examples of human annotation of tweets

	H_1	H_2	H_3
H_1	–	0.61	0.48
H_2	0.61	–	0.51
H_3	0.48	0.51	–

Table 3: Cohen's Kappa for three annotators H_1, H_2 and H_3

texts belonging to the suicidal ideation class and less frequently in the non-ideation class. These terms play a role in differentiating between the two classes. Finally, manual annotators were asked to remove any terms from this list which were not based on suicidal intent as well as duplicate terms. This gave a final lexicon of 108 terms consisting of but not limited to the phrases/words of Table 1.

The public Streaming API [2] offered by the microblogging website Twitter allows programmatic collection of tweets as they occur, filtered by specific criteria. Using the same, anonymized data was collected from Twitter. This content contained self-classified suicidal ideation (i.e. text posts tagged or 'hash-tagged' with a word or phrase present in the generated corpus).

[2]https://developer.twitter.com/en/docs

The tweets retrieved from Twitter using the API contain extraneous information. It can be associated with a URL, user mention, media files(image, audio, and video), timestamp, number of retweets. For the tasks in this paper, the text from each tweet was extracted while the rest of the information about the tweet was discarded. Although the tweets were collected from the 'Stream' based on a suicidal language earlier developed, the exact sentiment of the tweets was unknown. Tweets consisting of suicidal terms could be related to other things as well. Eg. *suicidal awareness campaign and prevention, a news report consisting of a third person's suicide, sarcasm* etc. This made a manual annotation of the dataset imperative for better accuracy.

3.2 Data Annotation

The final dataset consisting of 5213 text sentences from different tweets was then, manually annotated. Three human annotators were asked to classify the texts from the dataset based on binary criterion (*Does this text imply self-harm inflicting tendencies or suicidal intent?*). This means that the annotators were asked to select one of the two categories (**Suicidal** or **Non-suicidal**) and to select **Suicidal** in case of ambiguity. The suicidal criterion means that the tweet is a clear display of suicidal intent by the user. The suicide is imminent and not conditional unless some event is a clear risk factor eg: depression, bullying, substance abuse. On the other hand, the non-suicidal criteria is the default category for all the texts, i.e. they show no evidence or ambiguous evidence towards suicidal intent. They might include sarcasm, news reports or suicidal awareness texts. The classification is more clearly explained using examples in Table 2.

A satisfactory agreement between the annotators (e.g., 0.51 for H_2 and H_3) can be inferred from Table 3.

As a result, 822 tweets in the dataset (ie., 15.76% of the dataset) were annotated to be suicidal while the rest were classified into 'Non-Suicidal'.

4 Methodology

4.1 Preprocessing

Preprocessing involves filtering the input text to improve the accuracy of the proposed methodology by eliminating redundant features and noise. This is achieved by applying a series of filters, based on Xiang et al. (2012), in the order given below to process the raw tweets prior to learning the word embeddings.

1. Removal of non-English tweets using Ling-Pipe (Baldwin and Carpenter, 2003) with Hadoop.

2. Removal of URLs in tweets.

3. Identification and elimination of user mentions in tweet bodies having the format of @username as well as retweets in the format of RT.

4. Removal of all hashtags with length > 10 due to a great volume of hashtags being concatenated words, which tends to amplify the vocabulary size inadvertently and leads to redundant features.

5. Condensation of three or more than three repetitive letters into a single letter, e.g. *dieeee* to *die*. Similar heuristics have been used in other work such as (Go et al., 2009).

6. Stopword removal.

7. Removal of tokens that are not a sequence of letters, - or '. This includes removal of numbers, terms such as *h3110Ooo*, etc, which do not represent words.

4.2 Distributed Word Representation

A distributed language representation X consists of an embedding for every vocabulary word in space S with dimension D, the dimension of the latent representation space. The embeddings are learned to optimize an objective function defined on the original text, such as the likelihood of word occurrences. An interesting implementation to get the word embeddings is the word2vec model (Mikolov et al., 2013a) which is used here.

word2vec is a group of related models that are used to produce word embeddings. These models are shallow, two-layer neural networks that are trained to reconstruct linguistic contexts of words. word2vec takes as its input a large corpus of text and produces a vector space, typically of several hundred dimensions, with each unique word in the corpus being assigned a corresponding vector in the space. Word vectors are positioned in the vector space such that words that share common contexts in the corpus are located in close proximity to one another in the space.

Generating word embeddings from text corpus is an unsupervised process. To get high-quality embedding vectors, a large amount of training data is necessary. After training, each word, including all hashtags, is represented by a real-valued vector which can be given as input to a deep learning based model.

4.3 Deep Learning Models

An efficient model to classify sequential information of arbitrary length is a Recurrent Neural Network(RNN) (Elman, 1990) model.

However, the gradient vector of RNNs with transition functions of this form can grow or decay exponentially over long sequences (Hochreiter et al., 2001) which makes it difficult to learn long distance correlations.

Long Short Term Memory (Hochreiter and Schmidhuber, 1997) prevents this vanishing or explosion gradient seen in the RNN and is thus, preferred over RNN. The LSTM has a memory cell which consists of four main components: input, output, forget gates and candidate memory cell. The forget gates control the information that

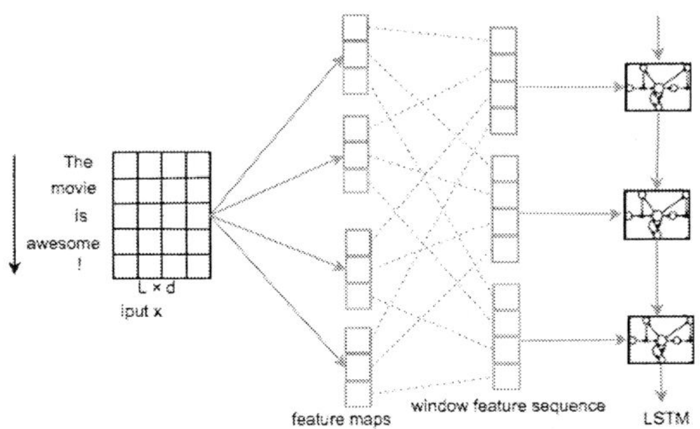

Figure 1: The architecture of C-LSTM for sentence modeling taken from (Zhou et al., 2015). Blocks of the same color in the feature map layer and window feature sequence layer corresponds to features for the same window. The dashed lines connect the feature of a window with the source feature map. The final output of the entire model is the last hidden unit of LSTM.

is to be sent to the next time step. The memory cell stores the data at each step and thus ensures long-distance correlations. The output at each time step depends on the input of that step, the output from the previous time step, the forget gates and the data in the memory cell.

The LSTM architecture is similar to a standard RNN. At each time step, the output of the module is controlled by a set of gates in R^d as a function of the old hidden state h_{t1} and the input at the current time step x_t: the forget gate f_t, the input gate i_t and the output gate o_t. These gates collectively decide how to update the current memory cell C_t and the current hidden state h_t. We use d to denote the memory dimension in the LSTM and all vectors in this architecture share the same dimension.

LSTMs are well-suited to classify, process and predict time series and capture long-term dependencies in sentences along with a relative insensitivity to gap length unlike alternative models such as RNNs and hidden Markov Models (Eddy, 1996) make it an excellent choice for the identification of suicidal ideation in tweets.

In a C-LSTM Model (Zhou et al., 2015), CNN and LSTM are stacked in a semantic sentence modelling. As is shown in Figure 1, the CNN is applied to text data and consecutive window features which are extracted are fed into the LSTM

model which enables it to learn long-range dependencies from higher-order sequential features. The one-dimensional convolution involves a filter vector sliding over a sequence and detecting features at different positions. The C-LSTM model uses multiple filters to generate multiple feature maps which are rearranged as feature representations for each window. The new successive higher-order window representations then are fed into LSTM. The output of the hidden state at the last time step of the LSTM is regarded as the document representation. The efficient spatial encoding and automatic feature extraction by the CNN layer combined with the efficient text classification by LSTMs motivate this study to explore the C-LSTM model for suicidal ideation identification.

4.4 Classification

Suicidal Ideation detection is formulated as a supervised binary classification problem. For every tweet $t_i \in D$, the dataset, a binary valued variable $y_i \in \{0, 1\}$ is introduced, where $y_i = 1$ denotes that the tweet t_i exhibits Suicidal Ideation. To learn this, the classifier must determine whether any sentence in t_i possesses a certain structure or keywords that mark the existence of any possible Suicidal thoughts. The word embeddings derived from the previous step are used to train a classification model to identify tweets exhibiting suicidal ideation. Three Deep Learning based architectures, namely, vanilla RNN, vanilla LSTM and C-LSTM, are explored for the suicidal ideation detection task. The architectural is presented in the following section.

The following steps are executed on every tweet $t_i \in D$:

1. *Word Embeddings.* Top-N frequent words occurring in a tweet are encoded to form an embedding layer utilizing the 300-dimensional word2vec embeddings.

2. *Sentence Embeddings.* For the C-LSTM model, a one dimensional CNN and max-pooling layer are added after the embedding layer. These sentence embeddings are then fed into the LSTM layer.

3. *Classification.* Ultimately, the model feeds the learned sentence embeddings *(C-LSTM)* or word embeddings *(Vanilla RNN or LSTM)* to a deep neural network *(RNN or LSTM)*.

Model	Accuracy	Precision	Recall	F1 Score
LR: Character n-grams	0.669	0.663	0.753	0.702
LR: TF-IDF	0.727	0.767	0.778	0.772
LR: Bag of Words	0.737	0.712	0.788	0.748
SVM: Character n-grams	0.682	0.676	0.763	0.713
SVM: TF-IDF	0.732	0.724	0.793	0.758
SVM: Bag of Words	0.730	0.712	0.801	0.733
RNN	0.737	0.720	0.817	0.753
LSTM	0.789	0.745	**0.874**	0.796
C-LSTM	**0.812**	**0.787**	0.872	**0.827**

Table 4: Classification Results in terms of Evaluation metrics.

5 Experiment Settings

5.1 Baselines

In order to offer fair comparisons to other competitive models, and validate the proposed Deep Learning model, experiments are conducted with baselines. Hand-crafted features are extracted from tweets and are fed into a linear classifier. Multinomial logistic regression (Böhning, 1992) is used as a classifier with the three feature extraction models given below. Support Vector Machines have also been used for feature extraction based suicide-ideation classification problems, and hence are also used as baselines to compare performance. 10-fold cross-validation is performed to report results in terms of the evaluation metrics presented in the following subsections.

1. *Character n-grams*. State-of-the-art method (Cavnar et al., 1994) for sentence level classification using up to 3-grams from each tweet.

2. *TF-IDF*. Text Frequency - Inverse Document Frequency (TF-IDF) are commonly used features for text classification.

3. *Bag of Words*. A bag-of-words model (Sriram et al., 2010) is constructed by selecting the 50,000 most frequent words from the training tweets. The count of each word is used to create a feature vector for classification.

5.2 Model Architectures and Parameters

For the classification task, both a RNN and a LSTM are trained using 10-fold cross-validation to identify the best hyper-parameter settings. Pre-Trained word2vec word embeddings that were trained on 100 billion words from Google News are employed as features for classification. These vectors have a dimensionality of 300 and were trained using the continuous bag-of-words architecture (Mikolov et al., 2013b). The experiment settings pertaining to both are presented below:

1. *RNN*. Vanilla RNN with $h = 128$ units, 32 dense units, a dropout rate of 0.1.

2. *LSTM*. Vanilla LSTM with $h = 128$ memory units, 32 dense units, a dropout probability of 0.2.

3. *C-LSTM*. Convolution Layer (mask size = 5, filter maps= 128)$\rightarrow$ Max-Pooling Layer (mask size = 2) $\rightarrow$ LSTM layer ($h = 128$) $\rightarrow$ Dropout Layer with dropout probability = 0.2.

ReLU (Nair and Hinton, 2010) was used for activation the CNN layers in C-LSTM, and Dense layer with single neuron and sigmoid activation was used for all the models. Dropout layers were added to all models to avoid over-fitting. A batch size of 64 was chosen, and the models were trained for a total of 10 epochs. The Adam Optimizer (Kingma and Ba, 2014) was used to minimize log loss.

5.3 Evaluation Metrics

The Baselines and Deep learning models above are compared with each other in terms of the following metrics:

1. **Precision** $= \frac{t_p}{t_p + f_p}$

2. **Recall** $= \frac{t_p}{t_p + f_n}$

3. **F1 score** $= \frac{2t_p}{2t_p + f_p + f_n}$

4. **Accuracy** $= \frac{t_p + t_n}{t_p + t_n + f_p + f_n}$

where, t_p is the number of true positives, t_n is the number of true negatives, f_p is the number of false positives, and f_n is the number of false negatives.

5.4 Results and Analysis

Table 4 shows the results of the baselines as well as deep learning models on the suicide ideation detection task in terms of the evaluation metrics. The first six rows show results for baseline methods, whereas the bottom three rows focus on proposed deep learning models. The results shown are obtained using 10-fold cross validation.

As the table shows, C-LSTM perform performs significantly better than the baseline methods as well as vanilla LSTM and RNN. This is attributed to the ability of LSTMs to learn how to forget past observations makes them more robust to noise, and better able to capture long-term dependencies in a tweet combined with the efficient encoding of the one-dimensional spatial structure in the sequence of words for tweets which further serve as input to the LSTM layer. RNNs are comparable to both TF-IDF and Bag of words models with Multinomial logistic Regression and Support Vector Machines. Among the baselines, the TF-IDF model combined with multinomial logistic regression is better than the others. Surprisingly, standard feature extraction methods coupled with a linear classifier perform comparatively well as compared to RNNs that involve a much larger amount of computation. However, there is a vast improvement with the incorporation of LSTM and C-LSTM which easily compensates for the additional computation involved.

5.5 Error Analysis

A brief error analysis is presented in this subsection to highlight some of the tweets both annotators and the proposed models that gave erroneous results.

- **Subtle references** *Life is so meaningless to me right now, should prolly end it* The models were unable to identify the subtle hints towards suicidal ideation.

- **Uncertainty** *Friends are worrying about me committing suicide.* It is unclear for both annotators and the system to identify the nature of this tweet due to the lack of explicit suicidal intent.

- **Unfamiliarity** *I finally found a whole bottle full of pills, im sorry* The current training dataset lacks in terms of suicidal ideation phrases and would need updates to cover broader aspects and learn the context between topics such as pill overdose and suicides.

6 Conclusion and Future Work

In this paper, three Deep Learning based models, particularly RNN, LSTM, and C-LSTM are employed for the task of suicidal ideation detection in tweets. For this purpose, a lexicon of terms was first generated by scraping and manually annotating anonymized data from known suicide Web forums. A dataset of tweets was collected using the Twitter REST API by using search queries corresponding to the generated lexicon. Human annotators labeled tweets with suicidal intent present or absent, which were then used to train both three machine learning-based baseline models as well as the three proposed deep learning models. A quantitative comparison between the various models revealed the effectiveness of a C-LSTM based model in suicidal ideation detection in tweets. This was attributed to the ability of CNNs to spatially encode the tweets into a one-dimensional structure to be fed into LSTMs along with the ability of LSTMs to capture long-term dependencies. In the future, this work can be extended by investigating other deep learning based architectures for the tasks of suicidal ideation detection on Twitter as well as other Web forums and Social media. Also, nature-inspired heuristics can be explored for efficient feature selection as done by Sawhney et al. (2018b,c).

References

Breck Baldwin and Bob Carpenter. 2003. Lingpipe. *Available from World Wide Web: http://alias-i. com/lingpipe.*

Dankmar Böhning. 1992. Multinomial logistic regression algorithm. *Annals of the Institute of Statistical Mathematics*, 44(1):197–200.

Pete Burnap, Walter Colombo, and Jonathan Scourfield. 2015. Machine classification and analysis of suicide-related communication on twitter. In *Proceedings of the 26th ACM conference on hypertext & social media*, pages 75–84. ACM.

William B Cavnar, John M Trenkle, et al. 1994. N-gram-based text categorization. *Ann arbor mi*, 48113(2):161–175.

Gualtiero B Colombo, Pete Burnap, Andrei Hodorog, and Jonathan Scourfield. 2016. Analysing the connectivity and communication of suicidal users on twitter. *Computer communications*, 73:291–300.

Kate Daine, Keith Hawton, Vinod Singaravelu, Anne Stewart, Sue Simkin, and Paul Montgomery. 2013. The power of the web: a systematic review of studies of the influence of the internet on self-harm and suicide in young people. *PloS one*, 8(10):e77555.

Bart Desmet and VéRonique Hoste. 2013. Emotion detection in suicide notes. *Expert Systems with Applications*, 40(16):6351–6358.

Sean R Eddy. 1996. Hidden markov models. *Current opinion in structural biology*, 6(3):361–365.

Jeffrey L Elman. 1990. Finding structure in time. *Cognitive science*, 14(2):179–211.

Alec Go, Richa Bhayani, and Lei Huang. 2009. Twitter sentiment classification using distant supervision. *CS224N Project Report, Stanford*, 1(12).

Martin Grandjean. 2016. A social network analysis of twitter: Mapping the digital humanities community. *Cogent Arts & Humanities*, 3(1):1171458.

Sepp Hochreiter, Yoshua Bengio, Paolo Frasconi, Jürgen Schmidhuber, et al. 2001. Gradient flow in recurrent nets: the difficulty of learning long-term dependencies.

Sepp Hochreiter and Jürgen Schmidhuber. 1997. Long short-term memory. *Neural computation*, 9(8):1735–1780.

Xiaolei Huang, Lei Zhang, David Chiu, Tianli Liu, Xin Li, and Tingshao Zhu. 2014. Detecting suicidal ideation in chinese microblogs with psychological lexicons. In *Ubiquitous Intelligence and Computing, 2014 IEEE 11th Intl Conf on and IEEE 11th Intl Conf on and Autonomic and Trusted Computing, and IEEE 14th Intl Conf on Scalable Computing and Communications and Its Associated Workshops (UTC-ATC-ScalCom)*, pages 844–849. IEEE.

Jared Jashinsky, Scott H Burton, Carl L Hanson, Josh West, Christophe Giraud-Carrier, Michael D Barnes, and Trenton Argyle. 2014. Tracking suicide risk factors through twitter in the us. *Crisis: The Journal of Crisis Intervention and Suicide Prevention*, 35(1):51.

Diederik P Kingma and Jimmy Ba. 2014. Adam: A method for stochastic optimization. *arXiv preprint arXiv:1412.6980*.

Debanjan Mahata, Jasper Friedrichs, Rajiv Ratn Shah, and Jing Jiang. 2018. Did you take the pill?-detecting personal intake of medicine from twitter. *arXiv preprint arXiv:1808.02082*.

Puneet Mathur, Meghna Ayyar, Sahil Chopra, Simra Shahid, Laiba Mehnaz, and Rajiv Shah. 2018a. Identification of emergency blood donation request on twitter. In *Proceedings of the Third Workshop On Social Media Mining for Health Applications*.

Puneet Mathur, Ramit Sawhney, Meghna Ayyar, and Rajiv Shah. 2018b. Did you offend me? classification of offensive tweets in hinglish language. In *Proceedings of the Second Workshop on Abusive Language Online*.

Puneet Mathur, Rajiv Shah, Ramit Sawhney, and Debanjan Mahata. 2018c. Detecting offensive tweets in hindi-english code-switched language. In *Proceedings of the Sixth International Workshop on Natural Language Processing for Social Media*, pages 18–26.

Tomas Mikolov, Ilya Sutskever, Kai Chen, Greg S Corrado, and Jeff Dean. 2013a. Distributed representations of words and phrases and their compositionality. In C. J. C. Burges, L. Bottou, M. Welling, Z. Ghahramani, and K. Q. Weinberger, editors, *Advances in Neural Information Processing Systems 26*, pages 3111–3119. Curran Associates, Inc.

Tomas Mikolov, Ilya Sutskever, Kai Chen, Greg S Corrado, and Jeff Dean. 2013b. Distributed representations of words and phrases and their compositionality. In *Advances in neural information processing systems*, pages 3111–3119.

Vinod Nair and Geoffrey E Hinton. 2010. Rectified linear units improve restricted boltzmann machines. In *Proceedings of the 27th international conference on machine learning (ICML-10)*, pages 807–814.

Bridianne O'Dea, Stephen Wan, Philip J Batterham, Alison L Calear, Cecile Paris, and Helen Christensen. 2015. Detecting suicidality on twitter. *Internet Interventions*, 2(2):183–188.

Juan Ramos et al. 2003. Using tf-idf to determine word relevance in document queries. In *Proceedings of the first instructional conference on machine learning*, volume 242, pages 133–142.

Patricia R Recupero, Samara E Harms, and Jeffrey M Noble. 2008. Googling suicide: surfing for suicide information on the internet. *The Journal of clinical psychiatry*.

Ramit Sawhney, Prachi Manchanda, Raj Singh, and Swati Aggarwal. 2018a. A computational approach to feature extraction for identification of suicidal ideation in tweets. In *Proceedings of ACL 2018, Student Research Workshop*, pages 91–98.

Ramit Sawhney, Puneet Mathur, and Ravi Shankar. 2018b. A firefly algorithm based wrapper-penalty feature selection method for cancer diagnosis. In *International Conference on Computational Science and Its Applications*, pages 438–449. Springer.

Ramit Sawhney, Ravi Shankar, and Roopal Jain. 2018c. A comparative study of transfer functions in binary evolutionary algorithms for single objective optimization. In *International Symposium on Distributed Computing and Artificial Intelligence*, pages 27–35. Springer.

Bharath Sriram, Dave Fuhry, Engin Demir, Hakan Ferhatosmanoglu, and Murat Demirbas. 2010. Short text classification in twitter to improve information filtering. In *Proceedings of the 33rd international ACM SIGIR conference on Research and development in information retrieval*, pages 841–842. ACM.

Hajime Sueki. 2015. The association of suicide-related twitter use with suicidal behaviour: a cross-sectional study of young internet users in japan. *Journal of affective disorders*, 170:155–160.

Michiko Ueda, Kota Mori, Tetsuya Matsubayashi, and Yasuyuki Sawada. 2017. Tweeting celebrity suicides: Users' reaction to prominent suicide deaths on twitter and subsequent increases in actual suicides. *Social Science & Medicine*, 189:158–166.

Guang Xiang, Bin Fan, Ling Wang, Jason Hong, and Carolyn Rose. 2012. Detecting offensive tweets via topical feature discovery over a large scale twitter corpus. In *Proceedings of the 21st ACM international conference on Information and knowledge management*, pages 1980–1984. ACM.

Chunting Zhou, Chonglin Sun, Zhiyuan Liu, and Francis C. M. Lau. 2015. A C-LSTM neural network for text classification. *CoRR*, abs/1511.08630.

UTFPR at IEST 2018:
Exploring Character-to-Word Composition for Emotion Analysis

Gustavo H. Paetzold

Federal University of Technology - Paraná / Brazil

ghpaetzold@utfpr.edu.br

Abstract

We introduce the UTFPR system for the Implicit Emotions Shared Task of 2018: A compositional character-to-word recurrent neural network that does not exploit heavy and/or hard-to-obtain resources. We find that our approach can outperform multiple baselines, and offers an elegant and effective solution to the problem of orthographic variance in tweets.

1 Introduction

Emotion analysis has become one of the most prominent tasks in Natural Language Processing (NLP) in recent years. It can be framed as either a regression task, where one wants to gauge the degree of some emotion, such as how optimistic a certain opinion is with respect to a given matter, or a classification task, where one wants to decide on which type of emotion is being conveyed, such as happiness, fear, anger, etc. The task is particularly interesting for industry applications, since it can potentially allow for institutions to automatically assess the public opinion on things like initiatives, products, etc. The task can also be applied in many interesting natural language domains. For instance, one can try to determine whether a certain restaurant review posted in a major news outlet favors the establishment, or whether a certain tweet about a celebrity or institution conveys support or disdain.

The type of target domain can greatly influence how an emotion analysis system is structured. If the targets are formally written and well revised

articles from newspapers and magazines, then one can expect to find only orthographically correct words and appropriately structured sentences in the input. The authors of tweets, on the other hand, often use many distinct orthographic variants of the same word (ex: you, u, youu), tend to have less regard for form, and use non-textual symbols to express meaning, such as emojis. Also, articles tend to be much longer than tweets, which have a size limit of just a few hundred characters. Systems for the later type of domain must address a lot of challenges that systems for the former do not have to, which can compel them to be much more complex.

The SeerNet system (Duppada et al., 2018), one of the best performing systems of the SemEval 2018 shared task on affect in tweets (Mohammad et al., 2018), is a great example of that. In this shared task, participants were asked to create both regression (for emotion intensity) and classification (for emotion decision) systems for emotion analysis in English, Arabic, and Spanish. In order to overcome the challenge of analyzing tweets, the SeerNet system resorts to a wide range of specialized resources, such as special tokenizers and embedding models for tweets, emoji analyzers, and even off-the-shelf systems trained on large amounts of curated data. Though undoubtedly effective, the SeerNet has a very complex architecture that would be difficult to replicate, specially for under-resourced languages.

In an effort to offer a simpler solution to emotion analysis in tweets, we present the UTFPR system submitted to Implicit Emotions Shared Task (IEST) of 2018 (Klinger et al., 2018). Ours is a character-to-word recurrent neural network architecture that offers an elegant solution to orthographic variance within tweets, and does not rely

Proceedings of the 9th Workshop on Computational Approaches to Subjectivity, Sentiment and Social Media Analysis, pages 176–181
Brussels, Belgium, October 31, 2018. ⓒ2018 Association for Computational Linguistics
https://doi.org/10.18653/v1/P17

on any resources other than the input provided by the shared task organizers. We describe our approach in what follows.

2 Task Description

The UTFPR system is a contribution to the IEST 2018 shared task, hosted at the 9th Workshop on Computational Approaches to Subjectivity, Sentiment & Social Media Analysis (WASSA 2018). In this shared task, participants were tasked with classifying tweets with respect to the emotion they convey.

The task organizers provided participants a training set composed of $153,383$ instances, a trial set with $9,591$ instances, and an unlabeled test set with $28,757$ instances. Each instance is composed of a tweet with a target emotion word replaced with a [#TRIGGERWORD#] marker, and an emotion label. There are six possible emotions in this setup: joy, sad, disgust, anger, surprise, and fear.

The organizers also provided a wide array of external resources that could complement the systems created, such as emotion dictionaries, lexicons, datasets from previous tasks, etc.

3 Preliminary Experiment

Before conceiving the final version of the UTFPR system, we conducted a preliminary experiment with baseline classification models in order to test some model design options, and hence guide the creation of the UTFPR approach. More specifically, we assessed two design options with respect to input:

- **Structure:** Since each instance contains an omitted target emotion word, we tested whether it is more productive to address the entire tweet as a bag of words, or to individually model the words to the left and right of the target.

- **Enhancement:** We also tested whether or not it is helpful to complement the training set with data gathered in unsupervised fashion.

3.1 Experimental Setup

In this section, we delve into the details of how our preliminary experiment was structured.

Data: We used 90% of the training data from the shared task for training, and 10% for testing. Notice that we did not use the trial data for testing

because the labels had not been made available at the time this experiment was conducted.

Models: We tested three types of machine learning models; logistic regression, decision trees, and random forests. All these models were implemented with the help of scikit-learn[1].

Input Features: We tried two types of features; TF-IDF weights from a bag-of-words model trained over our input training data (TF-IDF), and the average word embedding values of the words in the tweet (Embeddings). We used the 300-dimension word embeddings model of Paetzold and Specia (2016), which was trained using the CBOW model (Mikolov et al., 2013) over a corpus of $\tilde{7}$ billion words from assorted sources, such as news articles, subtitles, tweets, etc.

Input Structure: We tested two types of inputs to the models; one in which we calculate and concatenate two separate feature representations of the words to the left and right of the target (Separate), and another in which we calculate only one feature representation of all words in the tweet aside from the target (Joint).

Input Enhancement: We tested two variants of each model; one trained only on our training data (TR), and another trained on the training data plus a set of $1,774,423$ automatically extracted complementary instances (TR+E). To produce the complementary instances we first extracted all morphological variants and synonyms of the words "joy", "sad", "disgust", "anger", "surprise", and "fear", then looked for sentences containing these words in the same 7 billion word corpus used to train our embeddings. Finally, we replaced the emotion word in each sentence with [#TRIGGER-WORD#], and assigned the appropriate emotion label to the instance.

3.2 Preliminary Results

The macro F-score obtained by each variant tested is featured in Table 1. The results reveal that, across almost all scenarios, modeling the words to the left and right of the target (Separate) without data enhancement (TR) yields the most promising results.

---

[1]http://scikit-learn.org

| | TF-IDF | | | | Embeddings | | | |
| | Joint | | Separate | | Joint | | Separate | |
	TR	TR+E	TR	TR+E	TR	TR+E	TR	TR+E
Logistic Regression	0.270	0.406	0.277	0.220	0.139	0.095	0.160	0.058
Decision Trees	0.201	0.165	0.213	0.191	0.112	0.101	0.155	0.145
Random Forests	0.228	0.186	0.243	0.219	0.122	0.096	0.177	0.166

Table 1: Preliminary experiment results. Each cell represents the macro F-score obtained by a given model.

4 The UTFPR System

The UTFPR system is a compositional character-to-word recurrent neural network model that attempts to address the challenges of working with tweets in an elegant way. Guided by the findings from our preliminary experiment, we structured our as illustrated in Figure 1.

First, the words to the left and right of the target word, which we henceforth refer to as left and right contexts, are passed through a character embedding layer. The embeddings are then passed onto a bidirectional GRU network that produce a numerical representation for each word in the sentence. The representations of the words in the left and right contexts are then passed on to two separate bidirectional GRU networks, which in turn produce a final representation of each context. Finally, these representations are concatenated and passed on to a final perceptron layer, which predicts the most likely emotion based on softmax.

The model uses no external resources other than the sentence itself as input, and because it is a neural model, it can be configured with respect to the size of embeddings, type of recurrent layers used, number of layers, activation function, etc. We describe our experiments and configuration of the UTFPR system in what follows.

5 Experimental Setup

For our experiments, we configure the UTFPR system as follows:

- **Character embedding size:** 25

- **RNN layer type:** Gated Recurrent Units (GRU)

- **RNN layer depth:** 2

- **RNN layer size:** 50

- **Dropout proportion:** 50%

- **Loss function:** Cross-entropy

- **Framework used:** PyTorch[2]

As mentioned in section 2, we submited the UTFPR system to the IEST 2018 shared task. We trained the UTFPR system over the entire training set provided by the organizers, and validated it over the trial set. Our final submission was the model resulting from iteration with the lowest cross-entropy error on the trial set.

In order to offer some points of comparison and highlight the importance of some design decisions made when creating UTFPR, we trained two other variants of UTFPR:

- **UTFPR-C**: A version of UTFPR without the character-to-word layers. Instead, it uses as input word embeddings extracted from the word embeddings model described in section 3.

- **UTFPR-CD**: A version of UTFPR-C trained without dropout.

Due to the limited amount of computing resources available to us, we were not able to train any more variants of UTFPR. We also include in our performance comparison all the baseline models described in section 3, the baselines provided by the IEST 2018 organizers, and the 5 systems with the highest macro F-scores in the shared task.

6 Results

Table 2 showcases the micro and macro Precision, Recall, and F-scores of our UTFPR variants, as well the IEST 2018 baselines and top 5 systems. Although our approach did not manage to reach the top of the leaderboards, the results do highlight the impact of some design decisions made when creating the final UTFPR system. As it can be noticed, incorporating dropout and adding a character-to-word encoder to our model slightly increases its performance. While the complete UTFPR system

---
[2]https://pytorch.org

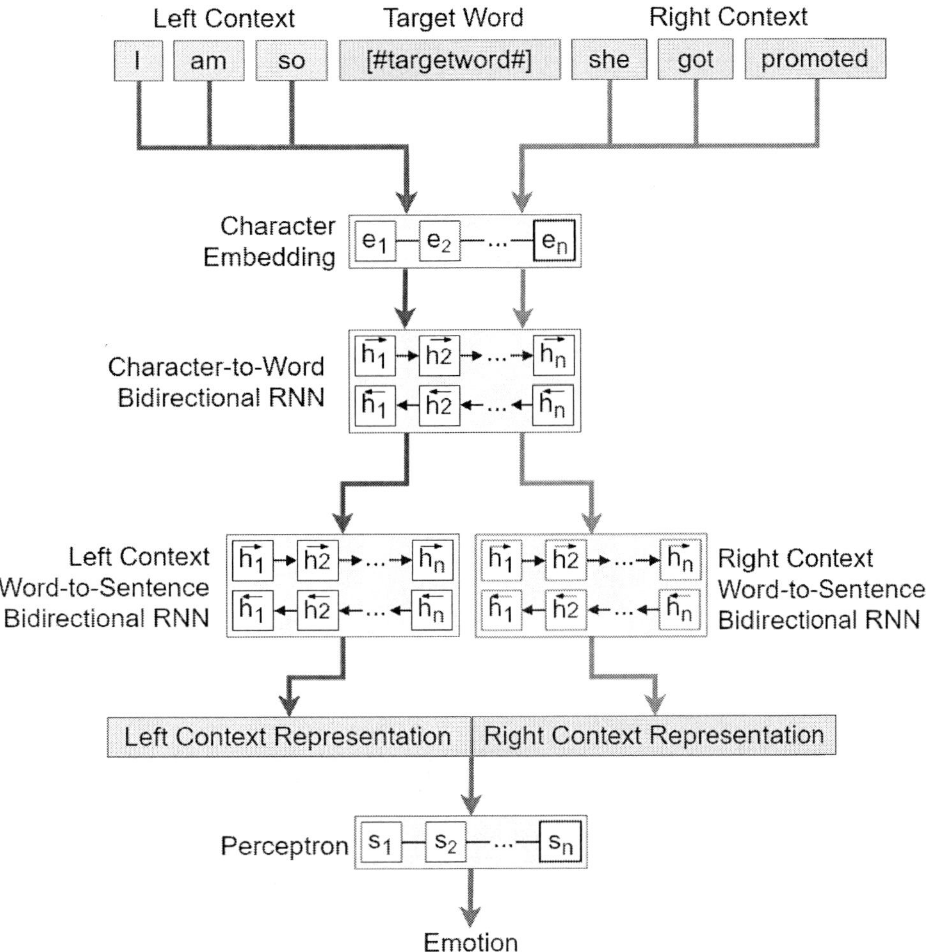

Figure 1: Architecture of the UTFPR system

	Micro			Macro		
	P	R	F	P	R	F
Amobee	-	-	-	-	-	0.714
IIIDYT	-	-	-	-	-	0.710
NTUA-SLP	-	-	-	-	-	0.703
UBC-NLP	-	-	-	-	-	0.693
Sentylic	-	-	-	-	-	0.692
BOW MaxEnt	-	-	-	-	-	0.599
"Joy" Always	-	-	-	-	-	0.051
UTFPR-CD	0.541	0.541	0.541	0.550	0.544	0.541
UTFPR-C	0.545	0.545	0.545	0.551	0.546	0.545
UTFPR	**0.568**	**0.568**	**0.568**	**0.575**	**0.569**	**0.569**

Table 2: Official micro and macro scores obtained by the UTFPR systems. Bold-case scores showcase the highest scores obtained by the UTFPR systems. The first five lines showcase the scores for the top 5 IEST 2018 systems, and the following two the ones for the IEST 2018 baselines.

| | TF-IDF | | | | Embeddings | | | |
| | Joint | | Separate | | Joint | | Separate | |
	TR	TR+E	TR	TR+E	TR	TR+E	TR	TR+E
Logistic Regression	0.496	0.403	0.500	0.406	0.255	0.093	0.293	0.104
Decision Trees	0.369	0.304	0.387	0.351	0.211	0.188	0.284	0.267
Random Forests	0.418	0.346	0.449	0.405	0.232	0.182	0.332	0.310

Table 3: Macro F-scores obtained by our baseline models on the official IEST 2018 test set.

managed to place 23rd in the competition, either of its two variants would place 26th.

Table 3 features the macro F-score results obtained by the baseline systems described in section 3 on the IEST 2018 test set. The results are consistent with the ones in Table 1, which brings some reassurance with respect to the usefulness of our preliminary experiment. Nonetheless, none of the baseline systems managed to outperform the more elaborate UTFPR systems.

7 Analysis

In addition to our performance comparison, we also conducted complementary analyses that allowed us to delve into the merits and limitations of the UTFPR system. First we produced its confusion matrix, which is illustrated in Table 4. Although the mistakes made by the UTFPR system are well spread out throughout the matrix, it can be noticed that, despite the labels in the reference set being present in even proportions, the UTFPR model is slightly biased towards the anger and surprise labels.

Finally, we conducted an experiment comparing the robustness of the three UTFPR variants described in section 5 (UTFPR, UTFPR-C, UTFPR-CD). For this experiment, we first created an orthographically "jammed" version of the IEST 2018 test set. For each tweet in the test set, we randomly selected 75% of its words, and then either duplicated (50% chance) or removed (50% chance) a randomly selected letter. We then trained the UTFPR variants on the regular IEST 2018 training and trial set, and tested them over our jammed test set.

The results in Table 5 show that adding the compositional character-to-word encoder to our model greatly increases its robustness with respect to orthographic variance. While jamming the words cost the UTFPR-C and UTFPR-CD variants upwards of 14, 3% in macro F-score, the performance of our complete UTFPR system only dropped by

2, 2%.

8 Conclusions

In this contribution, we introduced the UTFPR emotion analysis system for the IEST 2018 shared task. Unlike current state-of-the-art approaches, our model does not rely on external resources, and employs instead a single compositional recurrent neural network that learns representations of sentences based on its words, and of words based on its characters.

Through our experiments we found that, although the UTFPR system cannot compete with more elaborate, resource-heavy approaches, it does offer a promising solution to the task that is very robust to orthographic variance. In the future, we aim to create more sophisticated variants of the UTFPR approach that incorporate other cost-effective sources of information to better inform the model and hence increase its performance.

9 Acknowledgments

We would like to thank the Federal University of Technology - Paraná for supporting this contribution.

References

Duppada, Venkatesh, Royal Jain, and Sushant Hiray. 2018. Seernet at semeval-2018 task 1: Domain adaptation for affect in tweets. In *Proceedings of The 12th International Workshop on Semantic Evaluation*, pages 18–23. Association for Computational Linguistics.

Klinger, Roman, Orphée de Clercq, Saif M. Mohammad, and Alexandra Balahur. 2018. Iest: Wassa-2018 implicit emotions shared task. In *Proceedings of the 9th Workshop on Computational Approaches to Subjectivity, Sentiment and Social Media Analysis*. Association for Computational Linguistics.

Mikolov, Tomas, Kai Chen, Greg Corrado, and Jeffrey Dean. 2013. Efficient estimation of word representations in vector space. *CoRR*, abs/1301.3781.

	joy	sad	disgust	anger	surprise	fear	% Ref.
joy	2790	595	295	646	563	357	18.24%
sad	343	2582	451	467	316	181	15.09%
disgust	203	524	2784	429	677	177	16.67%
anger	399	417	435	2530	686	327	16.67%
surprise	290	296	478	442	2971	315	16.66%
fear	323	326	275	523	660	2684	16.66%
% Pred.	15.12%	16.48%	16.41%	17.52%	20.42%	14.05%	-

Table 4: Confusion matrix of the UTFPR system. Lines represent reference labels and columns represent predictions. The last column and line feature the occurrence proportion of each emotion in the reference and predicted label set, respectively.

	Micro			Macro		
	P	R	F	P	R	F
UTFPR-CD	0.400	0.400	0.400	0.414	0.403	0.398
UTFPR-C	0.408	0.408	0.408	0.414	0.407	0.404
UTFPR	**0.546**	**0.546**	**0.546**	**0.552**	**0.547**	**0.547**

Table 5: Official micro and macro scores obtained by the UTFPR systems on the jammed test set. Bold-case scores showcase the highest scores obtained by the UTFPR systems.

Mohammad, Saif, Felipe Bravo-Marquez, Mohammad Salameh, and Svetlana Kiritchenko. 2018. Semeval-2018 task 1: Affect in tweets. In *Proceedings of The 12th International Workshop on Semantic Evaluation*, pages 1–17. Association for Computational Linguistics.

Paetzold, Gustavo H. and Lucia Specia. 2016. Unsupervised lexical simplification for non-native speakers. In *Proceedings of the 13th AAAI Conference on Artificial Intelligence*, pages 3761–3767.

HUMIR at IEST-2018: Lexicon-Sensitive and Left-Right Context-Sensitive BiLSTM for Implicit Emotion Recognition

Behzad Naderalvojoud, Alaettin Ucan and Ebru Akcapinar Sezer
Department of Computer Engineering
Hacettepe University, Turkey
{n.behzad, aucan, ebru}@hacettepe.edu.tr

Abstract

This paper describes the approaches used in HUMIR system for the WASSA-2018 shared task on the implicit emotion recognition. The objective of this task is to predict the emotion expressed by the target word that has been excluded from the given tweet. We suppose this task as a word sense disambiguation in which the target word is considered as a synthetic word that can express 6 emotions depending on the context. To predict the correct emotion, we propose a deep neural network model that uses two BiLSTM networks to represent the contexts in the left and right sides of the target word. The BiLSTM outputs achieved from the left and right contexts are considered as context-sensitive features. These features are used in a feed-forward neural network to predict the target word emotion. Besides this approach, we also combine the BiLSTM model with lexicon-based and emotion-based features. Finally, we employ all models in the final system using Bagging ensemble method. We achieved macro F-measure value of 68.8 on the official test set and ranked sixth out of 30 participants.

1 Introduction

Textual emotion recognition has received increasing attention in the natural language processing and computational linguistics in the recent decade. It aims to identify the emotion expressed by the given text based on two emotion models: *categorical model* and *dimensional model* (Russell 2003). While the categorical one uses discrete emotional categories such as Ekman's six basic emotions (Ekman, 1992), the dimensional one defines emotions in a *k-dimensional* space; each dimension represents an attribute of the emotion such as *valence*, *arousal* and *dominance*. However, the objective of the Implicit Emotion Shared Task (IEST) is to predict the emotion expressed

by the target word excluded from the given tweet instead of the emotion expressed by the tweet (Klinger et al., 2018). This task is organized based on the categorical model over 6 emotion categories as *anger*, *disgust*, *fear*, *joy*, *sadness*, and *surprise*.

Many approaches have been proposed for textual emotion recognition task. In general, these approaches can be grouped into 3 main categories: rule-based approaches, machine learning approaches and deep learning approaches. Rule based approaches exploit linguistic lexical resources like WordNet-Affect (Strapparava et al., 2004) as well as unsupervised techniques such as Latent Semantic Analysis (LSA) in rule-based classifiers (Kim et al., 2010; Lee et al., 2010). The second group of the approaches employs machine learning algorithms –such as support vector machines, naive Bayes, random forest, logistic regression, etc– to classify a text into emotion categories (Liew and Turtle, 2016). This group of approaches needs an extensive feature engineering as well as domain knowledge. Furthermore, in this group, many of emotion lexicons which are generated manually or automatically play an important role in extracting emotion-specific features. For instance, (Mohammad et al., 2013) proposes an SVM classifier based on a variety of feature sets extracted from manually and automatically generated sentiment lexicons and (Köper et al., 2017) exploits several lexicon-based features and employs them in the random forest classifier.

Unlike the previous approach, deep learning methods do not require any extensive feature engineering and can automatically extract features from raw text. Long Short-Term Memory (LSTM) and Convolutional Neural Network (CNN) are the basis of many approaches in deep learning for emotion recognition (Abdul-Mageed and Ungar, 2017; Kalchbrenner et al., 2014). The key objective of the both LSTM and CNN methods is

Proceedings of the 9th Workshop on Computational Approaches to Subjectivity, Sentiment and Social Media Analysis, pages 182–188
Brussels, Belgium, October 31, 2018. ©2018 Association for Computational Linguistics
https://doi.org/10.18653/v1/P17

to handle the semantic compositionality and to model the compositional changes on the text semantic according to its syntactic and semantic structure. However, some methods train CNN and LSTM models jointly (Stojanovski et al., 2016) or use a CNN followed by a LSTM (Wang et al., 2016; Köper et al., 2017).

In this paper, we suppose the target word as a synthetic ambiguous word that can express 6 emotions depending on the context. To predict the correct emotion, we propose 7 deep neural network models that use three *context-sensitive, lexicon-based* and *emotion-weight* features. The influence of these features is investigated over the proposed deep neural network models where they are employed to identify the context-dependent emotion of the target word.

2   System Description

In this section, we describe our proposed system to predict the emotion expressed by the target word which has been excluded from the tweet. In this system, we employ 6 deep neural network models along with a multi-layer perceptron (MLP) and combine them into a single predictive model using an ensemble method. All the models are obtained from 4 different approaches namely BiLSTM, Lexicon-BiLSTM, Left-Right BiLSTM and Lexicon-MLP. In these models, three kinds of features are extracted from a tweet and feed into a feed forward neural network: (1) *context-sensitive* features that are extracted from hidden state vectors of the BiLSTM network, (2) *lexicon-based* features that are obtained from AffectiveTweets Weka package (Mohammad and Bravo-Marquez, 2017) and (3) *emotion-weight* features that are computed by a feature evaluation metric proposed in (Naderalvojoud et al., 2015). In the following sections, we will describe our models and explain how they use these features to predict the emotion of the target word.

2.1   Feature Sets

The first feature set is obtained from the output of the Bidirectional Long Short-Term Memory (BiLSTM) network. BiLSTM is a variant of Recurrent Neural Network that uses LSTM cells to model a sequence. It encodes a tweet once from the beginning to end (left-to-right) and once from end to beginning (right-to-left). As a result, it maps a tweet to a pair of hidden state vectors. These vectors are used as context-sensitive features in our system to learn the semantic composition effects. The second kind of features are extracted from different sentiment and emotion lexicons. We have used 45 lexicon-based features extracted from the AffactiveTweet of Weka package. The details of these features can be found in (Mohammad and Bravo-Marquez, 2017). We also propose 6 emotion-weight features (corresponding to 6 emotion classes) as the third feature set. This feature set indicates the emotional weights of a certain tweet with respect to emotion classes. We first calculate the relatedness degree of words to each emotion class using PNF metric proposed in (Naderalvojoud et al., 2015) as Eq. 1:

$$PNF(t,c) = 1 + \frac{P(t|c) - P(t|\bar{c})}{P(t|c) + P(t|\bar{c})} \qquad (1)$$

In Eq. 1, $P(t|c)$ and $P(t|\bar{c})$ denotes the occurrence probability of term t given and not given emotion class c, respectively. Thus, each word in the vocabulary set is represented by a *6-dimensional* emotion-vector. Finally, to calculate the emotion-weight features for a tweet, we sum up the emotion vectors of individual words within the tweet.

2.2   Emotion-Specific Word Embedding

In our system, we have employed *200-dimensional* pre-trained word embeddings which have been trained on 2B tweets using GloVe embedding model[1] (called as TwitterGloVe). The distributed representation of words (also called as word embedding) is the basis of deep learning methods in NLP applications. Word embeddings represent words in the compact real value vectors in which the semantic and syntactic information of words are embedded into the vector space. This kind of representation provide us an inherent notion of relationships between words and we can detect words that are semantically similar to each other. However, the words that express opposite sentiment/emotion may have similar vectors in this space (Tang et al., 2014; Yu et al., 2017). At the same time, the lexical variations in the social media data make a challenge for dealing with out-of-vocabulary (OOV) words. For example, almost 3.5K out of 25K words in our vocabulary set were not matched to any word embedding.

---

[1] http://nlp.stanford.edu/data/glove.twitter.27B.zip

To deal with these two problems, we generate a simple BiLSTM model (which will be further presented in Section 2.4) to predict the emotion of the target word. In this model, we initialize the weight-matrix of the embedding layer with pre-trained word embeddings and assign to all OOV words random vectors created from a uniform distribution over [-0.25, 0.25]. We tune the embedding matrix during training. Finally, we employ the embedding matrix of the models achieved from epochs 1, 2 and 5 as our emotion-specific embeddings. We then repeat the same experiment using our emotion-specific embeddings with 50 epochs, however they are not tuned during training. Table 1 shows the results obtained from 3 emotion-specific embeddings as well as the TwitterGloVe. From this table, the embeddings achieved from the first epoch is the best. As the embeddings have been trained over the training data, well-tuned embeddings cause model to be overfit. Thus, we consider the embeddings achieved from the first epoch as the final system embeddings.

Model-WordEmbedding	Acc %
BiLSTM-Emotion-Specific-WE-1	**66.53**
BiLSTM-Emotion-Specific-WE-2	66.30
BiLSTM-Emotion-Specific-WE-5	62.62
BiLSTM-TwitterGloVe	66.35

Table 1: The accuracy of BiLSTM model using 4 word embeddings on the development set

2.3 Lexicon-based Multi-Layer Perceptron

To evaluate the importance of *lexicon-based* features as well as *emotion-weight* features, we use a simple multi-layer perceptron (MLP) model with 3 *input*, *hidden* and *output* layers. Two different models are trained by using two sets of features. While a tweet is represented using 45 lexicon-based features in the first model, they are represented by adding emotion-weight features into our prior feature set in the second one. Thus, the inputs of the first and the second models are 45 and 51-dimensional vectors. We set the number of hidden units as twice the input and assign them ReLU activation function. Finally, we apply dropout with a rate of 0.5 to the output of the hidden layer and pass them to the output. The output layer consists of 6 units with sigmoid activation function. Table 2 shows the best accuracy

achieved from each of two models on the development set. From this table, we observe that adding 6 emotion-weight features to our lexicon-based features increases the accuracy from 37.54 to 49.81. Hence, we select the second model for the final system and also consider both feature sets in the other models. In order to make a comparison with linear models, we also used libSVM with linear kernel function in this experiment. As seen, MLP outperforms SVM when using 45 lexicon-based features.

Model	Acc %
libSVM with 45 features	34.71
MLP with 45 features	37.54
MLP with 51 features	**49.81**

Table 2: The accuracy of SVM and MLP on the development set

2.4 Lexicon-Sensitive BiLSTM

In this section, we describe 2 types of deep neural network models using BiLSTM to predict the target word emotion. First, we create a simple 4-layer neural network namely *input*, *embedding*, *BiLSTM* and *output* layers. Each tweet is represented sequentially using 25K most frequent words. Those words out of vocabulary are treated as unknown word (UNK). However, the target word is not considered as UNK. In all tweets, the target word is supposed as a single particular word that can express all of the 6 emotions. In this model, pre-trained emotion-specific word vectors (described in Section 2.2) are used in the embedding layer. Here, a tweet which is represented as a sequence of word vectors is given to the BiLSTM layer in which the dimension of the hidden vectors in LSTM is 256. In order to avoid overfitting, we apply dropout (Srivastava et al., 2014) with a rate of 0.5 to the input of the BiLSTM layer. Finally, the output layer with 6 softmax units predicts the emotion of the target word.

In the second model, the lexicon-based and emotion-weight features are fed into the prior BiLSTM model. The output of the BiLSTM layer is concatenated with *51-dimensional* feature vector described in Section 2.3. Here, we actually employ all the three kinds of feature sets stated in Section 2.1 and predict the emotion of the target word by using these features through a feed forward neural network. We again apply dropout with a rate of 0.4 to the input of the feed forward

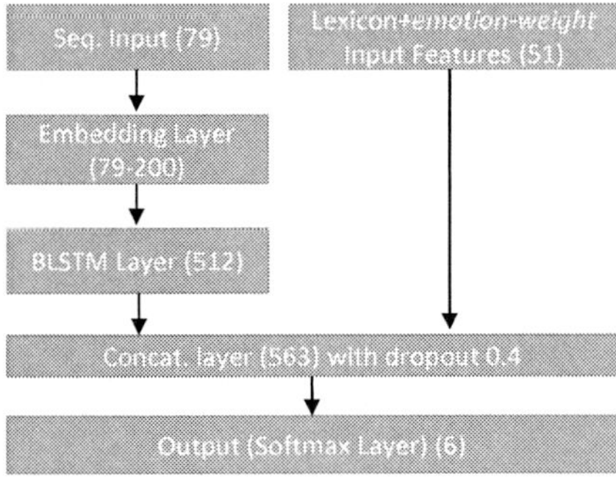

Figure 1: The architecture of Lexicon-BiLSTM approach

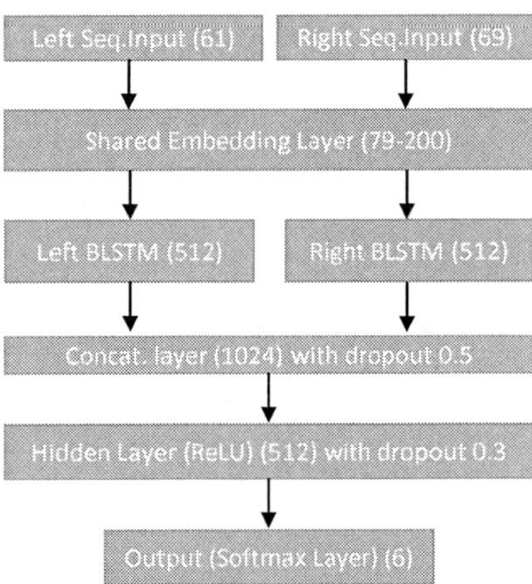

Figure 2: The architecture of LR-BiLSTM approach

neural network. Figure 1 depicts the overall architecture of the proposed model. This approach is called as Lexicon-BiLSTM in our experiments.

2.5 Left-Right Context-Sensitive BiLSTM

In the three previous approaches, we actually classified each tweet according to the emotion of the target word. However, in the fourth approach, we suppose the target word as a synthetic ambiguous word that can express 6 emotions depending on the context. Thus, our objective is to disambiguate the emotion expressed by this synthetic word in the given context (tweet). To this end, we consider the left and the right sides of the target word separately. We extract two semantic vectors from the context of the target word by applying BiLSTM model to its left and right sides. Hence, we call this approach as Left-Right context-sensitive BiLSTM (LR-BiLSTM). This exactly corresponds to the output of the BiLSTM layer in the two previous models when only left or right context of the target word is considered as input. These two vectors together represent the semantic signature of the context in which target word has been occurred. By relying on these two vectors, we create a feed forward neural network to predict the emotion of the target word. In this network, the concatenation of two semantic vectors are considered as input. The input is given to a hidden layer in which the number of units is the half of the input length. ReLU activation function is used in the hidden layer as well as two dropouts over its input and output with rates of 0.5, 0.3 respectively. Finally, the output layer using 6 softmax units predicts the emotion of the target word given its left and right contexts. Figure 2 summarizes this approach and shows the architecture of this model.

2.6 Ensemble Approach-Final System

We proposed 4 different approaches in three previous subsections. While 2 approaches leverage lexicon-based and emotion-weight features, two others only use hidden state vectors of the BiLSTM model. In order to use the advantages of all proposed models in the final system, we combine them using Bagging ensemble method (Breiman, 1996) to obtain an aggregated predictor. In this method, we take an average of the outputs of the proposed models and make a vote when predicting the emotion of the target word. Here, the output of each model is a *6-dimensional* vector (one output per class). Thus, N models generate a matrix $\mathbf{M}$ with the shape of $N \times 6$. The output of the ensemble method is a *6-dimensional* vector which is obtained by taking average of each column of matrix $\mathbf{M}$. The class voting is done according to the maximum value of the result vector.

For the final system, we create 7 models based on 4 approaches proposed in Sections 2.3, 2.4 and 2.5: Four models are generated from LR-BiLSTM approach using different settings and three models are generated from each of Lexicon-MLP, BiLSTM and Lexicon-BiLSTM approaches. The four models of the LR-BiLSTM approach is generated by the 4 following settings: (1) without hidden layer, with GloVeTwitter embedding (called as LR-BiLSTM-1); (2) without hidden layer, with emotion-specific embedding (called as LR-BiLSTM-2); (3) hidden layer with 300 units and emotion-specific embedding (called as LR-BiLSTM-3); (4) hidden layer with 512 units and emotion-specific embedding (called as LR-

BiLSTM-4). The architecture of LR-BiLSTM-4 is exactly the same as Figure 2. We use all these models in our final system since all of them increases the overall accuracy. For example, the system accuracy decreases to 67.4 without using Lexicon-MLP model.

3 Implementation Details

We used Keras library[2] with TensorFlow backend to implement all the proposed models. Before training, we removed all urls, usernames and newlines inside a tweet and employed NLTK toolkit[3] to tokenize tweets. All hyperparameters were tuned based on the development set with 50 epochs. We trained all models over training data provided by the shared task organizer (Klinger et al., 2018) and selected the best model based on the accuracy achieved from the development set. Table 3 shows the best results obtained by each of the proposed models.

Model	Dev-Macro F1	Dev-Acc
Lex-BiLSTM	66.5	66.68
LR-BiLSTM-1	65.4	65.49
LR-BiLSTM-2	65.7	65.81
LR-BiLSTM-3	66.8	66.94
LR-BiLSTM-4	**67.3**	**67.38**
BiLSTM	66.4	66.53
Lex-MLP	49.7	49.81
Final-system	**67.9**	**68.02**

Table 3: The best results on the development set

4 Empirical Evaluation and Discussion

We evaluate the proposed models on the shared task official test set. Table 4 shows the results according to the shared task evaluation measures – micro and macro averaged F-measure– over all 6 emotion classes. According to the results, the proposed Left-Right context-sensitive BiLSTM approach (i.e. LR-BiLSTM-3 and LR-BiLSTM-4) achieves the best official score of 67.8 among other individual models. The macro F1-score increases to 68.6 when using all models in our ensemble system.

According to the macro-F1 score achieved from BiLSTM and Lexicon-BiLSTM models, we can observe that two sets of lexicon-based and

emotion-weight features improve the performance of BiLSTM model. However, this growth is not seen in all classes. For example, in two *joy* and *sad* classes, BiLSTM model performs better than Lexicon-BiLSTM. In addition, the macro and micro averaged F-measure values obtained from the Lexicon-MLP (see Table 4) indicate that the lexicon-based and emotion-weight features are effective on less than 50% of test instances. This can raise two facts about the test set (1) a small number of affective clue words are used in the tweets (2) the syntactic structure of the context changes the emotions expressed by the affective clue words in the tweets. This issue will be further discussed in Section 4.1.

Another important finding is that all models give a weak performance on the *anger* and *surprise* emotions. The confusion matrix shown in Table 5 indicates that our final system predicts tweets as *anger* instead of *surprise* in 402 cases and vice versa in 519 cases. These are the highest False Negative (FN) errors with respect to *anger* and *surprise* emotion classes and show that these two emotions occur in similar contexts. It means that the senses expressed by these two emotion classes are much similar to each other in some tweets in which our system cannot distinguish them from each other. Moreover, from Table 5, *anger* and *surprise* emotions constitute the highest portion of the FN errors in the other emotion classes. They are bold in Table 5.

4.1 Error Analysis

We analyze the errors of the final system from two different aspects. In the first one, none of the models predict the correct emotion, whereas in the second one at least one model predict correctly. Here, we give two examples for each case, respectively:

- Ex.1 "I don't understand why everyone's [#TRIGGERWORD#] when Miley shows her body she's comfortable so why should it matter to you?"

- Ex.2 "it is quite [#TRIGGERWORD#] that you think that is awesome."

- Ex.3 "Cold coffee is really only [#TRIGGERWORD#] when you expect it to be hot. Otherwise, it's just as good."

- Ex.4 "@USERNAME making me [#TRIGGERWORD#] because she's better than me at everything"

[2]https://keras.io/
[3]https://www.nltk.org/

Models	F1-score over emotion classes						Mic-avg	Mac-avg (official)
	surp.	disg.	sad	fear	anger	joy		
Lex-BiLSTM	63.7	67.5	64.9	70.3	60.5	76.2	67.4	67.2
LR-BiLSTM-1	61.8	65.5	63.6	68.2	58.6	75.1	65.6	65.5
LR-BiLSTM-2	61.7	66.3	62.8	68.9	59.1	74.9	65.8	65.6
LR-BiLSTM-3	63.8	68.1	**66.3**	**71.0**	60.2	**77.3**	**68.0**	**67.8**
LR-BiLSTM-4	**64.2**	**68.3**	65.6	70.8	**60.9**	76.9	67.9	**67.8**
BiLSTM	63.6	67.0	65.2	69.5	59.5	76.3	67.0	66.9
Lex-MLP	42.7	53.5	45.4	50.8	43.2	61.1	49.6	49.4
Final-system	**64.9**	**69.0**	**66.4**	**71.6**	**62.3**	**77.6**	**68.8**	**68.6**

Table 4: The performance of all models on the official test set

Real	Predict					
	surp.	disg.	sad	fear	anger	joy
surp.	3310	367	183	303	**402**	227
disg.	**554**	3246	312	158	380	144
sad	236	384	2762	207	**430**	321
fear	**494**	177	192	3337	368	223
anger	**519**	336	297	326	3033	283
joy	289	103	228	203	**336**	4087

Table 5: Confusion matrix for final system

Table 6 indicates the predictions of the proposed models for the four above examples along with their true emotion labels. From the confusion matrix (Table 5) the biggest number of errors occurs when our system predict a tweet as *surprise*, whereas the true emotion is *disgust* (554 cases). Hence, the three of above examples were selected from the *disgust* class and last one was selected from *sad*. In Ex.1, it is observed that most of the models predict the emotion of the target word as *surprise*. However, Lexicon-MLP and LR-BiLSTM-2 predict it as *joy* and *anger*, respectively. Since Lexicon-MLP only use the lexicon-based and emotion-weight features, it cannot predict correctly when the emotion of the target word depends on the syntactic and semantic structures of the tweet. Thus, it predicts an opposite emotion (i.e. *joy*) for Ex.1. Moreover, you can see an ambiguity among *surprise*, *anger* and *disgust* in this example. In Ex.2, there is an irony that makes difficult the recognition of the target word emotion. Although the Ex.3 is similar to Ex.1, our context-sensitive BiLSTM approach (LR-BiLSTM-4) predicts the correct emotion. In Ex.4, you can see a challenge between *anger* and *sad* emotions. All the proposed models predict the emotion of the target word as *anger* except for LR-BiLSTM-3

which correctly predicts the target word emotion as *sad*. Here, we believe that a mixed emotion is inferred from the given context in Ex.4. However, the length of tweets is limited, thus it makes difficult the disambiguation task for the implicit emotion recognition.

Predictor	Ex.1	Ex.2	Ex.3	Ex.4
Lex-BiLSM	surp.	sad	surp.	anger
LR-BiLSTM-1	surp.	surp.	surp.	anger
LR-BiLSTM-2	anger	surp.	**disg.**	anger
LR-BiLSTM-3	surp.	surp.	**disg.**	**sad**
LR-BiLSTM-4	surp.	sad	**disg.**	anger
BiLSTM	surp.	surp.	surp.	anger
Lex-MLP	joy	surp.	surp.	anger
Final-sys	surp.	surp.	surp.	anger
True emotion	**disg.**	**disg.**	**disg.**	**sad**

Table 6: The predictions of models on 4 samples of tweets in the test set

5 Conclusion

In this paper, we proposed 6 deep neural network models as well as a MLP based on 3 kinds of feature sets, *lexicon-based*, *emotion-weight* and *context-sensitive*. The combination of all these models in our ensemble system achieved the best result on the official test set of IEST shared task. However, the results indicate that the model obtained from our proposed LR-BiLSTM approach outperforms the other individual models on the implicit emotion recognition task. Our results also showed that the Lexicon-BiLSTM approach performs better than BiLSTM by relying on the both *lexicon-based* and *emotion-weight* features.

References

Muhammad Abdul-Mageed and Lyle Ungar. 2017. Emonet: Fine-grained emotion detection with gated recurrent neural networks. In *Proceedings of the 55th Annual Meeting of the Association for Computational Linguistics (Volume 1: Long Papers)*, volume 1, pages 718–728.

Leo Breiman. 1996. Bagging predictors. *Machine learning*, 24(2):123–140.

Paul Ekman. 1992. An argument for basic emotions. *Cognition & emotion*, 6(3-4):169–200.

Nal Kalchbrenner, Edward Grefenstette, and Phil Blunsom. 2014. A convolutional neural network for modelling sentences. *arXiv preprint arXiv:1404.2188*.

Sunghwan Mac Kim, Alessandro Valitutti, and Rafael A Calvo. 2010. Evaluation of unsupervised emotion models to textual affect recognition. In *Proceedings of the NAACL HLT 2010 Workshop on Computational Approaches to Analysis and Generation of Emotion in Text*, pages 62–70. Association for Computational Linguistics.

Roman Klinger, Orphée de Clercq, Saif M. Mohammad, and Alexandra Balahur. 2018. IEST: WASSA-2018 Implicit Emotions Shared Task. In *Proceedings of the 9th Workshop on Computational Approaches to Subjectivity, Sentiment and Social Media Analysis*, Brussels, Belgium. Association for Computational Linguistics.

Maximilian Köper, Evgeny Kim, and Roman Klinger. 2017. IMS at EmoInt-2017: emotion intensity prediction with affective norms, automatically extended resources and deep learning. In *Proceedings of the 8th Workshop on Computational Approaches to Subjectivity, Sentiment and Social Media Analysis*, pages 50–57.

Sophia Yat Mei Lee, Ying Chen, and Chu-Ren Huang. 2010. A text-driven rule-based system for emotion cause detection. In *Proceedings of the NAACL HLT 2010 Workshop on Computational Approaches to Analysis and Generation of Emotion in Text*, pages 45–53. Association for Computational Linguistics.

Jasy Suet Yan Liew and Howard R Turtle. 2016. Exploring fine-grained emotion detection in tweets. In *Proceedings of the NAACL Student Research Workshop*, pages 73–80.

Saif M Mohammad and Felipe Bravo-Marquez. 2017. WASSA-2017 shared task on emotion intensity. *arXiv preprint arXiv:1708.03700*.

Saif M Mohammad, Svetlana Kiritchenko, and Xiaodan Zhu. 2013. NRC-Canada: Building the state-of-the-art in sentiment analysis of tweets. *arXiv preprint arXiv:1308.6242*.

Behzad Naderalvojoud, Ebru Akcapinar Sezer, and Alaettin Ucan. 2015. Imbalanced text categorization based on positive and negative term weighting approach. In *International Conference on Text, Speech, and Dialogue*, pages 325–333. Springer.

Nitish Srivastava, Geoffrey Hinton, Alex Krizhevsky, Ilya Sutskever, and Ruslan Salakhutdinov. 2014. Dropout: a simple way to prevent neural networks from overfitting. *The Journal of Machine Learning Research*, 15(1):1929–1958.

Dario Stojanovski, Gjorgji Strezoski, Gjorgji Madjarov, and Ivica Dimitrovski. 2016. Finki at semeval-2016 task 4: Deep learning architecture for twitter sentiment analysis. In *Proceedings of the 10th International workshop on semantic evaluation (SemEval-2016)*, pages 149–154.

Carlo Strapparava, Alessandro Valitutti, et al. 2004. Wordnet affect: an affective extension of wordnet. In *Lrec*, volume 4, pages 1083–1086. Citeseer.

Duyu Tang, Furu Wei, Nan Yang, Ming Zhou, Ting Liu, and Bing Qin. 2014. Learning sentiment-specific word embedding for twitter sentiment classification. In *Proceedings of the 52nd Annual Meeting of the Association for Computational Linguistics (Volume 1: Long Papers)*, volume 1, pages 1555–1565.

Jin Wang, Liang-Chih Yu, K Robert Lai, and Xuejie Zhang. 2016. Dimensional sentiment analysis using a regional CNN-LSTM model. In *Proceedings of the 54th Annual Meeting of the Association for Computational Linguistics (Volume 2: Short Papers)*, volume 2, pages 225–230.

Liang-Chih Yu, Jin Wang, K Robert Lai, and Xuejie Zhang. 2017. Refining word embeddings for sentiment analysis. In *Proceedings of the 2017 Conference on Empirical Methods in Natural Language Processing*, pages 534–539.

NLP at IEST 2018: BiLSTM-Attention and LSTM-Attention via Soft Voting in Emotion Classification

Qimin Zhou, Zhengxin Zhang, Hao Wu*

School of Information Science and Engineering, Yunnan University

Chenggong Campus, Kunming, P.R. China

`{zqmynu,zzxynu}@gmail.com, haowu@ynu.edu.cn`

Abstract

This paper describes our method that competed at WASSA2018 *Implicit Emotion Shared Task*. The goal of this task is to classify the emotions of excluded words in tweets into six different classes: sad, joy, disgust, surprise, anger and fear. For this, we examine a BiLSTM architecture with attention mechanism (BiLSTM-Attention) and a LSTM architecture with attention mechanism (LSTM-Attention), and try different dropout rates based on these two models. We then exploit an ensemble of these methods to give the final prediction which improves the model performance significantly compared with the baseline model. The proposed method achieves 7th position out of 30 teams and outperforms the baseline method by 12.5% in terms of *macro F1*.

1 Introduction

Sentiment analysis is a hot and vital research area in the field of natural language processing. It aims at detecting the sentiment expressed in the context written by the authors. Many advanced deep learning models have been exploited to address this issue in recent years (Cambria, 2016; Kim, 2014). The rise of social media, such as twitter and facebook, has fueled the interest of researchers in this field. Twitter is one of the most popular and influential social media all over the world, which attracts over more than 300 million users with over 500 million tweets every day [1]. Therefore, it has received great attention in research communities as a data source due to its easy accessibility of data and diversity of the content (Pak and Paroubek, 2010).

In this shared task, given tweets are incomplete because that certain emotion words are removed from these tweets. These words belong to one of the following classes: sad, happy, disgusted, surprised, anger and afraid, or a synonym of one of them. The goal of the task of WASSA2018 is to classify the emotion of the excluded words into one of the above-mentioned emotions according to the incomplete tweets. All the data given by WASSA2018 are in English.

For this task, we put forward to two different models: one is LSTM-Attention which mainly consists of LSTM (Li and Qian, 2016) and attention mechanism (Bahdanau et al., 2014; Lai et al., 2015), the other is BiLSTM-Attention which mainly consists of BiLSTM and attention mechanism. We have tried different dropout (Srivastava et al., 2014) rates to get different classification results on each model. To further better the predictive performance, our final method employs an ensemble of these models, with a strategy called *soft voting*.

The remainder of the paper is structured as follows: we provide the detailed architecture of proposed methods in Section 2. We present evaluation metrics and experimental results in Section 3. And we conclude our works and point to the future works in Section 4.

2 Methodology

In this section, we describe the details of our proposed methods, including data preprocessing, neural networks and ensemble strategy.

2.1 Data Preprocessing

As data released by WASSA2018 is crawled from the internet, raw tweets may contain a lot of useless (even misleading) information, such as some punctuations and abbreviations. Therefore, we perform a few preprocessing steps to improve the quality of raw data for the ongoing study: (1) The positions in the tweets where the emotion words have been removed are marked with [#TRIG-

---

[1] http://www.internetlivestats.com/twitter-statistics/

189

Proceedings of the 9th Workshop on Computational Approaches to Subjectivity, Sentiment and Social Media Analysis, pages 189–194

Brussels, Belgium, October 31, 2018. ©2018 Association for Computational Linguistics

https://doi.org/10.18653/v1/P17

GERWORD#] (see Figure 1), so we remove them from the raw data. (2) We remove the useless link *"http : //url.removed"* and some meaningless punctuations such as semicolon and colon. (3) We restore some abbreviations in the tweets, e.g., substituting *"have"* for *"'ve"*. (4) All characters are then transformed into lowercase. (5) The TweetTokenizer [2] tool is used to split tweets into a list of words. We try to remove stopwords via nltk.corpus [3], but there is no performance improvement, so we ignore this processing.

I was absolutely [#TRIGGERWORD#] when I heard about what happened yesterday. It astounds me that some people··· http://url.removed

Figure 1: An example of raw tweets

2.2 Neural Networks

Our models consist of an embedding layer, a LSTM or BiLSTM layer, an attention layer and two dense layers. Figure 2 shows the architecture of the BiLSTM-Attention model. For the LSTM-Attention model, it shares the same architecture with the BiLSTM-Attention model, except that the BiLSTM layer is replaced with the LSTM layer.

2.2.1 Embedding Layer

To extract the semantic information of tweets, each tweet is firstly represented as a sequence of word embeddings. Denote s as a tweet with n words and each word is mapping to a global vector (Mikolov et al., 2013), then we have:

$$s = [\vec{e_1} \parallel \vec{e_2} \parallel \vec{e_3} \parallel ... \parallel \vec{e_n}], \qquad (1)$$

where vector $\vec{e_i}$ represents the vector of i-th word with a dimension of d. The vectors of word embeddings are concatenated together to maintain the order of words in a tweets. Consequently, it can overcome deficits of *bag-of-words* techniques. For our methods, Word2vec-twitter-model, a pretrained word embedding model using Word2vec technique (Mikolov et al., 2013) on tweets is exploited. The embedding dimension of Word2vec-twitter-model is d=400.

2.2.2 LSTM/Bidirectional-LSTM Layer

In this emotion classification task, we model the twitter messages using *Recurrent Neural Network*

(RNN), to be exact, we respectively examine LSTM and Bidirectional LSTM (Zeng et al., 2016) to process the tweets. LSTM firstly introduced by (Hochreiter and Schmidhuber, 1997) has proven to be stable and powerful for modeling long-time dependencies in various scenarios such as speech recognition and machine translations. Bidirectional LSTM (Graves and Schmidhuber, 2005; Graves et al., 2013) is an extension of traditional LSTM to train two LSTMs on the input sequence. The second LSTM is a reversed copy of the first one, so that we can take full advantage of both past and future input features for a specific time step. We train both LSTM and Bidirectional LSTM networks using back-propagation through time (BPTT) (Chen and Huo, 2016). After the embedding layer, the sequence of word vectors is fed into a single-layer LSTM or Bidirectional LSTM to achieve another representation of $h = LSTM/BiLSTM(s)$. In order to maintain consistency of dimensions, the number of neurons is configured as 400 in both the LSTM Layer and the BiLSTM Layer.

2.2.3 Attention layer

Generally, not all words in a tweet contribute equally to the representation of tweet, so we leverage word attention mechanism to capture the distinguished influence of the words on the emotion of tweet, and then form a dense vector (Yang et al., 2017) considering the weights of different word vectors. Specifically, we have:

$$\begin{aligned} u_{ti} &= \tanh(W h_{ti} + b), \\ \alpha_{ti} &= \frac{\exp(u_{ti}^T u_w)}{\sum_{j=1}^{n} \exp(u_{tj}^T u_w)}, \\ s_t &= \sum_i \alpha_{ti} h_{ti}. \end{aligned} \qquad (2)$$

t represents t-th tweet, i represents i-th word in the tweet and n is the number of words in a tweet. h_{ti} represents the word annotation of the i-th word in the t-th tweet which fed to a one-layer MLP to get u_{ti} as a hidden representation of h_{ti}. More specifically h_{ti} is the concatenation output of the LSTM/BiLSTM layer in our model. W is a weight matrix of the MLP, and b is a bias vector of the MLP. Then we measure the importance of words through the similarity between u_{ti} and a word level context vector u_w which is randomly initialized. And after that, we get a normalized importance weight α_{ti} through a softmax function. α_{ti} is the weight of the i-th word in the t-th tweet. The bigger α_{ti} is, the more important the i-th word is

---

[2] http://www.nltk.org/api/nltk.tokenize.html
[3] http://www.nltk.org/api/nltk.corpus.html

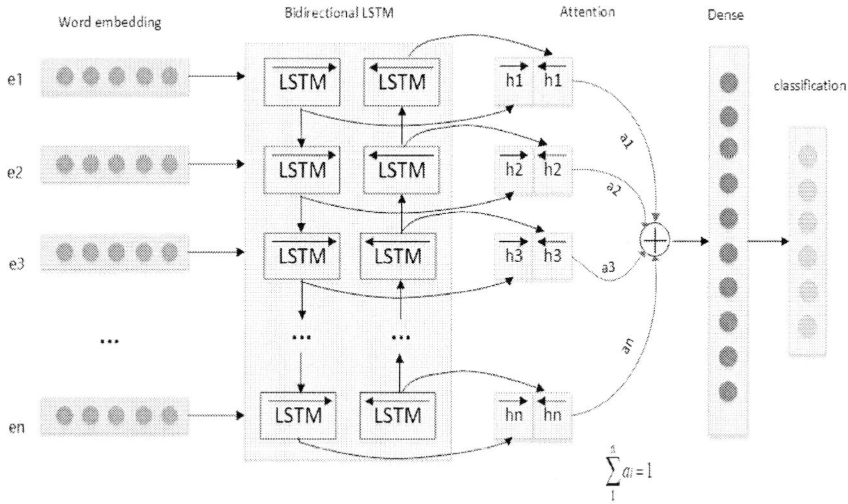

Figure 2: The architecture of BiLSTM-Attention model

for emotion representation. Finally, we represent the sentence vector s_t as a weighted sum of the word annotations.

2.2.4 Dense Layers

The attention layer is followed by two dense layers with different sizes of neurons. The output of attention layer is fed into the first dense layer with 400 hidden neurons. The activation function of this layer is *tanh*. And in order to avoid potential overfitting problem, *dropout* is utilized between these two dense layers. And we try different dropout rates to find the best configurations. The output is then fed into the second dense layer with 6 hidden neurons, and the activation function in this layer is *softmax*. So we can obtain the probability that the excluded word belongs to each of the six classes.

2.3 Ensemble Strategy

Ensemble strategies (Dietterich, 2000) have been widely used in various research fields because of their ascendant performance. Ensemble strategies train multiple learners and then combine them to achieve a better predictive performance. Many ensemble strategies have been proposed, such as Voting, Bagging, Boosting, Blending, etc [4]. In our methods, a simple but efficient ensemble strategy called soft voting is utilized. It means that for a classification problem, soft voting returns the class label of the maximum of the weighted sum

of the predicted probabilities. We assign a weight equally to each classifier, then the probability that a sample belongs to a certain class is the weighted sum of probabilities that this sample belongs to this class predicted by all classifiers. And the class with the highest probability is the final classification result. It can be defined as Eq.3 (Zhou, 2012):

$$H^j(x) = \frac{1}{T} \sum_{i=1}^{T} h_i^j(x). \tag{3}$$

i represents i-th classifier, T is the total number of classifier. j is the class label where j is an integer between 0 and 5, because there are 6 classes in our task. x is a sample. $h_i^j(x)$ represents the i-th classifier's predictive probability towards the sample x on the j-th class label, it is a probability which is between 0 and 1. Finally, $H^j(x)$ represents the probability that the sample x belongs to j-th class after ensembling.

3 Experiments

3.1 Evaluation Metrics

To evaluate the classification performance, there are two available metrics: *macro average* and *micro average*. In this task, we use macro average to measure the performance of proposed methods. Macro average is the arithmetic mean of the performance metrics for each class, e.g. precision and recall (Ting, 2011). *Precision* is the fraction of relevant instances among the retrieved instances, while *recall* is the fraction of relevant instances

---

[4]http://scikit-learn.org/stable/modules/ensemble.html

that have been retrieved over the total amount of relevant instances [5]. More specifically, *macro F1* score is utilized as a measurable indicator of classification performance. The F1 score can be interpreted as a weighted average of the precision and recall. The relative contributions of precision and recall to the F1 score are equal. The formula of F1 score can be defined as Eq.4:

$$F1 = \frac{2 * precision * recall}{precision + recall}.\tag{4}$$

3.2 Experiment Results

Our system is implemented on Keras with a Tensorflow backend [6]. For experiments, we use the datasets downloaded from WASSA2018, they mainly include three splits: 153,383 tweets in the training set, 9,591 tweets in the validation set and 28,757 tweets in the test set. We train our model on the training set, and then tune the hyper parameters of models on the validation set.

For training, the mini-batch size is set at 128 and the max length of sentences (namely, the number of words in a tweet) is configured as 37 to ensure the same length of each tweet. Namely, if the length of a tweet is less than 37, it will be padded with zero; otherwise, it will be truncated from the tail. And the dropout rates that we have tried are ranged from 0.1 to 0.6 with a step of 0.1. In our models, the categorical-crossentropy based loss function and the gradient descent algorithm with *Adaptive Moment Estimation* (Kingma and Ba, 2014) are used to learn the model parameters of neural networks as well as the word vectors. The default parameters of *Adaptive Moment Estimation* is $learning\_rate$=0.001, $beta\_1$=0.9, $beta\_2$=0.999, $eposilon$=1e-08.

The experimental results on different emotion classes are shown in Table 1. There are three evaluation metrics of each emotion class, namely precision, recall and F1 score. Apparently, our system works best on the emotion class named joy in term of all the metrics. And the F1 score on the class called anger is the lowest.

The experimental results of different models in our system are shown in Table 2. Obviously, all of our models outperform the baseline model dramatically. More specifically, the BiLSTM-Attention model performs slightly better than the LSTM-Attention model because BiLSTM can learn more features than LSTM.

Classes	Precision	Recall	Macro average F1
sad	0.685	0.622	0.652
joy	0.773	0.778	0.776
disgust	0.701	0.673	0.687
surprise	0.620	0.683	0.650
anger	0.618	0.627	0.623
fear	0.722	0.722	0.722

Table 1: Experimental Results on Different Classes

Model	Dropout	Macro average F1
Baseline	-	0.599
BiLSTM-Attention	0.1	0.659
	0.2	0.662
	0.3	0.655
	0.4	0.659
	0.5	0.658
	0.6	0.659
LSTM-Attention	0.1	0.656
	0.2	0.659
	0.3	0.661
	0.4	0.660
	0.5	0.652
	0.6	0.654
Ensemble	-	0.685

Table 2: Experimental Results on Different Models

To achieve better performance, we utilize a simple ensemble method called *soft voting*. Briefly speaking, if a class gets the highest weighted sum of probabilities from various models, then it is the final class which our sample belongs to. After ensembling the LSTM-Attention model and the BiLSTM-Attention model with different dropout rates, the macro F1 score reaches to 0.685. These results demonstrate that the ensemble approach boosts the classification performance dramatically.

Figure 3 shows the predictive accuracy which is measured by F1 score as a function of epoch when dropout rate is 0.2. The accuracy of our model is optimal when the epoch is equal to 2, so we set the epoch to 2 in our final model.

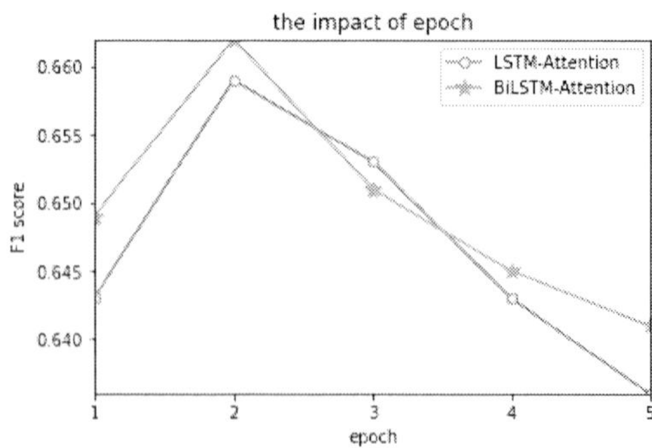

Figure 3: impact of epoch

4   Conclusion & Future work

We have presented a deep learning based approach for implicit emotion analysis task which can be seen as a classification task. We explore LSTM model and BiLSTM model both equipped with attention mechanism using different dropout rates and leverage ensemble method to boost the classification performance. Experimental results demonstrate that our system is effective for this implicit emotion classification task.

As for future works, it can follow three directions. Firstly, we intend to try different ensemble methods like hard voting and stacking to find which one is the most suitable for our task. Secondly, we would like to combine word embedding and char embedding (Santos and Guimaraes, 2015) together with different weights. Also we can utilize some new embedding algorithms like ELMo embeddings [7]. Finally, we plan to explore more textual features like emotion icons to gain better performance.

Acknowledgments

This work is partially supported by the National Natural Science Foundation of China (61562090) and the Graduate Research Innovation Found Projects of Yunnan University (YDY17113).

References

Dzmitry Bahdanau, Kyunghyun Cho, and Yoshua Bengio. 2014. Neural machine translation by jointly learning to align and translate. *arXiv preprint arXiv:1409.0473*.

Erik Cambria. 2016. Affective computing and sentiment analysis. *IEEE Intelligent Systems*, 31(2):102–107.

Kai Chen and Qiang Huo. 2016. Training deep bidirectional lstm acoustic model for lvcsr by a context-sensitive-chunk bptt approach. *IEEE/ACM Transactions on Audio, Speech and Language Processing (TASLP)*, 24(7):1185–1193.

Thomas G Dietterich. 2000. Ensemble methods in machine learning. In *International workshop on multiple classifier systems*, pages 1–15. Springer.

Alex Graves, Abdel-rahman Mohamed, and Geoffrey Hinton. 2013. Speech recognition with deep recurrent neural networks. In *Acoustics, speech and signal processing (icassp), 2013 ieee international conference on*, pages 6645–6649. IEEE.

Alex Graves and Jürgen Schmidhuber. 2005. Framewise phoneme classification with bidirectional lstm and other neural network architectures. *Neural Networks*, 18(5-6):602–610.

Sepp Hochreiter and Jürgen Schmidhuber. 1997. Lstm can solve hard long time lag problems. In *Advances in neural information processing systems*, pages 473–479.

Yoon Kim. 2014. Convolutional neural networks for sentence classification. In *Proceedings of the 2014 Conference on Empirical Methods in Natural Language Processing, EMNLP 2014, October 25-29, 2014, Doha, Qatar, A meeting of SIGDAT, a Special Interest Group of the ACL*, pages 1746–1751.

Diederik P Kingma and Jimmy Ba. 2014. Adam: A method for stochastic optimization. *arXiv preprint arXiv:1412.6980*.

Siwei Lai, Liheng Xu, Kang Liu, and Jun Zhao. 2015. Recurrent convolutional neural networks for text classification. In *AAAI*, volume 333, pages 2267–2273.

Dan Li and Jiang Qian. 2016. Text sentiment analysis based on long short-term memory. In *IEEE International Conference on Computer Communication and the Internet*, pages 471–475.

Tomas Mikolov, Kai Chen, Greg Corrado, and Jeffrey Dean. 2013. Efficient estimation of word representations in vector space. *arXiv preprint arXiv:1301.3781*.

Alexander Pak and Patrick Paroubek. 2010. Twitter as a corpus for sentiment analysis and opinion mining. In *LREc*, volume 10, pages 1320–1326.

Cicero Nogueira dos Santos and Victor Guimaraes. 2015. Boosting named entity recognition with neural character embeddings. *arXiv preprint arXiv:1505.05008*.

Nitish Srivastava, Geoffrey Hinton, Alex Krizhevsky, Ilya Sutskever, and Ruslan Salakhutdinov. 2014. Dropout: a simple way to prevent neural networks from overfitting. *The Journal of Machine Learning Research*, 15(1):1929–1958.

Kai Ming Ting. 2011. Precision and recall. In *Encyclopedia of machine learning*, pages 781–781. Springer.

Zichao Yang, Diyi Yang, Chris Dyer, Xiaodong He, Alex Smola, and Eduard Hovy. 2017. Hierarchical attention networks for document classification. In *Conference of the North American Chapter of the Association for Computational Linguistics: Human Language Technologies*, pages 1480–1489.

Ying Zeng, Honghui Yang, Yansong Feng, Zheng Wang, and Dongyan Zhao. 2016. A convolution bilstm neural network model for chinese event extraction. In *Natural Language Understanding and Intelligent Applications*, pages 275–287. Springer.

---

[7]https://allennlp.org/elmo

Zhi-Hua Zhou. 2012. *Ensemble methods: foundations and algorithms.* Chapman and Hall/CRC.

SINAI at IEST 2018: Neural Encoding of Emotional External Knowledge for Emotion Classification

Flor Miriam Plaza-del-Arco[†] **Eugenio Martínez-Cámara**[♣]
M. Teresa Martín-Valdivia[†] **L. Alfonso Ureña- López**[†]
[†]Department of Computer Science,
Advanced Studies Center in ICT (CEATIC)
Universidad de Jaén, Campus Las Lagunillas, 23071, Jaén, Spain
[♣]Andalusian Research Institute in Data Science and Computational Intelligence (DaSCI)
University of Granada, Spain
{fmplaza, maite, laurena}@ujaen.es, emcamara@decsai.ugr.es

Abstract

In this paper, we describe our participation in WASSA 2018 Implicit Emotion Shared Task (IEST 2018). We claim that the use of emotional external knowledge may enhance the performance and the capacity of generalization of an emotion classification system based on neural networks. Accordingly, we submitted four deep learning systems grounded in a sequence encoding layer. They mainly differ in the feature vector space and the recurrent neural network used in the sequence encoding layer. The official results show that the systems that used emotional external knowledge have a higher capacity of generalization, hence our claim holds.

1 Introduction

Emotions play an important role in human beings due to what we notice and remember is not the mundane but events that evoke feelings like joy, sadness, surprise, and disgust. Emotions relate us to others as a form of interpersonal communication, they introduce us to the world as well as the motivational force for what is best and worst in human behavior.

Emotion mining is part of the Sentiment Analysis (SA) and consists of recognizing emotions mainly from text. According to Ekman (1992), the basic emotions expressed by humans are: joy, sadness, surprise, fear, disgust and anger. Emotion recognition is still in its infancy and still has a ling way to proceed (Yadollahi et al., 2017). The high rate at which users share their opinions on news articles, blogs, microblogs and social networking sites, make this king of media even more attractive to measure specific emotions towards current affairs. Recognizing emotion is extremely important for some text-based communication tools (Wu et al., 2006), e.g., the dialog system is a kind of human machine communication system that uses only text input and output. Recognizing the users emotional states enables the dialog system to change the response and answer types (Lee et al., 2002). Text is still the main communication tool on the Internet. In online chat, the users emotional states can be used to control the dialog strategy.

In this paper, we describe the four systems submitted to the IEST shared-task of the WASSA Workshop (Klinger et al., 2018). The shared task consists of predicting the implicit emotion expressed in a tweet, and the labels of emotion are: sadness, joy, disgust, surprise, anger, or fear. We tackled the challenge as a multi-classification task, and we claim that the use of emotional external knowledge may enhance the performance and the capacity of generalization of the classification systems. We submitted four systems based on deep learning. Two of them do not use emotional external knowledge, and the other two do. The official results show that those systems with emotional external knowledge have a higher capacity of generalization as we hypothesized.

The rest of the paper is organized as follows. Section 2 describes the dataset used by our systems. Section 3 presents the details of the proposed systems. Section 4 displays the results and analyses them. We conclude in Section 5 with remarks and future work.

2 Dataset

The evaluation dataset (Klinger et al., 2018) is annotated on a scale of six emotions, namely: sadness, joy, disgust, surprise, anger, or fear. To run our experiments, we used this dataset as follows. During pre-evaluation period, we trained our models on the *train* set, and evaluated our different approaches on the *dev* set. During evaluation period, we trained our models on the *train* and *dev* sets,

Proceedings of the 9th Workshop on Computational Approaches to Subjectivity, Sentiment and Social Media Analysis, pages 195–200
Brussels, Belgium, October 31, 2018. ©2018 Association for Computational Linguistics
https://doi.org/10.18653/v1/P17

Dataset	Tweets
Train	153383
Dev	9591
Test	28757

Table 1: Number of tweets for each dataset.

and tested the model on the *test* set. The size of the datasets is in Table 1.

3 System description

The aim of the shared task is the classification of the implicit emotion of an input tweet. However, the word that explicitly expresses the emotion was remove from the input tweets. Accordingly, two specific features may be incorporated in the classification system: (1) the position of the removed word with emotion meaning; and (2) emotional external knowledge. Since our claim is that the use of emotional external knowledge can enhance the classification of emotions, we only considered the second specific feature, namely the incorporation of emotional external knowledge.

We designed a neural architecture built upon a sequence encoding approach, which is able to perform the classification with or without emotional external knowledge. We submitted four systems, which share a common structure composed of three modules: (1) language representation or features lookup module; (2) sequence encoding module; and (3) non linear classification module. The four systems differ in the first and second modules. The details of the modules and the differencies of the four systems are described in the following subsections.

3.1 Features lookup module

Regarding our claim, we defined a feature vector space for the training and the evaluation that is composed of: (1) unsupervised vectors of word embeddings; and (2) one-hot vector representation of emotional features.

Vectors of word embeddings A set of vectors of word embeddings is the representation of the ideal semantic space of words in a real-valued continuous vector space, hence the relationships between vectors of words mirror the linguistic relationships of the words. Vectors of word embeddings are a dense representation of the meaning of a word, thus each word is linked to a real-valued continuous vector of dimension d_{emb}.

There are freely available several pre-trained sets of vectors of word embeddings grounded in different approaches to represent the context of a word, such as C&W (Collobert et al., 2011), word2vect (Mikolov et al., 2013) and Glove (Pennington et al., 2014). Since the genre of the input documents is social media, Twitter, the use of a set of embeddings trained on tweets is advisable. Therefore, we specifically used the set of pre-trained vectors of word embeddings of Glove[1] that is trained on tweets. The most relevant characteristics of that set are: (1) the size of the vocabulary is 1.2 million of words; (2) all the words are lower-case.

Emotional external knowledge Two of the submitted systems used emotional external knowledge. We encoded the external emotional knowledge with a one-hot encoding approach, hence the emotional categories considered were represented as a one-hot vector. Accordingly, the feature vector space is enlarged with the size of the additional components or dimensions corresponding to the emotional categories ($d=d_{emb}+d_{emo}$).

To obtain the emotional external knowledge we use the following emotional lexicons:

NRC Word-Emotion Association Lexicon (EmoLex) (Mohammad and Turney, 2010). This lexicon has a list of English words associated to one or more of the following emotions: anger, fear, anticipation, trust, surprise, sadness, disgust, joy. Since the emotional external knowledge is encoded as one-hot vector, the corresponding emotion is set to 1 of those words that are in the lexicon. The results is a vector of eight emotion values. In case the word belongs to one or more emotions, all the emotions to which it belongs are taken into account.

Emoji lexicon We use this lexicon to identify the emojis present in text using some faces of an emoji lexicon.[2] This lexicon contains a list of emojis but it is not labeled with emotion. Thus, we manually annotated some emojis to one of the Ekman emotions: joy, anger, fear, disgust, surprise, sadness (Ekman, 1992). After this process, we obtained

---

[1] https://nlp.stanford.edu/projects/glove/

[2] https://github.com/erunion/emoji-lexicon

a lexicon with 72 emojis labelled by the Ekman emotions. The distribution of emojis by Ekman emotions is shown in Table 2.

Emotion	Number of Emojis
Joy	39
Sad	15
Anger	8
Fear	6
Surprise	3
Disgust	1

Table 2: Number of emojis for each Ekman emotion.

We tokenized the input tweets with the Twitter-aware tokenizer of NLTK[3] in order to project them in the feature vector space defined by the vector of word embeddings and emotional features. Consequently, each tweet (t) is transformed in a sequence of n words ($w_{1:n} = \{w_1, \ldots, w_n\}$). The size of the input sequence (n) was defined by the mode of the lengths of the inputs in the training data, hence sequences shorter than n were truncated. After the tokenization, the first layer of our architecture model is an feature lookup layer, which makes the projection of the sequence of tokens into the feature vector space. Therefore, the output of the features lookup layer is the matrix $\mathbf{WE} \in \mathbb{R}^{d \times n}$, $\mathbf{WE}_{1:n}^{\mathbf{T}} = (\mathbf{we}_1, \ldots, \mathbf{we}_n)$, where $\mathbf{we}_i \in \mathbb{R}^d$. The parameters of the embedding lookup layer are not updated during the training.

3.2 Sequence encoding module

The aim of the sequence encoding layer is the generation of high level features, which condense the semantic meaning of the entire sentence. We used an RNN layer because RNNs can represent sequential input in a fixed-size vector and paying attention to the structured properties of the input (Goldberg, 2017). RNN is defined as a recursive R function applied to a input sequence. The input of the function R is an state vector s_{i-1} and an element of the input sequence, in our case a word vector ($\mathbf{we}_i$). The output of R is a new state vector (s_i), which is transformed to the output vector $\mathbf{y}_i$ by a deterministic function O. Equation 1 summa-

[3] https://www.nltk.org/api/nltk.tokenize.html#nltk.tokenize.casual.TweetTokenizer

rizes the former definition.

$$RNN(\mathbf{we}_{1:n}, \mathbf{s}_0) = \mathbf{y}_{1:n}$$
$$\mathbf{y}_i = O(\mathbf{s}_i) \qquad (1)$$
$$\mathbf{s}_i = R(\mathbf{we}_i, \mathbf{s}_{i-1});$$

$$\mathbf{we}_i \in \mathbb{R}^{d_{in}}, \mathbf{s}_i \in \mathbb{R}^{f(d_{out})}, \mathbf{y}_i \in \mathbb{R}^{d_{out}}$$

From a linguistic point of view, each vector ($\mathbf{y}_i$) of the output sequence of an RNN condenses the semantic information of the word w_i and the previous words ($\{w_1, \ldots, w_{i-1}\}$). However, according to the distributional hypothesis of language (Harris, 1954), semantically similar words tend to have similar contextual distributions, roughly speaking, the meaning of a word is defined by its contexts. An RNN can only encode the previous context of a word when the input of the RNN is the sequence $\mathbf{we}_{1:n}$. However, the input of the RNN can be also the reverse of the previous sequence ($we_{n:1}$). Consequently, we can elaborate a composition of two RNNs, the first one encode the sequence from the beginning to the end (*forward*, f), and a second one from the end to the beginning (*backward*, b), therefore the previous and the following context of a word is encoded. This elaboration is known as *bidirectional* RNN (biRNN), whose definition is in Equation 2.

$$biRNN(\mathbf{we}_{1:n}) = [RNN^f(\mathbf{we}_{1:n}, s_0^f);$$
$$RNN^b(\mathbf{we_a n} : \mathbf{1}, s_0^b)] \qquad (2)$$

The four systems submitted are based on the use of a specific gated-architecture of RNN, namely Long Short-Term Memory (LSTM) (Hochreiter and Schmidhuber, 1997). Figure 1 shows the architecture of these models. The specific details of the sequence encoding layer of each submitted system are described as what follows.

NoEMoLSTM The sequence encoding layer is composed of one LSTM RNN. The input is the feature space only defined by the matrix of vectors of word embeddings ($\mathbf{WE} \in \mathbb{R}^{d_{emb}}$). The output is all the output vectors of all the words of the sequence, hence the output is the sequence $\mathbf{y}_{1:n}$, $y_i \in \mathbb{R}^{d_{out}}$.

EmoLSTM This sequence encoding layer is similar to the previous one, however the input is a feature space composed of vectors of word embeddings and emtotional features, mathematically

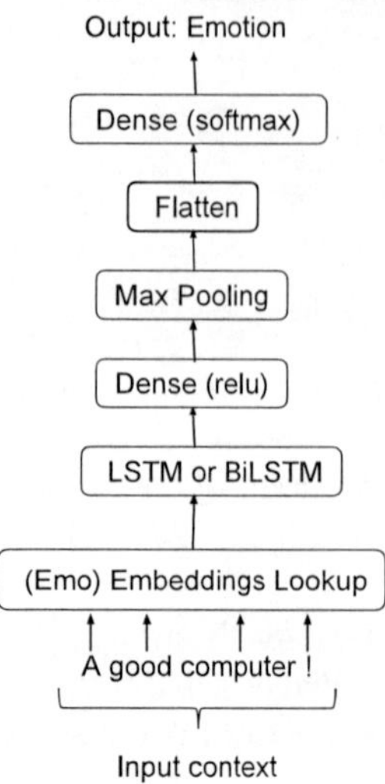

Figure 1: Neural model, where Emo represents the EmoLSTM and EmoBiLSTM models.

$\mathbf{WE} \in \mathbb{R}^{d_{emb}+d_{emo}}$. As NoEMoLSTM, the output is all the output vectors of all the words of the sequence, hence the output is the sequence $\mathbf{y}_{1:n}$, $y_i \in \mathbb{R}^{d_{out}}$.

NoEMoBiLSTM It only differs from NoEMoL-STM in the RNN layer. In this case the RNN layer is an BiLSTM layer. Since an BiLSTM is the composition of two LSTMs, the output units returned of NoEMoBiLSTM is larger than the one of NoE-MOLSTM, specifically $\mathbf{y}_{1:n}$, $y_i \in \mathbb{R}^{d_{out} \cdot 2}$.

EmoBiLSTM As EmoLSTM, it incorporates emotional external knowledge ($\mathbf{WE} \in \mathbb{R}^{d_{emb}+d_{emo}}$), and as NoEMoBiLSTM, the encoding layer is an BiLSTM RNN, therefore the output is the sequence $\mathbf{y}_{1:n}$, $y_i \in \mathbb{R}^{d_{out} \cdot 2}$.

3.3 Non linear classification module

The sequence representation of the tweets is then classified by two fully connected layers with ReLU as activation function, and additional layer activated by the softmax function. The layers activated by ReLU have different hidden units or output neurons ($dense^1$ and $dense^2$, see Table 3). With the aim of selecting the most relevant features, the output of the first full connected layer is processed by a max pooling layer. The size of the pooling layer was 2, and it was applied to every step, i.e. the strides size is 1. Since the four sequence encoding layers return an output se-

Hyper	NoEMo-LSTM	EMo-LSTM	NoEMo-BiLSTM	EMo-BiLSTM
n	27	27	27	27
$d_{emb}+d_{emo}$	200	214	200	214
d_{out}	128	128×2	128	128×2
$dense^1$	128	128	128	128
$dense^2$	64	64	64	64
dr^1	0.5	0.5	0.5	0.5
dr^2	0.5	0.5	0.5	0.5
$L_2\ r$	0.0001	0.0001	0.0001	0.0001

Table 3: Hyperparater values of the systems submitted.

quence $\mathbf{y}_{1:n} \in \mathbb{R}^{n \times d_{out}}$, after the max pooling layer, the sequence is flattened to a single vector $\mathbf{y} \in \mathbb{R}^{n \cdot d_{out}}$. The number of hidden units of the softmax layer matches the number of emotion categories of the task.

In order to avoid overfitting, we add a dropout layer (Hinton et al., 2012) after each fully connected layer with a dropout rate value dr. Besides, we applied an L_2 regularization function to the loss function with a regularization value (r). Moreover, the training is stopped in case the loss value does not improve in 3 epochs.

The training of the network was performed by the minimization of the cross entropy function, and the learning process was optimized with the Adam algorithm (Kingma and Ba, 2015) with its default learning rate. The training was performed following the minibatches approach with a batch size of 64, and the number of epochs was 30.

For the sake of the replicability of the experiments, Table 3 shows the values of the hyperparaments of the network, and the source code of our experiments is publicly available.[4]

3.4 Internal baseline

We also developed an internal baseline for evaluating the performance of the neural networks models. Our internal baseline was a linear classification system, namely Support Vector Machines (SVM). The feature space is composed of the unigrams of the training set weighted by the TF-IDF metric, and the number of unigrams of each emotional category considered. The results reached by our internal baseline are in Table 4 with the name EmoSVM.

---

[4] https://github.com/fmplaza/WASSA-2018

	Development			Test		
System	M. Prec	M. Recall	M. F1	M. Prec	M. Recall	M. F1
Amobee[1]	-	-	-	-	-	71.4%
EmoSVM	49.99%	50.1%	50.02%	49.77%	49.84%	49.69%
EmoLSTM[21]	56.11%	56.13%	55.96%	58.41%	58.3%	58.30%
NoEMoLSTM[21]	56.60%	56.46%	56.43%	58.25%	58.17%	58.11%
EmoBiLSTM[22]	56.42%	56.3%	56.17%	57.92%	57.97%	57.94%
NoEMoBiLSTM[26]	55.17%	55.24%	55.12%	56.41%	54.7%	54.68%

Table 4: Dev. and Test results reached by our systems and by the best system in the competition. The superscripts specify the rank of the systems in the competition.

4 Analysis of results

We performed our experiments in the pre-evaluation phase and evaluation phase, and we used the official competition metric macro-averaged F1-score as evaluation measure. Moreover, we computed the Macro Precision, Macro Recall and Macro F1. This results are shown in Table 4.

First, we assessed our internal baseline (EmoSVM), which set a lower bound during the development or pre-evaluation phase. Since the number of classes is 6, the performance of our internal baseline is acceptable, and we also conclude the its generalization capacity is acceptable.

The submitted systems, which are based on deep learning, outperformed EmoSVM with the development and test data. Regarding the results reached with the development subset, the models that did not use emotional external knowledge reached higher results that those ones that used external knowledge. However, those systems that used emotional external knowledge (EmoLSTM and EmoBiLSTM) outperformed the ones that did not use external knowledge on the evaluation data, which means that the emotional external knowledge enhance the capacity of generalization of the classification models, as we expected.

Regarding the performance of LSTM and BiLSTM, the use of LSTM as sequence encoding module resulted in a higher capacity of generalization, because BiLSMT reached higher results with the development data, but LSTM reached higher results with the evaluation data. Therefore, we conclude that the use of LSTM as sequence encoding module and emotional external knowledge allow to reach good results in the task of emotion classification, which allow us to confirm our claim.

Finally, the best system of the task (Amobee) has reached 71.4% of F1-score in the evaluation phase, since we do not know the evaluation measures corresponding to the pre-evaluation phase, in Table 4 they appear as "-". Our best system (EmoLSTM) hold the 22 position in the ranking with 58.3% in F1-score.

5 Conclusions

We described the participation of the SINAI lab in the IEST shared task of the WASSA Workshop. We submitted four systems based on deep learning. The systems mainly differ in the sequence encoding module, and the feature vector space. We compare the performance of LSTM and BiLSTM as sequence encoding module, and the use of emotional external knowledge. The results show that the use of LSTM and emotional external knowledge give a higher capacity of generalization to the classification model.

As future work, we will study how to improve the use of external knowledge in the task of emotion classification, as well as, how to automatically select the most relevant features. Hence, we will study the development of an Attention module in our models. Furthermore, we will research how to add relevant linguistic information to our models, as the influence of negation in the classification of emotions.

Acknowledgments

This work has been partially supported by Fondo Europeo de Desarrollo Regional (FEDER), REDES project (TIN2015-65136-C2-1-R) and SMART-DASCI project (TIN2017-89517-P) from the Spanish Government. Eugenio Martínez

Cámara was supported by the Juan de la Cierva Formación Programme (FJCI-2016-28353) from the Spanish Government.

References

Ronan Collobert, Jason Weston, Léon Bottou, Michael Karlen, Koray Kavukcuoglu, and Pavel Kuksa. 2011. Natural language processing (almost) from scratch. *Journal of Machine Learning Research*, 12:2493–2537.

Paul Ekman. 1992. An argument for basic emotions. *Cognition & emotion*, 6(3-4):169–200.

Yoav Goldberg. 2017. *Neural Network Methods for Natural Language Processing*. Morgan & Claypool Publishers.

Zellig S. Harris. 1954. Distributional structure. *WORD*, 10(2-3):146–162.

Geoffrey E Hinton, Nitish Srivastava, Alex Krizhevsky, Ilya Sutskever, and Ruslan R Salakhutdinov. 2012. Improving neural networks by preventing co-adaptation of feature detectors. *arXiv preprint arXiv:1207.0580*.

Sepp Hochreiter and Jürgen Schmidhuber. 1997. Long short-term memory. *Neural Computation*, 9(8):1735–1780.

Diederik P. Kingma and Jimmy Ba. 2015. Adam: A method for stochastic optimization. In *3rd International Conference for Learning Representations, San Diego, 2015*.

Roman Klinger, Orphée de Clercq, Saif M. Mohammad, and Alexandra Balahur. 2018. Iest: Wassa-2018 implicit emotions shared task. In *Proceedings of the 9th Workshop on Computational Approaches to Subjectivity, Sentiment and Social Media Analysis*, Brussels, Belgium. Association for Computational Linguistics.

Chul Min Lee, Shrikanth S Narayanan, and Roberto Pieraccini. 2002. Combining acoustic and language information for emotion recognition. In *Seventh International Conference on Spoken Language Processing*.

Tomas Mikolov, Ilya Sutskever, Kai Chen, Greg S Corrado, and Jeff Dean. 2013. Distributed representations of words and phrases and their compositionality. In C. J. C. Burges, L. Bottou, M. Welling, Z. Ghahramani, and K. Q. Weinberger, editors, *Advances in Neural Information Processing Systems 26*, pages 3111–3119. Curran Associates, Inc.

Saif M Mohammad and Peter D Turney. 2010. Emotions evoked by common words and phrases: Using mechanical turk to create an emotion lexicon. In *Proceedings of the NAACL HLT 2010 workshop on computational approaches to analysis and generation of emotion in text*, pages 26–34. Association for Computational Linguistics.

Jeffrey Pennington, Richard Socher, and Christopher Manning. 2014. Glove: Global vectors for word representation. In *Proceedings of the 2014 Conference on Empirical Methods in Natural Language Processing (EMNLP)*, pages 1532–1543. Association for Computational Linguistics.

Chung-Hsien Wu, Ze-Jing Chuang, and Yu-Chung Lin. 2006. Emotion recognition from text using semantic labels and separable mixture models. *ACM transactions on Asian language information processing (TALIP)*, 5(2):165–183.

Ali Yadollahi, Ameneh Gholipour Shahraki, and Osmar R Zaiane. 2017. Current state of text sentiment analysis from opinion to emotion mining. *ACM Computing Surveys (CSUR)*, 50(2):25.

EmoNLP at IEST 2018: An Ensemble of Deep Learning Models and Gradient Boosting Regression Tree for Implicit Emotion Prediction in Tweets

Man Liu

liumanlalala@gmail.com

Abstract

This paper describes our system submitted to IEST 2018, a shared task (Klinger et al., 2018) to predict the emotion types. Six emotion types are involved: anger, joy, fear, surprise, disgust and sad. We perform three different approaches: feed forward neural network (FFNN), convolutional BLSTM (ConBLSTM) and Gradient Boosting Regression Tree Method (GBM). Word embeddings used in convolutional BLSTM are pre-trained on 470 million tweets which are filtered using the emotional words and emojis. In addition, broad sets of features (i.e. syntactic features, lexicon features, cluster features) are adopted to train GBM and FFNN. The three approaches are finally ensembled by the weighted average of predicted probabilities of each emotion label.

1 Introduction

Twitter is an active social networking platform. It is estimated that nearly 500 million tweets are sent per day[1]. As a short message where people can convey their emotions, twitter data is particular interesting for emotional detection. The task of WASSA 2018 Implicit Emotion Shared Task is aimed to predict the emotion underlying in the tweets. The emotional types that are supposed to predict are "Anger, Fear, Sadness, Joy, Surprise, Disgust". In each tweet, the emotional expression is implicit, that is, a certain emotional word is removed. The removed emotional words could be one of the following:"sad", "happy", "disgusted", "surprised", "angry", "afraid" or a synonym of one of them. For example, given the tweet "It's [#TARGETWORD#] when you feel like you are invisible to others.", the system should predict the label of this tweet as "Sadness". Moreover, the

system can not only be useful for implicit emotion detection but also for various NLP applications. For example, this system can be used to detect the emotions in movie reviews which do not have the sentimental word but actually express sentimental polarities. In this paper, we describe our approaches and experiments to solve this problem. Our system is an ensemble of three classification approaches combined with a weighted average of predicted probabilities. Whilst, two of the three approaches are neural network models and the other is a gradient boosting regression tree model (Section 3). The rest of the paper is structured as follows: Section 2 discusses in brief the dataset for the task. Section 3 gives an explanation about the details of various approaches used in our system. Section 4 shows the results and discussions about them. Finally, we draw the conclusion about our participation in the Section 5.

2 Data

The dataset provided in this task contains the tweet text and the target emotions which are the predicted labels. The gold labels of test set are given only in the evaluation period. In the training data, there are 153383 tweets for training, 9591 tweets in the development dataset and 28757 in the test dataset. We also make use of external dataset which contains 640 million tweets. The external data is used for training the word embedding as the input of the deep learning model.

3 Proposed system

Our system is an ensemble of three different models. We demonstrate the separate models followed by the ensemble method. We tokenize each tweet with the tokenization tool **tweetokenize** [2]. Since

---

[1] https://en.wikipedia.org/wiki/Twitter

[2] https://github.com/jaredks/tweetokenize

Proceedings of the 9th Workshop on Computational Approaches to Subjectivity, Sentiment and Social Media Analysis, pages 201–204
Brussels, Belgium, October 31, 2018. ©2018 Association for Computational Linguistics
https://doi.org/10.18653/v1/P17

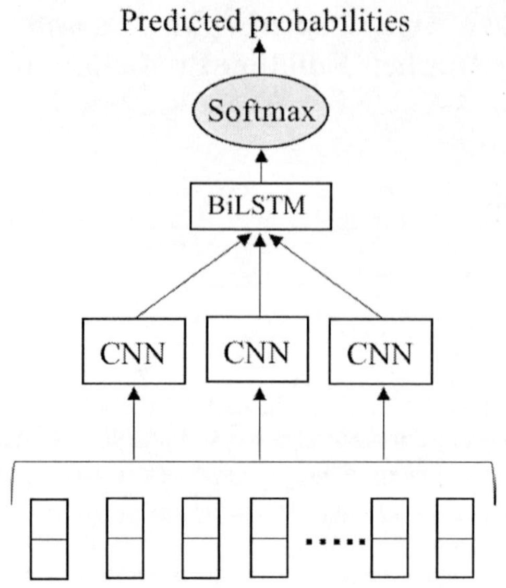

Figure 1: Architecture of ConBLSTM.

all the hashtags have been removed, we make no changes about hashtags.

3.1 Approach 1: convolutional BLSTM

To capture the sentence-level features and lexical information hiding in the tweets, we utilize a convolutional BLSTM model without any hand-crafted features. convolutional BLSTM has showed strong advancement in various NLP domains (Zeng et al., 2016), (Eger et al., 2017).

Input features: We trained word embedding on 470 million emotion related tweets using GloVe method. The 470 million emotion related tweets are filtered from 640 million tweets. The filtering process are based on a pre-built emotion word list which was extracted from NRC Word-Emotion Association Lexicon (Mohammad and Turney, 2013). With NRC Word-Emotion Association Lexicon, we extract the word which has at least one positive emotion. In addition, emojis are incorporated into the pre-built emotion word list because emojis as another expression of emotions are helpful for the emotion prediction. The emoji list is extracted from python package *emoji*[3]. Then the filtered tweets are used to train the word embedding. Considering the experiment efficiency and performance, we finally select the trained word embedding with dimension 100.

---

[3]https://pypi.org/project/emoji/

Architecture: After loading the pre-trained GloVe word embedding, we apply 3 convolutional layers with filter sizes 3, 5, 7. We concatenate the respective vectors and feed them into the forward and backward LSTM layers. The output of the BLSTM layer is put into the softmax layer to compute the probabilities of each emotion. The final predicted emotion type is the one with the max probabilities. Figure 1 is used to illustrate the architecture of this model.

Training: The epoch and filter number in each layer in the final experiment are chosen based on the result of pre-experiments. The epoch is 100 and the filter number in the 3 convolutional layers are 512. The output dimension of BLSTM is 128 which is also selected based on pre-experiments.

3.2 Approach 2: Feed-forward neural neural network

Inspired by the previous work of Pranav et al. 2017 (Goel et al., 2017), which is a system to predict the emotional intensity, we choose feed forward neural network due to its advantage of efficiency and effectivity in the classification task. We spell out the architecture as follows:

Input features: Given a tokenized sentence with words $\{w_0, w_1, w_2..., w_n\}$, the first step is to extract word-level and character-level representations by vectorizing word and character ngrams. The next step is to extract a fixed length sentiment feature representation. Each tweet is represented as a sentence vector by concatenating broad sets of character-level representations, word-level representations and sentiment feature representations. To handle with the problem that the length of each tweet vector varies, we utilize the SciKit-Learn tool **DictVectorizer**[4] and **CountVectorizer**[5]. We adopted features including character ngram feature, POS feature, cluster feature, negation feature, word ngram feature, counting feature and lexicon feature. Details of these features are explained in Liu (2018). A variety of sentiment lexicons are explored in the lexical features[6]. All these features are concatenated as the input features. Dimension

---

[4]http://scikit-learn.org/stable/modules/generated/ sklearn.feature_extraction.DictVectorizer.html

[5]http://scikit-learn.org/stable/modules/generated/ sklearn.feature_extraction.text.CountVectorizer.html

[6]NRC Emotion Lexicon; NRC Hashtag Sentiment Lexicon; MaxDiff Twitter Lexicon; MPQA Effect Lexicon; MPQA Subjectivity Lexicon; Harvard Inquirer Lexicon; Bing Liu Lexicon; Loughran McDonald Lexicon; Amazon Laptop Review Lexicon; Sentiment140 Lexicon.

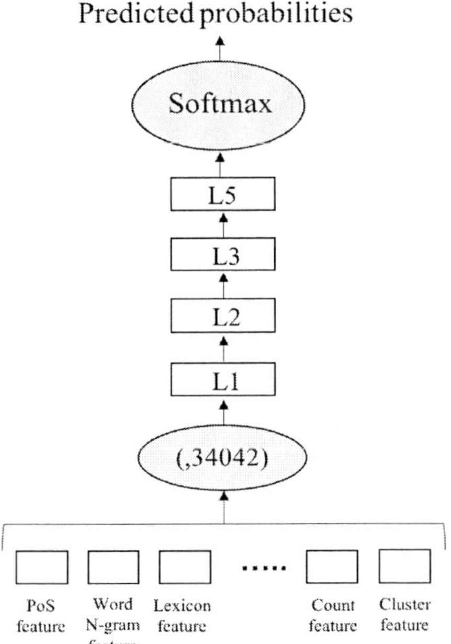

Figure 2: Architecture of feed forward neural network (FFNN). 34042 shows the number of input tweets.

of each sentence vector is not fixable and dependent on the corpus. For the training dataset with 153383 samples, the dimension of each sentence vector is 41298.

Architecture: Firstly, sentence vectors are fed into the input layer and then passed to four hidden layers (L_1, L_2, L_3, L_4). L_1, L_2 and L_3 are all followed by dropout *(p=0.5)* to avoid over-fitting and co-adaptation of features (Srivastava et al., 2014). Activation functions in the hidden layers are *Relu* (Maas et al., 2013). L_4 is followed by a softmax neuron which predicts the probability of each emotion. We use Figure 2 to illustrate the architecture of this network.

Training: Parameters are optimized in the neural network by performing 5-fold cross validation. We use a batch size of 128 and 100 epochs. The optimization algorithm is Adam (Kingma and Ba, 2014) with the default parameter setting in Keras[7].

3.3 Approach 3: GBM

The input features of this models are same with those of the previous model feed forward neural network. Input features are concatenated and fed into the model Gradient Boosting Regression Tree (GBM). GBM previously shows efficiency

---

[7]https://keras.io

and power to take use of broad sets of sentimental features in predicting the type of emojis (Liu, 2018). In this task, despite of implication of the emotion words, GBM still has a comparable performance. From the previous experiments, we choose two hyperparameters to tune and use 300 trees and 64 leaves per tree in this model. Besides, we set learning rate to 0.1 and minimal number of data in one leaf to 20. The tool we used to build GBM model is lightGBM (Ke et al., 2017).

3.4 Ensemble of the three approaches

Out final submitted system is ensembled by the previously described three approaches. We compute the weighted average of the predicted probabilities and determine the final label using the max probability. Due to the time limit, our submitted system does not use the global optimization of ensemble weights. After submitting, we tune the weights of each model with intensive experiments. The final weights for our system are: 2 (FFNN), 2 (ConBLSTM) and 1 (GBM), while the weights of submitted system are 4 (FFNN), 2 (ConBLSTM) and 1 (GBM).

4 Result and discussion

We compare the results achieved by our individual approaches, the ensemble system and the WEKA Baseline system which is the official baseline model for this task. The official score of our submitted system is 0.621. Table 1 and 2 shows the results of our systems with the best weight settings on development and test dataset. From table 1, we can find the ensemble model achieves the best performance compared with the single model and FFNN+BLSTM ensemble model. Approach 1 (ConBLSTM) achieves the lowest scores among the three approaches. Table 2 illustrates that among all the individual emotions, our system performs best on "Joy" which has the most labels in both the development dataset and the test dataset.

5 Conclusion and future work

In this paper, we propose an ensemble system to predict the implicit emotion of tweets. Three approaches are exploited: convolutional BLSTM, feed forward neural network and gradient boosting regression tree. To ensure the replicability, each approach is detailed about the architecture and the input features. In the future work, we will carry

	Development			Test		
System	P	R	F1	P	R	F1
Feed Forward NN	0.61	0.61	0.61	0.62	0.61	0.62
ConBLSTM	0.55	0.55	0.55	0.55	0.55	0.55
GBM	0.62	0.62	0.62	0.62	0.62	0.62
Feed Forward NN + BLSTM	0.61	0.61	0.61	0.63	0.63	0.63
Ensemble Model	0.64	0.63	0.63	0.64	0.64	0.64
Baseline	0.60	0.60	0.60	0.60	0.60	0.60

Table 1: Test and Development results on our system.

	Development			Test		
Label	P	R	F1	P	R	F1
Anger	0.57	0.57	0.57	0.53	0.53	0.53
Disgust	0.65	0.62	0.64	0.66	0.66	0.66
Fear	0.64	0.68	0.66	0.65	0.70	0.67
Joy	0.78	0.72	0.75	0.76	0.72	0.74
Sadness	0.65	0.58	0.61	0.65	0.57	0.61
Surprise	0.56	0.64	0.60	0.56	0.64	0.60

Table 2: Results on different labels.

out experiments with different dimensions of word embedding as well as different embedding methods, i.e. word2vector. Due to the time limit, the experiments lack feature analysis with which the final result may be improved. We plan to experiment different sets of features to find out which feature sets are more helpful. Finally, we would test more ensemble methods as well as the effectiveness of each approach in the ensemble system.

References

Steffen Eger, Erik-Lân Do Dinh, Ilia Kuznetsov, Masoud Kiaeeha, and Iryna Gurevych. 2017. Eelection at semeval-2017 task 10: Ensemble of neural learners for keyphrase classification. In *Proceedings of the 11th International Workshop on Semantic Evaluation (SemEval-2017)*, pages 942–946.

Pranav Goel, Devang Kulshreshtha, Prayas Jain, and Kaushal Kumar Shukla. 2017. Prayas at emoint 2017: An ensemble of deep neural architectures for emotion intensity prediction in tweets. In *Proceedings of the 8th Workshop on Computational Approaches to Subjectivity, Sentiment and Social Media Analysis*, pages 58–65.

Guolin Ke, Qi Meng, Thomas Finley, Taifeng Wang, Wei Chen, Weidong Ma, Qiwei Ye, and Tie-Yan Liu. 2017. Lightgbm: A highly efficient gradient boosting decision tree. In *Advances in Neural Information Processing Systems*, pages 3146–3154.

Diederik P Kingma and Jimmy Ba. 2014. Adam: A method for stochastic optimization. *arXiv preprint arXiv:1412.6980*.

Roman Klinger, Orphée de Clercq, Saif M. Mohammad, and Alexandra Balahur. 2018. Iest: Wassa-2018 implicit emotions shared task. In *Proceedings of the 9th Workshop on Computational Approaches to Subjectivity, Sentiment and Social Media Analysis*, Brussels, Belgium. Association for Computational Linguistics.

Man Liu. 2018. Emonlp at semeval-2018 task 2: English emoji prediction with gradient boosting regression tree method and bidirectional lstm. In *Proceedings of The 12th International Workshop on Semantic Evaluation*, pages 390–394.

Andrew L Maas, Awni Y Hannun, and Andrew Y Ng. 2013. Rectifier nonlinearities improve neural network acoustic models. In *Proc. icml*, volume 30, page 3.

Saif M. Mohammad and Peter D. Turney. 2013. Crowdsourcing a word-emotion association lexicon. 29(3):436–465.

Nitish Srivastava, Geoffrey Hinton, Alex Krizhevsky, Ilya Sutskever, and Ruslan Salakhutdinov. 2014. Dropout: a simple way to prevent neural networks from overfitting. *The Journal of Machine Learning Research*, 15(1):1929–1958.

Ying Zeng, Honghui Yang, Yansong Feng, Zheng Wang, and Dongyan Zhao. 2016. A convolution bilstm neural network model for chinese event extraction. In *Natural Language Understanding and Intelligent Applications*, pages 275–287. Springer.

HGSGNLP at IEST 2018: An Ensemble of Machine Learning and Deep Neural Architectures for Implicit Emotion Classification in Tweets

WenTing Wang[1], Man Lan[2]
[1]Alibaba Group, WenYi West Road #969, Hangzhou City
[2]Department of Computer Science and Technology,
East China Normal University, Shanghai, P.R.China
`nantiao.wwt@alibaba-inc.com, mlan@cs.ecnu.edu.cn`

Abstract

This paper describes our system designed for the WASSA-2018 Implicit Emotion Shared Task (IEST). The task is to predict the emotion category expressed in a tweet by removing the terms *angry*, *afraid*, *happy*, *sad*, *surprised*, *disgusted* and their synonyms. Our final submission is an ensemble of one supervised learning model and three deep neural network based models, where each model approaches the problem from essentially different directions. Our system achieves the macro F1 score of 65.8%, which is a 5.9% performance improvement over the baseline and is ranked 12 out of 30 participating teams.

1 Introduction

In Natural Language Processing, emotion recognition is concerning of associating words, phrases or documents with predefined emotion categories, such as Anger, Anticipation and Sadness (Ekman, 1999; Plutchik, 2001). Most of previous research works on emotion recognition (Wang et al., 2012; Bestgen and Vincze, 2012; Suttles and Ide, 2013; Recchia and Louwerse, 2015; Hollis et al., 2017) presumes emotion words or their representations are accessible. Such models might fail to learn associations for more subtle descriptions and therefore fail to predict the emotion when overt emotion words are not available.

The WASSA-2018 Implicit Emotion Shared Task (IEST) (Klinger et al., 2018) aims to predict the emotion category of a given tweet when the explicit emotion word, or *trigger words*, is removed. The emotion category can be one of six classes: *Anger*, *Disgust*, *Fear*, *Joy*, *Sadness* and *Surprise*. For examples:

1. "It's [#TARGETWORD#] when you feel like you are invisible to others."

2. "We are so [#TARGETWORD#] that people must think we are on good drugs or just really good actors."

In the above 2 examples, with the help of common sense or world knowledge, implicit emotion still can be inferred from context as *Sadness* and *Joy*. The [#TARGETWORD#] tokens in the examples indicate the position of the removed word in the given tweet.

Our submitted system is an ensemble of four broad sets of approaches combined using a weighted average of the separate predictions. One approach uses traditional lexicon-based method to train a logistic regression classifier, while the remaining three approaches rely on representing the input tweet as a word vector and using neural network based architectures to give the emotion category for the tweet.

The rest of the paper is structured as follows. Section 2 describes the features used in our system. Section 3 explains the various approaches used by our ensemble model and the way we combined the predictions. Section 4 states the experiment results and discusses the implications of those results. We conclude our work in Section 5.

2 Features

2.1 Word

The current word and its lowercase format are used as features. To provide additional context information, word n-grams and character n-grams are also used.

2.2 Word Embeddings

Word embeddings are trained from large unlabeled raw tweets to be used as input to neural network model as well as for generating word clusters.

From an initial collection of 1.6 billion tweets, the collection is filtered to only include tweets that

Proceedings of the 9th Workshop on Computational Approaches to Subjectivity, Sentiment and Social Media Analysis, pages 205–210
Brussels, Belgium, October 31, 2018. ©2018 Association for Computational Linguistics
https://doi.org/10.18653/v1/P17

Arguments	Value
–oaa	6
–loss_function	logistic
–passes	10
–ngram	b3
–skips	b2
–affix	+3b,-1b
-l	0.3

Table 1: Vowpal Wabbit command line arguments used to train the model. The namespace b denotes lowercase word feature.

contain emotion word found in the NRC Emotion Lexicon. In addition, the word to the left and right of the emotion word are constrained to those words found in the training data. This constraint is used to remove tweets containing generic context such as "happy birthday". After filtering, the final tweet collection contains 11 million tweets.

From this tweet collection, word embeddings are generated following the steps described in Toh and Su (2016). Besides using the previous two approaches (Gensim and GloVe tool), the fastText tool (Bojanowski et al., 2017)[1] is also used to generate word embeddings.

2.3 Word Cluster

K-means clusters are generated from the word embeddings using the K-means implementation of Apache Spark MLlib. From the K-means clusters, word cluster features are generated. For each word, the cluster id that the word belongs to is used as a feature.

3 Approaches

This section describes the four approaches used to generate the emotion predictions.

3.1 Approach 1: Lexicon Model

The Vowpal Wabbit tool[2] is used to train a multiclass classifier using the one-against-all setting (`--oaa`).

The features used to train the classifier include the words in the tweet (both original and lowercase format) and word clusters where 5 different word clusters are used.

Table 1 shows the command line arguments used to train the Vowpal Wabbit model.

Arguments	Value
-lr	0.05
-epoch	40
-loss	softmax
-neg	5
-wordNgrams	5
-bucket	30000000
-dim	100
-minn	10
-maxn	10

Table 2: fastText command line arguments used to train the model.

3.2 Approach 2: fastText Model

The fastText tool is used to train a text classifier using the `supervised` subcommand (Joulin et al., 2017).

The lowercase words in the tweet are used to train the classifier.

Table 2 shows the command line arguments used to train the fastText model.

3.3 Approach 3: Convolutional Neural Network Model

Convolutional Neural Network (CNN) has been shown to work well for sentence-level classification tasks (Kim, 2014). Here we detail the architecture of our network.

Input and Embedding Layer: Each tweet is preprocessed by (1) normalizing emoji to text[3]; (2) normalizing hyper links and @mentions to *someurl* and *someuser*; and (3) splitting hashtag chunks into separate words[4]. Then the tweet is converted into a concatenated vector and padded to an equal length (or truncated if the tweet is longer than the pre-defined length). The input vector is fed to the embedding layer (i.e. pretrained glove.twitter.27B vectors), which converts each word into a distributional vector.

CNN Layer: The concatenated vector representation of the tweet is then fed to CNN. The number of hidden units is set to be 256. We apply *tanh* as activation and dropout with a rate of 0.2.

Output Layer: The output of CNN is flattened and then passed to a fully connected layer. Finally, a softmax layer was added on top of the fully connected layer. The network is trained by minimiz-

---

[1]https://fasttext.cc/
[2]https://github.com/JohnLangford/vowpal_wabbit/wiki

[3]https://pypi.org/project/emoji
[4]https://pypi.python.org/pypi/wordsegment

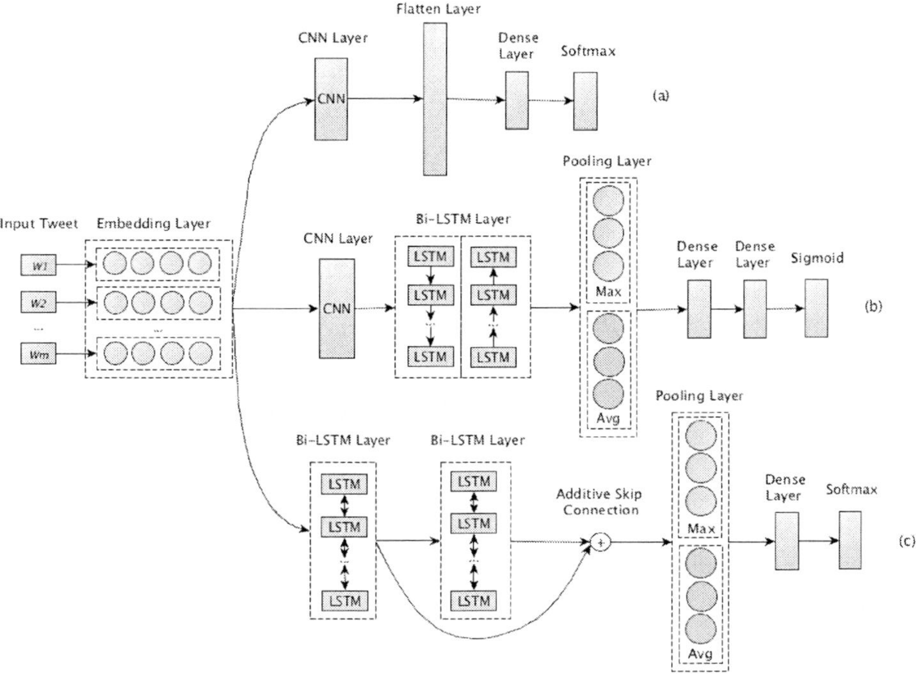

Figure 1: The architectures of our three neural models. (a) is the neural model for Approach 3. (b) is the neural model for Approach 4. (c) is the neural model for Approach 5.

ing the categorical cross-entropy error with RM-SProp for parameter optimization.

Figure 1 (a) shows the model architecture of the CNN model.

3.4 Approach 4: Sequence Modeling using CNN and LSTM

Long-short Term Memory (LSTM) (Hochreiter and Schmidhuber, 1997) architecture is an advanced version of RNN and has been successful in the NLP domain on various tasks (Graves and Schmidhuber, 2005; Graves and Jaitly, 2014). Combining CNN and LSTM has also been found to be quite successful in (Zhou et al., 2015; Goel et al., 2017). In this approach, we attempt to use CNN to extract regional features and then use Bi-LSTM to capture compositional semantics from both forward and backward directions of word sequence.

Since the input, embedding, CNN layers are the same as Approach 2, we only detail the architectures of the following different layers.

Bi-LSTM with Pooling Layer: We use bidirectional LSTMs followed by some pooling layer to model the output from CNN layer. The number of hidden units is set to be 300. We apply relu as activation and dropout with a rate of 0.2. The outcomes from max pooling and average pooling are concatenated.

Output Layer: The concatenated output of Bi-LSTM with Pooling layer is then passed to a fully connected layer. Finally, a sigmoid layer was added on top of the fully connected layer. The network is trained by minimizing the categorical cross-entropy error with Adam for parameter optimization.

Figure 1 (b) shows the model architecture of the sequence model.

3.5 Approach 5: Residual LSTM Model

Residual LSTM (Kim et al., 2017) adds an additional spatial shortcut path from lower layers to better deal with vanishing gradients. It provides efficient training of deep networks with multiple LSTM layers and has been successfully applied to speech recognition and NER tasks (Tran et al., 2017). The formulation is as follows:

$$i_t^l = \sigma(W_{xi}^l x_t^l + W_{hi}^l h_{t-1}^l + w_{ci}^l c_{t-1}^l + b_i^l) \quad (1)$$

System	anger	disgust	fear	joy	sadness	surprise	macro average
Lexicon	0.58	0.65	0.68	0.74	0.61	0.62	0.65
fastText	0.55	0.63	0.66	0.72	0.59	0.60	0.62
CNN	0.56	0.58	0.63	0.68	0.55	0.55	0.60
CNN-LSTM	0.57	0.63	0.66	0.70	0.58	0.59	0.62
Res-LSTM	0.48	0.58	0.58	0.68	0.50	0.52	0.56
Ensemble (excluding Res-LSTM)	0.58	0.67	0.69	0.74	0.63	0.64	0.66

Table 3: Performance comparison between individual models and ensemble model on trial data. Our final ensemble model includes lexicon, fastText, CNN and CNN-LSTM models.

$$f_t^l = \sigma(W_{xf}^l x_t^l + W_{hf}^l h_{t-1}^l + w_{cf}^l c_{t-1}^l + b_f^l) \quad (2)$$

$$c_t^l = f_t^l \cdot c_{t-1}^l + i_t^l \cdot tanh(W_{xc}^l x_t^l + W_{hc}^l h_{t-1}^l + b_c^l) \quad (3)$$

$$o_t^l = \sigma(W_{xo}^l x_t^l + W_{ho}^l h_{t-1}^l + w_{co}^l c_t^l + b_o^l) \quad (4)$$

$$r_t^l = tanh(c_t^l) \quad (5)$$

$$m_t^l = W_o^l \cdot r_t^l \quad (6)$$

$$h_t^l = o_t^l \cdot (m_t^l + x_t^l) \quad (7)$$

Where l represents layer index and i_t^l, f_t^l and o_t^l are input, forget and output gates respectively. x_t^l is an input from $(l-1)^{th}$ layer, h_{t-1}^l is a output layer at time $t-1$ and c_{t-1}^l is an internal cell state at $t-1$. And a short cut from a prior output layer h_t^{l-1} is added to a projection output m_t^l via $W_h^l x_t^l = W_h^l h_t^{l-1}$

Figure 1 (c) shows the model architecture of our residual LSTM model. Two Bi-LSTM layers are included and the number of hidden units is set to be 512. We apply relu as activation and dropout with a rate of 0.2. The network is then trained by minimizing the categorical cross-entropy error with Adam for parameter optimization.

3.6 Ensemble Model

To combine the predictions of the five models mentioned above, we compute the weighted average of the category probabilities of the four models. The trial data is used to select the optimal weight of each model. The selected emotion category is the category that has the highest weighted average.

4 Experiments and Results

4.1 Dataset and Evaluation Metric

The task organizers provide a training dataset (i.e. 153k instances) and a small blind trial dataset (i.e. 9.6k instances) for system building. Then a period of 1 week is given for submitting the predictions on a blind test dataset (i.e. 29k instances).

Macro-averaged F1 score is chosen to be the official evaluation metric.

4.2 Results on Trial Data and Analysis

The optimal setting for each model is decided using cross validation on training dataset. Then the weighted average is computed from individual predictions to generate the predictions for the final ensemble model using trial dataset as described in Section 3.6. Table 3 shows the trial results for all individual models and ensemble model.

We observe that the Lexicon approach achieves the best score among all approaches. Among the four deep neural models, CNN+LSTM and fastText achieve better score of 62% compared to CNN and Residual-LSTM, which demonstrates that both the combination of long sequence and regional features and the word n-grams capture effective information. Since the residual LSTM network does not perform as expected, we did not include it into our final ensemble model.

We also observe that the ensemble model achieves the best performance compared with each individual model and offers equal or better performance across all the emotions, which indicates that the four approaches do complement each other quite well.

4.3 Official Results on Test Data

Table 4 reports our official results on test data. Among the individual emotions, our ensemble

Label	TP	FP	FN	Precision	Recall	F1
anger	2814	1922	1980	0.594	0.587	0.591
disgust	3168	1537	1626	0.673	0.661	0.667
fear	3292	1455	1499	0.693	0.687	0.690
joy	3949	1342	1297	0.746	0.753	0.750
sad	2547	1290	1793	0.664	0.587	0.623
surprise	3212	2229	1580	0.590	0.670	0.628
Micro Average	18982	9775	9775	0.660	0.660	0.660
Macro Average				0.660	0.657	0.658

Table 4: Official results for our submission.

System	anger	disgust	fear	joy	sadness	surprise	macro average
Our Submission	0.59	0.67	0.69	0.75	0.62	0.63	0.658 (12)
Baseline	0.52	0.62	0.63	0.70	0.56	0.57	0.599
Amobee	0.64	0.72	0.75	0.82	0.69	0.68	0.714 (1)
IIIDYT	0.64	0.71	0.75	0.80	0.69	0.68	0.710 (2)
NTUA-SLP	0.63	0.71	0.74	0.79	0.69	0.67	0.703 (3)

Table 5: Performance comparison between our system, official baseline system and top-ranked systems on IEST shared task. The number in parentheses are the official rankings.

model gives the best performance for *Joy*, followed by *Fear* and *Disgust*.

We also compare the results achieved by our submitted ensemble system, official baseline system and top-ranked systems in Table 5. Our ensemble model achieves average f1-macro score of 65.8%, which beats the baseline model by 5.9%. However, the top-ranked systems all incorporate models trained in previous emotion related tasks (e.g. SemEval 2018: Affective in Tweets) as additional features. This probably is the reason for our performance gap.

5 Conclusion and Future Work

In this paper, we propose a hybrid framework to predict the emotion category in tweets when no explicit emotion words are presented. The proposed approach combines lexicon based logistic regression classifier, fastText, Convolutional Neural Networks and Sequence Modeling using CNN and LSTM, allowing us to explore the different directions each methodology can take. Our system HGSGNLP, submitted to the IEST 2018 Shared Task, beats the baseline system by 5.9% on the test set.

Compared to the best systems, there is still room for improvement. In the future, we would like to experiment with some other filters provided in AffectiveTweets package (Mohammad and Bravo-Marquez, 2017) such as `TweetToSentiStrengthFeatureVector`. We would also experiment with incorporating lexicon features to existing neural networks.

References

Yves Bestgen and Nadja Vincze. 2012. Checking and bootstrapping lexical norms by means of word similarity indexes. *Behavior research methods*, 44(4):998–1006.

Piotr Bojanowski, Edouard Grave, Armand Joulin, and Tomas Mikolov. 2017. Enriching word vectors with subword information. *Transactions of the Association for Computational Linguistics*, 5:135–146.

Paul Ekman. 1999. Basic emotions. *Handbook of cognition and emotion*, pages 45–60.

Pranav Goel, Devang Kulshreshtha, Prayas Jain, and Kaushal Kumar Shukla. 2017. Prayas at emoint 2017: An ensemble of deep neural architectures for emotion intensity prediction in tweets. In *Proceedings of the 8th Workshop on Computational Approaches to Subjectivity, Sentiment and Social Media Analysis*, pages 58–65.

Alex Graves and Navdeep Jaitly. 2014. Towards end-to-end speech recognition with recurrent neural networks. In *International Conference on Machine Learning*, pages 1764–1772.

Alex Graves and Jürgen Schmidhuber. 2005. Frame-wise phoneme classification with bidirectional lstm and other neural network architectures. *Neural Networks*, 18(5-6):602–610.

Sepp Hochreiter and Jürgen Schmidhuber. 1997. Long short-term memory. *Neural computation*, 9(8):1735–1780.

Geoff Hollis, Chris Westbury, and Lianne Lefsrud. 2017. Extrapolating human judgments from skip-gram vector representations of word meaning. *The Quarterly Journal of Experimental Psychology*, 70(8):1603–1619.

Armand Joulin, Edouard Grave, Piotr Bojanowski, and Tomas Mikolov. 2017. Bag of tricks for efficient text classification. In *Proceedings of the 15th Conference of the European Chapter of the Association for Computational Linguistics: Volume 2, Short Papers*, pages 427–431. Association for Computational Linguistics.

Jaeyoung Kim, Mostafa El-Khamy, and Jungwon Lee. 2017. Residual lstm: Design of a deep recurrent architecture for distant speech recognition. In *INTER-SPEECH*.

Yoon Kim. 2014. Convolutional neural networks for sentence classification. In *Proceedings of the 2014 Conference on Empirical Methods in Natural Language Processing (EMNLP)*, pages 1746–1751. Association for Computational Linguistics.

Roman Klinger, Orphée de Clercq, Saif M. Mohammad, and Alexandra Balahur. 2018. Iest: Wassa-2018 implicit emotions shared task. In *Proceedings of the 9th Workshop on Computational Approaches to Subjectivity, Sentiment and Social Media Analysis*, Brussels, Belgium. Association for Computational Linguistics.

Saif Mohammad and Felipe Bravo-Marquez. 2017. Wassa-2017 shared task on emotion intensity. In *Proceedings of the 8th Workshop on Computational Approaches to Subjectivity, Sentiment and Social Media Analysis*, pages 34–49. Association for Computational Linguistics.

Robert Plutchik. 2001. The nature of emotions: Human emotions have deep evolutionary roots, a fact that may explain their complexity and provide tools for clinical practice. *American scientist*, 89(4):344–350.

Gabriel Recchia and Max M Louwerse. 2015. Reproducing affective norms with lexical co-occurrence statistics: Predicting valence, arousal, and dominance. *The Quarterly Journal of Experimental Psychology*, 68(8):1584–1598.

Jared Suttles and Nancy Ide. 2013. Distant supervision for emotion classification with discrete binary values. In *International Conference on Intelligent Text Processing and Computational Linguistics*, pages 121–136. Springer.

Toh, Zhiqiang and Su, Jian. 2016. NLANGP at SemEval-2016 Task 5: Improving Aspect Based Sentiment Analysis using Neural Network Features. In *Proceedings of the 10th International Workshop on Semantic Evaluation (SemEval-2016)*, pages 282–288. Association for Computational Linguistics.

Quan Tran, Andrew MacKinlay, and Antonio Jimeno Yepes. 2017. Named entity recognition with stack residual lstm and trainable bias decoding. In *Proceedings of the Eighth International Joint Conference on Natural Language Processing (Volume 1: Long Papers)*, pages 566–575. Asian Federation of Natural Language Processing.

Wenbo Wang, Lu Chen, Krishnaprasad Thirunarayan, and Amit P Sheth. 2012. Harnessing twitter" big data" for automatic emotion identification. In *Privacy, Security, Risk and Trust (PASSAT), 2012 International Conference on and 2012 International Confernece on Social Computing (SocialCom)*, pages 587–592. IEEE.

Chunting Zhou, Chonglin Sun, Zhiyuan Liu, and Francis Lau. 2015. A c-lstm neural network for text classification. *arXiv preprint arXiv:1511.08630*.

DataSEARCH at IEST 2018: Multiple Word Embedding based Models for Implicit Emotion Classification of Tweets with Deep Learning

Yasas Senarath
University of Moratuwa,
Sri Lanka
`wayasas.13@cse.mrt.ac.lk`

Uthayasanker Thayasivam
University of Moratuwa,
Sri Lanka
`rtuthaya@cse.mrt.ac.lk`

Abstract

This paper describes an approach to solve implicit emotion classification with the use of pre-trained word embedding models to train multiple neural networks. The system described in this paper is composed of a sequential combination of Long Short-Term Memory and Convolutional Neural Network for feature extraction and Feedforward Neural Network for classification. In this paper, we successfully show that features extracted using multiple pre-trained embeddings can be used to improve the overall performance of the system with Emoji being one of the significant features. The evaluations show that our approach outperforms the baseline system by more than 8% without using any external corpus or lexicon. This approach is ranked 8th in Implicit Emotion Shared Task (IEST) at WASSA-2018.

1 Introduction

Emotion classification is a major area of interest within the field of Sentiment Analysis (SA). Social media is a great source of emotional content since people are willing to publish their views on them. Twitter is one such platform which enables users to publish micro-blogs otherwise known as Tweets. Although, the tweets are limited by the number of characters, when viewed as a group it can be very significant. Every day, on average, around 500 million tweets are tweeted on Twitter. This has attracted much interest from both academia and industries to study about opinions in tweets.

Tweets can generally be considered to contain textual content. However, tweet text is usually informal containing much casual forms and emoji, thus bringing challenges in research.

Implicit emotions play a major challenge in emotion identification process in tweets. This is due to the informal nature of the tweet and lack of methods to properly model such sentences. Here the term "implicit emotion" can be defined as the emotion conveyed in the text without stating the words denoting the emotion directly.

There is an effect of implicit emotions on opinion analysis tasks such as emotion identification and emotional intensity prediction. However, techniques for modeling implicit emotions in tweets lack the sufficient performance. Therefore, this study makes a major contribution to research by exploring methods for properly modeling a tweet.

Implicit Emotion Shared Task (IEST) (Klinger et al., 2018) hosted by WASSA-2018[1] poses a similar task of finding the emotion expressed in a tweet out of six basic emotions without the use of the word denoting the emotion. This paper presents our approach to solve the above problem. We were ranked 8th in the competition related to this task.

Artificial Neural Networks (ANN) has shown to perform better than conventional machine learning algorithms and has been used in variety of Natural Language Processing tasks (Young et al., 2017). One of the primary objectives of using neural networks is to model the non-linear relationships in data, which is observed in textual content frequently. Up to now, a number of studies confirmed the effectiveness of neural networks as feature extractors rather than the final classifier for opinion mining. A variety of neural network classifiers has been applied to similar tasks such as emotion identification, polarity classification, and other text classification tasks. Feedforward Neural Networks (FNN), Convolutional Neural Networks (CNN) (Kim, 2014), Long Short-Term Memory (LSTM) (Tran and Cheng, 2018; Socher et al.,

---

[1]http://implicitemotions.wassa2018.com

Proceedings of the 9th Workshop on Computational Approaches to Subjectivity, Sentiment and Social Media Analysis, pages 211–216
Brussels, Belgium, October 31, 2018. ©2018 Association for Computational Linguistics
https://doi.org/10.18653/v1/P17

2013) networks are commonly used in recent related work. Furthermore, researchers have studied much complex forms of Neural Networks by combining CNN and LSTM in different ways.

The rest of the paper is organized as follows: Section 2 will provide a brief description on the dataset, Section 3 describes the system architecture, Section 4 reports the results and analysis of our system, finally we conclude our work in Section 5 along with a discussion on further improvements.

2 Dataset

The dataset is labeled based on the emotion word present in the tweet before replacing that emotion word in the text with a placeholder. The dataset is labeled for six basic emotions: Anger, Sad, Joy, Fear, Disgust and Surprise. The complete details of the dataset can be found in the task description paper (Klinger et al., 2018).

3 System Description

The system consists three different components: the preprocessor, feature extractor and classifier. In this study we considered that effective classifier trained on the training dataset could be used as a feature extractor as well. This section will be subdivided to accommodate the stated components separately.

3.1 Preprocessing

The tweets contained in the dataset are preprocessed to an extent. In the dataset, the URLs were replaced with "http://url.removed", mentions with "@USERNAME" and new lines with "[NEWLINE]". Additionally, we have performed following preprocessing on the dataset: changing target term "[#TRIGGERWORD#]" to "__trigger__" and "[NEWLINE]" to "__newline__". These changes were performed to correct the tokenization. We have used TweetTokenizer [2] available in python NLTK library for tokenization. In addition to NLTK tokenizer we evaluated our system using a dictionary based tokenizer.

3.2 Feature Extraction

A number of techniques have been developed to extract features for the classifier, some of which are trained on the dataset in order to create features explicitly. The most basic feature unit is the

ID	Model	Corpus	Corpus Size	Dim
TW2V	Word2Vec	Twitter	400M tweets	400
GW2V	Word2Vec	Google News	100B words	300
WFT	fastText	Wiki	16B tokens	300
WSFT	fastText	Wiki Subword	16B tokens	300
TGv	Glove	Twitter	2B tweets	200
E2V	Word2Vec	Twitter	1661 emoji	300

Table 1: Embedding Models used in Experiments

words. We used words to obtain the Word Vectors from multiple word embedding models trained on different corpses. Although our best performing system was based on word embeddings we developed and evaluated other features as well. In this section we will describe all the features that we have tried out.

Word Vectors: Table 1 summarizes all of the word embedding models we used in our implementation. It illustrates the word embedding techniques and the dataset it is trained on and its specific features as well. Additionally, it provides an identifier which we will be using to identify that word embedding in the next sections. Tweets can be represented as a word vector using the word2vec approach (Mikolov et al., 2013). GW2V has been obtained by training Word2vec on part of Google News dataset [3]. Similarly, Godin et al. (2015) has provided a word2vec model trained on twitter dataset (TW2V) [4]. Furthermore, fastText (Joulin et al., 2016) models are trained on trained on UMBC webbase corpus and statmt.org news dataset with and without subword infomation (WSFT and WFT) [5] (Mikolov et al., 2018). Glove (Pennington et al., 2014) embedding (TGv) has been trained on twitter corpus containing two billion tweets [6]. Eisner et al. (2016) has released emoji2vec (E2V) [7] a pre-trained embedding model for all Unicode emoji. Intended means of using E2V is as an extension to GW2V.

Transfer Features: Features generated by training a neural classifier on the training dataset, obtained from the last layer (layer before the output later).

---

[2] https://www.nltk.org/api/nltk.tokenize.html
[3] https://code.google.com/archive/p/word2vec/
[4] https://www.fredericgodin.com/software/
[5] https://fasttext.cc/docs/en/english-vectors.html
[6] https://nlp.stanford.edu/projects/glove/
[7] https://github.com/uclmr/emoji2vec

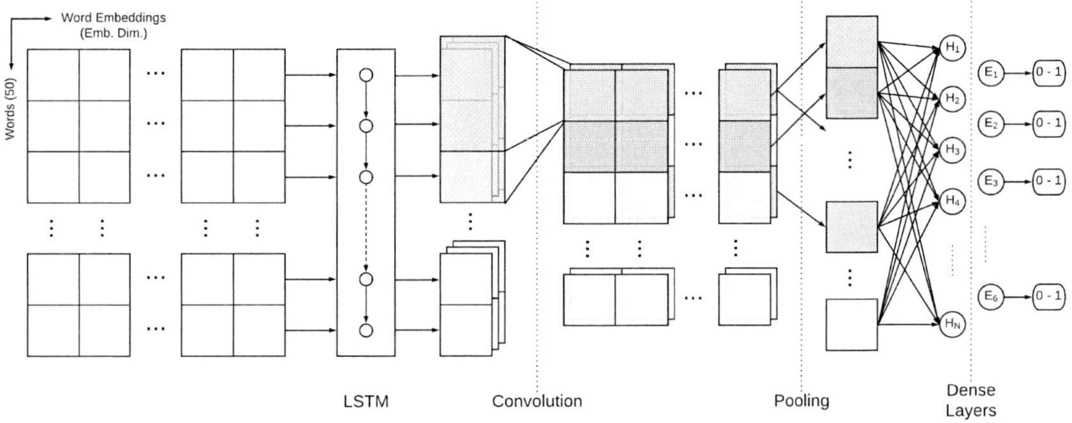

Figure 1: High-level LSTM-CNN Architecture

Section	Parameter	Value
LSTM	Num. of units	250
CNN	Num. of filters	350
	Kernel Sizes	2, 3, 5
Pooling	Method	Max
Dense Layer	Num. of units	50
	Activation	ReLU
Output Layer	Num. of Units	6
	Activation	Softmax

Table 2: Network Parameters for LSTM-CNN

Section	Parameter	Value
Hidden Layer 1	Num. of Units	50
	Activation	ReLU
Hidden Layer 2	Num. of Units	25
	Activation	ReLU

Table 3: Network parameters for FNN

3.3 Classifiers

The trial data provided in the competition is reasonably large for evaluating the model performance. As described in Section 3.2, different combinations of feature extractors were used. Following the feature extraction process, extracted features were used to train various neural networks.

3.3.1 LSTM-CNN

Two of the commonly used techniques to model text documents are Convolutional Neural Networks (CNN) and Long short-term memory (LSTM) networks. Rather than developing the neural network with CNN and LSTM separately, the proposed system is developed using a combination of CNN and LSTM. Figure 1 illustrates the proposed LSTM-CNN architecture. The hyper parameters selected for this network are tabulated in Table 2.

The network parameters are learned by optimizing the categorical cross-entropy between actual and predicted category. Optimization is per-

formed through back propagation via mini-batch gradient descent. A batch size of 256 was used with 5 epochs to train the network. Furthermore, a dropout layer with dropout rate 0.2 is used before the dense layer when training. Adam optimization algorithm (Kingma and Ba, 2014) is used in this study for optimization . We have trained and evaluated the system with each of the word embedding models stated in Table 1.

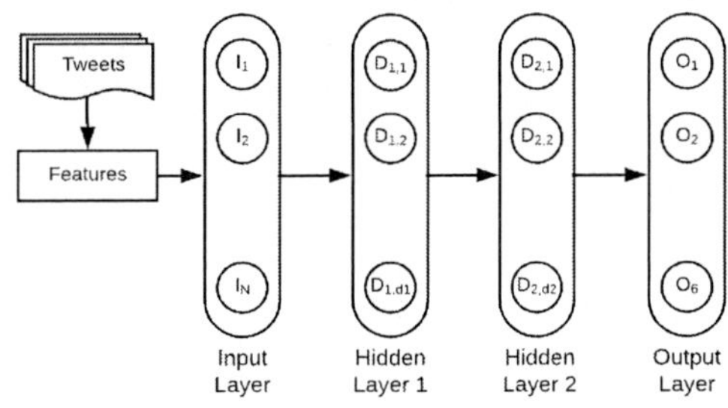

Figure 2: High-level FNN Architecture

3.3.2 Feed-forward neural network

Previous studies has shown that feed-forward neural network (FNN), can be used for modeling text

ID	Features	Trial Set			Test Set		
		Macro Precision	Macro Recall	Macro F_1	Macro Precision	Macro Recall	Macro F_1
M_{TW2V}	$TW2V$	**65.9**	**65.5**	**65.5**	**67.1**	**67.0**	**67.0**
M_{E2V}	$GW2V + E2V$	63.7	63.6	63.6	65.6	65.1	65.2
M_{GW2V}	$GW2V$	64.4	62.6	62.9	65.4	63.7	63.8
M_{WTF}	WTF	65.3	64.1	64.3	65.5	65.1	65.2
M_{WSTF}	$WSTF$	62.5	62.0	62.0	63.9	62.2	62.5
M_{TGv}	TGv	63.4	63.2	63.2	63.9	63.9	63.9
Baseline		60.1	60.1	60.1	-	-	59.8

Table 4: Evaluation of LSTM-CNN for different word embeddings

Features	Macro Precision	Macro Recall	Macro F_1
$F(M_{TW2V})$ ++ $F(M_{E2V})$	68.0	67.8	67.8
$F(M_{TW2V})$ ++ $F(M_{WTF})$	67.9	67.8	67.8
$F(M_{E2V})$ ++ $F(M_{WTF})$	67.1	66.7	66.8
$F(M_{E2V})$ ++ $F(M_{TW2V})$ ++ $F(M_{WTF})$	**68.3**	**68.1**	**68.1**
Baseline	-	-	59.8
IEST@WASSA 2018 Best	-	-	71.45

Table 5: Results of FNN for different feature combinations

documents (Bengio et al., 2003). Furthermore, Tang et al. (2014) has used deep neural network for learning sentiment-specific word embedding.

The proposed architecture of FNN is shown in Figure 2 and related hyper-parameters used in final system are provided in Table 3.

Training parameters of the FNN is similar to that of LSTM-CNN model. Dropout layers were used in training after each hidden layer with dropout rate of 0.5. Features used to train the FNN are transfered from dense layer of LSTM-CNN models trained with different embedding models. Several feature vectors obtained from LSTM-CNN are concatenated and provided as input to FNN. The final system used features from LSTM-CNN models trained with embeddings: TW2V, GW2V + E2V and WFT.

3.3.3 Optimization

Hyper-parameters of the neural networks should be optimized to gain better performance. They were selected based on the results on the trial set and were optimized with both manual processes and with Tree of Parzen Estimators (TPE) (Bergstra et al., 2011). However, due to the lack of processing power and time limitations we were not able to perform a comprehensive analysis on different hyper-parameter variations.

3.3.4 Implementation Details

Python is used to implement the system with Keras (Chollet et al., 2015) with Tensorflow (Abadi et al.) as the backend and Scikit-learn (Pedregosa et al., 2011) being the mostly used external libraries. Hyper-parameter optimization is performed with Hyperopt library (Bergstra et al., 2013). Any hyper-parameter not mentioned in Section 3 defaults to their default values in respective library. Furthermore, we made our source code and trained models available online [8].

4 Evaluation and Discussion

The first set of analyses examined the impact of LSTM-CNN models trained with different word embedding models. The results of the LSTM-CNN analysis are set out in Table 4. The train set evaluation is performed by training model on training dataset evaluating on trial set. Test set training data comprised of both training data and trial data.

It is apparent from this Table 4 that the model has performed similarly for both trial dataset and test dataset, achieving similar/ better F_1 scores and variations from one feature to another. We observe

---

[8]https://github.com/ysenarath/opinion-lab

the best performance of the system when using Word2vec trained on twitter. This could be due to the fact that it contains in-domain vocabulary. What stands out in the table is the improvement of results of M_{GW2V} with inclusion of Emoji2Vec. It can thus be suggested that Emoji provide a substantial support to finding emotion in implicit context. Furthermore, we observe that M_{WTF} performs better than M_{WSTF} and can be suggested that sub-word information provided by the embedding is not important in crating the model. Another noteworthy observation is that all the models indicated in Table 4 outperforms the baseline model in both trial and test cases, thus proving the effectiveness of the proposed model itself for implicit emotion prediction task.

In the next part of the analysis we used FNN trained using features extracted from LSTM-CNN models. Table 5 provides the evaluation results of these models on the test set. '++' is used to represent vector concatenation operation and $f(M)$ denotes a function that extracts the learned features form model M from the last dense layer in the neural network for a given input text. The evaluations are performed using the three best performing LSTM-CNN models: M_{TW2V}, M_{WTF} and M_{E2V}. We have omitted M_{GW2V} for this analysis since the word vector used to train M_{GW2V} is already contained in M_{E2V}.

Results from Table 4 can be compared with the results in Table 5 which shows that the performance (precision, recall and F_1) of models in the latter has improved than the individual model variants. Closer inspection of the Table 5 shows that the best models are obtained when features from M_{TW2V} and M_{E2V} are used together. The overall best performance is obtained when features from M_{TW2V}, M_{E2V} and M_{WTF} are concatenated together.

5 Conclusion

This study is set out to propose a system for implicit emotion classification with state-of-the-art neural network classifiers. Additionally we investigate the effectiveness of combinations of different pre-trained embedding for implicit emotion classification of Tweets. In this study, a LSTM and a CNN are combined sequentially and trained with different pre-trained word embeddings to be used as a feature generator for a secondary feedforward neural network classifier to make the final classi-fication. The results of this study indicate that the system performs well in implicit emotion identifi-cation and beats the baseline system by about 8% on the test set.

Furthermore the experiments support the idea that features extracted from several pre-trained word embedding models can be effectively combined to improve the overall classification performance . The most obvious finding to emerge from this study are that in-domain word embeddings and Emoji embeddings contribute in improving performance of implicit emotion classification. The generalisability of these results is subject to certain limitations. For instance, this research does not focus on fine-tuning the model architectures to different word-embeddings. Although this gives a general ground in comparing word-embeddings for this task, it does not provide the justification for individual capabilities. Further research will have to be conducted in order to determine the best configurations for individual word embeddings and feature combinations to improve the overall performance of the system.

Acknowledgments

The research was supported by the DataSEARCH research centre for data science, engineering, and analytics at University of Moratuwa, Sri Lanka. We thank all the contributions made by the group to this research. We would also like to thank the organizers of IEST at WASSA-2018 for organizing this shared task.

References

Martín Abadi, Paul Barham, Jianmin Chen, Zhifeng Chen, Andy Davis, Jeffrey Dean, Matthieu Devin, Sanjay Ghemawat, Geoffrey Irving, Michael Isard, et al. Tensorflow: a system for large-scale machine learning.

Yoshua Bengio, Réjean Ducharme, Pascal Vincent, and Christian Jauvin. 2003. A neural probabilistic language model. *Journal of machine learning research*, 3(Feb):1137–1155.

James Bergstra, Dan Yamins, and David D Cox. 2013. Hyperopt: A python library for optimizing the hyperparameters of machine learning algorithms. Citeseer.

James S Bergstra, Rémi Bardenet, Yoshua Bengio, and Balázs Kégl. 2011. Algorithms for hyper-parameter optimization. In *Advances in neural information processing systems*, pages 2546–2554.

François Chollet et al. 2015. Keras. `https://github.com/fchollet/keras`.

Ben Eisner, Tim Rocktäschel, Isabelle Augenstein, Matko Bošnjak, and Sebastian Riedel. 2016. emoji2vec: Learning emoji representations from their description. *arXiv preprint arXiv:1609.08359*.

Fréderic Godin, Baptist Vandersmissen, Wesley De Neve, and Rik Van de Walle. 2015. Multimedia lab @ acl wnut ner shared task: Named entity recognition for twitter microposts using distributed word representations. In *Proceedings of the Workshop on Noisy User-generated Text*, pages 146–153.

Armand Joulin, Edouard Grave, Piotr Bojanowski, and Tomas Mikolov. 2016. Bag of tricks for efficient text classification. *arXiv preprint arXiv:1607.01759*.

Yoon Kim. 2014. Convolutional neural networks for sentence classification. *arXiv preprint arXiv:1408.5882*.

Diederik P Kingma and Jimmy Ba. 2014. Adam: A method for stochastic optimization. *arXiv preprint arXiv:1412.6980*.

Roman Klinger, Orphée de Clercq, Saif M. Mohammad, and Alexandra Balahur. 2018. Iest: Wassa-2018 implicit emotions shared task. In *Proceedings of the 9th Workshop on Computational Approaches to Subjectivity, Sentiment and Social Media Analysis*, Brussels, Belgium. Association for Computational Linguistics.

Tomas Mikolov, Kai Chen, Greg Corrado, and Jeffrey Dean. 2013. Efficient estimation of word representations in vector space. *arXiv preprint arXiv:1301.3781*.

Tomas Mikolov, Edouard Grave, Piotr Bojanowski, Christian Puhrsch, and Armand Joulin. 2018. Advances in pre-training distributed word representations. In *Proceedings of the International Conference on Language Resources and Evaluation (LREC 2018)*.

F. Pedregosa, G. Varoquaux, A. Gramfort, V. Michel, B. Thirion, O. Grisel, M. Blondel, P. Prettenhofer, R. Weiss, V. Dubourg, J. Vanderplas, A. Passos, D. Cournapeau, M. Brucher, M. Perrot, and E. Duchesnay. 2011. Scikit-learn: Machine learning in Python. *Journal of Machine Learning Research*, 12:2825–2830.

Jeffrey Pennington, Richard Socher, and Christopher Manning. 2014. Glove: Global vectors for word representation. In *Proceedings of the 2014 conference on empirical methods in natural language processing (EMNLP)*, pages 1532–1543.

Richard Socher, Alex Perelygin, Jean Wu, Jason Chuang, Christopher D Manning, Andrew Ng, and Christopher Potts. 2013. Recursive deep models for semantic compositionality over a sentiment treebank. In *Proceedings of the 2013 conference on empirical methods in natural language processing*, pages 1631–1642.

Duyu Tang, Furu Wei, Bing Qin, Ting Liu, and Ming Zhou. 2014. Coooolll: A deep learning system for twitter sentiment classification. In *Proceedings of the 8th international workshop on semantic evaluation (SemEval 2014)*, pages 208–212.

Nam Khanh Tran and Weiwei Cheng. 2018. Multiplicative tree-structured long short-term memory networks for semantic representations. In *Proceedings of the Seventh Joint Conference on Lexical and Computational Semantics*, pages 276–286.

Tom Young, Devamanyu Hazarika, Soujanya Poria, and Erik Cambria. 2017. Recent trends in deep learning based natural language processing. *arXiv preprint arXiv:1708.02709*.

NL-FIIT at IEST-2018: Emotion Recognition utilizing Neural Networks and Multi-level Preprocessing

Samuel Pecar, Michal Farkas, Marian Simko, Peter Lacko, Maria Bielikova
Slovak University of Technology in Bratislava
Faculty of Informatics and Information Technologies
lkovičova 2, 842 16 Bratislava, Slovakia
`{samuel.pecar, michal.farkas, marian.simko, peter.lacko`
`maria.bielikova}@stuba.sk`

Abstract

In this paper, we present neural models submitted to Shared Task on Implicit Emotion Recognition, organized as part of WASSA 2018. We propose a Bi-LSTM architecture with regularization through dropout and Gaussian noise. Our models use three different embedding layers: GloVe word embeddings trained on Twitter dataset, ELMo embeddings and also sentence embeddings. We see preprocessing as one of the most important parts of the task. We focused on handling emojis, emoticons, hashtags, and also various shortened word forms. In some cases, we proposed to remove some parts of the text, as they do not affect emotion of the original sentence. We also experimented with other modifications like category weights for learning and stacking multiple layers. Our model achieved a macro average F1 score of 65.55 %, significantly outperforming the baseline model produced by a simple logistic regression.

1 Introduction

Both text reconstruction and sentiment analysis are well studied and highly practical areas of research in the field of natural language processing. Recently, there have been significant advances and improvements (Buechel and Hahn, 2017), at least partly due to the wider adoption of neural networks (Köper et al., 2017).

As it is, Implicit Emotion Recognition, as proposed by organizers of WASSA 2018 workshop (Klinger et al., 2018), can be seen both as a text reconstruction and as a sentiment analysis task. This is possible because, in this task, sentiment of a sentence should be equal to the missing word. In practice, the difference is marginal, nevertheless for both these tasks bi-directional LSTMs are widely used.

In recent years, there have been several competitions, papers and shared tasks dealing with

emotion recognition and classification (Mohammad et al., 2018; Mohammad and Bravo-Marquez, 2017). Dealing with noisy and ungrammatical user-generated text can be also challenging in other high-level NLP tasks like summarization (Pecar, 2018).

In this paper, we present a neural network architecture with special focus on the preprocessing phase. We believe preprocessing can have significant impact on accuracy of each system in natural language processing. We explored many setups and also different types of regularization as dropout, Gaussian noise, kernel and activity regularization – L1 and L2, and also recurrent dropout within LSTM cells. We also experimented with three different types of embedding layers – GloVe, ELMo and various sentence representations. Finally, we explored impact of different setups on model accuracy. In this paper, we report on results of these experiments.

2 Preprocessing

We are aware that preprocessing of input is one of the most important phases in natural language processing. This need is also highlighted when using user generated content which is more difficult to process. We can distinguish our preprocessing in a few stages displayed in Figure 1. We also evaluate different setups of our preprocessing in the results section.

Word-level Cleaning Word-level cleaning consists of several rules to handle various forms of words in language. Especially, we focused on handling short forms of auxiliaries and also its negative variations. We split negative auxiliaries into its full form (e.g. *don't* as *do not*, *isn't* as *is not*). We also handled non negative auxiliaries and expanded them into their full form (e.g. *'ll* as *will*). In analysis of original dataset we decided to also

217

Proceedings of the 9th Workshop on Computational Approaches to Subjectivity, Sentiment and Social Media Analysis, pages 217–223
Brussels, Belgium, October 31, 2018. ©2018 Association for Computational Linguistics
https://doi.org/10.18653/v1/P17

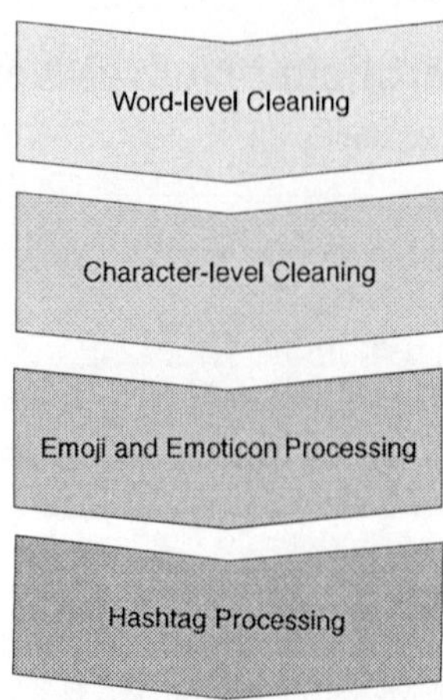

Figure 1: Preprocessing pipeline

omit some of the words which do not affect classification (e.g. @username, http://url.removed). The [NEWLINE] sign was replaced by sentence endings followed by space.

Character-level Cleaning Similarly to word-level cleaning, this phase consists of several rules operating on character-level preprocessing. We can describe this preprocessing in several categories, such as: currency handling, character escaping, replacing, and removing. In currency handling, we replaced signs for pounds, dollars, euros and yens with its word form. Other currency signs were replaced with the word 'currency'. Character replacing consists of unification of different forms used for apostrophe and as quotation marks. In character escaping, we surrounded characters like apostrophe, quotation mark, colon, dash, and caret with white-spaces to separate them from words and make tokenization easier. Finally, we decided to remove other unmentioned punctuation marks. We also considered removing all numbers as they often do not determine any sentiment.

Emoji and Emoticons Processing Handling emoticons and emojis is a more extensive part in our preprocessing phase. The first step consists of replacing emoticons (punctuation, numbers and characters used to create pictorial icons) with their emoji equivalent (only one unicode character). In phase of handling emojis, we removed all characters which modify original emoji with gender or skin color. We also tried to categorize emoji into categories (Figure 2). This step helped us to reduce amount of emojis used in text. We re-

placed emojis symbolizing sport, moon, earth, animal, fruit, food, lag, music, flower, plant, drink, dress, money with their category word surrounded by colon (Figure 2). Another categories were produced by unification of different emojis with similar sense.

Figure 2: Emoji categorization

Finally, we surround all emojis with white-spaces. This step can significantly help in tokenization, as emojis were sometimes recognized as part of words and also group of emojis were recognized as one token.

Hashtags Processing The last phase of preprocessing consists of handling hashtags. We examined different options of hashtag handling. In our final setup, we replaced only those hashtags, which can be found in word embeddings in their form without hash sign. We suppose removing other, unknown hashtags should be also considered as one of the step within hashtag processing. We also considered splitting hashtags into words but some of the separated words can bring different sentiment as the original hashtag. Hence, we decided to omit this step.

Figure 3: Emoji replacing

Examples of preprocessed texts are displayed in Figure 4. We can see examples of each preprocessing step described in this chapter.

3 Model

In this shared task, we experimented with many different setups, based on a different embedding layer and also different neural layers on top of an embedding layer.

3.1 Embedding Layer

We experimented some of the commonly used embedding layers like Word2Vec (Mikolov et al., 2013), GloVe (Pennington et al., 2014) or ELMo (Peters et al., 2018) but also sentence embeddings like Universal Sentence Encoder (Cer et al., 2018) and InferSent (Conneau et al., 2017). For encoding input words, we used various pre-trained word embeddings available online like GloVe embeddings[1]. With GloVe embeddings, we experimented with domain specific embeddings trained on Twitter data but also with embeddings trained on data extracted by CommonCrawl. We have also experimented with recent ELMo embeddings,

however these experiments were done additionally, after submission deadline. We used pre-trained model of ELMo available online[2].

Both GloVe and ELMo embeddings were included in model in such way that they can be further fine-tuned. However, available implementation of InferSent is done in Torch and integrating that model into Keras model proved to be problematic, this is mainly due to their use of custom layer. Hence, we encoded sentences into their vectors outside of the model and stored it in a separate file. We are considering a whole tweet as a single sentence and have a file that has a label and an embedding of the entire tweet. On the other hand, both variants of USE are available as a Tensorflow module[3] [4]. This enables us to use them as an embedding layer, although without any fine tuning.

3.2 Hidden Layers

Embedding layer is followed by several Bi-LSTM layers, when sentence embeddings were not used. We have experimented with up to two stacked layers. In case of sentence embedding models, we have experimented with several architectures with varying number of layers, however in the end we have settled on simple feed-forward network with one hidden layer, which uses parametric rectified linear unit.

We experimented with a different size of each layer and also a different number of stacked layers.

While using 1024 units in each of hidden layers was the best option, we also tested a much bigger model with sentence embeddings containing more units within each layer and also more stacked layers.

3.3 Activation

We experimented with several different activation functions, but their impact was either insignificant or obvious. Hence, all our results use the same configuration as far as activation functions are concerned.

In LSTM cells, we use typical activation functions – hard sigmoid and hyperbolic tangent. In case of models that utilize sentence embeddings, we use parametric rectified linear activation, although its contribution is uncertain.

---

[1]https://nlp.stanford.edu/projects/glove/

[2]https://tfhub.dev/google/elmo/2

[3]https://tfhub.dev/google/universal-sentence-encoder/2

[4]https://tfhub.dev/google/universal-sentence-encoder-large/3

Figure 4: Examples of preprocessed sentences

Since we use categorical crossentropy as our loss function, choice of softmax activation function for the last layer is natural.

3.4 Regularization

In training stage, we discovered a problem with over-fitting on training dataset and some regularization was needed. We experimented with different types of regularization like dropout, Gaussian noise and also applying L1 and L2 norm to different types of regularization, such as: bias, kernel, recurrent or activation. We found out that using combined L1 and L2 regularization often causes learning to stop. Although we fine-tuned L1 and L2 weight parameters, it failed to achieve better results than a model without this kind of regularization.

Unsurprisingly, we have utilized early stopping technique to halt training when validation accuracy has not improved at least by 0.001% two times in a row. Although we experimented with different configurations, such as monitoring validation loss and tweaking patience, we did not observe any improvement and in most cases we even observed detrimental effect.

While L1 and L2 regularization had no positive effect on accuracy of our model, application of dropout and Gaussian noise significantly improved accuracy of tested models. We experimented with different setups and the most accurate combination was with the use of dropout with rate of 0.3 after each layer or replacing dropout after embedding layer with dropout with rate 0.2 and Gaussian noise on the embeddings with standard deviation 0.2. That being said, we have found out that applying these regularizations on sentence embeddings proved to be more challenging and the same settings often were too much for the neural network to handle.

4 Evaluation

In this section, we briefly summarize evaluation metrics for this task and also basic information about used dataset and embeddings. Later, we describe different setups of our model.

For evaluation, standard measures like precision, recall and f-score were used. Then micro and macro measures were computed. As final official result, macro F1 was taken.

4.1 Dataset

The dataset for emotion recognition shared task consists of tweets where emotion word was removed. The dataset contains six different categories: anger, disgust, fear, joy, sadness, and surprise. The train dataset contains approximately 150 thousands of tweets and test contains more than 30 thousands of tweets. Detailed information can be found in the main paper of the shared task (Klinger et al., 2018).

4.2 Results

Our experiments show that the effect of LSTM size is apparent up to 1024 units. After that, it has negligible or even detrimental effect. Similarly, our experiments with two-layer Bi-LSTM achieved worse or same results as single-layer only. Our results are shown in Table 1. Setup for Glove and also ELMo was set as follows[5]:

- batch size: 64

- gaussian noise after embedding layer: 0.2

---

[5]default attributes from keras were used if not specified otherwise

- dropout after embedding layer: 0.2

- dropout after recurrent layer: 0.3

- loss function: categorical cross entropy

- optimizer: adam

- early stopping value: 0.01

- early stop patience: 1

- embeddings dimension: 200

The same setup, except for regularization, was used also for sentence embedding approach. Regularization did not seem to improve generalization and results, hence we did not include it in our model. It is highly probable that regularization was not needed, because, as we reported earlier, sentence embedding methods are applied in such way that they cannot be fine-tuned.

Model	P	R	F1
GloVe			
Bi-LSTM-256	0.6	0.598	0.599
Bi-LSTM-2x256	0.601	0.599	0.6
Bi-LSTM-1024	**0.657**	**0.655**	**0.655**
Bi-LSTM-2x1024	0.643	0.64	0.638
ELMo			
Bi-LSTM-1024	0.665	0.666	0.665
Bi-LSTM-2048	0.661	0.661	0.661
Bi-LSTM-2x1024	0.666	0.665	0.664
Sentence embeddings			
InferSent	0.564	0.536	0.537
USE-small	0.504	0.501	0.5
USE-large	0.544	0.544	0.542

Table 1: Comparison between different models.

Various variants of GloVe, even those trained on Twitter data, did not show much variance. On the other hand, ELMo embeddings did slightly improve our results as was expected.

There are several possible reasons why sentence embedding methods failed. First, the provided dataset is actually quite substantial and does not need such methods. Secondly, these methods cannot work well on Twitter data. Finally, the way we have included both InferSent and USE into our models does not enable fine tuning. Of course we cannot rule out a bug in our code as well.

Preprocessing had far greater impact on results than fine tuning our model. Details shown in Table

2 clearly demonstrate that text cleaning with emoji processing can improve classification of emotion. In the setup *Text cleaning*, only word-level and character-level cleaning were used. In the *Emoji processing* setup, we used previous features along with emoji processing and in *Hashtag processing* we used only text cleaning with hashtag processing. Finally, in the last setup, all previous setups were combined.

Setup	P	R	F1
No preprocessing	0.630	0.626	0.626
Text cleaning	0.645	0.639	0.641
Emoji processing	0.657	0.655	0.655
Hashtags processing	0.648	0.647	0.647
Combined	**0.657**	**0.655**	**0.655**

Table 2: Comparison of different preprocessing setups.

To see how our best model performed on different classes, we can take a look at Table 3. It is apparent that we have achieved best results on 'joy' class and worst results on 'anger' class. Precision metric of class 'surprise' is particularly noteworthy, due to it being considerably lower than other classes. This suggests that our model often classified other labels as 'surprise' class.

Confusion matrix, shown in Table 4, depicts accuracy of our official results (columns represent predicted classes while rows represent true labels). Quite surprisingly, false positives are more or less balanced across all categories. Nevertheless, we can see that our model rarely misclassified 'joy' as 'disgust', 'fear', and vice versa. We can glean more findings from this confusion matrix, but they may be just a noise.

5 Conclusion

In this paper, we discussed different neural models for emotion recognition based on word and sentence embeddings followed by stacked Bi-LSTM layers and dense layers, respectively. We also discussed need of preprocessing that can significantly improve accuracy.

We observed that false negative and also false positive examples were equally distributed between classes. We tried also set sample weights for classes with the best and worst F1, but no combination brought any overall improvement.

In our preprocessing, we also removed all numbers as they do not contain any sentiment. After

Label	TP	FP	FN	P	R	F
anger	2717	1713	2077	0.613	0.567	0.589
disgust	3013	1368	1781	0.688	0.628	0.657
sad	2793	1722	1546	0.619	0.644	0.631
joy	3893	1193	1353	0.765	0.742	0.754
surprise	3124	2297	1668	0.576	0.652	0.612
fear	3345	1578	1446	0.679	0.698	0.689
MicAvg	18885	9871	9871	0.657	0.657	0.657
MacAvg				**0.657**	**0.655**	**0.655**

Table 3: Official results over classes.

Class	anger	disgust	fear	joy	sadness	surprise
anger	**2717**	345	437	310	397	588
disgust	352	**3013**	196	146	457	630
fear	314	169	**3345**	223	275	465
joy	303	119	266	**3893**	337	328
sadness	388	364	234	274	**2793**	286
surprise	356	371	445	240	256	**3124**

Table 4: Confusion matrix of official results.

this preprocessing some of the sentences can be recognized as the same. An interesting point of research can be deduplication of these examples and examination of overall impact of these duplicated examples.

We made our code publicly available at GitHub[6].

Acknowledgments

This work was partially supported by the Slovak Research and Development Agency under the contract No. APVV-17-0267 - Automated Recognition of Antisocial Behaviour in Online Communities, the Scientific Grant Agency of the Slovak Republic, grant No. VG 1/0667/18 and VG 1/0646/15 and the Cultural and Educational Grant Agency of the Slovak Republic, grant No. KEGA 028STU-4/2017

References

Sven Buechel and Udo Hahn. 2017. Emobank: Studying the impact of annotation perspective and representation format on dimensional emotion analysis. In *Proceedings of the 15th Conference of the European Chapter of the Association for Computational Linguistics: Volume 2, Short Papers*, pages 578–585. Association for Computational Linguistics.

Daniel Cer, Yinfei Yang, Sheng-yi Kong, Nan Hua, Nicole Limtiaco, Rhomni St John, Noah Constant, Mario Guajardo-Cespedes, Steve Yuan, Chris Tar, et al. 2018. Universal sentence encoder. *arXiv preprint arXiv:1803.11175.*

Alexis Conneau, Douwe Kiela, Holger Schwenk, Loïc Barrault, and Antoine Bordes. 2017. Supervised learning of universal sentence representations from natural language inference data. In *Proceedings of the 2017 Conference on Empirical Methods in Natural Language Processing*, pages 670–680, Copenhagen, Denmark. Association for Computational Linguistics.

Roman Klinger, Orphée de Clercq, Saif M. Mohammad, and Alexandra Balahur. 2018. Iest: Wassa-2018 implicit emotions shared task. In *Proceedings of the 9th Workshop on Computational Approaches to Subjectivity, Sentiment and Social Media Analysis*, Brussels, Belgium. Association for Computational Linguistics.

Maximilian Köper, Evgeny Kim, and Roman Klinger. 2017. IMS at EmoInt-2017: Emotion intensity prediction with affective norms, automatically extended resources and deep learning. In *Proceedings of the 8th Workshop on Computational Approaches to Subjectivity, Sentiment and Social Media Analysis*, Copenhagen, Denmark. Workshop at Conference on Empirical Methods in Natural Language Processing, Association for Computational Linguistics.

Tomas Mikolov, Ilya Sutskever, Kai Chen, Greg S Corrado, and Jeff Dean. 2013. Distributed representations of words and phrases and their compositional-

[6]https://github.com/SamuelPecar/nl-fiit-wassa-emotion

ity. In *Advances in neural information processing systems*, pages 3111–3119.

Saif Mohammad and Felipe Bravo-Marquez. 2017. Wassa-2017 shared task on emotion intensity. In *Proceedings of the 8th Workshop on Computational Approaches to Subjectivity, Sentiment and Social Media Analysis*, pages 34–49. Association for Computational Linguistics.

Saif M. Mohammad, Felipe Bravo-Marquez, Mohammad Salameh, and Svetlana Kiritchenko. 2018. Semeval-2018 Task 1: Affect in tweets. In *Proceedings of International Workshop on Semantic Evaluation (SemEval-2018)*, New Orleans, LA, USA.

Samuel Pecar. 2018. Towards opinion summarization of customer reviews. In *Proceedings of ACL 2018, Student Research Workshop*, pages 1–8. Association for Computational Linguistics.

Jeffrey Pennington, Richard Socher, and Christopher D. Manning. 2014. Glove: Global vectors for word representation. In *Empirical Methods in Natural Language Processing (EMNLP)*, pages 1532–1543.

Matthew Peters, Mark Neumann, Mohit Iyyer, Matt Gardner, Christopher Clark, Kenton Lee, and Luke Zettlemoyer. 2018. Deep contextualized word representations. In *Proceedings of the 2018 Conference of the North American Chapter of the Association for Computational Linguistics: Human Language Technologies, Volume 1 (Long Papers)*, pages 2227–2237. Association for Computational Linguistics.

UWB at IEST 2018: Emotion Prediction in Tweets with Bidirectional Long Short-Term Memory Neural Network

Pavel Přibáň[1,2] and **Jiří Martínek**[1,2]

[1]NTIS – New Technologies for the Information Society,
Faculty of Applied Sciences, University of West Bohemia, Czech Republic
[2]Department of Computer Science and Engineering,
Faculty of Applied Sciences, University of West Bohemia, Czech Republic
{pribanp, jimar}@kiv.zcu.cz
http://nlp.kiv.zcu.cz

Abstract

This paper describes our system created for the WASSA 2018 Implicit Emotion Shared Task. The goal of this task is to predict the emotion of a given tweet, from which a certain emotion word is removed. The removed word can be *sad*, *happy*, *disgusted*, *angry*, *afraid* or a synonym of one of them. Our proposed system is based on deep-learning methods. We use Bidirectional Long Short-Term Memory (BiLSTM) with word embeddings as an input. Pre-trained DeepMoji model and pre-trained emoji2vec emoji embeddings are also used as additional inputs. Our System achieves 0.657 macro F_1 score and our rank is 13th out of 30.

1 Introduction

Emotions, especially on the social media and social networks, as an immediate response to a specific object or a situation, are a significant part of the communication between people. Even for a human, it is sometimes challenging to describe or recognize an emotion without imminent contact with a subject (e.g. idioms or sarcasm). One of the most important ways to express an emotion in a text is an emoji. Emojis are small ideograms depicting objects, people and scenes (Barbieri et al., 2018). Emojis try to capture a facial expression of a subject, which is determining for emotion detection.

This paper describes our system created for the WASSA 2018 Implicit Emotion Shared Task (Klinger et al., 2018). The goal of this task is to predict the emotion of a given tweet, from which a certain emotion word is removed, for example:

```
It is [#TARGETWORD#] when you feel
like you are invisible to others.
```

The removed word can be *sad*, *happy*, *disgusted*, *surprised*, *angry*, *afraid* or a synonym of

one of them. The possible emotions are Sadness, Joy, Disgust, Surprise, Anger, and Fear. The `[#TARGETWORD#]` token in the example indicates a position of the removed word in the given tweet.

1.1 Related Work

As we mentioned before emojis are an important part of expressing emotions. Barbieri et al. (2017) investigated the relationship between words and emojis. They also proposed an approach to predict the most probable emoji that is associated with a tweet. The mentioned approach uses a Bidirectional Long Short–Term Memory networks (BiLSTM) (Graves and Schmidhuber, 2005).

Pre-trained word embeddings (word representations) such as (Mikolov et al., 2013; Pennington et al., 2014) are currently standard part in most of the state-of-the-art solutions for key NLP tasks.

Tang et al. (2014) propose a method that can learn sentiment–specific word embeddings, which are able to improve performance by combining with other existing feature sets.

There are also some previously submitted systems in similar SemEval shared tasks using deep learning models. Cliche (2017) uses a CNN and LSTM for Sentiment Analysis SemEval–2017 task 4 (Rosenthal et al., 2017). Another approach with a deep LSTM with Attention mechanism is used by Baziotis et al. (2017) for the same task. Most of the best performing submitted systems (Baziotis et al., 2018; Gee and Wang, 2018; Park et al., 2018) in SemEval-2018 Task 1: Affect in Tweets (Mohammad et al., 2018) also use deep learning models with LSTM or BiLSTM neural networks.

2 Overview

Our approach is based on the artificial neural network that combines word embeddings and emoji–

Proceedings of the 9th Workshop on Computational Approaches to Subjectivity, Sentiment and Social Media Analysis, pages 224–230
Brussels, Belgium, October 31, 2018. ©2018 Association for Computational Linguistics
https://doi.org/10.18653/v1/P17

based features as input. We use Weka machine learning workbench (Hall et al., 2009) for preprocessing. Our submitted model combines BiLSTM layer for word embeddings input and dense layers for the other inputs (emoji2vec (Eisner et al., 2016) and DeepMoji (Felbo et al., 2017) features, see 2.2) connected to one dense layer, see the Figure 2 with a model architecture. Outputs of these three layers are concatenated and then a dropout (Srivastava et al., 2014) technique is applied. After the concatenating a next dense layer is employed. An output from the previous dense layer is then passed to a fully-connected softmax layer. An output of the softmax layer is a probability distribution over all six possible classes.

We trained several modified versions of our submitted model and we evaluated these models on the development data. The model with the highest macro F_1 score on the development data was then trained again on the training data extended by the development data. This model was used for test data predictions. All models were implemented by using Keras (Chollet et al., 2015) with TensorFlow backend (Abadi et al., 2015).

2.1 Tweets Preprocessing

Tweets often contain slang expressions, misspelled words, emoticons or abbreviations and it is needed to make some preprocessing steps before training and making predictions. We use a similar approach to Přibáň et al. (2018).

At first, we remove the [#TARGETWORD#] token, that represents a position of the removed word with a certain emotion and every tweet is tokenized using *TweetNLP twokenizer* (Gimpel et al., 2011). Then the following steps are applied on tokens:

1. Tokens are converted to lowercase

2. Tokens containing sequences of letters occurring more than two times in a row are replaced with two occurrences of them (e.g. *huuuungry* is reduced to *huungry*, *looooove* to *loove*)

3. From hashtags (tokens starting with #) the # character is removed.

4. Common sequences of words and emojis are separated by space (e.g. token *"nice:D:D"* is split into three tokens *"nice"*, *":D"* and *":D"*)

5. Characters &_– in tokens are replaced with space

Weka machine learning workbench is used to perform the mentioned steps. After tokenization and mentioned preprocessing the tweet is padded to 50 tokens. Tweets longer than 50 words are shortened, while to the shorter tweets padding tokens are added.

2.2 Features

We use three types of input features – word embeddings, emoji embeddings and an emotional representation of a sentence. **Word embeddings** are representations of words usually expressed as pre-trained dense real vectors (Mikolov et al., 2013; Pennington et al., 2014) with a fixed dimension size. We use pre-trained Ultradense Word Embeddings (Rothe et al., 2016) that were trained on Twitter domain corpus. The number of dimensions for this embedding is 400.

Pre-trained emoji2vec (Eisner et al., 2016) **emoji embeddings** (300-dimensional) are used as another input to our model. We average vectors for each emoji in a tweet and the resulting averaged vector is used as an input. The mentioned emoji2vec embeddings contain vectors for all Unicode emojis which were learned from their description in the Unicode emoji standard[1], see the (Eisner et al., 2016) for details. Emoji2vec embeddings can be used only for some tweets because not every tweet contains some emojis, but we suppose that using emoji2vec will lead to an overall performance improvement.

We also use DeepMoji (Felbo et al., 2017) as an **emotional sentence representation**. The DeepMoji model is able to predict emoji that is included with a given sentence and thus the model has also an understanding of the emotional content of that sentence. The model was trained on a dataset of 1.2 billion tweets. As an input for our model, we use the 2304-dimensional vector from the attention layer in the pre-trained DeepMoji model.

2.3 Recurrent Neural Network

The Recurrent Neural Network (RNN) extends the classic (feed–forward) neural network. An RNN is intended for sequential data. The actual hidden state h_t of the RNN depends on the previous hidden state h_{t-1} (see Figure 1). An RNN takes the input sequence $x_1, x_2 \ldots x_T$ and for each element, at the time step t computes new hidden state h_t

---

[1] http://www.unicode.org/emoji/charts/emoji-list.html

from the input x_t and from the previous hidden state h_{t-1}. The new hidden state h_t is computed by hidden layer function $\mathcal{H}$.

$$h_t = \mathcal{H}(x_t, h_{t-1}) \tag{1}$$

In the simplest case, the hidden layer function $\mathcal{H}$ is defined as:

$$h_t = \sigma \left(W_{xh} x_t + W_{hh} h_{t-1} + b_h \right) \tag{2}$$

where the W terms correspond to weight matrices (e.g. W_{xh} is the input-hidden weight matrix) and b_h term is hidden bias vector. The concrete implementation of the $\mathcal{H}$ function depends on the type of the used RNN unit (Graves et al., 2013), for example Long Short-Term Memory (LSTM) unit (Hochreiter and Schmidhuber, 1997) or Gated Recurrent Unit (GRU) (Cho et al., 2014).

In our case, the input x_t denotes the word embedding vector for each word in the tweet and T is a length of the tweet. Every tweet is also padded to the length T. As mentioned, the new hidden state h_t depends on the previous hidden state and hence the word order is also taken into account in the RNN.

2.4 Long Short-Term Memory

The Long Short-Term Memory (Hochreiter and Schmidhuber, 1997) allows learning (remember) long-term dependencies from the input sequence. The LSTM unit consists of cell state (cell activation vector) input, forget and output gates. These gates control how the cell state is updated. The $\mathcal{H}$ function of the LSTM unit is defined as:

$$i_t = \sigma \left(W_{xi} x_t + W_{hi} h_{t-1} + b_i \right) \tag{3}$$

$$f_t = \sigma \left(W_{xf} x_t + W_{hf} h_{t-1} + b_f \right) \tag{4}$$

$$o_t = \sigma \left(W_{xo} x_t + W_{ho} h_{t-1} + b_o \right) \tag{5}$$

$$c_t = f_t * c_{t-1} + i_t * \tanh \left(W_{xc} x_t + W_{hc} h_{t-1} + b_c \right) \tag{6}$$

$$h_t = o_t * \tanh \left(c_t \right) \tag{7}$$

where the W terms correspond to weight matrices and b terms are bias vectors, i, f, o are the input, forget and output gates, c denotes cell state (activation vector), σ is sigmoid function and $*$ character means element-wise multiplication.

It is a common practice to use Bidirectional LSTM (BiLSTM) (Graves and Schmidhuber, 2005). The BiLSTM consists of two LSTMs, one LSTM process the input sequence from the first

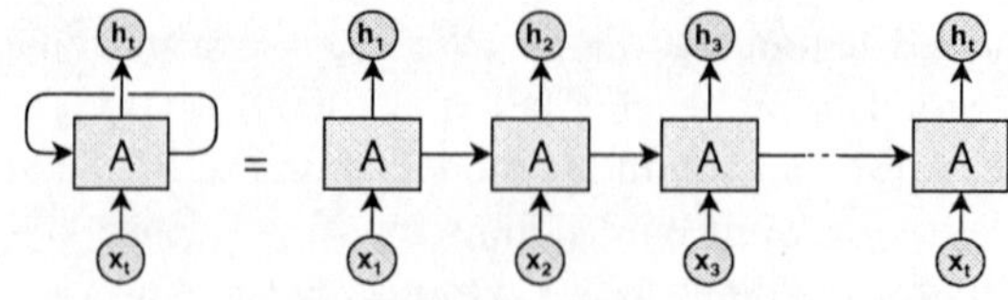

Figure 1: Basic RNN architecture[2]

element x_1 to x_T and produces output vector $\overrightarrow{h_t}$. The second LSTM process the input sequence in reverse order e.g. from the last element x_T to x_1 and produces output vector $\overleftarrow{h_t}$. Both output vectors have dimension D. The final output vector h_t from BiLSTM with dimension $2D$ is then created by concatenating two vectors $\overrightarrow{h_t}$ and $\overleftarrow{h_t}$.

Dropout (Srivastava et al., 2014) is a technique for improving neural networks by reducing overfitting. The dropout technique randomly drops out units (hidden and visible) during training and thus prevents co-adaption of neurons from training data.

3 Model Description

The proposed model has three inputs. Figure 2 shows the model architecture. The first input (**word embeddings**) represents tweet as a sequence of $t = 50$ tokens. We use the Ultradense Word Embeddings (Rothe et al., 2016) to obtain a vector of dimension $d = 400$ for each token from the tweet. The whole tweet is then represented as a matrix $M \in \mathbb{R}^{t \times d}$. The vectors are obtained only for 50,000 most frequent words in the training dataset. If the tweet word is not present in a vocabulary of 50,000 most frequent words, the randomly initialized vector of the same dimension is used. The **word embeddings** input is followed by a BiLSTM layer with 1200 units, respectively every single LSTM has 600 units. We also use a dropout to recurrent connections in BiLSTM layer.

The **emoji embeddings** input is based on emoji2vec (Eisner et al., 2016). For each emoji in the tweet, a 300-dimensional vector is produced by the pre-trained model. All emoji vectors for the tweet are then averaged to a single vector. If the tweet does not contain any emoji a zero vector is used. The resulting averaged **emoji embeddings** vector $E \in \mathbb{R}^{300}$ is used as an input to a dense layer with 300 units.

[2]Image is based on: http://colah.github.io/ posts/2015-08-Understanding-LSTMs/

226

Our last input uses a pre-trained DeepMoji (Felbo et al., 2017) model for an **emotional sentence representation**. The DeepMoji model generates for each tweet vector $D \in \mathbb{R}^{2304}$ which represents the emotional content of the tweet. The **emotional sentence representation** input is followed by a dense layer with 2304 units.

All three output vectors of the BiLSTM and two dense layers are concatenated into one vector $C \in \mathbb{R}^{3804}$ that is passed to a next dense layer with 400 units. We also use a dropout after the concatenating. An output of the last dense layer is passed to a final fully-connected softmax layer. An output of the softmax layer is a probability distribution over all six possible classes. The class with the highest probability is predicted as a final output of our model.

3.1 Model Training & Hyper-Parameters

We trained our model using mini-batches of size 1024 for 5 epochs and we used the Adam (Kingma and Ba, 2014) optimizer with learning rate 0.001 the other parameters of the Adam optimizer follow those provided in the cited paper. As an activation function in the BiLSTM and in the dense layers, we used a Rectified Linear Unit (ReLu). Dropout of 0.2 is used for the recurrent connections in BiLSTM layer and in all dense layers.

We trained the model on the provided training dataset and we evaluated the trained model on the development dataset. We experimented with different settings of the hyper-parameters (learning rate, mini-batch size etc.) but the mentioned settings showed to be the best one on the development data. These hyper-parameters settings were also used for final submission.

4 Experiments & Results

All presented experiments were evaluated on the provided development and test datasets. Table 1 shows the results for the different model settings.

We performed ablation study to see which features are the most beneficial (see Table 2). Numbers represent the performance change when the given feature is removed [3].

We also modified our model and we experimented with an attention mechanism (Rocktäschel et al., 2015; Raffel and Ellis, 2015). The atten-

[3]The lowest number denotes the most beneficial feature

	Macro F_1	
Model Settings	**dev data**	**test data**
Ultradense + DeepMoji + emoji2vec[†]	0.657	0.657
Ultradense + DeepMoji	**0.661**	**0.660**
Ultradense + emoji2vec	0.653	0.658
Ultradense	0.648	0.650
DeepMoji + emoji2vec	0.556	0.547
DeepMoji	0.560	0.552
emoji2vec	0.151	0.154
Ultradense + DeepMoji + emoji2vec[*]	0.661	0.656
Ultradense + DeepMoji[*]	0.654	0.653

[*]Model with added attention mechanism to BiLSTM layer
[†]Model used for the final submission

Table 1: Results for individual model settings

tion mechanism was added to our BiLSTM layer[4] (see Table 1 with results obtained by the modified model).

Our results for the WASSA 2018 Implicit Emotion Shared Task are shown in Table 3 along with some other teams. Table 4 contains the confusion matrix obtained from the submitted predictions and Table 5 contains Recall, Precision an F_1 measures that are computed from the confusion matrix.

Feature	dev data	test data
Ultradense + DeepMoji + emoji2vec[*]	0.657	0.657
Ultradense	**-0.101**	**-0.110**
DeepMoji	-0.004	-0.001
emoji2vec	0.004	-0.003

[*]Values used to calculate ablation results

Table 2: Feature ablation study

Team	Macro F_1	Rank
Amobee	0.714	1
IIIDYT	0.710	2
NTUA-SLP	0.703	3
hgsgnlp	0.658	12
UWB	**0.657**	**13**
NL-FIIT	0.655	14
BASELINE	0.599	20

Table 3: WASSA 2018 Implicit Emotion Shared Task official results

4.1 Discussion

Thanks to the ablation study (see Table 2) and results from Table 1 we can observe that the **Ultradense Word Embeddings** are the most important features for our model. The **DeepMoji** and the

[4]We experimented with an attention mechanism after the submission deadline and therefore the modified model cannot be used to make predictions for the final submission

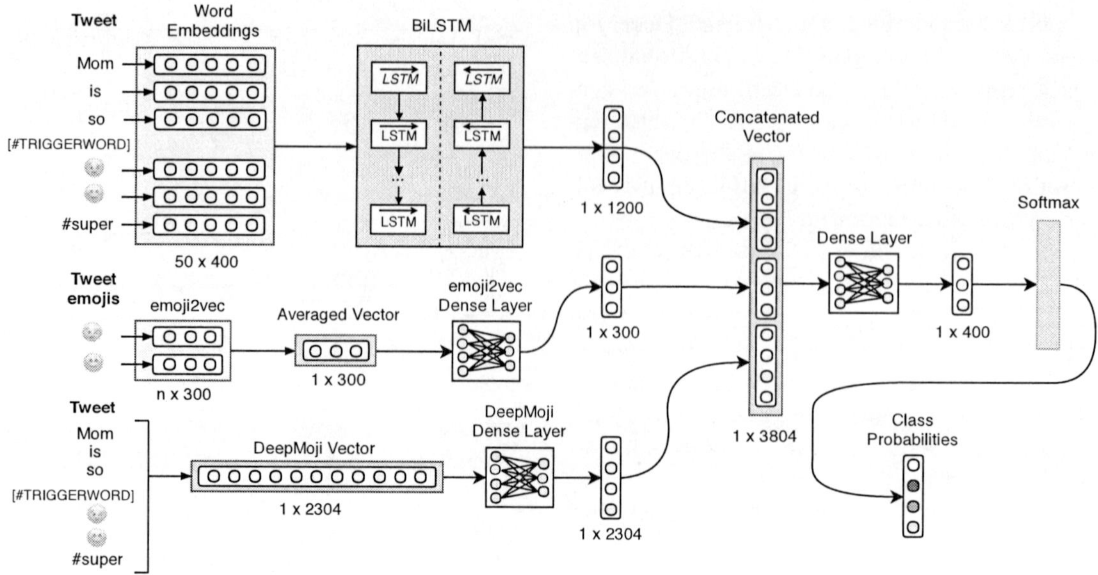

Figure 2: System architecture

		Predicted Labels				
	A	**D**	**F**	**J**	**Sa**	**Su**
A	3011	250	441	326	431	335
D	484	2807	274	204	596	429
F	461	119	3484	243	210	274
J	336	76	319	4021	304	190
Sa	439	206	266	345	2939	145
Su	530	331	569	315	345	2702

(Row labels at left: **Gold Labels**)

Table 4: Confusion Matrix on the test dataset (A, D, F, J, Sa, and Su are abbreviations for anger, disgust, fear, joy, sadness, and surprise respectively)

Emotion	**Recall**	**Precision**	**F$_1$ score**
Anger	0.628	0.572	0.599
Disgust	0.586	**0.741**	0.654
Fear	0.727	0.651	0.687
Joy	**0.766**	0.737	**0.752**
Sadness	0.677	0.609	0.641
Surprise	0.564	0.663	0.609

Table 5: Recall, Precision and F$_1$ score for each emotion of the test dataset

emoji2vec features also increase the performance of our model for the test dataset, but the contribution is insignificant and it is not so important as the word embeddings. So our assumption, that the emoji2vec feature will lead to a more significant overall performance improvement for the test dataset, is not correct. It would be more beneficial to use a simpler model without an emoji2vec feature.

The modified models with the attention mechanism did not improve the performance. The possible explanation is that it is caused by the missing emotion word in the classified tweet. The missing word carries probably the most information about the emotion. If the word was present in the classified tweet the attention mechanism would pay most attention to the missing word and thus the attention mechanism would improve the perfor-

mance of our model.

Our model performs best for the joy and fear emotions (see Table 5). On the other hand, we obtained worst results for the anger emotion. Our model produces the most false positive predictions for the anger emotion (tweet is classified as anger but the true emotion is different). From the confusion matrix (Table 4), we can see that for our model it is difficult to distinguish especially between disgust and sadness, disgust and anger, fear and anger, surprise and anger, and between surprise and fear.

Table 1 shows that there are no important differences between the development dataset and test dataset results. So our decision to select the second best model (evaluated on the development dataset) for the final submission based on the results for the development dataset was suitable.

5   Conclusion

In this paper we described our UWB deep-learning system created for the WASSA 2018 Implicit Emotion Shared Task. Our system uses Bidirectional Long Short-Term Memory (BiLSTM) with word embeddings as an input. Pre-trained DeepMoji model and pre-trained emoji2vec emoji embeddings are also used as additional inputs. The proposed system performs best for the joy emotion. Our System achieves 0.657 macro F_1 score and our rank is 13th out of 30.

We performed ablation study and showed that the most beneficial features are word embeddings. The emotional sentence representation (DeepMoji feature) and the averaged emoji vectors (emoji2vec feature) did not much improve the performance of our model.

In the future work, we would like to try another approach employing a twitter specific language model to predict probabilities for each emotion class for the missing target emotion word in the provided data. These probabilities could be used as input features to our model.

Acknowledgments

This work was partly supported from ERDF "Research and Development of Intelligent Components of Advanced Technologies for the Pilsen Metropolitan Area (InteCom)" (no.: CZ.02.1.01/0.0/0.0/17_048/0007267) and by Grant No. SGS-2016-018 Data and Software Engineerig for Advanced Applications.

References

Martín Abadi, Ashish Agarwal, Paul Barham, Eugene Brevdo, Zhifeng Chen, Craig Citro, Greg S. Corrado, Andy Davis, Jeffrey Dean, Matthieu Devin, Sanjay Ghemawat, Ian Goodfellow, Andrew Harp, Geoffrey Irving, Michael Isard, Yangqing Jia, Rafal Jozefowicz, Lukasz Kaiser, Manjunath Kudlur, Josh Levenberg, Dandelion Mané, Rajat Monga, Sherry Moore, Derek Murray, Chris Olah, Mike Schuster, Jonathon Shlens, Benoit Steiner, Ilya Sutskever, Kunal Talwar, Paul Tucker, Vincent Vanhoucke, Vijay Vasudevan, Fernanda Viégas, Oriol Vinyals, Pete Warden, Martin Wattenberg, Martin Wicke, Yuan Yu, and Xiaoqiang Zheng. 2015. TensorFlow: Large-scale machine learning on heterogeneous systems. Software available from tensorflow.org.

Francesco Barbieri, Miguel Ballesteros, and Horacio Saggion. 2017. Are emojis predictable? *arXiv preprint arXiv:1702.07285.*

Francesco Barbieri, Jose Camacho-Collados, Francesco Ronzano, Luis Espinosa Anke, Miguel Ballesteros, Valerio Basile, Viviana Patti, and Horacio Saggion. 2018. Semeval 2018 task 2: Multilingual emoji prediction. In *Proceedings of The 12th International Workshop on Semantic Evaluation*, pages 24–33.

Christos Baziotis, Athanasiou Nikolaos, Alexandra Chronopoulou, Athanasia Kolovou, Georgios Paraskevopoulos, Nikolaos Ellinas, Shrikanth Narayanan, and Alexandros Potamianos. 2018. Ntua-slp at semeval-2018 task 1: Predicting affective content in tweets with deep attentive rnns and transfer learning. In *Proceedings of The 12th International Workshop on Semantic Evaluation*, pages 245–255. Association for Computational Linguistics.

Christos Baziotis, Nikos Pelekis, and Christos Doulkeridis. 2017. Datastories at semeval-2017 task 4: Deep lstm with attention for message-level and topic-based sentiment analysis. In *Proceedings of the 11th International Workshop on Semantic Evaluation (SemEval-2017)*, pages 747–754.

Kyunghyun Cho, Bart Van Merriënboer, Caglar Gulcehre, Dzmitry Bahdanau, Fethi Bougares, Holger Schwenk, and Yoshua Bengio. 2014. Learning phrase representations using rnn encoder-decoder for statistical machine translation. *arXiv preprint arXiv:1406.1078.*

François Chollet et al. 2015. Keras. `https://keras.io`.

Mathieu Cliche. 2017. Bb_twtr at semeval-2017 task 4: Twitter sentiment analysis with cnns and lstms. *arXiv preprint arXiv:1704.06125.*

Ben Eisner, Tim Rocktäschel, Isabelle Augenstein, Matko Bošnjak, and Sebastian Riedel. 2016. emoji2vec: Learning emoji representations from their description. *arXiv preprint arXiv:1609.08359.*

Bjarke Felbo, Alan Mislove, Anders Søgaard, Iyad Rahwan, and Sune Lehmann. 2017. Using millions of emoji occurrences to learn any-domain representations for detecting sentiment, emotion and sarcasm. In *Conference on Empirical Methods in Natural Language Processing (EMNLP)*.

Grace Gee and Eugene Wang. 2018. psyml at semeval-2018 task 1: Transfer learning for sentiment and emotion analysis. In *Proceedings of The 12th International Workshop on Semantic Evaluation*, pages 369–376. Association for Computational Linguistics.

Kevin Gimpel, Nathan Schneider, Brendan O'Connor, Dipanjan Das, Daniel Mills, Jacob Eisenstein, Michael Heilman, Dani Yogatama, Jeffrey Flanigan, and Noah A. Smith. 2011. Part-of-speech tagging for twitter: Annotation, features, and experiments. In *Proceedings of the 49th Annual Meeting of the*

Association for Computational Linguistics: Human Language Technologies: Short Papers - Volume 2, HLT '11, pages 42–47, Stroudsburg, PA, USA. Association for Computational Linguistics.

Alex Graves, Abdel-rahman Mohamed, and Geoffrey Hinton. 2013. Speech recognition with deep recurrent neural networks. In *Acoustics, speech and signal processing (icassp), 2013 ieee international conference on*, pages 6645–6649. IEEE.

Alex Graves and Jürgen Schmidhuber. 2005. Framewise phoneme classification with bidirectional lstm and other neural network architectures. *Neural Networks*, 18(5-6):602–610.

Mark Hall, Eibe Frank, Geoffrey Holmes, Bernhard Pfahringer, Peter Reutemann, and Ian H. Witten. 2009. The WEKA data mining software: An update. *SIGKDD Explorations*, 11(1):10–18.

Sepp Hochreiter and Jürgen Schmidhuber. 1997. Long short-term memory. *Neural computation*, 9(8):1735–1780.

Diederik P Kingma and Jimmy Ba. 2014. Adam: A method for stochastic optimization. *arXiv preprint arXiv:1412.6980*.

Roman Klinger, Orphée de Clercq, Saif M. Mohammad, and Alexandra Balahur. 2018. Iest: Wassa-2018 implicit emotions shared task. In *Proceedings of the 9th Workshop on Computational Approaches to Subjectivity, Sentiment and Social Media Analysis*, Brussels, Belgium. Association for Computational Linguistics.

Tomas Mikolov, Ilya Sutskever, Kai Chen, Greg S Corrado, and Jeff Dean. 2013. Distributed representations of words and phrases and their compositionality. In *Advances in neural information processing systems*, pages 3111–3119.

Saif M. Mohammad, Felipe Bravo-Marquez, Mohammad Salameh, and Svetlana Kiritchenko. 2018. Semeval-2018 Task 1: Affect in tweets. In *Proceedings of International Workshop on Semantic Evaluation (SemEval-2018)*, New Orleans, LA, USA.

Ji Ho Park, Peng Xu, and Pascale Fung. 2018. Plusemo2vec at semeval-2018 task 1: Exploiting emotion knowledge from emoji and #hashtags. In *Proceedings of The 12th International Workshop on Semantic Evaluation*, pages 264–272. Association for Computational Linguistics.

Jeffrey Pennington, Richard Socher, and Christopher Manning. 2014. Glove: Global vectors for word representation. In *Proceedings of the 2014 conference on empirical methods in natural language processing (EMNLP)*, pages 1532–1543.

Pavel Přibáň, Tomáš Hercig, and Ladislav Lenc. 2018. Uwb at semeval-2018 task 1: Emotion intensity detection in tweets. In *Proceedings of The 12th International Workshop on Semantic Evaluation*, pages 133–140. Association for Computational Linguistics.

Colin Raffel and Daniel PW Ellis. 2015. Feedforward networks with attention can solve some long-term memory problems. *arXiv preprint arXiv:1512.08756*.

Tim Rocktäschel, Edward Grefenstette, Karl Moritz Hermann, Tomáš Kočiskỳ, and Phil Blunsom. 2015. Reasoning about entailment with neural attention. *arXiv preprint arXiv:1509.06664*.

Sara Rosenthal, Noura Farra, and Preslav Nakov. 2017. SemEval-2017 task 4: Sentiment analysis in Twitter. In *Proceedings of the 11th International Workshop on Semantic Evaluation*, SemEval '17, Vancouver, Canada. Association for Computational Linguistics.

Sascha Rothe, Sebastian Ebert, and Hinrich Schütze. 2016. Ultradense word embeddings by orthogonal transformation. *arXiv preprint arXiv:1602.07572*.

Nitish Srivastava, Geoffrey Hinton, Alex Krizhevsky, Ilya Sutskever, and Ruslan Salakhutdinov. 2014. Dropout: a simple way to prevent neural networks from overfitting. *The Journal of Machine Learning Research*, 15(1):1929–1958.

Duyu Tang, Furu Wei, Nan Yang, Ming Zhou, Ting Liu, and Bing Qin. 2014. Learning sentiment-specific word embedding for twitter sentiment classification. In *Proceedings of the 52nd Annual Meeting of the Association for Computational Linguistics (Volume 1: Long Papers)*, volume 1, pages 1555–1565.

USI-IR at IEST 2018: Sequence Modeling and Pseudo-Relevance Feedback for Implicit Emotion Detection

Esteban A. Ríssola, Anastasia Giachanou and Fabio Crestani
Faculty of Informatics
Università della Svizzera italiana (USI)
{esteban.andres.rissola, anastasia.giachanou, fabio.crestani}@usi.ch

Abstract

This paper describes the participation of USI-IR in WASSA 2018 Implicit Emotion Shared Task. We propose a relevance feedback approach employing a sequential model (biLSTM) and word embeddings derived from a large collection of tweets. To this end, we assume that the top-k predictions produce at a first classification step are correct (based on the model accuracy) and use them as new examples to re-train the network.

1 Introduction

Recent years have seen the rapid growth of social media platforms (*e.g.*, Facebook, Twitter, several blogs) that has changed the way that people communicate. Many people express their opinion and emotions on blogs, forums or microblogs. Detecting the emotions that are expressed in social media is a very important problem for a wide variety of applications. For example, enterprises can detect complains of customers about their products or services and act promptly.

Emotion detection aims at identifying various emotions from text. According to (Plutchik, 1980) there are eight basic emotions: anger, joy, sadness, fear, trust, surprise, disgust and anticipation. Considering the abundance of opinions and emotions expressed in microblogs, emotion and sentiment analysis in Twitter has attracted the interest of the research community (Giachanou and Crestani, 2016). In particular, *Implicit Emotion Shared Task (IEST)* is a shared task by WASSA 2018 that focuses on emotion analysis. In this task, participants are asked to develop tools that can predict the emotions in tweets from which a certain emotion word is removed. This is a very challenging problem since the emotion analysis needs to be done without access to an explicit mention of an emotion word and consequently taking advantage of context that surrounds the target word.

In this paper, we describe our submitted system to the *IEST: WASSA-2018 Implicit Emotion Shared Task*. Our system is based on a bidirectional Long Short-Term Memory (biLSTM) network on top of word embeddings which is later inserted in a pseudo-relevance feedback schema. Our results show that even though the model still need more refinement it offers interesting capabilities to address the task at hand.

2 Dataset

To train our model, we employ the dataset provided within the shared task. It is worth mentioning that no other external datasets are used during the training and development phases. There are roughly 153K tweets in the training set, 10K in the development set and 28K in the test set. Each data instance includes the tweet and the emotion class of the word which has been extracted from the text. The test set's golden labels were provided only after the evaluation period. The complete description of the dataset can be found in (Klinger et al., 2018)

3 Proposed Approach

In recent years, Recurrent Neural Networks (RNN) have risen in popularity among different NLP tasks (Mikolov et al., 2010; Graves et al., 2013; Filippova et al., 2015). This success can be attributed to their inherent ability to capture temporal information and learn features directly from the data. In other words, the time based sequentially connected structure of these networks is intuitive to use for sequential inputs, such as sentences or words. For this reason, we decide to model the tweets employing bidirectional Long Short-Term Memory (biLSTM) networks (Graves and Schmidhuber, 2005), which are an alternative RNN architecture that incorporates additional

Proceedings of the 9th Workshop on Computational Approaches to Subjectivity, Sentiment and Social Media Analysis, pages 231–234
Brussels, Belgium, October 31, 2018. ©2018 Association for Computational Linguistics
https://doi.org/10.18653/v1/P17

structures, called gates, to better control the information across sequential inputs and deal with issues that may arise during training, like the vanishing gradient problem. Moreover, each training sequence is presented forwards and backwards and the output combined at each timestep allowing to improve the overall performance of the network.

In the context of Information Retrieval (IR), relevance feedback refers to a technique designed to refine a query, either automatically or through user interaction. The goal of this process is to construct a query that is a better representation of the information need, and therefore to retrieve better documents (Manning et al., 2008). In particular, pseudo-relevance feedback automates the manual part of relevance feedback as the system simply assumes that the initial top-ranked documents are relevant and uses them to produce a new result set. In order to increase the accuracy of the biLSTM network we develop a pseudo-relevance feedback schema where we assume that the top-k predictions produce at a first classification step are correct (based on the model accuracy) and use them as new examples to re-train the network.

4 Experimental Setup

Preprocessing and tokenization are crucial steps of the pipeline involved in the development of a model: the output produced has an immediate effect in the features learned by the model. This task could turn to be particularly challenging in Twitter since the vocabulary results quite unstable over time and the way that users expressed does not follow traditional patterns. In order to preprocess and tokenize the collection of tweets we employ a python library[1] developed for that purpose which applies different regular expressions to extract particular units, such as hashtags, and separates them from the rest of the tokens. We only conserve words, hashtags, mentions, emojis and smileys. The remaining tokens outside these categories are discarded given that their inclusion did not prove to be useful for the task. Some examples of such tokens are URLs (they were originally replaced with `http://url.removed`), numbers and the unit `[NEWLINE]`. Furthermore, we remove the hash symbols from the hashtags and split the words when possible using the Viterbi algorithm. The prior probabilities are obtained from word statistics from Google Ngram corpus. In par-

ticular, we observed a positive impact on the training accuracy of the network. One possible reason could be that the terms contained in the hashtags were probably present in the word embeddings but not as a singular unit (*e.g., #classyCouple*). All the tokens are transformed to lowercase and words which were completely in capitals, emulating a yell in the social media language, were doubled. It is important to remark that stopwords are not removed.

The model is comprised of an embedding layer, a biLSTM layer and a softmax layer. It receives as input a tokenized twitter message treated as a sequence of words. Since the length of different tweets can vary, we set the length of each message to 99 (the maximum message length across training and development data according to the operations performed in the preprocessing step). Tweets that are shorter than this length are zero-padded. It should be noted that the network will ignore everything that goes beyond the last word in the text, *i.e.*, the padding. The weights of the embedding layer are initialized using word2vec (Mikolov et al., 2013) embeddings trained on 400 million tweets (Godin et al., 2015) from the ACL W-NUT share task (Baldwin et al., 2015). We also tried to use the 300-dimensional pre-trained vector trained on Google News dataset[2] combined with emojis pre-trained embeddings (Eisner et al., 2016). However, the performance was slightly worse and for that reason we decided not to employ them. Words out of the embeddings are conserved, albeit their weights are randomly initialize and learn from scratch. A single biLSTM layer with a hidden layer size of 128 neurons follows in the architecture and feeds a softmax layer in order to obtain the final prediction. The network parameters are learned by minimizing Cross-Entropy and by backpropagating the error through layers over 5 epochs, with a batch size of 128, using RMSprop optimization algorithm. Moreover, a dropout rate (Srivastava et al., 2014) of 0.5 is used to address overfitting issues. The aforementioned model was implemented in Python using Tensorflow library (Abadi et al., 2015).

Lastly, as introduced in Section 3, we propose a pseudo-relevance feedback scheme as follows: (a) A first instance of the network is trained using the training and development sets; (b) Sub-

---

[1]See: `https://github.com/s/preprocessor`

[2]See: `https://code.google.com/archive/p/word2vec/`

Emotion	I	you	shehe	adverb	posemo	insight	cause	focuspresent	focusfuture	swear
Anger	7.43	2.21	**2.24**	8.53	2.65	1.9	**3.55**	14.78	1.08	0.85
Disgust	6.63	2.33	1.58	8.98	2.7	**2.54**	2.8	15.15	0.73	**1.08**
Fear	**9.36**	2.64	1.82	7.1	2.69	2.03	2.68	15.95	**2.95**	0.49
Joy	9.11	**3.4**	1.69	**9.54**	**4.58**	1.78	2.94	15.59	1.43	0.47
Sadness	7.35	2.56	1.38	8.85	3.35	2.18	2.95	**16.37**	1.49	0.54
Surprise	7.13	1.95	1.96	8.56	3.1	2.09	2.94	13.18	0.89	0.58

Table 1: LIWC selected categories for the six emotions. The values represent percentages over total words.

sequently, the k percentage of the tweets with the highest class probability is extracted with the corresponding labels to create a new set examples; (c) Finally, the training and development sets along with the new examples are used to re-train the model from scratch and obtain the final predictions. It should be noted that the same hyperparameters are employed at both training and re-training steps.

5 Results and Discussion

Overall, we observe that the effectiveness obtained on the test set by the proposed approach is not as satisfactory as expected (see Table 2). As can be noticed the performance diminishes as the relevance set used to re-trained the network increases in size. One of the reason could be that even though the majority of the new examples are accurately classified the remaining ones correspond to misclassification errors. Consequently, this might introduce certain noise and affect the performance of the model. One possible way to overcome this issue could be to define a threshold and select the cases whose class probability exceeds this limit, instead of just taking the k percentage with the highest chance of being correctly classified. Another reason, could reside in the fact that different training parameters, like the number of epochs, should be again optimized given that the size and content of the new training data has changed.

In addition to the previously mentioned pseudo-relevance feedback schema, we also explore the use of the information provided by a tool known as Linguistic Inquiry and Word Count (LIWC) (Pennebaker et al.). This software is equipped with a series of dictionaries which allows to obtain different psychometric properties that may arise from language use. More specifically, it was developed by psychologists with focus on studying the various emotional, cognitive, and structural components present in individuals' verbal and written speech samples. Interesting findings arose after analyzing the training set with this tool. In particular, the selected categories showed noticeable differences between the tweets expressing different emotions (See Table 1). For instance, the use of the word I in the tweets expressing fear, which could correlate with the fact that individuals tend to refer more to themselves when they expressed the perceived danger, threat or even concerns, or the high use of she/he pronouns and causation words (because, hence, thus) when conveying anger. We attempted to incorporate this information to our model by repeating the words in the tweets that were included in a set of selected dictionaries for each emotion. It is clear that the chosen dictionaries should not overlap so as to emphasize the differences among the emotions. Nonetheless, only in the training (and development) set the labels are known in advance, and consequently only these instances can be expanded in this way. The results obtained by following with this approach were not promising and for that reason, we decided to expand the tweets using the dictionaries disregarding of the emotion. Given that the improvement was almost marginal we decided not to include the results in the paper.

k%	%Correct	MacAvg
10	63.72	0.60
20	64.08	0.59
30	64.22	0.58
40	64.35	0.57
50	64.13	0.58

Table 2: Pseudo-relevance feedback schema results on the test set

6 Conclusions

In this work, we introduced a relevance feedback schema employing a sequential model (biLSTM) in order to predict the class of a certain emotion that has been removed from a tweet. Despite the fact that the performance did not improve as expected, we consider that the method still needs further improvement. For instance, by employing a probability threshold to create a more accurate expansion set. Furthermore, we would like to continue exploring different ways to incorporate LIWC's output to the network. Promising features can be extracted from the presented analysis which might allow to emphasize the differences between the emotions conveyed in the tweets.

References

Martín Abadi, Ashish Agarwal, Paul Barham, Eugene Brevdo, Zhifeng Chen, Craig Citro, Greg S. Corrado, Andy Davis, Jeffrey Dean, Matthieu Devin, Sanjay Ghemawat, Ian Goodfellow, Andrew Harp, Geoffrey Irving, Michael Isard, Yangqing Jia, Rafal Jozefowicz, Lukasz Kaiser, Manjunath Kudlur, Josh Levenberg, Dandelion Mané, Rajat Monga, Sherry Moore, Derek Murray, Chris Olah, Mike Schuster, Jonathon Shlens, Benoit Steiner, Ilya Sutskever, Kunal Talwar, Paul Tucker, Vincent Vanhoucke, Vijay Vasudevan, Fernanda Viégas, Oriol Vinyals, Pete Warden, Martin Wattenberg, Martin Wicke, Yuan Yu, and Xiaoqiang Zheng. 2015. TensorFlow: Large-scale machine learning on heterogeneous systems. Software available from tensorflow.org.

Timothy Baldwin, Marie Catherine de Marneffe, Bo Han, Young-Bum Kim, Alan Ritter, and Wei Xu. 2015. Shared tasks of the 2015 workshop on noisy user-generated text: Twitter lexical normalization and named entity recognition. ACL Association for Computational Linguistics.

Ben Eisner, Tim Rocktäschel, Isabelle Augenstein, Matko Bosnjak, and Sebastian Riedel. 2016. emoji2vec: Learning emoji representations from their description. In *Proceedings of The Fourth International Workshop on Natural Language Processing for Social Media*, pages 48–54. Association for Computational Linguistics.

Katja Filippova, Enrique Alfonseca, Carlos A. Colmenares, Lukasz Kaiser, and Oriol Vinyals. 2015. Sentence compression by deletion with lstms. In *Proceedings of the 2015 Conference on Empirical Methods in Natural Language Processing*, pages 360–368. Association for Computational Linguistics.

Anastasia Giachanou and Fabio Crestani. 2016. Like it or not: A survey of twitter sentiment analysis methods. *ACM Computing Surveys*, 49(2):28.

Fréderic Godin, Baptist Vandersmissen, Wesley De Neve, and Rik Van de Walle. 2015. Multimedia lab @ acl w-nut ner sharedtask: named entity recognition for twitter microposts using distributed word representations. In *ACL 2015 Workshop on Noisy User-generated Text, Proceedings*. Association for Computational Linguistics.

A. Graves, N. Jaitly, and A. r. Mohamed. 2013. Hybrid speech recognition with deep bidirectional lstm. In *2013 IEEE Workshop on Automatic Speech Recognition and Understanding*.

A. Graves and J. Schmidhuber. 2005. Framewise phoneme classification with bidirectional lstm networks. In *Proceedings. 2005 IEEE International Joint Conference on Neural Networks, 2005.*, volume 4, pages 2047–2052 vol. 4.

Roman Klinger, Orphée de Clercq, Saif M. Mohammad, and Alexandra Balahur. 2018. Iest: Wassa-2018 implicit emotions shared task. In *Proceedings of the 9th Workshop on Computational Approaches to Subjectivity, Sentiment and Social Media Analysis*, Brussels, Belgium. Association for Computational Linguistics.

Christopher D. Manning, Prabhakar Raghavan, and Hinrich Schütze. 2008. *Introduction to Information Retrieval*. Cambridge University Press, New York, NY, USA.

Tomas Mikolov, Kai Chen, Greg Corrado, and Jeffrey Dean. 2013. Efficient estimation of word representations in vector space. In *ICLR Worshop*, Scottsdale, AZ, USA.

Tomas Mikolov, Martin Karafit, Luks Burget, Jan Cernock, and Sanjeev Khudanpur. 2010. Recurrent neural network based language model. In *INTERSPEECH*, pages 1045–1048. ISCA.

James W. Pennebaker, Cindy K. Chung, Molly Ireland, Amy Gonzales, and Roger J. Booth. The development and psychometric properties of liwc2015. Technical report, The University of Texas at Austin.

Robert Plutchik. 1980. Emotion: Theory, research, and experience: Vol. 1. theories of emotion. In R. Plutchik and H. Kellerman, editors, *Approaches to Emotion*, pages 3–33. Academic press.

Nitish Srivastava, Geoffrey Hinton, Alex Krizhevsky, Ilya Sutskever, and Ruslan Salakhutdinov. 2014. Dropout: A simple way to prevent neural networks from overfitting. *Journal of Machine Learning Research*, 15:1929–1958.

EmotiKLUE at IEST 2018: Topic-Informed Classification of Implicit Emotions

Thomas Proisl, Philipp Heinrich, Besim Kabashi, Stefan Evert

Friedrich-Alexander-Universität Erlangen-Nürnberg

Lehrstuhl für Korpus- und Computerlinguistik

Bismarckstr. 6, 91054 Erlangen, Germany

{thomas.proisl,philipp.heinrich,besim.kabashi,stefan.evert}@fau.de

Abstract

EmotiKLUE is a submission to the Implicit Emotion Shared Task. It is a deep learning system that combines independent representations of the left and right contexts of the emotion word with the topic distribution of an LDA topic model. EmotiKLUE achieves a macro average F_1 score of 67.13%, significantly outperforming the baseline produced by a simple ML classifier. Further enhancements after the evaluation period lead to an improved F_1 score of 68.10%.

1 Introduction

The aim of the Implicit Emotion Shared Task (IEST; Klinger et al., 2018) is to infer emotion from the context of emotion words. The working definition of emotion for the shared task implies that emotion is triggered by the interpretation of a stimulus event (Scherer, 2005, 697), i. e. the cause of the emotion. Consequently, the data for the shared task have been compiled with the aim of including a description of the cause of the emotion. This has been accomplished by using distant supervision: The organizers collected tweets that contain exactly one of 21 emotion words belonging to six emotions (anger, fear, disgust, joy, sadness, surprise), where the emotion word has to be followed by *that*, *because* or *when* as likely indicators for a description of the cause of the emotion. The corpus collected this way comprises more than 190.000 tweets and is split into three data sets: 80% training, 5% trial and 15% test. The emotion words in the tweets are masked and participants of the shared task have to predict the emotion of the masked emotion word from its context.

EmotiKLUE, our submission to the shared task, is a deep learning system that learns independent representations of the left and right contexts of the emotion word, similar to Saeidi et al. (2016), who use n-gram representations for both the right and the left context around triggerwords in aspect-based opinion mining. Our intuition is that the distribution of the emotions is dependent on the topics of the tweets, therefore we train a Twitter-specific LDA topic model and explore different ways of combining the topic distributions with the left and right contexts in order to predict the emotions. EmotiKLUE is available on GitHub.[1]

2 Related Work

Emotion detection has been an important topic in natural language processing, particularly in the subfield of opinion mining, for several years. The shallowest approaches deal with sentiment polarity detection, either classifying utterances into categories ranging from *negative* via *neutral* to *positive*, or regressing towards a score typically ranging from -1 to 1 (see, for example, Proisl et al., 2013; Evert et al., 2014). Further tasks involve the automatic computation of stances (*in favor of* vs. *against*) towards pre-specified topics (Mohammad et al., 2017). Predicting more sophisticated categories of emotion than in the task at hand has been a more recent phenomenon. Generally, the approaches can be classified into two groups, namely rule-based approaches on the one hand and the far more common machine learning approaches on the other.

We give a short list of related work here, for a more comprehensive listing see the task description (Klinger et al., 2018). A survey of emotion detection from text and speech is given by Sailunaz et al. (2018). For a linguistic analysis of implicit emotions see Lee (2015). An approach to implicit emotion detection based on textual inference is presented by Ren et al. (2017).

---

[1] https://github.com/tsproisl/EmotiKLUE

Proceedings of the 9th Workshop on Computational Approaches to Subjectivity, Sentiment and Social Media Analysis, pages 235–242

Brussels, Belgium, October 31, 2018. ©2018 Association for Computational Linguistics

https://doi.org/10.18653/v1/P17

As an example for rule-based emotion detection we mention Udochukwu and He (2015), who use a pipeline approach based on the OCC-Model (Ortony et al., 1988), without emotion-bearing words.

More recent work deals with ML and deep learning approaches. Rout et al. (2018) use both unsupervised and supervised approaches with different machine learning algorithms such as multinomial naive bayes, maximum entropy, and support vector machines on unigram feature matrices and report F_1-scores of above 99% when disambiguating tweets according to seven emotion categories. However, since their text data are selected via a keyword-filter containing exactly the words representing the emotion which in turn can be used as features by the machine learner at hand, their high accuracy values are unsurprising.

Other tasks, such as detecting the emotion *stimulus* in emotion-bearing sentences are more challenging; Ghazi et al. (2015) e. g. use a conditional random fields classifier and report F_1-scores of up to 60% for finding the stimulus in their self-constructed data set. Finally, Firdaus et al. (2018) use different latent features such as emotion and sentiment as input to predict user behaviour (e. g. the act of *retweeting*).

3 System Description

3.1 Data Preprocessing and Additional Data

The data sets released by the organizers of the shared task contain the full text of the tweets, with the emotion word, usernames and URLs being substituted by placeholders. We tokenize the text with the web and social media tokenizer SoMaJo[2] (Proisl and Uhrig, 2016) and convert it to lowercase.

In addition to the official data sets, we use two resources: ENCOW14[3] (Schäfer and Bildhauer, 2012; Schäfer, 2015) and an in-house collection of 114 million deduplicated English tweets (see Schäfer et al. (2017) for the deduplication algorithm), collected between February 2017 and June 2018.[4] We tokenize the tweets with SoMaJo (but not ENCOW14, which is already tokenized), mask

usernames and URLs and convert the text to lowercase.

3.2 Representations derived through unsupervised methods

We use our in-house collection of tweets to create Twitter-specific word embeddings and topic models.

Using the Gensim[5] (Řehůřek and Sojka, 2010) implementation of word2vec (Mikolov et al., 2013a,b), we create four sets of embeddings for all words with a minimum frequency of 5: 100- and 300-dimensional vectors using the skip-gram approach and 100- and 300-dimensional vectors using the CBOW approach.

Our intuition is that the distribution of the emotion words depends on the topics of the tweets. To capture these topics, we use Gensim and create an LDA topic model (Blei et al., 2003) with 100 topics based on the most recent 10 million tweets in our collection (ignoring words that only occur once).

3.3 Additional Data for Pretraining

We compile an additional data set from EN-COW14 and our collection of tweets that we use to pretrain our model. To this end, we select tweets and ENCOW14 sentences with a maximum length of 110 words that contain a single emotion word from the following set of emotion words: *afraid*, *angry*, *disgusted*, *disgusting*, *happy*, *sad*, *surprised*, *surprising*. This list of emotion words was determined by a cursory glance at the official training data and happens to be a subset of the 21 emotion words used by the task organizers (which were only revealed after the evaluation period). Note that we do not restrict the contexts in which the emotion words occur, i. e. the emotion words do not have to be followed by *that*, *because* or *when*. After balancing the data, we have approximately 159.000 items per class.

3.4 Network Architecture

We experiment with three variants of a neural network architecture implemented using Keras[6] (Chollet et al., 2015) and visualized in Figure 1.

The word-level representations for the left and right contexts of the emotion word that are returned by the embedding layers are fed into

---

[2]https://github.com/tsproisl/SoMaJo
[3]http://corporafromtheweb.org/encow14
[4]The overlap of the released data sets with our in-house collection of tweets is negligible. Our collection contains less than 0.6% of the tweets from the released data sets: 775 from the training set (0.51%), 49 from the trial set (0.51%) and 163 from the test set (0.57%).

[5]https://radimrehurek.com/gensim
[6]https://keras.io

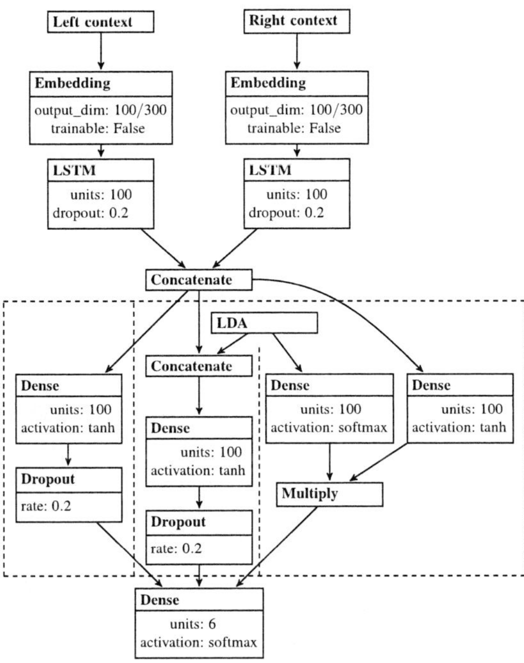

Figure 1: Architecture of the three model variants

model	trial	test
train-skip100-nolda	64.06	65.14
train-skip100-ldafeat	64.46	65.10
train-skip100-ldafilt	64.56	65.03
train-skip300-nolda	65.93	66.33
train-skip300-ldafeat	66.05	66.35
train-skip300-ldafilt	65.18	65.79
add-skip100-nolda	52.01	52.12
add-skip100-ldafeat	52.49	52.84
add-skip100-ldafilt	51.29	51.88
add-skip300-nolda	55.28	55.49
add-skip300-ldafeat	55.22	55.11
add-skip300-ldafilt	52.76	52.68
add+train-skip100-nolda	65.19	66.55
add+train-skip100-ldafeat	65.71	66.02
add+train-skip100-ldafilt	65.67	65.94
add+train-skip300-nolda	67.05	**67.50**
add+train-skip300-ldafeat	**67.17**	67.08
add+train-skip300-ldafilt	66.43	67.00
add+train+trial-skip300-ldafeat (subm.)		67.13

Table 1: Results for models using skip-gram-based embeddings (macro F_1)

two unidirectional LSTM layers (Hochreiter and Schmidhuber, 1997; Gers et al., 2000): A left-to-right layer for the left context from the beginning of the tweet to the masked emotion word, and a right-to-left layer for the right context from the end of the tweet to the masked emotion word. The hidden states of the two LSTM layers are concatenated. Now, we explore three variants of incorporating the 100-dimensional LDA topic distribution into the model:

1. We do not use LDA topics. The output of the LSTMs is fed to a dense layer, followed by a dropout layer and finally a softmax output layer.

2. We use LDA topics as features alongside the LSTM output. The LDA topic distribution and the output of the LSTMs are concatenated. The result is fed to a dense layer, followed by a dropout layer and finally a softmax output layer.

3. We use LDA topics as filter. The output of the LSTMs is fed to a dense layer to reduce dimensionality. The LDA topic distribution is fed to a softmax layer. The output of the two layers is combined using element-wise multiplication. The result is fed to the final softmax output layer.

We train each model for a maximum of 20 epochs with a batch size of 160, using the Adam optimizer (Kingma and Ba, 2014) to minimize categorical crossentropy. If the validation loss (determined on the trial data) fails to improve for two consecutive epochs, training stops early.

4 Results and Error Analysis

4.1 Experiments

We have three different network architectures that differ in the way they use LDA topic distributions. We have four sets of embeddings that differ in size and training objective. And we have three options for the training data (only the official training data, only our additional data, or training on the latter and retraining on the former). In order to quantify the impact of the individual choices, we train and evaluate all 36 possible models. Results for models using skip-gram-based embeddings are shown in Table 1 and results for models using CBOW-based embeddings in Table 2. The evaluation metric used is the macro average of the F_1 scores of the six classes.

The exact numbers listed in Tables 1 and 2 should not be taken too seriously as they are subject to some small amount of random variation due

model	trial	test
train-cbow100-nolda	63.75	64.07
train-cbow100-ldafeat	62.81	63.20
train-cbow100-ldafilt	63.39	63.24
train-cbow300-nolda	64.09	63.91
train-cbow300-ldafeat	64.00	63.94
train-cbow300-ldafilt	63.61	63.49
add-cbow100-nolda	49.64	50.14
add-cbow100-ldafeat	48.16	48.55
add-cbow100-ldafilt	48.69	48.81
add-cbow300-nolda	51.26	50.70
add-cbow300-ldafeat	51.25	51.48
add-cbow300-ldafilt	49.31	49.01
add+train-cbow100-nolda	63.10	64.03
add+train-cbow100-ldafeat	64.46	64.08
add+train-cbow100-ldafilt	63.42	63.60
add+train-cbow300-nolda	64.34	64.74
add+train-cbow300-ldafeat	64.26	64.66
add+train-cbow300-ldafilt	63.83	63.64

Table 2: Results for models using CBOW-based word embeddings (macro F_1)

to differences in the initialization of the weights and the shuffling of the training data.[7] However, since all the individual options have been used at least nine times, we can still make some fairly reliable claims about their usefulness.

The most obvious observation is that the official training data lead to much better results than our additional data (+12.97 on average). This is probably due to two reasons: We only use a subset of the emotion words that have been used in the official data sets and, more importantly, we use all instances of the emotion words and not only those that are followed by something that is likely to be a description of the cause of the emotion. However, first training the model on the additional data and then retraining it on the official training data is benefitial (+1.96).

We can also see that word embeddings based on the skip-gram approach consistently outperform those based on the CBOW approach (+2.55). 300-dimensional embeddings are notably better than 100-dimensional embeddings (+1.19), an effect that is more pronounced for the skip-gram-based embeddings (+1.57) than for the CBOW-based ones (+0.80).

The LDA topic distributions only have a positive effect when used as additional features alongside the LSTM output – and even then the effect is small and only positive for models using skip-gram-based embeddings (+0.08) and negative for models using CBOW-based embeddings (−0.24). Using the LDA topic distribution as a filter usually has a negative effect (−0.76).

Consequently, for our submission to the shared task, we chose the second network architecture (LDA topic distribution as feature), used 300-dimensional skip-gram embeddings and trained the model first on our additional data and retrained it on the official training and trial data. That model achieved a macro average F_1 score of 67.13 on the test data and took the tenth place in the shared task. For comparison, Klinger et al. (2018) report that human performance on this task is approximately 45%, the MaxEnt uni- and bigram classifier used as a baseline system achieved 59.88% and the best submission (Rozental et al., 2018) 71.45%.

4.2 Error Analysis

We present detailed error analyses in Table 3 in form of an extensive confusion matrix including label confusion per triggerword in the test data. We downloaded all available tweets used in the shared task via the Twitter API[8] to gain access to the actual triggerwords. For reasons of interpretability we report absolute marginal frequencies and relative frequencies of predicted label per real label and triggerword.[9] This corresponds to recall (true-positive-rate) for those cases where the prediction equals the true label and false-negative-rate (FNR) per class for all other cases.

Recall is rather similar across labels: The highest rate can be achieved for *joy* (78%), the lowest is achieved for *sad* (59%). High FNRs have to be reported for confusing *anger*, *disgust*, and *fear* with *surprise* (11% and 10%), as well as *sad* with *anger* and *disgust* (each 11%).

Looking at the recall values per triggerword, explanations for the macro-values are not far to seek:

1. Performance is generally higher for those triggerwords that have been manually se-

---

[7]The 95%-confidence interval for the performance of the add+train-skip300-ldafeat model on the test data is 67.12 ± 0.34, for example (estimated from 20 instances of the model).

[9]The difference in absolute numbers between label-based confusions and triggerword-based confusions are due to the fact that not all tweets can be retrieved from the API – once a tweet is e. g. deleted by a user, it is no longer accessible for others either.

	anger	disgust	fear	joy	sad	surprise	total
anger	**0.61**	0.09	0.08	0.06	0.06	0.11	**4794**
angry	*0.62*	*0.07*	*0.08*	*0.07*	*0.06*	*0.09*	*2893*
furious	*0.57*	*0.11*	*0.06*	*0.04*	*0.05*	*0.18*	*1292*
disgust	0.08	**0.67**	0.04	0.03	0.07	0.11	**4794**
disgusted	*0.14*	*0.53*	*0.06*	*0.05*	*0.03*	*0.19*	*2065*
disgusting	*0.03*	*0.79*	*0.01*	*0.01*	*0.10*	*0.05*	*2398*
fear	0.08	0.04	**0.69**	0.05	0.04	0.10	**4791**
afraid	*0.05*	*0.02*	*0.76*	*0.04*	*0.03*	*0.08*	*1693*
fearful	*0.10*	*0.03*	*0.69*	*0.05*	*0.03*	*0.10*	*315*
frightened	*0.11*	*0.11*	*0.49*	*0.05*	*0.04*	*0.20*	*324*
scared	*0.10*	*0.05*	*0.62*	*0.06*	*0.05*	*0.12*	*1648*
joy	0.06	0.02	0.04	**0.78**	0.04	0.06	**5246**
cheerful	*0.09*	*0.05*	*0.05*	*0.64*	*0.07*	*0.09*	*56*
happy	*0.06*	*0.02*	*0.04*	*0.79*	*0.04*	*0.06*	*4215*
joyful	*0.05*	*0.04*	*0.08*	*0.61*	*0.09*	*0.12*	*97*
sad	0.11	0.11	0.06	0.07	**0.59**	0.06	**4340**
depressed	*0.21*	*0.08*	*0.09*	*0.10*	*0.46*	*0.06*	*642*
sad	*0.09*	*0.12*	*0.05*	*0.06*	*0.62*	*0.06*	*2751*
sorrowful	*0.00*	*0.12*	*0.00*	*0.50*	*0.25*	*0.12*	*8*
surprise	0.08	0.09	0.07	0.05	0.03	**0.68**	**4792**
astonished	*0.08*	*0.13*	*0.07*	*0.04*	*0.01*	*0.66*	*350*
astounded	*0.07*	*0.17*	*0.09*	*0.03*	*0.01*	*0.63*	*263*
shocked	*0.12*	*0.06*	*0.08*	*0.06*	*0.03*	*0.65*	*1021*
startled	*0.10*	*0.06*	*0.22*	*0.04*	*0.01*	*0.57*	*228*
stunned	*0.12*	*0.10*	*0.08*	*0.07*	*0.01*	*0.62*	*500*
surprised	*0.07*	*0.05*	*0.06*	*0.06*	*0.01*	*0.74*	*1223*
surprising	*0.02*	*0.11*	*0.01*	*0.01*	*0.12*	*0.74*	*805*
total	**4841**	**4801**	**4633**	**5305**	**3732**	**5445**	**28757**

Table 3: Confusion Matrix for the six predicted emotion categories (columns) for each real emotion and each triggerword (rows) in the test data

lected by us for producing additional training data (see Section 3.3): *angry* (62%) shows higher recall than *furious* (57%), *afraid* (76%) and *happy* (79%) perform best in the *fear* and *joy* categories, respectively, and *surprised* and *surprising* (each 74%) are the best predictors for *surprise*.

2. Rare triggerwords generally lead to worse results. The most obvious example is *sorrowful*, which we only observed 28 times in the training data (8 times in the test data) and which yields 25% recall for predicting category *sad*, confusing it in half of the cases with *joy*. Additionally, *cheerful* and *joyful* (361 and 536 observations in the training data, re-

spectively) perform lower than *happy* (22348 observations) – although admittedly *happy* had already been pre-selected for additional training as mentioned above.

3. Many confusions can also be explained from a psycho-linguistic point of view when looking at the actual corpus. Instances involving the triggerword *disgusted* e. g. are frequently categorized as *anger* by our system. Corpus evidence shows that these words are hard to disambiguate:

- Hindu women should be [#TRIGGER-WORD#] when Law Panel says Father-In-Law should pay alimony, what next

model	trial	test
add2-skip300-ldafeat	56.66	56.98
add2+train-skip300-ldafeat	67.34	67.47
300-train-skip300-ldafeat	66.14	66.68
300-add-skip300-ldafeat	57.10	57.29
300-add+train-skip300-ldafeat	67.89	68.06
300-add2-skip300-ldafeat	58.35	58.49
300-add2+train-skip300-ldafeat	67.98	68.10

Table 4: Results for the post-analysis experiments (macro F_1)

women are property of Father-In-Law?

- I wake up [#TRIGGERWORD#] because I know you doin me wrong but u dont think its nothing wrong with being in a verbal relationship with another gal

It is hard to see how one could reliably predict the "real" emotion (*disgust*) in the above examples, since *anger* – as predicted by our system – seems to be an equally sensible guess. Similar instances can be found for other confusions, most notably when predicting *anger* in case of the triggerword *depressed*.

4.3 Post-analysis experiments

The analysis in the previous section has shown that our system performs better on the more frequent words that we used for compiling our additional data than on the less frequent words. Therefore, we recompile our additional data as described in Section 3.3 but for all of the 21 emotion words that occur in the official data. After balancing the data, this results in approximately 163.000 items per class.

We take the model versions from Section 4.1 that are the basis for our submission and replace the additional data with the updated version. The new models (prefixed with "add2" in Table 4) improve on the old ones both when using only the additional data (+1.66) and when retraining on the official training data (+0.28).

It is also worth pointing out that so far we have not fine-tuned the hyperparameters of our model. As a first step in that direction, we try to use more units in the hidden layers and increase the size of all hidden layers to 300 units (models prefixed with "300-add" in Table 4). This boosts the performance both when using only the additional data

(+2.03) and when retraining on the official training data (+0.85).

Combining the recompiled additional data and the larger hidden layers yields further improvements (models prefixed with "300-add2" in Table 4). The retrained model is approximately 1 point better than our submission and would have taken the eighth place in the shared task.

A further error analysis shows that the additional training data indeed yield the desired effect: Recall for category *angry* improves from 61% to 66%, largely due to better recall in the case of the triggerword *furious* (rising from 57% to 65%). Further improvements can be found in almost all categories, namely for *fear* (69% to 72%, especially *frightened*: 49% to 53%), *joy* (78% to 79%, with recall for *joyful* rising from 61% to 65% and for *cheerful* from 64% to 70%), and *sad* (59% to 62%, triggerword *depressed* up two points from 46% to 48%). However, the additional training data had an adverse effect on category *surprise*; here recall falls from 68% to 65%, with almost all triggerwords dropping a couple of points, the worst being *surprised*, falling from 74% to 69%.

Finally, we want to take a closer look at the contribution of the LDA topic distribution. To this end, we have trained 20 instances of the 300-add2+train-skip300-ldafeat and 300-add2+train-skip300-nolda models and have calculated the means and 95%-confidence intervals. As it turns out, both model variants perform identically on the trial data. On the test data, there are some minor differences but the performance means lie within one standard deviation of each other. This means that our choice of concatenating the LDA topic distribution of the tweet to the LSTM does not have a statistically significant result..

5 Conclusion

We presented EmotiKLUE, a topic-informed deep learning system for detecting implicit emotion. Our experiments showed that for this task skip-gram-based word embeddings outperform CBOW-based embeddings. Additional data, that – on their own – yield rather poor results, improve the performance when used for pretraining the model. LDA topic models, that we initially believed to have a small positive effect, turned out to not contribute significantly.

The error analysis shows that the objective as set in the shared task at hand is rather difficult: With many instances of tweets showing prima facie ambiguous emotions, it is unsurprising that even perfectly trained classifiers will not be able to achieve 100% accuracy when using the textual data alone.

Future work could nonetheless involve more experimentation with the hyperparameters of the network, e. g. number, size and activation of the hidden layers, choice of regularization strategy and optimizer, etc.

The software is available on GitHub.[10]

References

David M. Blei, Andrew Y. Ng, and Michael I. Jordan. 2003. Latent dirichlet allocation. *Journal of Machine Learning Research*, 3:993–1022.

François Chollet et al. 2015. Keras. `https://keras.io`.

Stefan Evert, Thomas Proisl, Paul Greiner, and Besim Kabashi. 2014. SentiKLUE: Updating a polarity classifier in 48 hours. In *Proceedings of the 8th International Workshop on Semantic Evaluation (SemEval 2014)*, pages 551–555, Dublin. Association for Computational Linguistics.

Syeda Nadia Firdaus, Chen Ding, and Alireza Sadeghian. 2018. Topic specific emotion detection for retweet prediction. *International Journal of Machine Learning and Cybernetics*, pages 197–203.

Felix A. Gers, Jürgen Schmidhuber, and Fred A. Cummins. 2000. Learning to forget: Continual prediction with LSTM. *Neural Computation*, 12(10):2451–2471.

Diman Ghazi, Diana Inkpen, and Stan Szpakowicz. 2015. Detecting emotion stimuli in emotion-bearing sentences. In *Computational Linguistics and Intelligent Text Processing. CICLing 2015*, pages 152–165.

Sepp Hochreiter and Jürgen Schmidhuber. 1997. Long short-term memory. *Neural Computation*, 9(8):1735–1780.

Diederik P. Kingma and Jimmy Ba. 2014. Adam: A method for stochastic optimization. *CoRR*, abs/1412.6980.

Roman Klinger, Orphée de Clercq, Saif M. Mohammad, and Alexandra Balahur. 2018. IEST: WASSA-2018 Implicit Emotions Shared Task. In *Proceedings of the 9th Workshop on Computational Approaches to Subjectivity, Sentiment and Social Media Analysis*, Brussels. ACL.

Sophia Yat Mei Lee. 2015. A linguistic analysis of implicit emotions. In *Chinese Lexical Semantics - 16th Workshop, CLSW 2015, Beijing, China, May 9-11, 2015, Revised Selected Papers*, pages 185–194.

Tomas Mikolov, Kai Chen, Greg Corrado, and Jeffrey Dean. 2013a. Efficient estimation of word representations in vector space. *CoRR*, abs/1301.3781.

Tomas Mikolov, Ilya Sutskever, Kai Chen, Gregory S. Corrado, and Jeffrey Dean. 2013b. Distributed representations of words and phrases and their compositionality. In *Advances in Neural Information Processing Systems 26: 27th Annual Conference on Neural Information Processing Systems 2013. Proceedings of a meeting held December 5-8, 2013, Lake Tahoe, Nevada, United States.*, pages 3111–3119.

Saif M. Mohammad, Parinaz Sobhani, and Svetlana Kiritchenko. 2017. Stance and sentiment in tweets. *Special Section of the ACM Transactions on Internet Technology on Argumentation in Social Media*, 17(3).

A. Ortony, G. Clore, and A. Collins. 1988. *Cognitive Structure of Emotions*. Cambridge University Press.

Thomas Proisl, Paul Greiner, Stefan Evert, and Besim Kabashi. 2013. KLUE: Simple and robust methods for polarity classification. In *Proceedings of the 7th International Workshop on Semantic Evaluation (SemEval 2013)*, pages 395–401, Atlanta, GA. Association for Computational Linguistics.

Thomas Proisl and Peter Uhrig. 2016. SoMaJo: State-of-the-art tokenization for German web and social media texts. In *Proceedings of the 10th Web as Corpus Workshop (WAC-X) and the EmpiriST Shared Task*, pages 57–62, Berlin. ACL.

Han Ren, Yafeng Ren, Xia Li, Wenhe Feng, and Maofu Liu. 2017. Natural logic inference for emotion detection. In *Proceedings of CCL 2017 and NLP-NABD 2017*, pages 424–436.

Jitendra Kumar Rout, Kim-Kwang Raymond Choo, Amiya Kumar Dash, Sambit Bakshi, Sanjay Kumar Jena, and Karen L. Williams. 2018. A model for sentiment and emotion analysis of unstructured social media text. *Electronic Commerce Research*, 18(1):181–199.

Alon Rozental, Daniel Fleischer, and Zohar Kelrich. 2018. Amobee at IEST 2018: Transfer learning from language models. In *Proceedings of the 9th Workshop on Computational Approaches to Subjectivity, Sentiment and Social Media Analysis*, Brussels. ACL.

Marzieh Saeidi, Guillaume Bouchard, Maria Liakata, and Sebastian Riedel. 2016. Sentihood: Targeted aspect based sentiment analysis dataset for urban neighbourhoods. In *Proceedings of COLING 2016, the 26th International Conference on Computational Linguistics: Technical Papers*, pages 1546–1556, Osaka, Japan. The COLING 2016 Organizing Committee.

[10]`https://github.com/tsproisl/EmotiKLUE`

Kashfia Sailunaz, Manmeet Dhaliwal, Jon Rokne, and Reda Alhajj. 2018. Emotion detection from text and speech: a survey. *Social Network Analysis and Mining*, 8(1):28:1–28:26.

Klaus R. Scherer. 2005. What are emotions? And how can they be measured? *Social Science Information*, 44(4):695–729.

Fabian Schäfer, Stefan Evert, and Philipp Heinrich. 2017. Japan's 2014 General Election: Political Bots, Right-Wing Internet Activism and PM Abe Shinzō's Hidden Nationalist Agenda. *Big Data*, 5(4):294–309.

Roland Schäfer. 2015. Processing and querying large web corpora with the COW14 architecture. In *Proceedings of Challenges in the Management of Large Corpora 3 (CMLC-3)*, pages 28–34, Lancaster. UCREL, IDS.

Roland Schäfer and Felix Bildhauer. 2012. Building large corpora from the web using a new efficient tool chain. In *Proceedings of the Eighth International Conference on Language Resources and Evaluation (LREC 2012)*, pages 486–493, Istanbul. ELRA.

Orizu Udochukwu and Yulan He. 2015. A rule-based approach to implicit emotion detection in text. In *Proceedings of NLDB 2015*, pages 197–203.

Radim Řehůřek and Petr Sojka. 2010. Software framework for topic modelling with large corpora. In *Proceedings of the LREC 2010 Workshop on New Challenges for NLP Frameworks*, pages 46–50, Valletta. ELRA.

BrainT at IEST 2018: Fine-tuning Multiclass Perceptron For Implicit Emotion Classification

Vachagan Gratian
Universität Stuttgart
vgratian@utopianlab.am

Marina Haid
Universität Stuttgart
haidmarina@gmail.com

Abstract

We present *BrainT*, a multi-class, averaged perceptron tested on implicit emotion prediction of tweets. We show that the dataset is linearly separable and explore ways in fine-tuning the baseline classifier. Our results indicate that the bag-of-words features benefit the model moderately and prediction can be improved with bigrams, trigrams, *skip-one-* tetragrams and POS-tags. Furthermore, we find preprocessing of the n-grams, including stemming, lowercasing, stopword filtering, emoji and emoticon conversion generally not useful. The model is trained on an annotated corpus of 153,383 tweets and predictions on the test data were submitted to the WASSA-2018 Implicit Emotion Shared Task. BrainT[1] attained a Macro F-score of 0.63.

1 Introduction

Our task is to predict emotions of tweets in a dataset where words explicitly mentioning the emotion are masked (Figure 1 and 2). Following the definition of Ekman (1992), there are six "basic" emotions, these tweets have the labels joy, fear, surprise, disgust, anger or sadness. As the model has no access to the *explicit* emotion word, it has to detect it from its *implicit* context, i.e. the situational or causal description of the event. This aspect of the task makes it comparable to centre word prediction from context words.

Twitter language distinguishes itself by a heterogeneous variety of internet vernaculars, abundance of abbreviations, emojis, hashtags and deviation from conventional spelling, grammar, syntax and lexicon. This makes recognition of emotions intricate even for human readers as evident from the noticeably low inter-annotator agreement reported by Balabantaray et al. (2012) or the

---

09.08.17, 02:45

Figure 1: Example of a tweet expressing *joy*.

Figure 2: The tweet in the dataset: the gold label (left) and the tweet text (right) where the emotion word is masked.

"testing" of the IEST dataset on English native-speakers which resulted in an F-score of 0.45 (Klinger et al., 2018).

2 Related Work

Previous research on sentiment analysis and emotion analysis of Twitter data often disagrees on the benefits or disadvantages of the various approaches, algorithms and feature models.

In Psomakelis et al. (2014) linear and multi-layer classifiers are evaluated on sentiment analysis of tweets and is found that learning-based approaches outperform lexicon-based approaches explaining this chiefly by the lack of contextual information that lexical entries (such as polarity scores) express in the unigram model. Kouloumpis et al. (2011) found a mixed feature set of unigrams and n-grams beneficial for sentiment analysis, but found that adding POS-tags to the feature set drops the model's performance and questioned its usefulness specifically on Twitter data. Aston et al. (2014) observe that the voted perceptron performs quite well using only character n-grams and propose a feature-reduction method that dramatically decreases runtime with-

---

[1] Source code is publicly available at:
https://github.com/ims-teamlab2018/
BrainT

Proceedings of the 9th Workshop on Computational Approaches to Subjectivity, Sentiment and Social Media Analysis, pages 243–247
Brussels, Belgium, October 31, 2018. ©2018 Association for Computational Linguistics
https://doi.org/10.18653/v1/P17

out compromising performance. Conversely, Balabantaray et al. (2012) evaluate a "greedy" feature model, including n-grams, POS-tags, bigram POS-tags, dependency tags, affection labels etc. Interestingly, the authors of this paper add a seventh class, *no emotion* to the six basic emotion classes and find that the multi-class SVM attains a high accuracy score with a panoramic feature model.

3 Methods

3.1 Multi-class Perceptron

We design our model following the "one-against-all" approach described in Allwein et al. (2001) by reducing the multi-class prediction task into $k = 6$ binary classification problems. We add weight vectors for each emotion class ($w^{joy}, w^{fear}, ...$). Prediction is made by assigning each tweet vector x_i the label that gets the highest confidence:

$$\hat{y} = argmax\, w^y \cdot x$$

$$y \in \{sad, joy, disgust, fear, surprise, anger\}$$

For each incorrect prediction, the model is updated by adding the tweet vector x_i to the true label's weights y_i and subtracting it from all the other weights:

$$if\ \hat{y} \neq y_i :$$

$$w^y \leftarrow w^y + x_i$$

$$w^{\hat{y}} \leftarrow w^{\hat{y}} - x_i$$

After our first experiments we upgraded our model to the averaged perceptron as defined in Collins (2002) and as discussed in Kazama and Torisawa (2007). Doing so, we set the final weights to be the average of all updated weights during training. Additionally, we randomize the order of tweets before each training epoch to reduce overfitting.

3.2 Features

Our feature set consists of unigrams, bigrams, trigrams and what we call *skip-one*-tetragrams. We use a combination of n-grams as our feature set and optionally add POS-tags.

The unigrams are modified depending on the selected preprocessing mode. This can be either *reductive* (surface word is reduced to its stem or lowercased, stop words and punctuation are removed, emojis and emoticons are replaced by labels, numbers are replaced by $\langle NUM \rangle$ tag) or *additive* in which case stems, labels and tags are added to the feature set alongside the surface form. Bigrams and trigrams are added to the feature set as they are. Tetragrams are duplicated and respectively the second and the third tokens[2] are replaced with $\langle SKIP \rangle$. We expect that this will generalize phrases that only differ in one token. E.g., "he loves red apples" with *skip-one* is "he loves $\langle SKIP \rangle$ apples" and will match with "he loves green apples" in another tweet.

We calculate the feature values using one of the following measures: binary (0 or 1), count, frequency or tf-idf.

4 Experiments

4.1 Dataset

The dataset we use is provided by the WASSA 2018 Implicit Emotion Shared Task[3]. It is a corpus of 153,383 tweets annotated with distant supervision where each tweet originally contained one of the six emotion words (joy, fear, surprise, disgust, anger, sadness) or their synonyms. These words are masked in the dataset, as are usernames and URLs. The dataset is described in detail in Klinger et al. (2018). We use a test set consisting of 28,757 tweets, provided by the IEST as well.

4.2 Preprocessing

We tokenize and normalize tweets using methods that allow for the orthographic anomalies of tweets (e.g., missing space between words and punctuation marks; use of punctuation marks as emoticons). Tokens are labelled by their type (word, punctuation, numerical, emoji, emoticon, hashtag or URL). Depending on our choice between the reductive or additive modes, word tokens are replaced or complemented with stems, all other types by a label or tag. For example, the emoji 😄 and the emoticon :)))) both are replaced or complemented by *laughing*[4]. Numbers like e.g. *1948* are replaced or complemented by $\langle NUM \rangle$.

We also add counts of word classes in the tweet using the NLTK[5] part-of-speech tagger. Option-

---

[2] Doing the same with the first and last tokens would reduce it to a trigram.

[3] Available at: http://implicitemotions.wassa2018.com/data/

[4] We created our own libraries for common emojis and emoticons. For not common emojis we used the Python library *emoji*.

[5] https://www.nltk.org/

Feature vectors	Conv	Macro F
Binary	0.8	**0.382**
Count	0.78	**0.412**
Freq	0.57	**0.436**
TF-IDF	0.79	**0.401**

Table 1: Results of testing the baseline with unigrams. $T = 150$.

ally stopwords and punctuation marks can be removed and tokens can be lowercased.

These preprocessing options are only applied to unigrams, since they would otherwise disturb the word order in n-grams.

4.3 Experimental Setup

We evaluate our model on the test data described in section 4.1. We consider Macro F-score as the evaluation metric and calculate Precision and Recall scores for each emotion class. We run our experiments with learning rates ranging from 0.1 to 0.5, but choose for 0.3 in later experiments as the model seems to converge slightly better in this case. For the initial model we set the number of epochs $T = 150$, but with averaging of the weights, $T = 50$ seems reasonable as the learning curve plateaus already after 30-35 epochs. During each epoch we calculate the accuracy of the predictions on the train data (we refer to this measure as *Convergence* or *Conv*).

Additionally, after each epoch the model is evaluated on the test data whereby the weights are not adjusted so the test data remains unseen. With these two measures we can track how the model adapts to the train data in comparison to its performance on the test data.

4.4 Results

We conduct four groups of experiments in increasing complexity of the feature set.

Group 1. First, we test the "vanilla" perceptron with unigrams and with minimal preprocessing (only tokenization). We try all four vector value calculations, but since frequency attains the highest score, we choose only that one for the next experiments. Results of this group of experiments are shown in table 1.

Group 2. We then update our model to the averaged perceptron and shuffle tweets before each epoch. This raises the F-score from 0.44 to 0.52. Subsequently we evaluate the model with more advanced preprocessing options. Both reductive and additive modes are considered. Results of Group 2

reductive options	Conv	Macro F
none	0.47	**0.519**
replace emoji/emoticon with label	0.47	**0.516**
replace number with tag	0.47	**0.519**
remove stopwords	0.50	**0.481**
remove punctuation	0.48	**0.511**
lowercase	0.46	**0.511**
replace word with stem	0.49	**0.529**
all of the above	0.52	**0.468**

Table 2: Results of *reductive* preprocessing options using unigram frequencies. $T = 50$.

additive options	Conv	Macro F
add emoji/emoticon label	0.50	**0.545**
add number tag	0.50	**0.545**
add covercased token	0.50	**0.546**
add stem	0.49	**0.536**
add stem + emoji/emoticon label	0.49	**0.537**
add stem + emoji/emoticon label + number tag	0.50	**0.546**
all of the above	0.49	**0.537**

Table 3: Results of *additive* preprocessing options using unigram frequencies. $T = 50$.

experiments are included in Tables 2 and 3. Since the impact of these options is either negative or positive but negligible, we choose for no unigram preprocessing options in the next experiments.

Group 3. In Group 3 of the experiments we incrementally add bigrams, trigrams, skip-one-tetragrams and POS-tags to the feature set (Table 5 and Figure 3).

Group 4. Finally, we repeat the experiments of Group 3 non-incrementally. Table 5 shows the results.

4.5 Discussion

We observe a strong improvement of the averaged perceptron with shuffling over the baseline perceptron. Predictions get better as more n-grams are added to the feature set, which is self-evident as they capture more contextual information. The learning curve converges on the training data after trigrams are added, which indicates that the dataset is linearly separable.

As it was found by Saif et al. (2014), we

Feature vectors	Conv	Macro F
Unigram	0.50	**0.546**
Bigram	0.88	**0.607**
Trigram	0.99	**0.616**
Skip-one-Tetragram	1.00	**0.625**
POS-tags	0.99	**0.632**

Table 4: Results of third group of experiments: Feature sets are added incrementally. $T = 50$.

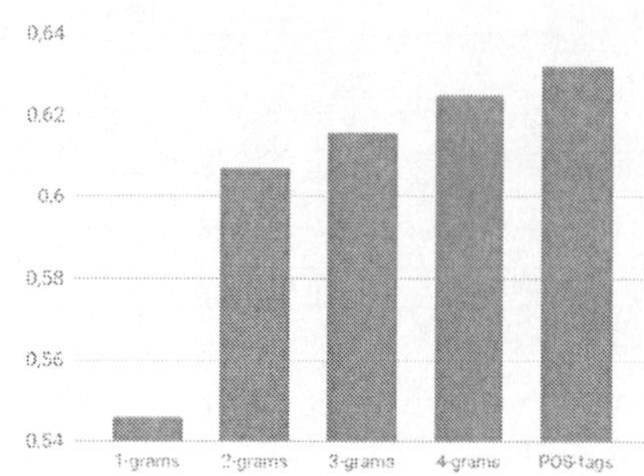

Figure 3: Macro F-scores obtained on different feature sets. Feature sets are added incrementally (i.e. the feature type on the right contains all on its left).

Feature vectors	Conv	**Macro F**
Unigram	0.50	**0.546**
Bigram	0.90	**0.585**
Trigram	0.99	**0.571**
Skip-one-Tetragram	1.00	**0.559**
POS-tags	0.99	**0.301**

Table 5: Group 4 experiments: feature set includes only one n-gram or the POS-tags. $T = 50$.

confirm that classic stopword filtering decreases performance and observe that similarly lowercasing, punctuation removal, stemming and emoji/emoticon conversion have a negative or neutral impact.

5 Future Work

The model and approaches described in this paper can be improved in two directions: enhancing the feature set and addressing the limitations of the multi-class perceptron. In the "one-against-all" model the output of each classifier is treated as a confidence measure, for a more precise prediction this score can be calibrated into probability. As demonstrated in Figure 4, models trained on different feature sets show different strengths and weaknesses in their predictions. This disparities can be exploited by adding "redundant" classifiers for the same emotion class and train them differently. A final prediction can be made based on a simple majority vote or a distance measure between the individual predictions. As described in Garcia Cifuentes (2009), this can improve the models performance. In this scenario, the preprocessing options described in 4.2 could also prove to be helpful.

We would also like to try other multi-class reduction approaches on the same implicit emo-

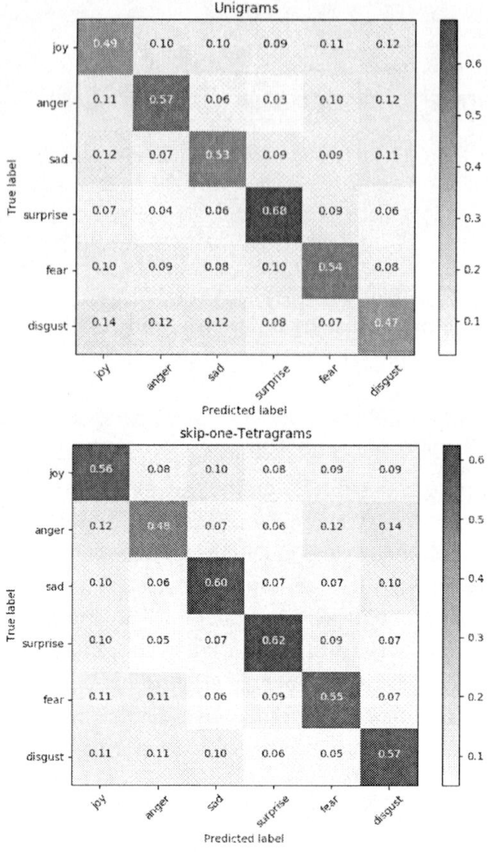

Figure 4: Confusion matrix of two models trained on Unigram and skip-one-Tetragram features.

tion prediction task, such as "all-pairs" or "error-correcting code", both known to perform better than the "one-against-all" approach (Allwein et al., 2001).

6 Conclusion

In this paper we evaluate a multiclass averaged perceptron on implicit emotion detection in tweets. We discuss how different preprocessing options and feature sets affect its performance. In particular, we demonstrate that the bag-of-words model enhanced with bigrams, trigrams, skip-one-tetragrams and POS-tags shows strong improvements over the initial baseline. Conversely, stopword filtering, lowercasing, stemming, emoji and emoticon conversion, proved not to be helpful in our experimental settings.

References

Erin L Allwein, Robert E Schapire, and Yoram Singer. 2001. Reducing multiclass to binary: a unifying approach for margin classifiers. *The Journal of Machine Learning Research*, 1:113–141.

Nathan Aston, Jacob Liddle, and Wei Hu. 2014. Twitter sentiment in data streams with perceptron. *Journal of Computer and Communications*, 2(03):11.

Rakesh C Balabantaray, Mudasir Mohammad, and Nibha Sharma. 2012. Multi-class twitter emotion classification: A new approach. *International Journal of Applied Information Systems*, 4(1):48–53.

Michael Collins. 2002. Discriminative training methods for hidden markov models: Theory and experiments with perceptron algorithms. In *Proceedings of the ACL-02 conference on Empirical methods in natural language processing-Volume 10*, pages 1–8. Association for Computational Linguistics.

Paul Ekman. 1992. An argument for basic emotions. *Cognition & emotion*, 6(3-4):169–200.

Cristina Garcia Cifuentes. 2009. Multi-class classification with machine learning and fusion.

Junichi Kazama and Kentaro Torisawa. 2007. A new perceptron algorithm for sequence labeling with non-local features. In *Proceedings of the 2007 Joint Conference on Empirical Methods in Natural Language Processing and Computational Natural Language Learning (EMNLP-CoNLL)*.

Roman Klinger, Orphée de Clercq, Saif M. Mohammad, and Alexandra Balahur. 2018. Iest: Wassa-2018 implicit emotions shared task. In *Proceedings of the 9th Workshop on Computational Approaches to Subjectivity, Sentiment and Social Media Analysis*, Brussels, Belgium. Association for Computational Linguistics.

Efthymios Kouloumpis, Theresa Wilson, and Johanna D Moore. 2011. Twitter sentiment analysis: The good the bad and the omg! *Icwsm*, 11(538-541):164.

Evangelos Psomakelis, Konstantinos Tserpes, Dimosthenis Anagnostopoulos, and Theodora Varvarigou. 2014. Comparing methods for twitter sentiment analysis. In *Proceedings of the International Joint Conference on Knowledge Discovery, Knowledge Engineering and Knowledge Management-Volume 1*, pages 225–232. SCITEPRESS-Science and Technology Publications, Lda.

Hassan Saif, Miriam Fernández, Yulan He, and Harith Alani. 2014. On stopwords, filtering and data sparsity for sentiment analysis of twitter.

Disney at IEST 2018: Predicting Emotions using an Ensemble

Wojciech Witon[1*]   Pierre Colombo[1*]   Ashutosh Modi[1]   Mubbasir Kapadia[1,2]

[1]Disney Research Los Angeles, [2]Rutgers University

{wojtek.witon, pierre.colombo}@disneyresearch.com
{ashutosh.modi, mubbasir.kapadia}@disneyresearch.com

Abstract

This paper describes our participating system in the WASSA 2018 shared task on emotion prediction. The task focuses on implicit emotion prediction in a tweet. In this task, keywords corresponding to the six emotion labels used (anger, fear, disgust, joy, sad, and surprise) have been removed from the tweet text, making emotion prediction implicit and the task challenging. We propose a model based on an ensemble of classifiers for prediction. Each classifier uses a sequence of Convolutional Neural Network (CNN) architecture blocks and uses ELMo (Embeddings from Language Model) as an input. Our system achieves a 66.2% F1 score on the test set. The best performing system in the shared task has reported a 71.4% F1 score.

1   Introduction

Besides understanding the language humans communicate in, AI systems that naturally interact with humans should also understand implicit emotions in language. To be consistent and meaningful, an AI system conversing with humans should reply while taking into account the emotion of the utterance spoken by the human. If the user appears to be unhappy, a subsequent joyful response from the system would likely detract from the engagement of the user in the conversation. In recent years, several researchers have attempted to address this problem by developing automated emotion prediction for text (Medhat et al., 2014).

Predicting emotions implicit in natural language is not trivial. A naïve attempt to classify text based on emotion keywords may not always work due to the presence of various linguistic phenomena (e.g., negation, ambiguities, etc.) in the text. Moreover, emotion may be triggered by a sequence of words and not just a single keyword, requiring an

automated system to understand the underlying semantics of the text. In the WASSA shared task, keywords describing the emotion label have been removed, making the emotion implicit in the text. This makes the task more challenging.

Typically, a system developed for implicit emotion prediction must understand the meaning of the entire text and not just predict using a few keywords. We propose a model which uses a CNN based architecture (Gehring et al., 2017) for emotion prediction. The model stacks CNN blocks on ELMo (Embeddings from Language Model), as introduced by Peters et al. (2018). Additionally, we include word level Valence, Arousal, and Dominance (VAD) features for guiding our model towards prediction. We describe our model in detail in Section 4. As described in Section 6, our model achieves 66% accuracy on the WASSA task. We further investigate the generalizability of our model by experimenting on the Cornell movie dataset as shown in Section 7.

2   Related Work

Emotion prediction is related to the task of sentiment analysis. The best performance in sentiment analysis has been attained using supervised techniques as outlined in a survey by Medhat et al. (2014). Recent breakthroughs in deep learning have shown strong results in sentence classification (Joulin et al., 2016), language modeling (Dauphin et al., 2016) and sentence embedding (Peters et al., 2018). Our emotion prediction model is also based on deep learning techniques. Recently, fastText (Joulin et al., 2016) has been proposed for generating word representations which have shown state-of-the-art performance on a number of text related tasks. Our model makes use of a fastText model for emotion classification.

---

* indicates equal contribution.

248

Proceedings of the 9th Workshop on Computational Approaches to Subjectivity, Sentiment and Social Media Analysis, pages 248–253
Brussels, Belgium, October 31, 2018. ©2018 Association for Computational Linguistics
https://doi.org/10.18653/v1/P17

Chen et al. (2018) introduce an emotion corpus based on conversations taken from Friends TV scripts and propose a similar emotion classification model using a CNN-BiLSTM. Our model is similar to the model proposed by (Chen et al., 2018), but we use a pre-trained ELMo instead of a BiLSTM.

Mohammad (2018) have proposed a VAD lexicon for emotion detection systems. We use VAD features together with ELMo (Peters et al., 2018). Recently, the ELMo model has been shown to boost performance on a number of Natural Language Processing (NLP) tasks. To the best of our knowledge, we are the first to make use of VAD features in a deep learning setting for emotion prediction.

3 Task Description

The WASSA 2018 shared task[*] (Klinger et al., 2018) is about predicting implicit emotion in a given tweet. The task is challenging because the keyword indicative of the emotion has been removed from the tweet. The participating system is required to predict the implicit emotion based on the remaining context using world knowledge or statistical techniques.

3.1 Emotion Corpus

The corpus provided for the competition has around 188,000 tweets ($\sim$150,000 for training, $\sim$9,000 for validation, $\sim$28,000 for testing) annotated with 6 emotion labels (anger, surprise, joy, sad, fear, disgust). The dataset has a balanced distribution of examples for the six label classes (see Table 1).

Emotion	Train	Val	Test
Joy	27762	1719	5246
Disgust	25541	1595	4794
Surprise	25449	1595	4794
Anger	25439	1592	4792
Fear	24435	1520	4791
Sad	22836	1443	4340
Total	**151462**	**9464**	**28757**

Table 1: Label distribution of the provided corpus.

4 Emotion Prediction Model

Our model has two sets of classifiers at its disposal: an ensemble of CNN-based classifiers and a fastText classifier (Joulin et al., 2016). A CNN-based

[*]http://implicitemotions.wassa2018.com

classifier requires a fixed length input. Since tweets have a variable number of words, padding is typically added to the shorter word sequences in order to have equal lengths across the mini-batch. In practice, having long sequences may not work well due to noise introduced by padding. Based on tweet length distribution (see Figure 1) and our experiments, we set the maximum length of a tweet to 40 words. These tweets were classified using CNN based models. For longer tweets (> 40), we used a fastText classifier. FastText works by averaging word representations into a text representation using bag of words (BoW) and bag of n-grams. The text representation is then fed into a linear classifier with a hierarchical softmax on top. FastText was chosen based on its simplicity and efficiency.

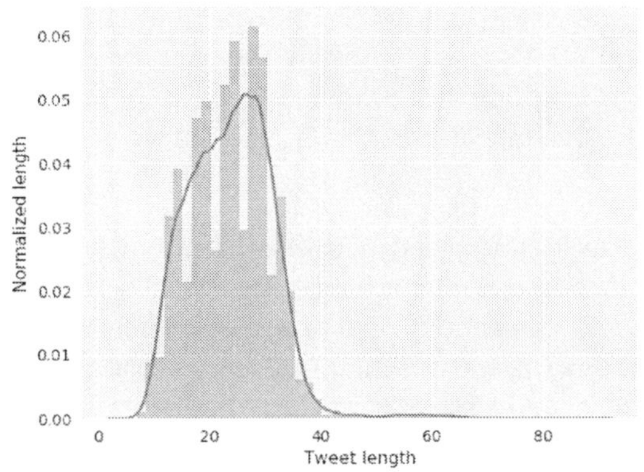

Figure 1: Raw tweet length distribution used for setting a maximum length of input sequence for the classifier.

4.1 Deep CNN Classifier

We use an ensemble of CNN-based classifiers for shorter ($<$ 41 words) tweets. Each of the CNN-based classifiers in the ensemble has a network architecture as shown in Figure 2. The CNN classifier has two sub-modules:

- **Text sub-module**: At the lowest level, this module captures the dependencies between the words of the tweet using a Bi-Directional LSTM model with sub-word information (extracted via character-level CNN) as introduced in ELMo by Peters et al. (2018). The weights of this recurrent network were initialized with values provided by the authors (pre-trained on a 1 billion word benchmark), and updated during training. The next layers of the classifier are CNN blocks (see §4.2).

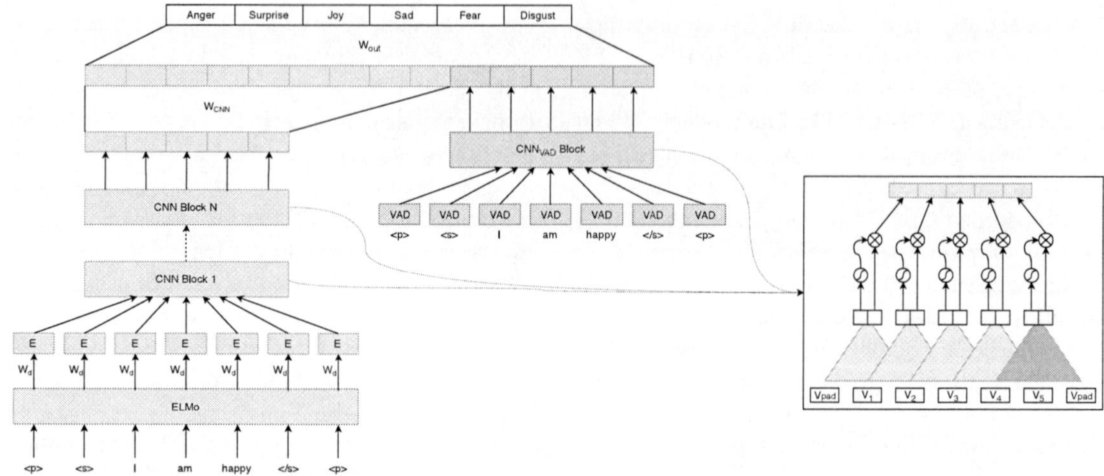

Figure 2: *Left*: the proposed emotion classifier architecture. *Right*: CNN block structure.

- **Emotion sub-module**: In this sub-module, the model uses VAD emotion values (see §4.3), this is followed by a CNN block layer.

Outputs from both networks are mapped to constant size layers, concatenated, mapped to the output (classification) layer of size 6 and normalized using a softmax function. An overview of the system is presented in Figure 2.

4.2 Convolutional Block Structure

We base our network on Convolutional Blocks introduced by Gehring et al. (2017). We make use of a CNN encoder, which consists of several convolutional layers (blocks), followed by Gated Linear Units (GLU) layers introduced by Dauphin et al. (2016), and residual connections. The architecture of the CNN block is presented in Figure 2 (*right*).

Inputs to the first convolutional block are ELMo representations $w = (w_1, ..., w_m)$, mapped to size d, for a given input sequence of length m. Each convolution kernel takes as input $X \in \mathcal{R}^{m \times d}$ and outputs a single element $Y \in \mathcal{R}^{2d}$. This output is then mapped to $Y' \in \mathcal{R}^d$ using GLU. We use m different kernels, which are concatenated to form a final output matrix $Z \in \mathcal{R}^{m \times d}$ that serves later as an input to the next block. The output of the last block is mapped to a one dimensional vector using a linear layer.

4.3 VAD Lexicon

To model the emotions carried by each tweet at a word level we use VAD features extracted from an external lexicon introduced by Mohammad (2018). Each of the 14,000 words in the lexicon is represented by a vector in the VAD space ($v \in [0, 1]^3$) and each sentence is associated with a matrix resulting from concatenation of VAD vectors for words in the sentence ($V \in \mathcal{R}^{m \times 3}$). To label out-of-vocabulary (OOV) words, the closest word in the dictionary is found using a difflib library[†] in python (algorithm based on the Levenshtein distance). If no word with more than 90% of similarity is found, a default VAD value ($v = [0.5, 0.5, 0.5]$) is assigned. At the end of the process, around 50% of words of the training set are labeled with VAD values.

4.4 Classifier Ensemble

The model ensemble consists of a 6-emotion (general) CNN classifier and six binary CNN classifiers (e.g., "happy" vs all other emotions). The final prediction is made by looking for an agreement between binary classifiers − 5 classifiers predict the "negative" class and the other one predicts the "positive" class with a confidence score for the "positive" class that is over a certain threshold T. If the conditions are not met, the tweet is classified using the 6-emotion classifier. The threshold T is tuned based on validation accuracy.

[†]https://docs.python.org/3/library/difflib.html

5   Experiments

In this section, we describe the procedure for training classifiers as part of the Ensemble Classifier. The parameters were tuned based on both validation loss and accuracy.

5.1   Preprocessing

Each tweet in the dataset is first tokenized using the Spacy tokenizer[‡]. Then, each of the 6 most common emojis is mapped into a sequence of ASCII characters (e.g., 😃 is mapped to ":d"). As the last step, the start and end of sentence tokens (<SOS>, <EOS>) are added, together with pad tokens (<PAD>) to match the maximum sequence length.

5.2   Training Procedure

Our Deep emotion classifier is composed of 2 CNN blocks ($N = 2$) stacked on top of ELMo and 1 CNN block stacked on top of VAD features. We set the window size of the Convolutional Block to 5, ELMo size to 1024 (mapped to $d = 256$), initial learning rate for ADAM optimizer (Kingma and Ba, 2014) to 0.001, dropout rate to 0.5, batch size to 128, and the threshold T to 0.86.

Each batch of samples used for training the binary classifiers is balanced by randomly sampling half of the batch from positive labels and half of the batch from negative labels (the number of negative labels is 5 times larger). Sampling using this process makes the training more robust to overfitting. Additionally, noise is added to the training samples; a small amount of negative labels are sampled and presented as positive labels to the classifier (Section 6.1).

6   Implicit Emotion Prediction Results

In this section we present the results on the Implicit Emotion Prediction task. The six binary classifiers and the 6-emotion classifier used in the Ensemble Classifier were chosen based on validation accuracy presented in Table 2. Our system achieved a macro F1 Score of 66.2%, whereas the top 3 participating systems have reported a score of 71.4%, 71% and 70.3%, respectively.

6.1   Analysis

Table 2 shows that some emotions (e.g., joy, fear) are easier to predict. In some cases we see improve-

[‡]https://spacy.io

Emotion	No noise	Noise 5%	Noise 10%
Joy	91.4%	91.0%	**92.2%**
Disgust	89.4%	**89.7%**	89.6%
Surprise	87.7%	87.1%	**87.9%**
Anger	**86.9%**	86.4%	86.5%
Fear	**90.9%**	**90.9%**	90.8%
Sad	89.0%	**89.6%**	87.7%
6 emotions	64.8%	**65.5%**	64.5%

Table 2:   Validation accuracy for each classifier (note: high accuracy scores for binary classifiers come from unbalanced classes).

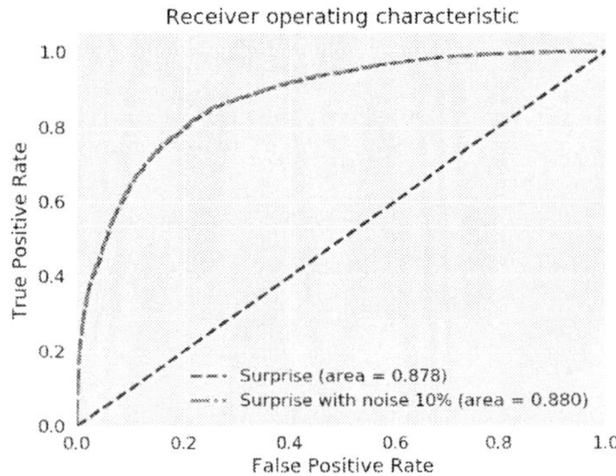

Figure 3:   ROC curve for predicting surprise emotion on the test set (predictions are made on a balanced dataset).

ment in validation accuracy after adding noise. Surprisingly, this does not lead to statistically significant improvement (Figure 3).

Results for the 6-emotion classifier and the Ensemble Classifier are presented in Table 3. Some emotions are easier to predict than others, this is corroborated by the confusion matrix in Figure 4. Joy is easier to predict, whereas predicting anger remains a difficult task (also shown in Table 2). Some emotions are harder to distinguish (surprise with fear and disgust), whereas some emotions are very unlikely to be confused with each other (e.g., joy with disgust). Our model probably commits errors because firstly, emotions are not disjoint – a sentence can express more than one emotion at the same time (i.e., a sentence can be classified as either "disgust" or "fear"), and secondly, several emotion labels could be assigned to the same sentence by changing only the trigger words (e.g., the sentence "I am #TRIGGERWORD to see you here." can be classified both by anger and surprise,

Classifier	F1 Score
fastText	50.0%
6-emotion classifier	65.2%
Ensemble classifier	**66.2%**

Table 3: F1 Score on test set.

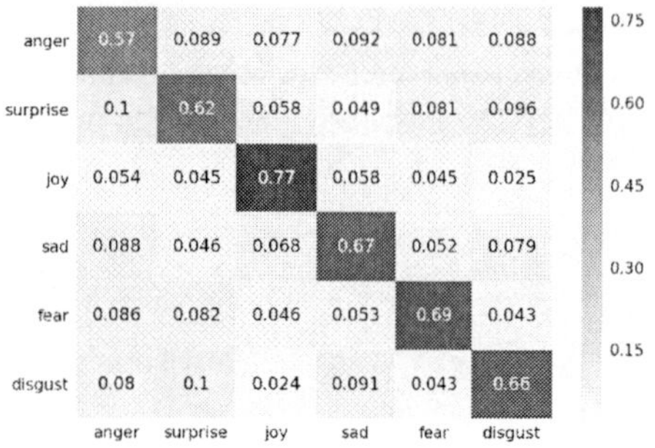

Figure 4: Confusion Matrix for the Ensemble Classifier.

depending on whether the trigger word was "happy" or "surprised").

7 Model Generalization

In order to have a better understanding of the performance of our system for real world applications, we tested our system on an explicit emotion prediction task.

7.1 Dataset and Task

For our experiments, we used the Cornell Movie Corpus built by Danescu-Niculescu-Mizil and Lee (2011), which is composed of around 300,000 utterances extracted from 600 movies. A group of internal annotators manually annotated a subset of 58,000 lines, with at most 2 of 7 emotion labels (fear, surprise, anger, disgust, joy, sad, neutral). We use this data for two experiments. In the first experiment, we measure how well the classifier predictions correlate with human annotation for the 6 emotions. For this experiment we create the dataset $\mathcal{D}_1$ by randomly sampling 4800 lines consisting of 800 samples for each emotion class (except for the neutral class). In the second experiment, we measure how well the classifier is able to predict a neutral emotion. We create the dataset $\mathcal{D}_2$ by extracting a subset of 45,000 neutral lines.

Emotion	F1 Score
Joy	52.1%
Disgust	48.2%
Surprise	52.0%
Anger	50.0%
Fear	50.1%
Sad	44.2%
Total	**49.4%**

Table 4: F1 Score on Cornell dataset.

7.2 Prediction on 6 emotions

In the first experiment, we take the top 2 emotions predicted by the final system on $\mathcal{D}_1$ and check if at least one of the predicted labels matches one of the golden labels. F1 Scores are presented in Table 4.

7.3 Prediction on neutral emotion

In the second experiment, we determine that the classifier predicts a neutral emotion if each emotion is predicted with low confidence (confidence lower than 0.5). We evaluate our system on $\mathcal{D}_2$. The final system predicts a neutral emotion for 85% of sentences, whereas fastText only reaches 4% of accuracy. FastText misclassifies those neutral lines as joy with high confidence ($> 80\%$).

In conclusion, the results show that our model generalizes well on the Cornell Movie corpus when compared to a fastText classifier, pre-trained similarly on the task dataset. While we do not expect to reproduce precisely the same performance on the Cornell Movie Corpus, since the word distribution and writing style are very different, the system generalizes reasonably well.

8 Conclusion

In this paper, we presented a system making use of state-of-the-art techniques for Natural Language Processing, such as ELMo and a CNN encoder for emotion classification. We have designed a robust classifier for sentences without any assumptions about the intrinsic properties of the task which make it generalizable to other tasks (e.g., explicit emotion prediction) on other datasets.

References

Sheng-Yeh Chen, Chao-Chun Hsu, Chuan-Chun Kuo, Ting-Hao Huang, and Lun-Wei Ku. 2018. Emotionlines: An emotion corpus of multi-party conversations. *CoRR*, abs/1802.08379.

Cristian Danescu-Niculescu-Mizil and Lillian Lee. 2011. Chameleons in imagined conversations: A new approach to understanding coordination of linguistic style in dialogs. In *Proceedings of the Workshop on Cognitive Modeling and Computational Linguistics, ACL 2011*.

Yann N. Dauphin, Angela Fan, Michael Auli, and David Grangier. 2016. Language modeling with gated convolutional networks. *CoRR*, abs/1612.08083.

Jonas Gehring, Michael Auli, David Grangier, Denis Yarats, and Yann N. Dauphin. 2017. Convolutional sequence to sequence learning. *CoRR*, abs/1705.03122.

Armand Joulin, Edouard Grave, Piotr Bojanowski, and Tomas Mikolov. 2016. Bag of tricks for efficient text classification. *CoRR*, abs/1607.01759.

Diederik P. Kingma and Jimmy Ba. 2014. Adam: A method for stochastic optimization. *CoRR*, abs/1412.6980.

Roman Klinger, Orphée de Clercq, Saif M. Mohammad, and Alexandra Balahur. 2018. Iest: Wassa-2018 implicit emotions shared task. In *Proceedings of the 9th Workshop on Computational Approaches to Subjectivity, Sentiment and Social Media Analysis*, Brussels, Belgium. Association for Computational Linguistics.

Walaa Medhat, Ahmed Hassan, and Hoda Korashy. 2014. Sentiment analysis algorithms and applications: A survey. *Ain Shams Engineering Journal*, 5(4):1093–1113.

Saif M. Mohammad. 2018. Obtaining reliable human ratings of valence, arousal, and dominance for 20,000 english words. In *Proceedings of The Annual Conference of the Association for Computational Linguistics (ACL)*, Melbourne, Australia.

Matthew E. Peters, Mark Neumann, Mohit Iyyer, Matt Gardner, Christopher Clark, Kenton Lee, and Luke Zettlemoyer. 2018. Deep contextualized word representations. In *Proc. of NAACL*.

Sentylic at IEST 2018: Gated Recurrent Neural Network and Capsule Network Based Approach for Implicit Emotion Detection

Prabod Rathnayaka, Supun Abeysinghe, Chamod Samarajeewa
Isura Manchanayake, Malaka Walpola
Department of Computer Science and Engineering
University of Moratuwa, Sri Lanka
{prabod.14,supun.14,chamod.14,isura.14,malaka}@cse.mrt.ac.lk

Abstract

In this paper, we present the system we have used for the Implicit WASSA 2018 Implicit Emotion Shared Task. The task is to predict the emotion of a tweet of which the explicit mentions of emotion terms have been removed. The idea is to come up with a model which has the ability to implicitly identify the emotion expressed given the context words. We have used a Gated Recurrent Neural Network (GRU) and a Capsule Network based model for the task. Pre-trained word embeddings have been utilized to incorporate contextual knowledge about words into the model. GRU layer learns latent representations using the input word embeddings. Subsequent Capsule Network layer learns high-level features from that hidden representation. The proposed model managed to achieve a macro-F1 score of 0.692.

1 Introduction

Emotion is a complex aspect of the human behavior which makes the humanity distinguishable from other biological behaviors of creatures. Emotions are typically originated as a response to a situation. Since the emergence of social media, people often express opinions as responses to daily encounters by posting on these platforms. These microblogs contain emotions related to the topics the author have discussed. Thus emotion detection is useful to understand more specific sentiments held by the author towards the discussed topics. Hence this is a challenge with a significant business value.

Emotion analysis can be considered as an extension of sentiment analysis. Even though there has been a notable amount of research in sentiment analysis in the literature, research on emotion analysis has not gained much attention. The related work suggests this task can be handled us-

ing emojis or hashtags present in the text i.e. distance supervision techniques (Felbo et al., 2017). However, these features can be unreliable due to noise, thus affect the accuracy of the results.

Although explicit words related to emotions (happy, sad, etc.) in a document directly affect the emotion detection task, other linguistic features play a major role as well. Implicit Emotion Recognition Shared Task introduced in Klinger et al. (2018) aims at developing models which can classify a text into one of the emotions; *Anger, Fear, Sadness, Joy, Surprise, Disgust* without having access to an explicit mention of an emotion word. Participants were given a tweet from which any of the above emotion terms or one of their synonyms is removed. The task is to predict the emotion that the excluded word expresses.

E.g.:

It's [#TARGETWORD#] when you feel like you are invisible to others.

The [#TARGETWORD#] in the given example corresponds to sadness ("sad").

In this paper, we propose an approach based on Gated Recurrent Units (GRU) (Cho et al., 2014) followed by Capsule Networks (Sabour et al., 2017) to tackle the challenge. This model managed to achieve a macro-F1 score of **0.692** and ranked **5th** in WASSA 2018 implicit emotion detection task.

2 Methodology

We have used a sentence classification model which is based on bidirectional GRUs and Capsule networks. First, the raw tweets are preprocessed, then mapped into a continuous vector space using an embedding layer. Afterward, we used a Bidirectional Gated Recurrent Unit (Bi-GRU) (Cho et al., 2014) layer to encode sentences into a fixed length representation. The fixed length represen-

Proceedings of the 9th Workshop on Computational Approaches to Subjectivity, Sentiment and Social Media Analysis, pages 254–259
Brussels, Belgium, October 31, 2018. ©2018 Association for Computational Linguistics
https://doi.org/10.18653/v1/P17

tation is then fed into a Capsule Network (Sabour et al., 2017) where it will learn the features and emotional context of the sentences. Finally, the Capsule network is followed by a fully connected dense layer with softmax activation for the classification.

2.1 Preprocessing

Microblogs typically contain informal language usages such as short terms, emojis, misspellings, and hashtags. Hence, preprocessing steps should be employed in order to clean these informal and noisy text data. Moreover, efficient preprocessing plays a vital role in achieving a good performance. Ekphrasis tool (Baziotis et al., 2017) is used for initial preprocessing of the tweets. Tweet tokenizing, word normalization, spell correcting and word segmentation for hashtags are done as preprocessing steps.

2.1.1 Tweet Tokenizing

Tokenizing is the first and the most important step of preprocessing. Ability to correctly tokenize a tweet directly impacts the quality of a system. Since there is a large variety of vocabulary and expressions present in short texts such as Twitter, it is a challenging task to correctly tokenize a given tweet. Twitter markup, emoticons, emojis, dates, times, currencies, acronyms, censored words (e.g. s**t), words with emphasis (e.g. *very*) are recognized during tokenizing and treated as a separate token.

2.1.2 Word Normalization

Upon tokenizing, set of transformations including converting to lowercase and transforming URLs, usernames, emails, phone numbers, dates, times, hashtags to a predefined set of tags (e.g @user1 → <user>) are applied. This method helps to reduce the vocabulary size and generalize the tweet.

2.1.3 Spell Correcting and Word Segmentation

As the last step in preprocessing, we apply spell correcting and word segmentation to hashtags. (e.g. #makeitrain → make it rain)

2.2 Model

An overview of the model is shown in figure 1 and each segment of the model is described in the following sub sections.

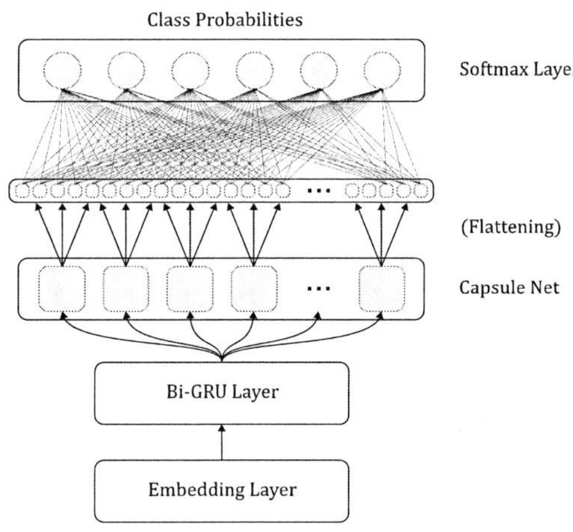

Figure 1: Overall model architecture

2.2.1 Word Embedding Layer

Word embedding layer is the first layer of the model. Each token will be mapped into a continuous vector space using a set of pretrained word embeddings. We used 300 dimensional, pretrained, Word2Vec embeddings introduced in Mikolov et al. (2013). Given an input tweet, $S = [s_1, s_2, ., s_i, .., s_n]$ where s_i is the token at position i, the embedding matrix W_e, the output of the embedding layer X is,

$$X = SW_e \tag{1}$$

2.3 Bidirectional GRU Layer

The word embedding layer is followed by a bidirectional GRU (Cho et al., 2014) layer. There is a forward GRU ($\overrightarrow{h_t}$) and a backward GRU ($\overleftarrow{h_t}$) and the latent representation output by the two GRUs is concatenated to get the final output ($\overrightarrow{h_t}, \overleftarrow{h_t}$) of the layer. Following set of equations follows the standard notation used in Cho et al. (2014).

$$r_t = \sigma(W_{ir}x_t + b_{ir} + W_{hr}h_{(t-1)} + b_{hr}) \tag{2}$$

$$z_t = \sigma(W_{iz}x_t + b_{iz} + W_{hz}h_{(t-1)} + b_{hz}) \tag{3}$$

$$n_t = \tanh(W_{in}x_t + b_{in} + r_t(W_{hn}h_{(t-1)} + b_{hn})) \tag{4}$$

$$h_t = (1 - z_t)n_t + z_t h_{(t-1)} \tag{5}$$

2.4 Capsule Layer

Features encoded by the bidirectional GRU layer is then passed to a Capsule Network (Sabour et al.,

2017). Capsule Network consists of a set of capsules where each capsule corresponds to a high level feature. Each capsule outputs a vector, of which the magnitude represents the probability of the corresponding feature existence. Following set of equations follows the standard notation used in Sabour et al. (2017).

Prediction vector $\hat{u}_{j|i}$ is calculated by multiplying the output h_i from the GRU layer with a weight matrix.

$$\hat{u}_{j|i} = W_{ij} h_i \tag{6}$$

Total input to a capsule s_j is a weighted sum over all the prediction vectors $\hat{u}_{j|i}$.

$$s_j = \sum_i c_{ij} \hat{u}_{j|i} \tag{7}$$

c_{ij} represents the coupling coefficients found through the iterative dynamic routing.

A non-linear *"Squash"* function is used to scale the vectors such that the magnitude is mapped to a value between 0 and 1.

$$v_j = \frac{\|s_j\|^2}{1 + \|s_j\|^2} \frac{s_j}{\|s_j\|} \tag{8}$$

Dynamic Routing process introduced by Sabour et al. (2017) is used as the routing mechanism between capsules.

2.5 Classification Layer

The flattened output from the capsule layer (Say C) is fed to a dense layer which has a softmax activation. It outputs a vector of size 6 (number of classes). The values in the vector components are probabilities for the presence of each of the six emotions. The emotion with the highest probability is selected as the output.

$$Y = W_{dense} C \tag{9}$$

For all $y_i \in Y$, f_i is calculated as follows.

$$f_i = \frac{e^{-y_i}}{\sum_{y_j \in Y} e^{-y_j}} \tag{10}$$

Then the class with highest f_i is taken as the output.

$$output = \arg\max_i f_i \tag{11}$$

2.6 Regularization

Gaussian noise is added to both the embedding layer and the softmax classification layer for the purpose of making the model more robust to overfitting. Further, dropout is applied to the Capsule network output and a spatial dropout is applied to the embedding Layer to reduce overfitting.

3 Experiments and Results

3.1 Experimental setup

3.1.1 Training

We used Adam optimizer (Kingma and Ba, 2014) for optimizing our network with a batch size of 512. Gradient Clipping (Pascanu et al., 2013) was employed to address the exploding gradient problem where all the gradients were clipped at 1. Keras (Chollet et al., 2015) was used to develop the model and experiments were done using both Tensorflow (Abadi et al., 2015) and Theano (Theano Development Team, 2016) backends. Google Colaboratory[1] was used as the runtime environment for training the model.

3.1.2 Hyper-Parameters

We have employed Word2Vec (Mikolov et al., 2013) embeddings of 300 dimensions for the embedding layer. The GRU layer consists of 128 cells for both directions. We have used 16 capsules each with an output size of 32 and 5 routing iterations. Spatial dropout of 0.3 is applied to the embeddings and dropout of 0.25 is applied to the Capsule network. Gaussian noise of 0.1 is added to both the embedding layer and the Capsule network.

3.2 Results

We ranked 5th among 30 contestants in the competition. We achieved a macro-F1 score of 0.692 which is 0.155 improvement compared to the baseline model (Maximum Entropy Model using bag of words (BoW) and bigrams). The top-ranked model has a 0.031 improvement compared to our model. Table 1 shows the macro-F1 scores of the top 10 competitors and the baseline model.

4 Analysis

4.1 Investigated Approaches

Recurrent Neural Networks (RNN) (Socher et al., 2013) based model achieves state-of-the-art in

---

[1] https://colab.research.google.com/

Team	Macro-F1
Amobee	**0.714**
IIIDYT	0.710
NTUA-SLP	0.703
UBC-NLP	0.693
Sentylic	**0.692**
HUMIR	0.686
nlp	0.685
DataSEARCH	0.680
YNU1510	0.676
EmotiKLUE	0.671
Baseline	**0.599**

Table 1: Competition results of top 10 competitors and the maximum entropy baseline classifier.

Model	Macro-F1
GRU + Hierarchical Attention	0.671
GRU + CNN	0.657
GRU + Capsnet	**0.692**

Table 2: Performance analysis of the best models in each investigated approaches.

Model	Macro-F1
GRU (1 layer) + Capsnet	**0.692**
LSTM (1 layer) + Capsnet	0.687
GRU (2 layers) + Capsnet	0.678

Table 3: Performance analysis of different variants of the proposed system

sentence classification tasks. RNNs have the capability to capture sequential features present in sentences. Further, when they are incorporated with attention mechanisms the accuracy of the models increases notably (Yang et al., 2016; Tang et al., 2015). Hence, we have first implemented a model which uses a bidirectional GRU (Cho et al., 2014) layer to learn latent representations followed by a hierarchical attention mechanism. Attention mechanisms have the ability to capture important keywords in sentences and give a higher weight to those words. This is one of the prominent approaches that typically results in a good performance in regular text classification tasks. Table 2 shows that this approach yielded a reasonable accuracy, yet it was not the best performing approach.

Another approach is to use a Convolution Neural Network (CNN) (Kim, 2014) layer on top of RNNs instead of attention mechanisms. Intuition is that the CNN layers will act as a different attention mechanism and captures high-level features from the features learned by the below layers. Hence, the second approach we investigated was using CNNs instead of the attention mechanism. As the table 2 shows, this approach resulted in a slight drop in performance compared to the previous approach.

Our next approach was to use Capsule networks (Sabour et al., 2017) instead of Convolution Neural Networks (CNN). Capsule networks have shown promising results in the field of computer vision. Sabour et al. (2017) argues that it is essential to preserve the hierarchical translational and rotational features of the identified high-level features in order to perform image classification and object detection in the field of computer vision. However, traditional CNNs with max-pooling layers tend to lose this spatial information related to identified features. Sabour et al. (2017) introduces capsule networks to tackle these issues identified in traditional CNNs. Nonetheless, the usability of Capsule networks has not researched much in the Natural Language Processing (NLP) community. Along the same lines, we can intuitively argue that CNN based models with pooling layers will cause loss of information in text related classification tasks as well. Hence, we have investigated the usability of capsule networks for improving the performance of text classification models. The use of Capsule networks instead of CNNs has improved the performance of the model slightly and assisted in gaining the best performing model.

4.2 Model Architecture Variants

We have tried several variants of the proposed model. Table 3 shows the performance of each of those variants. We have tried approaches using Long Short Term Memory networks (LSTM) (Hochreiter and Schmidhuber, 1997) which is one of the other prominent types of RNNs. However, the results showed a minor drop. Another variant is to use two layers of GRUs instead of using a single layer. Even this approach made the performance of the model slightly lesser. A potential reason for this could be model over-fitting. Using a single GRU layer followed by the Capsnet gave the best performance.

Emotion	Precision	Recall	F1-Score
Anger	0.631	0.614	0.622
Disgust	0.689	0.687	0.688
Fear	0.728	0.731	0.730
Joy	0.803	0.774	0.788
Sad	0.682	0.655	0.668
Surprise	0.625	0.689	0.656
Micro Avg.	0.694	0.694	0.694
Macro Avg.	0.693	0.692	0.692

Table 4: Precision, recall and F1-score of each class in test set using our proposed model.

4.3 Analysis on Predictions

Table 4 shows the performance of the proposed model for each class. As evident from the results, anger shows a significantly lower F1-score. Other emotions show similar results whereas joy stands out with a notably higher F1-score. Anger has been misclassified as sad in several examples.

e.g.- *Girls will get [#TARGETWORD#] that her man cheated with an ugly girl more than the fact he actually cheated.*

In the above example, it is unclear whether the emotion is anger or sadness. Such ambiguity of anger has affected the reduction of F1-score values. There were few other similar cases where it is challenging even for humans to clearly discriminate emotions due to nuance nature of emotions expressed.

5 Conclusion

WASSA 2018 Implicit Emotion Shared Task (Klinger et al., 2018) introduces a task to predict the emotion of a tweet of which the explicit mentions of emotion terms have been removed. We have experimented with several deep learning based approaches to tackle this task. We have used pre-trained Word2Vec embeddings. All the approaches we tried utilize an initial GRU layer which learns latent representations from the input word embeddings. Different alternative methods have been investigated for the subsequent layer. These methods include attention layer, CNN layer, and Capsnet layer. Model with the Capsnet layer achieved the best results among the experimented alternatives. Potential future work includes investigating the possibility of using Capsule networks for other tasks in Natural Language Processing, especially where CNNs are involved. Another line of future work could be to follow the approach mentioned in Felbo et al. (2017) and apply transfer learning on the model trained using this semi-automatically annotated dataset to test on human annotated datasets such as Mohammad et al. (2018).

References

Martín Abadi, Ashish Agarwal, Paul Barham, Eugene Brevdo, Zhifeng Chen, Craig Citro, Greg S. Corrado, Andy Davis, Jeffrey Dean, Matthieu Devin, Sanjay Ghemawat, Ian Goodfellow, Andrew Harp, Geoffrey Irving, Michael Isard, Yangqing Jia, Rafal Jozefowicz, Lukasz Kaiser, Manjunath Kudlur, Josh Levenberg, Dandelion Mané, Rajat Monga, Sherry Moore, Derek Murray, Chris Olah, Mike Schuster, Jonathon Shlens, Benoit Steiner, Ilya Sutskever, Kunal Talwar, Paul Tucker, Vincent Vanhoucke, Vijay Vasudevan, Fernanda Viégas, Oriol Vinyals, Pete Warden, Martin Wattenberg, Martin Wicke, Yuan Yu, and Xiaoqiang Zheng. 2015. TensorFlow: Large-scale machine learning on heterogeneous systems. Software available from tensorflow.org.

Christos Baziotis, Nikos Pelekis, and Christos Doulkeridis. 2017. Datastories at semeval-2017 task 4: Deep lstm with attention for message-level and topic-based sentiment analysis. In *Proceedings of the 11th International Workshop on Semantic Evaluation (SemEval-2017)*, pages 747–754, Vancouver, Canada. Association for Computational Linguistics.

Kyunghyun Cho, Bart Van Merriënboer, Caglar Gulcehre, Dzmitry Bahdanau, Fethi Bougares, Holger Schwenk, and Yoshua Bengio. 2014. Learning phrase representations using rnn encoder-decoder for statistical machine translation. *arXiv preprint arXiv:1406.1078.*

François Chollet et al. 2015. Keras. `https://keras.io`.

Bjarke Felbo, Alan Mislove, Anders Søgaard, Iyad Rahwan, and Sune Lehmann. 2017. Using millions of emoji occurrences to learn any-domain representations for detecting sentiment, emotion and sarcasm. *arXiv preprint arXiv:1708.00524.*

Sepp Hochreiter and Jürgen Schmidhuber. 1997. Long short-term memory. *Neural computation*, 9(8):1735–1780.

Yoon Kim. 2014. Convolutional neural networks for sentence classification. *arXiv preprint arXiv:1408.5882.*

Diederik P Kingma and Jimmy Ba. 2014. Adam: A method for stochastic optimization. *arXiv preprint arXiv:1412.6980.*

Roman Klinger, Orphée de Clercq, Saif M. Mohammad, and Alexandra Balahur. 2018. Iest: Wassa-2018 implicit emotions shared task. In *Proceedings of the 9th Workshop on Computational Approaches to Subjectivity, Sentiment and Social Media Analysis*, Brussels, Belgium. Association for Computational Linguistics.

Tomas Mikolov, Kai Chen, Greg Corrado, and Jeffrey Dean. 2013. Efficient estimation of word representations in vector space. *arXiv preprint arXiv:1301.3781*.

Saif M Mohammad, Felipe Bravo-Marquez, Mohammad Salameh, and Svetlana Kiritchenko. 2018. Semeval-2018 task 1: Affect in tweets. In *Proceedings of International Workshop on Semantic Evaluation (SemEval-2018), New Orleans, LA, USA*.

Razvan Pascanu, Tomas Mikolov, and Yoshua Bengio. 2013. On the difficulty of training recurrent neural networks. In *International Conference on Machine Learning*, pages 1310–1318.

Sara Sabour, Nicholas Frosst, and Geoffrey E Hinton. 2017. Dynamic routing between capsules. In *Advances in Neural Information Processing Systems*, pages 3856–3866.

Richard Socher, Alex Perelygin, Jean Wu, Jason Chuang, Christopher D Manning, Andrew Ng, and Christopher Potts. 2013. Recursive deep models for semantic compositionality over a sentiment treebank. In *Proceedings of the 2013 conference on empirical methods in natural language processing*, pages 1631–1642.

Duyu Tang, Bing Qin, and Ting Liu. 2015. Document modeling with gated recurrent neural network for sentiment classification. In *Proceedings of the 2015 conference on empirical methods in natural language processing*, pages 1422–1432.

Theano Development Team. 2016. Theano: A Python framework for fast computation of mathematical expressions. *arXiv e-prints*, abs/1605.02688.

Zichao Yang, Diyi Yang, Chris Dyer, Xiaodong He, Alex Smola, and Eduard Hovy. 2016. Hierarchical attention networks for document classification. In *Proceedings of the 2016 Conference of the North American Chapter of the Association for Computational Linguistics: Human Language Technologies*, pages 1480–1489.

Fast Approach to Build an Automatic Sentiment Annotator for Legal Domain using Transfer Learning

Viraj Salaka Gamage, Menuka Warushavithana, Nisansa de Silva,
Amal Shehan Perera, Gathika Ratnayaka and **Thejan Rupasinghe**
Department of Computer Science & Engineering
University of Moratuwa
`viraj.14@cse.mrt.ac.lk`

Abstract

This study proposes a novel way of identifying the sentiment of the phrases used in the legal domain. The added complexity of the language used in law, and the inability of the existing systems to accurately predict the sentiments of words in law are the main motivations behind this study. This is a transfer learning approach which can be used for other domain adaptation tasks as well. The proposed methodology achieves an improvement of over 6% compared to the source model's accuracy in the legal domain.

1 Introduction

As described by Esuli and Sebastiani (2007), sentiment analysis or *sentiment classification* is a recent methodology that aligns with information retrieval and computational linguistics which is focused on the opinion towards something which is represented by a certain text.

In many recent studies involving NLP in various domains, it is common to reuse the seminal RNTN (Recursive Neural Tensor Network) model (Socher et al., 2013b) trained on movie reviews for sentiment analysis. However, the trained model has bias towards the movie review domain.

We propose a novel methodology to perform transfer learning on the RNTN model mentioned in Socher et al. (2013b) and build a target model. Given that this is a transfer learning approach, the manually annotated data on movie reviews is used as the initial source model, rather than creating a new comparable manually annotated dataset for the legal domain.

In the proposed approach, the sentiment of a given phrase is classified into one of the two classes; *negative* and *non-negative*. This classification criterion is selected following the fact that the major use case aligns with classifying terms

and entities supporting/referring to either plaintiff or defendant. Therefore, the proposed methodology is focused on identifying the statements with negative sentiment as much as possible. This kind of sentiment classification is vital to identify the stakeholder-bias in legal case statements. Similarly, sentiment analysis in legal text can become useful in automating the identification of arguments, the supporting/opposing party for a given argument and counter arguments.

For the testing purposes, we created a manually annotated target domain test dataset such that the phrases belong to one of the two classes: *negative* or *non-negative*. The target system shows a recall of 0.7014 for identifying phrases with negative sentiment in the legal domain. Furthermore, the overall accuracy of the system is above 76% in classifying sentiments for a given phrase correctly. If this result is compared with the results of source RNTN model (Socher et al., 2013b), it is a 6% improvement in accuracy. The approach proposed in this study can be tried on other domain adaptation tasks related to sentiment classification as well.

2 Background

The legal vocabulary have words of mixed origin such as English and Latin has been raised as a reason for the difficulty of creating computing applications for the legal domain (Sugathadasa et al., 2018). However, recently, there have been attempts to involve and build legal ontologies (Jayawardana et al., 2017a,b,c). Given the popularity of knowledge embedding, a number of studies have also attempted to embed legal jargon in vector spaces (Sugathadasa et al., 2017; Nay, 2016). If we consider the research on sentiment analysis in legal domain, the study on *Opinion Mining* in legal blogs (Conrad and Schilder, 2007) is closest implementation for this study that we

Proceedings of the 9th Workshop on Computational Approaches to Subjectivity, Sentiment and Social Media Analysis, pages 260–265
Brussels, Belgium, October 31, 2018. ©2018 Association for Computational Linguistics
https://doi.org/10.18653/v1/P17

have found. But, the data set used for evaluation is based on movie reviews, customer reviews, and MPQA corpus (Wiebe et al., 2005).

There have been numerous studies that were built upon SentiWordNet (Esuli and Sebastiani, 2007; Baccianella et al., 2010) which attempts to classify sentiments of phrases and sentences. One such study by Ohana and Tierney (2009) proposes a methodology to perform opinion mining on movie reviews using support vector machine where some of the features were calculated using WordNet. This achieves an accuracy of 69.35% and claims that the inaccuracies in SentiWord-Net feature calculations are caused by the Senti-WordNet's reliance on glosses. Lu et al. (2012) evaluates the SentiWordNet for identifying opposing opinion networks in forum discussion. The average SentiWordNet opinion score of words is considered to identify whether a user's expressed comment for a given post has either *for* or *against* relationship. The achieved accuracy using the SentiWordNet opinion score of words is 0.56.

The method proposed by Socher et al. (2013b) provides an algorithm to identify the sentiment of a phrase or a sentence in a supervised manner using a deep learning model of the type Recursive Neural Tensor Network (RNN). It is claimed that this learning model has the capability to identify the sentiment considering the context of that word. A dataset which consists of movie reviews where each sentence in the data set was broken into phrases and each phrase is annotated by human judges were created for this study. The authors claim a testing accuracy of 80.7% in phrase level for a test set drawn from the same dataset. Further, the authors claim that the proposed model can be trained over any domain by following the provided methodology. While, theoretically, it is possible, following this for legal domain in a practical implementation which covers a corpus which is both significant and sufficient is difficult. This claim is substantiated by referring the dataset of the original research (Socher et al., 2013b) which utilized 215,154 manually annotated phrases (from 11,855 sentences) with over 5355 unique words. In comparison to this, the legal corpus used in our study has a vocabulary exceeding 17000 words. The difficulties are not mealy of scale given that the linguistic complexity of legal jargon exceeds that of the average text corpus (Jayawardana et al., 2017b,c; Sugathadasa et al., 2017, 2018).

Domain adaptation is a sub-category of *Transfer Learning* (Raina et al., 2007). There are several studies (Raina et al., 2007; Socher et al., 2013a) that claim the process of *domain adaptation* to be a suitable solution to perform transfer learning. While the generic process of transfer learning is defined as the process of "learning model is trained using data from a certain domain and tested with respect to a different domain" (Raina et al., 2007), the specific case of *domain adaptation* occurs when the task is similar in both source and target models. Quattoni et al. (2008) is a study based on domain adaptation in Image Classification.

3 Methodology

Given that the transfer learning process described in this study uses the Recursive Neural Tensor Network (RNTN) model proposed by Socher et al. (2013b) as the source model, we make numerous references to the aforementioned model throughout the paper. Therefore, to avoid clutter, from this point onward the model proposed by Socher et al. (2013b) is referred as **Socher Model** in the remainder of this paper.

3.1 Selecting the Vocabulary

Depending on the size of the corpus (phrases extracted from legal text), availability of human annotators and the time, it is not feasible to analyze and modify the sentiment of every word in a corpus. Therefore, it is required to select the vocabulary (unique words in the corpus) such that the end-model can correctly classify the sentiment of most of the phrases from the legal domain while not squandering human annotator time on words that occur rarely. To this end, first, the stopwords (Lo et al., 2005) are removed from the text by utilizing the classical stop-word list known as the Van stop-list (Van Rijsbergen, 1979). Next, the term frequencies for each word in the corpus is calculated and only the top 95% words of it are added to the vocabulary.

3.2 Assigning Sentiments for the Selected Vocabulary

The selected vocabulary (set of individual words) is given to the sentiment annotator *Socher Model* as input. From the model, sentiment is classified into one of the five classes as in table 3.2. This class scheme made sense for the movie reviews for which the *Socher Model* is trained and used for. However, in the application of this study, the basic requirement of finding sentiment in *court cases* in the legal domain is to identify whether a given statement is against the plaintiff's claim or not. Therefore, we define two classes for sentiment: *negative* and *non-negative*.

Three human judges analyze the selected vocabulary and classify each unique word into the two classes depending on its sentiment separately and independently. If at least two judges agree, the given word's sentiment is assigned as the class those two judges agreed. For the same word, the output from the sentiment annotator *Socher Model* belongs to one of the five classes mentioned in the preceding subsection. In this approach, we map the output from *Socher Model* to the two classes we define in Table 3.2.

	Human annotation	***Socher Model* output**
Class 1	Negative	Very negative, negative
Class 2	Non-negative	Neutral, Positive, very positive

Table 1: Sentiment Mapping

For a given word, if the two sentiment values assigned by the *Socher Model* and human judges do not agree with the above mapping, we define that the *Socher Model*'s output has deviated from its actual sentiment. For example:

Sentence: *Sam is charged with a crime.*
Socher Model's output: positive
Human judges' annotation: negative

The word *charged* has several meanings depending on the context. As the *Socher Model* was trained using movie reviews, the sentiment of the word *charged* is identified as positive. Although the sentiment of the term *crime* is recognized as negative, the sentiment of the whole sentence is output as positive. But in the legal domain, *charged* refers to a formal accusation. Therefore, the sentiment for the above sentence should have been negative. From the selected vocabulary, all the words with deviated sentiments are identified and listed separately for the further processing.

3.3 Brief description on the RNTN Model

In the preceding subsection, we came across a situation where the sentiment values from the *Socher Model* do not match the actual sentiment value because of the difference in domains. And there

are words like *insufficient*, which were not recognized by the model because those terms were not included in the training data-set. One approach to solve this is to annotate the phrases extracted from legal case transcripts manually as the *Socher Model* suggests, which will require a considerable amount of human effort and time. Instead of that, we can change the model such that the desired output can be obtained using the same trained *Socher Model* without explicitly training using phrases in the legal domain. Hence, this method is called a transfer learning method.

In order to change the model, first, it is required to understand the internals of the *Socher Model* model. When a phrase is provided as input, first it generates a binary tree corresponding to the input in which each leaf node represents a single word. Each leaf node is represented as a vector with d-dimensions. The parent nodes are also d-dimensional vectors which are computed in the bottom-up fashion according to some function g. The function g is composed of a neural tensor layer. Through the training process, the neural tensor layer and the word vectors are adjusted to support the relevant sentiment value. The neural tensor layer corresponds to identify the sentiment according to the structure of words representing the phrase. If we consider a phrase like *not guilty* ,both individual word elements have negative sentiments. But the composition of those words has the structure of negating a negative sentiment term or phrase. Hence the phrase has a non-negative sentiment. If the input was a phrase like *very bad*, the neural tensor layer has the ability to identify that the term *very* increases the negativity in the sentiment.

3.4 Adjusting Word Vector Values in RNTN Model

The requirement of the system is to identify the sentiment of a given phrase. The proposed approach is not to modify the neural tensor layer completely. We simply substitute the word vector values of individual words which are having deviated sentiments between *Socher Model* and human annotation (See sections 3.2). The vectors for the words which were not in the vocabulary of the training set which was used to train the RNTN model should be instantiated. The vectors of the words which are not deviated (according to the definition provided in the preceding subsection

3.3) will remain the same.

As the words with deviated sentiments (provided by the *Socher Model*) in the vocabulary are already known, we initialize the vectors corresponding to the sentiment annotation for those words. Since the model is not trained explicitly, the vector initialization is done by substituting the vectors of words in which sentiment is not deviated comparing the *Socher Model* output and its actual sentiment. After the substitution is completed, we consider the part-of-speech tag. For that purpose, the part-of-speech tagger mentioned in Toutanova et al. (2003) is used. The substitution of vectors is carried out as shown in Table 2.

POS Tag	Substituted word vector sentiment	
	non-negative	negative
NN	failure	thing
RB	insufficiently	naturally
VB	hate	do
VBZ	ignoring	doing

Table 2: Substituted Word Vectors for words which should be deviated

The number of words which have deviated sentiments is a considerably lower amount compared to the selected vocabulary. The rest of the words' vectors representing sentiments are not changed in the modification process. The neural tensor layer also remains unchanged from the trained *Socher Model* using movie reviews (Socher et al., 2013b). When the vectors for words with deviated sentiments are initialized according to the part-of-speech tag as shown in Table 2, it is possible to make a fair assumption that when deciding the sentiment with the proposed implementation, it does not harm the structure corresponding to the linguistic features of English. Consider the sentence "*evidence is insufficient.*" as an example.

The term "*insufficient*" is not in the vocabulary of the *Socher Model* due to the limited vocabulary in training data set. Therefore, the *Socher Model* provides the sentiment of that word as neutral which indicates as a word with a deviated sentiment. Following the Table 2, the sentiment related vector is instantiated by substituting the vector of **wrong** as the part-of-speech tag of **insufficient** is **JJ** (Santorini, 1990). Therefore the modified version of the RNTN model has the capability of identifying the sentiment of the above sentence as negative. The figure 1 shows how the sentiment is induced through the newly instantiated

word vector.

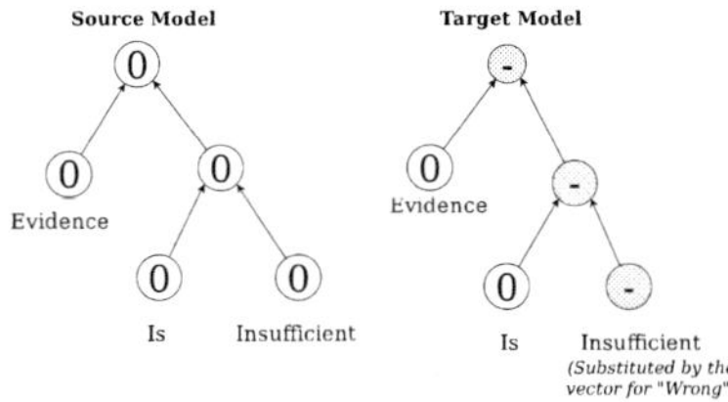

Figure 1: Sentiment Prediction for a phrase with words not in source's vocabulary but in target's vocabulary

And there are scenarios where the term is in the vocabulary of the *Socher Model* but has a different sentiment compared to the legal domain. Consider the sentence "*Sam is charged with a crime*" which was mentioned in section 3.2,

In section 3.2, we have identified that the term *charged* denotes a different sentiment in legal domain compared to movie reviews. The source RNTN model outputs a positive sentiment for that given sentence as the term *charged* is identified as having a positive sentiment according to movie reviews domain. And that term is the cause for having such an output from the source model. The figure 2 indicates how the change we introduced in the target model (in section 3.2) induce the correct sentiment up to the root level of the phrase. Therefore, the target model identifies the sentiment correctly for the given phrase.

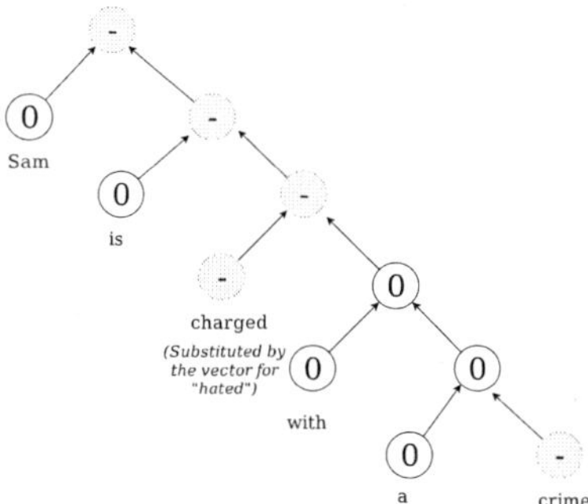

Figure 2: Sentiment Prediction for a phrase with words having deviated sentiment in two domains - target model

To improve the recall in identifying phrases with negative sentiment, we have added another rule to the classification criteria. The source RNTN model (*Socher Model*) provides the score for each of the five classes such that all those five scores sum up to 1. If the negative sentiment class has the highest score, the sentiment label of the phrase will be *negative*. Otherwise, the phrase again can be classified as having a *negative* sentiment if the score for negative sentiment class is above 0.4. If those two conditions are not met, the phrase will be classified as having a *non-negative* sentiment. Section 4 provides observations and results regarding the improved criteria.

4   Experiments and Results

The proposed approach in this paper is based on transfer learning. Therefore, we needed to create a golden standard for identifying sentiments of phrases and sentences in the legal domain in order to evaluate the model. The phrases and sentences for the test data set are randomly picked from legal case transcripts based on the United States Supreme Court. During the selection process, we have selected an equal amount of phrases for both classes according to the *Socher Model*. Each of these phrases and sentences is annotated by three human annotators. Since the classification process is binary, we pick the sentiment class for each test subject based on the maximum number of votes. In the end, we prepare the test data set containing nearly 1500 annotations to use in the evaluation process.

In the experiment, we compare the sentiment class picked by human judges and the modified RNTN model. As the baseline model, we use the source RNTN model (*Socher Model*) to check the impact caused by the proposed transfer learning approach. The acquired results from the baseline model is shown in Table 3 and results from the target model is shown in Table 4.

According to Table 3 and Table 4, there is a 10% improvement in identifying phrases with negative sentiment. The reason is that there are a lot of unknown words which are in the legal domain but not in movie reviews corpus. In addition, we have introduced new criteria based on a threshold for the score of negative class to improve the recall. Due to that reason, the precision in identifying phrases with a negative sentiment is 0.8441. But if we compare with the precision of the baseline model (*Socher Model*) for negative sentiment class is 0.7962 which is a lower value. Since the test dataset is not skewed a lot towards one class, it is fair to consider the accuracy of the system in predicting the sentiment for any given phrase. The baseline model shows the accuracy of 70.17% while the target model shows 76.80%. The im-

provement in accuracy is above 6%.

Predicted Actual	Negative	Non-negative	*Total*
Negative	60.43%	39.57%	278
Non-negative	18.29%	81.71%	235
Total	211	301	513

Table 3: Confusion Matrix for Results from the Baseline Model

Predicted Actual	Negative	Non-negative	*Total*
Negative	70.14%	29.86%	278
Non-negative	15.32%	84.68%	235
Total	231	282	513

Table 4: Confusion Matrix for Results from the Improved Model

The observed results in Table 3 and Table 4 show that there is a 6% improvement of the sentiment with respect to the baseline model. There are a few reasons behind the results. As we randomly selected phrases from the legal case transcripts corpus, only 45% of the phrases actually contained the words where we had substituted the vector regarding sentiment. Therefore, the output for 55% of the phrases from the baseline model and the target model was the same. If we compare the output provided by the baseline model and the target model, output of 9.5% of the total phrases are different to each other. Therefore the difference between the two models is based on that 9.5% of the total phrases.

5   Conclusion

This study is focused on building an automatic sentiment annotator for legal texts based on the *Recursive Neural Tensor Network (RNTN)* model mentioned in Socher et al. (2013b). Furthermore, this study can be identified as a transfer learning approach as it is not required to prepare a training data set for the legal domain specifically. Instead, this approach uses the same training data set stated in Socher et al. (2013b). This task can be recognized as a domain adaptation task. The proposed approach could achieve a 70.14% recall in identifying phrases with negative sentiments (improvement is 10% compared to the source model). The accuracy of the target model is above 76% which is a 6% improvement over the source model.

References

Stefano Baccianella, Andrea Esuli, and Fabrizio Sebastiani. 2010. Sentiwordnet 3.0: an enhanced lexical resource for sentiment analysis and opinion mining. In *Lrec*, volume 10, pages 2200–2204.

Jack G Conrad and Frank Schilder. 2007. Opinion mining in legal blogs. In *Proceedings of the 11th international conference on Artificial intelligence and law*, pages 231–236. ACM.

Andrea Esuli and Fabrizio Sebastiani. 2007. Sentiwordnet: a high-coverage lexical resource for opinion mining. *Evaluation*, 17:1–26.

Vindula Jayawardana, Dimuthu Lakmal, Nisansa de Silva, Amal Shehan Perera, Keet Sugathadasa, and Buddhi Ayesha. 2017a. Deriving a representative vector for ontology classes with instance word vector embeddings. In *Innovative Computing Technology (INTECH), 2017 Seventh International Conference on*, pages 79–84. IEEE.

Vindula Jayawardana, Dimuthu Lakmal, Nisansa de Silva, Amal Shehan Perera, Keet Sugathadasa, Buddhi Ayesha, and Madhavi Perera. 2017b. Semi-supervised instance population of an ontology using word vector embedding. In *Advances in ICT for Emerging Regions (ICTer), 2017 Seventeenth International Conference on*, pages 1–7. IEEE.

Vindula Jayawardana, Dimuthu Lakmal, Nisansa de Silva, Amal Shehan Perera, Keet Sugathadasa, Buddhi Ayesha, and Madhavi Perera. 2017c. Word vector embeddings and domain specific semantic based semi-supervised ontology instance population. *International Journal on Advances in ICT for Emerging Regions*, 10(1):1.

Rachel Tsz-Wai Lo, Ben He, and Iadh Ounis. 2005. Automatically building a stopword list for an information retrieval system. In *Journal on Digital Information Management: Special Issue on the 5th Dutch-Belgian Information Retrieval Workshop (DIR)*, volume 5, pages 17–24.

Yue Lu, Hongning Wang, ChengXiang Zhai, and Dan Roth. 2012. Unsupervised discovery of opposing opinion networks from forum discussions. In *Proceedings of the 21st ACM international conference on Information and knowledge management*, pages 1642–1646. ACM.

John J Nay. 2016. Gov2vec: Learning distributed representations of institutions and their legal text. *arXiv preprint arXiv:1609.06616*.

Bruno Ohana and Brendan Tierney. 2009. Sentiment classification of reviews using sentiwordnet. In *9th. IT & T Conference*, page 13.

Ariadna Quattoni, Michael Collins, and Trevor Darrell. 2008. Transfer learning for image classification with sparse prototype representations. In *Computer Vision and Pattern Recognition, 2008. CVPR 2008. IEEE Conference on*, pages 1–8. IEEE.

Rajat Raina, Alexis Battle, Honglak Lee, Benjamin Packer, and Andrew Y Ng. 2007. Self-taught learning: transfer learning from unlabeled data. In *Proceedings of the 24th international conference on Machine learning*, pages 759–766. ACM.

Beatrice Santorini. 1990. Part-of-speech tagging guidelines for the penn treebank project (3rd revision). *Technical Reports (CIS)*, page 570.

Richard Socher, Milind Ganjoo, Christopher D Manning, and Andrew Ng. 2013a. Zero-shot learning through cross-modal transfer. In *Advances in neural information processing systems*, pages 935–943.

Richard Socher, Alex Perelygin, Jean Wu, Jason Chuang, Christopher D Manning, Andrew Ng, and Christopher Potts. 2013b. Recursive deep models for semantic compositionality over a sentiment treebank. In *Proceedings of the 2013 conference on empirical methods in natural language processing*, pages 1631–1642.

Keet Sugathadasa, Buddhi Ayesha, Nisansa de Silva, Amal Shehan Perera, Vindula Jayawardana, Dimuthu Lakmal, and Madhavi Perera. 2017. Synergistic union of word2vec and lexicon for domain specific semantic similarity. In *Industrial and Information Systems (ICIIS), 2017 IEEE International Conference on*, pages 1–6. IEEE.

Keet Sugathadasa, Buddhi Ayesha, Nisansa de Silva, Amal Shehan Perera, Vindula Jayawardana, Dimuthu Lakmal, and Madhavi Perera. 2018. Legal document retrieval using document vector embeddings and deep learning. *arXiv preprint arXiv:1805.10685*.

Kristina Toutanova, Dan Klein, Christopher D Manning, and Yoram Singer. 2003. Feature-rich part-of-speech tagging with a cyclic dependency network. In *Proceedings of the 2003 Conference of the North American Chapter of the Association for Computational Linguistics on Human Language Technology-Volume 1*, pages 173–180. Association for Computational Linguistics.

CJ Van Rijsbergen. 1979. Information retrieval. dept. of computer science, university of glasgow. *URL: citeseer. ist. psu. edu/vanrijsbergen79information. html*, 14.

Janyce Wiebe, Theresa Wilson, and Claire Cardie. 2005. Annotating expressions of opinions and emotions in language. *Language resources and evaluation*, 39(2-3):165–210.

What Makes You Stressed? Finding Reasons From Tweets

Reshmi Gopalakrishna Pillai, Mike Thelwall and Constantin Orasan
Research Institute in Information and Language Processing
University of Wolverhampton, UK
reshmi.g85@gmail.com, {m.thelwall,c.orasan}@wlv.ac.uk

Abstract

Detecting stress from social media gives a non-intrusive and inexpensive alternative to traditional tools such as questionnaires or physiological sensors for monitoring mental state of individuals. This paper introduces a novel framework for finding reasons for stress from tweets, analyzing multiple categories for the first time. Three word-vector based methods are evaluated on collections of tweets about politics or airlines and are found to be more accurate than standard machine learning algorithms.

1 Introduction

Stress is the manifestation of physical or emotional pressure, often as a bodily response to a real or perceived challenge. Selye (1936) defines it as non-specific response of the body to any demand for change. It is an important aspect of the mental state of people including business customers, citizens involved in political debates, and commuters. If detected automatically, it can be used to predict problems such as customer churn, threatening political events or transportation deadlocks in these contexts. In socio-political domains, such as politics, sports, and news, stress detection can help in understanding the stress trends to get a collective mental state of the target population. For example, increases in apparent stress, topics generating stress, or geographical stress hotspots might all have important consequences. Also, for service-centric businesses,

including hotels, airports and airlines, in which the owner's goal is to provide a stress-free stay, travel or transit, it is valuable to know the causes of stress for customers, which might point to issues requiring immediate attention.

Social media can be harnessed to discover trends in group or individual emotions and moods. Although previous studies (reviewed below) have developed methods to detect stress in social media, the causes of stress also need to be known so that remedial actions can be targeted more effectively. In response, this research implements a novel framework for finding the causes of stress expressed in tweets. This study introduces a method to classify stress causes from tweets belonging to two domains, one each from socio-political (Politics) and service-centric (Airlines) domains, to demonstrate the viability of the methods.

The contributions of this work are as follows:

1. This is the first multiple category study detecting reasons for stress expressed in tweets.
2. A dataset of tweets annotated with reasons for stress.

2 Related Work

2.1 Stress Detection from Social Media

In recent years, social media content analysis has emerged as a useful tool to evaluate the mental health of users. Internet usage patterns (Kotikalapudi et al, 2012) and status messages on Facebook (Moreno et al, 2011) have been demonstrated to be viable tools for evaluating

Proceedings of the 9th Workshop on Computational Approaches to Subjectivity, Sentiment and Social Media Analysis, pages 266–272
Brussels, Belgium, October 31, 2018. ©2018 Association for Computational Linguistics
https://doi.org/10.18653/v1/P17

depressive tendencies. Similarly, message content and interaction patterns on Twitter can also be harnessed to help identify depression (De Choudhury et al, 2013), Post Traumatic Stress Disorder (PTSD) (Coppersmith et al, 2014), and postpartum emotional and behavioral changes (De Choudhury et al., 2013).

TensiStrength (Thelwall et al, 2017) is the first lexical based program to detect the strength of stress and relaxation in tweets. Its lexicon is derived from LIWC (Tausczik and Pennebaker, 2010), General Inquirer (Stone et al, 1986) and emotion terms from the sentiment analysis software SentiStrength (Thelwall et al, 2010; Thelwall et al, 2012). TensiStrength estimates stress (on a scale of -1 to -5) and relaxation (on a scale of +1 to +5) with accuracy comparable to several general machine learning algorithms. The performance of this system was improved by adding word sense disambiguation as a preprocessing step for tweets (Gopalakrishna Pillai et al., 2018).

Though there is a growing interest in finding expressions of stress from social media content, as discussed above, the existing research does not, for the most part, discuss the reasons for stress. Our model, on the other hand, studies the reasons for stress in multiple categories.

2.2 Topic Modelling in Tweets

Topic modelling is the extraction of latent topics in documents, which may be helpful to find stress reasons from a collection of texts. Two common topic modelling methods for documents are Latent Dirichlet Allocation (LDA) (Blei et al, 2003) and Author Topic Models (ATM) (Rozen-Zvi et al., 2005).

The applicability of these methods to tweets is hindered by informal language, grammatical errors, slang and emoticons. To overcome these issues, aggregation of related tweets into individual documents has been proposed as a potential solution, called pooling.

Mehrotra et al (2013) proposed one of the most widely accepted pooling methods to overcome the limited coherence of LDA on Twitter data. It found that pooling tweets by hashtags performs better than other pooling schemes (author-wise, hourly, and burst-wise) based on Point-wise Mutual Information (PMI), NMI scores and purity scores.

Alvares-Melis and Saveski (2016) present a scheme for tweet pooling in which tweets and their replies are aggregated into a single document. The users who participate in the conversation are considered to be co-authors of this pooled document. We used an LDA-based topic modelling with hashtag pooling in our present study. Though conversation pooling was found to give better performance compared to hashtag pooling, it was not suitable for our datasets, which consisted of tweets having the relevant hashtags and could not be grouped into 'conversations'.

2.3 Word Vectors and its Application in Sentiment Analysis

Liu (2012) defines sentiment Analysis is as the field of study that analyses opinions or sentiments of people towards entities such as products, services, individuals and their attributes. Sentiments in text are most often expressed by opinion words which has positive (good, wonderful, fantastic) or negative (bad, poor, horrible) polarity. However, finding the inherent sentiment of a text from content words is not a straightforward problem, due to ambiguity of word meanings and complex sentiments such as sarcasm. Hence, efficient and accurate word representations which considers the context information also, become necessary.

Representation of words as real-valued vectors has been employed in sentiment analysis, as in other NLP problems. There are two common architectures for word vector representations: Word2Vec (Mikolov et al, 2013) and GloVe (Pennington et al, 2014). Word2Vec has two models: Skipgram where the objective is to predict a word's context given the word itself and Bag of Words (BoW) where the objective is to predict a word given its context. GloVe (Global Vectors) was proposed as an alternative model, in which the global corpus statistics are captured directly. Over the years, there have been attempts to incorporate the sentiment information of the words into these vectors, to make them more suitable for analysis of sentiment in documents and short texts such as tweets (Maas et al,2011, Tang et al., 2014). Our methods to find stress reasons from tweets also use word vector representations as illustrated in the next section.

3 Methods

3.1 Overview

The proposed method selects reasons for stress expressed in tweets from a pre-defined list of potential stressors for tweets belonging to two categories, politics and airlines, collected by the Tweepy API. Tweets with high stress scores, as judged by TensiStrength, were considered for creating this list of potential stressors. These high-stress tweets were subjected to topic modelling and k-means clustering to find the clusters of frequently occurring topics. Topic modelling provides a soft clustering of the topics, however we followed it with k-means clustering to obtain coherent collections of topics. These topic clusters were manually refined to generate title words that most aptly encompass each cluster. The title words constituted a list of potential stressors for the tweets of that category.

To automatically detect stress reasons, the tweets were processed by three new word-vector based methods to find a reason for the stress expressed within them. These were compared with reasons found by human coders to evaluate the accuracy.

3.2 Method details

Finding Potential Stressors: The first step is to form a list of potential reasons for stress in a given category/domain.

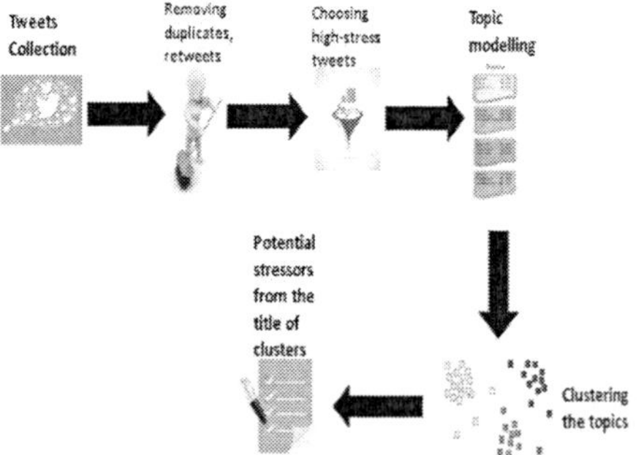

Figure 1: Finding potential stressors for a category/domain.

Word Vector Processing: The tweets were preprocessed to eliminate URLs, prepositions, interjections and conjunctions. Constituent words in hashtags were separated. The remaining words constitute the content words set. Three different word-vector based methods were used to find causes of stress from the list of potential stressors.

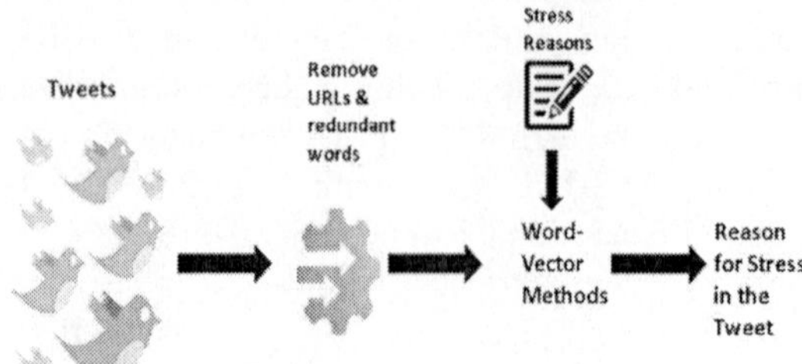

Figure 2: Finding reasons for stress in tweets.

Method 1 (maximum word similarity): The cosine similarity of each word in the content words set was calculated with each potential stressor. The stressor with highest similarity with any of the content words in the tweet was chosen as the stress cause.

Method 2 (context vector similarity): A context vector was found for each tweet by calculating the average of the word vectors of all words in the content words set. The stressor with highest cosine similarity with this context vector was chosen as the stress cause.

Method 3 (cluster vector similarity): Each stressor was represented by a cluster vector which is the average of vectors of all words in its topic cluster. The cosine similarity of each of these cluster vectors was calculated with the context vector and the cluster with maximum similarity was chosen as the stress cause.

3.3 Dataset and Annotation

Two different datasets of public Twitter posts were collected with the Tweepy API.

Politics: For political tweets, the search parameter was the hashtag "#politics AND #us" and #uspolitics from 14.04.2018 to 14.05.2018. This retrieved 22293 tweets, which were processed to remove duplicates, retweets and tweets with only URLs. The resulting dataset had 8163 tweets. The first task was to make a list of potential stressors for tweets which could be used for the further stressor identification tasks. The underlying assumption was that frequently discussed topics in tweets with very high stress scores were potential stressors.

Stress scores were assigned on a scale of -1 (no stress) to -5 (high stress) to each tweet in the dataset, using TensiStrength. The 2205 tweets having a stress score of -5 or -4 were filtered to form the corpus for further processing. They were then preprocessed by removing all URLs,

@usernames and stop words and divided into groups of 200 tweets each (11 groups, the last one having 205 tweets). The dominant topics in each group were found by an LDA-based topic modelling with hashtag pooling implementation in Python. These topics were aggregated and the k-means clustering algorithm used to separate them into 7 clusters. This number of clusters produced the most coherent and intuitive clusters for this collection.

The seven clusters were manually checked to find the most apt descriptive word for each one, after removing outliers, if any. For example, one cluster had topic modelling key terms: **rape, crime, rage, murder, terrorism, fight, chaos, avalanche, abuse.** We chose to describe this cluster by the word "violence". The title words for all 7 clusters constitute the list of potential stressors. Clusters and potential stressors emerging from them are listed in Table 1.

Example topics in the cluster	Stressor
Vote voter polls candidate race	Election
Public activity support boycott	Protest
Rape crime rage murder terrorism fight chaos avalanche abuse	Violence
Democrats Republican Trump	Person/ Party
Press report news scandal publicity editor	Media
Social system education act government	Policy
Wages inequality employed education college productivity	Economy

Table 1: Clusters and stressors (Politics)

To evaluate the new methods, out of the 8163 tweets obtained after duplicate removal, 4517 tweets with expressions of stress were selected (TensiStrength scores, -5, -4 or -3). 2000 tweets were randomly chosen from this collection and were annotated individually and independently by three human coders. Their task was to select the most appropriate stressor from the predefined list of potential stressors produced by the topic modeling. Coding guidelines were provided and inter-coder agreement scores were calculated using

Krippendorff's α (Krippendorff, 2004) and Pearson's correlation. The values, given in Table 2, were high enough to justify the use of the human codes.

Agreement Between	Krippendorff's α
A and B	72.54
B and C	75.95
A and B	73.17

Table 2: Inter-coder agreement for stressor annotation (Politics)

Airlines: A similar process was followed to create the Airlines dataset. The tweets were obtained by searching for hashtags belonging to 9 popular airlines (#gojetairlines, #allnipponairways, #airnewzealand, #swissair, #turkishairlines, #airfrance, #unitedairlines, #emirateairlines, #ryanair), during the same period as the political tweets. The search returned 31457 tweets and, after duplicates and retweets removal, 7965 tweets. Out of this, 3214 tweets were found to have expressions of high stress, (stress score -5 or -4) using TensiStrength system. These were analyzed by topic modelling to find out the list of potential stressors in the category, as detailed in the previous section.

The 3214 tweets having stress values of -5 or -4 were divided into groups of 300 (11 groups, the last group having 214 tweets) and using topic modelling with hashtag pooling we found out the topics in each groups; which was aggregated and further analyzed by k-means clustering to form five clusters after manual refining to remove the outliers. Examples of topics in the five detected clusters and the stressor title word corresponding to each of them are given in Table 2.

Example topics in the cluster	Stressor
Cost money ticket airline expensive	Cost
Delay delayed hours time today cancellation	Delay
Service customer staff food pilot	Service
Strike messed hijack attack	Violence
Luggage issue carry missing stolen	Luggage

Table 3: Clusters and stressors (Airlines)

Out of the 7965 tweets after duplicate removal, 4367 had stress scores of -3 or above, and we chose 2000 tweets from this randomly, to be annotated for stress reasons. The inter-coder agreement between the three coders is given below in Table 4.

Agreement Between	Krippendorff's α
A and B	71.23
B and C	76.19
A and B	78.23

Table 4: Inter-coder agreement for stressor annotation (Airlines)

High inter-coder agreement values in both categories denote that the problem definition and guidelines are well-defined and followed.

3.3 Experimental Setup

For training the word vectors used in the experiments, a Twitter Word2Vec model trained on 400 million tweets was used, released as part of an ACL W-NUT tasks (Godin et al, 2015).

We ran three machine learning algorithms as comparison baselines.

• AdaBoost: An adaptive boosting algorithm based on a simple classifier.

• Logistic Regression: Simple logistic regression.

• SVM: Support Vector Machines using sequential minimal optimization.

The classifiers were implemented using their default configurations in Weka 3.6. Term unigrams, bigrams and trigrams and their frequencies were the features used. Punctuation was included as a term, with consecutive punctuation treated as a single term (e.g., emoticons, multiple exclamation marks). Cross-sentence bigrams and trigrams were not allowed.

This feature selection was adapted from a similar task of finding the stress and relaxation magnitudes of tweets, in our previous research work TensiStrength (Thelwall, 2017).

4 Results

4.1 Results Summary

The stress reasons were found using the three methods discussed in the previous section. Based on Pearson correlations and exact match percentages with the human annotated scores, the cluster vector method best detects stress reasons (Tables 5, 6).

Method	Accuracy
max. word	47.81
context vector	54.63
cluster vector	**63.41**
SVM	52.48
AdaBoost	50.64
Logistic	49.23

Table 4: Performance of stress reason detection methods in Politics tweets

Method	Accuracy
max. word	50.13
context vector	59.74
cluster vector	**67.29**
SVM	58.13
AdaBoost	54.85
Logistic	52.15

Table 5: Performance of stress reason detection methods in Airlines tweets

4.2 Distribution of reasons

The percentage of tweets with different reasons of stress, according to the cluster vector method, are given in figures 3 and 4.

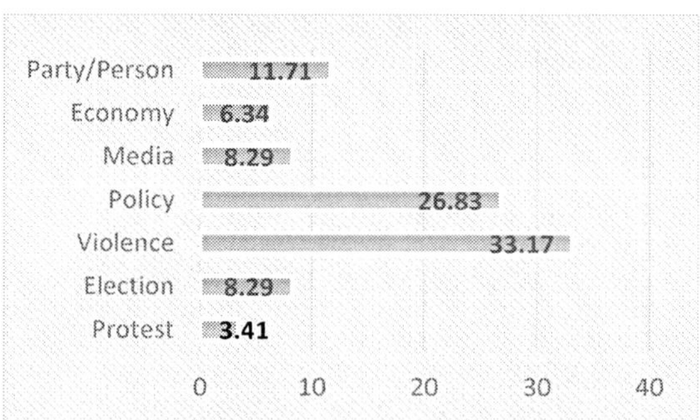

Figure 3: Stress reasons (%) – Politics.

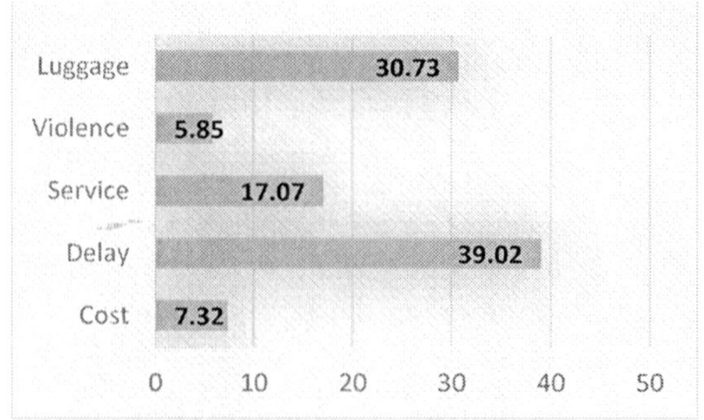

Figure 4: Stress reasons (%) – Airlines.

It is unsurprising that in many (34%) political tweets, violence is the cause of stress and in 39% of airline tweets, delay is the reason. This can be applied in identifying areas of urgent improvement in customer centric businesses.

4.3   Error analysis

There are some systematic reasons for the methods failing to find the correct stress reason.

Misleading hashtags or content words: "At least 14 killed in hockey team's bus crash #news #CNN" This tweet has hashtags #news #CNN which makes all word-vector based methods choose the reason as "media" instead of "violence". "Stocks dive amid fears of trade war" is another example. The human annotated stress reason is "economy" but, war is a misleading word which causes method 1 to choose "violence" as stressor. In methods 2 and 3 where the aggregated tweet vector instead of vectors of individual words are considered, the stressor economy is correctly identified.

Multiple stressors: Tweets in which there are multiple reasons for stress. E.g.: "Killing opponents is a ruthless way to win in elections" has two stressors, "election" and "violence". Expanding the methods to accommodate multiple stressors (by choosing all stressors with cosine similarity with the tweets/content words in tweets above a threshold) will improve its performance in such tweets.

5   Conclusion and Future Work

This paper described three new methods for finding reasons for stress in Tweets list. Datasets comprising of 2000 tweets for Politics and Airlines were manually annotated for stress reasons. The methods found stress reasons more accurately than standard machine learning, although it had problems when multiple causes were expressed in the same tweet, or when key words in the tweet were misleading.

This is the first multi-category study on finding stress reasons in tweets, though limited by the restriction to two domains (politics and airlines) and one source (Twitter). Future work needs to analyze the other domains and also automate the method to detect the potential stress reasons for different domains.

References

David Alvarez-Melis and Martin Saveski. 2016. Topic Modeling in Twitter: Aggregating Tweets by Conversations. ICWSM.

David M. Blei, Andrew Y. Ng, and Michael I. Jordan. 2003. Latent dirichlet allocation. J. Mach. Learn. Res. 3 (March 2003), 993-1022.

Glen A. Coppersmith, Craig T. Harman, and Mark Dredze. 2014. Measuring post-traumatic stress disorder in Twitter. In Proceedings of the International AAAI Conference on Weblogs and Social Media (ICWSM).

Munmun De Choudhury, Michael Gamon, Scott Counts, and Eric Horvitz. 2013. Predicting depression via social media. In Proceedings of the International AAAI Conference on Weblogs and Social Media (ICWSM).

Munmun De Choudhury, Scott Counts, and Eric Horvitz. 2013. Predicting postpartum changes in emotion and behavior via social media. In Proceedings of the ACM Annual Conference on Human Factors in Computing Systems (CHI), 3267–3276

Sally S. Dickerson and Margaret E. Kemeny. 2004 Acute Stressors and Cortisol Responses: A Theoretical Integration and Synthesis of Laboratory Research. Psychological Bulletin, 130, 355-391. http://dx.doi.org/10.1037/0033-2909.130.3.355

Frederic Godin, Baptist Vandersmissen, Wesley De Neve and Rik Van de Walle. 2015. Multimedia Lab@ ACL W-NUT NER shared task: Named entity recognition for Twitter microposts using distributed word representations. In: Proceedings of ACL-IJCNLP (p. 146).

Reshmi Gopalakrishna Pillai, Mike Thelwall, Constantin Orasan. 2018. Detection of Stress and Relaxation Magnitudes for Tweets. In The 2018 Web Conference Companion (WWW'18 Companion), April 23-27, 2018, Lyon, France, ACM, New York, NY, 8 pages. DOI: https://doi.org/10.1145/3184558.3191627

Elias Jónsson and Jake Stolee. "An Evaluation of Topic Modelling Techniques for Twitter."

Raghavendra Kotikalapudi, Sriram Chellappan, Frances Montgomery. 2012. Associating Internet usage with depressive behavior among college students. IEEE Technol SocMag.;31:73–80.

Klaus Krippendorff. 2004. Content analysis: An introduction to its methodology. Thousand Oaks, CA: Sage

Bing Liu. 2012. Sentiment Analysis and Opinion s Mining. Morgan & Claypool Publishers.

Andrew L. Maas, Raymond E. Daly, Peter T. Pham, Dan Huang, Andrew Y. Ng, and Christopher Potts. 2011. Learning word vectors for sentiment analysis. In Proceedings of the 49th Annual Meeting of the Association for Computational Linguistics: Human Language Technologies - Volume 1 (HLT '11), Vol. 1. Association for Computational Linguistics, Stroudsburg, PA, USA, 142-150.

Rishabh Mehrotra, Scott Sanner, Wray Buntine, and Lexing Xie. 2013. Improving LDA topic models for microblogs via tweet pooling and automatic labeling. In Proceedings of the 36th international ACM SIGIR conference on Research and development in information retrieval (SIGIR '13). ACM, New York, NY, USA, 889-892. DOI=http://dx.doi.org/10.1145/2484028.2484166

Tomas Mikolov, Chen Kai, Greg Corrado, and Jeffrey Dean. 2013 Efficient estimation of word representations in vector space. arXiv preprint arXiv:1301.3781

Tomas Mikolov, Ilya Sutskever, Kai Chen, Greg S. Corrado, and Jeff Dean. 2013. "Distributed representations of words and phrases and their compositionality." In Advances in neural information processing systems, pp. 3111-3119.

Megan A. Moreno, Lauren A. Jelenchick, Katie G. Egan, Elizabeth Cox, Henry Young, Kerry E. Gannon, Tara Becker. 2011. Feeling bad on Facebook: Depression disclosure by college students on a social networking site. Depression and Anxiety, 28(6), 447–455.

Jeffrey Pennington, Richard Socher, and Christopher Manning. "Glove: Global vectors for word representation." In Proceedings of the 2014 conference on empirical methods in natural language processing (EMNLP), pp. 1532-1543. 2014.

Michal Rosen-Zvi, Thomas Griffiths, Mark Steyvers, and Padhraic Smyth. 2004. The author-topic model for authors and documents. In Proceedings of the 20th conference on Uncertainty in artificial intelligence (UAI '04). AUAI Press, Arlington, Virginia, United States, 487-494.

Hans Selye. 1956. The Stress of Life. New York, McGraw-Hill Book Company, Inc.

Philip J. Stone, Dexter C. Dunphy, Marshall S. Smith and Daniel M. Ogilvie. 1966. The general inquirer: A computer approach to content analysis. Cambridge, MA: The MIT Press.

Duyu Tang, Furu Wei, Nan Yang, Ming Zhou, Ting Liu, Bing Qin. (2014). Learning Sentiment-Specific Word Embedding for Twitter Sentiment Classification. 52nd Annual Meeting of the Association for Computational Linguistics, ACL 2014 - Proceedings of the Conference. 1. 1555-1565. 10.3115/v1/P14-1146.

Yla R. Tausczik and James W. Pennebaker, 2010. The psychological meaning of words: LIWC and computerized text analysis methods. Journal of language and social psychology, 29(1), 24-54.

Mike Thelwall. 2017. TensiStrength: stress and relaxation magnitude detection for social media texts. Journal of Information Processing and Management. 53: 106–121

Mike Thelwall, Kevan Buckley Georgios Paltoglou, D. Cai and A. Kappas. 2010. Sentiment strength detection in short informal text. Journal of the American Society for Information Science and Technology, 61(12), 2544–2558.

Mike Thelwall, Kevan Buckley, and Georgios Paltoglou. 2012. Sentiment strength detection for the social web. J. Am. Soc. Inf. Sci. Technol. 63, 1 (January 2012), 163-173. DOI=http://dx.doi.org/10.1002/asi.21662

Liang-Chih Yu, Jin Wang, K. Robert Lai, and Xuejie Zhang. 2018. Refining Word Embeddings Using Intensity Scores for Sentiment Analysis. IEEE/ACM Trans. Audio, Speech and Lang. Proc. 26, 3 (March 2018), 671-681. DOI: https://doi.org/10.1109/TASLP.2017.2788182

EmojiGAN: learning emojis distributions with a generative model

Bogdan Mazoure[*]
Department of Mathematics & Statistics
McGill University

Thang Doan[*]
Desautels Faculty of Management
McGill University

Saibal Ray
Desautels Faculty of Management
McGill University

Abstract

Generative models have recently experienced a surge in popularity due to the development of more efficient training algorithms and increasing computational power. Models such as adversarial generative networks (GANs) have been successfully used in various areas such as computer vision, medical imaging, style transfer and natural language generation. Adversarial nets were recently shown to yield results in the image-to-text task, where given a set of images, one has to provide their corresponding text description. In this paper, we take a similar approach and propose a image-to-emoji architecture, which is trained on data from social networks and can be used to score a given picture using ideograms. We show empirical results of our algorithm on data obtained from the most influential Instagram accounts.

1 Introduction

The spike in the amount of user-generated visual and textual data shared on social platforms such as Facebook, Twitter, Instagram, Pinterest and many others luckily coincides with the development of efficient deep learning algorithms (Perozzi et al., 2014; Pennacchiotti and Popescu, 2011; Goyal et al., 2010). As humans, we can not only share our ideas and thoughts through any imaginable media, but also use social networks to analyze and understand complex interpersonal relations. Researchers have access to a rich set of metadata (Krizhevsky, 2012; Liu et al., 2015) on which various computer vision (CV) and natural language processing (NLP) algorithms can be trained.

For instance, recent work in the area of image captioning aims to provide a short description (i.e. caption) of a much larger document or image (Dai et al., 2017; You et al., 2016; Pu et al., 2016). Such

methods excel at conveying the dominant idea of the input. On the other hand, we use ideograms, also popular under the names of emojis or pictographs as a natural amalgam between annotation and summarization tasks. Note that, in this work, we use the terms emoji, ideogram and pictograph interchangeably to represent the intersection of these three domains. Ideograms bridge together the textual and visual spaces by representing groups of words with a concise illustration. They can be seen as surrogate functions which convey, up to a degree of accuracy, reactions of social media users. Furthermore, because each emoji has a corresponding text description, there is a direct mapping from ideograms onto the word space.

In this paper, we model the distribution of emojis conditioned on an image with a deep generative model. We use generative adversarial networks (GANs) (Goodfellow et al., 2014), which are notoriously known to be harder to train than other distributional models such as variational auto-encoders (VAEs) (Kingma and Welling, 2013) but tend to produce sharper results on computer vision tasks.

2 Related Work and Motivation

Since the release of word2vec by Mikolov and colleagues in 2013 (Mikolov et al., 2013), vector representations of language entities have become more popular than traditional encodings such as bag-of-words (BOW) or n-grams (NG). Because word2vec operations preserve the original semantic meaning of words, concepts like word similarity and synonyms are well-defined in the new space and correspond to closest neighbors of a point according to some metric.

The aforementionned word representation was followed by doc2vec (Le and Mikolov, 2014). Orig-

---

These authors contributed equally.

Proceedings of the 9th Workshop on Computational Approaches to Subjectivity, Sentiment and Social Media Analysis, pages 273–279
Brussels, Belgium, October 31, 2018. ©2018 Association for Computational Linguistics
https://doi.org/10.18653/v1/P17

inally, doc2vec was meant to efficiently encode collections of words as a whole. However, since empirical results suggest a similar performance for both algorithms, researchers tend to opt for the simpler and more interpretable word2vec model. One of the most recent and the most interesting vector embeddings has been emoji2vec (Eisner et al., 2016). It consists of more than 1,600 symbol-vector pairs, each associating a Unicode character to a real $300-$dimensional vector. The abundance of pictographs such as emojis on social communication platforms suggests that word-only analyses are limited in their scope to capture the full scale of interactions between individuals. Emojis' biggest advantage is their universality: no information is lost due to faulty translations, mistyped characters or even slang words. In fact, emojis were designed to be more concise and expressive than words. They, however, have been shown to suffer from varying interpretations which depend of factors such as viewing the pictograph on an iPhone or a Google Pixel (Miller et al., 2016). This in turn implies that the subject of conversation highly impacts the choice of media (text or emoji) picked by the user (Kelly and Watts, 2015). Reducing a whole media such as a public post or an advertisement image to a single emoji would almost certainly mean loosing the richness of information, which is why we suggest to instead model visual media as a conditional distribution over emojis that users employ to score the image.

Deep neural models have previously been used to analyse pictographic data: (Cappallo et al., 2015) used them to assign the most likely emoji to a picture, (Felbo et al., 2017) predicted the prevalent emotion of a sentence and (Zhao and Zeng, 2017) used recurrent neural networks (RNNs) to predict the emoji which best describes a given sentence. We build on top of this work to propose Emoji-GAN $-$ a model meant to generate realistic emojis based on an image. Since we are interested in modeling a distribution over image-emoji tuples, it is reasonable to represent it using generative adversarial networks. They have been shown to successfully memorize distributions over both text and images. For example, a GAN can be coupled with RNNs in order to generate realistic images based on an input sentence (Reed et al., 2016). We train our algorithm on emoji-picture pairs obtained from various advertisement posts on Insta-

gram. A practical application of our method is to analyze the effects of product advertisement on Instagram users. Previous works attempted to predict the popularity of Instagram posts by using surrogate signals such as number of likes or followers (Almgren et al., 2016; De et al., 2017). Others used social media data in order to model the popularity of fashion industry icons (Park et al., 2016). A thorough inspection of clothing styles around the world has also been conducted (Matzen et al., 2017).

3 Proposed Approach

3.1 Generative Adversarial Networks

Generative Adversarial Networks (GANs) (Goodfellow et al., 2014) have recently gained huge popularity as a blackbox unsupervised method of learning some target distribution. Taking roots in game theory, their training process is framed as a two player zero-sum game where a generator network G tries to fool a discriminator network D by producing samples closely mimicking the distribution of interest. In this work, we use Wasserstein-GAN (Arjovsky et al., 2017), a variant of the original GAN which uses the Wasserstein metric in order to avoid problems such as mode collapse. The generator and the discriminator are gradually improved through either alternating or simultaneous gradient descent minimization of the loss function defined as:

$$\min_{G} \max_{D} \ \mathop{\mathbb{E}}_{x \sim f_X(x)} [D(x)] + \mathop{\mathbb{E}}_{x \sim G(z)} [-D(x)] + p(\lambda),$$
$$(1)$$

where $p(\lambda) = \lambda(\|\nabla_{\tilde{x}} D(\tilde{x})\| - 1)^2$,
$\tilde{x} = \varepsilon x + (1 - \varepsilon)G(Z)$, $\varepsilon \sim \mathrm{Uniform}(0, 1)$,
and $Z \sim f_Z(z)$. This gradient penalized loss (Gulrajani et al., 2017) is now widely used to enforce the Lipschitz continuity constraint. Note that setting $\lambda = 0$ recovers the original WGAN objective.

3.2 Choice of embedding

Multiple embeddings have been proposed to encode language entities such as words, ideograms, sentences and even documents. A more recent successor of word2vec, emoji2vec aims to encode groups of words represented by visual symbols (ie ideograms or emojis). This representation is a fine-tuned version of word2vec which was trained on roughly 1,600 emojis to output a 300-dimensional real-valued vector. We experimented with both word2vec and emoji2vec by encoding each emoji through a sum of the word2vec representations of its textual description. We observed that both word2vec and emoji2vec embeddings yielded only a mild amount of similarity for most emojis. Moreover, dealing with groups of words requires to design a recurrent layer in the architecture, which can be cumbersome and yield suboptimal results as opposed to restricting the generator network to only Unicode characters. Bearing this in mind, we decided to use the emoji2vec embedding in all of our experiments.

3.3 Learning a skewed distribution

Just like in text analysis, some emojis (mostly emotions such as love, laughter, sadness) occur more frequently than domain-specific pictographs (for example, country flags). The distribution over emojis is hence highly skewed and multimodal. Since such imbalance can lead to a considerable reduction in variance, also known as mode collapse, we propose to re-weight each backward pass with coefficients obtained through either of the following schemes:

- term frequency-inverse document frequency (*tf-idf*) weights, a classical approach used in natural language processing (Salton and Buckley, 1988);

- Exponentially-smoothed raw frequencies:

$$w_s(e) = \frac{\exp^{-k \times freq(e)}}{\sum\limits_{i=1}^{N} \exp^{-k \times freq(e_i)}} \quad \forall e, k \geq 0 \quad (2)$$

where k is a smoothing constant and $freq(e) = \frac{count(e)}{N}$ is the frequency of emoji e and N is the total number of emojis.

3.3.1 Algorithm

Our method relies on the conditional version of WGAN-GP which accepts fixed size $(64 \times 64 \times 3)$ RGB image tensors. Our approach is presented in Algorithm. 1, shown below:

Algorithm 1 Conditional Wasserstein GAN

Input: Tuple of emojis and images (X, Y), the gradient penalty coefficient λ, the number of critic iterations per generator iteration n_{critic}, the batch size m, learning rate l_r and weight vector w.

Initialization: initialize generator parameters θ_{G_0}, critic parameters θ_{D_0}

for epoch $= 1, ..., N$ **do**
  for $t = 1, ..., n_{critic}$ **do**
    {Updating Discriminator}
    for $n = 1, ..., n_{disc}$ **do**
      Sample $\{x\}_{i=1}^{m} \sim X$, $\{y\}_{i=1}^{m} \sim Y$, $\{z\}_{i=1}^{m} \sim \mathcal{N}(0,1)$, $\{\epsilon\}_{i=1}^{m} \sim U[0,1]$
      $\tilde{x}_i \leftarrow \epsilon x_i + (1 - \epsilon_i) G(z_i | y_i)$
      $\mathcal{L}^{(i)} \leftarrow D(G(z_i | (y_i)) - D(x_i | y_i) + \lambda(|\nabla_{\tilde{x}_i} D(\tilde{x}_i | y_i)| - 1)^2$
      $\theta_D \leftarrow \text{Adam}(\nabla_{\theta_D} \sum_{i=1}^{m} w_i \mathcal{L}^{(i)}, l_r)$
    end for
    {Updating Generator}
    for $n = 1, ..., n_{gen}$ **do**
      sample a batch of $\{z^{(i)}\}_{i=1}^{m} \sim N(0,1)$
      $\theta_G \leftarrow \text{Adam}(-\nabla_{\theta_G} \sum_{i=1}^{m} w_i \mathcal{L}^{(i)}, l_r)$
    end for
  end for
end for

---

4 Experiments

4.1 Data collection

We used the (soon to be deprecated) Instagram API to collect posts from top influencers within the following categories: fashion, fitness, health and weight loss; we believe that user data across those domains share similar patterns. Here, *influencers* are defined as accounts with the highest combined count of followers, posts and user reactions; 166 influencers were selected from various ranking lists put together by Forbes and Iconosquare. The final dataset has 80,000 (image, pictograph) tuples and covers a total of 753 distinct symbols.

4.2 Architecture

Inspired from (Reed et al., 2016), we performed experiments using the following architecture: the generator has 4 convolutional layers with kernels of size 4 which output a 4×4 feature matrix with a fully connexted layer; the discriminator is identical to G but outputs a scalar softmax instead of a 300-dimensional vector. The structure of both D and G is shown in Fig. 1.

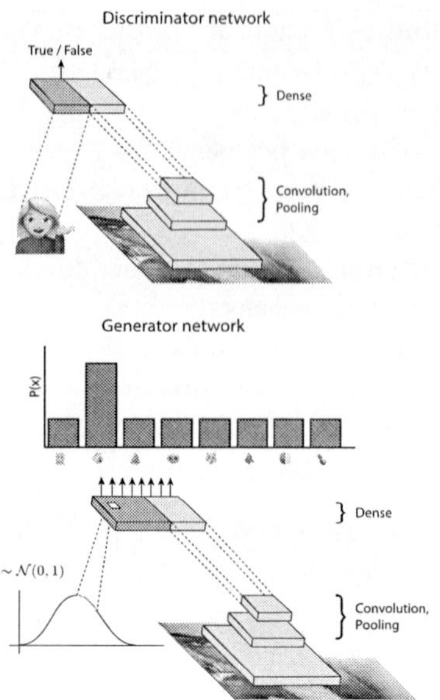

Figure 1: Illustration of how EmojiGAN learns a distribution. The generator learns the conditional distribution of emojis given a set of pictures while the discriminator assigns a score to each generated emoji.

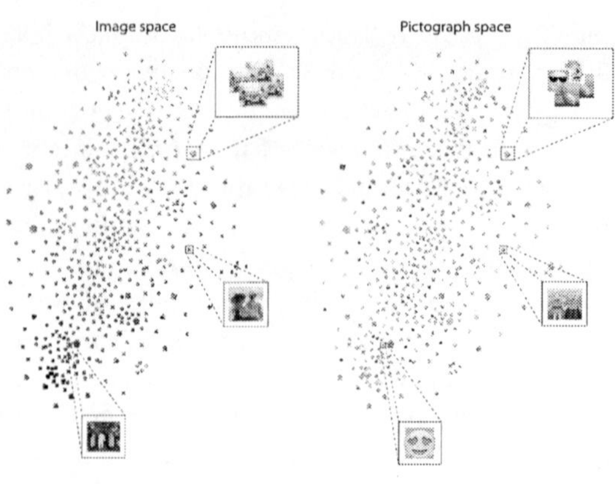

Figure 2: Visualization of t-SNE reduced images and their corresponding most frequent pictographs (emojis). The most popular emoji for each picture was obtained by sampling 50 observations from the generator and taking the mode of the sample. Note that even this technique has a stochastic outcome, meaning that if an image has a rather flat distribution, its mode will not be consistent across runs. The described behaviour can be observed in the upper right area of both space representations.

5   Results

A series of experiments were conducted on the data collected from Instagram. The best architecture was selected through cross-validation and hyperparameter grid search and has been previously discussed. The training process used minibatch alternating gradient descent with the popular Adam optimizer (Kingma and Ba, 2014) with a learning rate $l_r = 0.0001$ and $\beta_1 = 0.1$, $\beta_2 = 0.9$. We trained both G and D until convergence after aproximatively 10 epochs. Empirically, we saw that exponentially-smoothed raw frequencies weights (2) performed better than *tf-idf* weights.

In order to assess how closely the generator network approximates the true data distribution, we first sampled 750 images and obtained their respective emoji distribution by performing 50 forward passes through G. The *mode*, that is the most frequent observation in the sample, of the resulting distribution is considered as the most representative pictograph for the given image. We used t-SNE on the image tensor in order to visualize both the image and the emoji spaces (see Fig. 2). The purpose of the performed experiment was to assert whether two entities close to each other in the image space will also yield similar emojis. The top right corner of both clouds ex-

poses a shortcoming of the algorithm: if the distribution is flat (i.e. is multimodal), even large samples will yield different modes just by chance. This phenomenon is clearly present throughout the cloud of pictographs: four identical images yield three distinct emojis. On the other hand, the two remaining examples correctly capture the presence of two people in a single photo (middle section), as well expression of amazement (bottom section).

The performance of generative models is difficult to assess numerically, especially when it comes to emojis. Indeed, the Fréchet Inception Distance (Heusel et al., 2017) is often used to score generated images but to the best of our knowledge, no such measure exists for ideograms. As an alternative way to assess the performance of our method, we plotted the true and generated distributions over 30 randomly chosen emojis for 1000 random images (see Fig. 3). While our algorithm relied on raw (i.e. uncleaned and unprocessed) data, we still observe a reasonable match between both distributions.

Fig. 4 reports the fitted distribution of the top 10 most frequent observations for three randomly sampled images. The top image represents a fashion model in an outfit; our model correctly captures the concepts of woman, love, and overall

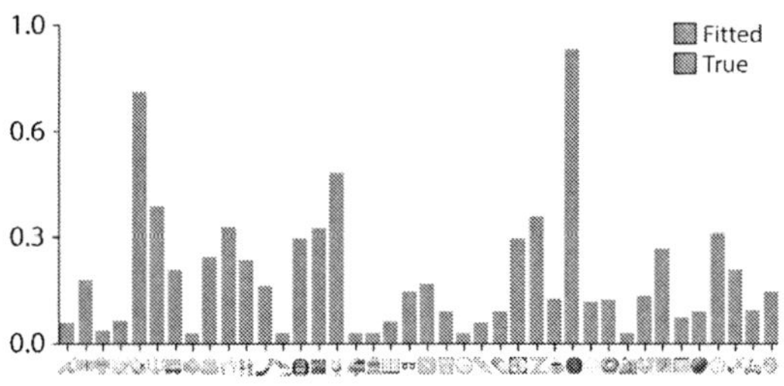

Figure 3: True and fitted distributions over 30 randomly sampled emojis for 500 randomly sampled images. Probabilities are normalized by the maximal element of the set.

positive emotion in the image. However, EmojiGAN can struggle with filtering out unrealistic emojis (in this case, pineapple and pig nose) for images with very few distinct ideograms. The bottom subfigure outlines another very common problem seen in GANs: mode collapse. While the generated emoji fits in the context of the image, the variance in this case is nearly zero and results in G learning a Dirac distribution at the most frequent observation.

The middle image also suffers from the above

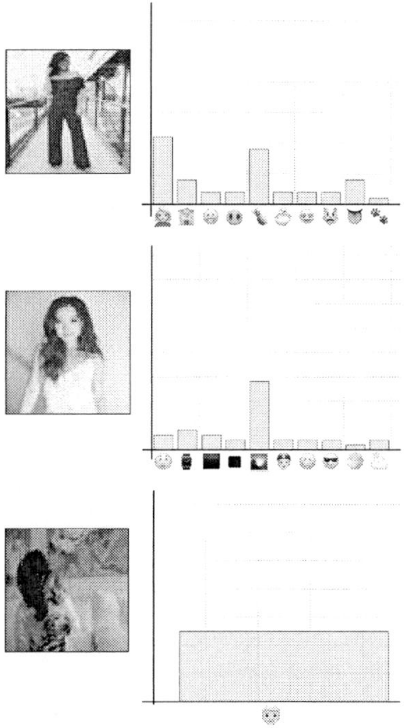

Figure 4: Emojis sampled for some Instagram posts: observe the mode collapse in the bottom subfigure as opposed to more equally spread out distributions.

problems (the sunset pictograph dominates the distribution). We note how algorithms based on unfiltered data from social networks are prone to ethical fallacies, as illustrated in the middle image. This situation is reminiscent of the infamous Microsoft chatbot Tay which started to pick up racist and sexist language after being trained on uncensored tweets and had to be shut down (Neff and Nagy, 2016). We ourselves experienced a similar behaviour when assessing the performance of EmojiGAN. One plausible explanation of this phenomenon would be that while derogatory comments are quite rare, the introduction of *exponential weight* or similar scores in the hope of preventing mode collapse to the most popular emoji has the side effect of overfitting least frequent pictographs.

6   Conclusion and Discussion

In this work, we proposed a new way of modeling social media posts through a generative adversarial network over pictographs. EmojiGAN managed to learn the emoji distribution for a set of given images and generate realistic pictographic representations from a picture. While the issue of noisy predictions still remains, our approach can be used as an alternative to classical image annotation methods. Using a modified attention mechanism (Xu et al., 2015) would be a stepping stone to correctly model the context-dependent connotations (Jibril and Abdullah, 2013) of emojis. However, the biggest concern is of ethical nature: training any algorithm on raw data obtained from social networks without filtering offensive and derogatory ideas is itself a debate (Islam et al., 2016; Davidson et al., 2017).

Future work on the topic should start with a thorough analysis of algebraic properties of emoji2vec similar to (Arora et al., 2016). For example, new Unicode formats support emoji composition, which is reminiscent of traditional word embeddings' behaviour and could be explicitly incorporated into a learning algorithm. Finally, the ethical concerns behind deep learning without limits are not specific to our algorithm but rather a community-wide discourse. It is thus important to work together with AI safety research groups in order to ensure that novel methods developed by researchers learn our better side.

References

Khaled Almgren, Jeongkyu Lee, et al. 2016. Predicting the future popularity of images on social networks. In *Proceedings of the The 3rd Multidisciplinary International Social Networks Conference on SocialInformatics 2016, Data Science 2016*, page 15. ACM.

Martín Arjovsky, Soumith Chintala, and Léon Bottou. 2017. Wasserstein GAN. *CoRR*, abs/1701.07875.

Sanjeev Arora, Yuanzhi Li, Yingyu Liang, Tengyu Ma, and Andrej Risteski. 2016. Linear algebraic structure of word senses, with applications to polysemy. *arXiv preprint arXiv:1601.03764*.

Spencer Cappallo, Thomas Mensink, and Cees G.M. Snoek. 2015. Image2emoji: Zero-shot emoji prediction for visual media. In *Proceedings of the 23rd ACM International Conference on Multimedia*, MM '15, pages 1311–1314, New York, NY, USA. ACM.

Bo Dai, Dahua Lin, Raquel Urtasun, and Sanja Fidler. 2017. Towards diverse and natural image descriptions via a conditional GAN. *CoRR*, abs/1703.06029.

Thomas Davidson, Dana Warmsley, Michael W. Macy, and Ingmar Weber. 2017. Automated hate speech detection and the problem of offensive language. *CoRR*, abs/1703.04009.

Shaunak De, Abhishek Maity, Vritti Goel, Sanjay Shitole, and Avik Bhattacharya. 2017. Predicting the popularity of instagram posts for a lifestyle magazine using deep learning.

Ben Eisner, Tim Rocktäschel, Isabelle Augenstein, Matko Bosnjak, and Sebastian Riedel. 2016. emoji2vec: Learning emoji representations from their description. *CoRR*, abs/1609.08359.

Bjarke Felbo, Alan Mislove, Anders Søgaard, Iyad Rahwan, and Sune Lehmann. 2017. Using millions of emoji occurrences to learn any-domain representations for detecting sentiment, emotion and sarcasm. *CoRR*, abs/1708.00524.

Ian J. Goodfellow, Jean Pouget-Abadie, Mehdi Mirza, Bing Xu, David Warde-Farley, Sherjil Ozair, Aaron C. Courville, and Yoshua Bengio. 2014. Generative adversarial networks. *CoRR*, abs/1406.2661.

Amit Goyal, Francesco Bonchi, and Laks VS Lakshmanan. 2010. Learning influence probabilities in social networks. In *Proceedings of the third ACM international conference on Web search and data mining*, pages 241–250. ACM.

Ishaan Gulrajani, Faruk Ahmed, Martín Arjovsky, Vincent Dumoulin, and Aaron C. Courville. 2017. Improved training of wasserstein gans. *CoRR*, abs/1704.00028.

Martin Heusel, Hubert Ramsauer, Thomas Unterthiner, Bernhard Nessler, Günter Klambauer, and Sepp Hochreiter. 2017. Gans trained by a two time-scale update rule converge to a nash equilibrium. *CoRR*, abs/1706.08500.

Aylin Caliskan Islam, Joanna J. Bryson, and Arvind Narayanan. 2016. Semantics derived automatically from language corpora necessarily contain human biases. *CoRR*, abs/1608.07187.

Tanimu Ahmed Jibril and Mardziah Hayati Abdullah. 2013. Relevance of emoticons in computer-mediated communication contexts: An overview. *Asian Social Science*, 9(4):201.

Ryan Kelly and Leon Watts. 2015. Characterising the inventive appropriation of emoji as relationally meaningful in mediated close personal relationships. *Experiences of Technology Appropriation: Unanticipated Users, Usage, Circumstances, and Design*.

Diederik P Kingma and Jimmy Ba. 2014. Adam: A method for stochastic optimization. *arXiv preprint arXiv:1412.6980*.

Diederik P Kingma and Max Welling. 2013. Auto-encoding variational bayes. *arXiv preprint arXiv:1312.6114*.

Alex Krizhevsky. 2012. Learning multiple layers of features from tiny images.

Quoc Le and Tomas Mikolov. 2014. Distributed representations of sentences and documents. In *International Conference on Machine Learning*, pages 1188–1196.

Ziwei Liu, Ping Luo, Xiaogang Wang, and Xiaoou Tang. 2015. Deep learning face attributes in the wild. In *Proceedings of International Conference on Computer Vision (ICCV)*.

Kevin Matzen, Kavita Bala, and Noah Snavely. 2017. Streetstyle: Exploring world-wide clothing styles from millions of photos. *CoRR*, abs/1706.01869.

Tomas Mikolov, Ilya Sutskever, Kai Chen, Greg Corrado, and Jeffrey Dean. 2013. Distributed representations of words and phrases and their compositionality. *CoRR*, abs/1310.4546.

Hannah Miller, Jacob Thebault-Spieker, Shuo Chang, Isaac Johnson, Loren Terveen, and Brent Hecht. 2016. Blissfully happy or ready to fight: Varying interpretations of emoji. *Proceedings of ICWSM*, 2016.

Gina Neff and Peter Nagy. 2016. Automation, algorithms, and politics— talking to bots: Symbiotic agency and the case of tay. *International Journal of Communication*, 10:17.

Jaehyuk Park, Giovanni Luca Ciampaglia, and Emilio Ferrara. 2016. Style in the age of instagram: Predicting success within the fashion industry using social media. In *Proceedings of the 19th ACM Conference on Computer-Supported Cooperative Work & Social Computing*, pages 64–73. ACM.

Marco Pennacchiotti and Ana-Maria Popescu. 2011. A machine learning approach to twitter user classification. *Icwsm*, 11(1):281–288.

Bryan Perozzi, Rami Al-Rfou, and Steven Skiena. 2014. Deepwalk: Online learning of social representations. In *Proceedings of the 20th ACM SIGKDD international conference on Knowledge discovery and data mining*, pages 701–710. ACM.

Yunchen Pu, Zhe Gan, Ricardo Henao, Xin Yuan, Chunyuan Li, Andrew Stevens, and Lawrence Carin. 2016. Variational autoencoder for deep learning of images, labels and captions. In *Advances in neural information processing systems*, pages 2352–2360.

Scott E. Reed, Zeynep Akata, Xinchen Yan, Lajanugen Logeswaran, Bernt Schiele, and Honglak Lee. 2016. Generative adversarial text to image synthesis. *CoRR*, abs/1605.05396.

Gerard Salton and Christopher Buckley. 1988. Term-weighting approaches in automatic text retrieval. *Information processing & management*, 24(5):513–523.

Kelvin Xu, Jimmy Ba, Ryan Kiros, Kyunghyun Cho, Aaron Courville, Ruslan Salakhudinov, Rich Zemel, and Yoshua Bengio. 2015. Show, attend and tell: Neural image caption generation with visual attention. In *International Conference on Machine Learning*, pages 2048–2057.

Quanzeng You, Hailin Jin, Zhaowen Wang, Chen Fang, and Jiebo Luo. 2016. Image captioning with semantic attention. In *Proceedings of the IEEE Conference on Computer Vision and Pattern Recognition*, pages 4651–4659.

Luda Zhao and Connie Zeng. 2017. Using neural networks to predict emoji usage from twitter data.

Identifying Opinion-Topics and Polarity of Parliamentary Debate Motions

Gavin Abercrombie and **Riza Batista-Navarro**
School of Computer Science
University of Manchester
Kilburn Building, Manchester M13 9PL
gavin.abercrombie@postgrad.manchester.ac.uk
riza.batista@manchester.ac.uk

Abstract

Analysis of the topics mentioned and opinions expressed in parliamentary debate motions– or proposals–is difficult for human readers, but necessary for understanding and automatic processing of the content of the subsequent speeches. We present a dataset of debate motions with pre-existing '*policy*' labels, and investigate the utility of these labels for simultaneous topic and opinion polarity analysis. For topic detection, we apply one-versus-the-rest supervised topic classification, finding that good performance is achieved in predicting the *policy* topics, and that textual features derived from the debate titles associated with the motions are particularly indicative of motion topic. We then examine whether the output could also be used to determine the positions taken by proposers towards the different policies by investigating how well humans agree in interpreting the opinion polarities of the motions. Finding very high levels of agreement, we conclude that the *policies* used can be reliable labels for use in these tasks, and that successful topic detection can therefore provide opinion analysis of the motions 'for free'.

1 Introduction

In the House of Commons of the UK Parliament, the topics contained in a debate's *motion*– a proposal one Member of Parliament (MP) puts to the other Members of the House–are the focus of opinions expressed during all subsequent speeches. These motions are therefore crucial for understanding the content of MPs' speeches and the opinions they convey.

It is often difficult for people to process debate motions due to the level of domain-specific knowledge related to the language and workings of Parliament they contain. Indeed, these motions are so hard for ordinary citizens to understand that parliamentary monitoring organisations like the Public Whip[1] and They Work for You[2] produce manually written summaries and annotated versions of them, which are written by crowd-sourced volunteers with domain expertise or interest.

Figure 1: Example of a debate motion as presented on the theyworkforyou.com website. Motions contain information about the topics of debates, as well as the proposer's opinions towards those topics, but can be difficult for human readers to process.

In conducting sentiment analysis of debate speeches, it has been observed that, when formulating these motions, the speakers that propose them themselves express sentiment towards the topics of the motions, and that these motions can act as polarity shifters for subsequent speeches in a debate–that is, depending on the sentiment polarity of a motion, the sentiment polarity of language used in subsequent speeches may be reversed (Abercrombie and Batista-Navarro, 2018). Identification of both the topics and polarity of motions is therefore crucial for any further investigation of debates, and is likely to be a key step in tasks such as sentiment or stance analysis of debate speeches.

Our contributions We create a dataset of UK parliamentary debate motions labelled with both topic

---

[1] http://www.publicwhip.org.uk
[2] https://www.theyworkforyou.com/

Proceedings of the 9th Workshop on Computational Approaches to Subjectivity, Sentiment and Social Media Analysis, pages 280–285
Brussels, Belgium, October 31, 2018. ©2018 Association for Computational Linguistics
https://doi.org/10.18653/v1/P17

and opinion polarity. We then investigate the utility of these labels for two tasks:

1) For motion topic detection, we treat the *policy* labels as topic classes and assess the performance of a multilabel classifier in predicting them.

2) We exploit the fact that the *policies* used as topic labels inherently incorporate information regarding the proposers' opinions towards those policies–that is their policy positions: whether they support or oppose them. We investigate whether, by correctly identifying a motion's *policy* category, we can also determine its position towards the policy in question, in effect obtaining opinion analysis of the motions 'for free'. We compare the output of this approach to human produced opinion polarity labels.

2 Background

2.1 Hansard debate transcripts

Debates in the House of Commons are of the following format: An MP proposes a *motion*, to which other MPs may respond when invited by the *Speaker* (the presiding officer of the chamber), either in support of, or opposition to the motion.

A domain with unique characteristics, the *Hansard* transcripts lie somewhere between formal written language and transcripts of spoken dialogue–they are near-verbatim transcriptions of almost everything that is said in Parliament, although disfluencies are removed and some contextual information (such as the names of the speakers) is added by the parliamentary reporters.

There exist a number of challenges associated with this domain. Here, analysis is complicated by the language employed by politicians, who tend to use: (1) little extreme or overtly polarised (especially negative) language, and (2) a tactical, political use of terminology–for example, policies that may be percieved as negative (such as cuts to services or tax increases) are generally not framed using those terms (Abercrombie and Batista-Navarro, 2018).

Additionally, the format of debates is complex, with manifold topics discussed by multiple participants. Motions may reference various entities, some of which may be described only within other debates or documents referred to in the motion (as in Figure 1).

Finally, the language used is often arcane, with much procedural terminology. In fact, many motions consist entirely of such language, giving little or no clue as to the topic under discussion (for further details see Section 3).

However, the existence of motions that have been manually labelled with 'policy votes' indicates that it may be feasible to train machine classifiers to conduct a form of motion topic detection. The fact that these labels also encompass policy positions suggests that they could also be used simultaneously for opinion analysis.

2.2 Opinion-topic labelling

Parliamentary monitoring website the Public Whip maintains a list of debates organised under '*policies*.'[3] These are sets 'of votes that represent a view on a particular issue' such as *European Union – For* and *Stop climate change*. Under each of these, members of the public are invited to submit debates–motions with vote outcomes– which match these descriptions.

We make use of these categorisations as labels for supervised topic classification. In many cases, it is not straightforward to determine a motion's *policy* label from the debate title–for example, for the *policy* '*More Powers for Local Councils*', debate titles include 'High Streets', 'Housing', 'Fixed Odds Betting Terminals', 'Local Bus Services'. Similarly, the text of a motion alone does not necessarily reveal its topic, with many motions consisting purely of procedural language, such as 'That the Bill be read a Second time'. As a result, human readers often require access to the title, motion, and sometimes other information found elsewhere in a debate in order to determine the motion's polarity.

While the *policies* represent both a policy topic and a polarised position towards it, this is a reflection of the vote outcome of the debate, not necessarily the position expressed in the motion. For example, if a motion proposed in support of a policy position is rejected, it will be labelled with a *policy* that reflects opposition to that position (see Figure 2).

In a further layer of complexity, the Public Whip also provides motions with a 'policy vote' label–the contributors' assessment of how somebody who supports each policy 'would have voted'–with the additional tags 'majority', 'minority', or 'abstain'. All in all, this means that each label has two potential polarity shifters (the vote

Angus Robertson Shadow SNP Westminster Group Leader 12:52 pm, 9th September 2015

I beg to move,

That this House
recognises the funding the Government has committed to the humanitarian initiatives to provide sanctuary in camps for refugees across the Middle East;
calls for a greater international effort through the United Nations to secure the position of such displaced people;
recognises that the Government has committed to accepting 20,000 vulnerable people from camps in Syria over the next five years but calls for a Government report to be laid before the House by 12 October 2015 detailing how that number can be increased, encompassing refugees already in Europe and including a plan for the remainder of this year to reflect the overwhelming urgency of this humanitarian crisis;
further notes that refugees arriving in European Union territory also have a moral and legal right to be treated properly;
and, given the pressure on Southern European countries, further calls for the UK to play its full and proper role, in conjunction with European partners, in providing sanctuary to our fellow human beings.

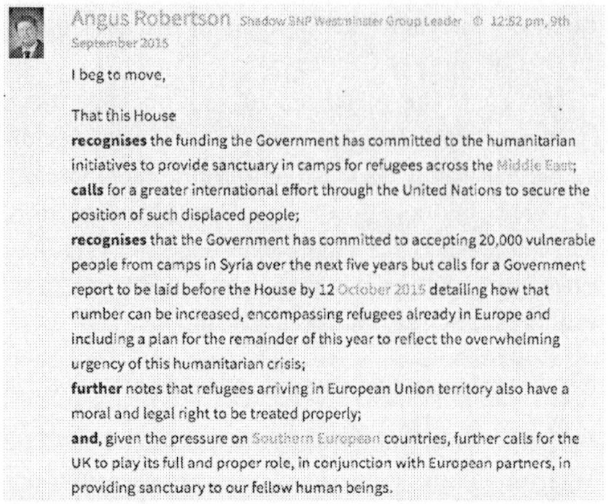

Figure 2: Motion from the *policy* category *Asylum System – More strict*. The motion, from a debate entitled '*Humanitarian Crisis in the Mediterranean and Europe*', opposes the idea of making the asylum system stricter, but the fact that it was rejected by the House, explains why it has been given this label.

outcome and the *policy vote*), which need to be taken into account if the Public Whip *policies* are to be used as labels for opinion polarity analysis.

3 Data

We present a dataset[4] of 592 UK parliamentary debate motions proposed in the House of Commons between 1997 and 2018.[5] We match these with the corresponding *policies* from the Public Whip for use as labels for supervised opinion-topic classification. We therefore include only those motions, which have been classified by *policy* on the Public Whip website. In order to provide sufficient examples to train a classifier we use only those debates for which there exist at least 20 examples per *policy* label. Because, for example, a debate may have been categorised with both the specific *policy* '*Higher taxes on alcoholic drinks*', as well as the more general label '*Increase VAT*' (Value Added Tax), motions may have been included in more than one *policy* category. The final dataset includes 13 different *policy* topic labels, with each applied to a minimum of 24 and a maximum of 129 motions ($\mu = 46.6$). 14 of the motions have two labels, while the remaining 578 have just one.

In addition to the Public Whip's crowdsourced labels, we provide a second set of manually annotated opinion polarity labels. For these, annotation was conducted by the first author of this paper, who read each example (motion, title, and supplementary information), and applied either *positive* or *negative* labels according to the opinion they perceived to be expressed towards the *policy* in question.

As potential machine classification features, we include the textual content of the motions as well as the following metadata information from the transcripts:

- *motion_speaker_name*: Some MPs are more or less likely to speak on various topics, depending on their interests and position.
- *motion_party*: Party affiliation of speakers is likely to be an indicator of both interest in topics and policy positions.
- *debate_title*: Titles are often, but not always, related to policy vote topics.
- *additional_information*: Information such as the names of relevant documents or explanations of amendments is often included in the transcripts, preceding the motion.

Motions in this dataset broadly follow one of the following three formats:

1. 'That this House {*verb*} {*argument*}; {*verb*} {*argument*}; ... and {*verb*} {*argument*}' –where the motion may contain several clauses (see examples in Figures 1 and 2).
2. That the {*legislation*} be now read {a Second/the Third} time. –where {*legislation*} is a Bill, Paper etc.
3. ...amendment {*number*}, page {*number*}, line {*number*}, leave out '{'*phrase*'}' and insert '{*phrase*}'.

Motions of type 2 and 3 contain very little topic information, so it may be necessary to make use of cues in the debate title or additional information provided in the transcript in order to determine the topic in such cases.

[4]Available at https://data.mendeley.com/datasets/j83yzp7ynz/1

[5]The transcripts were obtained from https://www.theyworkforyou.com/pwdata/scrapedxml/debates/

4 Method

Data pre-processing consisted of removal of stop-words, lowercasing and stemming of textual data, and binarization of metadata information.

In order to detect the topics of debate motions we employ a supervised machine classification approach. For this, we investigate the use of combinations of the following features:

— Textual features: uni-, bi-, and trigrams from the debate titles, motions and supplementary information.

— Metadata features: speaker name and party affiliation.

As some motions have more than one topic label, we apply one-vs-the-rest classification on a randomised 90-10% train-test split of the data. After initial experimentation with a range of algorithms, we apply a multilabel implementation of Support Vector Machine classification.

5 Results

Because we have 13 different classes, and therefore highly imbalanced datasets for each round of one-vs-the-rest classification, we use the F1 score as a performance metric. Strongest performance is achieved using n-gram features from both the debate motions and titles (F1 = 77.0).

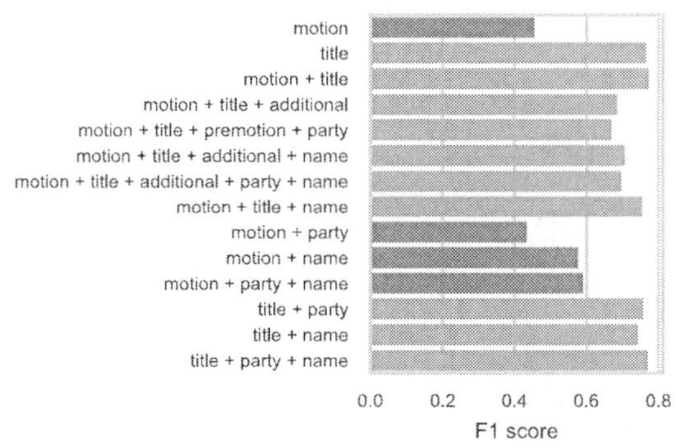

Figure 3: F1 score for different combinations of features used for topic classification. Highest performances (lighter, orange bars) are achieved when textual features derived from the debate titles are included.

Overall, use of the debate titles, with or without metadata features, produces the highest F1 scores, while the addition of other textual features does not generally lead to improvement, and in some cases results in losses in performance.

The motions themselves do not appear to provide particularly useful features for topic detec-

tion. Many consist solely of procedural terms that give no indication of the topics under discussion–such as motion types 2 and 3 (described in Section 3). Indeed, only 121 (20.8%) motions are of the more informative type 1.

Of the metadata features used, speaker name is more indicative of topic than party affiliation. This reflects the fact that each party is represented in most *policy* categories, but that individual MPs tend to be strongly associated with just a few, or in most cases, one single topic related to their particular role–of 234 MPs in the dataset, 163 (69.7%) propose motions on only one *policy*, and only one is represented in more than four.

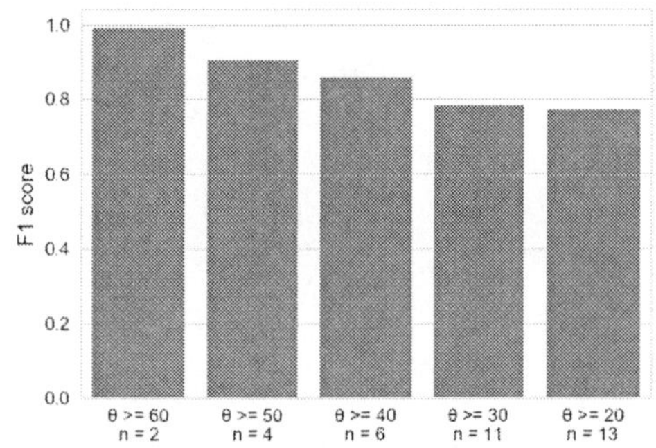

Figure 4: F1 scores for classification with different thresholds (θ) for the minimum number of example motions. As this threshold is lowered, the number of topic classes (n) increases and performance decreases.

As the threshold for the minumum number of examples per *policy* in the dataset is somewhat arbitary, we also test the system with a range of different thresholds. As the threshold decreases and the number of different topic classes increases, the F1 score drops, indicating that it may be challenging to obtain good results with a larger corpus and a greater number of topics (Figure 4).

6 Discussion

6.1 Topic detection

Considering the small number of training examples for each class, reasonable results are obtained using these labels for topic classification. However, it should be noted that many of the *policy* classes in this dataset feature debates with similar or even identical titles, in which cases the classifier is trained and tested on very similar data. While this is a common scenario in Parliament–the same pieces of legislation are debated mutiple times and often revisited year after year–it remains to be seen how well this system would perform on new, completely unseen examples from future debates.

6.2 Opinion polarity analysis

As Public Whip Policies are created with inbuilt policy positioning, we examine their use as opinion labels by comparing their polarity with the second set of manual annotations. We ignore cases labelled in the Public Whip with the *policy vote* 'abstain' (as these are assumed not to take a position towards the *policy* in question). We then treat the 'majority' motions as being labelled according to the vote outcome–those which were 'approved' by the vote are *positive*, while those which were 'rejected' are *negative*–and the 'minority' labels as polarity shifters–that is, the tag 'minority' reverses the label derived from the outcome, while a 'majority' tag preserves it (see Table 1).

	Outcome	Policy Vote	Opinion
Policy	Approved	'majority'	*positive*
		'minority'	*negative*
	Rejected	'majority'	*negative*
		'minority'	*positive*

Table 1: Interpretation of Policy labels for opinion analysis. For each of its *policy* labels, a motion also has two tags–*outcome* and *policy vote*–that can potentially reverse its opinion polarity.

To examine the utility of the output labels, we calculate inter-rater agreement between these and our own annotations, finding Cohen's kappa (κ) to be 94.2. This represents 'near-perfect' agreement,[6] indicating that the Public Whip's *policies* appear to be reliable labels for opinion position of motions towards the policies in question. Although these results are promising, it should be noted that the system used to interpret motion opinion from *policies* relies on the use of additional, manually applied *policy vote* tags. For use with future, unseen examples that do not have such tags, it would be necessary to reorganise the way that the Public Whip's *policies* are created, splitting those labelled 'majority' and 'minority' into different *for* and *against* Policy categories.

7 Related work

The legislative debates domain has attracted interest from researchers with a variety of backrounds, and there is a considerable body of work related to the analysis of both topics and speaker opinion contained in parliamentary and congressional debates, although these tasks have been tackled separately and from differing research perspectives.

For opinion analysis of US congressional debates, the dataset of Thomas et al. (2006) has been widely used (e.g. Balahur et al., 2009; Burfoot et al., 2011), and similar experiments have also been conducted on other legislatures such as the Dutch parliament (Grijzenhout et al., 2010), and the UK House of Commons (Salah, 2014).

Others have utilised similar techniques to facilitate other tasks. For example, Duthie et al. (2016) attempt to identify the 'ethos' of speakers in the UK Parliament, while Li et al. (2017) detect political ideology in those of the US Congress. Meanwhile, political scientists, such as Proksch and Slapin (2010) and Lauderdale and Herzog (2016) have analysed debates to position speakers on a range of scales related to policy and ideology.

While most work on this domain focuses on speeches, ignoring the role of motions in shaping the content of debates, Abercrombie and Batista-Navarro (2018) include analysis of the sentiment expressed in debate motions. However, they do not analyse the topics or identify the targets of sentiment in the motions.

Analysis of the topics contained within legislative debates has primarily focused on topic modelling based on speech content. For example, van der Zwaan et al. (2016) combine topic and political position analysis on Dutch parliamentary speech transcripts, while Zirn (2014) do similar for the German Bundestag. As far as we are aware, there exists no previous work on extracting topics from debate motions.

8 Conclusion

Opinion-topic labels derived from the Public Whip's *policies* can be used to train a classifier to achieve good performance in classifying the *policy* topics of parliamentary debate motions. These categories, which incorporate inbuilt policy position information, also appear to be reliable markers of opinion polarity, suggesting that we can use these labels to simultaneously obtain opinion analysis 'for free'. However, the ability of this approach to deal with new examples from future, unseen debates is uncertain, and it may be advisable to explore unsupervised methods of determining motion opinion-topics.

---

[6]Interpretation of κ: (Landis and Koch, 1977).

References

Gavin Abercrombie and Riza Batista-Navarro. 2018. 'Aye' or 'no'? Speech-level sentiment analysis of Hansard UK parliamentary debate transcripts. In *Proceedings of the Eleventh International Conference on Language Resources and Evaluation (LREC 2018)*, Miyazaki, Japan. European Language Resources Association (ELRA).

Alexandra Balahur, Zornitsa Kozareva, and Andrés Montoyo. 2009. Determining the polarity and source of opinions expressed in political debates. In *Computational Linguistics and Intelligent Text Processing. CICLing 2009. Lecture Notes in Computer Science*, pages 468–480. Springer.

Clinton Burfoot, Steven Bird, and Timothy Baldwin. 2011. Collective classification of congressional floor-debate transcripts. In *Proceedings of the 49th Annual Meeting of the Association for Computational Linguistics: Human Language Technologies*, pages 1506–1515. Association for Computational Linguistics.

Rory Duthie, Katarzyna Budzynska, and Chris Reed. 2016. Mining ethos in political debate. In *Computational Models of Argument: Proceedings from the Sixth International Conference on Computational Models of Argument (COMMA)*, pages 299–310. IOS Press.

Steven Grijzenhout, Valentin Jijkoun, Maarten Marx, et al. 2010. Opinion mining in Dutch Hansards. In *Proceedings of the Workshop From Text to Political Positions, Free University of Amsterdam*.

J Richard Landis and Gary G Koch. 1977. The measurement of observer agreement for categorical data. *Biometrics*, 4(1):159–174.

Benjamin E Lauderdale and Alexander Herzog. 2016. Measuring political positions from legislative speech. *Political Analysis*, 24(3):374–394.

Xilian Li, Wei Chen, Tengjiao Wang, and Weijing Huang. 2017. Target-specific convolutional bi-directional lstm neural network for political ideology analysis. In *Asia-Pacific Web (APWeb) and Web-Age Information Management (WAIM) Joint Conference on Web and Big Data*, pages 64–72. Springer.

Sven-Oliver Proksch and Jonathan B Slapin. 2010. Position taking in European Parliament speeches. *British Journal of Political Science*, 40(3):587–611.

Zaher Salah. 2014. *Machine learning and sentiment analysis approaches for the analysis of parliamentary debates*. Ph.D. thesis, University of Liverpool.

Matt Thomas, Bo Pang, and Lillian Lee. 2006. Get out the vote: Determining support or opposition from congressional floor-debate transcripts. In *Proceedings of the 2006 Conference on Empirical Methods in Natural Language Processing*, pages 327–335. Association for Computational Linguistics.

Cäcilia Zirn. 2014. Analyzing positions and topics in political discussions of the German Bundestag. In *Proceedings of the ACL 2014 Student Research Workshop*, pages 26–33. Association for Computational Linguistics.

Janneke M van der Zwaan, Maarten Marx, and Jaap Kamps. 2016. Validating cross-perspective topic modeling for extracting political parties' positions from parliamentary proceedings. In *Proceedings of ECAI: 22nd European Conference on Artificial Intelligence*, pages 28–36. IOS Press.

Homonym Detection For Humor Recognition In Short Text

Sven van den Beukel
Faculteit der Bèta-wetenschappen
VU Amsterdam, The Netherlands
sb1530@student.vu.nl

Lora Aroyo
Faculteit der Bèta-wetenschappen
VU Amsterdam, The Netherlands
l.m.aroyo@vu.nl

Abstract

In this paper, automatic homophone- and homograph detection are suggested as new useful features for humor recognition systems. The system combines style-features from previous studies on humor recognition in short text with ambiguity-based features. The performance of two potentially useful homograph detection methods is evaluated using crowdsourced annotations as ground truth. Adding homophones and homographs as features to the classifier results in a small but significant improvement over the style-features alone. For the task of humor recognition, recall appears to be a more important quality measure than precision. Although the system was designed for humor recognition in oneliners, it also performs well at the classification of longer humorous texts.

1 Introduction

Humor has the potential to help form, strengthen and maintain human relationships and could thus bring humans and computers closer to each other. It helps regulate conversations, builds trust between partners, facilitates self-disclosure and it is an important factor in social attraction (Nijholt et al., 2003). Furthermore, humans react in the same way to computers as they do to other human beings when it comes to psycho-social phenomena (Morkes et al., 1998; Reeves and Nass, 1996). Experiments have shown that people that received a joke, perceived the computer they interacted with as more likable and competent, reported greater cooperation and responded more sociable (Morkes et al., 1998). Automatic humor recognition could help computers respond more appropriately, making human-computer interaction feel more natural and enjoyable.

This paper focuses on humor recognition of written oneliners, which in this study are defined

as short jokes that are at most 140 characters long. The popularity of Twitter has likely caused an increase in availability of both humorous and non-humorous texts shorter than 140 tokens. The choice for oneliners increases difficulty of humor recognition as they contain less contextual information than longer humorous texts. The built classifier is also tested on humor recognition in larger texts. In this study, features that capture text style are selected from the State-of-the-Art on humor recognition in oneliners (Mihalcea and Strapparava, 2005), cartoon captions (Radev et al., 2015) and tweets (Zhang and Liu, 2014) and are combined with newly suggested ambiguity features. When referring to "The State-of-the-Art", we refer to Mihalcea and Strapparava (2005). This allows us to evaluate the usefulness of the style-features for application on humor recognition in oneliners (rather than cartoons or tweets), as well as the potential of automatic homophone and homograph detection as signalers of ambiguity, and subsequently humor.

The release of the datasets and code that were used (Appendix A) are also a valuable contribution, since it allows others to replicate the experiments and to explore further directions. The humorous oneliners and Reuters datasets themselves are not publicly released to prevent potential copyright infringements, but these can be requested from the authors. Two methods for detecting homophones and homographs are designed to detect ambiguity, after which the performance of the proposed methods is evaluated. In the remainder of this document these features might be referred to as "homonyms", the category of words to which homographs and homophones belong. The deployment of content-based features (e.g. LSA) are outside the scope of this study, despite their previously reported usefulness (Mihalcea and Strapparava, 2005; Sjöbergh and Araki, 2007). The per-

Proceedings of the 9th Workshop on Computational Approaches to Subjectivity, Sentiment and Social Media Analysis, pages 286–291
Brussels, Belgium, October 31, 2018. ©2018 Association for Computational Linguistics
https://doi.org/10.18653/v1/P17

formance achieved through content-based features might be unsustainable over time due to the changing nature of language. Style- and ambiguity-features have the potential to make classification results more sustainable. At the end of this paper, four research questions are answered.

1. How should high quality data for training a humor recognition system be gathered?

2. Which automatic homograph recognition method adds the highest information gain for humor recognition in oneliners?

3. Does the presence of automatically extracted homophones and homographs improve the accuracy of humor recognition in oneliners?

4. Can the proposed classification framework be used for recognizing humor in longer texts?

2 Related work

First of all, in this study the incongruity-resolution theory of humor is used as a frame for selecting useful stylistic features. It is argued to be the most influential theory used to study humor and laughter (Mulder and Nijholt, 2002). When one examines jokes according to the incongruity frame, two concepts within the joke are examined through one frame. When the recipient of the joke notices that the frame actually only applies to one of the objects, the difference between the two objects and the frame becomes apparent (incongruity). The humorous situation occurs when the recipient recognizes the congruous resolution of the apparent incongruity. This theory fits this study best, since it explains the structure of a joke. First there is an incongruity, then a congruous resolution is provided (Gruner, 2000).

2.1 Stylistic features

The stylistic features used in the State-of-the-Art are alliteration, antonymy and adult slang (Mihalcea and Strapparava, 2005). In this study, the features capturing alliteration and rhyme are separated, which was found to be useful by Zhang and Liu (2014). The reason these stylistic features are informative, could be that oneliners use rhyme or alliteration to create expectation and - if humorous - to break it. The expectation creates incongruity, which is resolved through breaking it. Secondly, negations (Mihalcea and Pulman, 2007) and antonyms (Mihalcea and Strappar-

ava, 2005) signal incongruity by having contradictions within a sentence. Thirdly, humorous one-liners were found to contain adult slang. Whereas the State-of-the-Art represented adult slang using sex-related words, insults and vulgar words are included in this study as well. Moreover, researchers have reported that negative and positive sentiment can help distinguish humorous from less humorous samples (Mihalcea and Pulman, 2007; Radev et al., 2015). Furthermore, humorous texts generally have higher sentiment polarity than non-humorous texts, which was found useful for classifying humorous tweets (Zhang and Liu, 2014). Additionally, the latter study found that the ratios of several Part of Speech tags are informative.

2.2 Ambiguity detection

Some types of humor (e.g. wordplay), owe their funniness directly to the presence of ambiguity (Taylor and Mazlack, 2004). In order to identify wordplays, the computer has to combine general knowledge of the world and of pronunciation. Wordplays surprise the recipient of the joke by breaking an expectation. This can be achieved through homographs (e.g. *"Cliford: The Postmaster General will be making the toast. Woody: Wow, imagine a person like that helping out in the kitchen!" (Taylor and Mazlack, 2004)*, in which toast is written the same yet has multiple meanings). Another possibility is the use of homophones, which are words that sound alike yet have different meanings (e.g. *"What is everybody's favorite aspect of mathematics? Knot theory, that's for sure."*, in which "knot" and "not" sound alike). Homophones are not necessarily spelled the same. Example previous attempts at ambiguity detection include a count of the number of senses available for a word (Barbieri and Saggion, 2014; Sjöbergh and Araki, 2007) and the number of parses possible for a sentence (Sjöbergh and Araki, 2007). Since ambiguity is such a complex problem to solve, there is room for improvement. Kao et al. (2015) have recently shown that homophones can be humorous, but only if both interpretations of the homophone are supported by the other words in the sentence. The more distinct the support for the multiple interpretations, the bigger the incongruity-resolution and thus the more humorous the oneliner is perceived. A similar observation has been reported for homographs (McHugh and Buchanan, 2016). However, to our knowledge no automatic homophone- or homograph-detection methods exist yet.

3 Approach

All sentences are at most 140 characters long, to prevent classification based on sentence length. In this study we used one humorous dataset, two non-humorous datasets that are stylistically similar to it (Reuters news headlines and English proverbs), and a third non-humorous dataset that has content comparable to the humorous dataset (wikipedia sentences).

3.1 Data gathering

Reuters news headlines were selected as they share the properties with humorous oneliners of being concise sentences that attract the attention of the reader to transfer a message. The second stylistically similar, non-humorous dataset consists of English proverbs. Proverbs are short texts that transmit facts or experiences of everyday life that many people consider to be true. Finally, the negative set containing short wikipedia sentences attempts to represent real-world scenarios. This set replaces the British National Corpus or the Open Mind Common Sense corpus used in the State-of-the-Art, which we were unable to collect.

Humorous oneliners are collected with a web-scraper designed for five manually selected web-sites dedicated to jokes[1]. The resulting dataset contains 12,046 oneliners and 5,606 jokes longer than 140 characters.

News Headlines are scraped from the website of publishing agency Reuters and were retrieved on August 15th, 2017. Headlines from multiple categories ("Business", "Politics", "World" and "Technology") were extracted to prevent topic-based classification. The full dataset contains 13,798 headlines.

English proverbs were collected manually [2], and due to scarcity this set is limited to 1,019 samples. The classifiers trained with proverbs as non-humorous samples, use an equal amount of humorous samples to prevent overfitting.

Wikipedia sentences were retrieved from a dataset provided in a study on text simplification (Kauchak, 2013), of which 12,046 items are selected based on size and content similarity (TF-IDF). This dataset is expected to be the hardest to classify due to the similarity in content with the humorous oneliners.

3.2 Detecting style and ambiguity

This paragraph lists the approaches for extracting the style- and ambiguity features. Since the approaches for extracting homonyms are designed from the ground up, they require evaluation.

Alliteration & Rhyme presence is measured through the CMUDict[3] phoneme dictionary. For alliterations, n-grams are considered an alliteration chain only if the first phoneme of a word is the same as the first one of one of the two next words. Rhymes are identified the same way, but consider the last phonemes rather than the first ones. For example, *goal* and *Glasgow* alliterate, and *score* rhymes with *more*. For both alliteration and rhyme, one feature is created containing the number of chains in a sentence, and a second consisting of the length of the longest chain in the sentence, divided by the number of words.

Sentiment polarity is the total sentiment score of a sentence, calculated using the Senticnet 4 package for Python (Cambria et al., 2016). The sentiment intensity scores ranging from very negative (-1) to very positive (+1) are used to calculate the total sentiment polarity of a sentence. A sentence that has both positive and negative parts in it, might result in a neutral score. In order to account for this, a second feature is introduced using only natural numbers. For example, a oneliner scoring -2 and +2 sentiment scores, is represented in the second feature with a value of 4.

Part of Speech-tag ratios are calculated using Stanford CoreNLP to tag sentences with Treebank pos-tags (Manning et al., 2014) and dividing the number of occurrences for each POS-category by the number of words in a sentence. The POS-tag categories included are pronouns, verbs, common nouns, proper nouns and modifiers.

Antonymy presence is evaluated using the WordNet "Antonymy"-relationship. Since not all antonyms are listed (Mihalcea and Strapparava, 2005), this set is expanded by also checking whether the antonyms of synonyms of any adjectives are present.

Adult Slang is identified in text, by putting all synsets that are hyponyms of the WordNet synsets 'sexuality' and 'sexual_activity' up to a depth of

---

three layers of hyponyms in a lexicon, and comparing the words in the sentence to it. Moreover, the definitions of each remaining word are scanned for phrases that signal adult slang, such as 'offensive word', 'obscene word' and 'vulgar term'.

Negations are identified by checking whether the word "not" or contraction "..n't" occurs.

Homophones are recognized using CMUDict to find words that have similar pronunciations. For each word in a sentence, another word is sought with the same pronunciation. A small experiment showed that this approach detects over 83% of the homephones found on an expert-created list[4], while capturing more than are on the list.

Homographs are identified using two methods. The first method matches words from sentences to a list of 160 common homographs retrieved from Wikipedia. The second method uses WordNet to extract the definitions of all senses found for a word and only keeps those definitions with no overlap in used vocabulary. A word is considered a homograph if more than two definitions remain.

3.3 Crowdsourcing homograph annotation

The performance of the two proposed homograph detection algorithms is measured by comparing the accuracy on a dataset containing 301 sentences with annotated homographs. The users of crowdsourcing platform Crowdflower[5] were presented with a sentence, and a list of answer options on clickable buttons. The 301 annotated sentences were randomly selected from the oneliners, reuters and wiki datasets and excluded for training.

For assessment of annotation quality, three metrics from the CrowdTruth approach were used (Dumitrache et al., 2015). This approach helps to extract more information from annotations by taking both annotator agreement and -disagreement into account, requiring less annotations for high quality results. The formulas for the used metrics can be found on GitHub[6].

First of all, the Media Unit Quality score (UQS) captures the level of agreement in annotation of a media unit. This metric helps identify ambiguity in the task of annotating specific sentences. Sentences that are hard to annotate, have a low UQS.

In this particular annotation task, this means that sentences with a low UQS likely contain homographs that are difficult to recognize or that are debatable. Secondly, the Worker Quality Score (WQS) assigns a score to each worker based on its annotation agreement with others that worked on the same sentences (Worker-Worker Agreement) and a workers' disagreement compared to the crowd, on a sentence basis. By using the weighted average, poor annotations of sentences that were found to be difficult to classify, have a lower impact on the final WQS of a worker. Finally, the UQS and WQS are combined into a weighted annotation score (Unit Annotation Score), giving better annotators more influence on the final annotation score of a sentence. The results are reported in sections 4.1 and 4.2.

3.4 Machine Learning algorithms

Three machine learning algorithms are deployed in this study, consisting of one Naive Bayes (Bernoulli NB) implementation and two Support Vector Machines (SVMs) with a linear and RBF kernel respectively. The main advantage NB classifiers have over their more sophisticated counterparts are its speed and reduced complexity. On the other hand, SVMs (Burges et al., 1996) outperformed other commonly used algorithms such as Naive Bayes, K-NN and C4.5 Decision Tree learners at the widely used benchmark task of text categorization of Reuters data (Joachims, 1998).

3.5 Experimental Setting

In the first experiment, all the style-features are used for training the classifiers. The classifier performance is reported by its average accuracy over 30 runs using 10-fold cross-validation, to minimize variability in results. This is repeated once with homographs extracted using the list-approach and once with the WordNet approach. Comparison with the State-of-the-Art is not useful, since different datasets were used.

4 Results

4.1 Homograph annotation

A total of 221 out of 301 sentences have a UQS below 0.5, meaning they were difficult to annotate. Since only people from natively English-speaking countries were invited, homograph annotation seems to be a difficult task for humans. The WQS are also low, with the best worker reaching

---

[4]www.singularis.ltd.uk/bifroest/misc/homophones-list.html

[5]www.elite.crowdflower.com

[6]https://github.com/CrowdTruth/CrowdTruth-core/blob/master/tutorial/ CrowdTruth%20metrics %202.0%20documentation.ipynb

a score of 0.7 and 70 workers achieving a score lower than 0.3. The annotators achieving a WQS lower than 0.1 are most likely spam-workers. For the Media Unit Annotation Score, we find 248 words with a score higher than 0.5 that are thus labeled a homograph.

4.2 Homograph recognition performance

The performance results of the two homograph recognition methods is reported in Table 1. The acceptance threshold of 0.5 indicates that only words with a weighted annotation value higher than 0.5 are labeled as homographs (weighted majority vote). The fixed list of homographs performs rather well on precision and accuracy, as the data contains much more non-homographs than it does homographs. The poor recall however, suggests that the list contains an insufficient number of homographs. Although its precision and accuracy are lower, the WordNet approach results in a higher recall and f-measure, but suffers from a low precision due to its high number of false positives.

Table 1: Homograph recognition results

	Homograph list	WordNet
Precision	82.6	35.3
Recall	8.2	82.5
F-Measure	14.9	49.5
Accuracy	85.9	74.6

4.3 Experiments

The results for the experiments are reported in Table 2. The table shows, per column and in this order, the results using 14) only style-features, 15) features in 14 + homophones, 16L) features in 15 + list-matched homographs and finally 16W) features in 15 + the WordNet-homograhps. Bold results have a significantly higher mean accuracy when compared with featureset 14 with probability P $\leq$ 0.025. The results of the system trained on oneliners an short wikipedia sentences and tested on humorous- and Wikipedia-texts longer than 140 characters, achieved a mean accuracy of 87.14%. All the results reported in Table 2 were achieved using the overall best performing classification algorithm (Linear SVM).

5 Discussion

The first research question concerned how high-quality data for training a humor recognition sys-

Table 2: Mean accuracy for each experiment

Featureset	14	15	16L	16W
Reuters	91.16%	91.11%	91.10%	**91.45%**
Wikipedia	69.66%	69.74%	69.66%	**69.94%**
Proverbs	75.78%	**75.98%**	75.97%	**76.91%**

tem should be gathered. Designing webscrapers targeting dedicated websites resulted in a dataset containing much less noise than the seedlist-webscraping approach reported in the State-of-the-Art (+-2% vs. +- 9% in a random 200 sentence sample) (Mihalcea and Strapparava, 2005). The second goal was to identify the best automatic homograph recognition method. For the task of humor recognition, the WordNet approach significantly outperforms the fixed list approach, which could suggest that recall is more important than precision for this task. The third goal was to evaluate whether automatically extracted homophones and homographs improve the accuracy of humor recognition in oneliners. Significant improvement in classification accuracy was found for homographs extracted through the WordNet approach, but not for homophones. Finally, the classifier trained on humorous and non-humorous oneliners performed well on humor classification in texts longer than 140 tokens (87.14% accuracy), suggesting the features are robust to variations in sentence length.

In future work, it might be interesting to find out through feature selection which features are most informative. Although the homophone detection seems to work well, homophone presence in a sentence does not seem to hold significant predictive value without a measure of strength of support for different senses of the homophone in question.

6 Conclusions

This paper presents a method (and code, see Appendix A) for gathering high-quality training data, a homograph recognition evaluation set and a set of features that can be used alongside content-features to achieve a robust high classification performance. Homographs help detect ambiguity in sentences, which in turn was found to slightly increase classification performance. Homophone detection is possible, but does not yet add significant predictive value in its current implementation. A humor recognition classifier trained on oneliners can also accurately label longer texts.

References

Francesco Barbieri and Horacio Saggion. 2014. Automatic detection of irony and humour in twitter. In *ICCC*, pages 155–162.

Christopher JC Burges et al. 1996. Simplified support vector decision rules. In *ICML*, volume 96, pages 71–77. Citeseer.

Erik Cambria, Soujanya Poria, Rajiv Bajpai, and Bjoern Schuller. 2016. Senticnet 4: A semantic resource for sentiment analysis based on conceptual primitives. In *Proceedings of COLING 2016, the 26th International Conference on Computational Linguistics: Technical Papers*, pages 2666–2677. The COLING 2016 Organizing Committee.

Anca Dumitrache, Lora Aroyo, and Chris Welty. 2015. Achieving expert-level annotation quality with crowdtruth. In *Proc. of BDM21 Workshop, ISWC*.

Charles R Gruner. 2000. *The game of humor: A comprehensive theory of why we laugh*. Transaction publishers.

Thorsten Joachims. 1998. Text categorization with support vector machines: Learning with many relevant features. In *European conference on machine learning*, pages 137–142. Springer.

Justine T Kao, Roger Levy, and Noah D Goodman. 2015. A computational model of linguistic humor in puns. *Cognitive science*.

David Kauchak. 2013. Improving text simplification language modeling using unsimplified text data. In *Proceedings of the 51st Annual Meeting of the Association for Computational Linguistics (Volume 1: Long Papers)*, pages 1537–1546. Association for Computational Linguistics.

Christopher Manning, Mihai Surdeanu, John Bauer, Jenny Finkel, Steven Bethard, and David McClosky. 2014. The stanford corenlp natural language processing toolkit. In *Proceedings of 52nd Annual Meeting of the Association for Computational Linguistics: System Demonstrations*, pages 55–60. Association for Computational Linguistics.

Tara McHugh and Lori Buchanan. 2016. Pun processing from a psycholinguistic perspective: Introducing the model of psycholinguistic hemispheric incongruity laughter (m. phil). *Laterality: Asymmetries of Body, Brain and Cognition*, 21(4-6):455–483.

Rada Mihalcea and Stephen Pulman. 2007. Characterizing humour: An exploration of features in humorous texts. In *International Conference on Intelligent Text Processing and Computational Linguistics*, pages 337–347. Springer.

Rada Mihalcea and Carlo Strapparava. 2005. Making computers laugh: Investigations in automatic humor recognition. In *Proceedings of Human Language Technology Conference and Conference on Empirical Methods in Natural Language Processing*.

John Morkes, Hadyn K Kernal, and Clifford Nass. 1998. Humor in task-oriented computer-mediated communication and human-computer interaction. In *CHI 98 Cconference Summary on Human Factors in Computing Systems*, pages 215–216. ACM.

Matthijs P Mulder and Antinus Nijholt. 2002. Humour research: State of art.

Anton Nijholt, Oliviero Stock, Alan Dix, and John Morkes. 2003. Humor modeling in the interface. In *CHI'03 Extended Abstracts on Human Factors in Computing Systems*, pages 1050–1051. ACM.

Dragomir Radev, Amanda Stent, Joel Tetreault, Aasish Pappu, Aikaterini Iliakopoulou, Agustin Chanfreau, Paloma de Juan, Jordi Vallmitjana, Alejandro Jaimes, Rahul Jha, et al. 2015. Humor in collective discourse: Unsupervised funniness detection in the new yorker cartoon caption contest. *arXiv preprint arXiv:1506.08126*.

Byron Reeves and Clifford Nass. 1996. *How people treat computers, television, and new media like real people and places*. CSLI Publications and Cambridge university press.

Jonas Sjöbergh and Kenji Araki. 2007. Recognizing humor without recognizing meaning. In *Proceedings of the 7th International Workshop on Fuzzy Logic and Applications: Applications of Fuzzy Sets Theory*, WILF '07, pages 469–476, Berlin, Heidelberg. Springer-Verlag.

Julia M Taylor and Lawrence J Mazlack. 2004. Computationally recognizing wordplay in jokes. In *Proceedings of the Annual Meeting of the Cognitive Science Society*, volume 26.

Renxian Zhang and Naishi Liu. 2014. Recognizing humor on twitter. In *Proceedings of the 23rd ACM International Conference on Conference on Information and Knowledge Management*, CIKM '14, pages 889–898, New York, NY, USA. ACM.

Appendix A. Github project depository

The code and datasets are available here: https://github.com/svenvdbeukel/Short-text-corpus-with-focus-on-humor-detection

Appendix B. Link to supplementary information

Supplementary information useful for reproduction of the described experiments can be found by copying the following link: http://bit.ly/2MuVQg1Humor

Emo2Vec: Learning Generalized Emotion Representation by Multi-task Training

Peng Xu, Andrea Madotto, Chien-Sheng Wu, Ji Ho Park and **Pascale Fung**
Center for Artificial Intelligence Research (CAiRE)
The Hong Kong University of Science and Technology, Clear Water Bay
`[pxuab,eeandreamad,cwuak,jhpark,pascale]@ust.hk`

Abstract

In this paper, we propose Emo2Vec which encodes emotional semantics into vectors. We train Emo2Vec by multi-task learning six different emotion-related tasks, including emotion/sentiment analysis, sarcasm classification, stress detection, abusive language classification, insult detection, and personality recognition. Our evaluation of Emo2Vec shows that it outperforms existing affect-related representations, such as Sentiment-Specific Word Embedding and DeepMoji embeddings with much smaller training corpora. When concatenated with GloVe, Emo2Vec achieves competitive performances to state-of-the-art results on several tasks using a simple logistic regression classifier.

1 Introduction

Recent work on word representation has been focusing on embedding syntactic and semantic information into fixed-sized vectors (Mikolov et al., 2013; Pennington et al., 2014) based on the distributional hypothesis, and have proven to be useful in many natural language tasks (Collobert et al., 2011). However, despite the rising popularity regarding the use of word embeddings, they often fail to capture the emotional semantics the words convey. For example, the GloVe vector captures the semantic meaning of "headache", as it is closer to words of ill symptoms like "fever" and "toothache", but misses the emotional association that the word carries. The word "headache" in the sentence "You are giving me a headache" does not really mean that the speaker will get a headache, but instead implies the negative emotion of the speaker.

To include affective information into the word representation, Tang et al. (2016) proposed Sentiment-Specific Word Embeddings (SSWE) which encodes both positive/negative sentiment

and syntactic contextual information in a vector space. This work demonstrates the effectiveness of incorporating sentiment labels in a word-level information for sentiment-related tasks compared to other word embeddings. However, they only focus on binary labels, which weakens their generalization ability on other affect tasks. Yu et al. (2017) instead uses emotion lexicons to tune the vector space, which gives them better results. Nevertheless, this method requires human-labeled lexicons and cannot scale to large amounts of data. Felbo et al. (2017) achieves good results on affect tasks by training a two-layer bidirectional Long Short-Term Memory (bi-LSTM) model, named DeepMoji, to predict emoji of the input document using a huge dataset of 1.2 billions of tweets. However, collecting billions of tweets is expensive and time consuming for researchers.

Furthermore, most works in sentiment and emotion analysis have focused solely on a single task. Nevertheless, as emotion is a complex concept, we believe that all emotion involving situations such as stress, hate speech, sarcasm, and insult, should be included for a deeper understanding of emotion. Thus, one way to achieve this is through a multi-task training framework, as we present here.

Contributions: 1) We propose Emo2Vec [1] which are word-level representations that encode emotional semantics into fixed-sized, real-valued vectors. 2) We propose to learn Emo2Vec with a multi-task learning framework by including six different emotion-related tasks. 3) Compared to existing affect-related embeddings, Emo2Vec achieves better results on more than ten datasets with much less training data (1.9M vs 1.2B documents). Furthermore, with a simple logistic regression classifier, Emo2Vec reaches competitive performance to state-of-the-art results on several

---

[1] https://github.com/pxuab/emo2vec_wassa_paper

Proceedings of the 9th Workshop on Computational Approaches to Subjectivity, Sentiment and Social Media Analysis, pages 292–298
Brussels, Belgium, October 31, 2018. ©2018 Association for Computational Linguistics
https://doi.org/10.18653/v1/P17

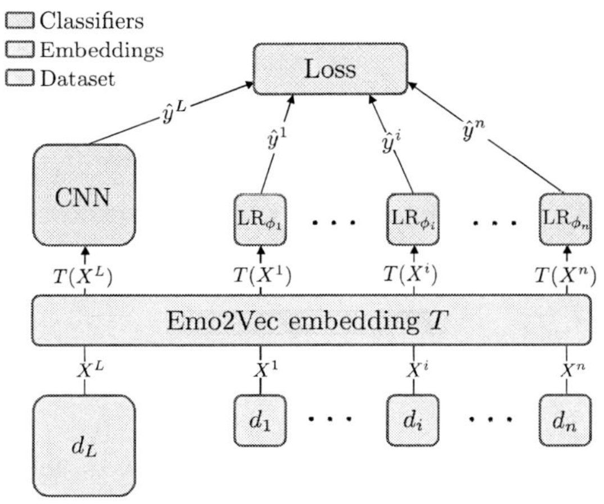

Figure 1: Multi-task learning diagram

datasets when combined with GloVe.

2 Methodology

We train Emo2Vec using an end-to-end multi-task learning framework with one larger dataset and several small task-specific datasets. The model is divided into two parts: a shared embedding layer (i.e. Emo2Vec), and task-specific classifiers. All datasets share the same word-level representations (i.e. Emo2Vec), thus forcing the model to encode shared knowledge into a single matrix. For the larger dataset, a Convolutional Neural Network (CNN) (LeCun et al., 1998) model is used to capture complex linguistic features present in the corpus. On the other hand, the classifier of each small dataset is a simple logistic regression.

Notation: We define $D = \{d_L, d_1, d_2, \cdots, d_n\}$ as the set of $n + 1$ datasets, where d_L is the larger dataset and the other d_i are the small datasets. We denote a sentence X^i with $i \in \{L, 1, 2, \cdots, n\}$ as $[w_{i,1}, w_{i,2}, \cdots, w_{i,N_i}]$ where $w_{i,j}$ is the j-th word in the i-th sample and N_i is the number of words. All the models' parameters are defined as $M_\Phi = \{T, \text{CNN}, \text{LR}_{\phi_1}, \ldots, \text{LR}_{\phi_n}\}$, where $T \in \mathbb{R}^{|V| \times k}$ is the Emo2Vec matrix, $|V|$ is the vocabulary size and k is the embedding dimension, CNN is a Convolutional Neural Network model and LR_{ϕ_i} for $i \in [1, n]$ is a logistic regression classifier parameterized by ϕ_i which is specific for the dataset d_i. We denote the embedded representation of a word $w_{i,j}$ with $e_{w_{i,j}}$.

2.1 CNN model

The CNN architecture used is illustrated in Figure 2. Firstly, 1-D convolution is used to extract n-

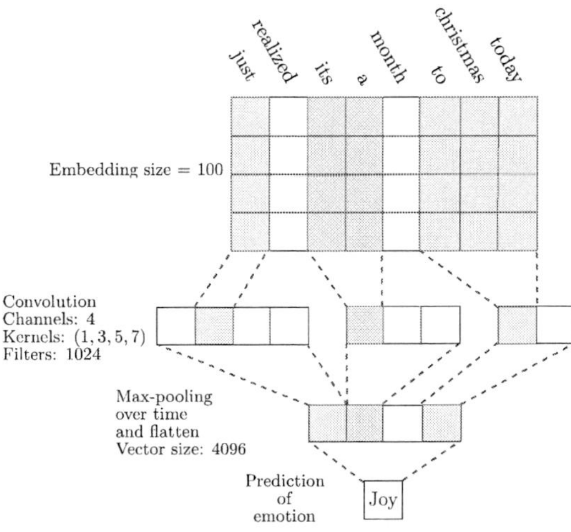

Figure 2: Structure of CNN model

gram features from the input embeddings. Specifically, the j-th filter denoted by F_j, is convolved with embeddings of words in a sliding window of size k_j, giving a feature value $c_{j,t}$. J filters are learned trough this process:

$$c_{j,t} = F_j * e_{w_{L,t:t+k_j-1}} + b_j$$

where $*$ is the 1-D convolution operation. This is followed by a layer of ReLU activation (Nair and Hinton, 2010) for non-linearity. After that, we add a max-pooling layer of pooling size $M - F_j + 1$ along the time dimension to force the network to find the most relevant feature for predicting y^L correctly. The result of this series of operations is a scalar output of fm_j. All fm_j for $j \in [1, J]$ are then concatenated together to produce a vector representation $fm_{1:J}$ of the whole input sentence.

$$fm_j = \text{Max\_Pooling}\left(\text{ReLU}\left(c_{j,t}\right)\right)$$

To make the final classification, the vector $fm_{i,1:J}$ is projected to the target label space by adding another fully connected layer (i.e. parameterized by W and b), with a softmax activation.

$$\hat{y}^L = \text{Softmax}(W \cdot [fm_{1:J}] + b)$$

2.2 Multi-task learning

Since collecting a huge amount of labeled datasets is expensive, we collect two types of corpora, one larger dataset (millions of training samples) and a set of small datasets (thousands of training samples each) with accurate labels. For small datasets, sentiment analysis, emotion classification, sarcasm detection, abusive language classification, stress detection, insult classification and personality recognition are included. The reason why we include many datasets is to 1) leverage different aspects of words emotion knowledge, which may not be present in single domain dataset; 2) create a more general embedding emotional space that can generalize well across different tasks and domains. To avoid over-fitting, L2 regularization penalty is added from the weights of all logistic regression classifiers ϕ_i for $i \in [1, n]$. Hence, we jointly optimize the following loss function:

$$L(M_\Phi) = \frac{1}{n} \sum_{j=1}^{n} L_j + \lambda \sum_{j=1}^{n} \|\mathrm{LR}_{\phi_j}\|_2$$

Where L_j is the negative log likelihood (NLL) between $\hat{y}^j$ and y^j, and λ an hyper-parameter for the regularization terms.

3 Experimental Setup

3.1 Dataset

Larger dataset

We collect a larger dataset from Twitter with hashtags as distant supervision. Such distant supervision method using hashtags has already been proved to provide reasonably relevant emotion labels by previous works (Wang et al., 2012).We construct our hashtag corpus from Wang et al. (2012), and Sintsova et al. (2017) [2]. More tweets between January and October 2017 are additionally added using the Twitter Firehose API by using the hashtags based on the hierarchy mentioned in Shaver et al. (1987). The hashtags are transformed into corresponding emotion labels of Joy, Sadness, Anger, and Fear. When extending the dataset, we only use documents with emotional hashtags at the end and filter out any documents with URLs, quotations, or less than five words as Wang et al. (2012) did. The total number of documents is about 1.9 million with four classes: joy (36.5%), sadness (33.8%), anger (23.5%), and fear (6%). The dataset is randomly split into a train (70%), validation (15%), and test set (15%) for experiments.

Small datasets

For sentiment, we include 8 datasets. (1,2) SST-fine and SST-binary (Socher et al., 2013) (3) OpeNER (Agerri et al., 2013) (4,5) tube_auto

and tube_tablet (Uryupina et al., 2014) (6) Se-mEval (Hltcoe, 2013) (7,8) SS-Twitter and SS-Youtube (Thelwall et al., 2010). For emotion tasks, we include 4 datasets, (1) ISEAR (Wallbott and Scherer, 1986) (2) WASSA (Mohammad and Bravo-Marquez, 2017) (3) Olympic Sintsova et al. (2013) (4) SE0714 (Staiano and Guerini, 2014). We further include 6 other affect-related datasets. (1,2) SCv1-GEN and SCv2-GEN for sarcasm detection, (3) Stress (Winata et al., 2018), (4) Abusive (Waseem, 2016; Waseem and Hovy, 2016). (5) Personality (Pennebaker and King, 1999) (6) Insult. The detailed statistics can be found in Table 4 and Table 5 in Supplemental Material.

3.2 Pre-training Emo2Vec

Emo2Vec embedding matrix and the CNN model are pre-trained using hashtag corpus alone. Parameters of T and CNN are randomly initialized and Adam is used for optimization. Best parameter settings are tuned on the validation set. For the best model, we use the batch size of 16, embedding size of 100, 1024 filters and filter sizes are 1,3,5 and 7 respectively. We keep the trained embedding and rename it as CNN embedding for comparison. 100-dim for Emo2Vec is used in all experiments.

3.3 Multi-task training

We tune our parameters of learning rate, L2 regularization, whether to pre-train our model and batch size with the average accuracy of the development set of all datasets. We early stop our model when the averaged dev accuracy stop increasing. Our best model uses learning rate of 0.001, L2 regularization of 1.0, batch size of 32. We save the best model and take the embedding layer as Emo2Vec vectors.

3.4 Evaluation

Baselines: We use 50-dimension Sentiment-specific Word Embedding (SSWE) (Tang et al., 2016) as our baseline, which is an embedding model trained with 10 millions of tweets by encoding both semantic and sentiment information into vectors. Also, lots of work about the detection/classification in sentiment analysis implicitly encodes emotion inside the word vectors. For example, Felbo et al. (2017) trains a two-layer bidirectional Long Short-Term Memory (bi-LSTM) model, named DeepMoji, to predict emoji of the

---

[2]http://hci.epfl.ch/sharing-emotion-lexicons-and-data#emo-hash-data

model	SS-T	SS-Y	SS-binary	SS-fine	OpeNER	tube_auto	tube_tablet	SemEval	average
SSWE	**0.815**	0.835	0.698	0.365	0.701	0.620	0.654	0.629	0.665
DeepMoji embedding	0.788	0.841	0.751	0.369	**0.754**	0.628	0.675	**0.676**	0.685
CNN embedding	0.803	**0.862**	0.734	0.369	0.713	0.605	0.667	0.622	0.672
Emo2Vec	0.801	0.859	**0.812**	**0.416**	0.744	**0.629**	**0.688**	0.638	**0.698**

Table 1: Comparison between different emotion representations on sentiment datasets, all results are reported with accuracy. The best results are highlighted with bold fonts. Emo2Vec achieves best average score.

model	ISEAR	WASSA	SE0714	Olympic	Stress	SCv1-GEN	SCv2-GEN	Insult	Abusive	Personality	average
SSWE	0.327	0.466	0.217	0.508	0.704	0.660	0.678	0.559	0.539	0.674	0.533
DeepMoji embedding	0.379	0.532	0.286	0.485	0.739	0.658	0.685	**0.666**	0.586	**0.678**	0.569
CNN embedding	**0.384**	0.549	0.259	0.480	**0.744**	0.657	0.707	0.623	0.560	0.676	0.564
Emo2Vec	0.372	**0.559**	**0.323**	**0.506**	**0.744**	**0.674**	**0.710**	0.647	**0.588**	0.675	**0.580**

Table 2: Comparison between different representations on other affect related datasets. All results are reported with f1 score. The best results are highlighted with bold fonts. On average, Emo2Vec achieves best f1 score.

input document using a huge dataset of 1.2 billion tweets. Their embedding layer is implicitly encoded with emotion knowledge. Thus, we use the DeepMoji embedding, the 256-dimension embedding layer of DeepMoji as another baseline.

Evaluation method: To make a fair comparison with other baseline representations, we first take one dataset d_i out from n small datasets as the test set. The remaining $n - 1$ small datasets and the larger dataset are used to train Emo2Vec through multi-task learning. We take the trained Emo2Vec as the feature for d_i and train a logistic regression on d_i to compare the performance with other baseline representations. The procedure is repeated n times to see the generalization ability on different datasets. We release Emo2Vec trained on all datasets. For sentiment tasks, accuracy score is reported. For other tasks, if it is binary task, we report f1 score for the positive class. If it is multi-class classification tasks, we make it binary classification problem for each class and report averaged f1 score.

4 Results

We compare our Emo2Vec with SSWE, CNN embedding, DeepMoji embedding and state-of-the-art(SOTA) results on 18 different datasets. The results can be found in Table 1 and Table 2.

Compared with CNN embedding: Emo2Vec works better than CNN embedding on 14/18 datasets, giving 2.6% absolute accuracy improvement for the sentiment task and 1.6% absolute f1-score improvement on the other tasks. It shows multi-task training helps to create better generalized word emotion representations than just using a single task.

Compared with SSWE: Emo2Vec works much better on all datasets except SS-T datasets, which gives 3.3% accuracy improvement and 4.7% f1

score improvement respectively on sentiment and other tasks. This is because SSWE is trained on 10M binary classification task on twitter which then over-fits on dataset SS-T, and generalizes poorly to other tasks.

Compared with DeepMoji embedding: Emo2Vec outperforms DeepMoji on 13/18 datasets despite the much smaller size of our training corpus (1.9M documents for us vs 1.2B documents for DeepMoji). On average, it gives 1.3% improvement in accuracy for the sentiment task and 1.1% improvement of f1-score on the other tasks.

Compared with SOTA results: We further compare the performance of Emo2Vec vectors with SOTA results on 14 datasets where the same split is shared. Since Emo2Vec is not trained by predicting contextual words, it is weak on capturing synthetic and semantic meaning. Thus, we concatenate Emo2Vec with the pre-trained GloVe vectors, which are trained on Twitter and Wikepedia [3]. Then, the concatenated vector of GloVe and Emo2Vec, the concatenated vector of GloVe and DeepMoji embeddings and GloVe are included for comparison with SOTA results. Note that SOTA results require complex bi-LSTM model while all these representations are trained and reported with a logistic regression classifier. Here, we want to highlight that solely using a simple classifier with good word representation can achieve promising results.

Table 3 shows that GloVe+Emo2Vec outperforms GloVe on 13/14 datasets. Compared with GloVe+DeepMoji, GloVe+Emo2Vec achieves same or better results on 11/14 datasets, which on average gives 1.0% improvement. GloVe+Emo2Vec achieves better performances on

---

[3] http://nlp.stanford.edu/data/glove.twitter.27B.zip and http://nlp.stanford.edu/data/glove.6B.zip

dataset	Previous SOTA results		GloVe	GloVe+DeepMoji	GloVe+Emo2Vec
SS-Twitter	bi-LSTM (Felbo et al., 2017)	0.88	0.78	**0.81**	**0.81**
SS-Youtube	bi-LSTM (Felbo et al., 2017)	0.93	0.84	0.86	**0.87**
SS-binary	bi-LSTM (Yu et al., 2017)	0.886	0.795	0.809	**0.823**
SS-fine	bi-LSTM (Yu et al., 2017)	0.497	0.414	0.421	**0.436**
OpeNER	bi-LSTM (Barnes et al., 2017)	0.825	0.750	**0.781**	0.778
tube_auto	SVM (Barnes et al., 2017)	0.662	0.630	0.628	**0.660**
tube_tablet	SVM (Barnes et al., 2017)	0.681	0.650	0.678	**0.684**
SemEval	bi-LSTM (Barnes et al., 2017)	0.685	0.671	**0.695**	0.680
ISEAR	bi-LSTM (Felbo et al., 2017)	0.57	0.41	0.43	**0.45**
SE0714	bi-LSTM (Felbo et al., 2017)	0.37	0.36	0.36	**0.43**
Olympic	bi-LSTM (Felbo et al., 2017)	0.61	0.52	0.52	**0.53**
stress	bi-LSTM (Winata et al., 2018)	0.743	0.759	**0.793**	0.770
SCv1-GEN	bi-LSTM (Felbo et al., 2017)	0.69	**0.69**	0.68	0.68
SCv2-GEN	bi-LSTM (Felbo et al., 2017)	0.75	0.73	**0.74**	**0.74**
Average			0.642	0.657	**0.667**

Table 3: Comparison between different word-level emotion representations with state-of-the-art results. The best results are in bold. New state-of-the-art results Emo2Vec that achieves are highlighted with boxes.

SOTA results on three datasets (SE0714, stress and tube_tablet) and comparable result to SOTA on another four datasets (tube_auto, SemEval, SCv1-GEN and SCv2-GEN). We believe the reason why we achieve a much better performance than SOTA on the SE0714 is that headlines are usually short and emotional words exist more commonly in headlines. Thus, to detect the corresponding emotion, more attention needs to be paid to words.

5   Related work

For sentiment analysis, numerous classification models (Kalchbrenner et al.; Iyyer et al., 2015; Dou, 2017) have been explored. Multi-modal sentiment analysis (Zadeh et al., 2017; Poria et al., 2017) extends text-based model to the combination of visual, acoustic and language, which achieves better results than the single modality. Various methods are developed for automatic constructions of sentiment lexicons using both supervised and unsupervised way (Wang and Xia, 2017). Aspect-based sentiment (Chen et al., 2017; Wang et al., 2016) is also a hot topic where researchers care more about the sentiment towards a certain target. Transfer learning from the large corpus is also investigated by Felbo et al. (2017) to train a large model on a huge emoji tweet corpus, which boosts the performance of affect-related tasks. Multi-task training has achieved great success in various natural language tasks, such as machine translation (Dong et al., 2015; Malaviya et al., 2017), multilingual tasks (Duong et al., 2015; Gillick et al., 2016), semantic pars-

ing (Peng et al., 2017). Hashimoto et al. (2017) jointly learns POS tagging, chunking, dependency parsing, semantic relatedness, and textual entailment by considering linguistic hierarchy and achieves state-of-the-results on five datasets. For sentiment analysis, Balikas et al. (2017) jointly trains ternary and fine-grained classification with a recurrent neural network and achieves new state-of-the-art results.

6   Conclusion and Future Work

In this paper, we propose Emo2Vec to represent emotion with vectors using a multi-task training framework. Six affect-related tasks are utilized, including emotion/sentiment analysis, sarcasm classification, stress detection, abusive language classification, insult detection, and personality recognition. We empirically show how Emo2Vec leverages multi-task training to learn a generalized emotion representation. In addition, Emo2Vec outperforms existing affect-related embeddings on more than ten different datasets. By combining Emo2Vec with GloVe, logistic regression can achieve competitive performances on several state-of-the-art results.

7   Acknowledgements

This work is partially funded by ITS/319/16FP of Innovation Technology Commission, HKUST 16248016 of Hong Kong Research Grants Council.

References

Rodrigo Agerri, Montse Cuadros, Sean Gaines, and German Rigau. 2013. Opener: Open polarity enhanced named entity recognition. *Procesamiento del Lenguaje Natural*, (51).

Georgios Balikas, Simon Moura, and Massih-Reza Amini. 2017. Multitask learning for fine-grained twitter sentiment analysis. In *Proceedings of the 40th International ACM SIGIR Conference on Research and Development in Information Retrieval*, SIGIR '17, pages 1005–1008, New York, NY, USA. ACM.

Jeremy Barnes, Roman Klinger, and Sabine Schulte im Walde. 2017. Assessing state-of-the-art sentiment models on state-of-the-art sentiment datasets. In *Proceedings of the 8th Workshop on Computational Approaches to Subjectivity, Sentiment and Social Media Analysis*, pages 2–12.

Steven Bird and Edward Loper. 2004. Nltk: the natural language toolkit. In *Proceedings of the ACL 2004 on Interactive poster and demonstration sessions*, page 31. Association for Computational Linguistics.

Peng Chen, Zhongqian Sun, Lidong Bing, and Wei Yang. 2017. Recurrent attention network on memory for aspect sentiment analysis. In *Proceedings of the 2017 Conference on Empirical Methods in Natural Language Processing*, pages 452–461.

Ronan Collobert, Jason Weston, Lon Bottou, Michael Karlen, Koray Kavukcuoglu, and Pavel Kuksa. 2011. Natural language processing (almost) from scratch. *Journal of Machine Learning Research*, 12(Aug):2493–2537.

Daxiang Dong, Hua Wu, Wei He, Dianhai Yu, and Haifeng Wang. 2015. Multi-task learning for multiple language translation. In *Proceedings of the 53rd Annual Meeting of the Association for Computational Linguistics and the 7th International Joint Conference on Natural Language Processing (Volume 1: Long Papers)*, volume 1, pages 1723–1732.

Zi-Yi Dou. 2017. Capturing user and product information for document level sentiment analysis with deep memory network. In *Proceedings of the 2017 Conference on Empirical Methods in Natural Language Processing*, pages 521–526.

Long Duong, Trevor Cohn, Steven Bird, and Paul Cook. 2015. Low resource dependency parsing: Cross-lingual parameter sharing in a neural network parser. In *Proceedings of the 53rd Annual Meeting of the Association for Computational Linguistics and the 7th International Joint Conference on Natural Language Processing (Volume 2: Short Papers)*, volume 2, pages 845–850.

Bjarke Felbo, Alan Mislove, Anders Sgaard, Iyad Rahwan, and Sune Lehmann. 2017. Using millions of emoji occurrences to learn any-domain representations for detecting sentiment, emotion and sarcasm. In *Proceedings of the 2017 Conference on Empirical Methods in Natural Language Processing*, pages 1616–1626.

Dan Gillick, Cliff Brunk, Oriol Vinyals, and Amarnag Subramanya. 2016. Multilingual language processing from bytes. In *Proceedings of the 2016 Conference of the North American Chapter of the Association for Computational Linguistics: Human Language Technologies*, pages 1296–1306.

Kazuma Hashimoto, Yoshimasa Tsuruoka, Richard Socher, et al. 2017. A joint many-task model: Growing a neural network for multiple nlp tasks. In *Proceedings of the 2017 Conference on Empirical Methods in Natural Language Processing*, pages 1923–1933.

J Hltcoe. 2013. Semeval-2013 task 2: Sentiment analysis in twitter. *Atlanta, Georgia, USA*, 312.

Mohit Iyyer, Varun Manjunatha, Jordan Boyd-Graber, and Hal Daumé III. 2015. Deep unordered composition rivals syntactic methods for text classification. In *Proceedings of the 53rd Annual Meeting of the Association for Computational Linguistics and the 7th International Joint Conference on Natural Language Processing (Volume 1: Long Papers)*, volume 1, pages 1681–1691.

Nal Kalchbrenner, Edward Grefenstette, and Phil Blunsom. A convolutional neural network for modelling sentences.

Yann LeCun, Léon Bottou, Yoshua Bengio, and Patrick Haffner. 1998. Gradient-based learning applied to document recognition. *Proceedings of the IEEE*, 86(11):2278–2324.

Chaitanya Malaviya, Graham Neubig, and Patrick Littell. 2017. Learning language representations for typology prediction. In *Proceedings of the 2017 Conference on Empirical Methods in Natural Language Processing*, pages 2529–2535.

Tomas Mikolov, Ilya Sutskever, Kai Chen, Greg S. Corrado, and Jeff Dean. 2013. Distributed representations of words and phrases and their compositionality. In *Advances in neural information processing systems*, pages 3111–3119.

Saif Mohammad and Felipe Bravo-Marquez. 2017. Wassa-2017 shared task on emotion intensity. In *Proceedings of the 8th Workshop on Computational Approaches to Subjectivity, Sentiment and Social Media Analysis*, pages 34–49.

Vinod Nair and Geoffrey E Hinton. 2010. Rectified linear units improve restricted boltzmann machines. In *Proceedings of the 27th international conference on machine learning (ICML-10)*, pages 807–814.

Hao Peng, Sam Thomson, and Noah A Smith. 2017. Deep multitask learning for semantic dependency parsing. In *Proceedings of the 55th Annual Meeting of the Association for Computational Linguistics (Volume 1: Long Papers)*, volume 1, pages 2037–2048.

James W Pennebaker and Laura A King. 1999. Linguistic styles: Language use as an individual difference. *Journal of personality and social psychology*, 77(6):1296.

Jeffrey Pennington, Richard Socher, and Christopher Manning. 2014. Glove: Global vectors for word representation. In *Proceedings of the 2014 conference on empirical methods in natural language processing (EMNLP)*, pages 1532–1543.

Soujanya Poria, Erik Cambria, Rajiv Bajpai, and Amir Hussain. 2017. A review of affective computing: From unimodal analysis to multimodal fusion. *Information Fusion*, 37:98–125.

Phillip Shaver, Judith Schwartz, Donald Kirson, and Cary O'connor. 1987. Emotion knowledge: Further exploration of a prototype approach. *Journal of personality and social psychology*, 52(6):1061.

Valentina Sintsova, Margarita Bolvar Jimnez, and Pearl Pu. 2017. Modeling the impact of modifiers on emotional statements. In *Proceedings of the 18th Int. Conference on Computational Linguistics and Intelligent Text Processing (CICLing)*.

Valentina Sintsova, Claudiu-Cristian Musat, and Pearl Pu. 2013. Fine-grained emotion recognition in olympic tweets based on human computation. In *4th Workshop on Computational Approaches to Subjectivity, Sentiment and Social Media Analysis*.

Richard Socher, Alex Perelygin, Jean Wu, Jason Chuang, Christopher D Manning, Andrew Ng, and Christopher Potts. 2013. Recursive deep models for semantic compositionality over a sentiment treebank. In *Proceedings of the 2013 conference on empirical methods in natural language processing*, pages 1631–1642.

Jacopo Staiano and Marco Guerini. 2014. Depeche mood: a lexicon for emotion analysis from crowd annotated news. In *Proceedings of the 52nd Annual Meeting of the Association for Computational Linguistics (Volume 2: Short Papers)*, volume 2, pages 427–433.

Duyu Tang, Furu Wei, Bing Qin, Nan Yang, Ting Liu, and Ming Zhou. 2016. Sentiment embeddings with applications to sentiment analysis. *IEEE Transactions on Knowledge and Data Engineering*, 28(2):496–509.

Mike Thelwall, Kevan Buckley, Georgios Paltoglou, Di Cai, and Arvid Kappas. 2010. Sentiment strength detection in short informal text. *Journal of the Association for Information Science and Technology*, 61(12):2544–2558.

Olga Uryupina, Barbara Plank, Aliaksei Severyn, Agata Rotondi, and Alessandro Moschitti. 2014. Sentube: A corpus for sentiment analysis on youtube social media. In *LREC*, pages 4244–4249. Citeseer.

Harald G. Wallbott and Klaus R. Scherer. 1986. How universal and specific is emotional experience? evidence from 27 countries on five continents. *Information (International Social Science Council)*, 25(4):763–795.

Leyi Wang and Rui Xia. 2017. Sentiment lexicon construction with representation learning based on hierarchical sentiment supervision. In *Proceedings of the 2017 Conference on Empirical Methods in Natural Language Processing*, pages 502–510.

Wenbo Wang, Lu Chen, Krishnaprasad Thirunarayan, and Amit P. Sheth. 2012. Harnessing twitter" big data" for automatic emotion identification. In *Privacy, Security, Risk and Trust (PASSAT), 2012 International Conference on and 2012 International Confernece on Social Computing (SocialCom)*, pages 587–592. IEEE.

Yequan Wang, Minlie Huang, Li Zhao, et al. 2016. Attention-based lstm for aspect-level sentiment classification. In *Proceedings of the 2016 Conference on Empirical Methods in Natural Language Processing*, pages 606–615.

Zeerak Waseem. 2016. Are you a racist or am i seeing things? annotator influence on hate speech detection on twitter. In *Proceedings of the first workshop on NLP and computational social science*, pages 138–142.

Zeerak Waseem and Dirk Hovy. 2016. Hateful symbols or hateful people? predictive features for hate speech detection on twitter. In *Proceedings of the NAACL student research workshop*, pages 88–93.

Genta Indra Winata, Onno Pepijn Kampman, and Pascale Fung. 2018. Attention-based lstm for psychological stress detection from spoken language using distant supervision. *2018 IEEE International Conference on Acoustics, Speech and Signal Processing*.

Liang-Chih Yu, Jin Wang, K Robert Lai, and Xuejie Zhang. 2017. Refining word embeddings for sentiment analysis. In *Proceedings of the 2017 Conference on Empirical Methods in Natural Language Processing*, pages 534–539.

Amir Zadeh, Minghai Chen, Soujanya Poria, Erik Cambria, and Louis-Philippe Morency. 2017. Tensor fusion network for multimodal sentiment analysis. In *Proceedings of the 2017 Conference on Empirical Methods in Natural Language Processing*, pages 1103–1114.

Learning representations for sentiment classification using Multi-task framework

Hardik Meisheri
TCS Research
Mumbai, India
`hardik.meisheri@tcs.com`

Harshad Khadilkar
TCS Research
Mumbai, India
`harshad.khadilkar@tcs.com`

Abstract

Most of the existing state of the art sentiment classification techniques involve the use of pre-trained embeddings. This paper postulates a generalized representation that collates training on multiple datasets using a Multi-task learning framework. We incorporate publicly available, pre-trained embeddings with Bidirectional LSTM's to develop the multi-task model. We validate the representations on an independent test Irony dataset that can contain several sentiments within each sample, with an arbitrary distribution. Our experiments show a significant improvement in results as compared to the available baselines for individual datasets on which independent models are trained. Results also suggest superior performance of the representations generated over Irony dataset.

1 Introduction

Sentiment analysis has attracted substantial research interest, especially in the field of social media, owing to the growing number of data and active users. In addition, the research community has gravitated towards a pragmatic characterization of language with the division into (and quantification of) specific emotions for sentiment analysis. This approach has come to prominence in recent times as a large number of enterprises (not just social media corporations) now rely on understanding customer sentiments for defining product and marketing strategies (Pang and Lee, 2004; Socher et al., 2012).

Beyond strategic inputs, sentiment analysis also performs a tactical role in the age of rapid (viral) increases and decreases in the visibility of specific events, with magnified consequences for corporations and communities at large. For example, United Airlines faced significant business impact due to a single (possibly isolated) passenger-related incident, due to its spread over Twitter[1]. It is conceivable that an automated system quickly alerting the management about the rate and depth of negative sentiments due to the incident, would have enabled them to produce a more amelioratory response from the outset.

Complementary to such motivating incidents is the recent availability of large datasets from social media sources. Twitter has become a go-to choice for scraping data due to its large user base and the easy accessibility of tweets through its API. The result is a large corpus of complex sentiments for identification and analysis. Tweets (the messages posted on Twitter) are limited to 140 characters, which creates a plethora of challenges as the users find new and innovative ways of condensing the messages using slang, hashtags, and emojis, often defying traditional grammatical rules of the language. This is further complicated by the fast, localized rise and decay of popular memes, slang, and hashtags.

Traditional sentiment analysis using dictionary-based methods has failed to capture these nuances, as the methods rely on grammatically correct, intact syntactic and semantic structures which are not followed in this space. Traditional sentiment analyzers such as (Akkaya et al., 2009; Poria et al., 2014; Sharma and Bhattacharyya, 2013) that worked well with well-written texts, face challenges at lexical, syntactic and semantic levels when dealing with tweets as analyzed in (Liu, 2012). Bag-of-words models and naive Bayes models are sequence-agnostic, and have therefore failed to generalize over a diverse distribution of sentiments, especially when multiple fine-grained emotions are compressed into a 140 character message. Word vectors trained on a large corpus to represent the word in dense representations have

---

[1] https://twitter.com/i/moments/851423833160634368

Proceedings of the 9th Workshop on Computational Approaches to Subjectivity, Sentiment and Social Media Analysis, pages 299–308
Brussels, Belgium, October 31, 2018. ©2018 Association for Computational Linguistics
https://doi.org/10.18653/v1/P17

proved to be efficient in handling sentiment analysis and effective emotions. Deep learning and specifically Recurrent Neural Networks have been extensively used with word vectors to achieve state of the art results on various sentiment analysis tasks. Although there are large datasets available on social media space, deep learning models require annotated data for supervised training. Annotation for such a large dataset is expensive, since multiple human annotators are required per sample for stable convergence.

A useful research question is how to leverage resources available on social media sites to improve sentiment classification across datasets by leveraging the generic representations and handling the noise present in the space. These challenges have led people to use transfer learning and multi-task learning approaches to transfer knowledge across different datasets and languages. Recently, neural-network-based models for multi-task learning have become very popular, ranging from computer vision (Misra et al., 2016; Nam and Han, 2016) to natural language processing (Collobert et al., 2011a; Luong et al., 2015), since they provide a convenient way of combining information from multiple tasks.

We propose a dual Attention based deep learning model which creates representations using Bidirectional LSTM. In particular, given an input tweet, our model first uses a pair of bidirectional LSTMs to learn a general representation. This portion of the model is trained in a multitask framework. The general sentence representation is then mapped into a task-specific representation through an attention mechanism, so that the most salient parts of the input are selected for each task. We achieve significant improvement over the baselines and obtain comparable results with the state of the art methods without any feature engineering.

We have selected datasets which classify a text into 3 classes, along with affect dataset. Affective dimensions provide much more granular analysis over emotions that are being conveyed. Affective emotions are classified along the valence, arousal and dominance axis according to circumplex model of affect, a well-established system for describing emotional states (Russell, 1980; Posner et al., 2005). Of these states, valence can directly be mapped to sentiment classification. These scales represent valence (or sentiment) and arousal

(or intensity), which defines each posts position on the circumplex of the 3 dimension

The major contributions of this paper are:

- Generating robust representation of a tweet from three different set of pre-trained embeddings which can handle emoji/smileys and out-of-vocabulary words in the dataset.

- Multi Task learning frame work using Bidirectional Long short Memory Networks (BiLSTM) and attention mechanism to effectively learn the representations across datasets.

We evaluate the effectiveness of the model with respect to both internal and external distribution. The former refers to the setting where distribution of the test data falls in one of the m training tasks, and the latter refers to the setting where task and data are different and we use just the representation to train the task-specific layers.

Rest of the paper is organized as follows, section 2 discusses works related to multi-task learning along the lines of sentiment analysis. We present our proposed approach in section 3, which details the system architecture and its key components. Two sets of experiments and results shown in section 4 and 5 respectively. Finally section 6 concludes the paper with future direction.

2   Related Work

The current state of the art models for classifying the sentiments over social media text specifically tweets use a mixture of handcrafted features and pre-trained embeddings. Lexicon-based features along with neural network models to predict intensity of emotions have been proposed (Mohammad et al., 2013; Wilson et al., 2005; Ding et al., 2008; Bravo-Marquez et al., 2016; Esuli and Sebastiani, 2007) which have proved successful. However, these representations do not generalize well when there is a change in the vocabulary and the distribution. In addition, refining and generating handcrafted features is an expensive and tedious process. Our model do not require any hand-crafted features and can work with raw text and hence it can generalize well.

Two most popular embeddings that are being used are word2vec (Mikolov et al., 2013) and Glove (Pennington et al., 2014). Although these embeddings have improved the baselines from the traditional bag-of-words model, they have been trained over large corpus in an unsupervised manner, they do not encode any sentiment information in them. The words like good and bad, due to their similar usage in the text appear to be close in the embedding space. To better represent the sentiment in the embeddings, several approaches to refine and learn embeddings have been reported. Learning of sentiment specific word embedding (SSWE) is presented in (Tang et al., 2014) where, embeddings were learned from a large corpus by incorporating the sentiment signal in the loss function. These embeddings are then used with different classifier such as convolutional Neural networks (CNN) followed by max-pooling (Collobert et al., 2011b; Socher et al., 2011; Mitchell and Lapata, 2010). We have considered this as one of our baselines.

Enriching of embedding using the distant-supervised method to learn set of embeddings using standard word2vec (Mikolov et al., 2013) and GLove (Pennington et al., 2014) is shown in (Deriu et al., 2016). Although this enrichment of embeddings is done using a large corpus of tweets, the basic assumption is that positive emoticons and emoji relate to the overall positive sentiment of the tweets create a lot of instability in the embedding space (Kunneman et al., 2014). This is due to the fact that, emoticons and emoji are used in various context and quite often in a polar opposite way to express sarcasm and irony (Poria et al., 2014). In addition, these methods are inefficient for more granular and fine-grained sentiment analysis.

3 Proposed Framework

In Figure 1 we present our generalized system diagram. Raw text is first preprocessed to normalize noise using standard text processing techniques.

3.1 Pre-processing

Tweets are essentially short text messages that are generated by humans to express their sentiments and reviews, and are known to be inherently noisy due to their condensed nature. This poses a challenge when trying to understand sentiment and affect. We have used standard text processing techniques with some modification to better suit the sentiment and affect domain:

- All the letters are converted to lower case form

- Significant amount of words are elongated with repeated number of characters such as "ANGRYYYYYYYYYYYY", we have limited these consequent characters to maximum of 2

- All the hyperlinks are removed as they do not serve the sentiment that is conveyed by the text itself and might relate to the sentiment pointed out by that links

- For words represented in hastags we remove "#" symbol, and if the word is not found in the vocabulary we try to segment it using Viterbi algorithm (Segaran and Hammerbacher, 2009)

- Usernames are replaced with "mention" token

- Compacted versions of word phrases such as "wasn't", "when's", etc., are replaced with corresponding expanded words

3.2 Embedding Generation

Processed text is then used to generate two sets of embeddings. First set of embeddings are generated by using three different pre-trained embeddings.

- Pre-trained embeddings which are generated from common crawl corpus have 6 Billion tokens which help in a better encoding of the syntactic and semantic structure of the language.

- Pre-trained emoji (Eisner et al., 2016) embeddings are used to represent the emojis and emoticons in the text. Emojis and emoticons are essential part of text which strongly convey the sentiments.

- To handle out of vocabulary words after the segmentations and the spelling corrections, we use character embedding[2] to generate a representations by summing all the character embeddings in that word. This helps in capturing sentiment related signals better than assigning it to the random tokens.

Pseudo code 1 details the process of generating first set of embedding which uses Glove embeddings trained over common crawl corpus of vector

---

[2]https://github.com/minimaxir/char-embeddings

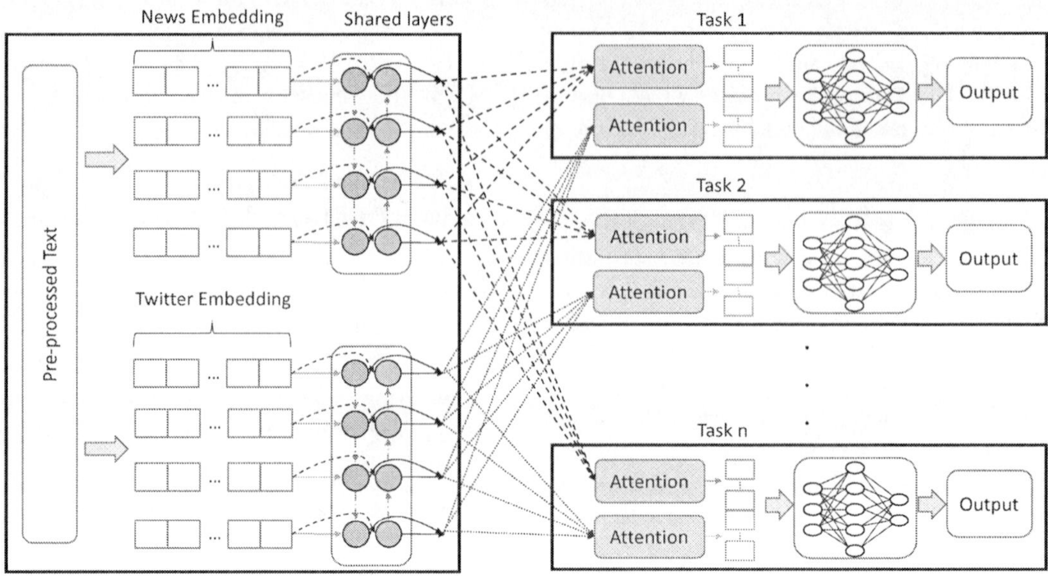

Figure 1: System Architecture

for each word. Second set of embeddings are extracted from pre-trained embeddings over Twitter corpus to get vectors that represents the nuances of the Twitter platform and in general of short and noisy text. These embeddings provide varied vector sizes, we use *300* and *200* dimensions of embedding for common crawl and twitter respectively.

```
word_token = Tokenize tweet
for each word in word_token do
    if word is in EmojiEmbb then
        word_vector =
        get_vector(EmojiEmbb,
        word_vector)
    else if word is in Glove then
        word_vector = get_vector(Glove,
        word_vector)
    else if word is in CharEmbb then
        word_vector = get_vector(charEmbb,
        word_vector)
    else
        chars = tokeinze word_token into
        character
        n = length(chars) word_vector =
        ∑ⁿ₁ get_vector(charEmbb, chars)
    end
end
```

Algorithm 1: Embedding Matrix generation

Embeddings are then zero padded to match the sequence length across the datasets of different task. We have used *90* words as the maximum sequence length to account for any variations in validation datasets. For generalization, single sample of processed text can be represented in form of two sets of matrix as $\langle n_w \times d_g \rangle$ and $\langle n_w \times d_t \rangle$, where n_w is maximum sequence length or maximum number of words present in the text and d_g, d_t are the dimension of each embeddings. In this paper $n_w = 90$, $d_g = 300$ and $d_t = 200$.

These embeddings are then fed into 2 separate BiLSTM layers for each set of embeddings.

3.3 Model Description

We use LSTM architecture that was proposed in (Graves, 2013), which is governed by following equations,

$$i_t = tanh(W_{xi}x_t + W_{hi}h_{t-1} + b_i)$$
$$j_t = sigm(W_{xj}x_t + W_{hj}h_{t-1} + b_j)$$
$$f_t = sigm(W_{xf}x_t + W_{hf}h_{t-1} + b_f)$$
$$o_t = tanh(W_{xo}x_t + W_{ho}h_{t-1} + b_o)$$
$$c_t = c_{t-1} \oplus f_t + i_t \oplus j_t$$
$$h_t = tanh(c_t) \oplus o_t$$

In these equations, the W_* are the weight matrices and b_* are biases. The operation $\oplus$ denotes the element-wise vector product. The variable c_t denotes memory of LSTM at time step t.

302

Bidirectional Long Short Term memory (BiL-STMs) are improvement over LSTM networks where, two LSTM layers are stacked over each other. One of the layer processes the sequence in the forward pass and another process the seqeunce in backward fashion. Equations for the LSTM layers remain same and training can be done using stochastic gradient descent. So at each time step t, we receive set of h_t, one from forward pass and one from backward pass in BiLSTM, we concatenate and term it as a single output h_t.

As can be seen from above equation, forget gate bias can prove to be inefficient if it is initialized to random value and might introduce problem of vanishing gradient problem by a factor of 0.5 (Hochreiter and Schmidhuber, 1997; Martens and Sutskever, 2011). This can adversely affect the long term dependencies, to address this problem we initialize forget gate bias b_f to value just above 1 to facilitate the gradient flow as suggested in (Gers et al., 2000; Jozefowicz et al., 2015). To further regularize and avoid over-fitting dropout is used.

The output of both BiLSTM layers is then fed into the task-specific layers. Figure 1 shows the task-specific layers, where attention is used over the output of each BiLSTM layer. Attention was initially proposed for Neural Machine Translation (NMT) for encoder-decoder architecture to provide a context in terms of weights to important words (Bahdanau et al., 2014). In our problem where the final goal is to classify or to predict the intensity, attention is only required at the encoding level. Context vector can be computed using for the output of RNNs are follows,

$$c_t = \sum_{j=1}^{T} \alpha_{tj} h_j$$
$$e_t = a_{(}h_t), a_t = \frac{exp(e_t)}{\sum_{k=1}^{T} exp(e_k)}$$

where T is the total number of time steps in the sequence(in our case maximum sequence length) and α_{tj} is the weight computed for hidden state h_j at each time step t. Context vector c_t are then used to compute new sequence using previous state in the sequence and the context vectors. This ensures the new sequences have direct access to the entire sequence h.

Output of the attention layer is then fed to the fully connected layers, and the size and activation of the final layer depends on the task at hand.

4 Experiments

In order to validate our approach we perform two experiments. In experiment-1 we train our model on mixture of regression and classification tasks and access its performance over the same task by fine tuning it for the same task. In experiment-2 we accesses the representations that are obtained during experiment-1 on a different task.

4.1 Experiment-1: Multi-task training

We train and evaluate our model on sentiment classification SemEval dataset obtained through shared task and affect emotion dataset from SemEval-2018. These tasks are based on Twitter text and align to our objective of classifying short and noisy text present in the social media space. Although sentiment and affect task require a varying degree of representation where sentiment classification in positive, negative and neutral space can be relatively easier, representations required for this tasks are not present in the pre-trained embeddings.

4.1.1 Datasets

For sentiment classification dataset we use SemEval-2017 Task 4 Subtask A dataset. It contains a tweet and its respective label from positive, negative and neutral in english language. From here on we refer to this dataset as Sem-3. The classes presented are imbalance and negative tweets are around *15%* in training set and *32%* in test set (Rosenthal et al., 2017).

For Affective emotion, we use dataset which was presented as in SemEval-2018 task 1 (Mohammad et al., 2018) subtask *EI-reg, EI-oc* contains tweets specific to 4 emotions namely, Anger, fear, Joy and Sadness for english language. Subtask *V-reg, V-oc* contains the tweets for valence denoting range of positive to negative of sentiment. In subtasks *EI-reg* and *V-reg*, Given a tweet and its corresponding emotion, predict the intensity score of that emotion between 0 to 1, 0 being lowest and 1 being highest. Whereas, for subtasks *EI-oc* and *V-oc* we need to classify them into predefined classes, where oc means ordinal classification. In this dataset, emotions are classified in 4 distinct labels from mildly felt emotion to strongly felt emotion, while valence is classified into 7 distinct classes. Distribution of the datasets into the train development and test set is presented in table 1.

Table 1: Data Distribution.

	Train	Dev	Test
Anger	1701	388	1002
Fear	2252	389	986
Joy	1616	290	1105
Sadness	1533	397	975
Valence	1181	449	937
Sem-3	50334	20632	12284

Predicting intensity for emotions and valence are considered as regression task, while classifying into one of the classes is considered as classification task. We have 5 regression tasks and 6 classification tasks across these two datasets.

4.1.2 Training Procedure

The sem-3 dataset have approximately 15 time more training samples on an average when compared to all the rest of tasks assuming regression and classification are different tasks for each emotions. We define a training algorithm mentioned in algorithm 2. We train for sem-3 task for 1 epochs while others are trained for 15 epochs to account for the sample imbalances. We have chosen to keep the validation and test dataset as it is to better compare over the baselines.

> **for** *episode in episodes* **do**
>   train sem-3 for 1 epoch
>   list = random order of task rest of 10
>   classes
>   **for** *task in list* **do**
> | train *task* for 15 epochs
>   **end**
> **end**

For classification tasks we have used categorical crossentropy as loss function, while for regression task we have defined a custom loss function as follows,

$$Loss = 0.7 \times (1 - pearson) + 0.3 \times MSE \quad (1)$$

where pearson is the pearson correlation and MSE is the mean squared error. As pearson correlation was the official metric for the regression task and has proven to be better representative than mean squared error. We have taken mean squared error into account to decrease the bias than creeps in due to batch size while training.

For classification tasks, class weights were applied in the loss function to handle class imbal-ances. Weights were set according to the inverse of their frequency.

Model hyper-parameters are shown in table 2. In addition, *0.5* and *0.35* dropout was used for fully connected layer and BiLSTM respectively. These parameters were chosen using grid search over validation dataset. We have used *Tanhyperbolic* as for BiLSTM and *Scaled Exponential Linear Units (selu)* (Klambauer et al., 2017) for fully connected layers as activation function. Fine tuning for each task is by freezing the shared layer weights after training to generate results for individual tasks.

Table 2: Details of layers

Layers	*Classification*	*Regression*
BiLSTM Layer 1	70	70
BiLSTM Layer 2	70	70
Fully connected layer 1	100	100
Fully connected layer 2	50	50
Fully connected layer 3	3/5/7	1

4.2 Experiment 2: Validating on external distribution

Irony detection in the social media is one such field which is correlated with the sentiment analysis. Although it requires different set of features, sentiment and affective emotions enhances the detection accuracies as reported in (Farías et al., 2016; Wallace, 2015). In this experiment, we apply representations generated earlier to irony classification to access its robustness. We have used irony detection dataset introduced in SemEval-2018 task 3 (Van Hee et al., 2018). Dataset was augmented and hashtags used to mine the tweets such as "#irony", "#sarcasm", etc., were omitted for testing. We have removed this hashtags during training as well to keep the dataset consistent.

This task contained two subtask, namely Subtask A and Subtask B. Objective of Subtask A was to classify whether a tweet contains irony or not, while of Subtask B was to classify into verbal irony (V-irony), situational irony (S-irony), other types of irony (O-irony) and non-ironic. Distribution of the dataset along the training and testing is presented in table 3.

Table 3: Distribution of Irony Dataset across train and test

	Subtask A		Subtask B			
	Ironic	Non-Ironic	V-irony	S-irony	O-irony	Non-ironic
Train	1911	1923	1390	316	205	1923
Test	311	473	164	85	62	473

For this we extract the representations from the model trained in experiment 1, specifically we take output of 2 BiLSTM layers. So for each sample in this dataset we have a 2D matrix of shape $\langle n_w \times b1 \rangle$, n_w is the maximum sequence length and $b1$ is the number of hidden units in the BiLSTM layer 1. Similarly we obtain the representation from BiLSTM layer 2. We concatenate this representation and pass it on to classification network consisting of single BiLSTM layer and two fully connected layers.

5   Results and Discussions

We ran our multi-task experiment for 10 episodes which translates to 100 training rounds. Figure 2 shows loss vs timesteps graph. Graphs are plotted differently to account for the different loss function scales. We can clearly observe the convergence over the time steps across tasks.

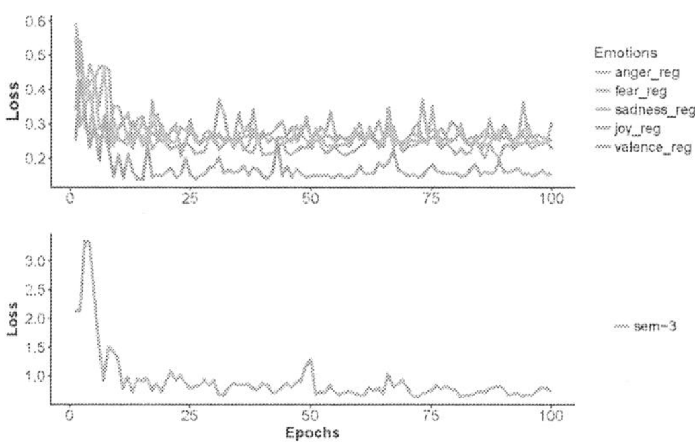

Figure 2: Upper graph shows the plot of loss vs episodes for regression task, while lower graph shows the corresponding plot for classification task for sem-3 task

For experiment 1, we use standard baselines as reported for the respective subtasks. In addition, we train a simple CNN classifier and LSTM classifier as our baselines. For *EI-reg, EI-oc, V-reg and V-oc*, baseline system was developed using wordvectors along with lexicons and support vector as final classification/regressor. We also compare the results with sentiment specific word embeddings (Tang et al., 2014), where we use Fully connected layers along with attention as the downstream model. For Sem-3 dataset we compare our results with RCNN (Yin et al., 2017) and Siamese network (Baziotis et al., 2017), which were top performing teams in the task. In addition, we separately train each task with same model parameters

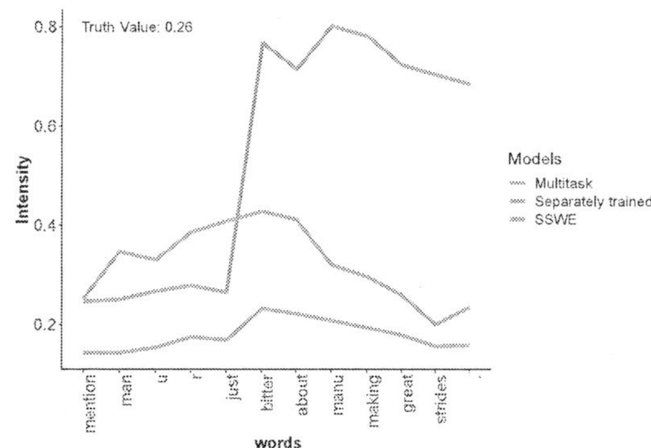

Figure 3: Plot of how intensity of the tweet changes with the words, signifying the importance of the sequence

without multi-task frame work, to observe the improvement due to multi-task and also to access the ability of the model architecture proposed. Results are shown in table 4, where for emotions and valence pearson correlation is reported and for sem-3 task accuracy and F1 score(F1 score is averaged for positive and negative class) is reported. Our model clearly out performs the baselines, and also provides significant increase over the recently proposed model architecture. Results also shows that separately trained model is able to beat the baselines, while adding the multi-task framework is able to boost the results further.

For experiment 2, baseline is unigram tf-idf features with Support vector classifiers. We compare it with the standard CNN and BiLSTM architectures. In addition, we also compare against recently proposed generalized representation for language modeling (Peters et al., 2018), which has been a state of the art for Yelp and IMDB dataset. These representations are available in two sets; a weighted sum of three layers of BiLSTMs (samples_size, max_length, 1024) refereed as ELMO-3D and fixed mean-pooling of all contextualized word representations (samples_size, 1024) refereed as ELMO-2D. For ELMO-3D embeddings we have used attention and fully connected layer as the classifier and for 2 dimension embeddings, we have used fully connected layers as classifiers. Results are shown in table 5, where F1-score is reported over the classes, for multiclass subtask average of F1 score for each class has been reported, this was the official metric of this task. We find that our framework out-performs all the baselines

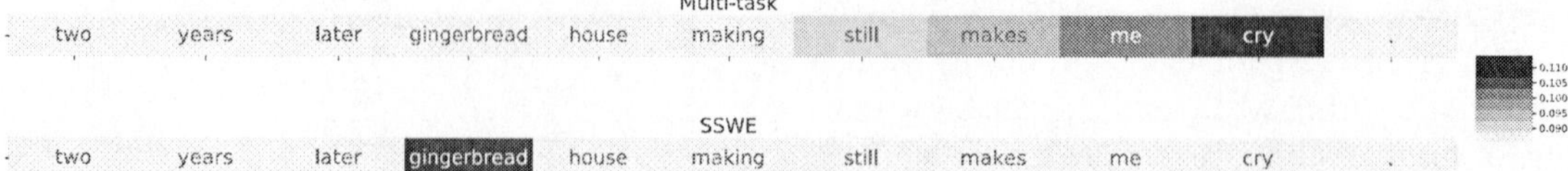

Figure 4: Attention weights comparison of Multi-task and SSWE

Table 4: Results of Experiment 1

	anger		fear		joy		sadness		valence		sem-3	
	reg	oc	reg	oc	reg	oc	reg	oc	reg	oc	Acc.	$F1_{PN}$
Baseline	0.526	0.382	0.525	0.355	0.575	0.469	0.453	0.370	0.585	0.509	0.333	0.162
CNN	0.556	0.445	0.579	0.462	0.601	0.534	0.573	0.459	0.714	0.591	0.545	0.556
BiLSTM	0.627	0.511	0.635	0.497	0.612	0.556	0.613	0.507	0.73	0.621	0.637	0.646
SSWE	0.641	0.498	0.637	0.483	0.655	0.60	0.623	0.539	0.784	0.634	0.639	0.645
RCNN Ensemble (Yin et al., 2017)	-	-	-	-	-	-	-	-	-	-	0.664	0.658
Siamese LSTM (Baziotis et al., 2017)	-	-	-	-	-	-	-	-	-	-	0.651	**0.677**
Separately trained	0.697	0.551	0.696	0.527	0.689	0.629	0.685	0.597	0.804	0.667	0.642	0.64
Multitask	**0.732**	**0.622**	**0.736**	**0.575**	**0.728**	**0.664**	**0.722**	**0.628**	**0.832**	**0.703**	**0.672**	0.670

reported. Results are averaged across *10* runs to reduce the variance.

Table 5: Irony Detection F1 score

	Subtask A	Subtask B
Baseline	0.585	0.327
CNN	0.535	0.329
BiLSTM	0.592	0.396
ELMO-2Dim	0.591	0.406
ELMO-3Dim	0.604	0.412
SSWE	0.557	0.361
Multitask Representation	**0.629**	**0.425**

A possible reason for the low performance of pre-trained SSWE might be narrow vocabulary. We have around 95K words in our vocabulary whereas, SSWE had 137052 words in its pre-trained vocabulary out of which only 33473 words were in overlap with the dataset vocabulary. Although the embeddings are refined for sentiment words, social media space often contains words which are not present in the formal dictionaries, here as our model was able to generate embeddings of out of vocabulary words using character embeddings. Figure 3 shows an example from fear emotion, where plot of how the final intensity of the sentence is changed over different model is shown. SSWE jumps on the word "bitter" as the word contains highly negative sentiment associated with it, whereas the true value is low for fear. Proposed model is able to normalize over the sequence as the jump is not that drastic. Figure 4 shows comparison of how our proposed model learns to put weights to the words as compared to SSWE model. We believe that adding the sentiment context over in the embedding through multi-task training aided in the Irony classification dataset.

6 Conclusion

In this paper, we present an approach for generating representations using sentiment and affect dataset in the multi-task framework. We present our deep learning based model with a dual attention over two sets of embedding space to capture more rich nuances of Twitter while still keeping the semantic and syntactic structure of language. In addition, we use emoji and character embeddings to help in getting better sentiment specific signals and to mitigate the effect of out of vocabulary problem. Our experiments over both internal and external distribution of data show the effectiveness of the representation. We observe that our model perform significantly better as compared to the baselines and the current state of the art methods for the tasks. Going further, it would be effective to devise an algorithm to modify these representations with minimum computation and still adapt to a different domain.

References

Cem Akkaya, Janyce Wiebe, and Rada Mihalcea. 2009. Subjectivity word sense disambiguation. In *Proceedings of the 2009 Conference on Empirical Methods in Natural Language Processing: Volume 1- Volume 1*, pages 190–199. Association for Computational Linguistics.

Dzmitry Bahdanau, Kyunghyun Cho, and Yoshua Bengio. 2014. Neural machine translation by jointly learning to align and translate. *arXiv preprint arXiv:1409.0473*.

Christos Baziotis, Nikos Pelekis, and Christos Doulkeridis. 2017. Datastories at semeval-2017 task 6: Siamese lstm with attention for humorous text comparison. In *Proceedings of the 11th International Workshop on Semantic Evaluation (SemEval-2017)*, pages 390–395, Vancouver, Canada. Association for Computational Linguistics.

Felipe Bravo-Marquez, Eibe Frank, Saif M Mohammad, and Bernhard Pfahringer. 2016. Determining word–emotion associations from tweets by multilabel classification. In *WI'16*, pages 536–539. IEEE Computer Society.

Ronan Collobert, Jason Weston, Léon Bottou, Michael Karlen, Koray Kavukcuoglu, and Pavel Kuksa. 2011a. Natural language processing (almost) from scratch. *Journal of Machine Learning Research*, 12(Aug):2493–2537.

Ronan Collobert, Jason Weston, Léon Bottou, Michael Karlen, Koray Kavukcuoglu, and Pavel Kuksa. 2011b. Natural language processing (almost) from scratch. *Journal of Machine Learning Research*, 12(Aug):2493–2537.

Jan Deriu, Maurice Gonzenbach, Fatih Uzdilli, Aurelien Lucchi, Valeria De Luca, and Martin Jaggi. 2016. Swisscheese at semeval-2016 task 4: Sentiment classification using an ensemble of convolutional neural networks with distant supervision. In *SemEval@ NAACL-HLT*, pages 1124–1128.

Xiaowen Ding, Bing Liu, and Philip S Yu. 2008. A holistic lexicon-based approach to opinion mining. In *Proceedings of the 2008 international conference on web search and data mining*, pages 231–240. ACM.

Ben Eisner, Tim Rocktäschel, Isabelle Augenstein, Matko Bosnjak, and Sebastian Riedel. 2016. emoji2vec: Learning emoji representations from their description.

Andrea Esuli and Fabrizio Sebastiani. 2007. Sentiwordnet: A high-coverage lexical resource for opinion mining. *Evaluation*, pages 1–26.

Delia Irazú Hernańdez Farías, Viviana Patti, and Paolo Rosso. 2016. Irony detection in twitter: The role of affective content. *ACM Transactions on Internet Technology (TOIT)*, 16(3):19.

Felix A. Gers, Jürgen A. Schmidhuber, and Fred A. Cummins. 2000. Learning to forget: Continual prediction with lstm. *Neural Comput.*, 12(10):2451–2471.

A. Graves. 2013. Generating Sequences With Recurrent Neural Networks. *ArXiv e-prints*.

Sepp Hochreiter and Jürgen Schmidhuber. 1997. Long short-term memory. *Neural Comput.*, 9(8):1735–1780.

Rafal Jozefowicz, Wojciech Zaremba, and Ilya Sutskever. 2015. An empirical exploration of recurrent network architectures. In *Proceedings of the 32nd International Conference on Machine Learning (ICML-15)*, pages 2342–2350.

G. Klambauer, T. Unterthiner, A. Mayr, and S. Hochreiter. 2017. Self-Normalizing Neural Networks. *ArXiv e-prints*.

FA Kunneman, CC Liebrecht, and APJ van den Bosch. 2014. The (un) predictability of emotional hashtags in twitter.

Bing Liu. 2012. Sentiment analysis and opinion mining. *Synthesis lectures on human language technologies*, 5(1):1–167.

Minh-Thang Luong, Quoc V Le, Ilya Sutskever, Oriol Vinyals, and Lukasz Kaiser. 2015. Multi-task sequence to sequence learning. *arXiv preprint arXiv:1511.06114*.

James Martens and Ilya Sutskever. 2011. Learning recurrent neural networks with hessian-free optimization. In *Proceedings of the 28th International Conference on Machine Learning (ICML-11)*, pages 1033–1040.

Tomas Mikolov, Ilya Sutskever, Kai Chen, Greg S Corrado, and Jeff Dean. 2013. Distributed representations of words and phrases and their compositionality. In *Advances in neural information processing systems*, pages 3111–3119.

Ishan Misra, Abhinav Shrivastava, Abhinav Gupta, and Martial Hebert. 2016. Cross-stitch networks for multi-task learning. *CoRR*, abs/1604.03539.

Jeff Mitchell and Mirella Lapata. 2010. Composition in distributional models of semantics. *Cognitive science*, 34(8):1388–1429.

Saif Mohammad, Felipe Bravo-Marquez, Mohammad Salameh, and Svetlana Kiritchenko. 2018. Semeval-2018 task 1: Affect in tweets. In *Proceedings of The 12th International Workshop on Semantic Evaluation*, pages 1–17. Association for Computational Linguistics.

Saif M Mohammad, Svetlana Kiritchenko, and Xiaodan Zhu. 2013. Nrc-canada: Building the state-of-the-art in sentiment analysis of tweets. *arXiv preprint arXiv:1308.6242*.

Hyeonseob Nam and Bohyung Han. 2016. Learning multi-domain convolutional neural networks for visual tracking. In *Proceedings of the IEEE Conference on Computer Vision and Pattern Recognition*, pages 4293–4302.

Bo Pang and Lillian Lee. 2004. A sentimental education: Sentiment analysis using subjectivity summarization based on minimum cuts. In *Proceedings of the 42nd annual meeting on Association for Computational Linguistics*, page 271. Association for Computational Linguistics.

Jeffrey Pennington, Richard Socher, and Christopher D. Manning. 2014. Glove: Global vectors for word representation. In *Empirical Methods in Natural Language Processing (EMNLP)*, pages 1532–1543.

Matthew E. Peters, Mark Neumann, Mohit Iyyer, Matt Gardner, Christopher Clark, Kenton Lee, and Luke Zettlemoyer. 2018. Deep contextualized word representations. *CoRR*, abs/1802.05365.

Soujanya Poria, Erik Cambria, Gregoire Winterstein, and Guang-Bin Huang. 2014. Sentic patterns: Dependency-based rules for concept-level sentiment analysis. *Knowledge-Based Systems*, 69:45–63.

Jonathan Posner, James A Russell, and Bradley S Peterson. 2005. The circumplex model of affect: An integrative approach to affective neuroscience, cognitive development, and psychopathology. *Development and psychopathology*, 17(3):715–734.

Sara Rosenthal, Noura Farra, and Preslav Nakov. 2017. Semeval-2017 task 4: Sentiment analysis in twitter. In *Proceedings of the 11th International Workshop on Semantic Evaluation (SemEval-2017)*, pages 502–518, Vancouver, Canada. Association for Computational Linguistics.

James A Russell. 1980. A circumplex model of affect. *Journal of personality and social psychology*, 39(6):1161.

Toby Segaran and Jeff Hammerbacher. 2009. *Beautiful data: the stories behind elegant data solutions.* " O'Reilly Media, Inc.".

Raksha Sharma and Pushpak Bhattacharyya. 2013. Detecting domain dedicated polar words. In *IJCNLP*, pages 661–666.

Richard Socher, Eric H Huang, Jeffrey Pennin, Christopher D Manning, and Andrew Y Ng. 2011. Dynamic pooling and unfolding recursive autoencoders for paraphrase detection. In *Advances in Neural Information Processing Systems*, pages 801–809.

Richard Socher, Brody Huval, Christopher D Manning, and Andrew Y Ng. 2012. Semantic compositionality through recursive matrix-vector spaces. In *Proceedings of the 2012 joint conference on empirical methods in natural language processing and computational natural language learning*, pages 1201–1211. Association for Computational Linguistics.

Duyu Tang, Furu Wei, Nan Yang, Ming Zhou, Ting Liu, and Bing Qin. 2014. Learning sentiment-specific word embedding for twitter sentiment classification. In *Proceedings of the 52nd Annual Meeting of the Association for Computational Linguistics (Volume 1: Long Papers)*, volume 1, pages 1555–1565.

Cynthia Van Hee, Els Lefever, and Veronique Hoste. 2018. Semeval-2018 task 3: Irony detection in english tweets. In *Proceedings of The 12th International Workshop on Semantic Evaluation*, pages 39–50. Association for Computational Linguistics.

Byron C Wallace. 2015. Computational irony: A survey and new perspectives. *Artificial Intelligence Review*, 43(4):467–483.

Theresa Wilson, Janyce Wiebe, and Paul Hoffmann. 2005. Recognizing contextual polarity in phrase-level sentiment analysis. In *Proceedings of the conference on human language technology and empirical methods in natural language processing*, pages 347–354. Association for Computational Linguistics.

Yichun Yin, Yangqiu Song, and Ming Zhang. 2017. Nnembs at semeval-2017 task 4: Neural twitter sentiment classification: a simple ensemble method with different embeddings. In *Proceedings of the 11th International Workshop on Semantic Evaluation (SemEval-2017)*, pages 621–625, Vancouver, Canada. Association for Computational Linguistics.

Super Characters: A Conversion from Sentiment Classification to Image Classification

Baohua Sun, Lin Yang, Patrick Dong, Wenhan Zhang, Jason Dong, Charles Young
Gyrfalcon Technology Inc.
1900 McCarthy Blvd. Milpitas, CA 95035
{baohua.sun,lin.yang,patrick.dong,wenhan.zhang}@gyrfalcontech.com

Abstract

We propose a method named Super Characters for sentiment classification. This method converts the sentiment classification problem into image classification problem by projecting texts into images and then applying CNN models for classification. Text features are extracted automatically from the generated Super Characters images, hence there is no need of any explicit step of embedding the words or characters into numerical vector representations. Experimental results on large social media corpus show that the Super Characters method consistently outperforms other methods for sentiment classification and topic classification tasks on ten large social media datasets of millions of contents in four different languages, including Chinese, Japanese, Korean and English.

1 Introduction

Sentiment classification is an interesting topic that has been studied for many years (Hatzivassiloglou and McKeown, 1997; Pang et al., 2002; Hong and Fang, 2015). Word embedding is a widely used technique for sentiment classification tasks, which embeds the words into numerical vector representation before the sentences are fed into models for classification (Mikolov et al., 2013; Le and Mikolov, 2014; Pennington et al., 2014; Yu et al., 2017; Cao et al., 2018). For sequential input, RNNs are usually used and have very good results for text classification tasks (Lai et al., 2015; Tang et al., 2015). Recently, there are also works using Convolutional Neural Networks (CNN) for text classification (Kim, 2014; Severyn and Moschitti, 2015; Vaswani et al., 2017; Bai et al., 2018). CNN models have feature extraction and classification in a whole model, which require no need of manually extracting features from images and

are proved to be successful in image classification tasks (LeCun et al., 1998; Krizhevsky et al., 2012; Simonyan and Zisserman, 2014; Szegedy et al., 2015; He et al., 2016a; Hu et al., 2017). There are also works on character level text classifications (Zhang et al., 2015; Zhang and LeCun, 2015; Kim et al., 2016). However, the input for CNNs are still using the embedding vectors.

Zhang and LeCun (2017) had studied the different ways of encoding Chinese, Japanese, Korean (CJK) and English languages for text classification. These encoding mechanisms include One-hot encoding, embedding and images of character glyphs. Comparisons with linear models, fastText (Joulin et al., 2016), and convolutional networks were provided. This work studied 473 models, using 14 large-scale text classification datasets in 4 languages including Chinese, English, Japanese and Korean.

Our work in this paper is based on the datasets provided in (Zhang and LeCun, 2017) and downloadable at (Zhang, 2017). Different from existing methods, our method has no explicit step of embedding the text into numerical vector representations. Instead, we project the text into images and then directly feed the images into CNN models to classify the sentiments.

Before introducing the details of our solution, let us first look at how humans read text and do sentiment analysis. Humans read sentences and can immediately understand the sentiment of the text; Humans can also read multiple lines at a first sight of paragraphs and get the general idea instantly. This fast process consists of two steps. First, the texts are perceived by human's eyes as a whole picture of text, while the details of this picture are block-built by many characters. Second, the image containing the texts are fed into the brain. And then the human brain processes the image of texts to output the sentiment classification

Proceedings of the 9th Workshop on Computational Approaches to Subjectivity, Sentiment and Social Media Analysis, pages 309–315
Brussels, Belgium, October 31, 2018. ©2018 Association for Computational Linguistics
https://doi.org/10.18653/v1/P17

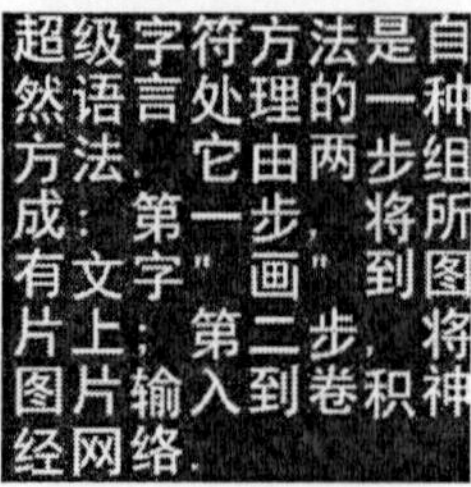

Figure 1: A Super Character example.

results. During the processing, the human brain may recognize words and phrases as the intermediate results, in order to further analyze the sentiment. However, if we treat the human brain as a black box system, its input is the image of texts received by the eyes, and its output is the sentiment classification result.

In this paper, we propose a two-step method that is similar to how humans do sentiment classification. We tested our method using the datasets provided by Zhang and LeCun (2017) on text classification tasks for social media contents from different countries in four languages, including English, Chinese, Japanese, and Korean. And compared with other existing methods, including fastText, EmbedNet, OnehotNet, and linear models. The results show our method consistently outperforms other method on these datasets for sentiment classification tasks.

2 Super Characters Method

The Super Characters method converts the sentiment classification problem into an image classification problem. It is defined in two steps.

- First, the texts, e.g. sentences or paragraphs, are "drawn" onto blank images, character by character. For example, a generated Super Characters image from Chinese text inputs (including punctuation marks) is shown in Figure 1. The Chinese text means "Super characters are a method for NLP. It consists of two steps: Frist, "draw" text onto images; second, feed images into CNN". Each generated Super Character image is attached with the same sentiment labels as its original text.

- Second, feed the generated Super Characters images with its labels to train CNN models.

The information embedded in the Super Characters image is near identical to that in the orig-

inal text, so we convert the sentiment classification problem into image classification problem. The Super Characters images are similar to how humans perceive text: as whole pictures containing text, whether printed on paper, projected on a screen, or written by hand. After the texts are converted to images, the performance of our text classification method is determined by the accuracy of image classification models. For large scale image classification tasks, CNN models such as ResNet(He et al., 2016b) have outperformed humans in image classification tasks as an end to end solution. Thus, if we feed the Super Characters images into CNN models such as ResNet, we expect the text classification using this 2-step pipeline to have a high accuracy.

For detailed implementation of projecting text into Super Characters image, there are a few settings to configure, including the image size of the whole Super Characters image; number of characters per row/column; size of each character; cut-length, which is the length of sentence to cut/padding in order to fit into the image; the fonts used to project each character into an image, and so on.

For Latin languages, we have the option of projecting text at the word level or at the alphabet level, which will make differences at some cases. For example, how to handle line-change if a word is at the end of a row in the Super Characters image and can't fit in the residual space in that row. If we separate the words into separate alphabets, we can fit as many characters in the residual space in that row and change to the next row for the rest of the alphabets in that word. Or, if we keep the word as a whole entity and avoid spliting, we have to change to the next line for that word.

For example, here are the settings used in one of our experiments in Section 3. We use a fixed image size of 224x224. And we also prefer integer numbers of characters in each row and having same-sized characters. Thus, we prefer to use 8x8=64, or 28x28=784, or 32x32=1024 characters per image. And we set the cut/padding length as the same. That also means, for 8x8 =64 settings, we will have 8 characters per row, and we have 8 rows in total. And each character is set to be of size 224/8=28 square pixels. The Arial_Unicode_MS font is selected as font to draw text onto image. For padding, we just draw nothing on the image.

From the definition and description of Super Character, we can see it has the following advantages. 1. Its speed is not sensitive to the length of the text input, so it can easily handle long and short texts input. This advantage will be more obvious when the input text is long, because super character using CNN as model will be parallel processing the input. And the processing time is invariant for training and inference. 2. The feature engineering work is no longer needed, which includes generating manmade features of each character related to the culture behind each language. The Super Characters image is treated as an input for CNN models, and the feature extraction task are handled automatically by CNN models. 3. Similar to image classification using CNN networks which requires large amount of labeled image data, this method of Super Characters for sentiment analysis also requires large amount of labeled text data.

3 Experiments

3.1 Sentiment Classification on Large Datasets from Online Social Media

Ten of 14 datasets provided by (Zhang and LeCun, 2017) were tested on, a brief description of which is provided:

Dianping: Chinese restaurant reviews were evenly split as follows: 4 and 5 star reviews were assigned to the positive class while 1-3 star reviews were in the negative class.

JD Full: Chinese shopping reviews wer evenly split for predicting full five stars. **JD Binary** Chinese shopping reviews are evenly split into positive (4-and-5 star reviews) and negative (1-and-2 star reviews) sentiments, ignoring 3-star reviews.

Rakuten Full Japanese shopping reviews were evenly split into predicting full five stars. **Rakuten Binary** Japanese shopping reviews were evenly split into positive (4-and-5 star reviews) and negative (1-and-2 star reviews) sentiments, removing duplicates and ignoring 3-star reviews.

11st Full Korean shopping reviews were evenly split into predicting full five stars. **11st Binary** Korean shopping reviews were evenly split into identifying positive (4-and-5 star reviews) or negative (1-3 star reviews) sentiments.

Amazon Full: English shopping reviews were evenly split into predicting full five stars.

Ifeng: First paragraphs of Chinese news articles from 2006-2016 were evenly split into 5 news channels.

Chinanews: Chinese news articles from 2008-2016 were evenly split into 7 news channels, removing duplicates.

The statistics of these datasets are given in Table 1. We can see that eight out of the ten datasets has more than millions of samples in training, and the largest datasets have 4 millions of samples in training set. The test datasets are in the range of 1/4 to 1/16 of the training datasets respectively. The languages used in these datasets include Chinese, Japanese, Korean, and English. And the number of classes ranges from 2, 5 to 7.

For each dataset, we generate Super Characters images first. We draw text with the Python Imaging Library (PIL) (Lundh, 2009), and set all the Super Character image sizes to 224x224 pixels, the background set to black. For long text inputs such as paragraphs or articles, the length of which is different so we set a cut-length from the beginning of the news article. Although we may forcely cut the input and ignore the rest, this cut-length still works well since the first few sentences usually convey the general information about the whole contents. For other text sources and tasks, the starting point of the text for the cut-length may change accordingly. For each experiment, we determine the estimated cut-length by using a threshold on sentence lengths. We have only tried one cut-length of 14x14=196 for every experimental data set. We set the size of each character as 224/14=16 square pixels.

And then, we feed the generated Super Characters to train CNN models. We use successful pretrained model SENet-154 (Hu et al., 2017) in the ImageNet competition (Russakovsky et al., 2015), which is the winner in ImageNet2017 competition and achieves 81.32% Top1 accuracy and 95.53% Top5 accuracy. We used pretrained model downloadable at (Hu, 2017) because it gave a good initialization for transfer learning tasks. We changed the last layer to the corresponding number of categories in each data set to train on the Super Characters images.

The sentiment classification results on test datasets are shown in Table 2. The accuracy numbers for the models of OnehotNet, EmbedNet, Linear Model, and fastText are given by (Zhang and LeCun, 2017). Note that in (Zhang and LeCun, 2017), each model is tried with different encoding methods. For example, OnehotNet uses 4 different encodings, EmbedNet uses 10, Linear Models uses 11, and fastText uses 10. We only listed the best results for each existing method across different encodings. And compare our results with the best of them. That means we compare our results with the finetuned best encoding of each existing model in 2. From the results we can see that our Super Characters method (short as S.C.) consistently outperforms other methods, even with their best encodings.

3.2 Experiments on THUCTC corpus

THUCTC (Sun et al., 2016) was provided by the Tsinghua University NLP lab in 2016. It totals 836075 documents after downloaded, covering 14 topics including 24373 Game, 37098 Finance, 63086 Politics, 50849 Society, 32586 Living, 20050 Real Estate, 7588 Lottery, 92632 Entertainment, 41936 Education, 13368 Fashion, 3578 Constellation, 162929 Technology, 131604 Sports and 154398 Stocks. The majority of the documents are long articles with hundreds or sometimes thousands of characters in multiple sentences or paragraphs. We use a cut-length of 28x28=784, each having an 8x8 pixel size and utilize simhei font for Super Characters on the THUCTC data. In Table 3, we showed our Super Character method using ResNet-50 (SC+ResNet50) attained an accuracy of 94.85% and our Super Character method using ResNet-152 (SC+ResNet152) attained an accuracy of 94.35%, while the result given by Sun et al. (2016) achieved only an accuracy of 88.6% using LibLinear. LibLinear (Fan et al., 2008) implements linear SVMs and logistic regression models trained using a coordinate descent algorithm. Our models reduce the error by 50.4% compared to this existing model.

3.3 Experiments on Fudan Corpus

The Fudan corpus (Li, 2011) contains 9804 documents of long sentences and paragraphs in 20 categories. We use the same split as (Xu et al., 2016; Cao et al., 2018) in selecting the same 5 categories: 1218 environmental, 1022 agricultural, 1601 economical, 1025 political and 1254 sport documents; 70% of the total data is used for training and the rest for testing.

- SC+ResNet-50: Using a ResNet-50 model pretrained on the ImageNet dataset, we fine-tuned the transfer learning model on the new generated super character dataset.

- SC+ResNet-50-THUCTC: Using a ResNet-50 model pretrained on THUCTC data, we fine-tuned the trasfere learning model on the new generated super character dataset.

We used a cut-length of 28x28=784 and words of pixel size 8x8 with the simhei font for our Super Characters in this experiment. In Table 4, the first 7 rows of model accuracies for different algorithms are given by (Cao et al., 2018). We can see that our SC+ResNet-50-THUCTC model attained an accuracy of 97.8% while the best existing method achieved only a 95.3% accuracy. Our SC+ResNet50-THUCTC model reduces the error by 53.2% compared with the best existing model. The SC+ResNet-50 model with 95.7% accuracy also outperforms the best existing model. The pretrained model on THUCTC dataset gives 2.1% accuracy improvement than SC+ResNet-50 model, which means pretrained models on the same language and a larger dataset will help for a better initialization and better model. For this data set, we did not delete the non-Chinese characters as (Cao et al., 2018) did. The result shows that our simple projection from text to Super Characters image is easy to implement and very robust. Users do not even need to perform complicated preprocessing techniques for the data.

3.4 Analysis on the Impact of the Cut-length for Configuring Super Characters Image

The cut-length determines how many characters in each generated Super Characters image. So it will impact if an input text needs clipping or padding, in order to have the same pixel size of each character and same length for all the text samples in the same dataset. The short cut-length may clip long sentences and cause information loss, which will decrease the sentiment classification accuracy. But increasing the cut-length of the text may prevent inadvertently clipping long sentences but also increases the number of blank spaces for short sentences. Thus it may impact the model and the sentiment analysis accuracy. The best setting for cut-length should be based on the dataset statistics. We have a study on different settings of cut-length using ResNet-50 on the Fudan corpus, and the results are given in Table 5. For this Fudan data, the average sentence length is 530, and the median sentence length is 509. It shows that the setting of cut-length=784 is the best configuration for this dataset compared with other options. This

Dataset	Short Name	Language	Classes	Train	Test
Dianping	D.P.	Chinese	2	2,000,000	500,000
JD full	JD.f	Chinese	5	3,000,000	250,000
JD binary	JD.b	Chinese	2	4,000,000	360,000
Rakuten full	RKT.f	Japanese	5	4,000,000	500,000
Rakuten binary	RKT.b	Japanese	2	3,400,000	400,000
11st full	11st.f	Korean	5	750,000	100,000
11st binary	11st.b	Korean	2	4,000,000	400,000
Amazon full	AMZ.f	English	5	3,000,000	650,000
Ifeng	Ifeng	Chinese	5	800,000	50,000
Chinanews	Cnews	Chinese	7	1,400,000	112,000

Table 1: Datasets statistics used in Table 2 and short names used for convenience.

Model	D.P.	JD.f	JD.b	RKT.f	RKT.b	11st.f	11st.b	AMZ.f	Ifeng	Cnews
OnehotNet	76.83	51.90	90.69	54.90	94.07	67.57	86.70	57.79	83.51	89.38
EmbedNet	76.40	51.71	90.81	54.80	93.93	67.71	86.75	56.30	82.99	89.45
Linear	76.97	51.82	91.18	54.74	93.37	56.58	86.60	57.30	81.70	89.24
fastText	77.66	52.01	91.28	56.73	94.55	61.42	86.89	59.98	83.69	90.90
S.C.(ours)	**77.80**	**54.10**	**92.20**	**57.70**	**94.85**	**68.70**	**87.60**	**60.70**	**84.40**	**92.00**

Table 2: Results of our Super Character (SC) method against other models on datasets provided by (Zhang and LeCun, 2017).

Model	Accuracy
LibLinear (Sun et al., 2016)	88.6%
SC+ResNet-50 (ours)	**94.85%**
SC+ResNet-152 (ours)	94.35%

Table 3: Results of our Super Character (SC) method against other models on THUCTC data set.

Cut-length	196	256	784	1024
Accuracy(%)	93.45	93.3	95.7	89.35

Table 5: Cut-length Impact on Accuracy.

Model	Accuracy
skip-gram (Mikolov et al., 2013)	93.4%
cbow (Mikolov et al., 2013)	93.4%
GloVe (Pennington et al., 2014)	94.2%
CWE (Chen et al., 2015)	93.2%
GWE (Su and Lee, 2017)	94.3%
JWE (Yu et al., 2017)	94.2%
cw2vec (Cao et al., 2018)	95.3%
SC+ResNet-50-THUCTC (ours)	**97.8%**
SC+ResNet-50 (ours)	95.7%

Table 4: Results of our Super Character (SC) method against other models on the Fudan dataset.

indicates that setting the cut-length according to the median or average sentence length could be a good option.

4 Conclusion and Future Work

In this paper, we proposed the Super Characters method for sentiment classification. It converts text into images and then applies CNN models to classify the sentiment. The text features are automatically extracted by CNN models. We have tested our method on social media text contents from four different languages. The experimental results showed that our method consistently outperforms other methods for Chinese, English, Japanese, and Korean text contents for sentiment classification tasks. We also showed that pre-trained Chinese text classification models on large datasets helps attain a higher accuracy for text classification on other Chinese datasets.

For future work, we can apply various preprocessing techniques such as the elimination of common words and other methods to further increase the accuracy of this method, and fine-tune the cut length to analyze its impact on different data sets. And we also need to compare with other RNN methods on the same datasets.

References

Shaojie Bai, J Zico Kolter, and Vladlen Koltun. 2018. An empirical evaluation of generic convolutional and recurrent networks for sequence modeling. *arXiv preprint arXiv:1803.01271*.

Shaosheng Cao, Wei Lu, Jun Zhou, and Xiaolong Li. 2018. cw2vec: Learning chinese word embeddings with stroke n-gram information.

Heng Chen, Junying Liang, and Haitao Liu. 2015. How does word length evolve in written chinese? *PloS one*, 10(9):e0138567.

Rong-En Fan, Kai-Wei Chang, Cho-Jui Hsieh, Xiang-Rui Wang, and Chih-Jen Lin. 2008. Liblinear: A library for large linear classification. *Journal of machine learning research*, 9(Aug):1871–1874.

Vasileios Hatzivassiloglou and Kathleen R McKeown. 1997. Predicting the semantic orientation of adjectives. In *Proceedings of the 35th annual meeting of the association for computational linguistics and eighth conference of the european chapter of the association for computational linguistics*, pages 174–181. Association for Computational Linguistics.

Kaiming He, Xiangyu Zhang, Shaoqing Ren, and Jian Sun. 2016a. Deep residual learning for image recognition. In *Proceedings of the IEEE conference on computer vision and pattern recognition*, pages 770–778.

Kaiming He, Xiangyu Zhang, Shaoqing Ren, and Jian Sun. 2016b. Deep residual learning for image recognition. In *Proceedings of the IEEE conference on computer vision and pattern recognition*, pages 770–778.

James Hong and Michael Fang. 2015. Sentiment analysis with deeply learned distributed representations of variable length texts. Technical report, Technical report, Stanford University.

Jie Hu. 2017. Senet-154. Github and model download: https://github.com/hujie-frank/SENet.

Jie Hu, Li Shen, and Gang Sun. 2017. Squeeze-and-excitation networks. *arXiv preprint arXiv:1709.01507*, 7.

Armand Joulin, Edouard Grave, Piotr Bojanowski, and Tomas Mikolov. 2016. Bag of tricks for efficient text classification. *arXiv preprint arXiv:1607.01759*.

Yoon Kim. 2014. Convolutional neural networks for sentence classification. *arXiv preprint arXiv:1408.5882*.

Yoon Kim, Yacine Jernite, David Sontag, and Alexander M Rush. 2016. Character-aware neural language models. In *AAAI*, pages 2741–2749.

Alex Krizhevsky, Ilya Sutskever, and Geoffrey E Hinton. 2012. Imagenet classification with deep convolutional neural networks. In *Advances in neural information processing systems*, pages 1097–1105.

Siwei Lai, Liheng Xu, Kang Liu, and Jun Zhao. 2015. Recurrent convolutional neural networks for text classification. In *AAAI*, volume 333, pages 2267–2273.

Quoc Le and Tomas Mikolov. 2014. Distributed representations of sentences and documents. In *International Conference on Machine Learning*, pages 1188–1196.

Yann LeCun, Léon Bottou, Yoshua Bengio, and Patrick Haffner. 1998. Gradient-based learning applied to document recognition. *Proceedings of the IEEE*, 86(11):2278–2324.

Ronglu Li. 2011. Fudan corpus for text classification. Data download: http://www.datatang.com/data/44139.

Fredrik Lundh. 2009. Python imaging library (pil). Webpage: http://www.pythonware.com/products/pil/.

Tomas Mikolov, Ilya Sutskever, Kai Chen, Greg S Corrado, and Jeff Dean. 2013. Distributed representations of words and phrases and their compositionality. In *Advances in neural information processing systems*, pages 3111–3119.

Bo Pang, Lillian Lee, and Shivakumar Vaithyanathan. 2002. Thumbs up?: sentiment classification using machine learning techniques. In *Proceedings of the ACL-02 conference on Empirical methods in natural language processing-Volume 10*, pages 79–86. Association for Computational Linguistics.

Jeffrey Pennington, Richard Socher, and Christopher Manning. 2014. Glove: Global vectors for word representation. In *Proceedings of the 2014 conference on empirical methods in natural language processing (EMNLP)*, pages 1532–1543.

Olga Russakovsky, Jia Deng, Hao Su, Jonathan Krause, Sanjeev Satheesh, Sean Ma, Zhiheng Huang, Andrej Karpathy, Aditya Khosla, Michael Bernstein, Alexander C. Berg, and Li Fei-Fei. 2015. ImageNet Large Scale Visual Recognition Challenge. *International Journal of Computer Vision (IJCV)*, 115(3):211–252.

Aliaksei Severyn and Alessandro Moschitti. 2015. Twitter sentiment analysis with deep convolutional neural networks. In *Proceedings of the 38th International ACM SIGIR Conference on Research and Development in Information Retrieval*, pages 959–962. ACM.

Karen Simonyan and Andrew Zisserman. 2014. Very deep convolutional networks for large-scale image recognition. *arXiv preprint arXiv:1409.1556*.

Tzu-Ray Su and Hung-Yi Lee. 2017. Learning chinese word representations from glyphs of characters. *arXiv preprint arXiv:1708.04755*.

Maosong Sun, Jingyang Li, Zhipeng Guo, Yu Zhao, Yabin Zheng, Xiance Si, and Zhiyuan Liu. 2016. Thuctc: An efficient chinese text classifier. Github and data download: https://github.com/thunlp/THUCTC.

Christian Szegedy, Wei Liu, Yangqing Jia, Pierre Sermanet, Scott Reed, Dragomir Anguelov, Dumitru Erhan, Vincent Vanhoucke, and Andrew Rabinovich. 2015. Going deeper with convolutions. In *Proceedings of the IEEE conference on computer vision and pattern recognition*, pages 1–9.

Duyu Tang, Bing Qin, and Ting Liu. 2015. Document modeling with gated recurrent neural network for sentiment classification. In *Proceedings of the 2015 conference on empirical methods in natural language processing*, pages 1422–1432.

Ashish Vaswani, Noam Shazeer, Niki Parmar, Jakob Uszkoreit, Llion Jones, Aidan N Gomez, Łukasz Kaiser, and Illia Polosukhin. 2017. Attention is all you need. In *Advances in Neural Information Processing Systems*, pages 6000–6010.

Jian Xu, Jiawei Liu, Liangang Zhang, Zhengyu Li, and Huanhuan Chen. 2016. Improve chinese word embeddings by exploiting internal structure. In *Proceedings of the 2016 Conference of the North American Chapter of the Association for Computational Linguistics: Human Language Technologies*, pages 1041–1050.

Jinxing Yu, Xun Jian, Hao Xin, and Yangqiu Song. 2017. Joint embeddings of chinese words, characters, and fine-grained subcharacter components. In *Proceedings of the 2017 Conference on Empirical Methods in Natural Language Processing*, pages 286–291.

Xiang Zhang. 2017. Which encoding is the best for text classification in chinese, english, japanese and korean? Github and data download: https://github.com/zhangxiangxiao/glyph.

Xiang Zhang and Yann LeCun. 2015. Text understanding from scratch. *arXiv preprint arXiv:1502.01710*.

Xiang Zhang and Yann LeCun. 2017. Which encoding is the best for text classification in chinese, english, japanese and korean? *arXiv preprint arXiv:1708.02657*.

Xiang Zhang, Junbo Zhao, and Yann LeCun. 2015. Character-level convolutional networks for text classification. In *Advances in neural information processing systems*, pages 649–657.

Learning Comment Controversy Prediction in Web Discussions
Using Incidentally Supervised Multi-Task CNNs

Nils Rethmeier, Mark Hübner, Leonhard Hennig
German Research Center for Artificial Intelligence (DFKI), Germany
`firstname.lastname@dfki.de`

Abstract

Comments on web news contain controversies that manifest as inter-group agreement-conflicts. Tracking such *rapidly evolving controversy* could ease conflict resolution or journalist-user interaction. However, this presupposes controversy online-prediction that scales to diverse domains using incidental supervision signals instead of manual labeling. To more deeply interpret comment-controversy model decisions we frame prediction as binary classification and evaluate baselines and multi-task CNNs that use an auxiliary news-genre-encoder. Finally, we use ablation and interpretability methods to determine the impacts of topic, discourse and sentiment indicators, contextual vs. global word influence, as well as genre-keywords vs. per-genre-controversy keywords – to find that the models learn plausible controversy features using only incidentally supervised signals.

1   Introduction

Online discussion comments are exchanged in parallel, creating redundancy that prohibits discussions from developing beyond a superficial stage of confirming previously held opinions. Instead, Mahyar et al. (2017) recently demonstrated that focusing users on controversial comments – i.e. comments that cause *inter-group agreement-conflicts* (Dori-Hacohen et al., 2015) – helps speed up inter-group consensus finding leading to improved group decisions. However, their system (ConsensUS) uses manual controversy labels which can not capture rapidly evolving comment-controversy at scale or over diverse domains. Hence, to fully automate comment-controversy prediction systems we contribute the following solutions to a number of challenges. **(I)** We extend controversy prediction to *comment-level*, and to *German news discussions*. We evaluate topic, sentiment and discourse importance

(Cramer, 2011) and analyze whether models plausibly capture controversy aspects using explainability methods (see Sec. 5.3). **(II)** We use comment vote-agreement to create an incidentally supervised (Roth, 2017) *controversy* signal as seen in Figure 1. Structural (output feature) signals like genre, are predicted by a sub-encoder (see Sec. 4) rather than required as input. **(III)** Sentiment and discourse *input feature* creation work on any tokenizable language (see Sec. 3).

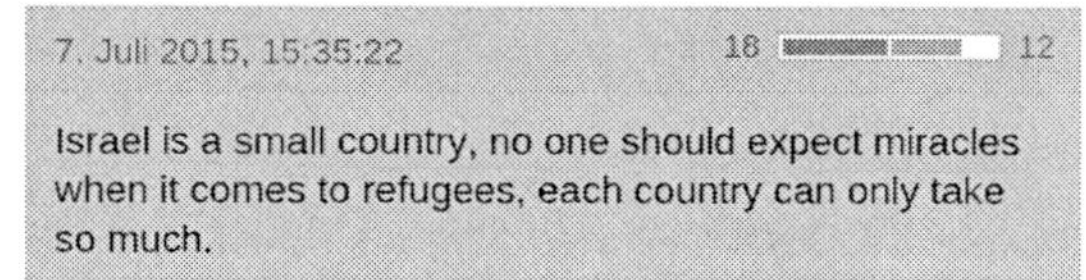

Figure 1: A comment is assumed controversial if its up and down votes show no clear $2/3$ majority decision.

2   Related Research

Since predicting user agreement-conflicts *upon web news* comments is a special case of controversy prediction, we list in the following related works that: (a) learn to predict controversy, using (b) incidental supervision, and (c) work on online (news) discussions. Chen et al. (2016) visualized *controversial words* using dissimilarities in pro vs. contra argument embeddings. Garimella et al. (2017) identified *controversial topics* using bipartite Twitter follower-graphs, while Dori-Hacohen and Allan (2015) proposed an incidentally supervised binary classification to predict controversial topics via Wikipedia tags. Jang et al. (2016) used language modeling to predict controversial documents, based on earlier hypotheses by Cramer (2011): "that language in *news discussions* is a good indicator of controversy". Choi et al. (2010) focused on using sentiment polarity indicators and

Proceedings of the 9th Workshop on Computational Approaches to Subjectivity, Sentiment and Social Media Analysis, pages 316–321
Brussels, Belgium, October 31, 2018. ©2018 Association for Computational Linguistics
https://doi.org/10.18653/v1/P17

subtopics, i.e. topically related phrases of nouns. *Vote-based learning signals* have been exploited by both Pool and Nissim (2016); Basile et al. (2017) who predict the sentiment distributions of news outlets or find controversial news pieces using Facebook-article emoticon-votes. Instead of predicting controversial topics (articles), we predict *controversial comments*, hence putting the focus on users (commentators) as curators of controversial content.

3   Incidental Supervision Signals

Controversy signal: We use comment vote-agreement ratios and news tags as incidental supervision signals (Roth, 2017) to label comments as controversial and by genre. Comments without a clear $2/3$ majority of either agreeing (up) or disagreeing (down) votes are considered controversial – i.e. of conflicted agreement. The ratio is calculated as $r = \min(up, down)/\max(up, down)$. Ratios below 0.5 mark a 2/3 majority. Ratios above 0.5 mark conflicted agreement. We reduce *labeling noise* via two noise margins: (a) controversial comments must have a vote-ratio $r > 0.6$ and (b) that both the up-votes (group) and down-votes (group) should each have more than 2 votes. **Article Genre signal:** Predicting controversy without context structure is difficult, hence we use article-genre (topic) prediction as an incidental structure signal. The data contains 15 genres – some of which are noisy mixes of others. However, to keep preprocessing general, we use genres "as-is". **Corpus:** We collected comments and the above training signals for every article published by the Austrian newspaper `DerStandard.at` in 2015. Each article has a news genre tag and user comments, that in turn receive up and down votes. The corpus contains 813k comments, from which we extracted 8.9k controversial and 12.6k non-controversial comments after removing duplicates and short comments with less than five words. **Text preprocessing:** is source agnostic without language-specific NLP. We remove noise like low-frequency words. We create special tokens for discourse (repeated punctuation) and reactionary sentiment (emoticons) by categorizing emoticons into four (non-overlapping) types using a Wikipedia emoticon list[1], see Table 1. We keep stop words, as they

often overlap with discourse markers (see Sec. 5). Compounds are separated with a \$comp\$ token. Finally, we pre-trained word2vec (Mikolov et al., 2013) embeddings on 3.35M preprocessed article and comment sentences to cover standard German and mixed (non)dialect.

Pattern	Replacement	Example
URL	\$url\$	`web.de`
happy	\$happy\$	:) :D
sad	\$sad\$	:(
skeptical	\$skeptical\$	:S, :/
unserious	\$unserious\$	:P ;p
rep. punct.	\$.\$, \$,\$, \$?\$, \$!\$	... !!!
compounds	word \$comp\$ word	Go-Fan

Table 1: Text normalization reduces vocabulary noise and creates *input features*.

4   Models

Baselines: As baselines we use Multinomial Naive Bayes (MNB) and Regularized Logistic Regression (LR) trained on TF or TFIDF Bag-of-Ngrams. FastText (FT) (Joulin et al., 2016) is trained on embedding 1-3grams.

Single / Multi-task CNNs : We also use convolutional neural nets (CNN) as they are widely used in text classification. Below, we describe how we modified the single-task model (ST) by Kim (2014) to create a multi-task architecture (MT) as follows. <u>ST:</u> A CNN that predicts comment-controversy only. It uses a deeper classifier, input-token dropout, custom word2vec embeddings and trains on comment, controversy label pairs via a binary cross-entropy – see *Controversy CNN* in Figure 2. <u>MT:</u> This model adds a genre-encoder to the ST. The encoder predicts multi-class genre via categorical cross-entropy and softmax on genre labels. Its penultimate activation map is fed to the ST's controversy classifier, to provide genre plus controversy features – see red downward arrow entitled *genre encoding* in Figure 2. The two losses are trained as a weighted sum. Thus, genre features are not required when predicting on new data.

MT modifications: Since feature extraction module design is central to CNNs, we evaluate a range of different design choices. We separate extraction modules into three categories from left to right: *convolution methods, activation schemes,*

---

[1] `https://en.wikipedia.org/wiki/List_of_emoticons`

and *pooling mechanisms* as seen in the upper and middle parts of Figure 2. White boxes are modules, dashed/dotted lines are module-combination options. Modules are marked by author, or with * for our own modifications. Module details are as follows:

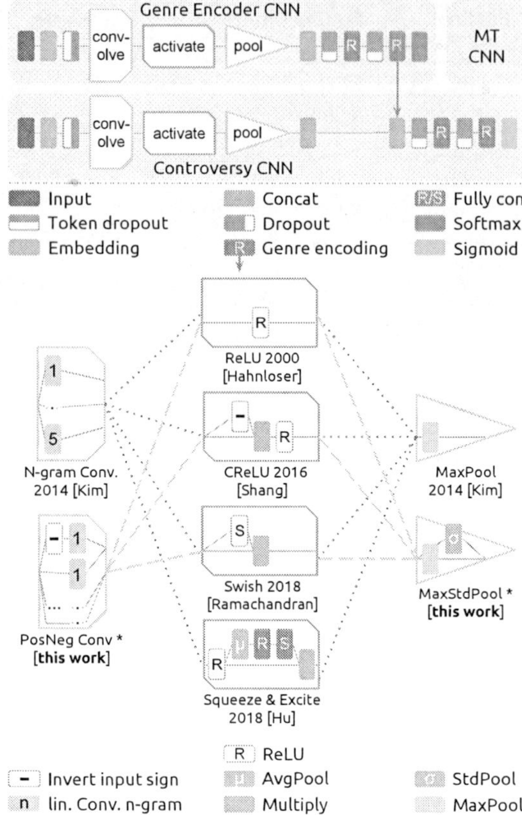

Figure 2: CNN modifications. Upper white box classifies genre to encode it, lower one classifies controversy. Colored rectangles are layers and operations as per the legend.

Conv: Kim (2014). CReLU Appends negated activations before applying ReLU (Shang et al., 2016). PosNeg Conv* (PNC): Learns separate convolutions for negated and positive embedding-activations, to extend CReLU. ReLU: (Hahnloser et al., 2000). Swish: Self-attention multiplying inputs x by their sigmoid $\sigma(x)$ (Ramachandran et al., 2018). Squeeze and Excite (SE): Bottle-necked multi-layer attention that learns convolution filter importances (Hu et al., 2018). MaxPool: (LeCun et al., 1998). Max(SPool)*: Appends per-filter Standard Deviation Pooling (SPool) to Max-Pool, to preserve variance info. In the next section we evaluate the most successful combinations.

5 Results and Discussion

We evaluate on 8.9k controversial and 12.6k non-controversial comments that each belong to exactly one genre. We created 5 randomly sampled (stratified) folds – 4 folds for cross validation (CV) and 1 as holdout set. MNB, LR, FT, Conv+ReLU (ST) only predict controversy. The MT models jointly predict controversy + genre and are tested for various modification combos. Finally, we investigate models decision semantics and feature type importances via ablation studies.

5.1 Baselines: MNB, LR, FT

In Table 2 we list F_1, area under the ROC curve (AUC) and accuracy (Acc) controversy prediction results on the holdout test set. We see that FastText is the best baseline[2]. Optimal hyperparameters from 4-fold CV were: word-embedding 1-3gram with 128 dimensional w2v embeddings for FT, and TFIDF 1+2grams with a maximum document-frequency of 100% and a minimum term frequency of 2 for MNB and LR.

5.2 ST, MT CNNs

Stopwords and punctuation are kept as they contain discourse and sentiment features – see sec. 5.3 for details. Low-frequency words are replaced with a pre-trained unknown word token (UNK). Conv+ReLU (ST): The controversy-only CNN outperformed FT at optimal CV parameters of: 1-5gram, global max pooling, 128 filters and 1k classifier widths. More filters or a 4k width decreased CV and test performance. Standard dropout (Hinton et al., 2012) and Batch Normalization (Ioffe and Szegedy, 2015) decreased performance, while 20% token-dropout (Gal and Ghahramani, 2016) led to consistent improvement. Conv+ReLU (MT): Adding a genre-task network to ST improved performances by 2 – 4 points each, despite working on halved hyper parameters – i.e. MTs performed best using only 64 filters and 512 classifier units, giving less model parameters than the ST, especially since increasing ST's parameters hurt its performance. MT modifications: Since some modifications underperformed we only list combinations that are top-3 in one of the measures. Notice-

---

[2]An always-controversial predictor gives $F_1 = 58\%$, $Acc = 42\%$ and sample weighted class average $\overline{F_1} = 24\%$. A always-non-controversial predictor gives $F_1 = 42\%$, $Acc = 58\%$ and $\overline{F_1} = 43\%$). Neither is useful in practice.

ably, the MT+PNC+SPool+Swish variant significantly improved AUC_{ROC} and Acc over the simpler Conv+ReLU (MT) model, which produced the best F_1. Overall, we see that adding more incidental supervision signals beats adding advanced network modules.

Model	AUC	F_1	Acc
MNB	59.84	55.72	57.44
LR	62.92	58.14	60.12
FT	65.06	60.57	63.82
Conv+ReLU (ST)	68.25	62.03	66.42
Conv+ReLU (MT↓)	_72.12_	**64.48**	68.37
PNC+CReLU	_72.06_	63.40	_68.72_
PNC+SPool+Swish	**72.28**	_64.21_	**68.82**
Conv+SE+ReLU	71.91	_63.93_	_68.76_

Table 2: Holdout performances for the *controversial class* (y=1). **Baselines:** top 3. **ST:** middle, **MT:** last 4 – only module combinations with top-3 performance in one measure are listed as: **best**, 2nd best, 3rd best.

5.3 Feature-type ablation

We ablated sentiment, discourse and topical features (Choi et al., 2010; Cramer, 2011). Then, we re-tuned the Conv+ReLU (MT) on the 4, now ablated, CV folds to measured test set performance changes as follows. *Three sentiment ablations*: (1) polarity words (sent ws by Waltinger (2010)), (2) repeated punctuation (punct.), and (3) emoticons (emotes) as mentioned in sec. 3. *Discourse:* Removal of German discourse markers (DiMLex) (Stede and Umbach, 1998). *Topic:* Noun removal as in Choi et al. (2010) to represent topical indicators. Figure 3 shows the relative percentual performance drop per ablation. Thus, for controversy prediction: *topic* was the most important, followed by *discourse* markers[3] and *sentiment* with repeated punctuation and emoticons being impactful style/sentiment features. Polarity words affect prediction, but are not language independent.

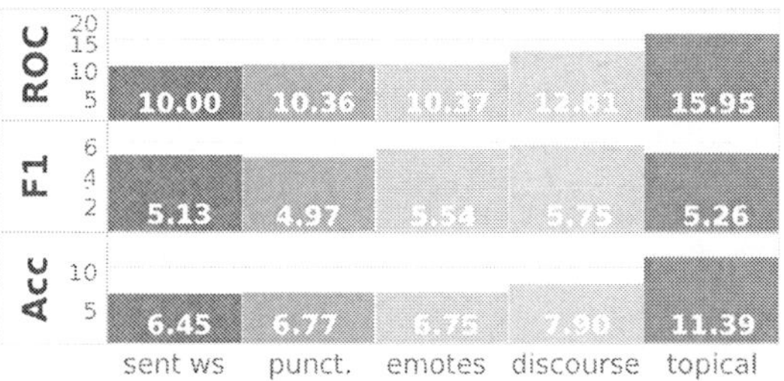

Figure 3: *Relative controversy prediction performance drop in %* for removal of: sentiment (blues), discourse (orange) and topic/nouns (red).

5.4 Per-word impacts

Inspired by explainability methods (Li et al., 2016; Arras et al., 2017) we also measured the controversy prediction-score change when replacing a token with a class neutral UNK token[4].

Discourse or punctuation ($):
Because it not_a UNK country but a dictatorship is
What UNK Putin of human_rights and peace $.$.
Had you the UNK or are you vaccinated $?$?

Emoticons:
They employ the same word_choice :((
Was easily UNK the tradition UNK ? ;)

Context dependent word influence:
Interestingly , if one something negative against ↵
Windows posts will one instantly_be with UNK ↵
bombarded .
But 2 years were we by Microsoft marketing ↵
and by Microsoft fan_boys UNK how cool yet not
Windows 8 and 8 .1 is .

Figure 4: $DE \rightarrow EN$ *Per-token controversy impacts:* Red is important for controversy. Blue lowers the controversy score. Last paragraph: *context dependent word influence* of the word Windows.

In Figure 4 we colored per-token score drops (red) or increases (blue) for German-to-English word-by-word translations on test set comments. We show examples by ablation types as described in section 5.3. As before, nouns and discourse markers increase controversy, while, expectedly, an (#unserious) ;) emoticon is strongly counter-indicative of controversy. *Repeated punctuation*, like $.$ or $?$, also impacts prediction. Finally, the model learned *context dependent con-*

---

[3]Markers overlap with a stop word list in approximately 49% of occurrences in our dataset. Stop words: `http://www.ranks.nl/stopwords/german`.

[4]Removing tokens would create unusual n-grams, and hence wrong results.

domestic politics		international politics		economy		panorama	
kpö	afd	ceasefire	poroschenko	bonds	tsipras	entry	pegida
pühringer	fpö	mariupol	separatists	rbi	troika	battery	prejudices
spö	grünen	rebels	putin	hedge funds	syriza	property dmg.	refugee policy
state elections	parties	hamas	arabs	budget	greece	passage	hate-monger
federal level	faymann	air raid	israelis	credits	varoufakis	tents	antisemitism
genre	+ controversy	genre	+ controversy	genre	+ controversy	genre	+ controversy

Table 3: Token importances in descending order. On the left **genre**: most important genre tokens. On the right (**+ controversy**): most controversial tokens per genre. Tokens are sorted by mean positive impact on genre and genre+controversy predictions.

troversy polarity for the word *Windows*, with has both strong positive and negative polarity.

5.5 Token impacts on genre and controversy

To generate keywords for **controversy** and **genre vs. controversy-per-genre**, we averaged UNK token-replacement prediction-impacts over all occurrences of a token t_i and calculated its impact mean $\mu(impacts(t_i))$ and standard deviation $\sigma(impacts(t_i))$, similar to how Horn et al. (2017) extract topic keywords.

Controversy keywords: In Table 4 we divided tokens into infrequent (top half) and common tokens (lower half). Infrequent tokens have over 10 occurrences, frequent ones at least 200.

(a) 0 con	(b) ↑↓ con	(c) ↑ con	(d) ↓ con
”	pkk	separatists	yet
.	kurds	putin	thx
;	crimea	pegida	has
−	tsipras	israelis	ain't
possibly	israelis	hamas	yeah
.	eu	eu	have
-	usa	usa	**#happy#**
?	**#unser.#**	country	**#unser.#**
”	**#happy#**	people	anyway
with	**$.$**	austria	from
$\sigma(impacts(token))$		$\mu(impacts(token))$	

(a) No impact := smallest $\sigma(impacts) \approx 0$ top.
(b) Impactful := largest $\sigma(impacts)$ top.
(c) Pro controv. := most positive $\mu(impacts)$ top.
(d) Contra cont. := most negative $\mu(impacts)$ top.

Table 4: Controversy impacts for seldom (upper half) and frequent token (lower half).

The tokens impact controversy either: (a) not at all, (b) positively or negatively, (c) generally increase it or (d) generally decrease it. We see that, standard punctuation has no impact on controversy (a), but repeated punctuation, emotes and political terms do (b). Expectedly, political terms generally increase controversy (c), while colloquialisms and friendly emotes lower it (d).

Genre vs. controversy-per-genre keywords: We examined mean token impacts $\mu(impacts)$ on *genre classification* vs. *per-genre controversy* in Table 3 for the four most interesting genres. The *domestic politics* genre is dominated by established Austrian parties or generic political terms, while right-wing, left-wing and liberal parties characterize domestic controversy. The *international* genre shows mostly war related terms. Its controversy focuses on the 2015 Ukraine and middle east conflicts. Keywords for the *economy* genre are general finance terms, whereas the Greek debt crisis dominates genre controversy. The *panorama* genre focuses on refugee-related terms, where the related right-wing issues caused controversy in 2015.

6 Conclusion

We proposed a fully automated, incidentally supervised, multi-task approach for comment-controversy prediction and showed that it successfully captures contextual controversy semantics despite only using minimal, language independent, preprocessing and feature creation. In the future, we aim to extend data collection to study controversy drift over time.

Acknowledgements

This work was supported by the German Federal Ministry of Education and Research (BMBF) through the project DEEPLEE (01IW17001).

References

Leila Arras, Franziska Horn, Grégoire Montavon, Klaus-Robert Müller, and Wojciech Samek. 2017. "What is relevant in a text document?": An interpretable machine learning approach. *PloS one* 12 (2017).

Angelo Basile, Tommaso Caselli, and Malvina Nissim. 2017. Predicting Controversial News Using Facebook Reactions.. In *CLiC-it*.

Wei-Fan Chen, Fang-Yu Lin, and Lun-Wei Ku. 2016. WordForce: Visualizing Controversial Words in Debates. In *COLING*.

Yoonjung Choi, Yuchul Jung, and Sung-Hyon Myaeng. 2010. Identifying Controversial Issues and Their Sub-topics in News Articles. In *PAISI*.

Peter A Cramer. 2011. *Controversy as news discourse.* Vol. 19. Springer Science & Business Media.

Shiri Dori-Hacohen and James Allan. 2015. Automated Controversy Detection on the Web. In *ECIR*.

Shiri Dori-Hacohen, Elad Yom-Tov, and James Allan. 2015. Navigating Controversy as a Complex Search Task. In *SCST@ECIR*.

Yarin Gal and Zoubin Ghahramani. 2016. A Theoretically Grounded Application of Dropout in Recurrent Neural Networks. In *NIPS*.

Venkata Rama Kiran Garimella, Gianmarco De Francisci Morales, Aristides Gionis, and Michael Mathioudakis. 2017. Reducing Controversy by Connecting Opposing Views. In *WSDM*.

Richard HR Hahnloser, Rahul Sarpeshkar, Misha A Mahowald, Rodney J Douglas, and H Sebastian Seung. 2000. Digital selection and analogue amplification coexist in a cortex-inspired silicon circuit. *Nature* 405, 6789 (2000).

Geoffrey E. Hinton, Nitish Srivastava, Alex Krizhevsky, Ilya Sutskever, and Ruslan Salakhutdinov. 2012. Improving neural networks by preventing co-adaptation of feature detectors. *CoRR* (2012).

Franziska Horn, Leila Arras, Grgoire Montavon, Klaus-Robert Mller, and Wojciech Samek. 2017. Discovering topics in text datasets by visualizing relevant words. *CoRR* (2017).

Jie Hu, Li Shen, and Gang Sun. 2018. Squeeze-and-Excitation Networks. *IEEE Conference on Computer Vision and Pattern Recognition* (2018).

Sergey Ioffe and Christian Szegedy. 2015. Batch Normalization: Accelerating Deep Network Training by Reducing Internal Covariate Shift. In *ICML*.

Myungha Jang, John Foley, Shiri Dori-Hacohen, and James Allan. 2016. Probabilistic Approaches to Controversy Detection. In *CIKM*.

Armand Joulin, Edouard Grave, Piotr Bojanowski, and Tomas Mikolov. 2016. Bag of Tricks for Efficient Text Classification. *arXiv preprint arXiv:1607.01759* (2016).

Yoon Kim. 2014. Convolutional Neural Networks for Sentence Classification. In *EMNLP*.

Yann LeCun, Léon Bottou, Yoshua Bengio, and Patrick Haffner. 1998. Gradient-based learning applied to document recognition. *Proc. IEEE* 86, 11 (1998).

Jiwei Li, Will Monroe, and Daniel Jurafsky. 2016. Understanding Neural Networks through Representation Erasure. *CoRR* (2016).

Narges Mahyar, Weichen Liu, Sijia Xiao, Jacob Browne, Ming Yang, and Steven Dow. 2017. ConsensUs: Visualizing Points of Disagreement for Multi-Criteria Collaborative Decision Making. In *CSCW Companion*.

Tomas Mikolov, Kai Chen, Greg Corrado, and Jeffrey Dean. 2013. Efficient estimation of word representations in vector space. *arXiv preprint arXiv:1301.3781* (2013).

Chris Pool and Malvina Nissim. 2016. Distant supervision for emotion detection using Facebook reactions. In *Proceedings of the Workshop on Computational Modeling of People's Opinions, Personality, and Emotions in Social Media (PEOPLES)*. The COLING Organizing Committee, Osaka, Japan. http://aclweb.org/anthology/W16-4304

Prajit Ramachandran, Barret Zoph, and Quoc V Le. 2018. Searching for activation functions. *ICLR* (2018).

Dan Roth. 2017. Incidental Supervision: Moving beyond Supervised Learning. In *AAAI*.

Wenling Shang, Kihyuk Sohn, Diogo Almeida, and Honglak Lee. 2016. Understanding and improving convolutional neural networks via concatenated rectified linear units. In *International Conference on Machine Learning*.

Manfred Stede and Carla Umbach. 1998. DiMLex: A lexicon of discourse markers for text generation and understanding. In *Proceedings of the 17th international conference on Computational linguistics-Volume 2*. Association for Computational Linguistics.

Ulli Waltinger. 2010. GERMANPOLARITYCLUES: A Lexical Resource for German Sentiment Analysis. In *Proceedings of the Seventh International Conference on Language Resources and Evaluation (LREC)*. electronic proceedings, Valletta, Malta.

Words Worth: Verbal Content and Hirability Impressions in YouTube Video Resumes

Skanda Muralidhar
Idiap and EPFL
Switzerland
smuralidhar@idiap.ch

Laurent Son Nguyen
Idiap
Switzerland
lnguyen@idiap.ch

Daniel Gatica-Perez
Idiap and EPFL
Switzerland
gatica@idiap.ch

Abstract

Automatic hirability prediction from video resumes is gaining increasing attention in both psychology and computing.Most existing works have investigated hirability from the perspective of nonverbal behavior, with verbal content receiving little interest.In this study, we leverage the advances in deep-learning based text representation techniques (like word embedding) in natural language processing to investigate the relationship between verbal content and perceived hirability ratings.To this end, we use 292 conversational video resumes from YouTube, develop a computational framework to automatically extract various representations of verbal content, and evaluate them in a regression task.We obtain a best performance of $R^2 = 0.23$ using GloVe, and $R^2 = 0.22$ using Word2Vec representations for manual and automatically transcribed texts respectively.Our inference results indicate the feasibility of using deep learning based verbal content representation in inferring hirability scores from online conversational video resumes.

1 Introduction

First impressions play an important role in many social interactions, be it in personal life (like a first date) or in the professional contexts (like job interviews) (Ambady and Skowronski, 2008).Psychologists define first impressions as the "mental image formed about something or someone after a first meeting".People form impressions about others' attractiveness, personality, hirability or trustworthiness within a very short amount of time; nonverbal cues have been shown to play an important role in the formation of first impressions (Ambady and Rosenthal, 1992; Willis and Todorov, 2006).Despite the importance of verbal content and its relationship with various social constructs, it has been studied relatively rarely in comparison

with nonverbal behavior.This work explores the relationship between verbal content and hirability impressions using a previously collected dataset consisting of noisy, real-world video resumes from YouTube (Nguyen and Gatica-Perez, 2016).

Literature in NLP and social computing have investigated the relation between verbal content and various social contrasts.In particular, Sinha et al. (Sinha et al., 2015) infered personality traits (HEXACO) of employees from Enterprise Social Media posts.Plank et al. (Plank and Hovy, 2015) collected a novel corpus of 1.2M English tweets annotated with Myers-Briggs personality type and reported the feasibility of using linguistic content from social media data to reliably predict some personality dimensions.Biel et al. (Biel et al., 2013), using 442 YouTube video blogs, investigated the relation between verbal content and personality impressions.The authors reported a performance of $R^2 = 0.31$ in inferring *Agreeableness* using manual transcriptions.

In the context of job interviews, literature has examined face-to-face interviews (Muralidhar and Gatica-Perez, 2017; Chen et al., 2016) and video interviews (Chen et al., 2017) to understand the relationship between verbal content and hirability impression.In this study, we investigate this relationship in the context of "in-the-wild", real-world conversational video resumes.To the best of our knowledge, we are the first to utilize advances in natural language processing (Doc2Vec, Word2Vec, GloVe) to understand verbal behavior in this context.In particular, using a dataset of 292 YouTube video resumes, we address three research questions; (1)How can verbal content be represented to infer hirability impressions in video resumes?(2)What is the effect of automatic speech recognition (ASR) on inference performance compared to manual transcription? (3)What is the im-

Proceedings of the 9th Workshop on Computational Approaches to Subjectivity, Sentiment and Social Media Analysis, pages 322–327
Brussels, Belgium, October 31, 2018. ©2018 Association for Computational Linguistics
https://doi.org/10.18653/v1/P17

pact of video duration on inferring hirability impressions using verbal content?

Towards this goal, we develop a computational model to automatically extract various verbal representations from text corpus and evaluate their performance in a regression task.The contribution of this work are: (1)We transcribe 292 videos both manually and automatically; (2) We extract various representations of verbal content (Doc2Vec, Word2Vec and GloVe); (3) For manual transcription, we evaluate the various representations in an inference task and observe best inference performance for *Overall Hirability* ($R^2 = 0.23$) using GloVe; (4) We then assess the performance of automatic transcription versus manual and observe comparable inference performances, with $R^2 = 0.21$ for *Overall Hirability*; (5) We assess the difference in performance between automatic transcription of 2 minutes versus full video duration and observe that inference performance improve slightly with $R^2 = 0.22$ for *Overall Hirability*.

2 Dataset

2.1 YouTube Video Resume Dataset

In this work, we use a dataset previously collected by our group (Nguyen and Gatica-Perez, 2016).Nguyen et al. collected 939 videos using various keywords (like video resume, video cv etc), collected these videos from YouTube.Of these, we randomly selected a subset of 313 videos (i.e. 1/3 of the data) as manual transcriptions is an expensive and time consuming process.Furthermore, of the 313 videos, 21 were discarded due to difficulty in transcription (due to music, accent of speakers) and missing annotations.Hence in this work, we use a corpus of 292 YouTube video resumes.

2.2 Annotations

The 292 videos were manually annotated for demographics and hirability impressions (on a $1 - 5$ Likert scale) by Amazon Mechanical Turkers (Nguyen and Gatica-Perez, 2016) with each video rated by at least 5 workers.We use Intraclass Correlation Coefficient (ICC) to measure inter rater agreement, a commonly used metric in psychology and social computing.ICC values were greater than 0.5 and is considered acceptable (Nguyen and Gatica-Perez, 2016).

2.3 Transcriptions

Manual Transcription: It was carried out by a native English speaker, who transcribed the videos

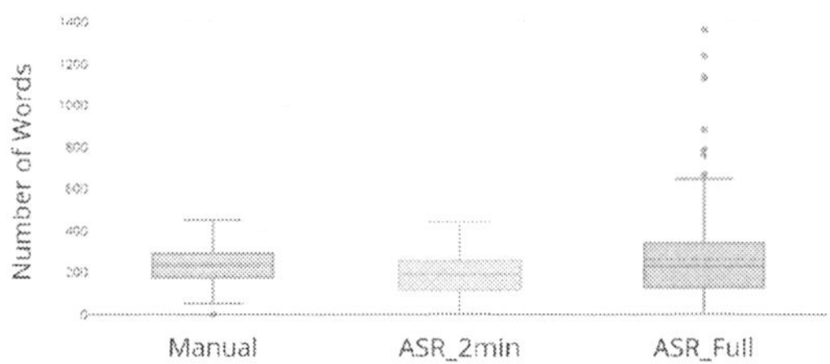

Figure 1: **Box plot illustrating the distribution of number of words obtained by (a) manual transcription [Man] (b) ASR for first 2 minutes [ASR-2min] (c) ASR for full video [ASR-Full] for a random subset of** 292 **videos. The dotted line indicates the mean value.**

as is (with no changes or corrections).As manual transcription is a tedious and expensive process, only the first 2 minutes were transcribed.These transcriptions constitute the "gold-standard" as they can be considered the output of an ideal, errorless ASR system.

Automatic Transcription: To address our research questions, we used an off-the-shelf ASR, Google Speech API (Cloud Services) for speech-to-text transcription.This API was selected as it is the best performing ASR system (Këpuska and Bohouta, 2017) and is readily available.Using Google Speech API, we generate two sets of transcriptions (a) first two minutes (to compare with manual transcription) (b) full video.Performance of the ASR was measured using word error rate (WER), and for this dataset was 41.5%.To put these results in perspective, Biel et al. reported an WER of 62.4% in their work (Biel et al., 2013) where the videos were comparable in terms of audio quality.Figure 1 shows the descriptive statistics of transcribed word count.

3 Method

Our methodology is illustrated in Figure 2. To obtain a feature representation of verbal content, we evaluated two distinct approaches: (a) representation at the document level; and (b) representation at the word level, followed by an aggregation step.For Doc2Vec and word-based representations, the text is pre-processed by converting them into lower case, removing the stop words, then stemmin and tokenizing.This was done using the Natural Language Toolkit (NLTK) python package (Bird et al., 2009).

3.1 Document-Based Representation

Linguistic Inquiry and Word Count (LIWC) is a software (Pennebaker and King, 1999) we use

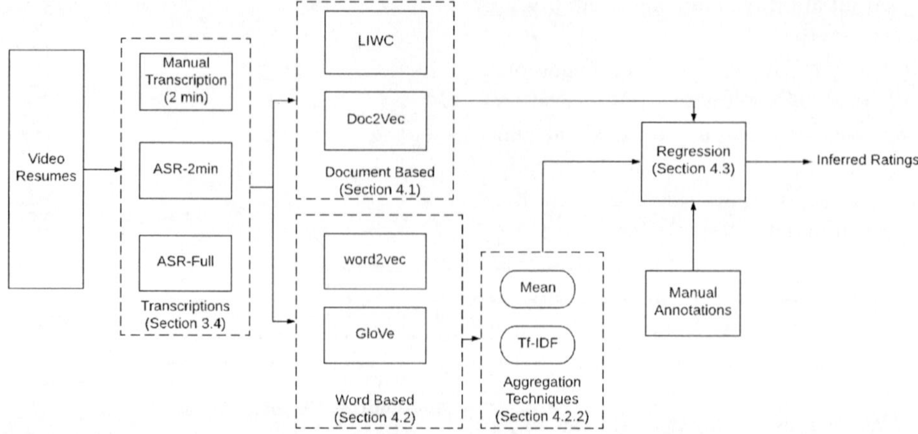

Figure 2: Overview of the work flow used in this study. The two classes of verbal content representation methods (a) document-based (b) word-based investigated is illustrated. For the document-based method, performance of LIWC and Doc2Vec in inferring hirability impressions is investigated. For the word-based method, all combinations of algorithm and aggregation techniques are investigated.

to extract lexical features.It computes these features by looking up each word in the transcript to the in-built English dictionary and is maps it to one of 70 categories.LIWC does not need text to be pre-processed and is a common text representation technique in computing literature (Muralidhar and Gatica-Perez, 2017; Biel et al., 2013).

Doc2Vec or paragraph vector was proposed by Le et al.(Le and Mikolov, 2014) to represent documents. After the text is pre-processed, we generate document vectors by training a model for word embedding using the Gensim package (Řehůřek and Sojka) in python. For the model generation, we use a constant learning rate for 10 epochs with 100 iterations and a vector of length 100. These numbers were empirically determined.

3.2 Word-Based Representations

For word-based representations, we use a two-step approach.First, word embedding from the transcripts are computed using pre-trained models (Word2Vec and GloVe).Next, these embedding are aggregated for a document level representation.

3.2.1 Word Representation

Word2Vec: developed by Mikolov et al., is an unsupervised learning algorithm that learns word embedding from a text corpus (Mikolov et al., 2013) with two models (a) continuous bag of words (CBOW) (b) continuous skip-gram (skip-gram).In both, the algorithm starts with a randomly initialized vectors and then learns the embedding by prediction.In this work, we use pre-trained CBOW model (300-dimensional) provided

by Google which is trained on the Google News Dataset consisting of 100 billion words and a vocabulary of 3 million words (Mikolov et al., 2013).

GloVe: is a statistical method to learn word embedding developed by Pennington et al. (Pennington et al., 2014).This algorithm uses the global co-occurrence statistics, i.e count of word co-occurrences in a text corpus.In this work, we use GloVe with two different pre-trained models (both 300-dimensional vector) provided by the authors; (a) GloVe(S) trained on 6 billion words of Wikipedia (2014) with a vocabulary size of 400K words, and (b) GloVe(B) trained on a larger corpus of 840 billion words with a vocabulary of 2.2 million words.

3.2.2 Aggregation Techniques

In order to use Word2Vec and GloVe for representing documents (document embedding), various aggregation techniques were applied as not all words represent a sentence equally.The most common aggregation techniques are averaging and term frequency-inverse document frequency (TF-IDF). They have been shown in literature to work better than Doc2Vec for short sentences and small documents (Kenter et al., 2016; De Boom et al., 2016; Yih et al., 2011).

3.3 Regression

We outline our proposed computational framework for evaluating the research questions posed as a regression task. We define this task as inferring the impressions of hirability and soft skills using various verbal content representations. Towards this, we evaluate two regression techniques (Support Vector Machines regression (SVM-R) and Random Forest regression (RF)) implemented in the "scikit-learn" package for Python (Pedregosa et al., 2011). The hyper-parameters of the machine learning algorithms were optimized for best performance using 10-fold inner cross-validation (CV) and grid search, while the performance was assessed using the 100 independent runs of Leave-one-video-out CV. The performance of machine learning algorithms was evaluated using the coefficient of determination (R^2). We report the best performing algorithm only (RF).

4 Results and Discussion

4.1 RQ-1: Manual Transcriptions

Regression results using manual transcriptions are presented in Table 1.We observe that in an ideal case (i.e. using manual transcriptions) best inference performance for *Overall Hirability* is obtained using GloVe(S) with $R^2 = 0.23$.This implies that raters, at least partially, formed their hirability impressions based on verbal content.

In terms of inference performance, Doc2Vec consistently performs worse for all the hirability variables with $R^2 = 0.08$ (*Overall Hirability*) being highest.We hypothesize that this poor results could be the relatively short length of the documents (mean number of words = 232.67; min=50; max=453).As the performance is much lower than the other representation methods, thereon we will not discuss the results of Doc2Vec.Competitive results were obtained for LIWC features, with highest inference performance for *Professional* ($R^2 = 0.24$), followed by *Overall Hirability*, indicating that simple features like LIWC captures some of the variances in data.

Using GloVe(B) (Tf-Idf), best performance was obtained for *Overall Hirability* ($R^2 = 0.19$), while GloVe(B) (Avg) performed little lower, (highest for *Overall Hirability* with $R^2 = 0.14$).The GloVe(S) (Avg), performed best amongst all the representations for all hirability variables except *Professional*.The best performance was achieved for *Overall Hirability* ($R^2 = 0.23$) and lowest for *Professional* and *Social* ($R^2 = 0.17$).It is interesting to note that GloVe(S) performed better than GloVe(B) trained on a much larger data.

The Word2Vec representation performed better than LIWC features for *Overall Impression, Social* and *Communication*, but slightly lower for *Overall Hirability* and *Professional*.Word2Vec (TF-IDF) performed better then Word2Vec (Avg) for *Overall Impression* ($R^2 = 0.2$ and $R^2 = 0.18$) and *Professional* ($R^2 = 0.20$ and $R^2 = 0.16$).In the context of existing works, these results are better than those reported in the literature.Muralidhar et al., (Muralidhar and Gatica-Perez, 2017) using LIWC features extracted from 169 videos, reported an inference performance of $R^2 = 0.11$.

Using 1891 video interviews, Chen et al. (Chen et al., 2017) obtained *Precision* and *Recall* of 0.67 and 0.66 respectively in a classification task.The authors obtained the text corpus using ASR provided by IBM Bluemix platform and representation was achieved using Bag-of-Words (BoW).Nguyen et al., (Nguyen and Gatica-Perez, 2016) investigated the impact of nonverbal behavior in inferring first impressionn and reported a inference performance of $R^2 = 0.15$ for *Overall Hirability* ($N = 939$).

In summary, using manually transcribed text, GloVe(S) (Avg) achieves the best inference performance for *Overall Hirability*.Our results indicate the improved performance of word-based representations of verbal content in inferring hirability impressions, thus answering RQ-1.

4.2 RQ-2: Effect of Automatic Transcriptions

We observe that for ASR-2min corpus, the best inference performance (*Overall Hirability* with $R^2 = 0.21$) is obtained using Word2Vec (Table 1).We also observe that LIWC features extracted from Manual perform slightly better than those from ASR-2min for *Overall Hirability* ($R^2 = 0.20$ compared to $R^2 = 0.17$). Interestingly, GloVe(S) model, which performed best for Manual, does not perform as well for the ASR-2min corpus with best performance for *Overall Impression* ($R^2 = 0.14$). Similarly, GloVe(B) model performs worse than other models individually and in comparison with results from Manual for *Overall Impression* ($R^2 = 0.12$).

Word2Vec (TF-IDF) representation performs best using ASR-2min text corpus with *Professional* ($R^2 = 0.26$) and worse for *Social* ($R^2 = 0.13$).We observe that except for *Communication* and *Overall Impression*, use of ASR-2min performs slightly better than manual transcriptions.We hypothesize that this improvement could be due to Word2Vec, being a predictive model is less sensitive to ASR errors (WER) than

Table 1: Results of the inference task using the random forest algorithm (N=292) using manually transcribed (Manual), automatically transcribed (ASR-2min and ASR-Full) text corpus.The best performance is highligted in bold.

	Overall Impression			Overall Hirability			Professional Skills			Social Skills			Communication Skills		
	Manual	ASR-2min	ASR-Full	Manual	ASR-2min	ASR-Full	Manual	ASR-2min	ASR-Full	Manual	ASR-2min	ASR-Full	Manual	ASR-2min	ASR-Full
LIWC	0.13	0.13	0.14	**0.20**	0.17	0.19	**0.24**	0.18	0.20	0.07	0.11	0.09	0.13	0.17	0.20
Doc2Vec	0.03	0.01	0.01	0.08	0.04	0.03	0.03	0.01	0.06	0.03	0.0	0.0	0.05	0.02	0.06
Word2Vec															
- Avg	0.18	0.09	0.16	0.18	0.08	**0.26**	0.16	0.17	0.13	0.14	0.09	**0.22**	0.22	0.14	0.21
- Tf-Idf	0.20	0.18	0.16	0.17	**0.21**	0.16	0.20	**0.26**	0.10	0.10	0.13	0.19	0.22	0.19	0.14
Glove(S)															
- Avg	0.21	0.14	0.19	**0.23**	0.12	0.14	0.17	0.12	0.09	0.17	0.13	0.11	0.20	0.07	0.12
- Tf-Idf	0.15	0.14	0.20	**0.23**	0.14	0.18	0.15	0.11	0.14	0.12	0.15	0.10	0.15	0.09	0.16
Glove(B)															
- Avg	0.12	0.13	0.16	0.14	0.09	0.12	0.11	0.06	0.12	0.14	0.11	0.14	0.16	0.08	0.16
- Tf-Idf	0.16	0.12	0.11	**0.19**	0.11	0.08	0.13	0.07	0.09	0.13	0.10	0.12	0.15	0.09	0.13

GloVe.Biel et al. (Biel et al., 2013) investigated the use of manual and automatic transcription to infer personality impressions in YouTube video blogs.The authors reported a much lower performance using ASR ($R^2 = 0.18$) as compared to manual transcriptions $R^2 = 0.31$ for *Agreeableness*.This can be attributed to the high WER (62.4%) of the ASR system used (Hain et al., 2012) rather than the text representation methods.

In summary, the results indicate that the performance of ASR-2min is slightly lower compared to Manual (albeit with a different representation (Word2Vec)), and suggest the potential of using this approach (RQ-2).

4.3   RQ-3: Effect of Duration

The best performance using LIWC features extracted from ASR-Full text corpus (Table 1) was obtained for *Communication* and *Professional* ($R^2 = 0.20$), and lowest for *Social* ($R^2 = 0.09$).This seems to suggest that transcription of the extra duration of the videos improves inference performance.Word2Vec (Avg) performed better than Word2Vec (TF-IDF) method for all social variables with best performances for *Overal Hirability* ($R^2 = 0.26$) and worse for *Professional* ($R^2 = 0.13$).Using this representation method, ASR-Full out-performed the ASR-2min corpus for all variables except *Professional* ($R^2 = 0.13$)

Inference performance of GloVe(S)(TF-IDF) performed slightly better than GloVe(S)(Avg) for all variables (best performance for *Overall Impression* ($R^2 = 0.20$), worse for *Social* ($R^2 = 0.10$)) and is better compared to ASR-2min (except *Social*).The performance of GloVe(B) was lower than that of all other representations with best results for *Overall Impression* and *Communication*($R^2 = 0.16$).Although the performance of GloVe(B) method was lower than other word-based representations, these results are better than those obtained using ASR-2min.

Overall, these inference results tend to be comparable to those obtained using 2-min manual transcriptions (gold standard) and are higher than those reported using nonverbal cues (Nguyen and Gatica-Perez, 2016). We observe a moderate improvement in inference performance with full video duration transcribed for Word2Vec (Avg), thus answering RQ3.

5   Conclusion

This work investigated the relationship between verbal content and the formation of hirability impressions in conversational video resumes from YouTube. To this end, we use 292 video resumes previously collected by Nguyen et al. (Nguyen and Gatica-Perez, 2016).These videos were transcribed into text using manual and automatic (Google Speech API) transcriptions.Various text representations (word2vec, GloVe) were computed from both manual and automatic transcripts.We then investigated the effect of various document-based and word-based representations on inference performance in the two text corpora.

To conclude, we acknowledge that there are certain limitations to this work.Firstly, our experiments would benefit from having more data. In particular, this could help in experiments with doc2vec, which requires large amounts of data for accurate document representation.In future work, we will investigate the connect between verbal content and personality impressions as well as fuse other non-textual predictors.We will also analyze the impact of verbal content on the hirability impressions using the complete dataset (939 videos).

Acknowledgments

This work was partially funded by the Swiss National Science Foundation (SNSF) through the UBImpressed project. We thank Lesly Miculicich and Nikolaos Pappas (Idiap) for discussions.

References

Nalini Ambady and Robert Rosenthal. 1992. Thin slices of expressive behavior as predictors of interpersonal consequences: A meta-analysis. *Psychological Bulletin*, 111(2).

Nalini Ambady and John Joseph Skowronski. 2008. *First impressions*. Guilford Press.

Joan-Isaac Biel, Vagia Tsiminaki, John Dines, and Daniel Gatica-Perez. 2013. Hi youtube! personality impressions and verbal content in social video. In *Proc. 15th ACM ICMI*, pages 119–126. ACM.

Steven Bird, Ewan Klein, and Edward Loper. 2009. *Natural language processing with Python: analyzing text with the natural language toolkit*. O'Reilly Media, Inc.

Lei Chen, Gary Feng, Chee Wee Leong, Blair Lehman, Michelle Martin-Raugh, Harrison Kell, Chong Min Lee, and Su-Youn Yoon. 2016. Automated scoring of interview videos using doc2vec multimodal feature extraction paradigm. In *Proc. 18th ACM ICMI*, pages 161–168. ACM.

Lei Chen, Ru Zhao, Chee Wee Leong, Blair Lehman, Gary Feng, and Mohammed Ehsan Hoque. 2017. Automated video interview judgment on a large-sized corpus collected online. In *Affective Computing and Intelligent Interaction (ACII), 2017 Seventh International Conference on*, pages 504–509. IEEE.

Google Cloud Services. Google Speech API.

Cedric De Boom, Steven Van Canneyt, Thomas Demeester, and Bart Dhoedt. 2016. Representation learning for very short texts using weighted word embedding aggregation. *Pattern Recognition Letters*, 80:150–156.

Thomas Hain, Lukáš Burget, John Dines, Philip N Garner, František Grézl, Asmaa El Hannani, Marijn Huijbregts, Martin Karafiat, Mike Lincoln, and Vincent Wan. 2012. Transcribing meetings with the amida systems. *IEEE Transactions on Audio, Speech, and Language Processing*, 20(2):486–498.

Tom Kenter, Alexey Borisov, and Maarten de Rijke. 2016. Siamese cbow: Optimizing word embeddings for sentence representations. *arXiv preprint arXiv:1606.04640*.

Veton Këpuska and Gamal Bohouta. 2017. Comparing speech recognition systems (microsoft api, google api and cmu sphinx). *Int. J. Eng. Res. Appl*, 7:20–24.

Quoc Le and Tomas Mikolov. 2014. Distributed representations of sentences and documents. In *Proc. 31st ICML*, pages 1188–1196.

Tomas Mikolov, Ilya Sutskever, Kai Chen, Greg S Corrado, and Jeff Dean. 2013. Distributed representations of words and phrases and their compositionality. In *Advances in neural information processing systems*, pages 3111–3119.

Skanda Muralidhar and Daniel Gatica-Perez. 2017. Examining Linguistic Content and Skill Impression Structure for Job Interview Analytics in Hospitality. In *Proc. 16th ACM MUM*.

Laurent Son Nguyen and Daniel Gatica-Perez. 2016. Hirability in the wild: Analysis of online conversational video resumes. *IEEE Transactions on Multimedia*, 18(7):1422–1437.

F. Pedregosa, G. Varoquaux, A. Gramfort, V. Michel, B. Thirion, O. Grisel, M. Blondel, P. Prettenhofer, R. Weiss, V. Dubourg, J. Vanderplas, A. Passos, D. Cournapeau, M. Brucher, M. Perrot, and E. Duchesnay. 2011. Scikit-learn: Machine learning in Python. *Journal of Machine Learning Research*, 12:2825–2830.

James W Pennebaker and Laura A King. 1999. Linguistic styles: language use as an individual difference. *J. Personality and Social Psychology*, 77(6):1296.

Jeffrey Pennington, Richard Socher, and Christopher Manning. 2014. Glove: Global vectors for word representation. In *Proceedings of the 2014 conference on empirical methods in natural language processing (EMNLP)*, pages 1532–1543.

Barbara Plank and Dirk Hovy. 2015. Personality traits on twitterorhow to get 1,500 personality tests in a week. In *Proceedings of the 6th Workshop on Computational Approaches to Subjectivity, Sentiment and Social Media Analysis*, pages 92–98.

Radim Řehůřek and Petr Sojka. Software Framework for Topic Modelling with Large Corpora. In *Proc. LREC 2010 Workshop on New Challenges for NLP Frameworks*. ELRA.

Priyanka Sinha, Lipika Dey, Pabitra Mitra, and Anupam Basu. 2015. Mining hexaco personality traits from enterprise social media. In *Proceedings of the 6th Workshop on Computational Approaches to Subjectivity, Sentiment and Social Media Analysis*, pages 140–147.

Janine Willis and Alexander Todorov. 2006. First impressions making up your mind after a 100-ms exposure to a face. *Psychological science*, 17(7):592–598.

Wen-tau Yih, Kristina Toutanova, John C Platt, and Christopher Meek. 2011. Learning discriminative projections for text similarity measures. In *Proceedings of the Fifteenth Conference on Computational Natural Language Learning*, pages 247–256. Association for Computational Linguistics.

Predicting Adolescents' Educational Track from Chat Messages on Dutch Social Media

Lisa Hilte, Walter Daelemans and **Reinhild Vandekerckhove**
CLiPS, University of Antwerp
Prinsstraat 13, 2000 Antwerp, Belgium
{firstname.lastname}@uantwerpen.be

Abstract

We aim to predict Flemish adolescents' educational track based on their Dutch social media writing. We distinguish between the three main types of Belgian secondary education: General (theory-oriented), Vocational (practice-oriented), and Technical Secondary Education (hybrid). The best results are obtained with a Naive Bayes model, i.e. an F-score of 0.68 (std. dev. 0.05) in 10-fold cross-validation experiments on the training data and an F-score of 0.60 on unseen data. Many of the most informative features are character n-grams containing specific occurrences of chat-speak phenomena such as emoticons. While the detection of the most theory- and practice-oriented educational tracks seems to be a relatively easy task, the hybrid Technical level appears to be much harder to capture based on online writing style, as expected.

1 Introduction

While some social variables, such as gender and age, have often been studied in author profiling (see e.g. the overview paper by Reddy et al. (2016)), educational track remains largely unexplored in this respect. The goal of this paper is twofold: we aim to develop a model that accurately predicts adolescents' educational track based on their language use in social media writing, and gain more insight in the linguistic characteristics of youngsters' educational background through inspection of the most informative features for this classification task.

The paper is structured as follows: we start by discussing related research (Section 2). Next, we describe the corpus, as well as the three main types of Belgian secondary education, i.e. the three class labels in the classification experiments (Section 3). Finally, we discuss our methodology (Section 4) and present the results (Section 5).

2 Related Research

Related work on this topic is scarce; only some studies in education profiling can be found, and they examine the impact of tertiary (and not secondary) education, on text genres other than social media writing. Furthermore, Dutch is never the language of interest. Estival et al. (2007), for instance, approached tertiary education profiling as a binary classification task (none versus some tertiary education) for a corpus of English emails. They obtained promising results with an ensemble learner (Bagging algorithm) using character-based, lexical and structural text features while explicitly excluding function words. Pennebaker et al. (2014), however, stressed the importance of function words in a related task: they linked students' writing in college admission essays to their later performance in college. Obtaining higher or lower grades appeared to be associated with the use of certain function words, belonging to either 'categorical' or 'dynamic' writing styles. In previous work on language and social status, Pennebaker (2011) had already pointed out the importance of pronouns: he described a more frequent use of you- and we-words as more typical of high status, as well as a less frequent use of I-words.

When we expand the scope of previous research from profiling studies to other related linguistic fields, we again conclude that this specific topic is underresearched. There are many studies on the characteristics of (youngsters') computer-mediated communication (CMC) (see e.g. Varnhagen et al. (2010), Tagliamonte and Denis (2008) and many more) and even some on the interaction between CMC and education (see e.g. Vandekerckhove and Sandra (2016) for the impact of CMC on school writing). However, the impact of educational track on adolescents' online writing is not addressed. For this specific topic, we can - to our

Proceedings of the 9th Workshop on Computational Approaches to Subjectivity, Sentiment and Social Media Analysis, pages 328–334
Brussels, Belgium, October 31, 2018. ©2018 Association for Computational Linguistics
https://doi.org/10.18653/v1/P17

Educational track	Participants	Posts	Tokens
General Secondary Education	596 (43%)	120 839 (28%)	739 831 (29%)
Technical Secondary Education	393 (28%)	197 534 (45%)	1 151 684 (46%)
Vocational Secondary Education	395 (29%)	116 164 (27%)	639 839 (25%)
Total	1 384	434 537	2 531 354

Table 1: Distributions in the corpus.

knowledge - only refer to our previous sociolinguistic work focusing on youngsters with distinct secondary education profiles, in which we have shown that teenagers in practice-oriented tracks tend to deviate more from formal standard writing on social media, by using more typographical chatspeak features (e.g. emoji), more non-standard lexemes (e.g. dialect words) and more non-standard abbreviations (Hilte et al., 2018a,b). While for all examined linguistic features, these differences were very consistent between the two 'poles' of the continuum between theory and practice, i.e. General and Vocational students, the Technical students did not always hold an intermediate position, but their chat messages showed a rather unpredictable linguistic pattern (Hilte et al., 2018a,b). We investigate in this paper whether these sociolinguistic results are confirmed in machine learning experiments.

3 Data Collection

Our corpus consists of Flemish[1] adolescents' private chat messages, written in Dutch on the social media platforms Facebook Messenger and WhatsApp. The data were collected through school visits during which the students were informed about the research, and could voluntarily donate chat messages. We asked for the students' (and for minors, their parents') consent to store and analyze their anonymized texts.

The final corpus contains 434 537 chat messages (2 531 354 tokens) by 1384 authors. All authors are Flemish high school students, aged 13-20, attending one of the three main types of Belgian secondary education: the theory-oriented General Secondary Education (which prepares for higher education), the practice-oriented Vocational Education (which prepares for a specific manual profession) and the hybrid Technical Education, which has both a strong theoretical and practical focus (Flemish Ministry of Education and Train-

ing, 2017). An overview of the distributions in the corpus can be found in Table 1.

We note that the Belgian secondary school system is similar to that of several other countries. The distinction between a vocational and an academic training is quite common (e.g. in Denmark, Finland, Croatia, France, Paraguay, China, etc.). The division between three main tracks (offering a more general, technical and vocational program respectively) is made in several countries as well (e.g. Czech Republic, Italy, Turkey, etc.)[2]. Consequently, the present classification task transcends the Belgian context and may be relevant in different countries and cultures, too.

4 Methodology

In this section, we describe the preprocessing of the data and the feature design (resp. Sections 4.1 and 4.2) as well as the experimental setup (Section 4.3).

4.1 Preprocessing

Since we will predict educational track on a participant-level, we must ensure to have sufficient data (and thus a fairly representative sample of online writing) for each participant. For this purpose, we deleted the participants who donated fewer than 50 chat messages. Next, we divided the remaining corpus in a training set (70% of the participants), and a test set (15%). A second test set (15%) was put aside for future experiments. This division was random but stratified, i.e. every subset contained the same proportion of participants per educational track.

4.2 Feature Design

The features used in the classification experiments consist of general textual features and features representing the frequency of typical chatspeak phenomena.

The general features include frequencies for token

---

[1]I.e. living in Flanders, the Dutch-speaking part of Belgium.

[2]en.wikipedia.org/wiki/List_of_secondary_education_systems_by_country

n-grams (uni-, bi- and trigrams) and character n-grams (bi-, tri- and tetragrams). In addition, average token and post length and vocabulary richness (type/token ratio) are taken into account as well. Finally, we use the dictionary-based computational tool LIWC (Pennebaker et al., 2001) in an adaptation for Dutch by Zijlstra et al. (2004) to count word frequencies for semantic and grammatical categories. While counts for individual words are already captured by the token unigrams, these counts per category can allow for broader generalizations for words which are semantically or functionally related. However, we note that the accuracy of this feature might not be optimal, as the social media texts are very noisy (and contain many non-standard elements, e.g. in terms of orthography or lexicon), whereas LIWC is based on standard Dutch word lists.

The set of chatspeak features contains counts for occurrences of several typographic phenomena. It includes the number of character repetitions (e.g. 'suuuuuper nice!!!') and combinations of question and exclamation marks (e.g. 'what?!'). The number of unconventionally capitalized tokens is added as well (alternating, inverse or all caps, e.g. 'AWESOME'). The final typographic features are emoticons and emoji (e.g. :), <3), the rendition of kisses and hugs (e.g. 'xoxoxo'), hashtags for topic indication (e.g. '#addicted') and 'mentions' for addressing a specific person in a group conversation (e.g. '@sarah'). We also add an onomatopoeic variable, i.e. the number of renditions of laughter (e.g. 'hahahah'). Another typical element of chatspeak are non-standard abbreviations and acronyms (e.g. 'brb' for 'be right back'). The final feature concerns language or register choice per token, in order to explicitly take into account the authors' use of words in a different language or linguistic variety than standard Dutch. We count the number of standard Dutch, English, and non-standard Dutch (e.g. dialect) lexemes. While the other chatspeak features are detected with regular expressions (typographic and onomatopoeic markers) or predefined lists (abbreviations), this lexical feature is extracted using a dictionary-based pipeline approach. For each token, we first checked if it was an actual word (and not e.g. an emoticon). Next, we checked if it occurred in a list of standard Dutch words and named entities. If not, we checked its presence in a standard English word list. Finally, if the token was

#verslaafd   ('#addicted')
Neeeeee   ('Noooooo')
Haha
HAHAHAHAHAHAHAHAHAHAHA

Figure 1: Example messages from the corpus.

absent again, it was placed in the 'non-standard Dutch' category. Figure 1 shows a sample of authentic chat messages from the corpus, illustrating the use of several chatspeak features.

For each participant, an individual feature vector was created containing the counts for all of these features. We proceeded with relative counts (to normalize for submission size) by dividing the absolute counts by the author's total number of tokens (e.g. for token unigrams, emoji,) or n-grams (for n-gram frequencies). For initial dimensionality reduction, we applied a frequency cutoff, only taking features into account that are used at least 10 times in the corpus, by at least 5 different participants.

4.3 Experimental Setup

We compared different models to predict Flemish adolescents' educational track based on their social media messages. The classification algorithms we tested were: Support Vector Machines, Naive Bayes (Multinomial, Gaussian and Bernoulli), Decision Trees, Random Forest, and Linear Regression. For all classifiers, we used the Scikit-learn implementation (Pedregosa et al., 2011). For each model, we searched for the optimal parameter settings through a randomized cross-validation search on the training data. We searched for optimal values for classifier-bound parameters (e.g. kernel for SVM), as well as an optimal feature scaler (no scaling, MinMax scaling or binarization) and an optimal percentile for univariate (chi-square based) feature selection, chosen from a continuous distribution. We compared the models' performance in 10-fold cross-validation experiments on the training data.

5 Results

In Section 5.1, we discuss the best model resulting from the 10-fold cross-validation experiments on the training data and compare it to different baseline models. In addition, we inspect the most informative features for the task. In Section 5.2, we discuss additional experiments which provide further insight in the classification problem.

Class levels	Precision	Recall	F-score
General	0.67	0.78	0.72
Technical	0.70	0.54	0.61
Vocational	0.68	0.71	0.70
Avg/total	0.68	0.68	0.68

Table 2: Classification report (in cross-validation).

Class levels	Precision	Recall	F-score
General	0.64	0.69	0.67
Technical	0.57	0.44	0.50
Vocational	0.58	0.68	0.63
Avg/total	0.60	0.61	0.60

Table 4: Classification report (on unseen data).

		Predicted class		
		Gen.	Tech.	Voc.
	Gen.	153	22	22
Actual class	Tech.	49	89	27
	Voc.	25	17	105

Table 3: Confusion matrix (in cross-validation).

5.1 Model Performance and Feature Inspection

The best performing model in CV-setting on the training data is a Multinomial Naive Bayes classifier, with optimized parameters: the value for the smoothing parameter alpha is 0.98, and the model uses the 12.50% best features (according to chi-square tests). The features were binarized. The classification report (Table 2) indicates that the performance is good, with a value of 0.68 for (prevalence-weighted macro-average) precision, recall and F-score (std. dev. 0.05). While precision is very similar for the three educational levels, recall is good for General Education, but slightly worse for the Vocational and much worse for the Technical level. Consequently, the model seems to miss many Technical profiles, confusing them with the other educational tracks. The confusion matrix (Table 3) shows that most (64%) misclassified Technical profiles were incorrectly labeled as the more theory-oriented General track, rather than as the more practice-oriented Vocational track (36%).

As Table 5 summarizes, the model strongly outperforms a probabilistic baseline (0.34) in cross-validation, as well as a simple bag-of-words model (which only uses token unigrams as features) without any parameter tuning, scaling or feature selection (F-score = 0.22). However, when parameter tuning, scaling and feature selection are introduced, the BoW-model obtains almost identical scores in cross-validation: it yields an overall precision, recall and F-score of 0.67 (std. dev. 0.03). There is, however, a difference in how well both models generalize to unseen data. While

the first model reaches an average F-score of 0.60 (see Table 4 for the detailed classification report), the BoW-model achieves a lower score of 0.55, and particularly underperforms in the detection of Technical profiles, with an F-score of 0.38 (vs 0.50 for the full model).

In order to better understand the differences and similarities between both models, we compared their feature sets (after feature selection was applied) and inspected the 1000 most informative ones, using information gain as ranking criterion. While we expected that the most informative features for the BoW-model would be lexical and the ones for the full model stylistic, this analysis suggests that in both models, many of the most informative selected features are specific occurrences of chatspeak markers. For the BoW-model, which uses only token unigrams as features, many of the most informative tokens contain one or more chatspeak features (e.g. colloquial register, a spelling manipulation, an emoticon, character repetition, etc.). Some other informative tokens seem to be more content- than style-related, revealing topics such as hobbies, specific locations, friends and school. Strikingly, although the full model contains abstraction of chatspeak phenomena (e.g. total count for emoticons), specific occurrences of these genre markers are still most informative. The 1000 most informative features are all character n-grams: only some reveal topics (e.g. school), but many more indicate the use of chatspeak features, and particularly combinations of emoji/emoticons. Other n-grams indicate the use of English and Arabic words, of colloquial terms, of chatspeak spelling, abbreviations and character repetition. As opposed to the BoW-model's token unigrams, these character n-grams allow the model to capture stylistic features on a sub-token level (e.g. the n-gram 'sss' captures repetition of the letter 's' in different words). We can illustrate a clear advantage by the Arabic word 'wallah' (meaning 'I swear on God's name'), which is often used by our participants with Ara-

Model	Cross-validation			Unseen data		
	Precision	Recall	F-score	Precision	Recall	F-score
Best model	**0.68**	**0.68**	**0.68**	**0.60**	**0.61**	**0.60**
BoW (non-finetuned)	0.15	0.39	0.22	0.15	0.39	0.21
BoW (finetuned)	0.67	0.67	0.67	0.55	0.55	0.55
Stylistic	0.65	0.64	0.64	0.59	0.60	0.59
Prob. baseline	0.34	0.34	0.34	0.34	0.34	0.34

Table 5: Comparison of the different models and baselines.

Class levels	Precision	Recall	F-score
General	0.86	0.80	0.83
Vocational	0.75	0.83	0.79
Avg/total	0.82	0.81	0.81

Table 6: Classification report for binary task (in cross-validation).

Class levels	Precision	Recall	F-score
General	0.82	0.79	0.80
Vocational	0.73	0.77	0.75
Avg/total	0.78	0.78	0.78

Table 7: Classification report for binary task (on unseen data).

bic roots, who spell it in many different ways. Because of these alternative spellings, 'wallah' does not appear among the most informative tokens in the BoW-model. However, for the full model, several related character n-grams (e.g. 'wlh', 'wll') do.

Next, we compared the full model to a stylistic model using only chatspeak features (both abstractions and specific occurrences), and no token or character n-grams. This stylistic model performs slightly worse on both the training set (F-score = 0.64, std. dev. 0.04) and unseen data (F-score = 0.59) (see Table 5). However, inspection of the most informative features in this feature set provides further insight in the education profiling task. Many of the most informative features are again specific occurrences of stylistic phenomena (e.g. specific emoticons, specific lexemes containing letter repetition). Some abstract representations of online writing style characteristics appear among the top-1000 features too (such as the total use of character repetition, of onomatopoeic laughter, acronyms, English words, mentions and hashtags, and emoticons), but much less prominently. These findings suggest that even in a purely stylistic model, abstract representation of certain style features is not informative enough for education profiling, and appears to be less important than the use of these features within specific tokens or contexts.

5.2 Additional Experiments

Additional experiments indicate that the task becomes much easier when the hybrid Technical Education level is not included. Performance for this binary classification task (distinguishing between General and Vocational students only) is much higher (F-score = 0.81 with std. dev. 0.04 in cross-validation, and 0.78 on unseen data; see Tables 6 and 7 for the classification reports), showing that Vocational and General students are not often linguistically confused by the model. Strikingly, in this setting, the purely stylistic model performs similarly on the training data (F-score = 0.81, std. dev. 0.08), and even better on the unseen data (F-score = 0.82) than the full model. This suggests that stylistic differences are more outspoken and consistent between General and Vocational students, and might be sufficient for classification.

Finally, first experiments with separate classifiers for girls and for boys, and for younger versus older teenagers, suggest interesting distinctions (see Table 8). It appears to be easier to correctly predict educational track for girls (F-score = 0.67 with std. dev. 0.07 in cross-validation; and 0.69 on unseen data) than for boys (F-score = 0.60 with std. dev. 0.09 in cross-validation; and 0.66 on unseen data). This suggests that more education-based linguistic variation can be found among girls than among boys. Similarly, better predictions could be made on unseen data for older teenagers, aged 17-20 (F-score = 0.62 in cross-validation, std. dev. 0.07; and 0.63 on unseen data), than for younger

Model	Cross-validation			Unseen data		
	Precision	Recall	F-score	Precision	Recall	F-score
Girls	0.67	0.67	0.67	**0.69**	**0.69**	**0.69**
Boys	0.61	0.61	0.60	0.67	0.67	0.66
Younger	**0.69**	**0.69**	**0.69**	0.55	0.55	0.55
Older	0.62	0.62	0.62	0.63	0.63	0.63

Table 8: Comparison of the models for separate groups.

adolescents, aged 13-16 (F-score = 0.69 in cross-validation, std. dev. 0.09; and 0.55 on unseen data). This might be due to the fact that the older teenagers have been together in the same peer networks and class groups for a longer time, and might write more similarly on social media. Furthermore, some of the younger students might actually still change educational track.

6   Conclusion

We conducted classification experiments to predict educational track for Flemish adolescents, based on their social media writing. These first results are promising and indicate that the task is doable. However, although the best model strongly outperforms a probabilistic baseline, its performance is similar to that of a simple BoW-model. This might give the impression that lexical features are still very important; however, inspection of the most informative features revealed that many of the most informative tokens contain stylistic features typical of the informal online genre. The most informative features for the full model suggest that abstraction of these stylistic chatspeak features (or at least, the current implementation) is still of lesser importance than specific occurrences.

While the distinction between General and Vocational high school students appears to be relatively easy to make, the detection of students in the intermediate Technical track is much harder. This could indicate that these students are truly a hybrid class with subsets of students that are simply not that different from their peers in more theory- or more practice-oriented tracks, respectively. In addition, related research shows that these students' online writing is rather unpredictable and does not follow a clear pattern (Hilte et al., 2018a,b).

In future work, we want to experiment with additional algorithms, such as ensemble methods, and with a post-level rather than a participant-level approach (in order to have more data samples at our disposal). We also want to improve the current feature design and particularly the abstract representation of style features, because as van der Goot et al. (2018) write, abstract features may increase generalizability to other corpora (and even genres and languages) in author profiling tasks, compared to lexical models. Finally, we want to further investigate the creation of different classifiers for different subgroups of participants (e.g. boys versus girls).

Finally, we stress that this profiling task is not only relevant in a Belgian context, since the educational tracks serving as class labels correspond to several countries' secondary education programs. Furthermore, the inclusion of stylistic features - i.e. chatspeak phenomena occurring in *any* language - adds to this generalizability. While specific lexemes or specific realizations of chatspeak markers may not always be relevant in other languages or corpora, the abstract stylistic features are more universal on social media. We argue that these models for education profiling, when further improved, could be used in different languages and applications. For instance, the addition of an educational compound can increase existing profiling tools' performance, which can be important in different tasks (e.g. the detection of fake accounts on social media, and many more).

7   Supplementary Materials

Because of the decision of our university's ethical committee, in line with European regulations to ensure the adolescents' privacy, we cannot make the dataset publicly available. The code will be made available.

8   Acknowledgments

We thank Stéphan Tulkens for his advice on the setup and analyses. We are also grateful towards the two anonymous reviewers for their feedback on a previous version of this paper.

References

Dominique Estival, Tanja Gaustad, Son Bao Pham, Will Radford, and Ben Hutchinson. 2007. Author profiling for English emails. In *Proceedings of the 10th Conference of the Pacific Association for Computational Linguistics*, pages 263–272.

Flemish Ministry of Education and Training. 2017. *Statistisch jaarboek van het Vlaams onderwijs. Schooljaar 2015-2016*. Department of Education and Training, Brussels.

Lisa Hilte, Reinhild Vandekerckhove, and Walter Daelemans. 2018a. Adolescents' social background and non-standard writing in online communication. *Dutch Journal of Applied Linguistics*, 7(1):2–25.

Lisa Hilte, Reinhild Vandekerckhove, and Walter Daelemans. 2018b. Social media writing and social class: A correlational analysis of adolescent CMC and social background. *International Journal of Society, Culture & Language*.

Fabian Pedregosa, Gaël Varoquaux, Alexandre Gramfort, Vincent Michel, Bertrand Thirion, Olivier Grisel, Mathieu Blondel, Peter Prettenhofer, Ron Weiss, Vincent Dubourg, et al. 2011. Scikit-learn: Machine learning in Python. *Journal of machine learning research*, 12(Oct):2825–2830.

James W Pennebaker. 2011. *The secret life of pronouns. What our words say about us*. Bloomsbury Press, New York.

James W Pennebaker, Cindy K Chung, Joey Frazee, Gary M Lavergne, and David I Beaver. 2014. When small words foretell academic success: The case of college admissions essays. *PloS one*, 9(12):e115844.

James W Pennebaker, Martha E Francis, and Roger J Booth. 2001. Linguistic inquiry and word count: LIWC 2001. *Mahway: Lawrence Erlbaum Associates*, 71(2001):2001.

T. Taghunadha Reddy, B. Vishnu Vardhan, and P. Vijayapal Reddy. 2016. A survey on authorship profiling techniques. *International Journal of Applied Engineering Research*, 11(5):3092–3102.

Sali A Tagliamonte and Derek Denis. 2008. Linguistic ruin? LOL! Instant messaging and teen language. *American speech*, 83(1):3–34.

Rob van der Goot, Nikola Ljubešić, Ian Matroos, Malvina Nissim, and Barbara Plank. 2018. Bleaching text: Abstract features for cross-lingual gender prediction. In *Proceedings of the 56th Annual Meeting of the Association for Computational Linguistics (Volume 2: Short Papers)*, volume 2, pages 383–389.

Reinhild Vandekerckhove and Dominiek Sandra. 2016. De potentiële impact van informele online communicatie op de spellingpraktijk van Vlaamse tieners in schoolcontext. *Tijdschrift voor Taalbeheersing*, 38(3):201–234.

Connie K Varnhagen, G Peggy McFall, Nicole Pugh, Lisa Routledge, Heather Sumida-MacDonald, and Trudy E Kwong. 2010. Lol: New language and spelling in instant messaging. *Reading and writing*, 23(6):719–733.

Hanna Zijlstra, Tanja Van Meerveld, Henriët Van Middendorp, James W Pennebaker, and RD Geenen. 2004. De Nederlandse versie van de 'linguistic inquiry and word count' (LIWC). *Gedrag Gezond*, 32:271–281.

Arabizi sentiment analysis based on transliteration and automatic corpus annotation

Imane Guellil[1,2], Ahsan Adeel[3], Faical Azouaou[2], Fodil Benali[2],ala-eddine Hachani[2],Amir Hussain[3]

1 Ecole Superieure des Sciences Appliquées d'Alger ESSA-alger
2 Laboratoire des Méthodes de Conception des Systèmes (LMCS),
Ecole nationale Supérieure d'Informatique,BP 68M, 16309, Oued-Smar, Alger, Algérie
3 Institute of Computing science and Mathematics, School of Natural Sciences
University of Stirling Stirling UK
`i.guellil@essa-alger.dz`
`{i_guellil,f_azouaou,df_benali,da_hachani}@esi.dz`
`{ahsan.adeel,ahu}@cs.stir.ac.uk`

Abstract

Arabizi is a form of writing Arabic text which relies on Latin letters, numerals and punctuation rather than Arabic letters. In the literature, the difficulties associated with Arabizi sentiment analysis have been underestimated, principally due to the complexity of Arabizi. In this paper, we present an approach to automatically classify sentiments of Arabizi messages into positives or negatives. In the proposed approach, Arabizi messages are first transliterated into Arabic. Afterwards, we automatically classify the sentiment of the transliterated corpus using an automatically annotated corpus. For corpus validation, shallow machine learning algorithms such as Support Vectors Machine (SVM) and Naive Bays (NB) are used. Simulations results demonstrate the outperformance of NB algorithm over all others. The highest achieved F1-score is up to 78% and 76% for manually and automatically transliterated dataset respectively. Ongoing work is aimed at improving the transliterator module and annotated sentiment dataset.

1 Introduction

Sentiment analysis (SA), also called opinion mining, is the field of study that analyzes people's opinions, sentiments, evaluations, appraisals, attitudes, and emotions towards entities such as products, services, organizations, individuals, issues, events, topics, and their attributes. It represents a large problem space(Liu, 2012). To determine whether a document or a sentence expresses a positive or negative sentiment, three main approaches are commonly used, the lexicon based approach (Taboada et al., 2011), machine learning (ML) based approach (Maas et al., 2011) and a hybrid approach (Khan et al., 2015). English has

the greatest number of sentiment analysis studies, while research is more limited for other languages including Arabic and its dialects (Alayba et al., 2017; Guellil and Boukhalfa, 2015).

ML based sentiment analysis is a more dominant approach in the literature but it requires annotated training data. One of the majors problems related to the treatment of Arabic and its dialect is the lack of resources. Other dominant problems include the non standard romanization (called Arabizi) that Arabic speakers often use in social media. Arabizi uses Latin alphabet, numbers, punctuation for writing an Arabic word (For example the word "mli7", combined with Latin letters and numbers, becomes the romanized form of the Arabic word "مليح" meaning "good"). To the best of our knowledge, limited work has been conducted on sentiment analysis of Arabizi ((Duwairi et al., 2016; Guellil et al., 2018)). The reason behind the lack of contribution is the complexity of Arabizi. Most researches are therefore moving towards the transformation of Arabizi into Arabic. This transformation or passage is recognized by the transliteration. Therefore, transliteration is only a process of passing from a written text in a given script or alphabet to another (Guellil et al., 2017c; Kaur and Singh, 2014). To bridge the gap, this paper proposes an approach determining the sentiment of Arabizi messages after transliterating them. This paper is organized as follows, Section 2 presents an overview of Arabizi. Section 3 presents the related work on SA and machine transliteration (MT). Section 4 presents the proposed approach and related components. Section 5 presents the simulation and experimentation. Finally, Section 6 presents the conclusion with some future directions.

335

Proceedings of the 9th Workshop on Computational Approaches to Subjectivity, Sentiment and Social Media Analysis, pages 335–341
Brussels, Belgium, October 31, 2018. ©2018 Association for Computational Linguistics
https://doi.org/10.18653/v1/P17

2 Arabizi: An overview

Arabic speakers on social media, discussion forums, Short Messaging System (SMS), and on line chat applications often use a non standard romanization called "Arabizi" (Darwish, 2013; Bies et al., 2014). For example, the sentence: "rani fer7ana" (which means I am happy and correspond to the arabic sentence: زَانِي فَرحَانة) is written in Arabizi. Hence, Arabizi is an Arabic text written using Latin characters, numerals and some punctuations (Darwish, 2013). The challenge behind Arabizi is the presence of many forms of the same word. For example the authors in (Ryan et al., 2014) argued that the word ان شَاء اللّه (meaning if the god willing) could be written in 69 different manners.

3 Related work

3.1 Machine learning Arabic sentiment analysis

ML based sentiment analysis requires annotated data. Among the corpora presented in the literature and focused on MSA, we cite: LABR (Aly and Atiya, 2013), AWATIF (Abdul-Mageed and Diab, 2012), ASTD (Nabil et al., 2015) and ArTwitter (Abdulla et al., 2013). LABR contains 63,257 comments annotated with stars ranging from 1 to 5. AWATIF is a multi-genre corpus containing 10,723 sentences manually annotated in objective and subjective sentences. ASTD contains 10,000 Arab Tweets classified into objective, subjective positive, subjective negative or subjective mixed. ArTwitter contains 2,000 tweets manually annotated into positive and negative. However, most of the aforementioned works suffer from manual annotation and almost all resources are not publicly available. In addition, constructed corpora are dedicated to some dialects, neglecting others (specially Maghrebi dialect such as Moroccan or Algerian dialect).

3.2 Arabizi Transliteration

The proposed approach is inspired by the work presented in (van der Wees et al., 2016), where the authors used a table extracted from Wikipedia[1] for the passage from Arabizi to Arabic. The originality of our transliteration approach compared to this work is the treatment of ambiguities related to Arabizi transliteration such as: (a) Am-

[1] https://en.wikipedia.org/wiki/Arabic_chat_alphabet

biguity of the vowels, where each vowels can be replaced by different letters or by NULL character (b) Ambiguity of the characters having the same sound or whose sounds are close, for example, the letters 's' and 'c' which can be replaced by the two letters س and ص (c) Ambiguity related to the transliteration direction, unlike the different works in (Guellil et al., 2017c,b), the rules of passage that we defined are from Arabizi to Arabic. The reverse passage may cause several ambiguities. The proposed approach is also inspired by the works presented in (Guellil et al., 2017c,b; Nouvel et al.) that uses a language model to determine the best possible candidate for a word in Arabizi. However, their work relies on a parallel corpus corresponding to the transliteration of a set of messages from Arabizi to Arabic. The realization of this corpus is usually done manually, which is a very time and effort consuming work. Hence, we avoid using a parallel corpus between Arabizi and Arabic and applied a language model (based on large corpus extracted from social media) to extract the best candidate.

3.3 Arabizi Sentiment Analysis

Different works have been proposed for handling Arabizi Darwish (2013); Guellil and Faical (2017); Azouaou and Guellil (2017); Guellil and Azouaou (2016). However, to the best of our knowledge, limited work has been conducted on sentiment analysis of Arabizi (Duwairi et al., 2016; Guellil et al., 2018). In (Duwairi et al., 2016), the authors presents a transliteration step before proceeding to the sentiment classification. However their approach present two majors drawbacks: (1) They rely on a very basic table for the passage from Arabizi to Arabic which cannot handle Arabizi ambiguities. (2) They construct a small annotated corpus manually (containing 3026 messages). This corpus contains Arabizi messages which therefore transliterated into Arabic. In (Guellil et al., 2018), the authors automatically construct an annotated sentiment Arabizi corpus and directly applied sentiment classification without calling the transliteration process. However, the authors confronted several ambiguity problems which resulted low F1-score of 66%. In contrast, the purpose of our paper is to present an approach dedicated to Arabizi sentiment analysis by calling transliteration process. The sentiment analysis corpus (training corpus) contains

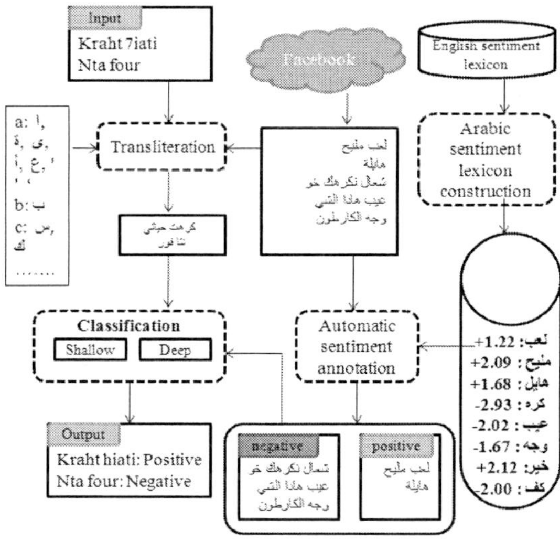

Figure 1: A general architecture of our approach for Arabizi sentiment analysis

Arabic messages (Modern Standard Arabic MSA and Dialectal Arabic DA, specially Algerian dialect) and it is constructed automatically. For transliteration step, this paper is focused on ambiguities treatment (especially vowels).

4 Methodology

This paper presents an approach for Arabizi Sentiment Analysis. Figure 1 summarizes the main steps of the proposed approach, including:

- Automatic construction of Arabic sentiment lexicon.

- Automatic annotation of Arabic messages

- Arabizi transliteration

- Sentiment classification of Arabic messages

4.1 Automatic construction of Arabic sentiment lexicon

In this study, the sentiment lexicon is constructed by translating an existing English lexicon, namely SOCAL (Taboada et al., 2011) to Arabic. We opt for using SOCAL rather than other lexicons such as SentiWordNet (Baccianella et al., 2010) or SentiStrength (Thelwall et al., 2010) because SOCAL contains a large number terms and in this study, we are not focusing on the context of terms but only on its global valence. The text is translated using the Glosbe API[2], which takes an English

[2]https://glosbe.com/en/arq/excellent

word as input and returns a set of equivalent in other languages. In this work we focus on Arabic and its dialect (MSA + dialect). We choose this API because, to the best of our language, it is the unique API dealing with some dialects with scarce resources such as the Algerian dialect. After the automatic translation, the same score is assigned to all the translated words. This score corresponds to the score of English word from which they are translated. For example, all the translations of the English word 'excellent' with a score of +5, such as بَاهي (bAhy), لطيف (lTyf), and 'مليح' (mlyH), are assigned a score of +5. 6 769 terms were obtained including negative sentiment terms (labels ranging between -1 and -5) and positive terms (labels ranging between +1 and +5). Since some Arabic sentiment words result from different English words having different sentiment scores, an average score is assigned to such English words. Lastly, the resulted lexicon is manually reviewed to retain correct sentiment words. The final lexicon contains 1 745 terms (in Algerian dialect) where 968 are negative, 6 are neutral and 771 are positives. We choose to apply our approach to Algerian dialect for comparing our results to those obtained in (Guellil et al., 2018).

4.2 Automatic Annotation of Arabic messages

The constructed lexicon is used to automatically provide a sentiment score for Arabic utterances. The lexicon is used to build a large sentiment corpus. To calculate the score, we considered: (1) Opposition (2) Multi-word expressions (because the constructed lexicon contains multi-word entries) (3) Handling Arabic morphology by employing a simple rule-based light stemmer that handles Arabic prefixes and suffixes (4) Negation which can reverse polarity. Negation in some Arabic dialect is usually expressed as an attached prefix, suffix, or a combination of both.

To score a message, the sentiment scores of all words in the message are averaged. Finally, balanced dataset is constructed by keeping the same number of messages in positive and negative dataset. The resulted corpus contains 255,008 messages (where both positive and negative corpus contains 127,504 messages).

4.3 Arabizi Transliteration

The proposed transliteration approach includes four important steps: (1) pretreatment of the Arabic corpus and the Arabizi message. (2) Proposal and application of the rules for the Algerian Arabizi. (3) Generating the different candidates. (4) Extraction of the best candidate. This part receives input, a set of messages written in Arabizi and a voluminous corpus written in DA extracted from Facebook. All these messages are pretreated (i.e. deleting exaggeration, etc). Afterwards, a set of passages rules are proposed (i.e. the letter 'a' could be replaces by 'ا، ة، ى، أ، ع', etc. It could also be replaced by '', none letters when it represents a diacritic). By applying different replacements, as well as different rules developed, each Arabizi word gives birth to several words in Arabic. For example the word "kraht" generates 32 possible candidates, such as: 'قرهت', 'كرهت', 'كرَاهت' etc. The correctly transliterated word is 'كرهت'. The word "7iati" has 16 candidates such as: 'حيَاطي', 'حيطي', 'حيطي'. The correctly transliterated word is 'حيَاتي'. To extract the best candidate for the transliteration of a given Arabizi word into Arabic, a language model is constructed and applied.

4.4 Sentiment classification of Arabic messages

In this paper, different classification models are compared. The document embedding vectorization (Doc2vec algorithm presented within (Le and Mikolov, 2014)) is used (with default parameters). For Doc2vec, the two methods presented in (Le and Mikolov, 2014) were applied: (1) Distributed Memory Version Of Paragraph Vector (PV-DM) and (2) Distributed Bag of Words Version of Paragraph Vector (PV-DBOW). Moreover, the implementation merging these two methods is used. For the classification part, five different classifiers are used: (1) Support Vector Machine (SVM) (2) Naive Bayes (NB) (3) Logistic regression (LR) (4) Decision Tree (DT) and 5) Random Forest (RF).

5 Experimentations and results

5.1 Experimental Setup

The proposed approach is applied on a Maghrebi dialect (i.e. Algerian Arabizi) which suffers from limited available tools and other handling resources required for automatic sentiment analysis. Algerian dialect (DALG) is largely presented in (Meftouh et al., 2012). However, the resources dedicated to the treatment of MSA cannot be directly applied to DALG. In this context, two large corpora were extracted from Facebook using RestFB[3]. The first one was extracted on September, 2017 which contains 8,673,285 messages with 3,668,575 written in Arabic letters. The second one was extracted on November, 2017 that contains 15,407,910 messages with 7,926,504 written in Arabic letters. The first one was used for transliteration task where the second one was used in sentiment annotation task. For testing our transliteration approach, we used Corpus_50 which is a part of Cottrell's corpus (Cotterell and Callison-Burch, 2014) used in (Guellil et al., 2017c,b,a). For testing our sentiment analysis approach, we used Corpus_500 (an Algerian Arabizi annotated corpus in (Guellil et al., 2018), containing 250 positives and negatives messages) .

5.2 Experimental results

The first experiment evaluates the transliteration module. The transliteration of Corpus_50 achieves an accuracy up to 74.76% (as compared to 45.35% in (Guellil et al., 2017c)). This results shows the efficacy of the proposed transliteration approach. For sentiment analysis, we used Corpus_500. This dataset was transliterated automatically with the transliterator module. To validate the quality of the automatic transliteration, this dataset was also transliterated manually by Algerian dialect's natives. The transliteration of this dataset achieves an accuracy up to 72.05%. Afterwards, we carried out two types of experiments: (1) SA on test corpus transliterated automatically (2) SA on test corpus transliterated manually. Table 1 presents the performance of different shallow classification algorithms in terms of Precision (P), Recall (R) and F1-score (F1) for Doc2vec methods (PV_DBOW, PV_DM and PV_DBOW + PV_DM) and for Tr_automatic and Tr_manual dataset (respectively referring to the dataset transliterated automatically and manually).

5.3 Results and errors analysis

Based on the simulations and analysis, three major observations are: (1) The results with

---

[3]http://restfb.com/

Vectorization	classifier	Tr_automatic			Tr_manual		
		P	R	F1	P	R	F1
PV_DBOW	SVM	0.67	0.82	0.74	0.68	0.84	0.75
	NB	**0.73**	0.80	**0.76**	**0.74**	0.83	**0.78**
	LR	0.66	**0.82**	0.73	0.68	**0.84**	0.75
	RF	0.70	0.79	0.75	0.72	0.82	0.77
	DT	0.63	0.71	0.68	0.64	0.69	0.67
PV_DM	SVM	0.68	0.82	0.74	0.66	0.79	0.72
	NB	0.66	0.77	0.71	0.68	0.76	0.72
	LR	0.66	0.82	0.73	0.66	0.8	0.72
	RF	0.69	0.78	0.73	0.72	0.79	0.75
	DT	0.60	0.68	0.64	0.60	0.63	0.61
PV_DBOW + PV_DM	SVM	0.64	0.79	0.71	0.67	0.83	0.74
	NB	0.68	0.78	0.72	0.69	0.80	0.75
	LR	0.63	0.80	0.70	0.67	0.84	0.75
	RF	0.68	0.74	0.71	0.72	0.84	0.77
	DT	0.61	0.69	0.65	0.62	0.70	0.65

Table 1: Classification results with shallow machine learning

Tr_manual are slightly better than Tr_automatic (because the mistake on transliteration generally appears on only one letter), (2) The implementation PV_DBOW of Doc2vec achieved best results, (3) For classification, NB performed the best. (4) The results presented in Table 1 largely outperform the resulted presented in (Guellil et al., 2018) (which are up to 66%). However, we were not able to compare our results to those presented in (Duwairi et al., 2016) because their data are not available.However, the most observed errors are as follow:

- The principal error appears in transliteration process is related to technique of choosing the best candidate. The idea of language model is to extract the candidate having the most important number of occurrence. However, in some cases, this techniques returns an incorrect candidate. For example the word "rakom" meaning "you are" is transliterated as "رقم" meaning "a number" rather than "راكم" (which is the correct transliteration). The solution to this problem is to integrate other parameters for determining the best candidate such as distance.

- Some sentiment classification errors are due to transliteration errors. For example, "khlwiya" meaning good and quiet is wrongly transliterated to "خليَا" (meaning empty) rather than خلوية. Improving transliteration will improve sentiment classification.

- Other sentiment classification errors are due to some errors occurred in the automatic annotated corpus (so the training corpus). For example, the messages جَابو فخَامة الأسم تكفي meaning *Djabou the excellency of the name is sufficient* was annotated negative (where it is positive). Manually reviewing the automatic annotation will definitely improve the results.

6 Conclusion

In this paper, we present an approach to automatically classify sentiments of Arabizi messages (extracted from Facebook). The proposed approach constitutes an automatic annotation and transliteration. An Arabic sentiment lexicon is automatically constructed followed by automatic annotation and transliteration (Arabizi to Arabic). The developed dataset is validated using shallow machine learning, where the highest achieved precision is up to 78% and 76% for manual and automatic transliteration respectively with NB classifiers and PV_DBOW vectorization method.In the future, we intend to further enhance the proposed approach by improving the transliteration module focusing the annotated corpus (i.e manually reviewing the automatic annotation).

Acknowledgment

Imane Guellil and Faical Azouaou are respectively supported by Ecole Superieure des Sciences Appliquées d'Alger ESSA-alger and Ecole nationale Supérieure d'Informatique. Amir Hussain and Ahsan Adeel were supported by the UK Engineering and Physical Sciences Research Council (EPSRC) grant No.EP/M026981/1.

References

Muhammad Abdul-Mageed and Mona T Diab. 2012. Awatif: A multi-genre corpus for modern standard arabic subjectivity and sentiment analysis. In *LREC*, pages 3907–3914. Citeseer.

Nawaf A Abdulla, Nizar A Ahmed, Mohammed A Shehab, and Mahmoud Al-Ayyoub. 2013. Arabic sentiment analysis: Lexicon-based and corpus-based. In *Applied Electrical Engineering and Computing Technologies (AEECT), 2013 IEEE Jordan Conference on*, pages 1–6. IEEE.

Abdulaziz M Alayba, Vasile Palade, Matthew England, and Rahat Iqbal. 2017. Arabic language sentiment analysis on health services. In *Arabic Script Analysis and Recognition (ASAR), 2017 1st International Workshop on*, pages 114–118. IEEE.

Mohamed Aly and Amir Atiya. 2013. Labr: A large scale arabic book reviews dataset. In *Proceedings of the 51st Annual Meeting of the Association for Computational Linguistics (Volume 2: Short Papers)*, volume 2, pages 494–498.

Faical Azouaou and Imane Guellil. 2017. Alg/fr: A step by step construction of a lexicon between algerian dialect and french. In *The 31st Pacific Asia Conference on Language, Information and Computation PACLIC 31 (2017)*.

Stefano Baccianella, Andrea Esuli, and Fabrizio Sebastiani. 2010. Sentiwordnet 3.0: an enhanced lexical resource for sentiment analysis and opinion mining. In *LREC*.

Ann Bies, Zhiyi Song, Mohamed Maamouri, Stephen Grimes, Haejoong Lee, Jonathan Wright, Stephanie Strassel, Nizar Habash, Ramy Eskander, and Owen Rambow. 2014. Transliteration of arabizi into arabic orthography: Developing a parallel annotated arabizi-arabic script sms/chat corpus. In *Proceedings of the EMNLP 2014 Workshop on Arabic Natural Language Processing (ANLP)*, pages 93–103.

Ryan Cotterell and Chris Callison-Burch. 2014. A multi-dialect, multi-genre corpus of informal written arabic.

Kareem Darwish. 2013. Arabizi detection and conversion to arabic. *arXiv preprint arXiv:1306.6755*.

Rehab M Duwairi, Mosab Alfaqeh, Mohammad Wardat, and Areen Alrabadi. 2016. Sentiment analysis for arabizi text. In *Information and Communication Systems (ICICS), 2016 7th International Conference on*, pages 127–132. IEEE.

Imane Guellil, Ahsan Adeel, Faical Azouaou, and Amir Hussain. 2018. Sentialg: Automated corpus annotation for algerian sentiment analysis. In *9th International Conference on Brain Inspired Cognitive Systems(BICS 2018)*.

Imane Guellil and Faiçal Azouaou. 2016. Arabic dialect identification with an unsupervised learning (based on a lexicon). application case: Algerian dialect. In *Computational Science and Engineering (CSE) and IEEE Intl Conference on Embedded and Ubiquitous Computing (EUC) and 15th Intl Symposium on Distributed Computing and Applications for Business Engineering (DCABES), 2016 IEEE Intl Conference on*, pages 724–731. IEEE.

Imane Guellil, Faiçal Azouaou, and Mourad Abbas. 2017a. Comparison between neural and sta-tistical translation after translitera-tion of algerian arabic dialect. In *WiNLP: Women & Underrepresented Minorities in Natural Language Processing (co-located withACL 2017)*.

Imane Guellil, Faical Azouaou, and Mourad Abbas. 2017b. Neural vs statistical translation of algerian arabic dialect written with arabizi and arabic letter. In *The 31st Pacific Asia Conference on Language, Information and Computation PACLIC 31 (2017)*.

Imane Guellil, Faiçal Azouaou, Mourad Abbas, and Sadat Fatiha. 2017c. Arabizi transliteration of algerian arabic dialect into modern standard arabic. In *Social MT 2017/First workshop on Social Media and User Generated Content Machine Translation*.

Imane Guellil and Azouaou Faical. 2017. Bilingual lexicon for algerian arabic dialect treatment in social media. In *WiNLP: Women & Underrepresented Minorities in Natural Language Processing (co-located with ACL 2017)*. http://www.winlp.org/wp-content/uploads/2017/final_papers_2017/92_Paper.pdf.

Imene Guellil and Kamel Boukhalfa. 2015. Social big data mining: A survey focused on opinion mining and sentiments analysis. In *Programming and Systems (ISPS), 2015 12th International Symposium on*, pages 1–10. IEEE.

Kamaljeet Kaur and Parminder Singh. 2014. Review of machine transliteration techniques. *International Journal of Computer Applications*, 107(20).

Aamera ZH Khan, Mohammad Atique, and VM Thakare. 2015. Combining lexicon-based and learning-based methods for twitter sentiment analysis. *International Journal of Electronics, Communication and Soft Computing Science & Engineering (IJECSCSE)*, page 89.

Quoc Le and Tomas Mikolov. 2014. Distributed representations of sentences and documents. In *International Conference on Machine Learning*, pages 1188–1196.

Bing Liu. 2012. Sentiment analysis and opinion mining. *Synthesis lectures on human language technologies*, 5(1):1–167.

Andrew L Maas, Raymond E Daly, Peter T Pham, Dan Huang, Andrew Y Ng, and Christopher Potts. 2011. Learning word vectors for sentiment analysis. In *Proceedings of the 49th annual meeting of the association for computational linguistics: Human language technologies-volume 1*, pages 142–150. Association for Computational Linguistics.

Karima Meftouh, Najette Bouchemal, and Kamel Smaïli. 2012. A study of a non-resourced language: The case of one of the algerian dialects. In *The third International Workshop on Spoken Languages Technologies for Under-resourced Languages-SLTU'12*.

Mahmoud Nabil, Mohamed Aly, and Amir Atiya. 2015. Astd: Arabic sentiment tweets dataset. In *Proceedings of the 2015 Conference on Empirical Methods in Natural Language Processing*, pages 2515–2519.

Houda Saâdane1 Damien Nouvel, Hosni Seffih, and Christian Fluhr. Une approche linguistique pour la détection des dialectes arabes. In *24e Conférence sur le Traitement Automatique des Langues Naturelles (TALN)*, page 242.

Cotterell Ryan, Adithya Renduchintala, Naomi Saphra, and Chris Callison-Burch. 2014. An algerian arabic-french code-switched corpus. In *Workshop on Free/Open-Source Arabic Corpora and Corpora Processing Tools Workshop Programme*, page 34.

Maite Taboada, Julian Brooke, Milan Tofiloski, Kimberly Voll, and Manfred Stede. 2011. Lexicon-based methods for sentiment analysis. *Computational linguistics*, 37(2):267–307.

Mike Thelwall, Kevan Buckley, Georgios Paltoglou, Di Cai, and Arvid Kappas. 2010. Sentiment strength detection in short informal text. *Journal of the American Society for Information Science and Technology*, 61(12):2544–2558.

Marlies van der Wees, Arianna Bisazza, and Christof Monz. 2016. A simple but effective approach to improve arabizi-to-english statistical machine translation. In *Proceedings of the 2nd Workshop on Noisy User-generated Text (WNUT)*, pages 43–50.

UBC-NLP at IEST 2018: Learning Implicit Emotion With an Ensemble of Language Models

Hassan Alhuzali   **Mohamed Elaraby**   **Muhammad Abdul-Mageed**

Natural Language Processing Lab

The University of British Columbia

{halhuzali,mohamed.elaraby}@alumni.ubc.ca,muhammad.mageeed@ubc.ca

Abstract

We describe UBC-NLP contribution to IEST-2018, focused at learning implicit emotion in Twitter data. Among the 30 participating teams, our system ranked the 4th (with 69.3% *F*-score). Post competition, we were able to score slightly higher than the 3rd ranking system (reaching 70.7%). Our system is trained on top of a pre-trained language model (LM), fine-tuned on the data provided by the task organizers. Our best results are acquired by an average of an ensemble of language models. We also offer an analysis of system performance and the impact of training data size on the task. For example, we show that training our best model for only one epoch with $< 40\%$ of the data enables better performance than the baseline reported by Klinger et al. (2018) for the task.

1 Introduction

Emotion is essential in human experience and communication, lending special significance to natural language processing systems aimed at learning it. Emotion detection systems can be applied in a host of domains, including health and well-being, user profiling, education, and marketing. There is a small, yet growing, body of NLP literature on emotion. Early works focused on creating and manually labeling datasets. The SemEval 2007 Affective Text task Strapparava and Mihalcea (2007) and Aman and Szpakowicz (2007) are two examples that target the news and blog domains respectively. In these works, data were labeled for the 6 basic emotions of Ekman (Ekman, 1972). More recent works exploit *distant supervision* (Mintz et al., 2009) to automatically acquire emotion data for training systems. More specifically, a number of works use hashtags like *#happy* and *#sad*, especially occurring finally in Twitter data, as a proxy of emotion (Wang

et al., 2012; Mohammad and Kiritchenko, 2015; Volkova and Bachrach, 2016). Abdul-Mageed and Ungar (2017) report state-of-the-art results using a large dataset acquired with hashtags. Other works exploit emojis to capture emotion carrying data (Felbo et al., 2017). Alhuzali et al. (2018) introduce a third effective approach that leverages first-person seed phrases like *"I'm happy that"* to collect emotion data.

Klinger et al. (2018) propose yet a fourth method for collecting emotion data that depends on the existence of the expression "emotion-word + one of the following words (when, that or because)" in a tweet, regardless of the position of the emotion word. In the "Implicit Emotion" shared task [1], participants were provided data representing the 6 emotions in the set (anger, disgust, fear, joy, sad, surprise). The trigger word was removed from each tweet. To illustrate, the task is to predict the emotion in a tweet like "Boys who like Starbucks make me *[#TRIGGERWORD#]* because we can go on cute coffee dates" (with the triggered word labeled as *joy*). In this paper, we describe our system submitted as part of the competition. Overall, our submission ranked the 4th out of the 30 participating teams. With further experiments, we were able to acquire better results, which would rank our model at top 3 (70.7% *F*-score).

The rest of the paper is organized as follows: Section 2 describes the data. Section 3 offers a description of the methods employed in our work. Section 3 is where we present our results, and we perform an analysis of these results in Section 5. We list negative experiments in Section 6 and conclude in Section 7.

---

[1] http://implicitemotions.wassa2018.com

Proceedings of the 9th Workshop on Computational Approaches to Subjectivity, Sentiment and Social Media Analysis, pages 342–347

Brussels, Belgium, October 31, 2018. ©2018 Association for Computational Linguistics

https://doi.org/10.18653/v1/P17

2 Data

We use the Twitter dataset released by the organizers of the "Implicit Emotion" task, as described in the previous section. The data are partitioned into $153,383$ tweets for training, 9591 tweets for validation, and $28,757$ data points for testing. The training and validation sets were provided early for system development, while the test set was released one week before the deadline of system submission. The full details of the dataset can be found in Klinger et al. (2018). We now describe our methods in the nesxt section.

3 Methods

3.1 Pre-processing

We adopt a simple pre-processing scheme, similar to most of the pre-trained models we employ. This involves lowercasing all text and filtering out urls and user mentions. We also split clusters of emojis into individual emojis, following Duppada et al. (2018). For our vocabulary V, we retain the top $100k$ words and then remove all words occurring < 2 times, which leaves $|V| = 23,656$.

3.2 Models

We develop a host of models based on deep neural networks, using some of these models as our baseline models. As an additional baseline, we compare to Klinger et al. (2018) who propose a model based on Logistic Regression with a bag of word unigrams (BOW). All our deep learning models are based on variations of recurrent neural networks (RNNs), which have proved useful for several NLP tasks. RNNs are able to capture sequential dependencies especially in time series data, of which language can be seen as an example. One weakness of RNNs, however, lies in gradient either vanishing or exploding during training. Long-short term memory (LSTM) networks were developed to target this problem, and hence we employ these in our work. We also use a bidirectional version (BiLSTM) where the vector of representation is built as a concatenation of two vectors, one that runs from left-to-right and another running from right-to-left. Ultimately, we generate a fixed-size representation for a given tweet using the last hidden state for the Fwd and Bwd LSTM. Our systems can be categorized as follows: (1) Systems tuning simple pre-trained embeddings, (2) Systems tuning embeddings from language models, and (3) Systems directly tuning language models. We treat #1 and #2 as baseline systems, while our best models are based on #3.

3.2.1 Systems With Simple Embeddings

Character and/or Word embeddings (Mikolov et al., 2013; Pennington et al., 2014; Bojanowski et al., 2016) have boosted performance on a host of NLP tasks. Most state of the art systems now fine-tune these embeddings as a simple transfer learning technique targeting the first layer of a network (McCann et al., 2017). We make use of one such pre-trained embeddings (fastText) to identify the utility of tuning its learned weights on the task.

FastText: The first embedding model is fastText [2](Bojanowski et al., 2016), which builds representations based on characters, rather than only words, thus alleviating issues of complex morphology charecetrestic of many languages like Arabic, Hebrew, and Swedish, but also enhancing representations for languages of simpler morphology like English. Additionally, fastText partially solves issues with out-of-vocabulary words since it exploits character sequences. FastText is trained on the Common Crawl dataset, consisting of 600B tokens.

For this and the next set of experiments (i.e., experiments in 3.2.2), we train both an LSTM and BiLSTM. Since we treat these as baseline systems, especially with our goal to report our experiments in available space for the competition, we try a small set of hyper-parameters, identifying best settings on our validation set. We train each network for 4 epochs each. For optimization, we use $Adam$ (Kingma and Ba, 2014). The model's weights W are initialized from a normal distribution $W \sim N$ with a small standard deviation of $\sigma = 0.05$. We apply two sources of regularization: $dropout$: we apply a dropout rate of 0.5 on the input embeddings to prevent co-adaptation of hidden units' activation, and $L2 - norm$: we also apply an L2-norm regularization with a small value (0.0001) on the hidden units layer to prevent the network from over-fitting on training set. Each of the networks has a single hidden layer. Network architectures and hyper-parameters are listed in Table 1.

3.2.2 Embedding From LMs

Peters et al. (2018) build embeddings directly from

---

[2]https://fasttext.cc/docs/en/
english-vectors.html

Hyper-Parameter	Value
Embed-dim-fastText	300
Embed-dim-ELMo	1024
layers	1
units	300
batch size	32
epochs	4
dropout	0.5

Table 1: Network architecture and hyper-parameters for experiments with simple pre-trained embeddings with fastText 3.2.1 and ELMo 3.2.2 across our LSTM and BiLSTM networks.

language models, which they refer to as ELMo. ELMo is shown to capture both complex characteristics of words (as syntax and semantics) as well as the usage of these words across various linguistic contexts, thanks to its language modeling component. ELMo is trained on a dataset of Wikipedia and is publicly available [3], which we use as our input layer. More specifically, we extract the weighted sum of the 3 layers (word embedding, Bi-lstm-outputs1, and Bi-lstm-outputs2) and follow the same network architectures and hyper-parameters employed with fastText as we explain before.

3.2.3 Fine-Tuning LMs: ULMFiT

Another recent improvement in training NLP systems is related to the way these systems are fine-tuned, especially vis-a-vis how different layers in the network operate during training time. Howard and Ruder (2018) present **ULMFiT**[4], an example such systems that is pre-trained on a language model exploiting Wikitext-103. Ultimately, ULMFiT employs a number of techniques for training. These include "gradual unfreezing", which aims at fine-tuning each layer of the network independently and then fine-tuning all layers together. Gradual unfreezing proves useful for reducing the risk of overfitting as also found in Felbo et al. (2017). ULMFiT also uses "discriminative fine-tuning", which tunes each layer with different learning rates, the idea being different layers capture different types of information (Howard and Ruder, 2018; Peters et al., 2018). Howard and Ruder (2018) also use different learning rates, which they refer to as "slanted triangular learning

rates", at different times of the training process. With ULMFiT, we experiment with different variations of LMs [5]: forward (**Fwd**), backward (**Bwd**), and an average of these (**BiLM (Fwd+Bwd)**). We follow Howard and Ruder (2018) in training each of the Fwd and Bwd models independently on the training data provided by the task organizers, and then combining their predictions using an ensemble averaging. This is the setting we refer to as BiLM. As we show in Section 3, this is a beneficial measure (similar to what Howard and Ruder (2018) also found). For our hyper-parameters for this iteration of experiments, we identify them on our validation set. We list the network architectures and hyper-parameters for this set of experiments in Table 2.

Hyper-Parameter	Value
dim-size	400
vocab	$23,656$
batches	64
layers	3
units	$1,150$
epochs	19

Table 2: Hyper-parameters for our submitted system exploiting fine-tuned language models from Howard and Ruder (2018).

4   Results

Table 3 shows results of all our models in F-score. As the Table shows, all our models achieve sizable gains over the logistic regression model introduced by (Klinger et al., 2018) as a baseline for the competition (F-score $= 60\%$). Even though our models trained based on fastText and ELMo each has a single hidden layer, which is not that deep, these at least 1.5% higher than the logistic regression model. We also observe that ELMo embeddings, which are acquired from language models rather than optimized from sequences of tokens, achieves higher performance than FastText embeddings. This is not surprising, and aligns with the results reported by Peters et al. (2018).

For results with ULMFiT, as Table 3 shows, it acquires gains over all the other models. As mentioned earlier, we experiment with different variations of LMs (Fwd, Bwd, and BiLM). Results in our submitted system are based on the Fwd model, and are at 69.4%. After system submission, we

[3]https://github.com/allenai/bilm-tf
[4]http://nlp.fast.ai/category/
classification.html.

[5]Fwd and Bwd LMs are offered by the authors of the ULMFiT model (Howard and Ruder, 2018).

also experimented with the Bwd and BiLM models and were able to acquire even higher gains, putting our best performance at 70.7% (which moves us to the top 3 position).

System	Dev	Test
Baseline (Klinger et al., 2018)		
BOW Log-Reg	0.601	0.601
Embeddings		
FastText (Bojanowski et al., 2016)		
LSTM	0.629	0.629
Bi-LSTM	0.628	0.626
Embed. from LM (ELMo) (Peters et al., 2018)		
LSTM	0.635	0.635
Bi-LSTM	0.615	0.614
Fine-Tuned LM (Howard and Ruder, 2018)		
Fwd LM (submitted system)	0.694	0.693
Bwd LM	0.686	0.693
BiLM	**0.707**	**0.707**

Table 3: Results: BiLM refers to an ensemble of both the Fwd and Bwd LMs.

5 Analysis

5.1 Error Analysis

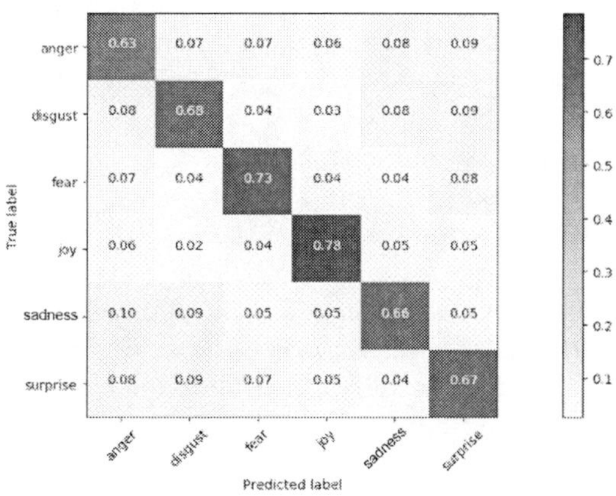

Figure 1: Confusion matrix of errors in F-score across the different emotion classes.

Using predictions from our best model (as described in Table 2), we investigate the extent with which each emotion is mislabeled and the categories with which it is confused. Figure 1 shows the confusion matrix of this analysis. As the Figure shows, *anger* is predicted with least F-score (% = 63), followed by *sadness* (% = 66). Figure

1 also shows that *anger* is most confused for *surprise* and *sadness* is most confused for *anger*. Additionally, *disgust* is the third most confused category (% = 66), and is mislabeled as *surprise* 9% of the time. These results suggest overlap in the ways each of the emotions is expressed in the training data.

To further investigate these observations, we measure the shared vocabulary between the different classes. Figure 2 shows percentages of lexical overlap in the data, and does confirm that some categories share unigram tokens to varying degrees. Lexical overlap between classes seem to align with the error matrix in Figure 1. For example, *anger* overlaps most with *surprise* (% = 9) and *sadness* overlaps most with *anger* (% = 10). These findings are not surprising, since our models are based on lexical input and do not involve other types of information (e.g., POS tags). Table 4 offers examples of overlap in the form of lexical sequences between test data and training data across a number of classes.

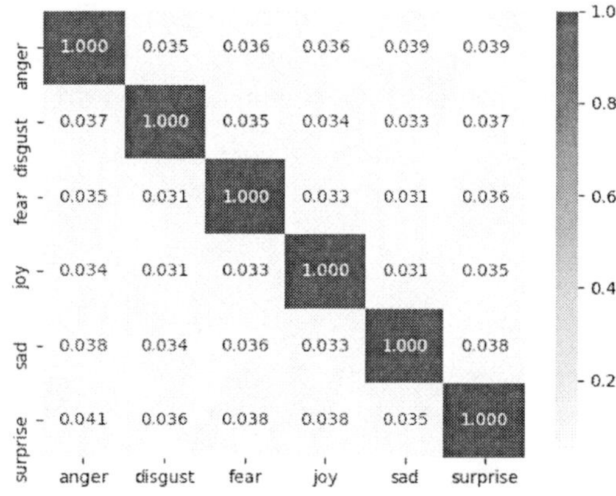

Figure 2: Heat Map for percentages of shared vocabulary between emotion classes.

5.2 Size of Training Data

We also investigate the impact of training data size on model accuracy. For this purpose, we train models with different data sizes with the best parameter settings shown in Table 2 [6]. Figure 3 shows the impact of different percentages of training examples on model performance. We test

---

[6]Due to the high computational cost of training these models, we only train each model with one epoch for this analysis.

Test Example	True	Predicted	Train Example	True
I'm [#TRIGGERWORD#] **that** **like none of** my friends at school have seen national lamoon's day	disgust	sad	[#TRIGGERWORD#] **that like** **none of** my videos from last night ..	sad
hey luke! I'm so [#TRIGGERWORD#] **because you** **don't follow me**, not lies, but please follow me	anger	sad	i'm so [#TRIGGERWORD#] **because** **you don't** **follow me**	sad

Table 4: Examples overlapping lexical sequences in test and training data.

model performance for this analysis on our validation data.

Interestingly, as Figure 3 shows, the model exceeds the baseline model reported by the task organizers (Klinger et al., 2018) when trained on only 10% of the training data. Additionally, the model outperforms the fastText and ELMo models by only seeing 40% of the training data. Once the model has access to 80% of the training data, its gains start to increase relatively slowly. In addition to the positive, yet unsurprising, impact that training data size has on performance, the results also reflect the utility of employing the pre-trained language model.

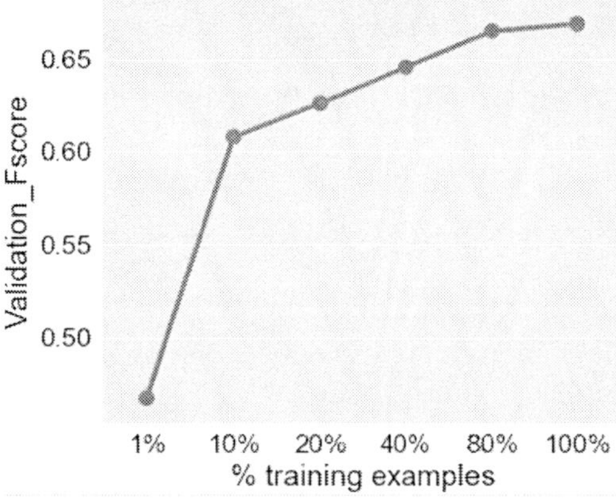

Figure 3: Impact of training data size on model performance, tested on our validation data. Results in *F*-score.

In order to further inspect this observation regarding the impact of language modeling, we use the same architecture reported in Table 2 to train a classifier that does not have access to the pre-trained LM. We find the classifier to achieve only 63.8 *F*-score. Again, this demonstrates the advantage of using the pra-trained LM.

6 Negative Experiments

We performed a number of negative experiments that we report briefly here. Our intuition is that training our models with Twitter-specific data should help classification. For this reason, we trained ULMFiT with 4.5 million tweets with the same settings reported in Table 2. We did not find this set of experiments to yield gains over the results reported in Table 3, however. For example, an Fwd LM trained on Twitter domain data yields 67.9% *F*-score, which is 1.4% less than the F-score obtained by the Wikipedia-trained Fwd LM in 3. The loss might be due to the smaller size of the Twitter data we train on, as compared to the Wikipedia data the ULMFiT is originally trained on (i.e., > 103 million tokens).

7 Conclusion

In this paper, we described our system submitted to IEST-2018 task, focused on learning implicit emotion from Twitter data. We explored the utility of tuning different word- and character-level pre-trained representations and language modeling methods to minimize training loss. We found that the method introduced by Howard and Ruder (2018) yields best performance on the task. We note that our baselines employing sub-word embeddings (fastText) and embeddings from language models (ELMo) can be improved by using deeper neural architectures with larger model capacity, which we cast for future work. We have also shown that the classifier confuses certain emotion classes with one another, possible due to overlap of lexical sequences between training and test data. This reflects the difficulty of the task.

8   Acknowledgement

We acknowledge the support of the Natural Sciences and Engineering Research Council of Canada (NSERC). The research was enabled in part by support provided by WestGrid (https://www.westgrid.ca/) and Compute Canada (www.computecanada.ca).

References

Muhammad Abdul-Mageed and Lyle Ungar. 2017. Emonet: Fine-grained emotion detection with gated recurrent neural networks. In *Proceedings of the 55th Annual Meeting of the Association for Computational Linguistics (Volume 1: Long Papers)*, volume 1, pages 718–728.

Hassan Alhuzali, Muhammad Abdul-Mageed, and Lyle Ungar. 2018. Enabling deep learning of emotion with first-person seed expressions. In *Proceedings of the Second Workshop on Computational Modeling of Peoples Opinions, Personality, and Emotions in Social Media*, pages 25–35.

Saima Aman and Stan Szpakowicz. 2007. Identifying expressions of emotion in text. In *Text, Speech and Dialogue*, pages 196–205. Springer.

Piotr Bojanowski, Edouard Grave, Armand Joulin, and Tomas Mikolov. 2016. Enriching word vectors with subword information. *arXiv preprint arXiv:1607.04606*.

Venkatesh Duppada, Royal Jain, and Sushant Hiray. 2018. Seernet at semeval-2018 task 1: Domain adaptation for affect in tweets. *arXiv preprint arXiv:1804.06137*.

P. Ekman. 1972. Universal and cultural differences in facial expression of emotion. *Nebraska Symposium on Motivation*, pages 207–283.

Bjarke Felbo, Alan Mislove, Anders Søgaard, Iyad Rahwan, and Sune Lehmann. 2017. Using millions of emoji occurrences to learn any-domain representations for detecting sentiment, emotion and sarcasm. In *Conference on Empirical Methods in Natural Language Processing (EMNLP)*.

Jeremy Howard and Sebastian Ruder. 2018. Fine-tuned language models for text classification. *arXiv preprint arXiv:1801.06146*.

Diederik Kingma and Jimmy Ba. 2014. Adam: A method for stochastic optimization. *arXiv preprint arXiv:1412.6980*.

Roman Klinger, Orphée de Clercq, Saif M. Mohammad, and Alexandra Balahur. 2018. Iest: Wassa-2018 implicit emotions shared task. In *Proceedings of the 9th Workshop on Computational Approaches to Subjectivity, Sentiment and Social Media Analysis*, Brussels, Belgium. Association for Computational Linguistics.

Bryan McCann, James Bradbury, Caiming Xiong, and Richard Socher. 2017. Learned in translation: Contextualized word vectors. In *Advances in Neural Information Processing Systems*, pages 6297–6308.

Tomas Mikolov, Ilya Sutskever, Kai Chen, Greg S Corrado, and Jeff Dean. 2013. Distributed representations of words and phrases and their compositionality. In *Advances in neural information processing systems*, pages 3111–3119.

Mike Mintz, Steven Bills, Rion Snow, and Dan Jurafsky. 2009. Distant supervision for relation extraction without labeled data. In *Proceedings of the Joint Conference of the 47th Annual Meeting of the ACL and the 4th International Joint Conference on Natural Language Processing of the AFNLP: Volume 2-Volume 2*, pages 1003–1011. Association for Computational Linguistics.

Saif M Mohammad and Svetlana Kiritchenko. 2015. Using hashtags to capture fine emotion categories from tweets. *Computational Intelligence*, 31(2):301–326.

Jeffrey Pennington, Richard Socher, and Christopher D Manning. 2014. Glove: Global vectors for word representation. In *EMNLP*, volume 14, pages 1532–1543.

Matthew E Peters, Mark Neumann, Mohit Iyyer, Matt Gardner, Christopher Clark, Kenton Lee, and Luke Zettlemoyer. 2018. Deep contextualized word representations. *arXiv preprint arXiv:1802.05365*.

Carlo Strapparava and Rada Mihalcea. 2007. Semeval-2007 task 14: Affective text. In *Proceedings of the 4th International Workshop on Semantic Evaluations*, pages 70–74. Association for Computational Linguistics.

Svitlana Volkova and Yoram Bachrach. 2016. Inferring perceived demographics from user emotional tone and user-environment emotional contrast. In *Proceedings of the 54th Annual Meeting of the Association for Computational Linguistics, ACL*.

Wenbo Wang, Lu Chen, Krishnaprasad Thirunarayan, and Amit P Sheth. 2012. Harnessing twitter" big data" for automatic emotion identification. In *Privacy, Security, Risk and Trust (PASSAT), 2012 International Conference on and 2012 International Confernece on Social Computing (SocialCom)*, pages 587–592. IEEE.

Author Index